THE UNCITRAL MODEL LAWS ON CROSS-BORDER INSOLVENCY AND ON THE RECOGNITION AND ENFORCEMENT OF INSOLVENCY-RELATED JUDGMENTS

An Article-by-Article Commentary

ELGAR COMMENTARIES IN CORPORATE AND COMPANY LAW

Volumes in this series provide comprehensive commentary on and analysis of key instruments in corporate and company law. From shareholders' rights and takeover bids to corporate sustainability and whistleblower protections, each *Commentary* provides a thorough examination of the context, interpretation and implementation of the relevant instrument. With a clear and structured format to facilitate easy navigation and pin-point searches, the series addresses a wide range of issues, covering the major directives, regulations, conventions and treaties in both EU and transnational law. Featuring the original text of the relevant instrument in situ alongside the analysis, and with detailed and extensive legal tables, the *Commentaries* form valuable reference works for both scholars who want a platform for their research, and practitioners who need clear guidance on interpreting the rules.

For a full list of Edward Elgar published titles, including the titles in this series, visit our website at www.e-elgar.com.

THE UNCITRAL MODEL LAWS ON CROSS-BORDER INSOLVENCY AND ON THE RECOGNITION AND ENFORCEMENT OF INSOLVENCY-RELATED JUDGMENTS

An Article-by-Article Commentary

Edited by

REINHARD BORK

Professor, University of Hamburg, Germany; Senior Research Fellow, Commercial Law Centre, Harris Manchester College, Oxford, UK and Visiting Professor, Radboud University, Nijmegen, the Netherlands

MICHAEL VEDER

Professor of Insolvency Law, Radboud Business Law Institute, Faculty of Law, Radboud University, the Netherlands and Attorney/Adviser, RESOR

ELGAR COMMENTARIES IN CORPORATE AND COMPANY LAW

EE Edward Elgar PUBLISHING

Cheltenham, UK • Northampton, MA, USA

Published by
Edward Elgar Publishing Limited
The Lypiatts
15 Lansdown Road
Cheltenham
Glos GL50 2JA
UK

Edward Elgar Publishing, Inc.
William Pratt House
9 Dewey Court
Northampton
Massachusetts 01060
USA

Authorised representative in the EU for GPSR queries only: Easy Access System Europe – Mustamäe tee 50, 10621 Tallinn, Estonia, gpsr.requests@easproject.com

A catalogue record for this book
is available from the British Library

Library of Congress Control Number: 2024952818

This book is available electronically in the **Elgar**online
Law subject collection
https://doi.org/10.4337/9781839102523

Printed on elemental chlorine free (ECF)
recycled paper containing 30% Post-Consumer Waste

ISBN 978 1 83910 251 6 (cased)
ISBN 978 1 83910 252 3 (eBook)

Printed and bound in the USA

CONTENTS

EXTENDED CONTENTS

Chapter IV Cooperation with foreign courts and foreign representatives

ARTICLE 11 PROCEDURE FOR SEEKING RECOGNITION AND ENFORCEMENT OF AN INSOLVENCY-RELATED JUDGMENT

ARTICLE 12 PROVISIONAL RELIEF

ARTICLE 13 DECISION TO RECOGNIZE AND ENFORCE AN INSOLVENCY-RELATED JUDGMENT

ARTICLE 14 GROUNDS TO REFUSE RECOGNITION AND ENFORCEMENT OF AN INSOLVENCY-RELATED JUDGMENT

CONTRIBUTORS

Reinhard Bork, Professor of Law, University of Hamburg, Germany; Visiting Professor, Radboud University, the Netherlands; Senior Research Fellow, Commercial Law Centre, Harris Manchester College, University of Oxford, UK

Stephan Madaus, Professor of Civil Law, Civil Procedure and Insolvency Law, Martin Luther University Halle-Wittenberg, Germany

Irit Mevorach, Professor of International Commercial Law, Warwick Law School, University of Warwick, UK

Rodrigo Rodriguez, Professor of Civil Procedure and Insolvency Law, University of Lucerne, Switzerland and Head of the Federal Supervisory Authority on Insolvency, Bern, Switzerland

Catarina Serra, Professor, School of Law, University of Minho, Portugal; Justice of the Portuguese Supreme Court

Christopher Symes, Professor Emeritus, Adelaide Law School, University of Adelaide, Australia

Virginia Torrie, Affiliated Researcher, Desautels Centre for Private Enterprise and the Law, Faculty of Law, University of Manitoba

Kristin van Zwieten, Clifford Chance Professor of Law and Finance and Gullifer Fellow, Harris Manchester College, University of Oxford, UK

Michael Veder, Professor of Insolvency Law, Radboud University, the Netherlands; attorney/adviser at RESOR, Amsterdam

G. Ray Warner, Professor of Law, St. John's University, New York, USA

Wan Wai Yee, Adjunct Professor, School of Law, City University of Hong Kong, Hong Kong SAR

TABLE OF CASES

Australia

Palmer (as trustee in the bankrupt estate of SLATER) v Registrar-General of Land Titles of the Australian Capital Territory and Others (2017) 181 ACTR 1 **1.11.01**
Tai-Soo Suk v Hanjin Shipping Co Ltd [2016] FCA 1404; [2017] FCA 404 **1.20.17**
Tucker, in the matter of Aero Inventory (UK) Limited v Aero Inventory (UK) Limited (2009) 76 ACSR 19; (2009) FCA 1354 **1.19.01, 1.19.08, 1.19.21, 1.19.23**
Wild v Coin Co International PLC [2015] FCA 354 **1.23.07, 1.23.20**
Yakushiji v Daiichi Chuo Kisen Kaisha (No 2) [2016] FCA 1277 **1.20.10**
Yakushiji v Kaisha; Fujita v Star Bulk Carrier Co SA (2015) 333 ALR 515 **1.20.17**
Yu v STX Pan Ocean Co Ltd (South Korea), in the matter of STX Pan Ocean Co Ltd (receivers appointed in South Korea)[2013] FCA 680, (2013) 223 FCR 189 **1.19.07, 1.19.09, 1.19.20, 1.20.17**

Canada

Hanjin Shipping Co., 2016 BCSC 2213 **1.20.10**
Hartford Computer Hardware Inc, Re, (2012) 94 CBR (5th) 20 **1.21.23**
Lightsquared LP 2012 ONSC 2994 **1.16.38, 1.16.42**
Massachusetts Elephant & Castle Group, Inc 2011 ONSC 4201 **1.16.38**
Nortel Networks Corporation (Re) 2015 ONSC 2987, Case No. 09-10138 (KG), 2015 WL 2374351 **1.32.21**
Probe Resources Ltd 2011 CarswellBC 1043, 79 CBR 5th 148 (BC SC) **1.15.26, 1.15.34**
Syncreon Group BV 2019 ONSC 5774 **1.2.13, 1.2.28**
Tucker v Aero Inventory (UK) Ltd, 2010 ONSC 1196 **1.11.14**
Zayed v Cook [2009] OJ No 5513 **1.2.20**

New Zealand

Chow Cho Poon (Private Limited) [2011] NSWSC 300 **1.1.06, 1.2.15**
Debis Financial Services (Aust) Pty Limited v Allied Bellambi Collieries Pty Limited [1999] NSWSC 935 **1.21.20**
Kim v STX Pan Ocean Co Limited [2014] NZHC 845 **1.20.21–1.20.25**
Whittman v UCI Holdings Ltd [2016] NZHC 1228 **1.19.04, 1.19.23**
Williams v Simpson (No 5) [2010] NZHC 1786 [2011] 2 NZLR 380 **1.7.4, 1.7.6, 1.16.35, 1.17.15**
Williams v Simpson HC Hamilton CIV 2010-419-1174 [2010] NZHC 1631 **1.19.01–1.19.02, 1.19.22, 19.07**

Singapore

Chang Chin Fen vs Cosco Sipping (Qidong) Offhore Ltd [2021] CSOH 94 **1.22.17**
Opti-Medix Ltd (in liquidation), In Re, [2016] 4 SLR 312 **1.16.29**
PT Garuda Indonesia (Persero) Tbk, In the Matter of [2024] SGHC (1) **1.6.19, 1.7.1, 1.7.5, 1.8.01, 1.8.04, 1.8.08, 1.15.20, 1.17.32**
Tantleff, Alan, Re [2022] SGHC 147 **1.21.28–1.21.31**
United Securities Sdn Bhd (in receivership and liquidation) v United Overseas Bank Ltd [2021] SGCA 78 **1.8.04, 1.8.08**
Zetta Jet Pte Ltd, Re, [2018] SGHC 16 **1.6.19, 1.8.04, 2.7.6**
Zetta Jet Pte Ltd (No. 2), Re, [2019] SGHC 53, [2019] 4 SLR 1343 **1.8.04, 1.16.45, 1.17.22**

United Kingdom

Agrokor dd, In re, [2017] EWHC 2791 (Ch), [2018] Bus LR 64 **1.1.18, 1.2.13, 1.2.16, 1.8.01, 1.8.04**
Akers & Anor v Deutsche Bank AG [2012] EWHC (Ch) 244 **1.21.21**
American Energy Group Ltd v Hycarbex Asia Pte Ltd (In Liquidation) [2014] EWHC 1091 (Ch) **1.4.6**
Aro Co. Ltd, Re, [1980] Ch 196 (CA) **1.20.24**
Atlantic Computer Systems, In Re, [1990] EWCA Civ 20, [1992] 2 WLR 367, [1990] BCC 859, [1992] Ch 505 **1.22.17**
Bakhshiyeva ex rel. Int'l Bank of Azerbaijan v. Sberbank of Russia [2018] EWCA (Civ) 2802, [2019] 1 BCLC 1, [2018] FCA 153, [2019] 2 All ER 713 **1.21.03, 1.22.17, 2.15.02, 2.X.15**
Banco de Portugal v. Waddell (1880) 5 App. Cass. 161 **1.32.10**
British & Commonwealth Holdings plc v Spicer & Oppenheim [1993] AC 426 **1.21.21, 1.21.27**
Buchler v Talbot [2004] UKHL 9, [2004] 2 AC 298 **1.2.09**
Cambridge Gas Transportation Corp v Official Committee of Unsecured Creditors of Navigator Holdings Plc [2006] 3 WLR 689, [2006] UKPC 26, [2007] 1 AC 508 **1.25.02**
Carter v Bailey and Hutchison [2020] EWHC 123 (Ch), [2020] 1 BCLC 600 **1.8.08**
Cherkasov v Olegovich, the Official Receiver of Dalnyaya Step LLC [2017] EWHC (Ch) 756, [2017] 1 WLR 4264 **2.7.3**
Cleaver v. Delta American Reinsurance [2001] UKPC 6, [2001] 2 AC 328, [2001] 2 WLR 1202 **1.32.04, 1.32.11**

Cooper, Leite v. Amicorp [2020] EWHC 3560 (Ch), (2021), 18 ICR, 137 **1.21.25–1.21.27**

Cosco Bulk Carrier v Armada Shipping [2011] EWHC 216 (Ch), [2011] BPIR 626, [2011] ArbLR 5 **1.22.17**

Doulgas ex parte Wilson , Re, (1872) LR 7 Ch App 490 **1.32.10**

England v Smith [2001] Ch 419, [2000] 2 WLR 1141 **1.7.5**

Fibria Celulose S.A v Pan Ocean [2014] EWHC 2124 (Ch); [2014] BUS LR 1041 **1.7.4, 1.8.04, 1.8.09, 1.21.06, 1.21.08, 1.21.22–1.21.24, 1.23.05, 2.7.4, P2.06**

Gategroup Guarantee Limited, In the Matter of [2021] EWHC 304 (Ch), [2022] 1 BCLC 98, [2021] BCC 549 **1.2.04, 1.2.06, 1.2.09**

Gibbs v La Societe Industrielle et Commercial des Metaux [1890] 25 QBD 399 **1.22.17, 2.15.02, 2.X.15–2.X.16**

International Bank of Azerbaijan OJSC, Re, Chancery Division (unreported, 6 June 2017) **1.1.18**

Kazakhstan Kagazy Plc and others v Zhunus and others [2021] EWHC 3462 **1.23.23**

Kireeva (Trustee & Bankruptcy Manager in Russia of Bedzhamov) v Bedzhamov [2022] EWCA Civ 35, [2022] 3 WLR 1253, [2022] BPIR 753, [2022] 4 All ER 192, [2022] BCC 603 **1.25.02**

Kireeva v Bedzhamov [2023] Ch 45, [2022] EWCA Civ 35 **1.7.5**

Larsen v Navios International Inc [2011] EWHC 878 (Ch), [2012] 1 BCLC 151, [2012] BCC 353 **1.7.4, 1.21.03**

Leite v. Amicorp (Re Industria De Alimentos Nilza Sa Buglin Participacoes Ltda) [2020] EWHC 3560 (Ch) **1.21.25–1.21.27**

McFadyen & Co, ex parte Vizianagaram Co Ltd, Re [1908] 1 KB 675 **1.27.11**

NMC Healthcare Limited (in Administration) [2021] EWHC 1806 (Ch) **1.2.12**

Nordic Trustee ASA v OGX Petróleo E Gás SA [2016] EWHC 25 (Ch); [2016] Bus LR 121 **1.6.20**

OGX Petroleo E Gas SA [2016] EWHC 25 (Ch), [2016] Bus LR 121 **1.17.14**

OJSC ANK Yugraneft [2008] EWHC 2614 (Ch) [2010] BCC 475 **1.11.16**

OJSC International Bank of Azerbaijan, Re [2018] EWCA Civ 2802, [2019] 2 All ER 713, [2019] 1 BCLC 1, [2018] FCA 153 **1.2.06, 1.7.5, P2.06**

Pan Ocean, Re [2014] Bus LR 1041; [2014] EWHC 2124 (Ch) **1.6.10, 1.7.5, 1.21.03**

Pan Ocean, Re [2018] BCC 4 **1.6.20**

Pan Oceanic Maritime Inc, Re [2010] EWHC 1734 **1.9.05**

Paramount Airways Ltd, In Re, [1993] Ch 223 (CA) **1.23.19, 1.23.23**

United States of America

European Cases

Other National Cases

Arcalon v Ramar of the Supreme Court of the Netherlands, HR 21 February 1986, NJ 1987 (Netherlands) **2.14.07**
Azabu Building Company Ltd, 2006 (shou) No. 1, 2007 (mi) No. 5, Tokyo District Court (Japan) **1.28.07**
HAHAP 20 (28 August 2008), Seoul Central District Court; RA 1524, Seoul High Court (South Korea) **1.28.07**
Jacobo Xacur Eljure, Felipe Xacur Eljure and Jose Maria Xacur Eljure (19 December 2002), Mexico City Federal District Court Proceedings no. 29.2001 (Mexico) **1.31.05**
John Hunt v Transworld Payment Solutions UK Ltd (in liquidation) [2020] Bda LR 17 (Bermuda) **1.25.02**
LATAM Finance Limited et.al, In the Matter of, FSD 105, 106 and 154 of 2020 (IKJ) (Cayman Islands) **1.27.28**
Rare Earth Magnesium Technology Group Holdings Ltd, Re [2022] HKCFI 1686 (Hong Kong) **1.22.17**
Sabena v. Swissair, Swiss Federal Court 137 III 268 and 140 III 320 (Switzerland) **2.14.41**
Singularis Holdings Ltd v PricewaterhouseCoopers (Bermuda) [2014] UKPC 36 (Bermuda) **1.25.02**
Think3, case nos. (shou) 3 and 5 of 2011, Tokyo District Court, ch 3, issue 2-2 (Japan) **1.16.08, 1.17.25**

UNCITRAL Cases

Amerindo, Re UN Doc A.CN.9.SER.C.ABSTRACTS.72 **1.9.02–1.9.03**
Lloyd, In Re, UN Doc A.CN.9.SER.C.ABSTRACTS.76 **1.10.01, 1.10.08**
North American Steamship UN Doc A.CN.9.SER.C.ABSTRACTS.72 **1.9.02–1.9.03**
Xacur UN Doc A.CN.9.SER.C.ABSTRACTS.64 **1.9.02**

TABLE OF LEGISLATION

UNCITRAL

Agreements and Conventions

European Union Legislation

National Legislation

Australia

Brazil

British Virgin Islands

Canada

China, People's Republic of

Enterprise Law 2006
Art. 7 **1.11.06**

Germany

Insolvency Code *(Insolvenzordnung)* **1.25.16**
Art. 17(2) **1.31.15**
Art. 39(1)(1) **1.13.16**
Art. 103 **1.22.11**
Art. 343 **2.14.58**

India

Insolvency and Bankruptcy Code 2016
Part Z **1.8.03**
Insolvency and Bankruptcy (Cross-Border Insolvency) Rules 2020
s. 6 **1.8.03**

Japan

Act on Recognition of and Assistance for Foreign Insolvency Proceedings, Act No. 129 of 2000 **2.7.6**

Mauritius

Insolvency Act 2009
s. 366 **1.1.08**

Mexico

Commercial Insolvency Law 2000
Art. 298 **1.19.12**
Art. 300 **1.19.12**

The Netherlands

Insolvency Act *(Faillissementswet)*
Art. 128 **1.13.16**

New Zealand

Admiralty Act 1973 **1.20.21**
Companies Act 1993
s. 248 **1.20.25**
Insolvency Act 1967
Art. 135 **1.7.4**
Insolvency (Cross-Border) Act 2006 **1.7.4, 1.14.12**
Art. 2(i) **1.11.18**
Art. 6 **1.6.20**
Art. 9 **1.9.10**
Art. 10 **1.10.07**
Art. 1 **1.11.09**
Art. 13(3) **1.13.20**

Portugal

Insolvency Code
Art. 20(1) **1.31.15**

Romania

Law 85/2014 on Insolvency Prevention Procedures and Insolvency Proceedings
Art 289 **1.1.08**

Singapore

Companies Act
s. 354B **1.2.05**
Art. 2(h) **1.2.05**
Art. 2(k) **1.11.18**
Art. 9 **1.9.10**
Art. 10 **1.10.07**
Art. 11 **1.11.09**

South Africa

Cross-Border Insolvency Act 42 of 2000
s. 2 **1.1.08**

South Korea

Debtor Rehabilitation Act and Bankruptcy Act, Act. No. 7428, Mar. 31, 2005 **2.7.6**

Miscellaneous

PART I

THE UNCITRAL MODEL LAW ON CROSS-BORDER INSOLVENCY (MLCBI)

MLCBI PREAMBLE

Reinhard Bork and Michael Veder

The purpose of this Law is to provide effective mechanisms for dealing with cases of cross-border insolvency so as to promote the objectives of:

(a) Cooperation between the courts and other competent authorities of this State and foreign States involved in cases of cross-border insolvency;
(b) Greater legal certainty for trade and investment;
(c) Fair and efficient administration of cross-border insolvencies that protects the interests of all creditors and other interested persons, including the debtor;
(d) Protection and maximization of the value of the debtor's assets; and
(e) Facilitation of the rescue of financially troubled businesses, thereby protecting investment and preserving employment.

A. BACKGROUND TO AND OBJECTIVES OF THE MLCBI

P1.01 The UNCITRAL Model Law on Cross-Border Insolvency ('MLCBI'), which was adopted in 1997,[1] is designed to assist States to equip their insolvency laws with an effective framework to address matters that arise in cross-border insolvency and restructuring proceedings.

P1.02 Work on the MLCBI was initiated by UNCITRAL, in close cooperation with INSOL International, in 1995, following two international colloquiums for

1 Report of the United Nations Commission on International Trade Law on the work of its thirtieth session, 12-30 May 1997, Official Records of the General Assembly, Fifty-second Session, Supplement No. 17 (A/52/17), paras. 12-225.

insolvency practitioners, judges, government officials and representatives of other interested sectors.[2]

An important driver for the work on the MLCBI was the acknowledgement that, while there was an increasing incidence of cross-border insolvencies, national insolvency laws were often ill-equipped to deal with cases of a cross-border nature. It was observed that this frequently resulted in inadequate and inharmonious legal approaches, which hampered the rescue of financially troubled businesses, were not conducive to a fair and efficient administration of cross-border insolvencies, impeded the protection of the assets of the insolvent debtor against dissipation and hindered the maximization of the value of those assets. Moreover, the absence of predictability in the handling of cross-border insolvency cases was held to impede capital flow and be a disincentive to cross-border investment.[3] **P1.03**

The objective of the MLCBI is modest. It respects the differences among national laws and does not attempt to harmonize or unify substantive or procedural insolvency law beyond the context of its scope. According to Art. 1, this scope is limited to certain procedural aspects of cross-border insolvency cases, and the MLCBI is intended to operate as an integral part of the existing insolvency law in enacting States. At the same time, it seeks to pursue an ambitious and important goal by providing a framework for cooperation between jurisdictions that seeks to facilitate and promote a uniform approach to cross-border insolvency. It does so in several ways.[4] It authorizes courts in enacting States and persons administering insolvency proceedings in enacting States, to the extent not already possible, to seek assistance abroad (Arts 9–14). It provides a foreign representative, that is, the person administering a foreign insolvency proceeding, with access to the courts of enacting States (Art. 9), thereby permitting him or her to seek relief and allowing the courts in an enacting State to determine what coordination among the jurisdictions concerned or other relief is warranted for an optimal disposition of the insolvency (Arts 19, 21). In that light it determines when a foreign insolvency proceeding should be granted recognition in enacting States and what the consequences of such recognition may be (Arts 15–24). Furthermore, it seeks to provide a transparent regime for the right of foreign creditors to commence, **P1.04**

---

2 The UNCITRAL–INSOL Colloquium on Cross-Border Insolvency (Vienna, 17 to 19 April 1994) and the UNCITRAL–INSOL Judicial Colloquium on Cross-Border Insolvency (Toronto, 22 to 23 March 1995); see further UNCITRAL Model Law on Cross-Border Insolvency with Guide to Enactment and Interpretation, United Nations Publications (New York), 2014, para. 13, footnote 5.

3 Guide to Enactment (n 2), para. 5.

4 Guide to Enactment (n 2), para. 4.

or participate in, an insolvency proceeding in enacting States (Arts 13, 14, 22). It also seeks to provide a mechanism that permits courts in enacting States to cooperate effectively with foreign courts and foreign representatives involved in an insolvency proceeding (Arts 25–32).

P1.05 The MLCBI is based on the idea that if there is a lack of communication and coordination among courts and insolvency practitioners from jurisdictions involved in (parallel) insolvency proceedings, it is more likely that assets would be dissipated, fraudulently concealed or possibly liquidated in a manner that is not in the best interest of the general body of creditors.[5] If there is a lack of cooperation and communication between jurisdictions involved in an insolvency matter the ability of creditors to receive payment may be diminished, as well as the possibility of rescuing financially viable businesses and, thereby, saving jobs. The coordinated administration of cases of cross-border insolvency should make it possible to adopt solutions that are sensible and in the best interest of the creditors and the debtor.[6] The introduction of a harmonized legal framework in the laws of enacting States that allows for and facilitates such cooperation and coordinated administration of an insolvency should also facilitate legal certainty for foreign investment and trade in enacting States.

P1.06 The instrument of a model law allows enacting States the flexibility that is necessary in order to make the MLCBI "fit into" the general system and structure of procedural and substantive insolvency law in place. Enacting States may therefore modify or leave out some of the provisions of the MLCBI, but, in order to achieve a satisfactory degree of harmonization and certainty across the States enacting the MLCBI, UNCITRAL recommends that States make as few changes as possible in incorporating the MLCBI into their legal systems:

> The flexibility to adapt the Model Law to the legal system of the enacting State should be utilized with due consideration for the need for uniformity in its interpretation [see paras 106–107 below] and for the benefits to the enacting State of adopting modern, generally acceptable international practices in insolvency matters. Thus it is advisable to limit deviations from the uniform text to a minimum. This will assist in making the national law as transparent as possible for foreign users (see also paras. 20 and 21 above). The advantage of uniformity and transparency is that it will make it easier for enacting States to demonstrate the basis of their national law on cross-border insolvency and obtain cooperation from other States in insolvency matters.[7]

---

5 Extensively on this idea Bork, *Principles of Cross-Border Insolvency Law*, Intersentia (Cambridge/Antwerp/Portland) 2017, para. 2.39 et seq.

6 Guide to Enactment (n 2), para. 9.

7 Guide to Enactment (n 2), para. 22.

B. GENERAL OVERVIEW OF THE MLCBI

The MLCBI focuses on four key elements: (i) access to local courts for foreign representatives and creditors, and authorization for representatives of local proceedings to seek assistance in other jurisdictions; (ii) recognition of certain orders issued by foreign courts; (iii) relief to assist foreign proceedings; and (iv) cooperation among the courts and insolvency practitioners of States where the debtor's assets are located and the coordination of parallel proceedings. **P1.07**

The provisions on access address both outbound and inbound cases. Article 5 authorizes an insolvency representative, that is, the person or body administering a reorganization or liquidation under the law of an enacting State, to act in a foreign State on behalf of those local proceedings. Pursuant to Art. 9, a foreign representative has direct access to the courts in an enacting State. A foreign representative may apply for recognition of the foreign proceeding in which he or she has been appointed (Art. 15), in particular in order to get the benefit of relief granted in accordance with Art. 20 or 21. Upon recognition, a foreign representative may participate in insolvency proceedings that are pending in an enacting State (Art. 12), initiate in the enacting State an action to avoid or otherwise render ineffective acts detrimental to creditors (Art. 23) and intervene in any local proceedings in which the debtor is a party (Art. 24). **P1.08**

Importantly, pursuant to Art. 13, foreign creditors, in principle, have the same right as local creditors to commence and participate in proceedings in enacting States. This holds true in particular for the right to apply for (or directly commence) insolvency proceedings, to participate in creditors' meetings and to lodge claims with the insolvency schedule. In order to enable foreign creditors to enforce these rights, Art. 14 provides that known foreign creditors are informed in the same way as domestic creditors. **P1.09**

One of the key objectives of the MLCBI is to establish simplified procedures for recognition of foreign insolvency proceedings. Pursuant to Art. 17, when the requirements of Art. 2 concerning the nature of the foreign proceeding (that is, that the foreign proceeding is a collective proceeding for the purposes of liquidation or reorganization under the control or supervision of the court) and the foreign representative are met and the evidence required by Art. 15 has been provided, the court should recognize the foreign proceeding without further requirement—subject to the public policy exception enshrined in Art. 6, of course. The process of application and recognition is assisted by the presumptions provided in Art. 16 that enable the court in the enacting State **P1.10** to presume the authenticity and validity of the certificates and documents originating in the foreign State.

P1.11 Under the MLCBI, a foreign proceeding may be recognized as either a main proceeding or a non-main proceeding. A main proceeding is a proceeding that has been commenced in the place where the debtor had its centre of main interests (COMI). COMI is not defined in the MLCBI, but, pursuant to Art. 16(3), is based on a presumption that it is the registered office or habitual residence of the debtor. In this respect, the MLCBI follows the lead of Art. 3 EIR.[8] A foreign proceeding may be recognized as a non-main proceeding if it is taking place in a State where the debtor has an establishment, that is "any place of operation where the debtor carries out non-transitory economic activity with human means and goods or services" (Art. 2(f)). Proceedings commenced in jurisdictions on a different basis, such as the presence of assets without a centre of main interests or establishment, would, according to the Guide to Enactment,[9] not qualify for recognition under the MLCBI. Recognition of foreign proceedings under the MLCBI has several effects, in particular concerning the availability of relief in accordance with Arts 20 and 21.

P1.12 Under the MLCBI, relief granted to foreign proceedings is considered necessary for the orderly and fair conduct of a cross-border insolvency. It is available to assist foreign proceedings, whether on an interim basis (Art. 19) or as a result of recognition (Art. 21). Accordingly, the MLCBI specifies the relief that is available in both of those instances. The MLCBI neither necessarily imports the consequences of the foreign law into the insolvency system of the enacting State nor applies to the foreign proceeding the relief that would be available under the law of the enacting State. Key elements of the relief accorded upon recognition of a foreign proceeding as a foreign main proceeding include a stay of actions of individual creditors against the debtor or a stay of enforcement proceedings concerning the assets of the debtor, and a suspension of the debtor's right to transfer or encumber its assets (Art. 21(1)(a)–(e)). Other remedies are at the discretion of the court (Art. 21(1)(g)).[10] With respect to interim and discretionary relief, the court can impose conditions and modify or terminate the relief to protect the interests of creditors and other interested persons affected by the relief ordered.

---

8 Regulation (EU) 2015/848 of the European Parliament and of the Council of 20 May 2015 on insolvency proceedings (recast) ('EU Insolvency Regulation' or 'EIR'). For details, see below Warner at para. 1.16.29.

9 Guide to Enactment (n 2), para. 32.

10 For details, see below Symes para. 1.21.20 et seq.

The MLCBI expressly empowers courts in enacting States to cooperate and to communicate directly with foreign courts (Art. 25). Cooperation between courts and foreign representatives and between foreign representatives is also provided for (Art. 26). Cooperation does not depend upon recognition of a foreign proceeding and may thus occur at an early stage and before an application for recognition is made. Cooperation is available in respect of not only applications for assistance made in an enacting State (inbound), but also applications from proceedings in an enacting State for assistance elsewhere (outbound). Moreover, cooperation is not limited to foreign proceedings that qualify as either main or non-main proceedings, but may also be available with respect to proceedings commenced on the basis of presence of assets. Article 27 sets out some of the possible means of cooperation (such as protocols). **P1.13**

Under the MLCBI, more than one insolvency proceeding may be pending in respect of one and the same debtor. The recognition of a foreign proceeding as a foreign main proceeding, for example, does not prevent commencement of local proceedings in the enacting State; nor does the commencement of local proceedings in the enacting State terminate or prevent recognition of foreign proceedings. Against this background, Arts 28–32 address the coordination of concurrent proceedings. They aim to foster decisions that would best achieve the objectives of all concurrent proceedings. **P1.14**

C. RECENT DEVELOPMENTS

It was clear from the outset that the MLCBI does not exhaustively regulate all issues of cross-border insolvencies. In particular, unlike the EIR,[11] there are no rules on the applicable law and other important features. This has gradually changed as UNCITRAL has adopted further Model Laws to complement the MLCBI. Particularly worth mentioning here are the Model Law on Recognition and Enforcement of Insolvency-Related Judgments of 2 July 2018[12] (which is explained in more detail in the second part of this commentary) and the Model Law on Enterprise Group Insolvency of 15 July 2019.[13] UNCITRAL's Working Group V, which is concerned with insolvency law,[14] is currently working on further Model Laws that will deal with asset tracing and, above all, the applicable law. As far as can currently be foreseen, these **P1.15**

11 For a comparison of the MLCBI and the EIR, see Reinhard Bork, The European Insolvency Regulation and the UNCITRAL Model Law on Cross-Border Insolvency, Int. Insolv. Rev. 26 (2017), 246–69.

12 Text available at https://uncitral.un.org/en/texts/insolvency/modellaw/mlij (last visited 14 June 2024).

13 Text available at https://uncitral.un.org/en/MLEGI (last visited 14 June 2024).

14 See https://uncitral.un.org/en/content/working-group-v-insolvency-law (last visited 14 June 2024).

matters will be regulated in separate Model Laws and will not be included as new chapters in the MLCBI.

D. ADOPTION OF THE MLCBI

P1.16 It is fair to say that the MLCBI has proven to be a success story when looking at its adoption across the globe. Legislation based on or influenced by the MLCBI has currently been adopted in 60 States in a total of 63 jurisdictions.[15] The decision of the OHADA (Organization for the Harmonisation of Business Law in Africa) in 2015 to transfer the Model Law to the laws of the member States with the *Acte uniforme portant organization des procédures collectives d'apurement du passif*, adopted on 10 September 2015,[16] provided a major boost. In the past ten years alone, more than 20 countries have decided to transpose the MLCBI into their national law. The vast majority of EU Member States[17] are however an exception, having decided to base their national cross-border insolvency law on the EIR rather than the MLCBI.

15 A current overview of the adoption of the MLCBI can be found at: https:// uncitral .un .org/ en/ texts/ insolvency/modellaw/cross-border_insolvency/status.

16 See www.ohada.org/en/insolvency-law/ (last visited 14 June 2024).

17 Exceptions are Greece, Poland, Romania, and Slovenia.

Chapter I Scope of application

Article 1

SCOPE OF APPLICATION

Irit Mevorach

1. This Law applies where: (a) Assistance is sought in this State by a foreign court or a foreign representative in connection with a foreign proceeding; or (b) Assistance is sought in a foreign State in connection with a proceeding under *[identify laws of the enacting State relating to insolvency]*; or (c) A foreign proceeding and a proceeding under *[identify laws of the enacting State relating to insolvency]* in respect of the same debtor are taking place concurrently; or (d) Creditors or other interested persons in a foreign State have an interest in requesting the commencement of, or participating in, a proceeding under *[identify laws of the enacting State relating to insolvency]*.
2. This Law does not apply to a proceeding concerning *[designate any types of entities, such as banks or insurance companies, that are subject to a special insolvency regime in this State and that this State wishes to exclude from this Law]*.

A. INTRODUCTION TO ARTICLE 1

1.1.01 Article 1 specifies the scope of the Model Law's application. Article 1(1) provides that the Model Law applies when assistance is sought in the State that enacted the Model Law (the 'enacting State') by a foreign court or a foreign representative in connection with a foreign proceeding; when assistance is sought in a foreign State in connection with a proceeding under the law of the enacting State relating to insolvency; when a foreign proceeding and proceeding under the law of the enacting State relating to insolvency in respect of the same debtor are taking place concurrently; and when creditors or other interested persons in a foreign State have an interest in requesting the commencement of, or participating in, a proceeding under the law of the enacting State relating to insolvency. Thus, the Model Law applies in *inbound* cases (when assistance is sought in the enacting State or foreign parties are interested in commencing or participating in proceedings in the enacting State), in *outbound* cases (when assistance is sought in a foreign State) and in regard to *concurrent* proceedings.

The Model Law seeks to, on the one hand, provide an effective framework, which promotes cooperation, assistance and deference to the proceeding pending in the debtor's centre of main interests[1] in various circumstances of cross-border cases, along the lines of the norm of modified universalism.[2] On the other hand, the Model Law restricts its scope to certain cross-border aspects (access, recognition, assistance, relief and cooperation). It does not attempt a comprehensive regulation of cross-border matters and notably does not address the issues of jurisdiction (direct competence) and applicable law.[3] It also focuses on single debtors and does not address the unique issues arising in relation to enterprise groups.[4] **1.1.02**

Article 1(2) further provides that the enacting State may exclude certain proceedings from its scope in regard to certain types of entities, for example banks **1.1.03**

1 See UNCITRAL Model Law on Cross-Border Insolvency (1997), *Guide to Enactment and Interpretation* (2013), para 1.

2 Namely a global approach to multinational default, modified to fit different business structures and insolvency scenarios (see JL Westbrook, 'A Global Solution to Multinational Default' (2000) 98 Mich L Rev 2276; I Mevorach, *The Future of Cross-Border Insolvency, Overcoming Biases and Closing Gaps* (OUP 2018), 12–28; I Mevorach, 'Modified Universalism as Customary International Law' 96 Texas Law Review (2018) 1403.

3 IF Fletcher, *Insolvency in Private International Law* (OUP 2007) 454–5. Another, complementary Model Law, however, addresses the recognition and enforcement of insolvency-related judgments (see UNCITRAL Model Law on Recognition and Enforcement of Insolvency-Related Judgments with Guide to Enactment (2018); I Mevorach, 'Overlapping International Instruments for Enforcement of Insolvency Judgments: Undermining or Strengthening Universalism?' (2021) 22(2) EBOR 301), and further ongoing work focuses on applicable law in insolvency proceedings (work on this topic commenced in December 2021 by UNCITRAL Working Group V: see https://uncitral.un.org/en/working_groups/5/insolvency_law.).

4 Nevertheless, the Model Law can apply in cases involving enterprise groups. The UNCITRAL Digest of Case Law on the UNCITRAL Model Law on Cross-Border Insolvency, United Nations, Vienna 2021 notes (at p 11) that the Model Law 'has found wide application in situations where there are multiple debtors that might be members of an enterprise group where each of those individual entities had their COMI or an establishment in the originating State'. See also I Mevorach, *The Future of Cross-Border Insolvency, Overcoming Biases and Closing Gaps* (OUP 2018), 227). Another Model Law now provides specific rules and mechanisms to address the insolvency of enterprise groups (UNCITRAL Model Law on Enterprise Group Insolvency with Guide to Enactment (2019)).

or insurance companies that are subject to a special insolvency regime in the enacting State. Enacting States have taken advantage of this option and have excluded a variety of entities from application of the MLCBI.[5]

B. APPLICATION OF THE MODEL LAW – INBOUND CASES

1.1.04 Article 1(1)(a), which provides that the assistance in the enacting State to foreign proceedings is within the scope of the instrument, reflects the main focus of the Model Law – the inbound effect of proceedings opened elsewhere. Thus, core articles in the Model Law provide harmonized rules concerning access, recognition, assistance, cooperation and relief[6] by relevant 'receiving' authorities in the enacting State to assist the 'foreign proceeding',[7] especially the 'main foreign proceeding'.[8] The definitions of 'foreign proceeding' and 'foreign representative' in the Model Law limit the scope of the Model Law, because proceedings and representatives that do not qualify will not be covered by the provisions on access, recognition, relief and cooperation.[9] The Model Law envisages that, in principle, collective reorganization or liquidation proceedings opened in the debtor's centre of main interests will have the main responsibility for managing the insolvency even though the debtor has assets or creditors in other countries.[10]

1.1.05 The United States Court of Appeal in *Trikona Advisers*[11] stressed the purpose and importance of the inbound assistance provisions. It noted that Chapter 15 US Bankruptcy Code (11 USC), which implements the Model Law in the United States (Chapter 15), provides for the coordination of domestic and foreign proceedings into a single bankruptcy 'in the interests of uniformity and efficiency' and in that regard 'allows foreign representatives appointed in connection with foreign proceedings to seek recognition of those proceedings

5 See UNCITRAL Digest of Case Law on the UNCITRAL Model Law on Cross-Border Insolvency, United Nations, Vienna 2021, 3–4. See further paras 1.15–1.16 below.

6 See UNCITRAL Model Law on Cross-Border Insolvency (1997), *Guide to Enactment and Interpretation* (2013), para 54 which notes that 'assistance' is intended to cover various situations dealt with in the Model Law where courts or insolvency representatives may request assistance in the enacting State.

7 See Commentary on Article 2 [1.2.02] regarding the meaning of 'foreign proceedings'.

8 See Commentary on Article 2 [1.2.21] regarding the meaning of 'foreign main proceeding'.

9 UNCITRAL Model Law on Cross-Border Insolvency (1997), *Guide to Enactment and Interpretation* (2013), para 63. See also Commentary on Article 2.

10 UNCITRAL Model Law on Cross-Border Insolvency (1997), *Guide to Enactment and Interpretation* (2013), para 1.

11 *Trikona Advisers, Ltd v Chugh*, 846 F.3d 22 (2d Cir. 2017). In this case, the instant non-bankruptcy action was unconnected to any foreign or United States bankruptcy proceeding and therefore Chapter 15 did not apply. See UNCITRAL Digest of Case Law on the UNCITRAL Model Law on Cross-Border Insolvency, United Nations, Vienna 2021, 4.

in United States courts as a means of requesting United States assistance in administering the main liquidation'.[12]

The UNCITRAL Digest of Case Law on the UNCITRAL Model Law on Cross-Border Insolvency notes that several cases suggest that the Model Law does not apply until assistance has been actively sought or a foreign representative has instigated recognition of foreign proceedings,[13] and that until that time, action could be brought locally to protect a party's interests.[14] **1.1.06**

Assistance by enacting States should promote 'an orderly and fair cross-border insolvency proceeding'.[15] Some assistance may also be granted to 'foreign non-main proceedings'.[16] Provisions in the Model Law specify some of the types of assistance that may be granted,[17] but the Model Law also anticipates that other possible means of assistance may be available in the enacting State.[18] Article 1(1)(d) further expands the scope of the Model Law in this respect to circumstances where creditors or other interested persons in a foreign State have an interest in requesting the commencement of, or participating in, a proceeding under the law of the enacting State relating to insolvency. **1.1.07**

The Model Law application is broad in this regard where it is not based on reciprocity and instead refers to assistance that may be sought by any foreign court or a foreign representative in connection with a foreign proceeding (as defined in Article 2[19]). However, some enacting States have restricted the scope and application of the Model Law where they have included reciprocity requirements.[20] **1.1.08**

---

12 Ibid. p 14, referring to In re *ABC Learning Centres Ltd.*, 728 F.3d 301, 14 No. 14-975-cv 1 305–06 (3d Cir. 2013) at [306].

13 UNCITRAL Digest of Case Law on the UNCITRAL Model Law on Cross-Border Insolvency, United Nations, Vienna 2021, 4, referring to: *Chow Cho Poon (Private Limited)* [2011] NSWSC 300; *Trikona Advisers, Ltd. v Chugh*, 846 F.3d 22 (2d Cir. 2017).

14 UNCITRAL Digest of Case Law on the UNCITRAL Model Law on Cross-Border Insolvency, United Nations, Vienna 2021, 4, referring to: *Winter v Winter and Ors* [2010] FamCA 933 [paras 208, 210–211]; *Bank of Western Australia v Henderson* (No. 3) [2011] FMCA 840 [para 15]; *United States v J.A. Jones Constr. Group, LLC* 333 B.R. 637, 638 (EDNY 2005).

15 UNCITRAL Model Law on Cross-Border Insolvency (1997), *Guide to Enactment and Interpretation* (n 4) (2013), para 178.

16 See Commentary on Article 2 [1.2.25].

17 See eg Articles 19(1)(a) and (b); 20(1)(a)–(c); 21(1)(a)–(f); Article 21(2); Article 27(a)–(e).

18 See eg Article 21(1)(g).

19 See Commentary on Article 2 [1.2.02].

20 See eg Romania (Law 85/2014 on insolvency prevention procedures and insolvency proceedings, art 289); South Africa (Cross-Border Insolvency Act 42 of 2000, s 2); Mauritius (Insolvency Act 2009, s 366).

1.1.09 Empirical studies that looked at the application of the Model Law in various jurisdictions which enacted it have shown that this aspect of the Model Law – the inbound aspect and especially the rules on recognition of foreign main proceeding and the ensuing automatic relief – has been enacted and operated quite consistently to promote the modified universalism norm.[21]

C. APPLICATION OF THE MODEL LAW – OUTBOUND CASES

1.1.10 Article 1(1)(b) refers to the corresponding scenario where a proceeding is opened in the enacting State and assistance is needed in relation to this proceeding in foreign jurisdictions where the debtor has some presence. The Model Law envisions that assistance may be needed abroad to allow reaching out to the debtor's assets or affairs outside the territory of the enacting State to promote a fair and efficient administration of the cross-border insolvency, maximize assets value or facilitate a rescue of the debtor's business. Courts or insolvency representatives in the enacting State may make outward-bound requests to courts in foreign jurisdictions for recognition of insolvency proceeding commenced under the laws of the enacting State and to apply for assistance and relief.[22] Provisions in the Model Law specifically authorize the representative or other authorities appointed in the enacting State to act abroad as permitted by the applicable foreign law.[23] The Model Law also provides rules and mechanisms regarding cooperation between courts and representatives of the enacting States and foreign courts and representatives.[24]

1.1.11 In this regard as well, the Model Law does not rely on reciprocity. The authority to act in a foreign country does not depend on whether that country has enacted legislation based on the Model Law.[25]

---

21 See JL Westbrook, 'An Empirical Study of the Implementation in the United States of the Model Law on Cross Border Insolvency' (2013) 87(2) Am Bankr LJ 247; I Mevorach, 'On the Road to Universalism: a Comparative and Empirical Study of UNCITRAL Model Law on Cross-Border Insolvency' (2011) 12 EBOR 517.

22 See UNCITRAL Model Law on Cross-Border Insolvency (1997), *Guide to Enactment and Interpretation* (2013), para 53.

23 See UNCITRAL Model Law on Cross-Border Insolvency (1997), *Guide to Enactment and Interpretation* (2013), para 53.

24 See also IF Fletcher, *Insolvency in Private International Law* (OUP 2007) 454.

25 UNCITRAL Model Law on Cross-Border Insolvency (1997), *Guide to Enactment and Interpretation* (2013), para 100.

D. APPLICATION OF THE MODEL LAW – CONCURRENT PROCEEDINGS

Article 1(1)(c) states that the Model Law applies when a foreign proceeding and a proceeding under the law of the enacting State in respect of the same debtor are taking place concurrently. The Model Law generally envisages scenarios where proceedings are taking place in two or more different jurisdictions,[26] and it devotes a chapter to the coordination of such concurrent proceedings.[27] **1.1.12**

E. EXCLUSIONS FROM THE MODEL LAW

Whilst the Model Law applies 'independently of the nature of the debtor or its particular status under national law',[28] consumers and certain types of entities, such as banks or insurance companies, may be excluded by enacting States. Article 1(2) provides that the Model Law does not apply to proceedings concerning 'types of entities, such as banks or insurance companies, that are subject to a special insolvency regime'. The Model Law does not require that such entities will be excluded from its scope and does not envisage that the regime it proposes would be completely irrelevant to such entities. On the contrary, the Guide to Enactment and Interpretation notes that it is not advisable to exclude all cases of insolvency of the entities mentioned in Article 1(2) and that even if entities are subject to a special regime, enacting States may consider whether it would be useful to leave certain features of the Model Law applicable also regarding such proceedings.[29] **1.1.13**

At the same time, the Model Law considers the fact that certain entities, including banks or insurance companies, may be subject to special regimes. It is widely acknowledged that the regulation and treatment of bank insolvency has certain specific objectives, and therefore bank insolvency may require special rules. Many countries have chosen to treat bank insolvencies differently from ordinary commercial insolvencies. Furthermore, the Model Law does not attempt to address the special circumstances of distressed financial institutions **1.1.14**

---

26 UNCITRAL Model Law on Cross-Border Insolvency (1997), *Guide to Enactment and Interpretation* (2013), para 53.

27 Chapter V, which also refers, in Articles 28–30, to seeking cooperation and coordination pursuant to Articles 25–27.

28 UNCITRAL Model Law on Cross-Border Insolvency (1997), *Guide to Enactment and Interpretation* (2013), para 55.

29 UNCITRAL Model Law on Cross-Border Insolvency (1997), *Guide to Enactment and Interpretation* (2013), paras 58–59.

and to provide the specific tools that may be required for their resolution across borders,[30] and enacting States typically exclude such entities from the Model Law's scope.[31]

1.1.15 For example, in Great Britain, the CBIR 2006[32] (Sch 1, art 1(2)(h)) excludes various categories of entities that are subject to special regimes from the application of the Model Law, including building societies, UK and EEA credit institutions and branches, third country credit institutions and UK and EEA insurers and reinsurers.[33]

1.1.16 In the United States, section 1501(c) of Chapter 15 excludes from the application of the Model Law a proceeding concerning an entity, other than a foreign insurance company, identified by exclusion in section 109(b). Section 109(b) excludes, among other entities, domestic insurance companies, banks, savings banks, cooperative banks, savings and loan associations, building and loan associations, foreign banks, savings banks, cooperative banks, savings and loan associations, building and loan associations or credit unions that have a branch or agency in the United States.[34] In Australia, a Regulation made under the Australian Cross-Border Insolvency Act also excludes specialist types of institutions including authorized deposit-taking institutions and insurance companies.[35]

1.1.17 There is, therefore, a gap in the international financial architecture whereby the Model Law may not apply in circumstances of financial institutions'

30 Including powers to recognize, enforce or give legal effect to specific foreign resolution measures employed in the home country of a financial institution, for example to operationalize a transfer of control in local branches to a bridge entity (see Financial Stability Board, 'Cross-border Recognition of Resolution Action' 29 September 2014, p 3). See also I Mevorach, *The Future of Cross-Border Insolvency, Overcoming Biases and Closing Gaps* (OUP 2018) 248, and R Davis, S Madaus, M Marcucci, I Mevorach, R Mokal, B Romaine, J Sarra and I Tirado, *Financial Institutions in Distress: Recovery, Resolution, Recognition* (Oxford University Press 2023) (proposing a special Model Law on the insolvency/resolution of banks and other financial institutions).

31 See also I Mevorach, *The Future of Cross-Border Insolvency, Overcoming Biases and Closing Gaps* (OUP 2018) 248.

32 In Great Britain, the Model Law is implemented by the Cross-border Insolvency Regulations 2006 ('CBIR 2006').

33 See in more detail LC Ho, 'England' in LC Ho (ed.), *A Commentary on the UNCITRAL Model Law*, 4th ed., Globe Law & Business (London), 2017, 164–8.

34 See PM Gilhuly, KA Posin and AE Malatesta, 'Bankruptcy without Borders: A Compehensive Guide to the First Decade of Chapter 15' ABI Law Review (2016) 47, 56–57.

35 See S Atkins, 'Australia' in LC Ho (ed.), *A Commentary on the UNCITRAL Model Law*, 4th ed., Globe Law & Business (London), 2017, 20–21. See also G McCormack and A Hargovan, 'Australia and the International Insolvency Paradigm' (2015) 37 Sydney LR 389, 410; EU Insolvency Regulation on Insolvency Proceedings (Regulation (EU) 2015/848 of the European Parliament and of the Council of 20 May 2015 on insolvency proceedings (recast)), Article 1(2) which excludes certain types of debtors from its scope of application.

cross-border insolvency, and at the same time these entities are not subject to any other special and comprehensive harmonized statutory framework to address their insolvency and resolution.[36]

The Model Law may, however, apply in certain circumstances of financial institutions' cross-border insolvency. For example, in *International Bank of Azerbaijan OJSC*,[37] recognition was granted by an English court regarding a restructuring proceeding opened against a foreign bank (*International Bank of Azerbaijan*) because the bank was not a UK, EEA or third country credit institution. In *Flynn v Wallace*,[38] a court in the United States granted recognition to an Irish liquidation proceeding for a failed bank, determining that this proceeding was not excluded from recognition since the bank had no branch or agency in the United States when the Chapter 15 petition was filed. In *PJSC Bank Finance and Credit*,[39] the High Court addressed an application for recognition of a liquidation proceeding of PJSC Bank Finance and Credit opened in Ukraine. The Court was satisfied that the debtor was not a 'third country credit institution'[40] and thus was not excluded from the scope of the CBIR, and recognized the proceedings as 'foreign main proceedings'. **1.1.18**

The Guide to Enactment and Interpretation of the Model Law explains that enacting States may also wish to exclude non-trader or natural persons (residing in the enacting State) whose debts have been incurred predominantly for personal or household purposes from the ambit of the Model Law.[41] For example, in the US, pursuant to section 1501(c)(2) of Chapter 15, individual consumer debtors who are citizens or long-term legal residents of the United States are excluded from the Model Law's scope.[42] In *Steadman*,[43] recognition **1.1.19**

---

36 See regarding the exclusions in Australia, G McCormack and A Hargovan, 'Australia and the International Insolvency Paradigm' (2015) 37 Sydney LR 389, 409–10 (arguing that the exclusions should be reviewed following the lessons from the global financial crisis and because a lot of cross-border insolvency cases have involved financial institutions, noting that 'Nobody seems to have taken the point that some of these institutions may have been denied the benefits of the Model Law because of the wording of the Australian exclusions'). See also I Mevorach, 'Beyond the Search for Certainty: Addressing the Cross-Border Resolution Gap', Brooklyn Journal of Corporate, Financial & Commercial Law (2015) 202.

37 *Re International Bank of Azerbaijan OJSC*, Chancery Division (unreported, 6 June 2017).

38 *Flynn v Wallace* (*In re Irish Bank Res Corp Ltd*), 538 BR 692, 696 (D Del 2015).

39 *In the Matter of PJSC Bank Finance and Credit (in liquidation)* [2021] EWHC 1100 (Ch).

40 See Credit Institutions (Reorganisation and Winding Up) Regulations 2004.

41 UNCITRAL Model Law on Cross-Border Insolvency (1997), *Guide to Enactment and Interpretation* (2013), para 61. It is also noted that enacting State may not exclude such persons where the total debts exceed a certain monetary ceiling.

42 See UNCITRAL Digest of Case Law on the UNCITRAL Model Law on Cross-Border Insolvency, United Nations, Vienna 2021, 4. See also C Martin, 'United States' in LC Ho (ed.), *A Commentary on the UNCITRAL Model Law*, 4th ed., Globe Law & Business (London), 2017, 638–40.

43 *Steadman*, 410 B.R. 397, 403 (Bankr. DNJ 2009).

was denied in the United States to a receiver of a United Kingdom debtor who had married an American and held a United States resident alien card with conditional permanent residence.[44]

1.1.20 The Guide to Enactment and Interpretation of the Model Law conclusively advises that, to promote transparency, exclusions from the Model Law's scope be expressly mentioned by the enacting State.[45]

44 See UNCITRAL Digest of Case Law on the UNCITRAL Model Law on Cross-Border Insolvency, United Nations, Vienna 2021, 4.

45 UNCITRAL Model Law on Cross-Border Insolvency (1997), Guide to Enactment and Interpretation (2013), para 60.

Article 2

DEFINITIONS

Irit Mevorach

For the purposes of this Law:

(a) 'Foreign proceeding' means a collective judicial or administrative proceeding in a foreign State, including an interim proceeding, pursuant to a law relating to insolvency in which proceeding the assets and affairs of the debtor are subject to control or supervision by a foreign court, for the purpose of reorganization or liquidation;
(b) 'Foreign main proceeding' means a foreign proceeding taking place in the State where the debtor has the centre of its main interests;
(c) 'Foreign non-main proceeding' means a foreign proceeding, other than a foreign main proceeding, taking place in a State where the debtor has an establishment within the meaning of subparagraph (f) of this article;
(d) 'Foreign representative' means a person or body, including one appointed on an interim basis, authorized in a foreign proceeding to administer the reorganization or the liquidation of the debtor's assets or affairs or to act as a representative of the foreign proceeding;
(e) 'Foreign court' means a judicial or other authority competent to control or supervise a foreign proceeding;
(f) 'Establishment' means any place of operations where the debtor carries out a non-transitory economic activity with human means and goods or services.

A. INTRODUCTION TO ARTICLE 2

1.2.01 Article 2 provides six definitions of terms specific to cross-border scenarios covered in the Model Law.[1] Thus, this Article defines the terms foreign proceeding, foreign main proceeding, foreign non-main proceeding, foreign representative, foreign court and establishment. The definitions also limit the scope of the Model Law by specifying the meaning of 'foreign proceeding' and a 'foreign representative' because proceedings and representatives that do not qualify will not be covered by the provisions on access, recognition, relief and cooperation.[2]

B. FOREIGN PROCEEDING

1.2.02 Article 2(a) defines 'foreign proceeding'. Such proceeding must be: (i) a collective proceeding, either judicial or administrative; (ii) taking place in a foreign State; (iii) pursuant to a law relating to insolvency; (iv) in which proceeding the assets and affairs of the debtor are subject to control or supervision by a foreign court; (v) for the purpose of reorganization or liquidation. The definition also covers 'interim proceedings'.

1.2.03 The definition of foreign proceeding is independent of the definitions of 'foreign main proceeding' and 'foreign non-main proceeding' (discussed below). Thus, a proceeding may qualify as a 'foreign proceeding' even if it is not a main or a non-main foreign proceeding, although the implications of

1 The Guide to Enactment and Interpretation of the Model Law (UNCITRAL Model Law on Cross-Border Insolvency (1997), Guide to Enactment and Interpretation (2013)) explains (in para 62) that because it is intended that the Model Law will be embedded in the national law, the Article only defines the terms relevant to the cross-border aspects.

2 UNCITRAL Model Law on Cross-Border Insolvency (1997), Guide to Enactment and Interpretation (2013), para 63. See also IF Fletcher, *Insolvency in Private International Law* (OUP 2007) 455–6.

qualifying as 'foreign proceeding' that is not main or non-main foreign proceeding is more limited.[3] To qualify for recognition and to be able to receive assistance and relief the proceedings will also need to meet the definition of either main or non-main foreign proceeding.

The definition of foreign proceeding is intended to be expansive and to encompass proceedings involving debtors that are in severe financial distress or insolvent, including proceedings accessible to debtors 'that are or will be generally unable to pay their debts as they mature'.[4] The Guide to Enactment and Interpretation of the Model Law explains that the definitions generally avoid using specific expressions that may have different technical meanings in different legal systems, and instead the Model Law adopts a functional approach.[5] The Guide to Enactment and Interpretation also refers in this respect to 'laws that prevent or address the financial distress of those debtors'.[6] Thus, in principle, the Model Law can accommodate a variety of proceedings, including preventive proceedings designed to help a debtor avoid insolvency.[7] **1.2.04**

There are some discrepancies in the enactment of this definition.[8] Thus, for example, while in Great Britain and in Australia the enactment has not altered the definition as prescribed in the Model Law,[9] in the United States the legislation adds to the definition that a foreign proceeding may relate to 'adjustment of debt'.[10] Japanese law defines a foreign proceeding as a proceeding which corresponds to a (Japanese) bankruptcy liquidation, civil rehabilita- **1.2.05**

---

3 It may be relevant in scenarios where a proceeding is opened pursuant to Article 28 of the Model Law on the basis of the location of assets (in the eyes of another enacting State), or where cooperation is sought in relation to a foreign proceeding which is not main or non-main proceeding (see UNCITRAL Model Law on Cross-Border Insolvency (1997), Guide to Enactment and Interpretation (2013), para 40).

4 UNCITRAL Model Law on Cross-Border Insolvency (1997), Guide to Enactment and Interpretation (2013), para 49.

5 UNCITRAL Model Law on Cross-Border Insolvency (1997), Guide to Enactment and Interpretation (2013), para 65.

6 UNCITRAL Model Law on Cross-Border Insolvency (1997), Guide to Enactment and Interpretation (2013), paras 67.

7 See I Mevorach and A Walters, 'The Characterization of Pre-insolvency Proceedings in Private International Law' (EBOR 2020), 870–2. See also *In the matter of Gategroup Guarantee Limited* [2021] EWHC 304 (Ch), 17 February 2021 at [95].

8 This paragraph draws on I Kokorin, S Madaus and I Mevorach, 'Global Competition in Cross-Border Restructuring and Recognition of Centralized Group Solutions' 56(2) Texas Journal of International Law (2021) 138.

9 See LC Ho, 'England' in LC Ho (ed.), *A Commentary on the UNCITRAL Model Law*, 4th ed., Globe Law & Business (London), 2017, 169; S Atkins, 'Australia' in LC Ho (ed.), *A Commentary on the UNCITRAL Model Law*, 4th ed., Globe Law & Business (London), 2017, 22.

10 11 USC § 101(23); NF Hannan, *Cross-Border Insolvency: The Enactment and Interpretation of the UNCITRAL Model Law* 65 (Springer, 1st ed. 2017) (noting that this addition anticipates recognition of proceedings that aim to restructure the debt of a company which may otherwise be solvent). See also Singapore Companies Act s 354B, Sch 10, art 2(h).

tion, corporate reorganization, corporate readjustment or special liquidation proceeding.[11] Korean law 'specifically refers to, among others, rehabilitation, bankruptcy and other similar proceedings'.[12]

1. Collective Judicial or Administrative Proceeding

1.2.06 To qualify for recognition and assistance under the Model Law the relevant proceeding must be collective (in addition to satisfying the other elements of the definition discussed further below), because, in line with the norm of modified universalism,[13] the Model Law aims to 'provide a tool for achieving a coordinated, global solution for all stakeholders of an insolvency proceeding'.[14] Various types of proceedings may qualify as collective, including compulsory or voluntary, corporate or individual, winding-up or reorganization proceedings;[15] proceedings where the debtor remains in control subject to court oversight;[16] or proceedings commenced under specific circumstances where the debtor is not in fact insolvent.[17]

1.2.07 A key consideration in this respect is whether substantially all of the assets and liabilities of the debtor are dealt with in the proceeding. Thus, the requirement for 'collectivity' rules out de facto collection proceedings that enable individual creditors or groups of creditors to enforce their claims, such as a receivership

---

11 K Yamamoto, 'New Japanese Legislation on Cross-border Insolvency as Compared with the UNCITRAL Model Law' 11 Int'l Insolvency Rev. 67, 71 (2002) (noting that a Japanese court would recognize as a foreign insolvency proceeding a proceeding that does not make debtor's insolvency a precondition for its commencement).

12 Wai Yee Wan and G. McCormack, 'Implementing Strategies for the Model Law on Cross-Border Insolvency: The Divergence in Asia-Pacific and Lessons for UNCITRAL' 36 Emory Bankr Dev J 59, 79 (2020) (arguing that schemes of arrangement are likely to be considered similar to rehabilitation proceedings in South Korea).

13 Namely a global approach to multinational default, modified to fit different business structures and insolvency scenarios (see JL Westbrook, 'A Global Solution to Multinational Default' (2000) 98 Mich L Rev 2276; I Mevorach, *The Future of Cross-Border Insolvency, Overcoming Biases and Closing Gaps* (OUP 2018), 12–28; I Mevorach, 'Modified Universalism as Customary International Law' 96 Texas Law Review (2018) 1403. See also *Re OJSC International Bank of Azerbaijan* [2018] EWCA Civ 2802 at [31]; *In the matter of gategroup Guarantee Limited* [2021] EWHC 304 (Ch) 17 February 2021 at [95].

14 UNCITRAL Model Law on Cross-Border Insolvency (1997), Guide to Enactment and Interpretation (2013), para 69.

15 UNCITRAL Model Law on Cross-Border Insolvency (1997), Guide to Enactment and Interpretation (2013), para 71.

16 UNCITRAL Model Law on Cross-Border Insolvency (1997), Guide to Enactment and Interpretation (2013), para 71. See also IF Fletcher, *Insolvency in Private International Law* (OUP 2007) 456.

17 UNCITRAL Model Law on Cross-Border Insolvency (1997), Guide to Enactment and Interpretation (2013), para 72 (noting, for example, 'cessation of payments by the debtor or certain actions of the debtor such as a corporate decision, dissipation of its assets or abandonment of its establishment'). See also G Ray Warner 'Comparative Collectivity – EU and US Approaches' (International Insolvency Review 2023).

instigated by a secured creditor.[18] In *Re ABC Learning Centres Limited*,[19] the United States bankruptcy court recognized a proceeding regarding an Australian company as a foreign proceeding even though the company's assets were under the control of a receiver acting for the secured creditors, because the receivership operated in conjunction with its voluntary winding up and therefore did not impact on the proceeding's collective nature.[20] In *Innua Can Ltd*[21] the United States bankruptcy court recognized a foreign receivership finding that it was a foreign proceeding because the originating court had declared the receiver to be the foreign representative of a foreign proceeding and authorized them to seek recognition of that proceeding in the receiving State.[22]

Financial adjustments on a purely contractual basis that do not lead to the opening of insolvency proceeding are ruled out.[23] The Guide to Enactment and Interpretation notes that such procedures 'would generally not satisfy the requirement for collectivity nor for control or supervision by the court'. Indeed, such arrangements are not 'proceedings'.[24] In *re Betcorp Ltd*,[25] the United States bankruptcy court noted in this respect that '[I]n the context of corporate insolvencies, the hallmark of a "proceeding" is a statutory framework that constrains a company's actions and that regulates the final distribution of a company's assets'.[26] **1.2.08**

However, proceedings are not necessarily ruled out because they leave a class of creditors' rights unaffected.[27] The Guide to Enactment and Interpretation gives the example of insolvency proceedings that exclude encumbered assets from the insolvency estate, leaving those assets unaffected by the commencement of the proceedings and allowing secured creditors to pursue their rights **1.2.09**

18 UNCITRAL Model Law on Cross-Border Insolvency (1997), Guide to Enactment and Interpretation (2013), para. 69. See also *In re Betcorp Ltd* 400 BR 266 (Bkrtcy D Nev 2009) p 281; *In re Gold & Honey, Ltd* 410 BR 357 (Bkrtcy EDNY 2009) pp 369–71; *In re Ashapura Minechem Ltd* 480 BR 129 (Bkrtcy SDNY 2012); I Mevorach and A Walters, 'The Characterization of Pre-insolvency Proceedings in Private International Law' (EBOR 2020), 871.

19 In *re ABC Learning Centres Ltd*, Case No 12-2808 (3rd Cir, 27 August 2013).

20 See S Atkins, 'Australia' in LC Ho (ed.), *A Commentary on the UNCITRAL Model Law*, 4th ed., Globe Law & Business (London), 2017, 25.

21 *Innua Can., Ltd.*, case No. 09-16362 (Bankr. DNJ Apr. 15, 2009).

22 Ibid, at p 4.

23 UNCITRAL Model Law on Cross-Border Insolvency (1997), Guide to Enactment and Interpretation (2013), para 78.

24 See I Mevorach and A Walters, 'The Characterization of Pre-insolvency Proceedings in Private International Law' (EBOR 2020), 871.

25 *In re Betcorp Ltd* 400 BR 266 (Bkrtcy D Nev 2009).

26 Ibid 278.

27 UNCITRAL Model Law on Cross-Border Insolvency (1997), Guide to Enactment and Interpretation (2013), para 70. I Mevorach and A Walters, 'The Characterization of Pre-insolvency Proceedings in Private International Law' (EBOR 2020) 871.

outside of the insolvency law.[28] Such is the case, for example, in the winding-up proceeding under the UK Insolvency Act 1986, which is regarded as a collective execution for unsecured creditors.[29] Various types of restructurings and arrangements may also qualify,[30] and collectivity may not rule out the type of restructuring that addresses balance sheet liabilities while leaving the claims of operating creditors untouched on the argument that the restructuring affects, and affords due process rights, to all creditors included within its scope.[31]

1.2.10 The collective proceeding should be judicial or administrative. This element of the definition has been interpreted broadly.[32] It is sufficient that the proceeding is either administrative or judicial.[33] The judicial character of the proceeding may be satisfied when representatives, such as managers, receivers, liquidators, or administrators, are appointed by the court,[34] or where there is an element of court supervision.[35]

2. In a Foreign State

1.2.11 The proceeding should take place in a foreign State. The critical factor in determining the (foreign) location of the proceedings has been the jurisdiction pursuant to whose law the proceedings is being conducted.[36]

---

28 UNCITRAL Model Law on Cross-Border Insolvency (1997), Guide to Enactment and Interpretation (2013), para 70.

29 See *Buchler v Talbot* [2004] UKHL 9, [2004] 2 AC 298, [28]–[30] (Lord Hofmann), [51]–[52] (Lord Millett).

30 See *In the matter of gategroup Guarantee Limited* [2021] EWHC 304 (Ch) 17 February 2021 at [100] where Mr Justice Zaccaroly stated with regard to the UK restructuring plan proceedings that 'proceedings designed to enable a company in financial difficulties to reach a composition or arrangement […] with its creditors involves the same peculiar feature as a straightforward bankruptcy or winding-up. The need for the composition or arrangement arises from the company's inability to satisfy the claims of all its creditors. There is inherently competition between the company's creditors, requiring a collective solution that is fair to all'.

31 See I Mevorach and A Walters, 'The Characterization of Pre-insolvency Proceedings in Private International Law' (EBOR 2020) 871 (referring to H Seife and F Vazquez, 'US Courts Should Continue to Grant Recognition to Schemes of Arrangement of Solvent Insurance Companies' (2008) 17 Norton J of Bankr L & P 571, 576 in relation to UK schemes of arrangement).

32 See LC Ho, 'England' in LC Ho (ed.), *A Commentary on the UNCITRAL Model Law*, 4th ed., Globe Law & Business (London), 2017, 181.

33 See eg *In re ABC Learning Centres Ltd*, 445 BR 318, 328 (Bankr D Del 2010), aff'd *In re ABC Learning Centres Ltd*, 728 F3d 301 (3d Cir Del 2013).

34 See eg *Re Stanford International Bank* [2010] EWCA Civ 137; [2011] Ch 33 at [27]; *In re British American Isle of Venice (BVI) Ltd*, 441 BR 713, 719 (Bankr SD Fla 2010).

35 *Re Stanford International Bank* [2010] EWCA Civ 137; [2011] Ch 33 at [15].

36 See *Re Stanford International Bank* [2010] EWCA Civ 137; [2011] Ch 33 at [27]; LC Ho, "England" in LC Ho (ed.), *A Commentary on the UNCITRAL Model Law*, 4th ed., Globe Law & Business (London), 2017, 183.

'Updates to UNCITRAL Model Law on Cross-Border Insolvency: The Judicial Perspective'[37] notes that very little consideration has been given to this element of the definition. It refers to *In the matter of NMC Healthcare Ltd*,[38] which has considered this term. In this case, recognition was sought in England of an administration taking place in the Abu Dhabi Global Market (ADGM) which is a special financial free zone within the United Arab Emirates (UAE) and which exists pursuant to the federal laws of the UAE. The court found that even though the ADGM was not itself a foreign State, the proceeding was taking place in a foreign State, namely the UAE, which had multiple applicable laws. **1.2.12**

3. Pursuant to a Law Related to Insolvency

The Model Law acknowledges that foreign proceedings which address the debtor's insolvency or severe financial distress may not necessarily take place pursuant to a law that is labelled insolvency law, and therefore the definition refers more broadly to 'a law related to insolvency'. The definition intends to capture a range of rules and laws which may not relate exclusively to insolvency.[39] Function carries more weight than form.[40] Thus, for example, a company law proceeding, such as a UK scheme of arrangement pursuant to Part 26 of the United Kingdom Companies Act 2006, when used for distressed/insolvent restructurings could be a proceeding pursuant to a law relating to insolvency under the Model Law.[41] In *Syncreon Group BV*[42] the Canadian court recognized an English scheme of arrangement as a foreign proceeding, concluding that the proceeding was pursuant to a law relating to insolvency. Insolvency was interpreted to include a company that 'was reasonably expected to run out of liquidity within reasonable proximity of time as compared with the time reasonably required to implement a restructuring'.[43] In *Re Avanti*,[44] the United States bankruptcy court recognized and enforced a scheme of arrangement **1.2.13**

37 UNCITRAL, Updates to 'UNCITRAL Model Law on Cross-Border Insolvency: The Judicial Perspective' A/CN.9/WG.V/WP.180, para 21.

38 *NMC Healthcare Limited* (in Administration) [2021] EWHC 1806 (Ch).

39 UNCITRAL Model Law on Cross-Border Insolvency (1997), Guide to Enactment and Interpretation (2013), para 73.

40 I Mevorach and A Walters, 'The Characterization of Pre-insolvency Proceedings in Private International Law' (EBOR 2020) 871.

41 See eg *In re Agrokor dd* [2017] EWHC 2791 (Ch), [2018] Bus LR 64 at [55]. It is doubtful, however, if a foreign scheme of arrangement of a solvent entity can qualify (see LC Ho, 'England' in LC Ho (ed.), *A Commentary on the UNCITRAL Model Law*, 4th ed., Globe Law & Business (London), 2017, 178).

42 *Syncreon Group BV* 2019 ONSC 5774.

43 Ibid at [28].

44 *Avanti Communications Group PLC*, 582 BR 603 (Bankr SDNY 2018).

from the United Kingdom, and in *Re Cell C Proprietary Ltd*,[45] the United States bankruptcy court recognized such proceedings from South Africa.

1.2.14 The definition does not intend, however, to refer to 'a simple proceeding for a solvent legal entity that does not seek to restructure the financial affairs of the entity, but rather to dissolve its legal status'.[46] As noted above,[47] some enactments of the Model Law have expanded the definition to explicitly include 'adjustment of debt' within its scope. 'Updates to UNCITRAL Model Law on Cross-Border Insolvency: The Judicial Perspective' notes that the 'addition of those words may affect the recognition of scheme proceedings in the United States'.[48] The legislative history indeed indicates that this addition reflects a wide scope of the Model Law; thus, Chapter 15 is not limited to proceedings involving only debtors which are technically insolvent.[49]

1.2.15 The law which enables the proceeding should relate to insolvency, but insolvency may not necessarily be the ground for opening the proceeding. In *Re Stanford International Bank Ltd*[50] the English Court of Appeal confirmed that the Antiguan winding up proceeding occurred pursuant to a law related to insolvency even though the relevant law included several possible grounds for winding up (including insolvency).[51] The Supreme Court of New South Wales has followed this approach in *Re Chow Cho Poon (Private) Limited*.[52] In *Re Betcorp Limited*,[53] the United States bankruptcy court concluded that an Australian members' voluntary winding up proceeding was a 'foreign proceeding' under Chapter 15.[54] Even though the debtor was not insolvent, the proceeding was considered to be one pursuant to a law related to insolvency because the relevant legislation contained provisions that dealt with corporate insolvency.[55] In *Sturgeon*,[56] the English court denied recognition to a procedure

45 *In re Cell C Proprietary Ltd* 571 BR 542 (Bankr SDNY 2017).

46 UNCITRAL Model Law on Cross-Border Insolvency (1997), Guide to Enactment and Interpretation (2013), para 73.

47 See n 10 above and accompanied text.

48 UNCITRAL, 'Updates to "UNCITRAL Model Law on Cross-Border Insolvency: The Judicial Perspective"' A/CN.9/WG.V/WP.180, fn 11.

49 See Martin, 'United States' in LC Ho (ed.), *A Commentary on the UNCITRAL Model Law*, 4th ed., Globe Law & Business (London), 2017, 642.

50 *Re Stanford International Bank Limited* [2010] EWCA Civ 137; [2010] 3 WLR 941.

51 Ibid at [15].

52 *Re Chow Cho Poon (Private) Limited* [2011] NSWSC 300.

53 *In re Betcorp Ltd* 400 BR 266 (Bkrtcy D Nev 2009).

54 Chapter 15 U.S. Bankruptcy Code (11 USC) implements the Model Law in the United States.

55 See also S Atkins, 'Australia' in LC Ho (ed.), *A Commentary on the UNCITRAL Model Law*, 4th ed., Globe Law & Business (London), 2017, 24–5.

56 *Sturgeon Central Asia Balanced Fund* [2020] EWHC 123.

regarding a solvent legal entity that did not seek to restructure the financial affairs of the entity but rather to dissolve its legal status.

4. Control or Supervision by a Foreign Court

The proceeding should be subject to formal control or supervision by a foreign court and such control/supervision should be with regard to both the assets and affairs of the debtor.[57] However, the Model Law does not prescribe the level of supervision or control required, nor does it prescribe the time at which that control/supervision should take place.[58] Thus, control/supervision may be potential rather than actual;[59] debtor-in-possession (full or partial) type of proceedings are covered, as well as expedited proceedings where a court exercises control at a late stage of the process, or proceedings where the control/supervision has occurred before the recognition application.[60] The control or supervision may not be exercised directly,[61] and a proceeding administered by an insolvency practitioner would still qualify as long as the insolvency practitioner is subject to court supervision.[62] **1.2.16**

5. For the Purpose of Reorganization or Liquidation

The foreign proceeding must also be for the purpose of liquidation or reorganization. Other procedures – for example, simply aimed at preserving assets, or preventing detriment to investors,[63] or merely to allow examination of the debtor,[64] or procedures in which the powers conferred on the foreign representative are more limited than the typical powers conferred in liquidation or reorganization – are not included.[65] As noted above, procedures for financial adjustments on a purely contractual basis that do not lead to the opening of **1.2.17**

57 UNCITRAL Model Law on Cross-Border Insolvency (1997), Guide to Enactment and Interpretation (2013), para 76. See also *In re Gold & Honey Ltd* 410 BR 357, 371 (Bkrtcy EDNY 2009).

58 UNCITRAL Model Law on Cross-Border Insolvency (1997), Guide to Enactment and Interpretation (2013), paras 74–75.

59 *Agrokor DD* [2017] EWHC 2791 (Ch) at [79].

60 GEI, paras 74–75.

61 *Agrokor DD* [2017] EWHC 2791 (Ch) at [79], [93].

62 UNCITRAL Model Law on Cross-Border Insolvency (1997), Guide to Enactment and Interpretation (2013), para 74.

63 UNCITRAL Model Law on Cross-Border Insolvency (1997), Guide to Enactment and Interpretation (2013), para 77. See also *Re Stanford International Bank Ltd* [2010] 3WLR 941.

64 See *In re British American Insurance Company Limited* 425 BR 884, 906, 907 (Bankr SD Fla 2010).

65 UNCITRAL Model Law on Cross-Border Insolvency (1997), Guide to Enactment and Interpretation (2013), para 77.

insolvency proceeding are also ruled out (these would also not satisfy the collectivity and court control/supervision requirements).[66]

1.2.18 But 'liquidation or reorganization' is otherwise broad and in conjunction with the other elements of the definition of 'foreign proceeding' seem to encompass a variety of proceedings.[67] In *Re British American Insurance Company Limited*,[68] the United States bankruptcy court held in relation to an application for recognition of Bahamas and Saint Vincent and the Grenadines as foreign proceedings that the determination whether the proceeding is for the purpose of liquidation or reorganization should consider circumstances arising after the filing of the recognition petition. The court also clarified that this element of the definition does not require that the proceeding results in an overall reorganization or winding up. Such interpretation would be too narrow, in particular in the context of recognition of a foreign non-main proceeding.[69] In *re Oversight and Control Commission of Avanzit SA*,[70] the United States bankruptcy court confirmed regarding this element of the definition that 'reorganization' can include the implementation stage of a plan.[71] In *Agrokor*,[72] the English court, applying the CBIR 2006,[73] recognized 'extraordinary administration proceedings' that were brought under special legislation to address the insolvency of the Croatian Agrokor group of companies. The court rejected the argument that recognition should be denied because the purpose of this proceeding was to protect a systemically important business rather than to reorganize the company's affairs. The court found that these two purposes were not incompatible.[74] The application also fell within the scope of the CBIR 2006, notwithstanding that in Croatia the proceedings encompassed not just the Agrokor company regarding which recognition was sought but also its affiliates, in a single group proceeding.[75]

66 UNCITRAL Model Law on Cross-Border Insolvency (1997), Guide to Enactment and Interpretation (2013), para 78.

67 See I Mevorach and A Walters, 'The Characterization of Pre-insolvency Proceedings in Private International Law' (EBOR 2020) 872 (arguing that the definition can cover proceedings that lead to one or more of a range of outcomes – break-up sales, going concern sales, wholesale restructurings, and skinny restructurings involving balance-sheet 'reorganization').

68 *In re British American Insurance Company Limited* 425 BR 884 (Bankr SD Fla 2010).

69 Ibid at pp 906–8.

70 *In re Oversight and Control Commission of Avanzit SA* 385 BR 525 (Bankr SDNY 2008).

71 Ibid at pp 533–4.

72 *Agrokor DD* [2017] EWHC 2791 (Ch).

73 In Great Britain, the Model Law is implemented by the Cross-Border Insolvency Regulations 2006 ('CBIR 2006').

74 *Agrokor DD* [2017] EWHC 2791 (Ch) at [100]–[108].

75 Ibid at [52]–[54].

6. Interim Proceeding

Foreign proceeding includes interim proceedings (and similarly, 'foreign representative' defined in Article 2(d), includes a representative 'appointed on an interim basis'). The Guide to Enactment and Interpretation explains the importance of including interim proceedings when enacting the definition even if it is not a known concept in the enacting State, because such proceedings are very common, and in many cases insolvency proceedings will initially be commenced and often for a prolonged period of time be conducted as interim proceedings. Such proceedings should meet all the other requirements of foreign proceedings and hence should not be distinguished from other insolvency proceedings.[76] **1.2.19**

Thus, for example, an English provisional liquidation qualifies for this purpose,[77] and a foreign provisional liquidation would be recognized as foreign proceeding under the CBIR 2006. In *Zayed v Cook*[78] the Canadian court recognized a United States receivership proceeding, concluding that it represented an initial stage of asset preservation that would lead to liquidation for the benefit of creditors.[79] **1.2.20**

C. FOREIGN MAIN PROCEEDING

Article 2(b) defines 'foreign main proceeding' as a 'foreign proceeding taking place in the State where the debtor has the centre of its main interests'. The concepts of 'main proceeding' and 'centre of main interests' (COMI) are also central to the framework prescribed by the EU Regulation on Insolvency Proceedings (EU Regulation).[80] Indeed, the Model Law has followed in this respect the developments in the EU and the formulation of these concepts that was initially adopted in the EU Convention on Insolvency Proceedings.[81] The Guide to Enactment and Interpretation also notes that jurisprudence **1.2.21**

76 UNCITRAL Model Law on Cross-Border Insolvency (1997), Guide to Enactment and Interpretation (2013), para 79.

77 See IF Fletcher, *Insolvency in Private International Law* (OUP 2007) 456–7; *In re Madoff Securities International Limited*, Case No 09-12998 (BRL) (Bankr SDNY 11 June 2009).

78 *Zayed v Cook* [2009] OJ No 5513.

79 Ibid at [10]–[11].

80 Regulation (EU) 2015/848 of the European Parliament and of the Council of 20 May 2015 on insolvency proceedings, Article 3.

81 UNCITRAL Model Law on Cross-Border Insolvency (1997), Guide to Enactment and Interpretation (2013), para 81.

interpreting the EU Regulation may also be relevant to interpretation of the Model Law.[82]

1.2.22 The determination that a foreign proceeding is a main proceeding is significant because the Model Law envisages that most of the assistance and relief will be granted to such proceedings.[83] Some of the relief is also automatic upon recognition of the proceeding as main proceeding.[84] It is also envisaged that the debtor will be subjected to only one foreign main proceeding.[85] This corresponds with the norm of modified universalism which is premised on deference to a global collective primary process that has a universal scope, with a secondary/ancillary role to other proceedings.[86]

1.2.23 COMI is not defined in the Model Law, except that Article 16 provides that COMI is presumed to be at the debtor's registered office, or habitual residence in the case of an individual. It was also not defined in the original formulation in the EU Regulation. However, the recast EU Regulation (2015) now provides that the COMI 'shall be the place where the debtor conducts the administration of its interests on a regular basis and which is ascertainable by third parties'.[87] This corresponds with the earlier explanation of the notion in the recitals of the original regulation,[88] and with the European Court of Justice decision in *Interedil*.[89] The Guide to Enactment and Interpretation of the Model Law in its revised version of 2013 also clarifies that the main factors for determining COMI are the location of the debtor's central administration which is readily ascertainable by creditors.[90] The concept of COMI, including

82 Ibid, para 82.

83 See eg Model Law, Article 21(3).

84 Model Law, Article 20.

85 See *In re British American Insurance Company Limited* 425 BR 884, 908 (Bankr SD Fla 2010) where the United States bankruptcy court noted that 'chapter 15 contemplates recognition of no more than one main proceeding…'.

86 See n 13 and accompanying text. See also *In re British American Insurance Company Limited* 425 BR 884, 908 (Bankr SD Fla 2010) where the United States bankruptcy court noted that 'A foreign main proceeding, by definition pending in the country where the debtor has its centre of main interest, is likely the primary tool for a reorganization or liquidation of the debtor…'.

87 Regulation (EU) 2015/848 of the European Parliament and of the Council of 20 May 2015 on insolvency proceedings, Article 3. Regarding the presumption, the Recast Regulation added that '[T]he presumption shall only apply if the registered office has not been moved to another member State within the 3-month period prior to the request for the opening of insolvency proceedings'. Or, regarding individuals, '[T]he presumption shall only apply if the habitual residence has not been moved to another member State within the 6-month period prior to the request for the opening of insolvency proceedings'.

88 COUNCIL REGULATION (EC) No 1346/2000, Recital 13.

89 Case C-396/09 *Interedil Srl, in liquidation v Fallimento Interedil Srl and Intesa Gestione Crediti SpA* ECLI:EU:C:2011:671.

90 UNCITRAL Model Law on Cross-Border Insolvency (1997), Guide to Enactment and Interpretation (2013), para 145. The Guide to Enactment and Interpretation continues to explain that when these main factors do not yield a clear answer a number of other factors may be considered (see paras 146–147).

the presumption, time of COMI assessment and movement of COMI, is discussed later in the Commentary in relation to Articles 16–17.

The definition refers to a proceeding 'taking place in the State…' (where the debtor has its COMI). In the United States, Chapter 15 uses the term 'pending' instead of 'taking place'. In *Oversight & Control Commission of Avanzit*,[91] the United States Bankruptcy Court indicated that presumably the same meaning was intended, and this phrase refers to the location of the foreign case, not to the stage (status) of the proceeding. Thus, assistance and cooperation should also be granted even if the foreign court had already approved a reorganization plan.[92] **1.2.24**

D. FOREIGN NON-MAIN PROCEEDING AND ESTABLISHMENT

Article 2(c) defines 'foreign non-main proceeding' as a foreign proceeding, other than a foreign main proceeding, taking place in a State where the debtor has an 'establishment'. Establishment is defined in Article 2(f) to mean any place of operations where the debtor carries out a non-transitory economic activity with human means and goods or services. These definitions are relevant for the operation of key provisions in the Model Law. Thus, Article 17, concerning the recognition of a foreign proceeding, requires that foreign proceedings be recognized as non-main proceedings if they take place in a State where the debtor has an establishment.[93] Article 21 provides that relief to foreign non-main proceedings is discretionary and when granted the court must be satisfied that the relief relates to assets that, under the law of the receiving State, should be administered in the foreign non-main proceeding or concern information required in that proceeding.[94] **1.2.25**

The definition of establishment was inspired by the equivalent definition in the EU Regulation,[95] and the Guide to Enactment and Interpretation refers in this respect to the Virgos-Schmit Report on the Convention (that preceded the Regulation), which emphasizes the need for 'a minimum level of organ- **1.2.26**

91 *Oversight & Control Commission of Avanzit, S.A* 385 BR 525, 535–538 (Bankr SDNY 2008).

92 See also UNCITRAL Digest of Case Law on the UNCITRAL Model Law on Cross-Border Insolvency, United Nations, Vienna 2021, pp 8, 14.

93 See Article 17(2)(b) of the Model Law.

94 See Article 21(3) of the Model Law.

95 The Recast EU Regulation on Insolvency Proceeding (2015), Article 2(10) now refers to the carrying on of non-transitory economic activity with human means and assets.

ization' and a 'certain stability' to qualify as an establishment.[96] The Guide to Enactment and Interpretation further explains that, unlike the notion of main proceeding determined by reference to the location of the COMI which is an undefined term, the enquiry concerning non-main proceedings and establishment is factual and is not assisted by any presumption.[97] However, like main proceedings and COMI, the enquiry must be based on objective criteria ascertainable by third parties.[98] According to the Guide to Enactment, it should be assessed in relation to the date of commencement of the foreign proceeding,[99] and should be a holistic consideration as the definition should be read as a whole rather than being broken down into discrete elements.[100] The timing of the COMI determination is discussed later in the Commentary in relation to Article 17.

1.2.27 Essentially, an establishment requires a fixed place of business and the mere presence of assets without any activity does not suffice.[101] Thus for example, in *Pirogova*,[102] a US court refused to recognize a foreign proceeding commenced in Russia as either a main or non-main proceeding, finding with regard to the existence of an establishment that even if the debtor owned an apartment in Russia this was insufficient as the debtor did not carry out non-transitory activities in that place and had no place of operations in Russia.[103]

1.2.28 The definitions of foreign non-main proceeding and establishment have been enacted with some modifications, for example in Great Britain, where the CBIR 2006 replaces 'goods' with 'assets' in the definition of establishment, to cover not only goods but also land and intangible property.[104] In Canada, the

---

96 UNCITRAL Model Law on Cross-Border Insolvency (1997), Guide to Enactment and Interpretation (2013), para 89 (referring to M Virgos and E Schmit, *Report on the Convention on Insolvency Proceedings*, Brussels 3 May 1996, para 7.1).

97 UNCITRAL Model Law on Cross-Border Insolvency (1997), Guide to Enactment and Interpretation (2013), para 90.

98 See Case C-396/09 *Interedil Srl, in liquidation v Fallimento Interedil Srl and Intesa Gestione Crediti SpA* ECLI:EU:C:2011:671 at [63]; LC Ho, 'England' in LC Ho (ed.), *A Commentary on the UNCITRAL Model Law*, 4th ed., Globe Law & Business (London), 2017, 174.

99 UNCITRAL Model Law on Cross-Border Insolvency (1997), Guide to Enactment and Interpretation (2013) para 159 (in relation to the relevant date for assessing COMI).

100 *Trustees of the Olympic Airlines SA Pension & Life Assurance Scheme v Olympic Airlines SA* [2015] UKSC 27; [2015] 1 WLR 2399 at [13].

101 See UNCITRAL Model Law on Cross-Border Insolvency (1997), Guide to Enactment and Interpretation (2013) para 90; *Trustees of the Olympic Airlines SA Pension & Life Assurance Scheme v Olympic Airlines SA* [2015] UKSC 27; [2015] 1 WLR 2399 at [13].

102 *In re Pirogova*, 593 B.R. 402 (Bankr. SDNY 2018).

103 See also UNCITRAL, Updates to 'UNCITRAL Model Law on Cross-Border Insolvency: The Judicial Perspective' A/CN.9/WG.V/WP.180, para 39.

104 See K van Zwieten, *Goode on Principles of Corporate Insolvency Law* (5th edition, Sweet and Maxwell 2019) 921.

Companies' Creditors Arrangement Act defines a foreign non-main proceeding as 'a foreign proceeding, other than a foreign main proceeding',[105] dropping the establishment requirement for qualification as a non-main proceeding. Thus, for example, in *Syncreon Group BV*,[106] the Canadian court granted recognition of an English scheme of arrangement adopted with respect to a Dutch incorporated company. It reasoned that since the debtor did not have a COMI in the UK, the foreign proceeding should therefore be recognized as a non-main proceeding.[107]

Recognition of a foreign non-main proceeding may also facilitate the centralization of group proceedings and their recognition abroad in countries that adopted the Model Law. In *Videology*[108] an English court, applying the CBIR, recognized US Chapter 11 proceedings in relation to Videology Inc, a company incorporated in the US, and its wholly-owned subsidiary Videology Ltd, a company incorporated in the UK. The court found that the COMI of the parent company, Videology Inc, was the US and the Chapter 11 proceeding in relation to this entity was recognized as a foreign main proceeding. In respect of Videology Ltd it was observed that the UK, as the place of its registered office, is also where its main assets, staff, and premises are located and where trading relationships are established – information that was also readily ascertainable by third parties. Thus, the court held that the COMI of Videology Ltd is the UK and rejected the application to recognize Chapter 11 proceedings as foreign main proceedings. Yet, it was observed that the connections with the US justified the proceedings to be recognized as foreign non-main proceedings.[109] The company carried out activities that were economic in nature through the human agency of the company's director and with the services of the senior management of the parent company, who were largely based at the group's head office.[110] **1.2.29**

105 Companies' Creditors Arrangement Act (S.C., 1985, c. C-36), at § 45(1).

106 *Syncreon Group B.V., Re*, 2019 ONSC 5774. See also I Kokorin, S Madaus and I Mevorach, 'Global Competition in Cross-Border Restructuring and Recognition of Centralized Group Solutions' 56(2) Texas Journal of International Law (2021) 136.

107 See I Kokorin, S Madaus and I Mevorach, 'Global Competition in Cross-Border Restructuring and Recognition of Centralized Group Solutions' 56(2) Texas Journal of International Law (2021) 136 (noting in regard to restructuring proceedings that due to the differences in transposition of the MLCBI and its interpretation, there could be a situation where the same scheme is eligible for recognition in some countries but cannot be recognized in others).

108 *Re Videology Limited* [2018] EWHC 2186 (Ch) [2019] BCC 195.

109 Ibid at [76].

110 Ibid at [80].

1.2.30 A different conclusion was reached by a US court in *Mood Media Corp.*[111] In this case a Canadian company, together with 14 direct and indirect US subsidiaries, was subject to an arrangement in Canada. In refusing recognition of the arrangement as applied to the US entities, the US court found that the US companies were beneficiaries rather than debtors in the foreign proceedings and had no office or physical presence in Canada. Therefore, they did not maintain a place of operations in Canada and did not have a COMI or establishment there.[112]

E. FOREIGN REPRESENTATIVE

1.2.31 Foreign representative is defined in Article 2(d) to mean 'a person or body, including one appointed on an interim basis, authorized in a foreign proceeding to administer the reorganization or liquidation of the debtor's assets or affairs or to act as a representative of the foreign proceeding'. Thus, as the Guide to Enactment and Interpretation explains, the definition refers either to persons generally authorized to administer the foreign proceeding or to persons specifically authorized to represent the foreign proceeding.[113] The definition is broad: it requires authorization, though not necessarily by a court. The representative may be appointed by a special agency, they may be appointed on an interim basis,[114] and they may be debtors who remain in possession after the commencement of the proceedings.[115] The definition is also broad where it refers to a person or 'body' and thus it covers foreign representatives that are legal persons.[116]

1.2.32 In *Stanford*,[117] an English Court of Appeal recognized liquidators appointed in Antigua as foreign representatives in regard to an Antiguan winding-up proceeding. The court found that the liquidators were directed by the winding-up order to collect all the debtor's assets and hold them for the benefit of the relevant stakeholders pursuant to Antiguan law, and they were authorized to

---

111 *In re Mood Media Corporation, et al.*, 569 BR 558 (Bankr. SDNY 2017).

112 Ibid at 561–2; see also I Kokorin, S Madaus and I Mevorach, 'Global Competition in Cross-Border Restructuring and Recognition of Centralized Group Solutions' 56(2) Texas Journal of International Law (2021).

113 UNCITRAL Model Law on Cross-Border Insolvency (1997), Guide to Enactment and Interpretation (2013), para 86.

114 See eg *United Drug (UK) Holdings v Bilcare Singapore* [2013] EWHC 4335 (Ch) (where interim judicial managers appointed in Singapore under Singapore insolvency law have been recognized as foreign representatives by an English Court).

115 Ibid.

116 See *In re Oversight and Control Commission of Avanzit SA* 385 BR 525, 540 (Bankr SDNY 2008).

117 Re *Stanford International Bank* [2010] EWCA Civ 137; [2011] Ch 33.

apply for recognition in other jurisdictions.[118] Less convincingly, the English Court of Appeal in *Stanford* affirmed a first instance decision that the US receiver applying for recognition in order to collect assets located in the UK is not a foreign representative. The court considered that the receiver appointed in regard to the US receivership had not yet been authorized to administer the debtor's liquidation or reorganization, even if the receivership is a foreign proceeding.[119] This decision has been criticized as wrongly applying the definition – if the receivership proceeding is categorized as a foreign proceeding then the receivership is a foreign representative, who indeed was appointed in this proceeding to collect assets wherever located and commence or become party to actions as necessary to preserve the estate and carry out the receiver's mandate.[120]

F. FOREIGN COURT

As discussed above, qualification as a foreign proceeding requires that the assets and affairs of the debtor are subject to control or supervision by a foreign court (for the purpose of reorganization or liquidation).[121] Article 2(e) defines foreign court as 'a judicial or other authority competent to control or supervise a foreign proceeding'. The definition is broad where it refers to both courts and non-judicial authorities (that are competent to control or supervise a foreign proceeding).[122] Thus, although the Model Law refers in short to the 'court' in various articles (for example concerning recognition or cooperation), pursuant to this definition it is in fact not necessarily a court that would supervise and apply the relevant law in the particular country where proceedings were commenced.[123] The Model Law accommodates varied scenarios in terms of the institutions involved.[124] However, mere supervision of an insolvency representative by a licensing authority would not be sufficient.[125] **1.2.33**

118 Ibid at [28].

119 Re *Stanford International Bank* [2010] EWCA Civ 137; [2011] Ch 33 at [29].

120 LC Ho, 'England' in LC Ho (ed.), *A Commentary on the UNCITRAL Model Law*, 4th ed., Globe Law & Business (London), 2017, 196.

121 See section B above.

122 See also UNCITRAL Model Law on Cross-Border Insolvency (1997), Guide to Enactment and Interpretation (2013), para 87.

123 See also IF Fletcher, *Insolvency in Private International Law* (OUP 2007) 459.

124 See also LC Ho, 'England' in LC Ho (ed.), *A Commentary on the UNCITRAL Model Law*, 4th ed., Globe Law & Business (London), 2017, 170 (noting that the definition would probably cover foreign regulatory authorities).

125 UNCITRAL Model Law on Cross-Border Insolvency (1997), Guide to Enactment and Interpretation (2013), para 74.

Article 3

INTERNATIONAL OBLIGATIONS OF THIS STATE

Irit Mevorach

To the extent that this Law conflicts with an obligation of this State arising out of any treaty or other form of agreement to which it is a party with one or more other States, the requirements of the treaty or agreement prevail.

A. INTRODUCTION TO ARTICLE 3

1.3.1 Article 3 explains that to the extent that legislation implementing the Model Law in the enacting State conflicts with any international obligation of the enacting State, the latter prevails and will displace the relevant provision in the national law. This article reflects the principle of supremacy of international obligations over domestic law and is consistent with provisions in other UNCITRAL model laws.[1]

1.3.2 The Guide to Enactment and Interpretation of the Model Law advises, however, to be cautious when enacting this Article to avoid excessive restriction of the effects of the legislation enacting the Model Law. International obligations may be given precedence only where there is a sufficient link between the international obligation concerned and the issue governed by the provision

1 See UNCITRAL Model Law on Cross-Border Insolvency (1997), Guide to Enactment and Interpretation (2013), para 91. See also UNCITRAL Digest of Case Law on the UNCITRAL Model Law on Cross-Border Insolvency, United Nations, Vienna 2021, 17.

of the national law enacting relevant articles of the Model Law.[2] The need to implement Article 3 (and the manner in which it may be implemented) may also depend on the way the enacting State deals with international treaties and agreements and whether binding treaties are self-executing or require internal legislation to become enforceable law.[3]

B. ENACTMENT AND APPLICATION OF ARTICLE 3

In Great Britain, prior to Brexit, the CBIR 2006[4] (Sch 1, art 3) governed the 'international obligations of Great Britain under the EC Insolvency Regulation' and provided that: 'To the extent that this Law conflicts with an obligation of the United Kingdom under the EC Insolvency Regulation, the requirements of the EC Insolvency Regulation prevail.' Article 3 could not be implemented verbatim because in the United Kingdom, international obligations based on treaties prevail only where the treaty obligations have already been enacted. The pre-Brexit implementation clarified the supremacy of EU law to the extent that there was conflict between the two regimes.[5] This article no longer features in the CBIR as (after 31 December 2020) the EU Regulation (Recast 2015) ceased to apply in the UK.[6] **1.3.3**

In the United States, Chapter 15 US Bankruptcy Code (11 USC)[7] implements Article 3 virtually verbatim in section 1503.[8] In Australia, Article 3 is enacted as drafted in the Model Law, via the Cross-Border Insolvency Act 2008 **1.3.4**

---

2 UNCITRAL Model Law on Cross-Border Insolvency (1997), Guide to Enactment and Interpretation (2013), para 92.

3 UNCITRAL Model Law on Cross-Border Insolvency (1997), Guide to Enactment and Interpretation (2013), para 93.

4 In Great Britain, the Model Law is implemented by the Cross-border Insolvency Regulations 2006 ("CBIR 2006").

5 See also LC Ho, 'England' in LC Ho (ed.), *A Commentary on the UNCITRAL Model Law*, 4th ed., Globe Law & Business (London), 2017, 197–8 commending this manner of implementation of Article 3 as it confirmed that 'the British Model Law and the EC Insolvency Regulation operate in parallel'. Courts had flexibility to apply the Model Law, including to cases where the Regulation applied, if there was no conflict with the Regulation. Ho criticized, however, the decision in *Re Stanford International Bank* (*Re Stanford International Bank)* [2010] EWCA Civ 137; [2011] Ch 33 where the court was not 'faithful to the tenor of parallel application' of the Model Law and the Regulation. It unnecessarily gave supremacy to the meaning of COMI based on the test promulgated by the European Court of Justice although there was no real conflict between the regimes in the circumstances.

6 See www .legislation .gov .uk/ uksi/ 2006/ 1030/ schedule/ 1/ part/ 1/ crossheading/ article -3 -international -obligations-of-great-britain-under-the-ec-insolvency-regulation.

7 Which implements the Model Law in the United States.

8 See https://usbankruptcycode.org/chapter-15-ancillary-and-other-cross-border-cases/subchapter-i-general -provisions/section-1503-international-obligations-of-the-united-states/.

(which enacted into Australian law the Model Law).[9] However, the intention is that 'the courts will attempt to read the Model Law and the international obligation so as not to conflict, especially if the international obligation addresses a subject matter less directly related than the Model Law to a case before the court'.[10] Australia is not a party to any such international agreement related to cross-border insolvency. Article 3 in any event has limited relevance in Australia because a treaty has effect only if implemented in internal law and in such a case 'the usual principles of statutory interpretation would apply to determine any questions of inconsistency'.[11]

1.3.5 The UNCITRAL Digest of Case Law on the UNCITRAL Model Law on Cross-Border Insolvency notes that there is no reported case law on issues of interpretation and application of Article 3.[12]

9 See www.legislation.gov.au/Details/C2021C00032 ('To the extent that this chapter conflicts with an obligation of the United States arising out of any treaty or other form of agreement to which it is a party with one or more other countries, the requirements of the treaty or agreement prevail').

10 C Martin, 'United States' in LC Ho (ed.), *A Commentary on the UNCITRAL Model Law*, 4th ed., Globe Law & Business (London), 2017, 642–3 (referring to House Report at 107).

11 S Atkins, 'Australia' in LC Ho (ed.), *A Commentary on the UNCITRAL Model Law*, 4th ed., Globe Law & Business (London), 2017, 27 (referring to Explanatory Memorandum, Cross-Border Insolvency Bill 2008, p 20).

12 The UNCITRAL Digest of Case Law on the UNCITRAL Model Law on Cross-Border Insolvency, United Nations, Vienna 2021, 17.

Article 4

[*COMPETENT COURT OR AUTHORITY*][1]

Irit Mevorach

The functions referred to in this Law relating to recognition of foreign proceedings and cooperation with foreign courts shall be performed by [*specify the court, courts, authority or authorities competent to perform those functions in the enacting State*].

---

[1] A State where certain functions relating to insolvency proceedings have been conferred upon government-appointed officials or bodies might wish to include in article 4 or elsewhere in chapter I the following provision:

Nothing in this Law affects the provisions in force in this State governing the authority of [*insert the title of the government appointed person or body*].

A. INTRODUCTION TO ARTICLE 4

Article 4 prompts enacting States to include in the legislation implementing the Model Law the relevant authorities that would perform the functions referred to in the Model Law in relation to recognition of foreign proceedings and cooperation with foreign courts, in particular if in the enacting State any of these functions are performed by an authority other than a court.[1] If the **1.4.1**

1 See UNCITRAL Model Law on Cross-Border Insolvency (1997), Guide to Enactment and Interpretation (2013), para 94.

competences of the various judicial functions lie in different courts, the enacting State may tailor the text to its own system of court competence.[2] The aim is to increase transparency and ease of use of the Model Law as implemented in the enacting State, especially by foreign representatives and foreign courts.[3]

1.4.2 The Guide to Enactment and Interpretation of the Model Law[4] also advises that in defining jurisdiction regarding the matters mentioned in this Article, the legislation should not 'unnecessarily limit the jurisdiction of other courts in the enacting State, in particular to entertain requests by foreign representatives for provisional relief'.[5]

1.4.3 Article 4 also notes in a footnote that if certain functions relating to insolvency proceedings have been entrusted to government-appointed officials or bodies, the enacting State might also wish to state that nothing in the legislation implementing the Model Law affects the provisions in force in the State governing the authority of such bodies. Government-appointed officials may typically be civil servants or judicial officers who may carry out their functions on a permanent basis, and the Model Law makes the point that it does not aim to restrict the authority of such officials.[6]

B. ENACTMENT AND APPLICATION OF ARTICLE 4

1.4.4 Enacting States have 'domesticated' Article 4 to identify the relevant authorities that shall perform the functions related to recognition of foreign proceedings and cooperation with foreign courts.

1.4.5 In Great Britain, the CBIR 2006[7] implements Article 4 and provides that the functions referred to in the law relating to recognition of foreign proceedings and cooperation with foreign courts shall be performed by the High Court and assigned to the Chancery Division, as regards England and Wales, and

---

2 See ibid, para 95.

3 Ibid. See also UNCITRAL Digest of Case Law on the UNCITRAL Model Law on Cross-Border Insolvency, United Nations, Vienna 2021, 18.

4 See n 1.

5 UNCITRAL Model Law on Cross-Border Insolvency (1997), Guide to Enactment and Interpretation (2013), para 96.

6 See also UNCITRAL Model Law on Cross-Border Insolvency (1997), Guide to Enactment and Interpretation (2013), paras 97–98.

7 In Great Britain, the Model Law is implemented by the Cross-border Insolvency Regulations 2006 ("CBIR 2006").

the Court of Session, as regards Scotland. Further subsections in the Article allocate jurisdiction within Great Britain.[8]

In *American Energy Group Ltd v Hycarbex Asia Pte Ltd*,[9] the English High Court considered an application to grant recognition to foreign winding-up proceedings opened in Singapore. The purpose of the application for recognition was to achieve a stay of an ICC arbitration brought by AEG to which Hycarbex was the third respondent. AEG therefore contested the application for recognition. One of the conditions of Article 17 of the Model Law as implemented in the CBIR is that the application for recognition has been submitted to the court referred to in Article 4. AEG argued that there was no sufficient jurisdictional connection to Great Britain per the connecting factors noted in the CBIR's implementation of Article 4. The court dismissed this argument. It concluded that on true construction of Article 4, it does not impose a threshold jurisdictional requirement. Rather, it specifies the courts which are competent to perform the functions relating to recognition of foreign proceedings and cooperation with foreign courts and it allocates jurisdiction as between the courts of England and Wales and the courts of Scotland.[10] **1.4.6**

In the United States, Chapter 15 US Bankruptcy Code (11 USC)[11] designates the court that is competent to exercise jurisdiction in aid of cases ancillary to foreign proceedings in accordance with Article 4. Section 1504 provides: 'A case under this chapter is commenced by the filing of a petition for recognition of a foreign proceeding under section 1515.' Jurisdiction regarding cases under the Bankruptcy Code is conferred on the US district courts, which, by designation, extend jurisdiction to the US bankruptcy courts.[12] **1.4.7**

In Australia, the Cross-Border Insolvency Act 2008 (which enacted into Australian law the Model Law) specifies in Section 10 the relevant information about the Australian courts that are competent to perform the functions mentioned in Article 3 of the Model Law. The Federal Court of Australia has jurisdiction in respect of individual debtor insolvency, and regarding jurisdiction under the Corporation Act the competent courts are the Federal **1.4.8**

8 See also LC Ho, 'England' in LC Ho (ed.), *A Commentary on the UNCITRAL Model Law*, 4th ed., Globe Law & Business (London), 2017, 198.

9 *American Energy Group Ltd v Hycarbex Asia Pte Ltd (In Liquidation)* [2014] EWHC 1091 (Ch).

10 Ibid [paras 7–13].

11 Which implements the Model Law in the United States.

12 C Martin, 'United States' in LC Ho (ed.), *A Commentary on the UNCITRAL Model Law*, 4th ed., Globe Law & Business (London), 2017, 643 (referring to 28 USC s 157, 1334).

Court of Australia and the Supreme Courts of the states and territories.[13] In *Bank of Western Australia v Henderson*,[14] the Federal Magistrates Court of Australia concluded that the reference, in section 10 implementing Article 4 of the Model Law, to the Federal Court of Australia or the Supreme Court of a State or Territory does not interfere with the Federal Magistrates Court's jurisdiction to make a sequestration order in a matter with a cross-border element: 'What is apparent, rather, is that when a local proceeding is occurring at the same time as one, or several, foreign proceedings (the case of concurrent proceedings) then the local court must cooperate with the foreign proceeding. As will be seen this does not mean that the local court is prevented from the making of a sequestration order.'[15]

13 See S Atkins, 'Australia' in LC Ho (ed.), *A Commentary on the UNCITRAL Model Law*, 4th ed., Globe Law & Business (London), 2017, 27.

14 *Bank of Western Australia v Henderson (No. 3)* [2011] FMCA 840.

15 Ibid [paras 12-13].

Article 5

AUTHORIZATION OF [*INSERT THE TITLE OF THE PERSON OR BODY ADMINISTERING REORGANIZATION OR LIQUIDATION UNDER THE LAW OF THE ENACTING STATE*] TO ACT IN A FOREIGN STATE

Kristin van Zwieten

A [*insert the title of the person or body administering a reorganization or liquidation under the law of the enacting State*] is authorized to act in a foreign State on behalf of a proceeding under [*identify laws of the enacting State relating to insolvency*], as permitted by the applicable foreign law.

A. INTRODUCTION

Most of the provisions of the Model Law are premised on the existence of foreign insolvency proceedings, and are concerned with the local treatment of such proceedings.[1] The Model Law makes provision for a 'court'[2] to recognise foreign proceedings[3] on the application of the 'foreign representative'[4] author- **1.5.1**

1 Provision is also made in Article 9 for 'direct access' to local courts by the 'foreign representative', that is, the person or body authorised to administer the reorganization or liquidation of the debtor's assets or affairs in a foreign proceeding or to act as a representative of the foreign proceeding (see Article 2(d)), and for the foreign representative to have standing to apply to commence local proceedings under the insolvency law of the enacting state (Article 11) and to participate in such proceedings (Article 12).

2 This body or bodies can be designated in Article 4, which expressly contemplates authorities other than national courts being designated. See Mevorach's commentary on Article 4.

3 As defined in the Model Law: see the commentary on Article 2(a) in this book.

4 Again, as defined: see above n1 and the commentary on Article 2(d). These definitions 'limit the scope of application of the Model Law': UNCITRAL, *Cross-Border Insolvency: Guide to Enactment of the UNCITRAL Model Law on Cross-Border Insolvency*, A/CN.9/442, 19 December 1997, [68].

ised to act in such proceedings, and for the extension of relief on recognition.[5] Provision is also made for cooperation with 'foreign courts' (the judicial or other authorities competent to control or supervise foreign proceedings)[6] and foreign representatives, and for direct communication with them,[7] and for coordination where there are local and foreign proceedings, or multiple foreign proceedings.[8] (Importantly, however, the Model Law also regulates the position of foreign creditors vis-à-vis local ones in local proceedings, and these provisions are not premised on the existence of foreign proceedings[9].)

1.5.2 It is, of course, unsurprising that the Model Law is primarily concerned with the local treatment of foreign proceedings. This reflects the nature of the instrument, and in particular the fact that the adoption of a model law by one state will affect the law of that state, but not the laws of other states (at least not directly).[10] An adopting state can require its courts to recognise foreign proceedings with particular characteristics, and make provision for certain relief to flow from recognition, but plainly cannot merely by doing so require the courts of some other place to do the same. Take-up might be nudged by conditioning the availability of relief on reciprocity, but this strategy might not be effective, and in the meantime, the application of the reciprocity condition may be costly.[11] These limitations were recognised in the early discussions of the UNCITRAL intergovernmental working group that developed the Model Law,[12] and the final text did not include a reciprocity condition.[13] Instead, the Group aimed at achieving greater harmonisation through the production of a Model Law 'modest'[14] enough to be capable of widespread unilateral take-up

5 Chapter III of the Model Law.

6 Article 2(e) of the Model Law.

7 Chapter IV of the Model Law. The cooperation duty arises irrespective of whether the foreign proceedings have been formally recognised for the purpose of the provisions of the Model Law on recognition and relief: *Guide to Enactment* (n 4) [177].

8 Chapter V of the Model Law.

9 Articles 13–14 of the Model Law.

10 Indirect effects are, however, conceivable through the operation of doctrines of international law: see I Mevorach, *The Future of Cross-Border Insolvency: Overcoming Biases and Closing Gaps* (OUP 2018).

11 Depending on its design: see JL Westbook, 'Theory and Pragmatism in Global Insolvencies: Choice of Law and Choice of Forum' 65(4) ABLJ 457.

12 See 'Report of the Working Group on Insolvency Law on the Work of the 18th Session', A/CN.9/419 (1 December 1995), [42]–[45]; see also 'Report of the Working Group on Insolvency Law on the Work of its 21st Session', A/CN.9/435 (19 February 1997), [86]–[89].

13 Of course, an adopting state may nevertheless choose to insert a reciprocity condition, as some states have done: see Mevorach on Article 1, para. 1.1.08, and Keith D. Yamauchi, 'Should Reciprocity Be a Part of the UNCITRAL Model Cross-Border Insolvency Law?' (2007) 16 Int. Insolv. Rev. 145. For an interesting discussion of the benefits and costs of reciprocity from a national perspective, see 'Report of the Insolvency Law Review Committee: Final Report' (2013) (Singapore) 235-238.

14 'Report of the Working Group on Insolvency Law on the Work of the 18th Session' (n 12) [16], [45]; *Guide to Enactment* (n 4) [3].

in relatively uniform form (that is, with little or no deviation from the model text).[15]

Against this backdrop, Article 5 of the Model Law is something of an outlier provision, being concerned exclusively with an 'outbound' question: that is, a question relating to the foreign treatment of local proceedings.[16] The question that Article 5 addresses is, however, a narrow one, namely the authority of the person or body appointed to administer local proceedings to act abroad, on behalf of those proceedings. And given the nature of the instrument, Article 5 is restricted to regulating the authority of the person or body to act as a matter of local, or domestic, law. Their treatment abroad will be a matter for the foreign law, although that law may first be concerned with eliminating the possibility that the person or body simply has no authority to act on behalf of the proceedings outside of the state of opening. This question can be answered by adopting Article 5. **1.5.3**

B. PURPOSE AND EFFECT OF ARTICLE 5

Article 1 of the Model Law provides that the Law applies not only in cases of 'inbound' requests for assistance – that is, where assistance is sought in the enacting State by a foreign court or foreign representative in connection with a foreign proceeding – but also to 'outbound' requests for assistance, where 'Assistance is sought in a foreign State in connection with a proceeding under [*identify laws of the enacting State relating to insolvency*]'.[17] The record of negotiations on the Model Law suggests that the reference to outbound requests was included primarily because of Article 5, and that Article 5 was agreed to be valuable because authority to seek assistance abroad was 'a question not adequately covered in some national laws'.[18] It was thought that in most states an office-holder's authority would not be restricted to being territorial in scope, but that this was nevertheless a question that could concern the courts of some **1.5.4**

15 *Guide to Enactment* (n 4) [12], [21], [53]. This assumes, of course, that text adopted in model form is also interpreted uniformly, which the Model Law itself exhorts: see Article 8, and *Guide to Enactment* (n 4) [91] ('a State enacting a model law also has an interest in its harmonized interpretation').

16 See to similar effect AJ Berends, 'The UNCITRAL Model Law on Cross-Border Insolvency: A Comprehensive Overview' (1998) 6 Tulane Journal of International and Comparative Law 309, 335.

17 Article 1(a) and (b). Sub-paragraphs (c) and (d) relate to concurrent local and foreign proceedings, and participation by creditors or other interested persons in a foreign State in local proceedings (see text to n9 above), respectively.

18 'Report of the Working Group on Insolvency Law on the work of its 19th Session', A/CN.9/422 (25 April 1996), [26], see also [73].

states.[19] An enacting state could address this potential challenge by providing assurance of authority to act abroad, thus clearing the way for an application for assistance.[20]

1.5.5 The Working Group was clear that 'the scope and exercise of power abroad would depend upon the foreign law and courts'.[21] Article 5 thus refers to the authority of designated persons or bodies to act in a foreign state on behalf of a local proceeding '*as permitted by the foreign law*'. The foreign law may, of course, itself include a version of the Model Law, and the person or body with authority to act abroad under the law of the enacting state may seek to rely on the foreign version of the Model Law's rules on recognition and relief.[22] Their ability to do so, however, will depend on them being characterised as a 'foreign representative' in 'foreign proceedings' by the court abroad.[23] This cannot be assumed, because the Model Law does not insist on a strict symmetry between the concepts of a 'foreign representative' in 'foreign proceedings' and the kinds of local representatives and proceedings that an enacting State could list for the purposes of filling out Article 5 (or any other provisions that require the designation of local persons 'administering a reorganisation or liquidation under the laws of the enacting State', or the identification of local laws 'relating to insolvency' under which proceedings may be opened that are regulated by the Model Law).[24] In practice, however, an enacting State does not appear to have any incentive to take a wider approach to local designation than it expects from the application of the concepts of 'foreign representative' and 'foreign proceedings' abroad, because local designation brings with it obligations – for example, the named 'person or body administering a reorganisation or liquida-

19 'Report of the Working Group on Insolvency Law on the work of the 18th Session', A/CN.9/419, [36].

20 ibid [37].

21 'Report of the Working Group on Insolvency Law on the work of its 19th Session', A/CN.9/422, [72].

22 As envisaged by the Commission when approving draft Article 5: 'Report of the United Nations Commission on International Trade Law on the work of its 30th Session', General Assembly Official Records, 52nd Session, Supplement No. 17 (A/52/17), [168]. See also Berends (n 16) 335.

23 Assuming the enactment of the Model Law in model form.

24 There is clearly some overlap between the references to 'administering a reorganisation or liquidation'/'laws relating to insolvency' and the definitions in Article 2, but the former were not intended to be read as shorthand for, or as somehow importing, the fuller definitions in Article 2. The Working Group did consider using a general definition of 'insolvency proceedings' that would apply to both foreign and local proceedings, and a definition of a local 'administrator' that would parallel the definition of the foreign representative. But in the end the 'mirror image' approach was rejected, on the basis that it was not necessary to introduce this complexity in an instrument primarily concerned with the recognition of foreign proceedings: 'Report of the Working Group on Insolvency Law on the work of its 19th Session' (n 18) [30]–[31], [38]–[39], [46]–[47]. Later, similar language to that used in the Model Law ('the person or body administering a reorganisation or liquidation') was used in the definition of the 'insolvency representative' in the *UNCITRAL Legislative Guide on Insolvency Law* (2005) at 5.

tion under the laws of the enacting State' is subject to a duty to cooperate with foreign courts and foreign representatives.[25]

The effect of listing a person or body as one 'administering a reorganisation or liquidation under the law of the enacting State' in Article 5 appears limited to providing that authority to act on behalf of the proceedings is not merely territorial in scope, or (put another way) may be exercised abroad as well as at home. Article 5 would therefore not function to cure (as a matter of domestic law, or as a matter for the law of the enacting State[26]) a wholesale lack of authority to act, nor to relax what would otherwise be a condition on the exercise of authority under the law of the enacting State (for example, a requirement that creditor approval is sought before the person or body takes a particular action on behalf of the proceeding): it is only the international question (the ability to exercise authority abroad) that is regulated by Article 5.[27] Moreover, an enacting State can further restrict Article 5 by making the ability to exercise authority abroad subject to some additional condition; for example, obtaining an order from a court to this effect.[28] **1.5.6**

There does appear to have been at least one enacting State that, in adopting Article 5, changed the prior law, relaxing a previous territorial limitation on authority to act on behalf of local proceedings.[29] In other States, where authority was already not limited in this way, the adoption of Article 5 will merely provide evidence of the *status quo*.[30] Still, that will provide reassurance to a court otherwise minded to interrogate this question at far lower cost than if expert evidence had been required to confirm the position. **1.5.7**

---

25 See Article 26 of the Model Law or, for another example, see Article 28 (restricting the commencement of those local proceedings identified by the enacting State as 'a proceeding under [*identify laws of the enacting State relating to insolvency*]' on recognition of a foreign main proceeding).

26 Of course, a lack of authority to act under the law of the enacting State may or may not be legally relevant in the foreign state – that would be a matter for the foreign law. See Berends (n 16) 336.

27 Consistently with this, see 'Report of the Working Group on Insolvency Law on the Work of its Twentieth Session' A/CN.9/433 (24 October 1996), [48]; see also 'Report of the Working Group on Insolvency Law on its work of the 19th Session' (n18) [72], though this is somewhat more obscure.

28 See for example s.442 of Part XVIII of the Insolvency Act of the British Virgin Islands as reported in P Kite, 'British Virgin Islands' in LC Ho (ed.), *A Commentary on the UNCITRAL Model Law*, 4th ed., Globe Law & Business (London), 2017.

29 See 'Greece' by D Passas, V Saliaris and M Passass in Ho (ed) (n 28) ('This covers a regulatory gap, insofar as the Code does not confer upon the receiver the authority to act in a foreign state'). There are also at least two other states where a change was reportedly made as part of a broader shift away from territorialism: see Shin-ichiro Abe, 'Japan' and C Rim, 'South Korea', in the same volume.

30 Guide to Enactment (n 4) [84].

Article 6

PUBLIC POLICY EXCEPTION

Kristin van Zwieten

Nothing in this Law prevents the court from refusing to take an action governed by this Law if the action would be manifestly contrary to the public policy of this State.

A. INTRODUCTION

1.6.01 Article 6 is a core provision of the Model Law, containing the 'public policy exception'[1] to the Model Law's provisions for the recognition of foreign proceedings, relief on recognition, and cooperation with foreign courts and foreign representatives. The 'public policy' with which Article 6 is concerned is that of the enacting State. Its purpose is to provide some protection in respect of 'matters of fundamental importance for the enacting State'[2] in the operationalisation of the Model Law's rules on the local treatment of foreign proceedings. The Guide to Enactment cautions that the provision should only be used in 'exceptional circumstances'.[3] Clearly, widespread and regular invocation of the provision would undo the gains expected to flow from the harmonisation of

1 UNCITRAL, *Cross-Border Insolvency: Guide to Enactment of the UNCITRAL Model Law on Cross-Border Insolvency*, A/CN.9/442, 19 December 1997, [20].

2 ibid [89].

3 ibid.

some 'basic principles' on access, recognition and cooperation in cross-border insolvencies.[4]

Article 6 is framed in the negative, providing that nothing in the Model Law prevents 'the court' from refusing to take an action governed by the Law if 'the action would be manifestly contrary to the public policy of this State'. The reference to 'the court' is a reference to the national authorities competent to perform the functions of the Model Law relating to recognition and cooperation.[5] These functions include determining whether a foreign proceeding should be recognised – and, if so, as a foreign main proceeding or as a foreign non-main proceeding[6] (recognition of the former bringing with it some automatic relief);[7] whether interim relief should be given pending a decision on recognition;[8] and whether additional relief should be awarded on recognition.[9] Whether or not a foreign proceeding is recognised, 'the court' must also cooperate with foreign courts and foreign representatives.[10] In adopting Article 6, an enacting State makes clear that these provisions for recognition and cooperation do not prevent the court from refusing to act where the action would be manifestly contrary to the enacting State's public policy. The provision can thus be characterised as a 'public policy reservation'; this is the way that UNCITRAL itself characterised it in the session in which the Model Law project was finalised.[11] **1.6.02**

4 See 'Report of the Working Group on Insolvency Law on the work of the 18th session' (Vienna, 30 October–10 November 1995) A/CN.9/419, 1 December 1995, [40], referring to the risk of 'defeating the objectives of the legal text being developed' in crafting the public policy exception, and [18], describing the work of the Working Group as directed to 'establishing a limited number of basic principles and threshold rules that would facilitate efficiency and speed in responding to cross-border insolvency cases'. More generally, see also A Mills, 'The Dimensions of Public Policy in Private International Law' (2008) 4 Journal of Private International Law 201, section 2.1: 'An excessive application of a public policy discretion could risk undermining the very existence of rules of private international law.'

5 See Mevorach's commentary on Article 4 in this book.

6 See Article 17. Main proceedings are those taking place in the place of the debtor's centre of main interests; non-main proceedings are those taking place in a place of establishment: see Article 2(b), (c). As to proceedings that are neither main nor non-main, see van Zwieten (ed), *Goode on Principles of Corporate Insolvency Law* (5th ed, 2018) at [16–31].

7 See the commentary on Article 20.

8 See the commentary on Article 19.

9 See the commentary on Article 21.

10 See the commentary on Article 25.

11 'Report of the United Nations Commission on International Trade Law on the work of its thirtieth session, 12-30 May 1997', General Assembly, Official Records, 52nd Session, Supplement No.17 (A/52/17), [32].

B. RATIONALE FOR THE INCLUSION OF A PUBLIC POLICY RESERVATION

1.6.03 In an important early paper on the Model Law,[12] Berends (who represented the Netherlands in the negotiation of the Model Law and of the European Insolvency Convention that became the European Insolvency Regulation[13]) wrote: 'One may ask whether this article [Article 6] is really necessary.'[14] Although UNCITRAL had hoped that the Model Law would be taken up by states in relatively uniform form,[15] it is inherent in the nature of the instrument that enacting States may adopt it in whole or only in part, and amend or add to the model text. Whether or not Article 6 was included in the Model Law, States could plainly have made any local legislation adopting the text subject to local public policy.[16] Indeed, Berends argued that in some jurisdictions this might have been the result even without an explicit public policy reservation: 'Even if it had not been included in the Model Law, in my view, no court would feel obliged to render a decision that is contrary to the public policy of its State.'[17]

1.6.04 In Berends' view, Article 6 was nevertheless a useful device to encourage take-up of the Model Law.[18] One barrier to take-up by states might be concerns of 'abuse':

> Some may fear the possibility of abuse of the Model Law. When a debtor is subjected to an insolvency proceeding in a country plagued with corruption, or where one must fear that the court is not independent from the government, concerns may arise over fairness. The fact that the debtor or other parties were not heard, or at least not afforded the opportunity to be heard, upon the request for opening the insolvency proceeding may cast some doubts upon the proceeding's fairness.[19]

1.6.05 Article 6 confirmed a court's ability to decline to act where doing so would be contrary to the State's 'fundamental principles of law'.[20] Other 'safeguards'

12 AJ Berends, 'UNCITRAL Model Law on Cross-Border Insolvency: A Comprehensive Overview' (1998) 6 Tulane Journal of International and Comparative Law 309.

13 Convention on insolvency proceedings, 23 November 1995; Council Regulation (EC) No 1346/2000 of 29 May 2000 on insolvency proceedings, OJ L 160, 30.6.2000, 1–18.

14 (n 12) 336.

15 See above, [1.5.2].

16 This is perhaps what Berends meant when he observed that 'these kinds of [public policy] articles seem to be more appropriate in a treaty than in a Model Law': (n 12) at 336.

17 ibid.

18 ibid.

19 ibid 373.

20 ibid 336. See also 'Report of the Working Group on Insolvency Law on the work of its 20th session' (Vienna, 7–18 October 1996), A/CN.9/433, 24 October 1996, [157]: 'The Working Group was informed that in certain jurisdictions the Model Provisions could only be enacted in such a way that they would not conflict

against abuse included that proceedings would only be entitled to recognition under the Model Law where certain conditions were satisfied,[21] that most forms of relief would not flow automatically from recognition[22] but instead only be available as a matter of discretion,[23] and that Article 22 made the availability of such relief conditional on the court being satisfied that the interests of the creditors and 'other interested persons' were adequately protected.[24]

In Berends' view, these safeguards were particularly important in a Model Law that did not insist on reciprocity.[25] In the absence of reciprocity, Berends reasoned, the safeguards worked to provide 'the cornerstone of a balance between all the interests involved' that would 'serve to convince legislators that the Model Law provides a satisfactory equilibrium'.[26] Fletcher,[27] Ho,[28] and Wan and McCormack similarly link the inclusion of Article 6 in the Model Law to the absence of a reciprocity condition.[29] Such a condition would not in and of itself appear to provide complete protection against the kinds of 'abuse' that Berends had in mind. But its inclusion would have functioned as a more general (and severe) limitation on the commitment made by any State when adopting the Model Law (particularly for the earliest adopters), and enabled adopters to signal to local constituencies (who might otherwise be concerned that access, recognition and relief in respect of foreign proceedings and foreign creditors might run counter to local interests) that the commitment was at least conditional on an expectation of reciprocal treatment abroad. The adoption by UNCITRAL of a Model Law without such a requirement was a major achievement. But producing an instrument capable of widespread, *unilateral* **1.6.06**

---

with certain fundamental rules and principles that formed the basis of their legal tradition. The Working Group took note of those remarks.'

21 See Article 17 of the Model Law.

22 The automatic relief provided by the Model Law being limited to the kind of stay on actions, execution and asset disposal that local law provides for, and only where the foreign proceedings are recognised as foreign main proceedings: see Article 20 of the Model Law.

23 See Article 21 of the Model Law.

24 Berends (n 12) 373–4.

25 ibid 373. As to the absence of a reciprocity condition, see above, [1.5.2].

26 ibid 374.

27 IF Fletcher, *Insolvency in Private International Law: National and International Approaches* (Clarendon Press, 1999) 362, describing Article 6 as attenuating the 'more extreme possibilities' to which 'international openness', 'without the prior condition of reciprocity, or mutual negotiation and agreement', could otherwise give rise.

28 Look Chan Ho (ed), *Cross-Border Insolvency* (4th ed), (Globe Law and Business, 2017) Ch 1, section 7, also discussing Article 22 in this context.

29 WY Wan and G McCormack, 'Implementing Strategies for the Model Law on Cross-Border Insolvency: The Divergence in Asia-Pacific and Lessons for UNCITRAL' (2020) 36 Emery Bankruptcy Developments Journal 59, 73–5, again also discussing Article 22.

take-up in relatively uniform form[30] required it to be 'realistic' in what was asked of enacting States,[31] and to temper these commitments with express provision for local interests and, more generally, local public policy.[32]

C. SCOPE

1.6.07 Article 17 of the Model Law, which stipulates that a foreign proceeding 'shall' be recognised if certain requirements are satisfied, is expressed to be 'subject to article 6'.[33] Working Group V had been clear from the outset that States ought to be able to 'withhold recognition on grounds of public policy'.[34] The retention of the proviso[35] in the final text, however, was presumably only for the avoidance of doubt, because on a plain reading Article 6 would apply to a decision of a court on an application for recognition, as well as to a range of other decisions: Article 6 is framed in general terms (providing that nothing in the Model Law prevents a court from refusing to take action where to do so would be manifestly contrary to the State's public policy) and is located in Chapter I of the Model Law, which is entitled 'General provisions'.

1.6.08 The decision to frame Article 6 in general terms was a deliberate one, the Working Group rejecting a suggestion to confine the public policy reservation to recognition decisions.[36] That is unsurprising against the backdrop of an

30 So as to achieve a greater degree of harmonisation: see above [1.5.2] and 'Report of the United Nations Commission on International Trade Law on the work of its 30th session, 12–30 May 1997', General Assembly, Official Records, 52nd Session, Supplement No.17 (A/52/17), [26] and [223].

31 ibid 'Report' [25] (referring to the draft text as constituting a 'realistic approach') and [97] (rejecting as unrealistic the suggestion that the opening of local proceedings after recognition of foreign main proceedings be limited to cases in which the debtor had a local establishment).

32 I Mevorach, 'On the Road to Universalism: A Comparative and Empirical Study of the UNCITRAL Model Law on Cross-Border Insolvency' (2011) 12 EBOR 517 at 527, characterising Arts 6 and 22 as 'safety valves'. Although Article 22 is not confined to requiring consideration of the interests of creditors and other interested persons in the enacting State (a deliberate choice: see 'Report of the United Nations Commission on International Trade Law on the work of its 30th session, 12–30 May 1997' (n 30) at [85]), the Guide to Enactment acknowledged 'In many cases the affected creditors will be "local" creditors': see (n 1) at [163]. Mevorach also draws attention to Article 21(2), which requires adequate protection for the interests of creditors in the enacting State in ordering turnover of assets for distribution in foreign main or non-main proceedings, also emphasised by Wan and McCormack (n 29) 76.

33 See Article 17(1) of the Model Law.

34 'Report of the Working Group on Insolvency Law on the work of the 18th session' (Vienna, 30 October–10 November 1995) A/CN.9/419, 1 December 1995, [40].

35 Which appears traceable to this document: 'Newly revised articles of the draft UNCITRAL Model Legislative Provisions on Cross-Border Insolvency: Note by the Secretariat' A/CN.9/WG.V/WP.48 (21 November 1996) (see comments on draft Art. 14).

36 'Report of the Working Group on Insolvency Law on the work of its 20th Session' (Vienna, 7–18 October 1996), A/CN.9/433, 24 October 1996, [158] (and see also 'Report of the Working Group on Insolvency Law in the Work of its 19th session', A/CN.9/422 (New York, 1–12 April 1996), [84]–[85]); 'Newly revised

instrument that provides for very limited relief to flow automatically from recognition, leaving much relief to be determined as a matter of discretion,[37] and which imposes cooperation duties on courts which are not dependent on prior recognition.[38] The overall effect of Article 6, read together with the proviso in Article 17, is that public policy may be relevant at both the recognition stage and at the relief stage (and, in any case, will also be relevant to the operationalisation of the Model Law's provisions on cooperation). In the revised Guide to Enactment issued by UNCITRAL in 2013, however, enacting States are encouraged to deny recognition on public policy grounds only very exceptionally: 'As a general rule, Article 6 should rarely be the basis for refusing an application for recognition, even though it might be a basis for limiting the nature of the relief accorded'.[39]

The Working Group gave as an example of a case in which denial of recognition would be appropriate one in which 'foreign proceedings were being pursued in collusion between the debtor and the foreign representative for the purpose of concealment of assets'.[40] **1.6.09**

There is one way in which the scope of the provision is arguably potentially limited. Article 6 provides that nothing in the Model Law prevents 'a court' from refusing to take an action governed by the Model Law if the action would be manifestly contrary to the enacting State's public policy. As explained above, the reference to 'the court' is a reference to the national authorities competent to perform the core functions of the Model Law relating to recognition, the extension of relief on recognition, and cooperation.[41] It may therefore be queried whether Article 6 applies to those parts of the Model Law which do not appear to require action by such authorities – most obviously, some of **1.6.10**

---

articles of the draft UNCITRAL Model Legislative Provisions on Cross-Border Insolvency: Note by the Secretariat', A/CN.9/WG.V/WP.48, 21 November 1996, Art. 6. The preliminary draft considered the year before had included public policy provisos at various points in the text (see 'Report of the Working Group on Insolvency Law on the Work of the 18th Session' (Vienna, 30 October–10 November 1995), A/CN.9/419), which the drafting group suggested be consolidated (A/CN.9/WG.V/WP.44 at 15).

37 *Cf* the position under the European Insolvency Regulation, which provides for automatic recognition and, in the case of main proceedings and except to the extent the Regulation otherwise provides, the extension of the effects provided by the *lex fori concursus* across Member States: see van Zwieten in Bork and van Zwieten (eds) *Commentary on the European Insolvency Regulation* (OUP 2022), 'Introduction', and below [1.6.17].

38 See Chapter IV of the Model Law, and below, commentary on Art.7, fn 7.

39 UNCITRAL, *UNICITRAL Model Law on Cross-Border Insolvency with Guide to Enactment and Interpretation* (2014), [161]. As to the revision of the Guide to Enactment, see below [1.8.08].

40 18th Session report (n 36) [186].

41 See above [1.6.02]. It is true that Chapter IV also makes provision for cooperation by a person or body administering a reorganisation or liquidation under the law of the enacting State, but this is expressed to be 'subject to the supervision of the court', as is the exercise of their power to communicate directly with foreign courts or foreign representatives: see Article 26.

the provisions of Chapter II ('Access of foreign representatives and creditors to courts in this State'). Some of these provisions involve 'the court' at some stage,[42] but others do not necessarily – for example, the provisions on rights of commencement and participation by, and notice to, foreign creditors.[43] Some scholarship appears to assume the possibility of Article 6 applying in this context,[44] and the historical materials on the negotiation of the Model Law provide some support for this interpretation, indicating an intention that all actions governed by the Model Law be subject to the public policy reservation.[45] In practice the question does not appear to have been litigated,[46] despite many jurisdictions using the language of 'the court' in local versions of Article 6.[47]

---

42 For example, Article 9, which provides that a foreign representative is entitled to apply directly to a court in the enacting State. In the view of UNCITRAL at the final session on the negotiation of the Model Law, Article 9 would be subject to Article 6: 'Report of the United Nations Commission on International Trade Law on the work of its 30th session', (n 11) [32]: 'It was said that it was not appropriate to subject to the reservation of public policy, for example, access by the foreign representative to courts of the enacting State, which was not conditioned on recognition of the foreign proceeding. The Commission, however, considered that article 6 should provide a general public policy reservation for any action governed by the Model Provisions.' The entitlement of the foreign representative to participate in a local proceeding (see Article 12) is conditional on recognition, which is subject to Article 6 (see Article 17(1), and above, text to [1.6.07]).

43 See Articles 13–14 of the Model Law. The fact that these provisions are largely designed to ensure that foreign creditors have the same rights as those creditors in the enacting State, under the law of the enacting State, may reduce the likelihood of a conflict with local public policy, but would not eliminate the possibility altogether.

44 See Fletcher (n 27) at 352, positing that Article 6 could be invoked to resist the admission of a foreign fiscal claim.

45 The record of discussions at the 30th session of UNCITRAL, during which draft articles of the Model Law were reviewed before the adoption of the instrument on the final day of the session, notes that it was suggested that the public policy reservation be restricted to be relevant only to decisions on recognition, rather than functioning as a 'general reservation applicable to other actions that might be taken under the Model Provisions', giving as an example the right of direct access of foreign representatives noted above (n 42). The suggestion was rejected: 'The Commission, however, considered that article 6 should provide a general public policy reservation for any action governed by the Model Provisions.' See 'Report of the United Nations Commission on International Trade Law on the work of its 30th session', 12–30 May 1997, (n 11) [32], and to similar effect: 'Report of the Working Group on the work of its 20th session', Vienna, 7–18 October 1996, A/CN.9/433, [158] (and relatedly 'Newly revised articles of the draft UNCITRAL Model Legislative Provisions on Cross-Border Insolvency: Note by the Secretariat' (n 35) Art. 6). As to the relevance of these materials to the interpretation of domestic legislation adopting the Model Law, see the commentary on Article 8. In the decision in the English High Court in *Re Pan Ocean Ltd* [2014] Bus. L.R. 1041, [2014] EWHC 2124 (Ch), Morgan J characterised Art. 6 as applying to 'all of the provisions' of the British version of the Model Law ([104]).

46 Based on the survey in the Digest of Case Law on the UNCITRAL Model Law on Cross-Border Insolvency (UNCITRAL, 2021).

47 See the survey of jurisdictions as at 2017 in Ho (ed) *Cross Border-Insolvency* (4th ed), (Globe Law and Business, 2017). *Cf* the position in Mexico, where the local version of Article 6 appears to have been framed more broadly, to expressly cover all action under the Model Law, so that the scope question appears to be moot: see P Perezalonso, 'Mexico' in the same volume.

D. INTERPRETATION

While a wide range of actions under the Model Law are subject to the public policy reservation (including but not limited to decisions on recognition), the intention was that the provision be given a 'restrictive interpretation',[48] so that national authorities would be slow to conclude that Article 6 was engaged on a particular set of facts. Clearly, the more the Model Law permits exceptions to the application of its 'basic principles and threshold rules' on access, recognition and cooperation, the less likely it is that the supply of these model provisions will function to increase legal certainty and promote 'efficiency and speed' in cross-border insolvency cases.[49] Recognising that the inclusion of a public policy reservation would bring with it the risk of 'defeating the objectives of the legal text being developed', but considering that *some* reservation was nevertheless required,[50] the Working Group on Insolvency Law considered whether it was 'feasible or advisable to qualify or define public policy considerations in a way that would ensure an appropriate application of the exclusion in view of the wide range of grounds that might arguably fall within such exclusion' but concluded that it was not possible to do so, 'in view of the extent to which the details of the notion of public policy differed from State to State'.[51] Instead, the Working Group deployed other strategies in a bid to minimise recourse to Article 6 in enacting States. **1.6.11**

Two important choices were made about the text of Article 6 itself. Firstly, the provision was deliberately framed in the negative, providing only that the Model Law does not prevent a court from declining to take action that is manifestly contrary to the enacting State's public policy, so as to avoid any suggestion that a court would have to positively determine that no such conflict was present before it could take an action governed by the Model Law. As the Working Group explained: **1.6.12**

> A suggestion was made to redraft article 6 in a positive manner along the following lines: 'The court may refuse to take an action governed by this Law if the action would be manifestly contrary to the public policy of this State.' The suggestion was objected to on the ground that the proposed wording might be interpreted as requiring the court

48 'Report of the Working Group on Insolvency Law on the work of its 21st session' (Vienna, 12–30 May 1997) A/CN.9/435, [126].

49 See 'Report of the Working Group on Insolvency Law on the work of its 18th session' (Vienna, 30 October–10 November 1995) A/CN.9/419, 1 December 1995, [18] and [16].

50 See above, section B.

51 A/CN.9/419 (n 49) at [40].

to ascertain whether each individual request for relief or other action under the Model Provisions was not manifestly contrary to the public policy of the enacting State.[52]

1.6.13 Secondly, the word 'manifestly' was included in the text of Article 6, so that the provision would only be engaged in the case of a 'manifest' conflict between the taking of an action governed by the Model Law and the enacting State's public policy. This qualifier was intended to work in two different ways, or at two different levels. Most obviously, it would signal that the mere presence of some 'technical' inconsistency between the way in which the foreign proceedings were being conducted and the mandatory requirements of local insolvency law was not itself a reason to resist the taking of an action under the Model Law.[53] But more fundamentally, it was hoped that the inclusion of the qualifier, which was noted to also feature in the public policy provisions of many other 'international legal texts', would be understood to import a very narrow conception of 'public policy' for the purposes of Article 6.[54]

1.6.14 One of the 'international legal texts' to which the Working Group had considerable regard in the preparation of the Model Law text was the draft European Convention on Insolvency Proceedings (which eventually entered into force in the form of an EC Regulation, the European Insolvency Regulation[55]). Article 26 of the Convention (see now Article 33 of the recast Regulation)[56] provided that a Contracting State could refuse to recognise insolvency proceedings under the Convention, or enforce a judgment handed down in the context of such proceedings, where the effects of recognition or enforcement would be 'manifestly contrary to that State's public policy, in particular its fundamental

52 A/CN.9/435 (n 48) at [128].

53 See 'Report of the United Nations Commission on International Trade Law on the work of its thirtieth session', 12–30 May 1997, General Assembly, Official Records, 52nd Session, Supplement No. 17 (A/52/17): 'The prevailing view, however, was that the qualifier [the word 'manifestly'] should be kept in order to facilitate international cooperation and to avoid a situation where cooperation under the Model Provisions would be frustrated because the particular step or measure was seen to be contrary to a mere technicality of a mandatory nature' ([172]), drawing on 'Report of the Working Group on Insolvency Law on the Work of its 20th session' (Vienna, 12–30 May 1997) A/CN.9/433, [160]. And see earlier 'Report of the Working Group on Insolvency Law on the Work of the 18th session' (n 4), recording the Working Group's agreement that any formulation of a public policy reservation in relation to the proposed cooperation duty should 'be sensitive to avoiding the suggestion that any and all cooperation should be withheld the instant a possible inconsistency, no matter how minor, with [...] public policy had been detected': [131].

54 A/52/17 ibid, again reflecting A/CN.9/433 (ibid) [160].

55 See (n 13) above.

56 Regulation (EU) 2015/848 of the European Parliament and of the Council of 20 May 2015 on insolvency proceedings. A public policy exception may also be found in the Brussels I Regulation (Regulation (EU) 1215/2012, 20.12.2012, OL J 351/1), which governs jurisdiction and the recognition and enforcement of judgments in civil and commercial matters other than bankruptcy (for the bankruptcy exception, see Art. 1(2)(b)): see Art. 45, P Oberhammer and F Scholz-Berger in Bork and van Zwieten (eds) *Commentary on the European Insolvency Regulation* (2nd ed, OUP 2022) [33.08] and as the historical development of the two instruments more generally, van Zwieten (n 37).

principles or the constitutional rights or liberties of the individual'.[57] The Report[58] that accompanied the Convention explained that while Article 26 could be engaged either by matters of (legal) substance or of procedure – the reporters giving as an example a denial of 'essential procedural guarantees such as the adequate opportunity to be heard'[59] – it was to operate 'only in exceptional cases'.[60] The concept of public policy was to be understood as one 'based on the fundamental principles of the law of the recognising State', involving 'in particular, constitutionally protected rights and freedoms' and other 'fundamental policies of the requested State'.[61]

The Commission had the same narrow conception in mind for Article 6, as the text of the Guide to Enactment (produced at the Commission's suggestion to 'assist States in enacting and applying the Model Provisions'[62]) makes clear. Drawing on the record of deliberations at the session at which the Commission decided to adopt the Model Law,[63] the Guide noted that 'in many States the public policy exception is construed to being restricted to fundamental principles of law, in particular constitutional guarantees',[64] and that 'a growing number of jurisdictions' distinguished between 'public policy' in a purely domestic context and 'public policy' on the international plane, using a narrower conception in the latter category of case ('This dichotomy reflects the realization that international cooperation would be unduly hampered if public policy would be understood in an extensive manner broadly [as encompassing essentially the mandatory law of the country]').[65] The word 'manifestly' had been included, the Guide explained, to signal to enacting States that 'public policy' was to be understood in the same restrictive sense in the Model Law: **1.6.15**

> The purpose of the expression 'manifestly', used also in many other international legal texts as a qualifier of the expression 'public policy', is to emphasize that public policy

57 The draft version of this clause was noted by the Secretariat in its initial preparatory note for the Working Group: 'Possible issues relating to judicial cooperation and access and recognition in cases of cross-border insolvency' A/CN.9/WG.V/WP.42, [38].

58 M Virgos and E Schmit, 'Report on the Convention on Insolvency Proceedings', EC Council Document 6500/96, Brussels, 3 May 1996.

59 ibid [206].

60 ibid [204].

61 ibid [205].

62 A/52/17 (n 53) [23].

63 See A/52/17, ibid [171]–[172], the language of which was then reflected in the text of the Guide. Compare with the draft version of the Guide considered by the Commission at the same session, which had a much briefer treatment of the public policy reservation: 'Draft Guide to Enactment of the UNCITRAL Model Legislative Provisions on Cross-Border Insolvency Note by the Secretariat', A/CN.9/436, [53].

64 UNCITRAL, *Cross-Border Insolvency: Guide to Enactment of the UNCITRAL Model Law on Cross-Border Insolvency*, A/CN.9/442, 19 December 1997, [87].

65 ibid [88].

exceptions should be interpreted restrictively and that article 6 is only intended to be invoked under exceptional circumstances concerning matters of fundamental importance for the enacting State.[66]

1.6.16 There are many difficult questions of policy to be answered in the design of any insolvency regime: when and under what conditions the debts of an insolvent individual should be deemed to be discharged; how shareholders and managers should be treated in a corporate insolvency; the extent to which transactions that would otherwise be settled at general law ought to be vulnerable to avoidance by reason of the fact that one of the parties to it was insolvent when entering into it, or in consequence of doing so; whether security interests should be respected when assets are insufficient to discharge liabilities and not all unsecured creditors are expected to have been able to adjust to their presence *ex ante*; whether and how (at whose expense) employees should be given special protection against the risk of enterprise failure; the order of priority as between other unsecured creditors. States answer these questions differently, informed by history and other aspects of the domestic context. How they do so is in one sense an expression of 'public policy'.[67] But this is not the sense in which the concept was used in Article 6 of the Model Law. UNCITRAL recognised and sought to respect, rather than to challenge, differences in national insolvency policy,[68] and when the guide to the enactment of Article 6 referred to matters of 'fundamental importance' to the enacting State, the drafters had in mind matters more fundamental than these choices – however politically salient they may be domestically. Writing on Article 33 of the recast European Insolvency Regulation, Oberhammer and Scholz-Berger have similarly argued:

> It is well known that the laws of the Member States differ strongly even with respect to such fundamental issues of insolvency law as the equal treatment of creditors... Insolvency lawyers, however, must understand that the 'fundamental' principles of their respective insolvency laws are not identical, and most likely – at least to a large extent – not even part of 'public policy' in the sense used in Article 33, and in particular not part of the fundamental principles or the constitutional rights or liberties of the individual that are protected by Article 33.[69]

---

66 ibid [89].

67 Indeed, Lord Millett wrote of insolvency law that 'No branch of the law is moulded more by considerations of national economic policy and commercial philosophy': (1997) 6 International Insolvency Review 99, 109; see also Gerard McCormack and Wan Wai Yee, 'The UNCITRAL Model Law on Cross-Border Insolvency Comes of Age: New Times or New Paradigms' (2019) 54(2) Texas International Law Journal 273, citing this passage and observing that 'Insolvency policies and procedures differ substantially between States' (at 287).

68 See A/CN.9/419 (n 49) at [18]: 'As a further aspect of keeping the project [the Model Law project] within the confines of feasibility, the Working Group was urged to keep in mind the inevitability that significantly differing policy approaches would continue to characterize national attitudes to matters of insolvency and that it was not the goal of the Commission's work to overcome or eliminate those differences.'

69 Oberhammer and Scholz-Berger (n 56) [1.33.04].

There are, of course, also obvious differences between Article 33 and Article 6. Article 33 is part of a Regulation that has direct effect in Member States of the EU (other than Denmark[70]), and national courts must strive to apply its provisions in a manner which ensures 'the effectiveness of the system established by the Regulation'.[71] Based on the principle of mutual trust,[72] this system is one which requires insolvency proceedings opened in one Member State to be automatically recognised by the courts of other Member States;[73] judgments concerning the course and closure of such proceedings, and for the approval of compositions in such proceedings, as well as judgments deriving directly from the proceedings and closely linked to them, must also be recognised with no further formalities.[74] In the case of 'main' proceedings (those opened in the place of the debtor's centre of main interests[75]), recognition of the opening of proceedings carries with it the extension, across the Union, of the effects provided by the (insolvency) law of the Member State of opening, except to the extent that the Regulation otherwise provides.[76] Jurisdiction to open proceedings to rival main proceedings is severely limited, and such 'secondary' proceedings are limited in territorial scope[77] and subject to rules designed to ensure their coordination with, and in some circumstances subordination to, main proceedings.[78] This sophisticated system for securing 'unity in the Union'[79] in the treatment of a cross-border insolvency would be undone if Member States could take a liberal approach to the construction of the public policy exception in Article 33, but this construction is not one that is open to Member States to adopt, and an attempt to do so could be corrected by the Court of Justice of the European Union: **1.6.17**

70 To which the European Insolvency Regulation has never applied: see van Zwieten in Bork and van Zwieten (eds) *Commentary on the European Insolvency Regulation* (2nd ed, OUP 2022) [0.31].

71 Case C-341/04, *Eurofood IFSC Ltd* ECLI:EU:C:2006:281, [52]–[53].

72 See Recital 65 of Regulation (EU) 2015/848 of the European Parliament and of the Council of 20 May 2015 on insolvency proceedings; *Eurofood* ibid [38]-[42]; and K van Zwieten, 'Case comment: *Apperley Investments Limited v Monsoon Accessorize Limited*' (2021) 34(3) Insolvency Intelligence 69.

73 See Article 19(1) of Regulation (EU) 2015/848 of the European Parliament and of the Council of 20 May 2015 on insolvency proceedings.

74 See Article 32(1) of Regulation (EU) 2015/848, providing that such judgments shall be enforced in accordance with Articles 39–44 and 47–57 of Regulation (EU) No 1215/2012.

75 See Article 3(1) of Regulation (EU) 2015/848.

76 And as long as no secondary proceedings are opened: see Article 20(1) of Regulation (EU) 2015/848, and as to secondary proceedings, text to n 77. See Veder's commentary on Article 20 in Bork and Zwieten (eds) *Commentary on the European Insolvency Regulation* (2nd ed, OUP 2022).

77 See Articles 3(2) and 20(2) of Regulation (EU) 2015/848.

78 See van Zwieten in Bork and van Zwieten (eds) *Commentary on the European Insolvency Regulation* (2nd ed, OUP 2022) [0.30] and [0.43].

79 See Recital 23 of Regulation (EU) 2015/848.

the starting point is that one generally needs to take into account that the EIR is intended to facilitate, to the greatest possible extent, the recognition of insolvency proceedings and free movement of judgments. The public policy exception must be interpreted strictly in as much as it constitutes an obstacle to the attainment of this fundamental objective and, therefore, is applicable only in exceptional cases. As a consequence, while Member States in principle remain free, by virtue of Article 33, to determine, according to their own concepts, what public policy requires, the limits of that concept are a matter of interpretation of the Regulation. Consequently, while it is not for the Regulation or the CJEU to define the content of the public policy of a Member State, the Court is nonetheless required to review – on the basis of European law – the limits within which the courts of a Member State may have recourse to that concept for the purpose of refusing recognition and enforcement.[80]

1.6.18 There is no equivalent mechanism for securing a restrictive interpretation of (local versions of) Article 6 of the Model Law. The Model Law exhorts enacting States to strive for a harmonised interpretation of local versions of the model provisions,[81] but it is inherent in the nature of the instrument that no outside institution can directly control any question of interpretation: that will be a matter for the domestic law.[82] Given this, the Working Group on Insolvency Law recognised that the realisation of its vision of a narrow public policy exception would depend on drafting choices made elsewhere in the instrument.[83] There were multiple rounds of negotiation on the drafting of the core provisions on recognition, relief and cooperation, and the result was 'threshold rules'[84] that are themselves, by design, highly sensitive to local policy choices, and accommodating of the local interests that such choices are constitutive of. Consider, for example, the fact that the relief that flows automatically from recognition (which is not itself automatic)[85] is limited to a stay on *individual* enforcement action (not the opening of rival *collective* proceedings[86]) when the proceedings are recognised as main proceedings,[87] and is

80 Oberhammer and Scholz-Berger in Bork and van Zwieten (eds) *Commentary on the European Insolvency Regulation* (2nd ed, OUP 2022) [33.09].

81 See the commentary in this book on Article 8.

82 *Gainsford, in the matter of Tannenbaum v Tannenbaum* [2012] FCA 904 (Australia), [37].

83 See for example A/CN.9/433, [36], and A/CN.9/422, [44] (n 36), both concerning questions of scope.

84 Above, text to n 49.

85 See A/CN.9/433 (n 36), [101]. But recognition should be given if the criteria specified in Article 17 are satisfied: see Guide to Enactment (n 1) [124].

86 See Article 20(4) of the Model Law and A/CN.9/422 (n 36), [104]: 'It was noted at the same time that the draft text did not disturb the rights that local creditors might have under the law of the enacting State to proceed collectively against the debtor, since collective actions were exempt from the stay.' The view had been formed early on that the Model Law should not seek to prevent the opening of local insolvency proceedings: see A/CN.9/419, (n 4), [72]. The Model Law does, however, stipulate that after recognition of a foreign main proceeding, the opening of local proceedings should be limited to cases in which the debtor has assets in the enacting State, and that such proceedings be restricted in scope to such assets: see Article 28.

87 See Article 20(1) of the Model Law and A/CN.9/422, (n 36) [94]–[103].

no more expansive than that which would apply if local collective proceedings were opened (thus securing respect for domestic policy choices on fundamental questions relating to the design of insolvency moratoria, such as the treatment of rights *in rem*),[88] and that the availability of discretionary relief depends on the court being satisfied that the interests of creditors and other interested persons, including the debtor, are adequately protected.[89] These are rules that were designed not only to be capable of unilateral legislative take-up,[90] but also to be capable of application without requiring regular recourse to the public policy exception: this is the special 'equilibrium' that Berends described.[91]

E. OPERATIONALISATION

Attempts to generalise about the operationalisation of Article 6 in enacting States are somewhat complicated by the fact that the provision has not been uniformly adopted in model form.[92] One reasonably common variation has been to omit the qualifier 'manifestly', so that the domestic provision simply refers to actions contrary to the public policy of the enacting State, rather than those that are 'manifestly contrary'.[93] In some jurisdictions, the omission does not appear to be regarded as significant;[94] in a smaller subset, however, the variation has been regarded as signalling some potential for a more expansive, **1.6.19**

88 See Article 20(2) of the Model Law and 'Report of the United Nations Commission on International Trade Law on the work of its thirtieth session', (n 11), [48]. The Working Group had considered attempting to align automatic relief with both or either of the local law and the law of the place in which the foreign proceedings had been commenced (see A/CN.9/422, (n 36) [94]–[118], A.CN.9/433, (n 36) [105]), but in the end resolved to focus only on ensuring local alignment, to minimise complexity and in view of the fact that an enacting State would be 'concerned primarily with the effects given to a foreign proceeding in its own territory': A/CN.9/435, (n 48) [26]. An early draft had featured a more general stay on 'the commencement of judicial, administrative or private actions against the debtor or its assets, except collective proceedings for liquidation or adjustment of debts'; the concern was expressed that this 'may be difficult to accept for jurisdictions that exempted enforcement of claims of secured creditors from treatment under insolvency proceedings': A/CN.9/419, (n 4), [134], [137] (see also at [150]).

89 See Article 22(1) of the Model Law and above, text to n 24.

90 Above, [1.6.05].

91 Above, [1.6.06], and see also the Guide to Enactment (n 1) at [161] referring to 'the balance' that is 'essential to achieve the objectives of cross-border insolvency legislation'.

92 As noted by Wan and McCormack (n 29) 77.

93 See for example the chapters on 'British Virgin Islands', 'Canada', 'Chile', 'Greece', 'Mexico', 'Serbia and Montenegro', 'Singapore' in Ho (ed) (n 28).

94 See e.g. D Passas and V Saliaris, 'Greece' in Ho (ed) (n 28): 'This enacts Article 6 of the Model Law almost verbatim; the omission of the word "manifestly" does not seem to correspond to any intention on the part of the legislature to depart from the Model Law. 'Public policy' is interpreted more restrictively when it comes to Greek private international law and procedural law…'; see also Michael A. Garza, 'When Is Cross-Border Insolvency Recognition Manifestly Contrary to Public Policy?' (2015) 38 Fordham International Law Journal 1587, 1596–7, suggesting that implementation in the British Virgin Islands, Greece, Mexico and Serbia (but as to this see immediately below), was in a form removing 'all adjectives and adverbs' from the model text.

or more liberal, approach to the application of the public policy reservation.[95] Latterly, however, a different approach has been taken in one of the jurisdictions in this subset (Singapore), with the Singapore International Commercial Court concluding that the omission of the qualifier in the domestic version of Article 6 was insufficient to support the conclusion that Parliament had intended to relax the threshold for invoking the public policy reservation.[96] In reaching this conclusion, the Court drew *inter alia* on the materials relating to the preparation of the Model Law, including the Guide to Enactment[97] – which made clear the intention that Article 6 be interpreted restrictively (a matter which, the Court reasoned, the qualifier was simply designed to emphasise)[98] – and the fact that other legal instruments featuring public policy provisions without the 'manifestly' qualifier had been interpreted similarly restrictively by the domestic courts, which could 'explain why Parliament did not think it necessary to include the word "manifestly" when adopting Article 6 of the Model Law'.[99]

1.6.20 Even among jurisdictions that have adopted Article 6 in model form, differences elsewhere in the instrument, and/or in its interpretation, may affect the likelihood of recourse to the public policy reservation.[100] It is, however, noteworthy that – notwithstanding this potential for heterogeneity – one important empirical study has found that, at least in relation to decisions on recognition (which on the model text, in the case of main proceedings, produces a stay),

95 See in Ho (ed) (n 28) S Golick, P Riesterer and M Wasserman, 'Canada' (but *cf Re Hartford Computer Hardware Inc* (2012) 94 CBR (5th) 20, [16]–[17] which appears to treat the Canadian provision as identical to the model text); A Lopez and J Munoz, 'Chile'; T Bubalo, V Janicijevic, M Novakov and B Vuckovic, 'Serbia and Montenegro' ('Unlike the Model Law, the Serbian legislation does not include the expression "manifestly" as a qualifier of public policy. Therefore, the public policy exceptions should not be interpreted restrictively'); Gerard McCormack and Wai Yee Wan (n 67) at 286–7 and *Re Zetta Jets Pte Ltd* [2018] SGHC 16 (Singapore), the court concluding that the omission of the qualifier must be taken to have been 'deliberate and conscious' ([22]), and that it followed from this that 'the standard of exclusion on public policy grounds in Singapore is lower' ([23]), but that the same result would have attained on the facts even if a more restrictive interpretation of Article 6 were adopted; Wan and McCormack (n 29) 75–6.

96 *In the matter of PT Garuda Indonesia (Persero) Tbk* [2024] SGHC (1).

97 Drawing on the passage from the Guide extracted above, [1.6.01]: see ibid [87].

98 ibid [88].

99 Ibid [93].

100 Consider, for example, differences in approach to the scope of Article 21, and in particular to the question of whether relief is limited to that which would be available in local proceedings: see G McCormack, 'US Exceptionalism and UK Localism? Cross-Border Insolvency Law in Comparative Perspective' (2016) 36(1) Legal Studies 136. Such a limitation would tend to reduce the potential for conflict with local public policy, a point made in argument in *Re Pan Ocean* [2018] BCC 4. Similarly, local provision for the modification of the stay that would otherwise arise automatically on recognition of foreign main proceedings may reduce the need to have recourse to Article 6: see *Nordic Trustee ASA v OGX Petróleo E Gás S.A.* [2016] Bus. L.R. 121 (High Court of England and Wales), Snowden J nevertheless considering it to be strongly arguable that the conduct of the applicant had been such as to warrant a refusal to recognise altogether on public policy grounds.

the public policy reservation has only been 'rarely applied'.[101] Certainly, there is nothing to suggest that the inclusion of Article 6 has functioned to 'defeat the objectives' of the Model Law project,[102] which again is testament to the careful and balanced approach taken to the drafting of the instrument, with multiple 'safety valves' for local interests.[103] Some jurisdictions have also adopted procedural mechanisms to deter unmeritorious attempts by counsel to invoke the public policy reservation.[104]

101 See Mevorach (n 32) 537.

102 See above, [1.6.11].

103 See above, [1.6.18] and n 32.

104 See J Clift, 'The UNCITRAL Model Law on Cross-Border Insolvency – A Legislative Framework to Facilitate Coordination and Cooperation in Cross-Border Insolvency' (2004) Tulane Journal of International and Comparative Law 307 at 338, reporting on the recommendation of the Law Commission of New Zealand that the legislation adopting the Model Law make provision for the court to involve the Solicitor-General in proceedings in which Article 6 was invoked. The Law Commission explained that this would give the court the benefit of 'independent argument' on the public policy question, and 'may also serve to deter counsel from raising public policy objections which have little or no merit': Report No 52, 'Cross-Border Insolvency: Should New Zealand adopt the UNCITRAL Model Law on Cross-Border Insolvency?', [152], and for the final legislative provision, Schedule 1, Article 6 of the Insolvency (Cross-Border) Act 2006. See also 'Report of Working Group V (Insolvency Law) on the work of its 39th session', Vienna, 6–10 December 2010, A/CN.9/715, [28].

Article 7

ADDITIONAL ASSISTANCE UNDER OTHER LAWS

Kristin van Zwieten

Nothing in this Law limits the power of a court or a [insert the title of the person or body administering a reorganization or liquidation under the law of the enacting State] to provide additional assistance to a foreign representative under other laws of this State.

A. INTRODUCTION AND RELATIONSHIP WITH ARTICLE 8

1.7.1 Articles 7 and 8 were late additions to the text of the Model Law, being proposed for inclusion only shortly before the adoption of the final text by the Commission at its 630th meeting on 30 May 1997.[1] Article 8 addresses how domestic versions of the Model Law are to be interpreted, with a view to ensuring that the overall objective of enabling states to coalesce around a set of 'basic principles and threshold rules'[2] on access, recognition, and cooperation is not undone by divergence in the interpretation of these rules at the national level.[3] Article 7 addresses the relationship between a domestic version of the Model Law, as interpreted at the national level, and other parts of the domestic

1 'Report of the United Nations Commission on International Trade Law on its work of its thirtieth session', 12-30 May 1997, General Assembly, Official Records, 52nd session, Supplement No. 17 (A.52/17), [174]–[175].

2 'Report of the Working Group on Insolvency Law on the Work of the 18th Session' (Vienna, 30 October–10 November 1995), A/CN.9/419, [18]; see also above, [1.6.11].

3 See further the commentary on Article 8 below; see also *Re PT Garuda Indonesia (Persero) Tbk* [2024] SGHC (1) at [90]–[91].

law,[4] providing that the former does not limit any power to offer 'additional assistance' – that is, assistance going beyond that for which the Model Law provides[5] – to the representative in foreign proceedings[6] under other parts of the domestic law.

Presented in this way, the two provisions appear complementary: Article 8 is directed to ensuring that the Model Law is capable of setting a 'common floor' as between enacting states,[7] while Article 7 is directed to ensuring that doing so does not inadvertently impose a 'ceiling' on the relief that any one enacting state can offer. Put differently, the Model Law project was aimed not at harmonisation *per se*, but at harmonisation with a view to *increasing* cooperation in cross-border cases,[8] against the backdrop of evidence that, at the time that the project was proposed, the laws of some states altogether precluded recognition of, and assistance in respect of, foreign proceedings.[9] Consistently with this, the Guide to Enactment of the Model Law provided the following guidance to states considering whether to enact a domestic version of Article 7: **1.7.2**

> The purpose of the Model Law is to increase and harmonise cross-border assistance available in the enacting State to foreign representatives. However, since the law of the enacting State may, at the time of enacting the Law, already have in place various provisions under which a foreign representative could obtain cross-border assistance, and since it is not the purpose of the Law to displace those provisions to the extent they provide assistance that is additional to or different from the type of assistance dealt with in the Model Law, the enacting State may consider whether Article 7 is needed to make that point clear.[10]

---

4 As to the relationship between a domestic version of the Model Law and a state's obligations under a treaty with other states, see the commentary on Article 3.

5 See 'Report of the United Nations Commission on International Trade Law on the work of its thirtieth session' (n 1) [175], describing the proposal for the inclusion of an article 'to the effect that nothing in the Model Provisions limited the power of the court to provide greater assistance to a foreign representative under any other laws of the enacting State'.

6 The 'foreign representative' is the person or body authorized in a 'foreign proceeding' to administer the reorganization or liquidation of the debtor's assets or affairs or act as a representative of the foreign proceeding: see the commentary on Article 2 and below, [1.7.3].

7 Consistently with this characterisation, see the various references to the provision of a 'minimum list' or 'minimum catalogue' in relation to relief following recognition in 'Report of the Working Group on Insolvency Law on the Work of its 21st Session' (New York, 20–31 January 1997), A/CN.9/435 (19 February 1997), and the record in the same document of 'wide opposition' to the suggestion that the draft provisions on cooperation be amended to make such cooperation contingent on prior recognition, on the grounds that the introduction of such a requirement 'would run counter to the current practice, pursuant to which judicial cooperation, when granted, was granted without prior recognition' ([196]) (or, put differently, could have functioned to reduce, rather than increase, the cooperation available).

8 See 'Report of the Working Group on Insolvency Law on the Work of the 18th Session' (n 2) [58], [75].

9 'Possible future work: Note by the Secretariat – Addendum – Cross-Border Insolvency', A/CN.9/378/Add.4, 23 June 1993, [18].

10 'Guide to the Enactment of the UNCITRAL Model Law on Cross-Border Insolvency' A/CN.9/442 (19 December 1997), [90].

B. SCOPE

1.7.3 Article 7 is concerned with the powers of a local 'court',[11] or of any person or body designated by the enacting State as one who administers a reorganisation or liquidation under local law,[12] to offer assistance to the 'foreign representative' under 'other laws' of the enacting State – that is, under laws other than the domestic version of the Model Law. The 'foreign representative' is the person or body authorised in a 'foreign proceeding'[13] to administer the reorganisation or liquidation of the debtor's assets or affairs or to act as a representative of the foreign proceeding.[14] The focus on the provision of assistance to a 'foreign representative' (rather than to a foreign court) suggests that Article 7 is primarily aimed at clarifying that the enactment of Chapter III of the Model Law – which makes provision for the recognition of foreign proceedings (see Arts 15–17)[15] and the (discretionary) grant of 'any appropriate relief' following recognition (see Art. 21),[16] on the application of the 'foreign representative' – should not be received as foreclosing the possibility that there will also be other routes to assistance available to the foreign representative elsewhere in the domestic law of the enacting State.

1.7.4 This interpretation would appear to leave open the question of the relationship between the provision made in Chapter IV of the Model Law for cooperation with foreign courts and foreign representatives and any provision elsewhere in the domestic law for such cooperation, but this is perhaps unsurprising once regard is had to the fact that Chapter IV simply requires cooperation 'to the maximum extent possible'.[17] While the interpretation of any domestic version of the Model Law will turn on domestic rules of statutory construction, it does not appear particularly plausible to posit that, merely by choosing to enact this provision mandating cooperation, the lawmaker risks inviting the conclusion that any pre-existing legal bases for cooperation must be taken to have been

11 See above, commentary on Article 5 at [1.5.1] and the commentary on Article 4.

12 See above, [1.5.5].

13 See Article 2(a) and the commentary on Article 2.

14 Article 2(d) of the Model Law, and above, [1.5.5], noting that the Model Law does not insist on a strict symmetry between the concepts of a 'foreign representative' in 'foreign proceedings' and the kinds of local representatives and proceedings that an enacting State could list for the purposes of filling out Articles 5 and 7.

15 Provision is also made for interim relief on the making of an application for recognition (see Art. 19), and for certain (limited) relief to flow automatically from the recognition of foreign proceedings as 'foreign main proceedings' (see Art. 20).

16 The list of forms of relief in Art. 21(1) was always intended to be inclusive rather than exhaustive: see 'Report of the Working Group on Insolvency Law on the work of its 20th Session' A/CN.9/433 (24 October 1996), [132].

17 See Article 25(1).

eliminated. In contrast, the provision in Article 21 of the Model Law for the grant of 'any appropriate relief' at the request of the foreign representative, following recognition of the foreign proceedings, is hemmed in by detailed conditions.[18] Absent a clarification of the kind offered by Article 7, it might be queried whether, in enacting these provisions,[19] the lawmaker must be taken to have replaced (rather than augmented) any existing and potentially overlapping bases for relief available elsewhere in the domestic law that may not necessarily be subject to precisely the same conditions.[20]

It may be, of course, that the relief that is available to the foreign representative under the domestic version of Chapter III of the Model Law goes well beyond anything that would have been available elsewhere in the domestic law, so that the problem to which Article 7 is addressed simply does not arise.[21] Clearly, the more broadly the provision for the grant of 'any appropriate relief' to the foreign representative is interpreted by domestic courts, the less likely it is that such representatives will seek to rely on alternative routes to assistance. If, on the other hand, the domestic version of Article 21 is construed narrowly, alternative routes to assistance will assume much greater practical significance. This is the position under English law, following a series of decisions in which courts held that, on a proper construction, various forms of relief sought by foreign representatives fell outside the scope of Article 21 as enacted in the Cross-Border Insolvency Regulations 2006 (UK).[22] The power of the court **1.7.5**

18 See Article 21(3) (where relief is sought in respect of foreign non-main proceedings), and Article 22(1) (in granting or denying relief, the court must be satisfied that the interests of creditors and other interested persons are 'adequately protected'). The relief that Article 21(1) provides for is relief 'where necessary to protect the assets of the debtor or the interests of the creditors', which at least in the English courts has been treated as a further control on the application of the British version of the provision: see *Fibria Celulose S/A v Pan Ocean* [2014] EWHC 2124 (Ch), [61], and *Larsen v Navios International Inc* [2011] EWHC 878 (Ch), [20].

19 Again, depending on the particular (domestic) rules of statutory construction.

20 It may also be the case that the particular way in which the Model Law is enacted leads domestic courts to conclude that while a pre-existing power to cooperate has been preserved, its application should now be understood to be subject to the same conditions that govern the availability of discretionary relief under the domestic version of the Model Law. This appears to be the case in New Zealand, where a pre-existing power was restated (and expanded) in the legislation that adopted the Model Law: see the carefully reasoned judgment of Heath J in *Williams v Simpson (No 5)* [2010] NZHC 1786; [2011] 2 NZLR 380 (also noted in Ho, 'England' in Look Chan Ho (ed), *Cross-Border Insolvency* (4th ed), (Globe Law and Business, 2017), commentary on Art.7), s. 8 and Schedule 1 of the Insolvency (Cross-border) Act 2006 (New Zealand), and previously s.135 of the Insolvency Act 1967 (New Zealand), as discussed in T Keeper, 'Applications for Aid and Assistance in Respect of Foreign Insolvency Proceedings in New Zealand since the Enactment of the Insolvency (Cross-Border) Act 2006 (NZ)' (2019) 27 Insolvency Law Journal 4.

21 Consistently with this, see 'Greece' and 'Japan' in Ho (ed) (ibid) (the latter reporting that Art. 7 was not taken up due to the absence of any other system for assistance under Japanese law).

22 See *Rubin v Eurofinance* [2013] 1 AC 236, [2012] UKSC 46; *Re Pan Ocean Ltd* [2014] Bus. L.R. 1041, [2014] EWHC 2124 (Ch); *Re OJSC International Bank of Azerbaijan* [2019] 2 All ER 713, [2018] EWCA Civ 2802, all noted in van Zwieten (ed) *Goode on Principles of Corporate Insolvency Law* (5th ed, 2018),

under section 426 of the Insolvency Act 1986 to grant assistance on a request by a foreign court is at least in one respect obviously wider than the British version of Article 21, as interpreted by the courts,[23] but section 426 is only available on receipt of a request from a foreign court in a designated country or territory.[24]

1.7.6 However broadly a domestic version of Article 21 is construed, this route to relief will only be available – assuming the enactment of the Model Law in model form – where a foreign proceeding has been recognised either as a 'foreign main proceeding' (that is, one taking place in the place of the debtor's centre of main interests) or as a 'foreign non-main proceeding' (that is, one taking place in a place where the debtor has an establishment). The provisions in Chapter III on recognition and relief following recognition are confined to 'main' and 'non-main' foreign proceedings.[25] Accordingly, a representative in foreign proceedings taking place in a jurisdiction in which the debtor has neither its centre of main interests nor any establishment (which might be, for example, in the case of a corporate debtor, the place in which a debtor has been incorporated) cannot rely on Chapter III, and must therefore look elsewhere for a basis on which the particular form of assistance sought may be given.[26] Although Article 7 appears primarily concerned with clarifying that the intro-

---

Ch. 16. The Insolvency Service has since proposed enacting Article X of the UNCITRAL Model Law on Recognition and Enforcement of Insolvency-Related Judgments as a response to *Rubin*: 'Implementation of two UNCITRAL Model Laws on Insolvency Consultation' (July 2023). *Cf* the position in Singapore as explored most recently in *PT Garuda Indonesia* (n 3), having regard to the legislative history of the enactment of the Model Law in Singapore.

23 Since section 426(5) makes express provision for the application of the foreign law: see *England v Smith* [2001] Ch. 419, [2000] 2 WLR 1141, and (on the British version of Art. 21), *Pan Ocean* ibid.

24 Jurisdiction to assist at common law is not so confined, but there are other (severe) limitations on the scope of this jurisdiction and the conditions under which it may properly be exercised: see most recently *Kireeva v Bedzhamov* [2024] UKSC 39, and earlier *Singularis Holdings Ltd v PricewaterhouseCoopers* [2015] A.C. 1675, [2014] UKPC 36.

25 See Article 2(a)–(c), Art.2(b) and (c) defining a foreign main proceeding as one taking place in the State where the debtor has its centre of main interests and a foreign non-main proceeding as one taking place in a State where the debtor has an establishment. For some of the background to this drafting decision, see 'Draft legislative provisions on judicial cooperation and access and recognition in cases of cross-border insolvency' A/CN.9/WG.V/WP.44 (8 March 1996); 'Report of the Working Group on Insolvency Law on the Work of its Nineteenth Session' (New York, 1–12 April 1996), A/CN.9/422; 'Revised articles of the draft UNCITRAL Model Legislative Provisions on Cross-Border Insolvency' A/CN.9/WG.V/WP.46 (6 September 1996), Art. 11; 'Report of the United Nations Commission on International Trade Law on the work of its 30th session', (n 1) [154]. In Canada, however, the legislator relaxed this restriction by defining foreign 'non-main' proceedings as any foreign proceedings other than main ones: see s.45 of the Companies' Creditors Arrangement Act R.S.C. 1985, c. C-36, and s.268 of the Bankruptcy and Insolvency Act RSC 1992, c. B-3, as noted by G. McCormack and A. Hargovan, 'Australia and the International Insolvency Paradigm' (2015) 37(3) Sydney Law Review 389, section B.

26 See *Williams v Simpson* as discussed above (n 20); *Gainsford* as noted below (n 28), and more generally the Australian decisions discussed by Scott Atkins in his commentary on Art. 7 in 'Australia' in Ho (ed) (n 20).

duction of a domestic version of Chapter III does not foreclose the possibility that there may be 'additional or different'[27] types of assistance available to the foreign representative in recognised 'main' or 'non-main' proceedings elsewhere in the domestic law, the presence of Article 7 may also offer domestic courts some comfort as they seek to identify bases for the grant of relief in cases that fall entirely outside the scope of Chapter III.[28]

C. TAKE-UP AND INTERPRETATION

Surveys by others of the take-up of the Model Law[29] suggest that in most cases,[30] Article 7 has been adopted in model form, and has not proved contentious in practice. The exceptional case is that of the United States, where there appears to have been considerable case law on the interpretation of the provision for 'additional assistance' in §1507 of the US Bankruptcy Code, which is understood to incorporate Article 7 of the Model Law,[31] and its relationship with the provision in §1521 of the Code for the grant of 'any appropriate relief' following recognition.[32] This appears to be a function, however, of the way in which the Model Law was enacted (in place of, rather than alongside, §304 of the US Bankruptcy Code), and of the particular choices made in the drafting of §1507, which unlike the model text is expressed to apply only after recognition and 'subject to the specific limitations' set out elsewhere in Chapter **1.7.7**

27 See above, [1.7.2] and [1.7.3].

28 As the Federal Court of Australia appeared to do in *Gainsford, in the matter of Tannenbaum v Tannenbaum* [2012] FCA 904, [55] (the reference to Art. 8 rather than Art. 7 here appearing to be a slip).

29 See Ho (ed) (n 20), in which take-up of the Model Law in Australia, British Virgin Islands, Canada, Cayman Islands, Chile, Colombia, England, Greece, Japan, Mauritius, Mexico, New Zealand, Philippines, Poland, Romania, Scotland, Serbia and Montenegro, Singapore, South Africa and OHADA Member States, South Korea and the United States is examined.

30 Steven Golick, Patrick Riesterer and Marc Wasserman have noted (in 'Canada' in Ho (ed) (n 20)) that the Canadian version of the Model Law did not include Article 7 in model form, but instead provided a 'conceptually similar' provision in Article 61(1) of the Companies' Creditors Arrangement Act RSC 1985, c. C-36, which under the heading 'Court not prevented from applying certain rules' provides that nothing in the relevant part of the statute 'prevents the court, on the application of a foreign representative or other interested person, from applying any legal or equitable rules governing the recognition of foreign insolvency orders and assistance to foreign representatives that are not inconsistent with the provisions of this Act'. (Notice, however, that the Canadian provisions on recognition and relief are wider than that contemplated under the Model Law in model form: see above, n 25). Michal Barlowski (in Ho (ed) (n 20)) notes that Poland did not enact Article 7 in model form, but that the same result is produced by another provision in the enacting legislation.

31 See Craig Martin, 'United States' in Ho (ed) (n 20).

32 See *Atlas Shipping A/S 404* B.R. 726, 741 (Bankr. SDNY 2009) and *Vitro S.A.B. de C.V.* 701 F.3d 1031, 1057 (5th Cir. 2013), and the other cases cited in UNCITRAL, 'Digest of Case Law on the UNCITRAL Model Law on Cross-Border Insolvency' (2021), Art.7.

15, and which requires the court to consider various factors in determining whether to provide additional assistance.[33]

1.7.8 In jurisdictions such as Australia and the UK, where the domestic version of the Model Law has been added to the existing 'menu' or suite of options available where assistance is sought in respect of foreign proceedings,[34] Article 7 has simply been enacted in model form. Both jurisdictions do also have an additional rule, set out elsewhere in the enacting instrument, to regulate cases of conflict between the provisions of the Model Law, as enacted, and other parts of the domestic insolvency law regime. The wider of the two rules – the UK rule – provides that where a conflict arises between the Cross-Border Insolvency Regulations (2006) (introducing the British version of the Model Law) and other parts of British insolvency law (as defined),[35] the Regulations shall prevail.[36] [37] But since the Regulations themselves contain the text of Article 7, which provides that nothing in the Law limits the power of a court or of a British insolvency officeholder to provide additional assistance to a foreign representative under other laws of Great Britain, the effect of the conflict rule in relation to the particular question of the relief available to a foreign representative[38] is that relief 'additional to or different from'[39] that for which the Regulations provides remains available,[40] in line with the original intention.

33 A point also made by McCormack and Hargovan (n 25) Part III. For the background to these drafting choices, see JL Westbrook, 'Chapter 15 At Last' (2005) 79(3) American Bankruptcy Law Journal 713, 720.

34 As to the tendency to add to the UK 'menu' more generally, see K van Zwieten, 'Mid-Crisis Restructuring Law Reform in the United Kingdom' (2023) 24 EBOR 287 and, critical of this choice in respect of Australia, McCormack and Hargovan (n 25) Part IV.

35 Or with Part 3 of the Insolvency Act 1986 (on receivership): see *Sealy & Milman: Annotated Guide to the Insolvency Legislation* (26th ed, 2023) vol 2.

36 See Reg. 3 of the Cross-Border Insolvency Regulations 2006 (UK). As to the position in relation to the European Insolvency Regulation in cases covered by the Brexit transitional arrangements, see Schedule 1, Art. 3 of the Regulations and *Goode* (n 22) [1.16.12].

37 The Australian rules focus more narrowly on inconsistency between the Model Law and particular (identified) parts of the domestic law relating to assistance (see Part 3 of the Cross-Border Insolvency Act 2008 (Australia)), but similarly provide for the Model Law, as enacted, to prevail.

38 As opposed to other areas of potential conflict: see *Goode* (n 22) [1.16.13].

39 Above, text to n 10.

40 See *Goode* (n 22) [1.16.13].

Article 8

INTERPRETATION

Reinhard Bork

In the interpretation of this Law, regard is to be had to its international origin and to the need to promote uniformity in its application and the observance of good faith.

A. INTRODUCTION TO ARTICLE 8

The reason for the rule contained in Article 8 arises from the fact that the MLCBI is not directly applicable law, but must first be transposed into national law by the national legislators. Insofar as this has been done, the national courts apply national law, which in and of itself must also be interpreted according to national criteria. However, such an approach is not compatible with the objective of harmonisation, since the risk that rules that apply in a large number of states are interpreted and applied differently cannot be denied.[1] If the MLCBI aims to harmonise cross-border insolvency law by providing a blueprint that is to be adopted by as many states as possible so that the same legal rules apply in as many states as possible, then these legal rules must also be interpreted and applied uniformly so that they are consistent with international understandings[2] and provide for 'commercial predictability'.[3] The aim of Article 8 is to achieve this by requiring the national rules of cross-border **1.8.01**

1 Bork, Cross-Border Insolvency Law, Edward Elgar Publishing (Cheltenham), 2023, 9.
2 *Betcorp Ltd* 400 BR 266 (Bankr. D.Nev. 2009) at fn. 23.
3 *Fogerty v Petroquest Resources, Inc. (Re Condor Ins. Ltd)* 601 F.3d 319, 322 (5th Cir. 2010).

insolvency law to be interpreted and construed not like 'an ordinary piece of domestic […] legislation'[4] but, in light of its international origins and of the aim of harmonisation, 'so as to provide for reciprocity between all the states which may incorporate [the] UNCITRAL [Model Law] into their domestic law'.[5] In this respect, Article 8 'is a license to depart where appropriate from the well-settled rule of statutory interpretation that a court should prefer specific provisions over the general when striving to uncover the meaning of a statute'.[6] Vice versa, as Ho put it, Article 8 'serves as a common thread uniting all local enactments of the Model Law'.[7] This is in the interest of all enacting states;[8] enforces the principles of universality, mutual trust, cooperation and coordination and legal certainty (predictability);[9] and is of utmost importance for the success of the intended harmonisation of international insolvency law.

1.8.02 Article 8 follows many international role models.[10] Corresponding rules can be found not only in some United Nations conventions,[11] but also in other model laws.[12] In particular, an identical provision is available in Article 8 UNCITRAL Model Law on Recognition and Enforcement of Insolvency-Related Judgments.[13] Also, in European law, the rules of cross-border insolvency law in the European Insolvency Regulation are, in principle, to be construed autonomously, that is, independent of the national understanding of terms contained in the EIR. This has been recognised by the CJEU[14] and is common practice in the application of the EIR.

---

4 *Re Agrocor DD* [2017] EWHC 2791 (Ch) para. 35.

5 *Re Stanford International Bank Ltd* [2010] EWCA Civ 137 para. 23 (expressions in brackets added by me, R.B.).

6 *JSC BTA Bank* 434 BR 334, 340 (Bankr. SDNY 2010).

7 Ho, The Revised UNCITRAL Model Law Enactment Guide – A Welcome Product?, Journal of International Banking Law and Regulation, 2014, 325–40 at 336.

8 Cf. *UNCITRAL Model Law on Cross-Border Insolvency with Guide to Enactment and Interpretation*, United Nations Publications (New York), 2014, para. 106 and above van Zwieten at para. 1.5.02 fn. 15.

9 See *Re PT Garuda Indonesia (Persero) Tbk* [2024] SGHC(I) 1 para. 91; Bork, *Principles of Cross-Border Insolvency Law*, Intersentia (Cambridge/Antwerp/Portland) 2016, para. 7.22, 7.24; Craig, United States, in: Ho (ed.), *Cross-Border Insolvency*, 4th ed., Globe Law and Business (Horsell) 2017, p.646 at para. 9.1; Golick/Riesterer/Wassermann, Canada, in: Ho (*ibid*), 95 at 9.1.

10 Cf. *Guide to Enactment and Interpretation* (above fn. 8), para. 106.

11 E.g. Article 7 para. 1 United Nations Convention on Contracts for the International Sale of Goods.

12 E.g. Article 3 para. 1 UNCITRAL Model Law on Electronic Commerce; Article 2A para. 1 UNCITRAL Model Law on International Commercial Arbitration.

13 See below the comments by Wan on Article 8 MLIJ.

14 Examples are *CJEU* Case C-341/04 *Eurofood IFSC Ltd*, ECLI:EU:C:2006:281 para. 31; Case C-116/11 *Bank Handlowy w Warszawie SA and PPHU 'ADAX'/Ryszard Adamiak v Christianapol sp. z o.o.*, ECLI:EU:C:2012:739 para. 49; Case C-195/15 *SCI Senior Home (in administration) v Gemeinde Wedemark/ Hannoversche Volksbank eG*, ECLI:EU:C:2016:804 para. 19 et seq.

Article 8 has been transposed in many national laws. For example, a literal adoption of the template from the Model Law can be found, among others, in the United Kingdom (Article 8 Sch. 1 Cross-Border Insolvency Regulation 2006), Australia (Article 8 Sch. 1 Cross-Border Insolvency Act 2008), and India (sec. 6 Insolvency and Bankruptcy [Cross-Border Insolvency] Rules 2020, Insolvency and Bankruptcy Code, 2016, Part Z). In the USA, Article 8 finds its equivalent in § 1508 Bankruptcy Code, albeit with a slightly different wording.[15] In other MLCBI-based jurisdictions, however, Article 8 has not been included in the national cross-border insolvency law.[16] **1.8.03**

The collection of Case Law on UNCITRAL Texts (CLOUT)[17] and the Digest of Case Law on the UNCITRAL Model Law on Cross-Border Insolvency[18] contain many examples. The Guide to Enactment and Interpretation has explicitly emphasised that these databases have a specific role to play in the unilateral application of the Model Law in general and Article 8 in particular.[19] National courts are encouraged to follow decisions of courts in other jurisdictions unless these decisions 'are based on different adaptations of the Model Law or do not accord with the preparatory materials (reports of working groups)'[20] that led to the final draft of the Model Law. National courts take this call very seriously,[21] but this does not exclude national divergences, not **1.8.04**

---

15 'In interpreting this chapter, the court shall consider its international origin, and the need to promote an application of this chapter that is consistent with the application of similar statutes adopted by foreign jurisdictions.'

16 Examples are Canada (see Golick/Riesterer/Wassermann in: Ho [above n. 9], 95 at para. 9.1; Hannan, Do Words Matter?, PhD thesis [available at https://research-repository.uwa.edu.au/files/5338528/Hannan_Neil_2015.pdf, last accessed 5 April 2024], 2015, 30; criticized by Ziegel, Canada-United States Cross-Border Insolvency Relations and the UNCITRAL Model Law, 32 (2007) Brook. J. Int'l l., 1041, 1056 et seq.), the Dominican Republic, Poland, the Philippines, the Republic of Korea ('for practical reasons': *Rim*, Cross-Border Insolvency Law in Korea [available at https://www.klri.re.kr:9443/bitstream/2017.oak/9807/1/18059k.pdf, last accessed 5 April 2024], 2017, 10), and Uganda.

17 Available at: https://uncitral.un.org/en/case_law (last accessed 5 April 2024).

18 Digest of Case Law on the UNCITRAL Model Law on Cross-Border Insolvency, United Nations Publications (New York), 2021, p.34.

19 *Guide to Enactment and Interpretation* (above n.8), para. 107.

20 *Re Agrocor DD* [2017] EWHC 2791 (Ch) para. 36; similarly *O'Sullivan v Loy* 432 B.R. 551, 560 et seq. (ED Va. 2010).

21 Cf. *Bear Sterns* 374 BR 122 (Bankr. SDNY 2007); *Betcorp Ltd* 400 BR 266 (Bankr. D.Nev. 2009); *Fibria Cellulose S/A v Pan Ocean Co Ltd* [2014] EWHC 2124 (Ch); *Fogerty v Petroquest Resources, Inc. (Re Condor Ins. Ltd.)* 601 F.3d 319 (5th Cir. 2010); *Gainsford, Re Tannenbaum v Tannenbaum* [2012] FCA 904; *JSC BTA Bank* 434 BR 334 (Bankr. SDNY 2010); *Kapila, Re Edelsten* [2014] FCA 1112; *Lavie v Ran*, 390 BR 257 (S.D. Tex. 2008) and 607 F.3d 1017 (5th Cir. 2010); *Morning Mist Holdings Ltd. v Krys (Re Fairfield Sentry Ltd.)* 714 F.3d 127 (2nd Cir. 2013); *OAS S.A.* 533 BR 83 (Bankr. S.D.N.Y. 2015); *O'Sullivan v Loy* 432 B.R. 551 (ED Va. 2010); *Re PT Garuda Indonesia (Persero) Tbk* [2024] SGHC(I) 1; *Re Sphinx* 371 BR 10 (SDNY 2007); *Re Tri-Continental Exchange Ltd.* 349 BR 627 (Bankr. Cal.); *Re Zetta Jet Pte Ltd and others (N. 2)* [2019] 4 SLR 1343; *Re Zetta Jet Pte Ltd and Others* [2018] SGHC 16; *Rubin & Anor v. Eurofinance SA and Ors* [2009] EWHC 2129, [2010] EWCA Civ 895, and [2012] UKSC 46; *United Securities Sdn Bhd (in receivership and liquidation) v United Overseas Bank Ltd* [2021] SGCA 78 (and on this case Teong Ying

least because the MLCBI has not been adopted word by word in all states and Article 8 has not been implemented in all jurisdictions.[22]

1.8.05 As elaborated in detail by van Zwieten above,[23] Article 8 is closely connected to Article 7. While the latter ensures that enactments do not set a ceiling (or cap) on the assistance available under national law, the former sets the floor by promoting harmonised interpretations of texts in model form. It has been used for many disputes on how to interpret and apply national cross-border insolvency laws that are built in the lead of the MLCBI – various examples of which can be found in this commentary.

B. CRITERIA FOR INTERPRETATION

1.8.06 Article 8 contains three criteria for the interpretation of terms transposed from the MLCBI into national laws: international origin, promotion of uniformity and observance of good faith.

1. International Origin

1.8.07 As regards international origin, courts – and the same holds true for all other persons and institutions applying the relevant norms – must have in mind that they are dealing with national provisions which have an international background, as they are stemming from the MLCBI. Judges are therefore encouraged to free themselves from the usual national understanding of the terms in question and instead take into account that these are rules which have been formulated with the intention of achieving harmonisation across a large number of jurisdictions and must therefore be interpreted against this background.

1.8.08 This requires, above all, interpretation guidance derived from the materials on the MLCBI, that is, from the drafts, the minutes of the discussions, and the Guide to Enactment and Interpretation,[24] which often provide indications

---

Keat, What Is Sauce for the Goose May Not Be Sauce for the Gander – Analysing the Principles Applicable to Recognition of Foreign Parallel Proceedings in Staying Local Proceedings, [2021], 34 Insolv. Int, 120 et seq.)

22 See above n.16.

23 At para. 1.7.01 et seq.

24 Here, a problem may arise from the fact that the revised *Guide to Enactment and Interpretation* (2013; above n.8) deviates in certain aspects from the original Guide to Enactment (1997); see for more details Ho, The Revised UNCITRAL Model Law Enactment Guide – A Welcome Product?, Journal of International Banking Law and Regulation, 2014, 325–40.

of how certain terms should be understood.[25] In English law, this is explicitly stated in the Cross-Border Insolvency Regulations 2006.[26] Further, the interpretation should not refer to the technical meaning of an expression as recognised in the national legal system but instead prefer arguments stemming from the purpose and function of the term in an international context.[27] In particular, courts are instructed to have in mind that the MLCBI – and, in its lead, many national cross-border insolvency laws – strives for international cooperation and coordination, which supports interpretations that facilitate rather than hinder such cooperation and coordination.[28]

For example, in the English case *Fibria Cellulose S/A v Pan Ocean Co Ltd*, the judge was tasked to decide whether 'any appropriate relief' in Article 21(1) Sch. 1 CBIR 2006 was to be construed broadly ('any possible relief') or narrowly ('any relief available in national insolvency proceedings') and decided for the latter by saying: **1.8.09**

> I am directed by reg. 2 of the CBIR to consider the documents relating to the working group on the Model Law. On my reading of the reports of the working group, it was not intended that 'any appropriate relief' would allow the recognising court to go beyond the relief it would grant in relation to a domestic insolvency. I do not think that there is sufficient in the discussion in those reports which would allow me to conclude (as the court concluded in *Re Condor Insurance Co Ltd*[29]) that the words 'any appropriate relief' were intended to replicate the position under section 304 of the former US Bankruptcy Code. I also note that whenever the legal position under article 21 has been described in an English case or in a textbook on the CBIR the discussion proceeds on the basis that 'any appropriate relief' allows the court to grant the same sort of relief as it would grant in relation to a domestic insolvency.[30]

---

25 *Carter v Bailey and Hutchison* [2020] EWHC 123 (Ch) para. 110; *Fibria Cellulose S/A v Pan Ocean Co Ltd* [2014] EWHC 2124 (Ch) para. 107; *OAS S.A.* 533 BR 83, 91 et seq. (Bankr. SDNY 2015).

26 Reg. 2(2)(b)/(c) CBIR 2006. For the USA, see – among others – *Morning Mist Holdings Ltd v Krys (Re Fairfield Sentry Ltd)* 714 F.3d 127 (2nd Cir. 2013); for Singapore *United Securities Sdn Bhd (in receivership and liquidation) v United Overseas Bank Ltd* [2021] SGCA 78 para. 28.

27 *Re PT Garuda Indonesia (Persero) Tbk* [2024] SGHC(I) 1 para. 91; *Re Stanford International Bank Ltd* [2010] EWCA Civ 137 para. 6, quoting the *Guide to Enactment and Interpretation* (above n.8) para. 71 (now: para. 65).

28 Cf. *Fogerty v Petroquest Resources, Inc. (Re Condor Ins. Ltd.)* 601 F.3d 319, 329 (5th Cir. 2010); *JSC BTA Bank* 434 BR 334, 340/342 (Bankr. SDNY 2010).

29 This refers to the judgment of the United States Court of Appeal in *Fogerty v Petroquest Resources, Inc. (Re Condor Ins. Ltd.)* 601 F.3d 319 (5th Cir. 2010).

30 *Fibria Cellulose S/A v Pan Ocean Co Ltd* [2014] EWHC 2124 (Ch) para. 107. For a more nuanced view, see above *van Zwieten* at para. 1.7.05.

2. Promotion of Uniformity

1.8.10 The second interpretation guideline is the reference to the promotion of uniformity. This means that courts should endeavour to interpret an expression originating from the MLCBI in the same way as courts in other countries whose cross-border insolvency law is based on the MLCBI have previously done,[31] unless these decisions are based on different adaptations of the MLCBI[32] or do not accord with the preparatory materials (reports of working groups) that led to the final draft of the MLCBI.[33]

3. Observance of Good Faith

1.8.11 The meaning of the reference to 'good faith' in Article 8 is entirely unclear. Firstly, it is ambiguous what the call to act in good faith refers to. Is it a third, independent criterion to the interpretation of rules modelled on the MLCBI or is it an explanatory auxiliary criterion to the consideration of international origin and the promotion of uniformity? Secondly, the purpose of this requirement remains in the dark. Thirdly, the addressee of the good faith-requirement is not obvious: does it call on the courts to rule in good faith, or should they ensure that cross-border insolvency proceedings are to be conducted in good faith?

1.8.12 The drafts and *travaux preparatoires* relating to Article 8 do not provide any information.[34] In a nutshell, it follows from the Guide to Enactment and Interpretation[35] that Article 8 has been modelled on Article 3 para. 1 UNCITRAL Model Law on Electronic Commerce which on its part has been adopted from Article 7 para. 1 United Nations Convention on Contracts for the International Sale of Goods (CISG). However, the materials relating to these provisions are not helpful either. In the Report of the UN Commission on International Trade Law (11th Session) the issue of good faith was addressed. Article 5 Draft CISG stated that parties must observe the principle of good faith in the course of contract formation, whereas Article 13 (now: Article 7) Draft CISG did not include such a requirement. When drafting the final version, there was a considerable amount of support for removing the good faith provision as it was a mere 'moral exhortation' and this would not

31 *Betcorp Ltd* 400 BR 266 (Bankr. D.Nev. 2009) at fn. 32.

32 On this aspect, see *Hannan* (above n.16), 70 et seq.

33 See above at para. 1.8.04.

34 For the following I am grateful to Daniel Jukes, PhD student at the University of Oxford, for helpful research assistance and contributions.

35 Cf. above at para. 1.8.02.

allow a coherent body of case-law to develop. It was also said to be unnecessary as the requirement of good faith was implicit in 'all laws regulating business activity' and thus the provision was superfluous. It was also said that such a principle should go to validity and not formation of contract. On the other hand, arguments were put forward that the principle of good faith was well recognised in public international law, and that extending a general norm that regulates commercial activity to international trade was a 'valuable extension of a widely recognised norm of conduct'. In the end, the compromise was to move the good faith requirement to (what is now) Article 7 CISG. A similar discussion followed in the working group on electronic data interchange.[36]

Against this background, it seems obvious that the wording of Article 8 does not make any sense at all. Firstly, the addressees of good faith requirements are the parties to contracts and not the courts. Secondly, it goes without saying that courts are required to interpret the law in good faith. Thirdly, the reference to good faith is too vague to add any sensible meaning to the two other criteria mentioned in Article 8. Hence, the reference to good faith is superfluous in and of itself.[37] If one wants to attach any meaning to the clause at all, then one has to look at the history of the law. As explained above,[38] Article 8 ultimately goes back to Article 7 CISG. However, this rule calls 'for the observance of good faith *in international trade*'.[39] In this version, the wording of the law can be accepted because it ultimately requires the courts – albeit perhaps unnecessarily – to interpret the text of the law in such a way as to ensure proper behaviour on the part of the parties involved in international trade.[40] Applied to Article 8 MLCBI, this means that this provision requires the courts to pay attention to decent behaviour of the parties involved in cross-border insolvency proceedings. Ultimately, however, this is also a matter of course, which would not have been necessary to include in the MLCBI. **1.8.13**

It does therefore not come as a surprise that there is nearly no case law on this prerequisite at all and that some legislators, when implementing Article 8 in their national law, have decided to forgo this criterion. This in particu- **1.8.14**

36 See the report A/CN.9/387 at para. 54, available at https://uncitral.un.org/fr/node/364 (last accessed 5 April 2024).

37 See also Wessels, International Insolvency Law Part I, 5th ed., Wolters Kluwer (Deventer) 2022, para. 10253 ('a hollow norm').

38 At para. 1.8.12.

39 Italics by me, R.B.

40 As revealed by the *Digest of Case Law on the United Nations Convention on Contracts for the International Sale of Goods*, United Nations Publications (New York), 2016, p.43 para. 13 et seq., the judgments referring to good faith address the parties and not the courts.

lar holds true for the USA.[41] Unfortunately, the materials relating to these national norms are not illuminating either. Remarkably, other international legal frameworks do also not refer to 'good faith' in their interpretation clauses. A good example is Article 5 para. 1 Cape Town Convention on International Interests in Mobile Equipment, which reads: 'In the interpretation of this Convention, regard is to be had to its purposes as set forth in the preamble, to its international character and to the need to promote uniformity and predictability in its application.'

41 See § 1508 U.S. Bankruptcy Code (cf. above n.15).

Chapter II Access of foreign representatives and creditors to courts in this state

Article 9

RIGHT OF DIRECT ACCESS

Virginia Torrie

A foreign representative is entitled to apply directly to a court in this State.

A. INTRODUCTION TO ARTICLE 9

1. Access Principle

1.9.01 The principle of direct access to courts in enacting States is a cardinal feature of the MLCBI.[1] Direct access allows those involved in foreign insolvency proceedings – including foreign representatives, creditors, and other stakeholders – to seek assistance from the courts in enacting States.[2] The two main access provisions are found in Article 5 and Article 9.[3] Article 5 focuses on *outbound* aspects of access, in which insolvency representatives appointed in the enacting

1 *UNCITRAL Model Law on Cross-Border Insolvency with Guide to Enactment and Interpretation: Part Two*, United Nations Publications (New York), 2014, para. 24.

2 *Guide to Enactment and Interpretation* (n 1), para. 24.

3 *Guide to Enactment and Interpretation* (n 1), para. 25.

State are empowered to act abroad as foreign representatives on behalf of the respective insolvency proceeding in foreign States.[4] Article 5 provides that the power exercised by an insolvency practitioner in a foreign country will depend on the foreign law and courts, but does not depend on whether the foreign country has enacted legislation based on the MLCBI.[5] Article 9 is concerned with *inbound* aspects of access, meaning requests from foreign representatives to recognize foreign proceedings locally, to request relief, or to commence local proceedings within enacting States.[6]

2. Mutual Trust and Cooperation

Providing expedited and direct access to foreign representatives through Article 9 is critical to achieving cooperation between courts involved in cases of cross-border insolvency.[7] The principles of mutual trust and cooperation are at the core of the EU Insolvency Regulation, which provides a simplified mechanism for recognition and enforcement of foreign insolvency proceedings.[8] The MLCBI encourages cooperation among states in insolvencies that cut across multiple jurisdictions, but it does not establish a principle of mutual trust as understood in the European context.[9] As seen in *Iida v Kitahara (In Re Iida)* (*'Re Iida'*),[10] enacting States, and specifically the United States, have shown a willingness to provide foreign representatives with access to their courts to seek relief, while continuing to show deference to foreign decisions and proceedings.[11] In general, the more closely Article 9 was implemented into the law of enacting States as compared to the MLCBI in granting court access, the fewer issues arose through case law.[12] The principle of cooperation **1.9.02**

4 *Guide to Enactment and Interpretation* (n 1), para. 25.

5 *Guide to Enactment and Interpretation* (n 1), para. 100; *UNCITRAL Model Law on Cross-Border Insolvency with Guide to Enactment and Interpretation: Part One*, United Nations Publications (New York), 2014, art. 5 [*MLCBI*]. In particular, Article 5 covers the authority of certain individuals or organizations to act in a foreign country on behalf of a local bankruptcy case, as allowed by the laws of that foreign country. If the foreign country has laws based on the Model Law, the person or organization authorized to act abroad may try to use those laws for recognition and help. However, whether they can do this depends on whether the court in the foreign country sees them as a 'foreign representative' in 'foreign proceedings'.

6 *Guide to Enactment and Interpretation* (n 1), para. 25.

7 *MLCBI* (n 5), preamble ss (a).

8 Regulation (EU) 2015/848 of the European Parliament and of the Council of 20 May 2015 on insolvency proceedings (recast) [2015] OJ L141/19 at 26, para 65 [*EIR*]; Veder in Bork and van Zwieten (eds), *Commentary on the European Insolvency Regulation* (2nd edn, Oxford University Press 2022), [19.03].

9 *MLCBI* (n 5), preamble ss (a) and ss (c); *Guide to Enactment and Interpretation* (n 1), para. 3.

10 *Iida v Kitahara (In Re Iida)*, 377 BR 243 (9th Cir 2007) (United States Bankruptcy Appellate Panel for the Ninth Circuit) [*Re Iida*].

11 Peter M Gilhuly, Kimberly A Posin and Adam E Malatesta, 'Bankruptcy Without Borders: A Comprehensive Guide to the First Decade of Chapter 15' (2016) 24 Am Bankr Inst L Rev 47, 53–4; *Re Iida* (n 10).

12 Look Chan Ho, *Cross Border Insolvency: A Commentary on the UNCITRAL Model Law* (4th edn, Globe and Law Business Ltd 2017), 31 (Australia), 73 (British Virgin Islands), 123 (Cayman Islands), 148-149

has a unique emphasis in the North American countries of the United States, Canada and Mexico, as their cross-border cooperation pre-dates the MLCBI through the North American Free Trade Agreement.[13] Multiple cases interpreting and applying the MLCBI have arisen between these three countries, but limited jurisprudence exists outside of North America.[14]

B. FOREIGN REPRESENTATIVES

1. Purpose

1.9.03 Foreign representatives are appointed by the court to represent a debtor or the estate to administer the reorganization or liquidation of the debtors' assets and affairs.[15] Without the assistance of the courts, foreign representatives lack enforceability of their claim to a debtor's assets, which may be in the possession of another interested party abroad.[16] Article 9 assists foreign representatives by allowing them to seek relief under Articles 19, 20 and 21.[17] Forms of relief available for foreign representatives include interim discretionary relief, relief upon recognition and additional discretionary relief.[18]

(Colombia), 209 (England), 300 (Greece), 324 (Japan), 342 (Mauritius), 363 (Mexico), 448 (Poland; even broader in scope than Art 9 MLCBI), 470 (Romania), 490 (Serbia and Montenegro), 524 (Singapore), 561 (South Africa).

13 *North American Free Trade Agreement Between the Government of Canada, the Government of Mexico and the Government of the United States*, 17 December 1992, Can TS 1994 No 2 Preamble (entered into force 1 January 1994); *Agreement between the United States of America, the United Mexican States, and Canada*, 13 December 2019, (entered into force 1 July 2020).

14 UNCITRAL, Case Law on UNCITRAL Texts (CLOUT) (2007) UN Doc A/CN.9/SER.C/ABSTRACTS/64 at 9–10 [*Xacur*]; UNCITRAL, Case Law on UNCITRAL Texts (CLOUT) (2007) UN Doc A/CN.9/SER.C/ABSTRACTS/72, 5–6 [*North American Steamship*]. In relation to Article 9, six cases were found on the UNCITRAL CLOUT Database, one arose in Mexico (*Xacur*) between the US and Mexico, five arose in the United States (*Re Iida, North American Steamship, Re Amerindo, Re Bancredit, Re Bear Stearns*); of these 5, *North American Steamship* arose between US and Canada.

15 *MLCBI* (n 5), art. 2(d).

16 *Guide to Enactment and Interpretation* (n. 1), paras 5–9, 34–36; UNCITRAL, Case Law on UNCITRAL Texts (CLOUT) (2007) UN Doc A/CN.9/SER.C/ABSTRACTS/72, 8 [*Re Amerindo*]; *North American Steamship* (n 14) 5–6.

17 *Guide to Enactment and Interpretation* (n 1), paras 25, 34–36.

18 *Guide to Enactment and Interpretation* (n 1), paras 34–36; Ishita Das, 'The Need for Implementing a Cross-Border Insolvency Regime within the Insolvency and Bankruptcy Code, 2016' (2020) 45:2 Vikalpa 104, 108; for further discussion on relief, see the relevant commentaries on Articles 19, 20 and 21.

2. Relief

(a) Interim and Discretionary Relief

Article 19 (discussed more extensively below) provides interim discretionary relief to ensure the assets of the debtor are maintained, or transferred to a foreign representative or other designated individual before a court grants recognition.[19] Examples of relief under Article 19 include staying proceedings against a debtor's assets, entrusting the administration of assets to a foreign representative or another designated party, suspending a debtor's transfer rights, allowing the examination of witnesses and evidence, and providing any additional relief available under the laws of an enacting State.[20] Article 21 provides discretionary relief that can extend Article 19 relief and supplement any relief offered by Article 19 or Article 20.[21] Article 19 and Article 21 apply to foreign main and non-main proceedings, but Article 20 only takes effect on the recognition of foreign main proceedings.[22] **1.9.04**

(b) Recognition Relief

Article 20 provides relief upon recognition of a foreign main proceeding.[23] Once recognized, an automatic stay of proceedings for any actions or proceedings filed against a debtor in the enacting State takes effect, and an automatic suspension of transfer rights prevents the debtor from transferring assets.[24] Article 20 is also supplemented by Article 19 and Article 21.[25] For example, it has been observed that the discretionary nature of Article 21 can provide relief in proceedings of a rescue or reorganization nature that would otherwise not be appropriate under the scope of the Article 20 automatic stay (designed for foreign liquidations).[26] **1.9.05**

19 Guide to Enactment and Interpretation (n 1), para. 36.

20 *MLCBI* (n 5), art. 19.

21 *Guide to Enactment and Interpretation* (n 1), paras. 36, 171.

22 *Guide to Enactment and Interpretation* (n 1), para. 36.

23 *MLCBI* (n 5), art. 20.

24 *MLCBI* (n 5), art. 20; *Guide to Enactment and Interpretation* (n 1), para. 37.

25 *Guide to Enactment and Interpretation* (n 1), paras 36, 171.

26 Gerard McCormack, *EU Insolvency Law: Cross Border Insolvency Law in Comparative Focus* (Edward Elgar Publishing Ltd 2022) at 243, 246; UNCITRAL, *Digest of Case Law on the UNCITRAL Model Law on Cross-Border Insolvency*, 2021, 61; *Re Pan Oceanic Maritime Inc* [2010] EWHC 1734.

C. RECOGNITION

1. Purpose

1.9.06 Another primary feature of the MLCBI is to provide a legal framework for the recognition of qualifying foreign proceedings.[27] In doing so, the MLCBI avoids the significant time and effort required to authenticate foreign proceedings.[28] However, not all foreign insolvency proceedings are to be recognized.[29] Article 15 and Article 17 list the requirements and procedural steps to acquire recognition of foreign proceedings.[30] The requirements in Article 15 and Article 17 are not onerous, but do restrict eligible claims for recognition.[31] The MLCBI differs from the EU Insolvency Regulation, which automatically recognizes decisions opening insolvency proceedings across European Union Member States when they become effective.[32] The MLCBI is a template provided by UNCITRAL and recommended for adoption in national insolvency laws. However, states have modified its provisions when adopting it into national insolvency law. Further, a guarantee of mutuality is not a condition for recognition under the MLCBI.[33] Whereas recital 65 of the Recast EIR specifically contemplates that the automatic recognition of insolvency proceedings should be based on the principle of mutual trust.[34] The EIR's framing of mutual trust is based on a guarantee of mutuality that is present throughout European law; this guarantee of mutuality has also been affirmed in European case law.[35] The MLCBI, however, guarantees neither recognition nor mutuality, and exists only to provide guidelines which may facilitate an easier process. This difference accounts for the fact that the MLCBI leads to a court decision for recognition of proceedings. An example of this relationship between cooperation and recognition can be seen in the outcome of the US decision in *In Re*

---

27 *Guide to Enactment and Interpretation* (n 1), paras 24, 29.

28 *Guide to Enactment and Interpretation* (n 1), para. 29; for more in-depth discussion on authentication, see relevant commentary on Article 16.

29 *Guide to Enactment and Interpretation* (n 1), para. 29; In general, Article 1(2) of the MLCBI sets out the principle that certain entities subject to special insolvency regimes in enacting States can be excluded from implementations of the MLCBI, see *MLCBI* (n 5), art. 1(2).

30 *Guide to Enactment and Interpretation* (n 1), paras 24, 29; Articles 17, 15 and 16 work together to establish a straightforward and quick process for recognizing foreign proceedings. They eliminate complex technical demands that could slow down the recognition process unnecessarily. Article 15 outlines the basic technical requirements for recognition applications, while Article 17 grants the receiving court the authority to recognize a foreign proceeding.

31 *Guide to Enactment and Interpretation* (n 1), paras 24, 29.

32 *EIR* (n 8); *MLCBI* (n 5), art. 19.

33 Reinhard Bork, "The European Insolvency Regulation and the UNCITRAL Model Law on Cross-Border Insolvency" (2017) 26 Int'l Insolvency Rev 246, 248.

34 *EIR* (n 8), para. 65.

35 *MG Probud Gdynia sp. z o.o.* [2010] CJEU-444/07, paras 27–29.

Bear Stearns, where it was held that recognition must be obtained in order for comity and cooperation to be granted instead of vice versa.[36]

2. Access

(a) Recognition and Access in the US

When implemented in the United States (discussion of implementation in other jurisdictions can be found below at [1.9.10]), Article 9 and Article 15 MLCBI were combined to create § 1509 Bankruptcy Code.[37] This combination made recognition a requirement before foreign representatives could access the courts in the United States, with the exception of an application to the court to gain recognition.[38] The recognition requirement imposed by § 1509 relies on the definition of foreign proceedings under § 101 (23) Bankruptcy Code, and the definition of foreign main and non-main proceedings under § 1502 (4)/(5) Bankruptcy Code and Article 2 of the MLCBI.[39] Foreign representatives may experience difficulties accessing courts due to the conditions imposed by § 1509 Bankruptcy Code.[40] In general, the recognition requirement imposed by 11 USC §1509(a) and §1509(b) means that court access is not guaranteed as set out in Article 9 of the MLCBI; court access is only guaranteed in applying for recognition, with further court access being gated behind a grant of recognition. As will be further discussed in [1.9.08] and [1.9.09], the way in which a recognition requirement has been implemented into 11 USC §1509 requires consideration of topics outside the scope of Article 9 in the MLCBI, for example, determining whether a case involves a foreign main or non-main proceeding for the purposes of recognition.[41] These extra steps in gaining court access are important in considering the aspects of comity and cooperation under 11 USC §1509, which relate to a foreign representative's ability to gain access to other courts.[42] When a foreign representative is granted recognition, an order of recognition is required when seeking comity and cooperation from courts other than the court that granted recognition (as per 11 USC **1.9.07**

36 *In Re Bear Stearns High-Grade Structured Credit Strategies Master Fund Ltd*, 389 BR 325 (Dist Ct SD NY 2008) (United States District Court for the Southern District of New York) [*Re Bear Stearns*]; Craig Martin, 'United States' in Ho (n 12), 617.

37 *Bankruptcy Code*, ch 15 tit 11 USC § 1509 (2005) [*Bankruptcy Code*].

38 *Re Bear Stearns* (n 36), 333–334; *Bankruptcy Code* (n 37), §101.

39 *Bankruptcy Code* (n 37), §101; Article 2 defines terms relevant to cross-border situations addressed in the Model Law.

40 *Bankruptcy Code* (n 37), §101.

41 *Re Bear Stearns* (n 36).

42 Sandeep Gopalan and Michael Guihot, 'Recognition and Enforcement in Cross-Border Insolvency Law: A Proposal for Judicial Gap-Filling' (2015) 48 Vand J Transnat'l 1225, 1246–7.

§1509(c)).[43] If denied recognition, a foreign representative may not only lack the order granting recognition, but the court denying recognition may also issue an order preventing a foreign representative from gaining cooperation from other courts under 11 USC §1509(d).[44]

3. Foreign Proceedings

(a) Interpretation of Proceedings Pursuant to Insolvency Law

1.9.08 Difficulties related to recognition and access result from different interpretations of proceedings under insolvency law. The United States and United Kingdom courts have different interpretations of proceedings pursuant to insolvency-related laws as included in the definition of foreign proceedings in Article 2.[45] In particular, the courts disagree over the inclusion of voluntary winding-ups of solvent companies as proceedings related to insolvency.[46] In *Re Sturgeon Central Asia Balanced Fund Ltd (in liquidation) Carter v Bailey and another (as foreign representatives of Sturgeon Central Asia Balanced Fund Ltd)* (‘*Re Sturgeon*’), the United Kingdom Court explains that because the debtor remains solvent, the voluntary winding up is not a proceeding relating to insolvency in the context of a foreign proceeding under the MLCBI.[47] The United Kingdom Court further explains that including solvent debtors as members of proceedings related to insolvency would be contrary to the objectives and purpose of the MLCBI.[48] In *In Re Betcorp Ltd*, the United States Court disagreed.[49] The United States Court held that a debtor does not have to be insolvent for the proceeding to be related to insolvency.[50] It is possible that this flows from the fact that the debtor need not be insolvent to access Chapter 11 proceedings. Similarly, the United Kingdom makes a distinction between members’ voluntary winding-ups and creditors’ voluntary winding-ups. The latter are usually considered an insolvent liquidation, but it has been observed that members’ voluntary winding-ups are a common solvent restructuring method usually undertaken to ensure that value is returned to shareholders.[51]

---

43 *Bankruptcy Code* (n 37), §1509(c).

44 *Bankruptcy Code* (n 37), §1509(d).

45 *Re Sturgeon Central Asia Balanced Fund Ltd (in liquidation) Carter v Bailey and another (as foreign representatives of Sturgeon Central Asia Balanced Fund Ltd)* [2020] EWHC 123 (Ch), para. 117 [*Re Sturgeon*]; *In Re Betcorp Ltd* 400 BR 266 (Bankr D N 2009) (United States Bankruptcy Court for the District of Nevada), 281–282 [*Re Betcorp*].

46 *Re Sturgeon* (n 45), paras 96, 121.

47 *Re Sturgeon* (n 45), paras 96, 121.

48 *Re Sturgeon* (n 45), para. 117.

49 *Re Betcorp* (n 45), 281–282.

50 *Re Betcorp* (n 45), 281–282.

51 Ho (n 12), 189.

Under this distinction, it is suggested that including members' voluntary liquidation under the umbrella of solvent debtors in foreign proceedings (as was done in *Betcorp*, due to lack of distinction in interpreting Australian insolvency legislation) is against the broad policy of the MLCBI.[52] Foreign representatives should be aware of the enacting State's interpretation of proceedings under insolvency law in the context of foreign proceeding determination when accessing their courts, as there are varying levels of restrictiveness.

(b) Foreign Main and Non-Main Proceedings

After being deemed a foreign proceeding, the court must also classify proceedings as either foreign main or non-main proceedings before granting recognition.[53] Classification of foreign main proceedings centres on the discussion of where a debtor's 'centre of main interest' ('COMI') is, while classification of foreign non-main proceedings are based around the location of a debtor's non-transitory economic activity ('establishment').[54] The effect of this requirement on foreign representative access to the courts appears in *In Re Bear Stearns High-Grade Structured Credit Strategies Master Fund Ltd* (*'Re Bear Stearns'*).[55] In *Re Bear Stearns*, the foreign representatives were denied access to the court because their proceedings could not be classified as either foreign main or non-main proceedings pursuant to § 1502 Bankruptcy Code and Article 2 MLCBI.[56] Specifically, it was held that the fund in question, although having a registered office in the Cayman Islands, did not meet the requirements of COMI under Articles 2(b) MLCBI and 11 USC §1502 for the purposes of determining foreign main proceedings. Various petitioners of the fund were based in the US, with only two investors being registered and two directors with residence in the Cayman Islands. Foreign non-main proceeding status was also not designated; the activities that occurred in the Cayman Islands (audits and preparation of incorporation documents) were held not to meet the definition of economic activity for the purposes of establishment.[57] As such, foreign representatives must take special care when applying to the US for relief in 'letter box' cases, that is, cases in which a debtor's registered office is located in a state where few operations occur.[58] **1.9.09**

52 Ho (n 12), 189.
53 Ho (n 12), 189.
54 Martin (n 36), 614.
55 *Re Bear Stearns* (n 36), 333–334.
56 *Re Bear Stearns* (n 36), 338–339.
57 Martin (n 36), 617.
58 G Ray Warner and Michael Veder, 'Enterprise Group Restructuring: Dutch Options and United States Enforcement' (2021) 7 EIRJ https://repository.ubn.ru.nl/bitstream/handle/2066/240749/240749.pdf?sequence=1&isAllowed=y 44.

4. Other Jurisdictions, Limitations, and Exception

(a) Other Jurisdictions

1.9.10 Similar to the United States, Canada has implemented a version of the MLCBI that has a recognition requirement for foreign representative court access.[59] Unlike the United States and Canada, countries such as the United Kingdom, Australia, New Zealand and Singapore have not added a recognition requirement.[60] While case law does not suggest that this recognition requirement has been abused, it is possible that this deviation from the MLCBI leaves the door open for a territorialist approach to foreign insolvency proceedings. Implementation of the MLCBI is based on the idea of harmonization of cross-border insolvency laws. Adding the extra requirement of recognition not only interferes with the simplified mechanism for recognition and enforcement as purported by the MLCBI, but also provides enacting States an additional option to deny universal relief, which may allow said states to prioritize local interests despite the objectives of the MLCBI.[61]

(b) Other Limitations

1.9.11 In addition to recognition, other requirements restrict foreign representative access to the courts in enacting States.[62] When considering a case in the United States, the courts require a live case or controversy.[63] In *Re Bancredit Cayman Ltd*, the foreign representatives sought an extension of the statute of limitations and recognition of foreign proceedings.[64] Extending the statute of limitations would apply to all the foreign representatives' activities as liquidators, including those which had not occurred.[65] The United States Court provided no relief, holding that there was no live case or controversy and explaining the inappropriateness of the request.[66] Foreign representatives should be aware of the live case and controversy requirement, as well as any other underlying provisions which could restrict foreign representative access to the courts when pursuing

59 *Bankruptcy and Insolvency Act*, RSC 1985, c B-3, s 269 ss (1); *Companies' Creditors Arrangement Act*, RSC 1985, c C-36, s 46 ss (1).

60 *MLCBI* (n 5), art. 9; *Cross-Border Insolvency Regulations 2006* (UK), SI 2006/1030, art. 9; *Cross-Border Insolvency Act 2008* (Cth), 2008/24, art 9; *Insolvency (Cross-Border) Act 2006* (NZ), 2008/171 57, art. 9; *Companies Act*, (Cap 50, 2006), art. 9.

61 Irit Mevorach, 'On the Road to Universalism: A Comparative and Empirical Study of the UNCITRAL Model Law on Cross-Border Insolvency' (2011) 12 Eur Bus Organization L Rev 517, 549.

62 *In Re Bancredit Cayman Ltd*, 2008 Bankr LEXIS 3544, 50 Bankr. Ct Dec 257 (Dist Ct SD NY 2008) (United States District Court for the Southern District of New York), 2–3 [*Re Bancredit Cayman*].

63 *Re Bancredit Cayman* (n 62), 2–3.

64 *Re Bancredit Cayman* (n 62), 2.

65 *Re Bancredit Cayman* (n 62), 2.

66 *Re Bancredit Cayman* (n 62), 2, 6.

relief in the United States. Foreign representatives should also be aware of any provisions that restrict access in other jurisdictions, as other enacting States may have additional requirements that are not part of the MLCBI.

(c) Exception

Although recognition is a requirement that restricts foreign representative access to the courts in the United States, foreign representatives may attain relief without engaging the court. *Re Iida* explains that foreign representatives do not always require court access to exercise rights that have been assigned to them by a foreign court, at least in the United States.[67] Foreign representatives can exercise the rights assigned to them if there is no challenge to their authority and capacity.[68] In *Re Iida*, the foreign representative acted as the debtor's trustee because they were authorized to do so by the Japanese Bankruptcy Court.[69] Upon authorization, the foreign representative began restructuring the company with no initial complaint filed by the debtor.[70] Months later, the debtor filed a complaint challenging the foreign representative's capacity and authority.[71] Upon the filing of the debtor's complaint, the foreign representative accessed the court to acquire recognition and seek relief.[72] It is important to note that, in the absence of the complaint, the foreign representative could take action as a trustee without having to access the courts.[73] **1.9.12**

It is also worth noting that 11 USC § 1509(f) provides an exception to the recognition requirement.[74] Under this section, failure to obtain recognition will not affect a foreign representative's right to sue in US Courts for collection or recovery of a property claim of the debtor.[75] As such, as long as the US Court has the jurisdiction over the subject matter, foreign representatives still have a right of access in this limited context.[76] **1.9.13**

---

67 *Re Iida* (n 10), 252–254.
68 *Re Iida* (n 10), 252–254.
69 *Re Iida* (n 10), 252.
70 *Re Iida* (n 10), 248, 250.
71 *Re Iida* (n 10), 250.
72 *Re Iida* (n 10), 258.
73 *Re Iida* (n 10), 258.
74 *Bankruptcy Code* (n 37), § 1509(f).
75 Gilhuly, Posin and Malatesta (n 11), 84.
76 Gilhuly, Posin and Malatesta (n 11), 84.

Article 10

LIMITED JURISDICTION

Virginia Torrie

The sole fact that an application pursuant to this Law is made to a court in this State by a foreign representative does not subject the foreign representative or the foreign assets and affairs of the debtor to the jurisdiction of the courts of this State for any purpose other than the application.

A. INTRODUCTION TO ARTICLE 10

1. Introduction

1.10.01 Article 10 of the MLCBI restricts exposure of foreign representatives to the jurisdiction of enacting States, while also protecting debtors' foreign assets and affairs.[1] Article 10 arises from the access principle and the right provided by Article 9.[2] In the absence of Article 10, foreign representatives

1 *UNCITRAL Model Law on Cross-Border Insolvency with Guide to Enactment and Interpretation: Part Two*, United Nations Publications (New York), 2014, para. 26.

2 *Guide to Enactment and Interpretation* (n 1), para. 26.

and debtors' foreign assets and affairs would be at risk of exposure from other interested parties within the enacting State they access.[3] In jurisdictions such as the United Kingdom, Canada, Australia, New Zealand and Singapore, no applications of Article 10 were found. There are several cases that reinforce the 'safe conduct' afforded to foreign representatives by Article 10, and fewer that mention its potential application in the US, further discussed in 1.10.09.[4] However, these cases do not include an actual application of Article 10.

2. Purposes

Article 10 limits the jurisdiction of enacting States over foreign representatives and the foreign assets and affairs of debtors.[5] Proceedings in an enacting State are limited to the application made by the foreign representative.[6] States may have legislation that provides court jurisdiction over any defendant that submits to the jurisdiction of said State's courts. As such, Article 10 provides that a foreign representative has not submitted to the court's jurisdiction solely because of an application that is made under implementations of the MLCBI.[7] Foreign representatives should not be subject to additional proceedings unless certain circumstances exist.[8] These circumstances could include, but are not limited to, a foreign representative committing misconduct, a tort or a crime in an enacting State; under these circumstances, a foreign representative may be subject to the jurisdiction of said State to address the consequences of such conduct.[9] **1.10.02**

Article 10 also limits debtor asset exposure to the assets included in the original application.[10] Any assets outside of the application's scope are protected unless an exception applies.[11] To illustrate: suppose a foreign representative is attempting to acquire possession of a debtor's asset that is currently in posses- **1.10.03**

3 *Guide to Enactment and Interpretation* (n 1), para. 26.

4 UNCITRAL, Digest of Case Law on the UNCITRAL Model Law on Cross-Border Insolvency, United Nations Publications (New York), 2021, 30 (footnote 2); UNCITRAL, Case Law on UNCITRAL Texts (CLOUT) (2007) UN Doc A/CN.9/SER.C/ABSTRACTS/76, 4 [*In Re Lloyd*]; *CSL Australia v Britannia Bulkers A/S* No. 08-15187 (SDNY 2009); *In Re Manley Toys Ltd*, 580 B.R. 632 (Bankr D NJ 2018) (United States Bankruptcy Court for the District of New Jersey) [*Re Manley Toys 2018*].

5 *Guide to Enactment and Interpretation* (n 1), para. 26.

6 *Guide to Enactment and Interpretation* (n 1), paras. 26, 110.

7 Andrew Chan, Alexander Yeo and Nigel Yeo, 'Singapore' in Look Chan Ho (ed), *Cross Border Insolvency: A Commentary on the UNCITRAL Model Law* (4th edn, Globe and Law Business Ltd 2017) 525.

8 Ho (n 7), 525.

9 *Guide to Enactment and Interpretation* (n 1), para 110; see also, Scott Atkins, 'Australia' in Ho (n 7) 32.

10 *Guide to Enactment and Interpretation* (n 1), para. 110.

11 *Guide to Enactment and Interpretation* (n 1), paras 26, 110.

sion of another interested party. In such an instance, the other interested party cannot begin to counterclaim for any of the debtor's other assets.

3. Objectives

(a) General Objective

1.10.04 Article 10 encourages foreign representatives to file for recognition by providing them with limited jurisdiction protection.[12] This Article ensures that an enacting State does not supersede jurisdiction over foreign proceedings.[13] This Article also prevents unnecessary litigation over a debtor's assets located outside of an enacting State.[14]

(b) Foreign Representatives

1.10.05 Article 9 allows foreign representatives to access courts in enacting States to assist them in reorganizing, liquidating or transferring a debtor's assets.[15] Article 10 ensures foreign representatives can fulfil their role as defined in the MLCBI.[16] In the absence of Article 10, a foreign representative's ability to reorganize, transfer or liquidate a debtor's assets may be frustrated, as they may face time-consuming suits from local creditors related to the aforementioned matters that would otherwise be addressed in ancillary proceedings.[17]

4. Limitations

(a) Limitation of Article 10 in the MLCBI

1.10.06 Another way in which the 'safe conduct' rule is not absolute is in relation to Article 22.[18] When foreign representatives seek recognition under Article 17, they may also seek discretionary relief under Article 19 or Article 21.[19] Article 22 allows a court to vary discretionary relief to protect interested parties from

---

12 *Guide to Enactment and Interpretation* (n 1), para. 24.

13 *Guide to Enactment and Interpretation* (n 1), para. 109.

14 *Guide to Enactment and Interpretation* (n 1), paras 109–110.

15 *Guide to Enactment and Interpretation* (n 1), para. 3; Article 9 focuses on the inbound dimension of access, which pertains to requests made by foreign representatives within enacting States.

16 *UNCITRAL Model Law on Cross-Border Insolvency with Guide to Enactment and Interpretation: Part One, United Nations Publications* (New York), 2014, art. 2(d) [*MLCBI*]; *Guide to Enactment and Interpretation* (n 1), paras 109–110.

17 *Guide to Enactment and Interpretation* (n 1), paras 109–110; Bryan Stark, 'Chapter 15 and the Advancement of International Cooperation in Cross-Border Bankruptcy Proceedings' (2006) 6 J Global L & Bus 203, 218.

18 *Guide to Enactment and Interpretation* (n 1), para. 110; Ho (n 7), 32.

19 *Guide to Enactment and Interpretation* (n 1), para. 36; Articles 19 and 21 permit the foreign representative to request various measures, with the court having discretion in granting them.

undue prejudice.[20] For example, a court may require foreign representatives to suspend the transfer of assets in a certain jurisdiction.[21] A foreign representative must follow the varied relief conditions, or they may be subject to other proceedings.[22] Alternatively, a court may impose consequences that impact a debtor's assets.[23]

B. IMPLEMENTATIONS OF ARTICLE 10

1. Implementations of Article 10

In jurisdictions such as the United Kingdom, Australia, New Zealand and Singapore, the implemented version of Article 10 remains in its original format and wording.[24] **1.10.07**

2. Modified Implementations of Article 10

Article 10 was implemented into the US Bankruptcy Code as 11 USC § 1510 with the minor modification that it applies to foreign representatives who file a petition for recognition under 11 USC § 1515.[25] As such, the implementation of Article 10 in the US has been considered to have little practical difference to that of the MLCBI.[26] However, the 'safe conduct' reinforced in US case law often includes mention of 11 USC § 306, upon which 11 USC § 1510 was modelled, which also protects foreign representatives who appear in connection with involuntary bankruptcy proceedings in the United States from the jurisdiction of US courts for any other purpose.[27] Unlike 11 USC § 306, § 1510 does not further provide the courts with the power to vary conditions **1.10.08**

---

20 *MLCBI* (n 16), art. 22; *Guide to Enactment and Interpretation* (n 1), para. 21. Article 22(1) establishes a compulsory provision stipulating that the interests of all interested parties must be sufficiently safeguarded when relief is granted, denied, or modified.

21 *In Re Ace Track Co*, 556 BR 887 (Bankr ND IL 2016) (United States Bankruptcy Court for the Northern District of Illinois, Eastern Division), 910–911.

22 *Guide to Enactment and Interpretation* (n 1), para. 110.

23 *Guide to Enactment and Interpretation* (n 1), para. 110; for further discussion on relief, see relevant commentary below.

24 *Cross-Border Insolvency Regulations 2006* (UK), SI 2006/1030, art. 10 [*CBIR*]; *Cross-Border Insolvency Act 2008* (Cth), 2008/24, art. 10; *Insolvency (Cross-Border) Act 2006* (NZ), 2008/171 57, art. 10; *Companies Act*, (Cap 50, 2006), art. 10; *MLCBI* (n 16), art. 10.

25 *Bankruptcy Code*, ch 15 tit 11 USC § 1510 (2005) [*Bankruptcy Code*]; *MLCBI* (n 16), arts. 9, 10, 15.

26 Neil Hannan, *Cross-Border Insolvency: The Enactment and Interpretation of the UNCITRAL Model Law* (Springer 2017) 94; Craig Martin, 'United States' in Ho (n 7), 647.

27 Peter M Gilhuly, Kimberly A Posin and Adam E Malatesta, 'Bankruptcy Without Borders: A Comprehensive Guide to the First Decade of Chapter 15' (2016) 24 Am Bankr Inst L Rev 47, 85; *Bankruptcy Code* (n 25), § 306; *In Re Lloyd* (n 4).

of discretionary relief, as similarly seen under Article 22 or 11 USC § 1522.[28] Additionally, it has been observed in the US context that, although previously mentioned that the safe conduct rule is not absolute in relation to Article 22, 11 USC § 1522 was not meant to be applied in a manner that imposes jurisdiction on foreign representatives for reasons beyond Chapter 15 and similar actions.[29]

1.10.09 Article 10 is also implemented into Canadian law with several minor modifications, which, similar to the US, have been observed to have little practical effect in the context of cross-border insolvency.[30] In particular, the modifications include exceptions to the safe conduct rule where foreign representatives may be subject to orders for costs of proceedings, or if Canadian courts make certain orders conditional upon compliance of the foreign representative with other court orders.[31] Although the Canadian legislation placed its Article 10 provisions in the 'Miscellaneous Provisions' sections, they will only apply to scenarios where foreign representatives acquire recognition of foreign proceedings.[32]

1.10.10 The MLCBI's Guide to Enactment explains that Article 10 is intended to apply upon an application for recognition, showing alignment between the MLCBI and legislation in the United States.[33] However, the language of the MLCBI refers to 'an application pursuant to this Law' with no explicit mention of an application for recognition.[34] As such, Article 10's original format is broader than the modified versions and may be used for other proceedings aside from an application for recognition.[35]

---

28 *Bankruptcy Code* (n 25), §§ 306, 1510; *MLCBI* (n 16), art. 22. Although this is not a modified implementation of Article 10, the fact that the safe conduct rule applies to both § 306 and § 1510 makes it a relevant distinction.

29 Gilhuly, Posin and Malatesta (n 27), 85.

30 *Bankruptcy and Insolvency Act*, RSC 1985, c B-3, s 269 ss (1) [*BIA*]; *Companies' Creditors Arrangement Act*, RSC 1985, c C-36, s 46 ss (1) [*CCAA*]; Steven Golick, Patrick Riesterer and Mark Wasserman, 'Canada' in Ho (n 7), 96.

31 Golick, Riesterer and Wasserman (n 30), 96.

32 *BIA* (n 30), s 280; *CCAA* (n 30), s 57.

33 *CCAA* (n 30), s 57; *Bankruptcy Code* (n 25), §§ 306, 1510; *Guide to Enactment and Interpretation* (n 1), para 109.

34 *MLCBI* (n 16), art. 10.

35 *MLCBI* (n 16), art. 10.

3. Potential Issue

(a) Recognition Requirement and Foreign Proceedings

A potential issue as it relates to Article 10 is its use outside of an application for recognition. 11 USC § 1510, like § 1509, relies on the classification of foreign proceedings under 11 USC § 101 (23) before granting recognition and providing foreign representatives with limited jurisdiction protection.[36] Classification of foreign proceedings, in turn, relies on court interpretation of proceedings related to insolvency law. As discussed in the previous chapter, the inclusion of voluntary windings-up of solvent companies as proceedings pursuant to insolvency law differs across jurisdictions.[37] In the US this will not be an issue, as the courts classify the voluntary winding-up of a solvent company as a proceeding under insolvency law for purposes of recognition.[38] In jurisdictions such as the United Kingdom, the courts disagree.[39] However, in the United Kingdom no recognition requirement exists, and Article 10 will apply to any foreign representative application made under the Cross-Border Insolvency Regulations 2006.[40] In the United States, if 11 USC § 1510 did not apply, 11 USC § 306 would provide protection whether recognition was sought or not.[41] For example, in instances where a creditor brings involuntary bankruptcy proceedings against a foreign debtor in the US, with no other ongoing proceedings in another jurisdiction, no recognition is available because there are no foreign proceedings and 11 USC § 306 would still apply to the foreign debtor, protecting them from additional proceedings in the US. **1.10.11**

C. APPLICATION OF ARTICLE 10

1. Jurisprudence

Due to the lack of case law on the application of Article 10 across jurisdictions, its application remains somewhat ambiguous. *In Re Manley Toys Ltd* ('*Re Manley Toys*') provides a scenario where 11 USC § 1510 may apply.[42] The **1.10.12**

---

36 *Bankruptcy Code* (n 25), §§§§ 101, 1509, 1510, 1515.

37 *Re Sturgeon Central Asia Balanced Fund Ltd (in liquidation) Carter v Bailey and another (as foreign representatives of Sturgeon Central Asia Balanced Fund Ltd)* [2020] EWHC 123 (Ch), para. 117 [*Re Sturgeon*]; *In Re Betcorp Ltd* 400 BR 266 (Bankr D N 2009) (United States Bankruptcy Court for the District of Nevada), 281–282 [*Re Betcorp*].

38 *Re Betcorp* (n 37), 281–282.

39 *Re Sturgeon* (n 37), paras. 96, 121.

40 *CBIR* (n 24), art. 10.

41 *Bankruptcy Code* (n 25), §§ 306, 1510.

42 *Re Manley Toys 2018* (n 4), 15.

debtor was a foreign company being wound up in Hong Kong.[43] The foreign representatives were appointed under the Hong Kong proceedings and applied for recognition as a foreign main proceeding in the United States.[44] The United States Court recognized the proceedings, automatically providing a stay order under 11 USC §§ 1520 and 362.[45] The creditor in *Re Manley Toys* sought to advance two causes of action against an affiliate of the debtor.[46] The creditor also requested a post-judgment discovery to collect information about the affiliate through the testimony of the foreign representatives.[47] Although the automatic stay would not apply to the affiliate in this case, the Court indicated that the foreign representatives may not have to comply with the request due to 11 USC § 1510.[48] However, this issue was not decided by the Court.[49] Due to the Court's inaction, the application of 11 USC § 1510 remains unclear.[50]

1.10.13 A very limited potential application of Article 10 has also been observed in the context of automatic Chapter 11 stays and Chapter 15 recognition.[51] In *Re Gold & Honey Ltd*, Gold & Honey Ltd and Gold & Honey LP filed for Chapter 11 reorganization.[52] Soon after, the First International Bank of Israel (FIBI) filed for a receivership proceeding at the District Court in Israel, despite the automatic worldwide stay on debtor assets stemming from the Chapter 11 proceedings. The Israeli court refused to recognize the stay orders, noting that while the US Courts have worldwide jurisdiction over a debtor's assets as a result of Chapter 11 proceedings, US Courts neither have control over the actions of foreign courts nor can exercise control over foreign assets without the assistance of foreign courts.[53] FIBI appeared in multiple related US proceedings and made petitions opposing the stay orders and was told by the US Court that they could proceed with the receivership proceedings at their own risk; further orders were also given reinforcing the automatic stay. Ultimately, when FIBI applied for recognition of the Israeli receivership proceedings under Chapter 15, it was determined (alongside a lack of foreign main/non-main designation) that the contempt of FIBI for the US stay order

43 *Re Manley Toys 2018* (n 4), 1.
44 *Re Manley Toys 2018* (n 4), 1–2.
45 *Re Manley Toys 2018* (n 4), 2, 4.
46 *Re Manley Toys 2018* (n 4), 2.
47 *Re Manley Toys 2018* (n 4), 14–15.
48 *Re Manley Toys 2018* (n 4), 15.
49 *Re Manley Toys 2018* (n 4), 15.
50 *Re Manley Toys 2018* (n 4), 15.
51 Hannan (n 26), 191–2.
52 *Re Gold & Honey Ltd* [2009] 410 BR 357 (Bankr ED NY 2009) [*Re Gold & Honey*].
53 *Re Gold & Honey* (n 52).

could not allow US Courts to recognize the receivership proceedings, as any actions taken contrary to the stay order are void.[54]

It has been suggested that FIBI could have avoided the negative situation and the jurisdiction of the US courts altogether by not appearing at the US proceedings and only filing for recognition of the Israeli proceedings.[55] In doing so, FIBI could have relied on Article 10 to support the argument that US Courts had no jurisdiction over them, as they would have submitted themselves to US Courts only for purposes of obtaining recognition.[56] That being said, this is a very niche potential application of Article 10 and is arguably meant to address a gap in how Chapter 11 operates. If FIBI had been allowed to proceed and assets particularly significant to the reorganization had been sold, the chance for a successful reorganization could have been severely compromised.[57] As such, this application of Article 10 may not be relevant nor appropriate, should the US remedy the deficiencies of the Chapter 11 automatic stay through more internationally cooperative means.[58] **1.10.14**

2. Orders Granting Recognition of Foreign Proceedings

Other applications of Article 10, and specifically 11 USC §§ 1510 and 306, are apparent in Orders Granting Recognition of Foreign Proceedings ('Orders Granting Recognition') in the United States.[59] 11 USC §§ 1510 and 306 are referenced and used as boilerplate language in Orders Granting Recognition.[60] **1.10.15**

Incorporating 11 USC §§ 1510 and 306 into Orders Granting Recognition establishes limited jurisdiction with respect to the foreign representative and the debtor and its assets.[61] This affirms that, leading up to recognition, the **1.10.16**

---

54 *Re Gold & Honey* (n 52).

55 Hannan (n 26), 192.

56 Hannan (n 26), 192.

57 Jonathan C Gordon, 'Crossing the Line in Cross-Border Insolvencies' (2019) 27 Am Bankr Inst L Rev 17, 36 (This essentially applies to lifting automatic stays in the context of reorganizations as well, which was at issue in *Re Manley Toys*).

58 Hannan (n 26), 192.

59 *In Re DTEK Fin Plc*, 2017 Bankr LEXIS 4545 (Bankr SD NY 2017) (United States Bankruptcy Court for the Southern District of New York) 1 (O) [*Re Dtek*]; *In Re Serviços De Petróleo Constellation SA*, 2020 Bankr LEXIS 909 (Bankr SD NY 2020) (United States Bankruptcy Court for the Southern District of New York) 4 (15) [*Re Serviços*]; *In Re Magyar Telecom BC*, 2013 Bankr Lexis 5716 (Bankr SD NY) (United States Bankruptcy Court for the Southern District of New York) 1 (N) [*Re Magyar*]; *In Re Amerindo Internet Growth Fund Ltd*, (Bankr SD NY 2007) (United States Bankruptcy Court for the Southern District of New York) (Order Granting Recognition of Foreign Main Proceeding Pursuant to Sections 1515 and 1517 of the Bankruptcy Code and Related Relief) 5 [*Re Amerindo*].

60 *Re Amerindo* (n 59), 5.

61 *Re Dtek* (n 59), 1 (O); *Re Amerindo* (n 59), 5.

court has no reason to waive protection under these sections of the Bankruptcy Code.[62] Due to the usage of 11 USC §§ 1510 and 306 in Orders Granting Recognition, potential waivers of protection may be an area of future litigation in the United States.

D. ALTERNATIVES

1. Barton Doctrine

1.10.17 In the United States, an alternative to 11 USC § 1510 may be the 'Barton Doctrine'. The Barton Doctrine is a common law doctrine that prevents adversary proceedings against court-appointed fiduciaries or equivalent positions unless the appointing court provides leave.[63] The Barton Doctrine applies to positions such as trustees, trustees' counsels, court-appointed administrators and liquidators and members of the unsecured creditors' committee.[64] However, its application to foreign representatives is yet to be determined.[65] The lack of determination may result from the fact that the United States courts are unable to appoint foreign representatives during foreign proceedings, as this is the responsibility of the foreign court.[66] The United States courts only recognize the foreign representative's appointment by the foreign courts.[67] To acquire relief under the Barton Doctrine, an interested party in the United States would have to receive permission from the foreign court to initiate proceedings against the foreign representative.[68] The complexity of this arrangement is likely a key reason for the present lack of determination as to the Barton Doctrine's extraterritorial application.

62 *Re Amerindo* (n 59), 5.

63 *McKillen v Wallace (In Re Ir Bank Resolution Corp)*, 2019 US Dist LEXIS 166153 (Dist Ct D 2019) (United States District Court of Delaware), 12–13 [*Re IBRC*].

64 *Allard v Weitzman (In Re DeLorean Motor Co)* 991 F2d 1236 (6th Cir 1993) (United States Court of Appeals for the Sixth Circuit), 1241; *Carter v Rodgers*, 220 F3d 1249 (11th Cir 2000) (United States Court of Appeals for the Eleventh Circuit), 1251–1255 [*Carter*]; *Lawrence v Goldberg*, 573 F3d 1265 (11th Cir 2009) (United States Court of Appeals for the Eleventh Circuit), 1270; *MF Global Holdings Ltd v Allied World Assur Co (In Re MF Global Holdings Ltd)* 562 BR 866 (Bankr SD NY 2017) (United States Bankruptcy Court for the Southern District of New York); *Blixseth v Brown (In Re Yellowstone Mt Club)*, 841 F3d 1090 (9th Cir 2016) (United States Court of Appeals for the Ninth Circuit), 1095.

65 *Re IBRC* (n 63), 12–13.

66 *Re IBRC* (n 63), 10.

67 *Re IBRC* (n 63), 10.

68 *Re IBRC* (n 63), 10.

2. Other Alternatives

An alternative to 11 USC § 1510 is the automatic stay of proceedings available after a court grants recognition to foreign main proceedings under 11 USC § 1520 and § 362.[69] 11 USC § 362 primarily protects debtors but may apply to non-debtors, such as foreign representatives, if it is necessary to protect the debtor's reorganization.[70] In previous cases, proceedings to remove foreign representatives have not been allowed due to the detrimental effects which may have followed.[71] Removing foreign representatives puts a debtor's assets in the United States at great risk, as US courts lack the power to appoint new foreign representatives.[72] However, the court may grant an exception to the automatic stay of proceedings, potentially subjecting the foreign representative to additional proceedings that could result in their removal.[73] In determining whether to grant an exception to 11 USC § 362, the court balances potential prejudice to the debtor, potential additional hardship to the non-bankrupt party and the creditor's likelihood of success.[74] **1.10.18**

Similar to the automatic stay of proceedings provided by 11 USC §§ 1520 and 362, a stay of proceedings may be available for foreign representatives as discretionary relief under 11 USC §§ 1519 and 1521.[75] The relief granted under § 1519 would be available upon an application for recognition, while relief under § 1521 would only be available after a court grants recognition.[76] **1.10.19**

69 *Bankruptcy Code* (n 25), §§ 1520, 362; Stark (n 17), 218.
70 *Re IBRC* (n 63), 17.
71 *Re IBRC* (n 63), 16.
72 *Re IBRC* (n 63), 17–18.
73 *Re IBRC* (n 63), 21–22.
74 *Re IBRC* (n 63), 21–22.
75 *Bankruptcy Code* (n 25), §§ 1519, 1521(a)(7).
76 *Bankruptcy Code* (n 25), §§ 1519, 1521(a)(7).

Article 11

APPLICATION BY A FOREIGN REPRESENTATIVE TO COMMENCE A PROCEEDING UNDER [*IDENTIFY LAWS OF THE ENACTING STATE RELATING TO INSOLVENCY*]

Virginia Torrie

A foreign representative is entitled to apply to commence a proceeding under [identify laws of the enacting State relating to insolvency] if the conditions for commencing such a proceeding are otherwise met.

A. INTRODUCTION TO ARTICLE 11

1. Introduction

1.11.01 As part of the access principle, commencing proceedings under Article 11 is essential to resolving cross-border insolvency issues.[1] Once provided with access to the court in an enacting State under Article 9, foreign representatives

1 *UNCITRAL Model Law on Cross-Border Insolvency with Guide to Enactment and Interpretation: Part Two*, United Nations Publications (New York), 2014, para. 25.

can apply to commence insolvency proceedings within an enacting State.[2] In some instances, a debtor may have interests or assets that are not accessible without assistance from the courts in an enacting State due to jurisdictional issues.[3] For example, in *Palmer (as trustee in the bankrupt estate of SLATER) v Registrar-General of Land Titles of the Australian Capital Territory and Others*, English foreign representatives were required to seek additional court orders in Australia to be entitled to the transfer of the debtor's property.[4] The English foreign representative's delay in commencing proceedings resulted in the entitlement of property to Australian representatives who had acted more swiftly in registering the property of the debtor.[5]

In jurisdictions such as the United Kingdom, the United States, Canada, Australia, New Zealand and Singapore, limited applications of Article 11 were found. Only one application of Article 11 was found on the UNCITRAL CLOUT Database, in the case *King (Trustee), in the Matter of Zetta Jet Pte Ltd v Linkage Access Limited* ('*Re Zetta Jet*'), which arose in Australia.[6] **1.11.02**

2. Purpose

Article 11 deals only with the standing of a foreign representative to apply for domestic insolvency proceedings.[7] As any other interested party, foreign representatives must therefore meet all other conditions within an enacting State to initiate insolvency proceedings under Article 11, which may deter potentially abusive applications.[8] The potential obstacle to efficiency that Article 11 presents in granting only standing is somewhat remedied by Article 31 of the MLCBI. Article 31 provides a presumption that the debtor is insolvent upon successful recognition of foreign insolvency proceedings.[9] **1.11.03**

Article 11 is similar to provisions found in the EU Insolvency Regulation (EIR), which allow for the opening of secondary proceedings in other EU **1.11.04**

2 *Guide to Enactment and Interpretation* (n 1), para. 25.

3 *Guide to Enactment and Interpretation* (n 1), para. 114.

4 *Palmer (as trustee in the bankrupt estate of SLATER) v Registrar-General of Land Titles of the Australian Capital Territory and Others* (2017) 181 ACTR 1, para. 42 [*Palmer*].

5 *Palmer* (n 4), paras 3–6, 42.

6 *King (Trustee), in the Matter of Zetta Jet Pte Ltd v Linkage Access Limited*, [2018] FCA 1979, paras 31–37 [*Re Zetta Jet*].

7 Gerard McCormack, *EU Insolvency Law: Cross Border Insolvency Law in Comparative Focus* (Edward Elgar Publishing Ltd 2022), 265.

8 *Re Zetta Jet* (n 6), paras 31–37; *Guide to Enactment and Interpretation* (n 1), para. 114.

9 McCormack (n 7), 265; For further discussion on Article 31, see relevant commentary below. Article 31 holds that if a local proceeding requires the debtor to be bankrupt to start, recognizing a foreign proceeding counts as proof the debtor is bankrupt for that purpose.

Member States alongside main proceedings, further discussed below at 1.11.04.[10] Both entitle a foreign Insolvency Practitioner to apply for domestic insolvency proceedings, albeit under different conditions.

3. Objectives

(a) Preamble

1.11.05 Enabling foreign representatives to commence proceedings assists in achieving a fair and efficient administration of cross-border insolvencies that protects the interests of all creditors and other interested persons, including debtors.[11] The MLCBI maintains fairness and efficiency for foreign representatives by providing them with the same ability as any interested party to apply to commence insolvency proceedings in an enacting State.[12]

(b) Foreign Representatives

1.11.06 To ensure an effective administration of a reorganization or liquidation of a debtor's assets, foreign representatives may need to access the courts to commence insolvency proceedings.[13] In the absence of Article 11, foreign representatives' claims to debtor assets may be unenforceable.[14] Depending on the case, unattainable assets – based on the foreign representative's lack of capacity to act according to jurisdictional rules in an enacting State – may be significant. In some jurisdictions, when listing the persons able to commence insolvency proceedings, the relevant insolvency statutes do not mention foreign representatives.[15] As a result, foreign representatives in those countries may be limited in their capabilities to seek relief in cross-border insolvencies.[16] This can be contrasted with the approach found in the EU Insolvency Regulation. While the EIR does not establish the persons with the right to apply for commencement of main insolvency proceedings, leaving this a matter for national laws, it

---

10 Cf. articles 3(2) and 34 et seq. of Regulation (EU) 2015/848 of the European Parliament and of the Council of 20 May 2015 on insolvency proceedings (recast) [2015] OJ L141/19 at 21, para 23 [*EIR*].

11 *UNCITRAL Model Law on Cross-Border Insolvency with Guide to Enactment and Interpretation: Part One*, United Nations Publications (New York), 2014, preamble ss (c), art. 11 [*MLCBI*].

12 *Guide to Enactment and Interpretation* (n 1), para. 113.

13 *Guide to Enactment and Interpretation* (n 1), paras 5–9.

14 *Guide to Enactment and Interpretation* (n 1), paras 5–9; *Palmer* (n 4), para. 42. Another scenario in which foreign representatives' claims to debtor assets may be unenforceable is a situation where recognition and relief of the foreign proceeding had not been sought and obtained.

15 *Guide to Enactment and Interpretation* (n 1), para. 112; Enterprise Insolvency Law of the People's Republic of China, art. 7 (2006), Database of Laws and Regulations, National People's Congress, 2; Lei Ordinária 11.101 de 09.02.05, art. 97. 34. St. 34 Federalnii zakon ot 30 dekabr 2008 г. N 296-Ф3 'O nesostoyatel'nosti (bankrotstve)' // Sobranie zakonodatel'stva Rossiiskoi Federatsii. 2008. N 43. st. 4190.

16 *Guide to Enactment and Interpretation* (n 1), para. 112.

does heavily regulate the right to open secondary insolvency proceedings.[17] As such, under Article 37(1) of the EIR, insolvency practitioners in main insolvency proceedings have standing to apply for commencement of secondary insolvency proceedings, as do any other persons or authorities empowered to open secondary insolvency proceedings under the laws of the relevant Member State.[18]

The MLCBI contemplates that foreign representatives may commence proceedings without first receiving recognition.[19] Similar to Article 19, Article 11 provides a solution for urgent matters concerning preservation of the debtor's assets.[20] In particular, it has been suggested that Article 11 allows foreign representatives to block sales initiated by local creditors in enacting States who seek enforcement of court orders or judgements in relation to the debtor's assets.[21] Articles 11 and 19 both provide solutions for foreign representatives participating in foreign main or non-main proceedings; however, Article 19 is only available upon an application for recognition.[22] **1.11.07**

B. IMPLEMENTATIONS OF ARTICLE 11

1. Implementations of Article 11

In jurisdictions such as Australia, New Zealand and Singapore, the implemented version of Article 11 remains in its original format.[23] **1.11.08**

In *Re Zetta Jet*, the Australian Court examined the application of Article 11.[24] In this case, the foreign representative of Zetta Jet sought a transfer of a luxury yacht purchased with allegedly misappropriated funds.[25] After the initial purchase, Zetta Jet resold the luxury yacht, and the foreign representative wished **1.11.09**

17 Remigijus Jokubauskas and Marek Świerczyński, 'The Coordination of Main and Secondary Insolvency Proceedings in European Union Insolvency Law' (2022) 8:1 Int'l Comparative Jurisprudence 1, 5.

18 Jokubauskas and Świerczyński (n 17), 1, 5; *EIR* (n 10), art. 37(1).

19 *Guide to Enactment and Interpretation* (n 1), para. 114.

20 *Guide to Enactment and Interpretation* (n 1), paras 114, 170; Article 19 provides the court with the discretion to issue interim relief promptly upon the application for recognition when it is deemed necessary.

21 Neil Hannan, *Cross-Border Insolvency: The Enactment and Interpretation of the UNCITRAL Model Law* (Springer 2017), 94.

22 *Guide to Enactment and Interpretation* (n 1), paras 36, 114.

23 *Bankruptcy Code*, c 15 tit 11 USC § 1511 (2005) [*Bankruptcy Code*]; *Bankruptcy and Insolvency Act*, RSC 1985, c B–3, s 274 [*BIA*]; *Companies' Creditors Arrangement Act*, RSC 1985, c C-36, s 51 [*CCAA*]; *Cross-Border Insolvency Act 2008* (Cth), 2008/24, art. 11 [*CBIA*]; *Insolvency (Cross-Border) Act 2006* (NZ), 2008/171 57, art. 11 [*ICBA*]; *Companies Act*, (Cap 50, 2006), art. 11 [*SGCA*]; *MLCBI* (n 11), art. 11.

24 *Re Zetta Jet* (n 6).

25 *Re Zetta Jet* (n 6), para. 1.

to transfer the yacht into its possession.[26] A disagreement arose over Zetta Jet's classification under the Corporations Act.[27] As stated in Article 11, foreign representatives must meet the conditions under the laws of the enacting State to commence proceedings.[28] For a foreign representative to commence proceedings in Australia, the debtor must be a 'company' as defined under the Corporations Act.[29] Due to Zetta Jet's lack of registration in Australia, they could not be classified as a 'company', resulting in the dismissal of proceedings.[30]

2. Modified Implementations of Article 11

1.11.10 The UK implementation of Article 11 follows the MLCBI closely but makes the additional minor clarification that Article 11 only applies to foreign representatives appointed in foreign main or non-main proceedings.[31]

1.11.11 In the United States, Article 11 has been modified in its implementation.[32] 11 USC § 1511 requires recognition before a foreign representative can commence insolvency proceedings.[33] After being granted recognition but before commencing insolvency proceedings, a foreign representative must advise the recognition granting court of its intentions to apply to commence insolvency proceedings.[34] 11 USC § 1511 also specifies what types of insolvency proceedings a foreign representative may apply for, including an involuntary case under 11 USC § 303, or a voluntary case under §§ 301 or 302.[35] To commence a voluntary case under §§ 301 or 302, the foreign proceedings must be classified as foreign main proceedings.[36]

1.11.12 11 USC § 1511 allows foreign representatives to commence insolvency proceedings under chapters of the Bankruptcy Code other than Chapter 15.[37] The MLCBI is implemented through Chapter 15 in the United States and

26 *Re Zetta Jet* (n 6), para. 1.
27 *Re Zetta Jet* (n 6), para. 14.
28 *MLCBI* (n 11), art. 11.
29 *Re Zetta Jet* (n 6), para. 32.
30 *Re Zetta Jet* (n 6), paras 15, 22.
31 *Cross-Border Insolvency Regulations 2006* (UK), SI 2006/1030, art. 11 [*CBIR*]; the significance of this difference is further discussed in [1.11.07].
32 *MLCBI* (n 11), art. 11; *Bankruptcy Code* (n 23), § 1511.
33 *Bankruptcy Code* (n 23), § 1511; S Chandra Mohan, 'Cross-border Insolvency Problems: Is the UNCITRAL Model Law the Answer?' (2012) 21 Int'l Insolv Rev 199, 213-214.
34 *Bankruptcy Code* (n 23), § 1511(b).
35 *Bankruptcy Code* (n 23), § 1511(b).
36 *Bankruptcy Code* (n 23), § 1511(a)(2).
37 *In Re AJW Offshore Ltd*, 488 BR 551 (Bankr ED NY 2013) (United States Bankruptcy Court for the Eastern District of New York), 559 [*Re AJW*].

offers a range of solutions and relief for cross-border insolvencies.[38] However, Chapter 15's relief is limited in that specific avoidance provisions are not available.[39] These avoidance provisions are typically reserved for trustees and creditors and are available under Chapter 7 for liquidations and Chapter 11 for reorganizations.[40] Foreign representatives can initiate proceedings under Chapters 7 and 11, using 11 USC §§ 1511 and 1523 to pursue the excluded relief provisions.[41] However, care must be taken when seeking relief under Chapter 11 and Chapter 7, as 11 USC § 1528 sets forth further limitations. In particular, § 1528 limits jurisdiction of US courts in post-recognition Chapter 11 or Chapter 7 plenary cases to assets within US territorial jurisdiction.[42] This jurisdiction can be extended to extraterritorial assets for purposes of cooperation with foreign courts and proceedings, but only if the extraterritorial assets are not subject to foreign proceedings that have been recognized under Chapter 15.

An additional requirement to commence proceedings is the presence of assets in the United States. For a foreign representative to bring proceedings under § 1528 Bankruptcy Code, a debtor must have assets in the United States.[43] This requirement is largely a non-issue in practice, as it has been observed that the interpretation of 'assets' is so broad that the intangible contract rights of a debtor under a debt instrument or even a retainer deposited with a US lawyer to obtain recognition will meet the asset requirement.[44] **1.11.13**

In Canada, under the *Bankruptcy and Insolvency Act* ('*BIA*') and *Canadian Companies Arrangement Act* ('*CCAA*'), recognition is also a requirement before foreign representatives can commence proceedings under Canadian insolvency **1.11.14**

38 *Awal Bank, BSC v HSBC Bank USA (In Re Awal Bank, BSC)*, 455 BR 73 (Bankr SD NY 2011) (United States Bankruptcy Court for the Southern District of New York) at 79–80 [*Re Awal*]; *Tacon v Petroquest Res. Inc (In Re Condor Ins Ltd)*, 601 F3d 319 (5th Cir 2010) (United States Court of Appeals for the Fifth Circuit), 322–323 [*Tacon*].

39 *Re Awal* (n 38), 79–80; *Tacon* (n 38), 322–323.

40 *Re AJW* (n 37), 559; *Tacon* (n 38), 323–324.

41 *Tacon* (n 38), 323–324.

42 *Bankruptcy Code* (n 23), § 1528; Craig Martin, 'United States' in Look Chan Ho (ed), *Cross Border Insolvency: A Commentary on the UNCITRAL Model Law* (4th edn, Globe and Law Business Ltd 2017) 647, 659 (It is, however, further contemplated that section 305 *Bankruptcy Code* allows the US court to stay, dismiss, or limit plenary domestic cases if cooperation and coordination with foreign courts and proceedings are needed, which is aligned with the purposes set out in § 1501); for further discussion on § 1528, see relevant commentary in Chapter V on Article 28.

43 *In Re Toft*, 453 BR 186 (Bankr SD NY 2011) (United States Bankruptcy Court for the Southern District of New York), 192.

44 Ray Warner and Michael Veder, 'Enterprise Group Restructuring: Dutch Options and United States Enforcement' (2021) 7 EIRJ <https:// repository .ubn .ru .nl/ bitstream/ handle/ 2066/ 240749/ 240749 .pdf ?sequence=1&isAllowed=y> 23.

law.[45] The Canadian legislation also contains additional restrictions. Under the BIA, foreign representatives possess the same abilities as a creditor of the debtor, or the debtor themselves.[46] Foreign representatives may file for a bankruptcy order against the debtor, appoint a receiver over the debtor's property, make a bankruptcy assignment for the debtor or commence restructuring proceedings for the debtor.[47] Under the CCAA, a foreign representative also possesses the same abilities as a creditor of the debtor, or the debtor itself, but is limited to commencing or continuing proceedings under the CCAA.[48] However, as seen in *Tucker v Aero Inventory (UK) Ltd*, foreign representatives may also commence or continue proceedings under the BIA to maximize a debtor's assets.[49] Since section 274 BIA and section 51 CCAA are not implemented identically to Article 11 of the MLCBI, the ability of foreign representatives to act without having obtained recognition is unclear in relation to the MLCBI Guide and urgency of protecting debtor assets. However, it has been suggested that section 284(1) BIA and section 61(1) CCAA allow Canadian courts the broad authority to grant relief to foreign representatives before obtaining recognition if the circumstances (possibly urgency) are appropriate.[50]

3. Potential Issues

(a) Recognition Requirement and Foreign Proceedings

1.11.15 The modified implementations of the MLCBI in Canada and the United States contradict the Guide to Enactment, which states that recognition requirements should not prevent a foreign representative from commencing proceedings under the insolvency laws of an enacting State.[51] Imposing a recognition requirement makes this intention impossible to achieve. However, Article 11 states that foreign representatives must abide by any conditions to commence proceedings in an enacting State.[52] Although there is conflict

45 *BIA* (n 23), s 274; *CCAA* (n 23), s 51.

46 *BIA* (n 23), s 274.

47 *BIA* (n 23), s 274.

48 *CCAA* (n 23), s 51.

49 *BIA* (n 23), s 275; *Tucker v Aero Inventory (UK) Ltd*, 2010 ONSC 1196, paras 29-30.

50 Steven Golick, Patrick Riesterer and Marc Wasserman, 'Canada' in Ho (n 42), 96; *BIA* (n 23), s 284(1); *CCAA* (n 23), s 61(1) ('Nothing in this Part prevents the court, on the application of a foreign representative or any other interested person, from applying any legal or equitable rules governing the recognition of foreign insolvency orders and assistance to foreign representatives that are not inconsistent with the provisions of this Act').

51 *CCAA* (n 23), s 51; *BIA* (n 23), s 274; *Bankruptcy Code* (n 23), § 1511; *Guide to Enactment and Interpretation* (n 1), para. 114.

52 *MLCBI* (n 11), art. 11.

between the MLCBI and the implemented versions of the MLCBI in Canada and the United States, recognition requirements may be allowed.[53]

Another issue relating to recognition requirements is the classification of foreign proceedings relating to insolvency. The recognition requirement of 11 USC § 1511 relies on the definition of foreign proceedings relating to insolvency under § 1501.[54] As discussed in the previous chapter, the inclusion of voluntary windings-up of solvent companies as foreign proceedings differs across jurisdictions.[55] For example, the voluntary winding-up of a company in the United States is a (foreign) proceeding relating to insolvency that may be recognized.[56] However, in the United Kingdom, a voluntary winding-up of a solvent company is not a (foreign) proceeding relating to insolvency capable of recognition.[57] Although recognition is not required for a foreign representative to commence proceedings under English insolvency law,[58] this difference in interpretation is still relevant, as the UK implementation of Article 11 specifically requires that the foreign representative be appointed in either a foreign main or non-main proceeding.[59] In this context and in relation to winding-up orders, it has been observed that an English court may be influenced by the views of the foreign representative when deciding whether to exercise its discretion to grant a winding-up order.[60] **1.11.16**

(b) Types of Proceedings

The types of insolvency proceedings that foreign representatives may initiate differ in each enacting State analysed. In the enacting States that use more specific language to indicate which insolvency proceedings are available, there is less ambiguity and a smaller likelihood of litigation. **1.11.17**

53 *CCAA* (n 23), s 51; *BIA* (n 23), s 274; *Bankruptcy Code* (n 23), § 1511.

54 *Bankruptcy Code* (n 23), §§§ 101, 1511, 1515.

55 *Re Sturgeon Central Asia Balanced Fund Ltd (in liquidation) Carter v Bailey and another (as foreign representatives of Sturgeon Central Asia Balanced Fund Ltd)* [2020] EWHC 123 (Ch) [117] [*Re Sturgeon*]; *In Re Betcorp Ltd* 400 BR 266 (Bankr D N 2009) (United States Bankruptcy Court for the District of Nevada), 281–282 [*Re Betcorp*].

56 *Re Betcorp* (n 55), 281–282.

57 *Re Sturgeon* (n 55), paras 96, 121.

58 Howard P Morres et al, 'Cross-border Insolvencies after Brexit: Views from the United Kingdom and Continental Europe' (Brexit: The International Legal Implications delivered at the Centre for International Governance Innovation, Waterloo, March 2018), 134.

59 *CBIR* (n 31), art. 11; *Bankruptcy Code* (n 23), § 1511; *MLCBI* (n 11), art. 11.

60 Look Chan Ho, 'England' in Ho (n 42), 210; in particular, it has been stated that 'It is one thing to decline to exercise the winding up jurisdiction in circumstances where the foreign liquidator is opposed to ancillary proceeding in England. It is quite another to decline to exercise the jurisdiction when the foreign liquidator, the principal creditor, and a 50% shareholder all invite its exercise', see *Re OJSC ANK Yugraneft* [2008] EWHC 2614 (Ch); [2010] BCC 475, para. 64.

1.11.18 In the United States, Canada and New Zealand, each jurisdiction specifies the types of proceedings which a foreign representative may commence.[61] In Australia, Singapore and the United Kingdom, each jurisdiction references or lists the applicable insolvency statutes and provisions, but does not specify the types of proceedings that may be commenced.[62] Future litigation in Australia, Singapore and the United Kingdom may occur due to the general and ambiguous references to the types of insolvency proceedings which may be initiated.[63] The United States, Canada and New Zealand may avoid this future litigation due to the higher specificity in their statutes.[64]

(c) Mixing and Matching

1.11.19 Article 11 presents another problem: the mixing and matching of different insolvency laws. The UNCITRAL Working Group on Insolvency Law raised this as a concern during the MLCBI's development.[65] Mixing and matching may arise as a problem because the MLCBI permits recognizing foreign courts to grant relief, while also granting standing for foreign representatives to bring actions under the laws of the enacting State.[66] The MLCBI leaves unresolved the question of which proceedings would apply in the event that an enacting State recognizes foreign proceedings *and* grants standing to a foreign representative to bring an action under the laws of the enacting State.[67] Courts in enacting States should be alive to the fact that foreign representatives may attempt to mix and match proceedings to achieve an optimal solution in a given case.[68]

1.11.20 The Australian case *Aquino (Trustee), Re McGowan (Bankrupt) v McGowan* ('*Re McGowan*') examines the conflicts that may arise between laws of enacting States.[69] The American foreign representative in *Re McGowan* requested the entrustment and administration of all of Mr McGowan's assets located in Australia to Australian representatives, the reason being that they would be more familiar with Australian insolvency law and procedure.[70] It was clarified that Article 11 and Article 23 provided the American foreign representative

61 *Bankruptcy Code* (n 23), § 1511; *BIA* (n 23), s 274; *CCAA* (n 23), s 51; *ICBA* (n 23), art. 2 (i).
62 *CBIA* (n 23), s (8); *SGCA* (n 23), art 2(k); *CBIR* (n 31), art 2 (a).
63 *CBIR* (n 31), art 2 (a).
64 *Bankruptcy Code* (n 23), § 1511; *BIA* (n 23), s 274; *CCAA* (n 23), s 51; *ICBA* (n 23), art. 2 (i).
65 *Guide to Enactment and Interpretation* (n 1), para. 113.
66 *Tacon* (n 38), 326–327.
67 *Tacon* (n 38), 326–327.
68 *Tacon* (n 38), 326–327.
69 *Aquino (Trustee), Re McGowan (Bankrupt) v McGowan*, [2020] FCA 221, para. 1 [*Re McGowan*].
70 *Re McGowan* (n 69), paras 2, 70.

with standing to commence insolvency proceedings against Mr McGowan.[71] The American foreign representative, in turn, also sought for all powers normally available to trustees under the Bankruptcy Act of Australia to be afforded to the Australian representatives by way of Articles 11 and 23.[72] However, Mr McGowan argued that the American foreign representative, and by extension the Australian representatives, lacked this standing due to a conflict between the specific nature of the intended proceedings, and principles of private international law and the US Bankruptcy Code.

In particular, it was argued that all representatives were subject to the US Bankruptcy Code due to lex fori concursus.[73] Therefore, they could not commence antecedent transaction avoidance proceedings under sections 120–122 of the Australian Bankruptcy Act because similar proceedings under the US Bankruptcy Code were statute-barred under limitation periods.[74] The Australian Court rejected the arguments after an analysis of the relevant sections of the US Bankruptcy Code, ultimately reiterating that the American foreign representative possessed the same capabilities as an Australian trustee.[75] Thus, the American foreign and Australian representatives had full standing to commence proceedings against Mr McGowan under Australian insolvency law.[76] While this example of mixing and matching of insolvency laws may have been limited to the scope of the intended proceedings, foreign representatives should still be alive to the possibility of conflict between the MLCBI and an enacted State's insolvency laws, especially in the context of the US. **1.11.21**

Further conflicts may occur in jurisdictions such as the United States where insolvency proceedings may proceed under multiple statutes.[77] In *Awal Bank, BSC v HSBC Bank USA (In Re Awal Bank, BSC)* ('*Re Awal*'), the foreign representative of Awal Bank pursued litigation against one of its largest creditors, HSBC.[78] The foreign representative sought to avoid or invalidate HSBC's set-off under Chapter 11 of the Bankruptcy Code.[79] In *Re Awal*, it is explained that no mixing and matching was present because the foreign representative's **1.11.22**

71 *Re McGowan* (n 69), para. 69; Article 23 provides the foreign representative with procedural standing to commence domestic avoidance actions.

72 *Re McGowan* (n 69), para. 71.

73 *Re McGowan* (n 69), para. 72.

74 *Re McGowan* (n 69), paras 72, 76.

75 *Re McGowan* (n 69), paras 69–71, 73–75, 99.

76 *Re McGowan* (n 69), paras 69–71.

77 *Tacon* (n 38), 326–327.

78 *Re Awal* (n 8), 76.

79 *Re Awal* (n 8), 76.

powers under Chapter 11 took priority over Chapter 15.[80] As a result, there was no conflict, as the foreign representative had no reason to use Chapter 15 for simultaneous relief.[81] Although there was no conflict in *Re Awal,* it has been observed that the modified implementation of Article 11 is an indication of US Congress trying to apply domestic and similar laws to foreign proceedings.[82] That being said, the modified aspects have not been strictly enforced and the US has been cooperative with foreign representatives and courts, although it has been noted that this cooperative stance could change according to public sentiment.[83] Further, disputes do arise between different insolvency statutes in the United States. *In Re AJW Offshore, Ltd* ('*Re AJW*'), foreign representatives sought turnover relief under § 1521 Bankruptcy Code.[84] Unlike the excluded specific avoidance provisions, turnover relief provisions are available as relief under § 1521.[85] However, in *Re AJW* their availability as relief was nevertheless debated due to the fact that the statutes potentially conflicted.[86]

80 *Re Awal* (n 8), 88–89.
81 *Re Awal* (n 8), 89.
82 Hannan (n 21), 95.
83 Hannan (n 21), 95.
84 *Re AJW* (n 37), 553.
85 *Re AJW* (n 37), 558.
86 *Re AJW* (n 37), 557–559.

Article 12

PARTICIPATION OF A FOREIGN REPRESENTATIVE IN A PROCEEDING UNDER [*IDENTIFY LAWS OF THE ENACTING STATE RELATING TO INSOLVENCY*]

Michael Veder

Upon recognition of a foreign proceeding, the foreign representative is entitled to participate in a proceeding regarding the debtor under [*identify laws of the enacting State relating to insolvency*].

A. INTRODUCTION TO ARTICLE 12

Chapter II of the MLCBI deals with the access of foreign representatives and creditors to courts in an enacting State. The access of foreign representatives to the courts in enacting States is addressed in Articles 9 to 12 MLCBI. Article 9 MLCBI provides that a foreign representative is entitled to apply directly to a court in an enacting State, in particular in view of obtaining recognition and relief of the foreign proceeding,[1] while Article 10 MLCBI restricts the exposure of foreign representatives to the jurisdiction of enacting States.[2] Pursuant to Article 11 MLCBI, a foreign representative is entitled to apply for the commencement of an insolvency proceeding in respect of the debtor in **1.12.01**

1 For details, see the commentary on Art. 9 MLCBI by Torrie.

2 For details, see the commentary on Art. 10 MLCBI by Torrie.

an enacting State.[3] Article 12 MLCBI addresses the participation of foreign representatives in insolvency proceedings opened in respect of the debtor in an enacting State. Article 13 MLCBI provides that, subject to certain limitations, foreign creditors have the same rights regarding the commencement of, and participation in, a proceeding opened in an enacting State as creditors in that State.[4] Article 14 MLCBI addresses the notification to be given to foreign creditors in respect of proceedings pending in an enacting State.[5]

1.12.02 Article 12 MLCBI seeks to ensure that a foreign representative is entitled to participate in an insolvency proceeding opened in the enacting State in respect of a debtor that is subject to the foreign proceeding. A foreign representative should not be prevented from participating in such proceedings by the sole fact that he or she is appointed in a foreign proceeding and not in the enacting State.[6]

1.12.03 The collection of Case Law on UNCITRAL Texts (CLOUT)[7] and the Digest of Case Law on the UNCITRAL Model Law on Cross-Border Insolvency[8] do not reveal any relevant case law relating to Article 12 MLCBI.

B. RECOGNITION AS A PRE-CONDITION

1.12.04 In line with the proposals in the initial stages of the drafting of the MLCBI,[9] Article 12 MLCBI restricts the right of the foreign representative to participate in local proceedings in the enacting State to cases where the foreign proceeding has been recognized. Recognition of the foreign proceeding as a prerequisite for the foreign representative undertaking certain actions in the enacting State can also be found in, for example, Article 21 (discretionary relief upon recognition), Article 23 (transactions avoidance) and Article 24 (intervention in proceedings to which the debtor is a party).

3 For details, see the commentary on Art. 11 MLCBI by Torrie.

4 For details, see the commentary on Art. 13 MLCBI by Veder.

5 For details, see the commentary on Art. 14 MLCBI by Veder.

6 Cf. A/CN.9/WG.V/WP.103, para. 100.

7 Available at: https://uncitral.un.org/en/case_law.

8 Digest of Case Law on the UNCITRAL Model Law on Cross-Border Insolvency, United Nations Publications (New York), 2021, 32.

9 Cf. A/CN.9/422, paras 94, 114 and 115, where Article 7(1)(d) of the then current draft is cited and (briefly) discussed. Article 7(1)(d) of that draft provided: '(1) For the purposes of providing assistance to a foreign proceeding, recognition of a foreign proceeding by a competent court [...] (d) authorizes the foreign representative to intervene in collective proceedings for liquidation or reorganization in the enacting State'.

At some point, it was discussed in Working Group V whether such right to participate, as well as the right to intervene in proceedings to which the debtor is a party as currently provided for in Article 24 MLCBI, should be broadened so as not to be conditioned on recognition of the foreign proceeding.[10] The optionality for enacting States that was included in an earlier draft of the MLCBI in this respect[11] has subsequently been dropped,[12] maintaining recognition as a pre-condition for the foreign representative to participate in local proceedings. **1.12.05**

Article 11 MLCBI, which confers on the foreign representative the right to apply to the courts in an enacting State for the opening of an insolvency proceeding in respect of the debtor, does not contain a similar requirement.[13] Even without recognition or the filing of an application for the recognition of a foreign proceeding, a foreign representative is entitled to apply for the opening of an insolvency proceeding in the enacting State. Whether such local proceedings are opened depends on whether the conditions for commencing such a proceeding are otherwise met. Notwithstanding that at some point it was observed that the authority of a foreign representative to participate in local proceedings was closely related to the power of the foreign representative to request the opening of insolvency proceedings in the enacting State,[14] as currently provided for in Article 11 MLCBI, the two provisions have not been aligned. **1.12.06**

C. FOREIGN MAIN AND NON-MAIN PROCEEDINGS

For the application of Article 12, it does not matter whether the foreign proceeding was recognized as a foreign main or foreign non-main proceeding. Any foreign representative is, upon recognition of the foreign proceeding, entitled to participate in an insolvency proceeding opened in respect of the debtor in the enacting State. **1.12.07**

10 Cf. A/CN.9/422, para. 149.

11 Cf. A/CN.9/WG.V/WP.46, 9. Article 6 (Access of foreign representatives to courts) of that draft reads: 'A foreign representative may [...] (c) [upon recognition,] intervene in collective or any other proceedings in the enacting State affecting the debtor or its assets'.

12 Cf. A/CN/WG.V/WP.48, 11.

13 See the commentary on Art. 11, where, in para. 1.11.06, reference is made to legislation in the USA and Canada, in which, contrary to Article 11 MLCBI, the right to request the opening of local proceedings is conferred on a foreign representative on the condition that the foreign proceeding has been recognized.

14 Cf. A/CN.9/433, para. 58.

1.12.08 During the negotiations leading up to the adoption of the MLCBI, the issue was raised whether the right to participate in local insolvency proceedings should not be restricted to foreign representatives that were appointed in foreign main proceedings.[15] This suggestion was made against the backdrop of the general debate in Working Group V concerning the extent to which foreign non-main proceedings should be recognized and, if so, what the scope of the effects of recognition of foreign non-main proceedings should be. Later, it was suggested to restrict the right of participation of representatives of foreign non-main proceedings to cases where the participation in the insolvency proceeding in the enacting State 'relates to assets falling under the authority of the foreign representative or concerns information required in that foreign non-main proceeding'.[16] This suggestion sought to align the right of foreign representatives to participate in local proceedings with the general limitation on the scope of the relief available to foreign non-main proceedings in, now, Articles 21(3) and 23(2) MLCBI. Pursuant to Article 21(3) MLCBI, in granting relief to a representative of a foreign non-main proceeding, the court must be satisfied that the relief relates to assets that, under the law of the enacting State, should be administered in the foreign non-main proceeding or concerns information required in that proceeding. Article 23(1) confers standing on a foreign representative to initiate transactions avoidance actions in an enacting State, but, when a foreign proceeding is a foreign non-main proceeding, the court must be satisfied that such actions relate to assets that, under the law of the enacting State, should be administered in the foreign non-main proceeding. The suggestion was not adopted. It was considered that it would be difficult, or inappropriate, to link proposals of the foreign representative to particular assets.[17]

D. RIGHT TO PARTICIPATE

1.12.09 Article 12 MLCBI is limited to giving the foreign representative standing. It only seeks to ensure that, when an insolvency proceeding concerning a debtor is taking place in an enacting State, the foreign representative will be given, as an effect of recognition of the foreign proceeding, standing to be heard and make petitions, requests or submissions concerning issues such as protection, realization or distribution of assets of the debtor or cooperation with the

15 Cf. A/CN.9/433, para. 52.
16 Cf. A/CN.9/435, para. 148.
17 Cf. A/CN.9/435, para. 148.

foreign proceeding.[18] However, it does not vest the foreign representative with any specific powers or rights. What the right to participate entails is left to the law of the enacting State. Article 12 MLCBI deliberately does not clarify what the right 'to participate' actually entails and does not specify the kinds of motions that the foreign representative might make and does not affect the provisions in the insolvency law of the enacting State that govern the fate of any such motions.[19]

The EU Insolvency Regulation[20] also confers on insolvency practitioners the right to participate in other insolvency proceedings pending in the EU in respect of the same debtor, but is more specific and elaborate in this respect. For example, the insolvency practitioner or debtor-in-possession in main insolvency proceedings must be given notice of and an opportunity to be heard on a request for the opening of secondary insolvency proceedings.[21] Insolvency practitioners in main and any secondary insolvency proceedings are entitled to, and under certain circumstances obliged to, lodge in other proceedings claims which have already been lodged in the proceedings for which they were appointed.[22] Article 45(3) EIR provides that insolvency practitioners in main or secondary insolvency proceedings are entitled to participate in other proceedings 'on the same basis as a creditor, in particular by attending creditor's meetings'.[23] Furthermore, insolvency practitioners appointed in main insolvency proceedings are given additional rights in secondary insolvency proceedings that seek to ensure the 'primacy' of main insolvency proceedings, such as the right to request a stay of the process of realization of assets in secondary insolvency proceedings[24] and the right to propose a restructuring plan in secondary insolvency proceedings.[25] 1.12.10

18 UNCITRAL Model Law on Cross-Border Insolvency with Guide to Enactment and Interpretation, United Nations Publications (New York), 2014, para. 115.

19 Cf. A/CN.9/435, para. 150; Guide to Enactment and Interpretation (n 18), para. 116.

20 Regulation (EU) 2015/848 of the European Parliament and of the Council of 20 May 2015 on insolvency proceedings (recast) ('EU Insolvency Regulation' or 'EIR').

21 Article 38(1) EIR.

22 Article 45(2) EIR.

23 On this provision, see Reinhard Dammann, in: Bork and van Zwieten, Commentary on the European Insolvency Regulation (2nd edition), Oxford University Press 2022, paras 45.25 et seq.

24 Article 46(1) EIR. On this provision, see Dammann (n 23), paras 46.07 et seq.

25 Article 47(1) EIR. On this provision, see Dammann (n 23), paras 47.12 et seq.

Article 13

ACCESS OF FOREIGN CREDITORS TO A PROCEEDING UNDER [*IDENTIFY LAWS OF THE ENACTING STATE RELATING TO INSOLVENCY*]

Michael Veder

1. Subject to paragraph 2 of this article, foreign creditors have the same rights regarding the commencement of, and participation in, a proceeding under [*identify laws of the enacting State relating to insolvency*] as creditors in this State.
2. Paragraph 1 of this article does not affect the ranking of claims in a proceeding under [*identify laws of the enacting State relating to insolvency*], except that the claims of foreign creditors shall not be ranked lower than [*identify the class of general non-preference claims, while providing that a foreign claim is to be ranked lower than the general non-preference claims if an equivalent local claim (e.g. claim for a penalty or deferred-payment claim) has a rank lower than the general non-preference claims*].[b]

[b] The enacting State may wish to consider the following alternative wording to replace paragraph 2 of article 13:

2. Paragraph 1 of this article does not affect the ranking of claims in a proceeding under [*identify laws of the enacting State relating to insolvency*] or the exclusion of foreign tax and social security claims from such a proceeding. Nevertheless, the claims of foreign creditors other than those concerning tax and social security obligations shall not be ranked lower than [*identify the class of general non-preference claims, while providing that a foreign claim is to be ranked lower than the general non-preference claims if an equivalent local claim (e.g. claim for a penalty or deferred-payment claim) has a rank lower than the general non-preference claims*].

A. INTRODUCTION TO ARTICLE 13

Article 13 MLCBI embraces the principle that foreign creditors, when they apply to commence an insolvency proceeding in the enacting State or file claims in such a proceeding, should not be treated differently than local creditors.[1] This principle of non-discrimination, that is dictated by the principles of equal treatment of creditors and procedural justice,[2] entails that all creditors, both local and foreign, should enjoy the same rights when it comes to the commencement of and participation in insolvency proceedings. The EU Insolvency Regulation[3] follows the same approach.[4] **1.13.01**

Participation in insolvency proceedings requires that creditors have access to or receive information about the opening and conduct of insolvency proceedings pending in an enacting State. This issue is addressed in Article 14 MLCBI, which deals with the duty to notify foreign creditors.[5] **1.13.02**

The principle of non-discrimination, as adopted in the MLCBI, is not absolute. This is reflected in Article 13(2) MLCBI, which allows foreign creditors to be treated worse than similarly situated local creditors with respect to the ranking of their claims and explicitly provides for the possibility to exclude foreign tax and social security claims from access to and participation in local insolvency proceedings. **1.13.03**

The working documents of Working Group V show that the adoption of the principle of non-discrimination in the MLCBI as such did not give rise to much debate. The debate in Working Group V focused on the treatment of **1.13.04**

1 *UNCITRAL Model Law on Cross-Border Insolvency with Guide to Enactment and Interpretation*, United Nations Publications (New York), 2014, para. 118. See also A/CN.9/WG.V/WP.44, 25–6: 'the thrust of the provision is to establish the principle of non-discrimination.'

2 Cf. Reinhard Bork, *Advanced Introduction to Cross-Border Insolvency Law*, Edward Elgar Publishing 2023, 114.

3 Regulation (EU) 2015/848 of the European Parliament and of the Council of 20 May 2015 on insolvency proceedings (recast) ('EU Insolvency Regulation' or 'EIR').

4 Cf. Recital 63 and Article 53 EIR.

5 See the commentary on Art. 14 MLCBI by Veder.

foreign public law claims, notably foreign tax and social security claims, and the ranking of foreign claims in local insolvency proceedings opened in an enacting State.

1.13.05 The collection of Case Law on UNCITRAL Texts (CLOUT)[6] and the Digest of Case Law on the UNCITRAL Model Law on Cross-Border Insolvency[7] do not reveal any relevant case law relating to Article 13 MLCBI.

B. PRINCIPLE OF NON-DISCRIMINATION

1.13.06 The character of insolvency proceedings as collective proceedings entails that all creditors are entitled to participate in an insolvency proceeding. In principle, no distinction ought to be made as to the nationality, domicile, residence or registered office of creditors holding the claims, or the law governing the claims. The principle of non-discrimination is reflected in Article 13(1) MLCBI and the EU Insolvency Regulation. It is accepted in many jurisdictions around the world that have not adopted the MLCBI.[8]

1.13.07 The absence of discrimination between creditors, for example, based on nationality, residence, domicile, or registered office, is an essential condition to ensure the equal treatment of creditors as a fundamental principle of insolvency law.[9] Accordingly, Article 13(1) MLCBI seeks to ensure that foreign creditors, when they apply to commence an insolvency proceeding in an enacting State or file claims in such a proceeding, should not be treated worse than local creditors.[10]

1.13.08 The principle of non-discrimination is effectively enshrined in the EU Insolvency Regulation. As a matter of general European law, any form of discrimination on the basis of nationality or residence is prohibited.[11] The

---

6 Available at: https://uncitral.un.org/en/case_law.

7 *Digest of Case Law on the UNCITRAL Model Law on Cross-Border Insolvency*, United Nations Publications (New York), 2021, 33.

8 This is, for example, the case in Germany and the Netherlands, see Michael Veder, Cross-Border Insolvency Proceedings and Security Rights, Series of Law of Business and Finance, volume 8, Kluwer Legal Publishers, 2004, Chapter II, para. 2.4. Some further, yet limited, information on the treatment of foreign claims in a number of jurisdictions may also be found in Dennis Faber et al (eds), *Ranking and Priority of Creditors, Oxford International and Comparative Insolvency Law Series*, Oxford University Press 2016.

9 Cf. Reinhard Bork, Principles of Cross-Border Insolvency Law, Intersentia, 2017, para. 2.62. On the principles of transparency and equal treatment of creditors, see also Reinhard Bork and Michael Veder, Harmonisation of Transactions Avoidance Laws, Intersentia 2022, paras 2.27–2.28 and 2.38–2.42.

10 Cf. *Guide to Enactment and Interpretation* (n 1), para. 118.

11 Cf. Article 18 of the Treaty on the Functioning of the European Union (OJ C 326 of 26 October 2012, 47 et seq.) and the interpretation given to that provision in, for example, Case C-43/95 Data Delecta Aktiebolag

right to request the opening of secondary insolvency proceedings under Article 37(1)(b) EIR must be determined on the basis of the law of the Member State where the opening of secondary insolvency proceedings is requested, but the Court of Justice of the European Union has held that the right to seek the opening of secondary proceedings cannot be restricted to creditors who have their domicile or registered office within the Member State in whose territory the relevant establishment is situated, or to creditors whose claims arise from the operation of that establishment.[12] The principle of non-discrimination is also reflected in Chapter IV of the EIR on the provision of information for creditors and lodgement of their claims. Articles 53–55 EIR, which contain uniform provisions of substantive law that prevail over any contrary provisions of the national laws of the EU Member States, seek to ensure that foreign creditors[13] are adequately informed of the opening of insolvency proceedings in the EU and are able to lodge their claims in any such proceedings without encountering undue obstacles.[14] Pursuant to Article 53 EIR, any foreign creditor may lodge claims in insolvency proceedings opened in the EU. While the admission of claims in insolvency proceedings is generally determined by the law of the Member State where the relevant insolvency proceeding has been opened,[15] Article 53 EIR ensures that the admission of a claim may not be denied on the ground that the creditor is located in another Member State. Article 53 explicitly provides that creditors may lodge their claims by any means of communication accepted by the law of the Member State where the relevant insolvency proceeding has been opened.[16] Submission of claims 'in writing', as provided for in Article 39 EIR 2000,[17] is (still) to be regarded as the maximum form requirement. No stricter form requirements may be imposed on foreign creditors for the lodgement of their claims.[18] In an effort to ensure that claims of foreign creditors may effectively be taken into account and to reduce unnecessary costs associated with the filing of claims in insolvency proceedings opened in other Member States of the EU, Article 53 now explicitly prohibits any domestic law requirement that creditors should be legally repre-

---

and Ronny Forsberg v MSL Dynamica Ltd, ECLI:EU:C:1996:357. Cf. Katja Lenzing, in: Bork and van Zwieten (eds), *Commentary on the European Insolvency Regulation* (2nd edn), Oxford University Press 2022, para. 53.04.

12 Cf. Case C-327/13 Burgo Group, ECLI:EU:C:2014:2158, para. 51.

13 As defined in Article 2(12) EIR.

14 Cf. Lenzing (n. 11), para. 53.01.

15 Cf. Article 7(2)(h) EIR.

16 This provision ties in with the trend in EU Member States to increasingly allow the use of electronic means of communication, including the electronic filing of claims. Cf. Lenzing (n 11), para. 53.16.

17 Council Regulation (EC) No. 1346/2000 of 29 May 2000 on insolvency proceedings, OJ L 160 of 30 June 2000, 1 et seq (EIR 2000).

18 Cf. Lenzing (n 11), para. 53.17.

sented for the sole purpose of lodging their claims and Article 55 establishes a set of uniform rules for the procedure for lodging claims by foreign creditors (by, for example, providing for the use of a standard form,[19] allowing creditors to file claims in any official language of the institutions of the EU[20] and establishing a minimum period for the filing of claims by foreign creditors[21]).

1.13.09 During the discussions leading up to the adoption of the MLCBI, the question was raised as to whether it would be advisable, in case of non-main proceedings, to limit the right to request the opening of such insolvency proceedings to local creditors.[22] Such a restriction has not been included in the MLCBI.[23] At the time this question was raised in Working Group V, a somewhat similar restriction on the right to request the opening of independent territorial insolvency proceedings[24] was found in Article 3(4) of the European Union Convention on Insolvency Proceedings.[25] That convention never entered into force, but the restriction reappeared as Article 3(4) EIR 2000. This provision sought to limit the opening of independent territorial insolvency proceedings to exceptional circumstances.[26] However, it did so in a manner that was clearly at odds with the principle of non-discrimination, in that it conferred the right to request the opening of such independent territorial insolvency proceedings on creditors who had their domicile, habitual residence or registered office in the Member State in which the debtor's establishment was located, regardless of whether their claims had arisen in connection with the operation of the establishment.[27] Article 3(4) EIR has narrowed and clarified this restriction

---

19 Cf. Article 55(1) EIR and Annex II to Commission Implementing Regulation (EU) 2017/1105 of 12 June 2017 establishing the forms referred to in Regulation (EU) 2015/848 of the European Parliament and of the Council on insolvency proceedings, OJ L 160 of 22 June 2017, 13.

20 Cf. Article 55(4) EIR.

21 Cf. Article 55(6) EIR.

22 Cf. A/CN.9/433, para. 85.

23 Cf. A/CN.9/433, para. 85 and André J. Berends, The UNCITRAL Model Law on Cross-Border Insolvency: A Comprehensive Overview, Tulane Journal of International and Comparative Law, 1998/6, 344.

24 That is, territorial insolvency proceedings that are opened in a Member State where the debtor has an establishment as defined in Article 2(10) EIR, prior to the opening of main insolvency proceedings in accordance with Article 3(1) EIR in the Member State where the debtor has its centre of main interests.

25 That provision read: 'Territorial insolvency proceedings referred to in paragraph 2 may be opened prior to the opening of main insolvency proceedings in accordance with paragraph 1 only:

(a) where insolvency proceedings under paragraph 1 cannot be opened because of the conditions laid down by the law of the Contracting State within the territory of which the centre of the debtor's main interests is situated, or

(b) where the opening of territorial insolvency proceedings is requested by a creditor who has his domicile, habitual residence or registered office in the Contracting State within the territory of which the establishment is situated, or whose claim arises from the operation of that establishment.

26 Cf. Virgós-Schmit Report, para. 84.

27 Cf. Georg Ringe, in: Bork and van Zwieten (eds), Commentary on the European Insolvency Regulation (2nd edn), Oxford University Press 2022, para. 3.214.

compared to the EIR 2000 and has brought it more in line with the principle of non-discrimination by stipulating that independent territorial proceedings may be opened if the request is made by 'a creditor whose claim arises from or is in connection with the operation of an establishment situated within the territory of the Member State where the opening of territorial proceedings is requested'. This may apply to local as well as foreign creditors.

C. FOREIGN CREDITORS

The MLCBI does not define the term 'foreign creditors'. This is different in the EIR. Pursuant to Article 2(12) EIR, 'foreign creditor' means a creditor which has its habitual residence, domicile or registered office in a Member State other than the State of the opening of proceedings, including the tax and social security authorities of Member States.[28] The working documents of Working Group V show that, even though references to residence, domicile or registered office were deleted in the course of the discussions, a similar interpretation must be given to the term 'foreign creditors' as included in the EIR. Also, the reference in Article 13(1) to 'creditors *in* this State' (emphasis added) suggests that in relation to foreign creditors, their residence, domicile or registered office are relevant. Earlier drafts contained language to this effect and there is nothing in the working documents that suggests that a different meaning was intended.[29] The omission of references to, for example, the residence, domicile or registered office of creditors rather seems to be due to the observation that it would not be realistic to attempt to formulate a uniform definition of the criteria that would distinguish 'foreign' from 'local' creditors.[30] **1.13.10**

Given the apparently perceived difficulties in providing a clear and uniform definition of 'foreign creditors' by reference to, for example, their residence, domicile or registered office, it was suggested to essentially limit paragraph 1 to a clear and simple reflection of the non-discrimination principle, that is, that all creditors should be treated in the same manner, without discrimination based on nationality or other grounds, except as provided in paragraph 2.[31] However, this proposal did not get enough support[32] and the current text was maintained in order to clarify the scope of the equal treatment of foreign and **1.13.11**

28 On the interpretation under EU law of the terms 'habitual residence', 'domicile' and 'registered office', see Lenzing (n 11), paras. 53.07-53.09.

29 Cf. A/CN.9/WG.V/WP.44, 25-26; A/CN.9/WG.V/WP.46, 11–12.

30 Cf. A/CN.9/435, para. 152.

31 Cf. A/CN.9/435, paras 152 and 156. See also, with respect to an earlier draft, A/CN.9/422, para. 179.

32 Cf. Berends (n 23), 343.

local creditors, that is, regarding the commencement of and participation in local insolvency proceedings.

D. RANKING OF CLAIMS HELD BY FOREIGN CREDITORS

1.13.12 The MLCBI does not contain conflict-of-laws provisions, but it is a widely accepted rule that, in principle, the law of the State where an insolvency proceeding is opened (the *lex fori concursus*) governs all aspects of the commencement, conduct, administration and closure of insolvency proceedings and their effects, including the ranking of claims.[33]

1.13.13 In applying the provisions of the *lex fori concursus* on the ranking of claims, issues of 'assimilation' may arise in cases where creditors' claims have been established in accordance with the laws of another State, such as the law chosen by the parties to apply to their contractual relationship. In such cases, it must be assessed whether claims created under foreign law can be regarded as equivalent to domestic law claims conferring certain privileges or priorities. The test to be applied here is whether a foreign claim, given its essential content and function, corresponds to a claim under domestic law to the extent that these claims can be considered as 'functionally interchangeable'. If the answer is in the affirmative, a claim established under foreign law should be considered equivalent and receive the same treatment in insolvency proceedings as the equivalent claim under domestic law. In the event that such equivalence cannot be established, and therefore a case for priority under the *lex fori concursus* cannot be made, a claim created under foreign law should be treated as an ordinary non-preference claim.[34]

1.13.14 An entirely different matter is how States deal with the ranking of claims that are held by foreign creditors. It follows from the principle of non-discrimination, which is also reflected in Article 13(1) MLCBI, that this should not matter. Claims held by foreign creditors should be dealt with on the same footing as similar claims held by local creditors. They ought to be treated alike, also as regards their ranking. However, the MLCBI leaves room for a different approach.

1.13.15 Pursuant to Article 13(2) MLCBI, the principle of non-discrimination embodied in Article 13(1) does not affect the ranking of claims in insolvency

33 Cf. Article 7(2)(i) EIR and Recommendation 31 of the UNCITRAL Legislative Guide on Insolvency Law, United Nations Publications (New York), 2005. See also A/CN.9/WG.V/WP.187, II (G).

34 Cf. UNCITRAL Legislative Guide on Insolvency Law (n 33), Part two, I, C, para. 84.

proceedings. It leaves intact the provisions on the ranking of claims in insolvency proceedings, including any provisions that might assign a special ranking to claims of foreign creditors.[35] The MLCBI thus allows States to treat claims held by foreign creditors differently from similar claims held by local creditors. This is clearly not in line with the principle of non-discrimination. However, Article 13(2) seeks to offer foreign creditors a certain degree of protection in cases where States assign a special – that is, lower – ranking to claims held by foreign creditors as compared to local creditors. In order not to completely rid the non-discrimination principle of its meaning by provisions giving the lowest ranking to claims of foreign creditors, Article 13(2) MLCBI establishes that as a minimum, foreign creditors should be given the rank of general unsecured claims.[36]

Article 13(2) MLCBI contains an exception to that minimum ranking for cases where the claim in question, if it were of a domestic creditor, would be ranked lower than general unsecured claims.[37] Such claims, if held by a foreign creditor, may rank below the general unsecured claims, but only for reasons other than the nationality or location of the creditor, as provided in the law of the enacting State.[38] This exception appears to be in line with the principle of non-discrimination as the ranking of the claim is determined by its nature, not by the nationality or the residence of the creditor holding it. **1.13.16**

E. EXCEPTION FOR FOREIGN TAX AND SOCIAL SECURITY CLAIMS?

The working documents of Working Group V reveal that a considerable amount of time was spent on deliberations on the position of claims held by foreign governmental authorities deriving from foreign public law, in particular foreign tax and social security claims.[39] These documents show the lack of consensus as to whether and to what extent foreign governmental authorities, in particular in relation to tax and social security claims, should also benefit from the principle of non-discrimination and be able to participate in local insolvency proceedings on the same basis as local creditors. **1.13.17**

---

35 *Guide to Enactment and Interpretation* (n 1), para. 119.

36 Cf. A/CN.9/433, para. 80.

37 For example, interest accrued on claims as from the opening of the insolvency proceeding that, under German law, are subordinated (cf. Article 39(1)(1) of the German *Insolvenzordnung*) or, under Dutch law, are not admissible in an insolvency proceeding at all (cf. Article 128 of the Dutch *Faillissementswet*).

38 Cf. *Guide to Enactment and Interpretation* (n 1), para. 119.

39 Cf. A/CN.9/WG.V/WP.44, 25-26; A/CN.9/422, paras. 180-183; A/CN.9/WG.V/WP.46, 11-12; A/CN.9/433, paras 82–83; A/CN.9/435, para. 155.

1.13.18 Within the EU, the principle of non-discrimination is applied consistently in respect of the treatment in insolvency proceedings of tax and social security claims emanating from other Member States.[40] However, in many jurisdictions, extending the principle of non-discrimination to foreign tax and social security claims may not be very straightforward as often such claims can only be enforced if a bi- or multilateral convention or other international regulation so provides.[41]

1.13.19 The debate in Working Group V has eventually led to the inclusion of a footnote to Article 13(2) MLCBI, containing an alternative to Article 13(2) MLCBI that allows States that refuse to recognize foreign tax and social security claims to continue to discriminate against such claims.

1.13.20 States that have implemented the MLCBI have dealt with this issue in varying manners. For example, Article 12 of the Australian Cross-Border Insolvency Act 2008 has simply implemented the solution suggested in the footnote to Article 13(2) MLCBI, leading to the exclusion of foreign tax and social security claims from the application of the non-discrimination principle. Pursuant to 11 USC § 1513 (b)(2)(B), allowance and priority as to a foreign tax claim or other foreign public law claim shall be governed by any applicable tax treaty of the United States, under the conditions and circumstances specified therein. In the UK, Article 13(3) of Schedule 1 to the Cross-Border Insolvency Regulations 2006 provides:

> A claim may not be challenged solely on the grounds that it is a claim by a foreign tax or social security authority but such a claim may be challenged
>
> (a) on the ground that it is in whole or in part a penalty, or
> (b) on any other ground that a claim might be rejected in a proceeding under British insolvency law.

1.13.21 An interesting case in this context is *Akers as joint foreign representative v Deputy Commissioner of Taxation* [2014] FCAFC 57.[42]

---

40 Cf. Articles 2(12) and 53 EIR. See also CJEU Case C-212/15 ENEFI, ECLI:EU:C:2016:841. However, this does not mean that Member States are obliged to grant similar priority to such foreign claims as available under domestic law, see, for example, Article 13 of Council Directive 2010/24/EU of 16 March 2010 concerning mutual assistance for the recovery of claims relating to taxes, duties and other measures (OJ L 84 of 31 March 2010, 1 et seq.).

41 Cf. Veder (n 8), Chapter II, para. 2.4.3.

42 On this decision, see Atkins/McCoy, 11 (2014) ICR, 304 et seq; Bork (n 9), para. 6.10.

Article 14

NOTIFICATION TO FOREIGN CREDITORS OF A PROCEEDING UNDER [*IDENTIFY LAWS OF THE ENACTING STATE RELATING TO INSOLVENCY*]

Michael Veder

1. Whenever under [*identify laws of the enacting State relating to insolvency*] notification is to be given to creditors in this State, such notification shall also be given to the known creditors that do not have addresses in this State. The court may order that appropriate steps be taken with a view to notifying any creditor whose address is not yet known.
2. Such notification shall be made to the foreign creditors individually, unless the court considers that, under the circumstances, some other form of notification would be more appropriate. No letters rogatory or other, similar formality is required.
3. When a notification of commencement of a proceeding is to be given to foreign creditors, the notification shall:

   (a) Indicate a reasonable time period for filing claims and specify the place for their filing;
   (b) Indicate whether secured creditors need to file their secured claims; and
   (c) Contain any other information required to be included in such a notification to creditors pursuant to the law of this State and the orders of the court.

A. INTRODUCTION TO ARTICLE 14

1.14.01 Article 14 MLCBI deals with the extent to and manner in which foreign creditors must be informed of the opening of an insolvency proceeding in an enacting State, and the information that must be provided to them. It is a logical corollary of the principle of non-discrimination embodied in Article 13(1) MLCBI, pursuant to which foreign creditors have the same rights to participate in an insolvency proceeding opened in an enacting State as creditors in that State. Foreign creditors will only effectively be in a position to participate in an insolvency proceeding opened in an enacting State if they are indeed made aware of the opening of such proceedings. The main purpose of notifying foreign creditors as provided in Article 14(1) MLCBI is to inform them of the commencement of the insolvency proceeding and of the time limit to file their claims.[1]

1.14.02 The collection of Case Law on UNCITRAL Texts (CLOUT)[2] and the Digest of Case Law on the UNCITRAL Model Law on Cross-Border Insolvency[3] do not reveal any relevant case law relating to Article 12 MLCBI.

B. PUBLICITY

1. Importance of Publicity

1.14.03 Given the impact of the opening of insolvency proceedings on, for example, the powers of the debtor in respect of its assets and the position of all (poten-

1 Cf. *UNCITRAL Model Law on Cross-Border Insolvency with Guide to Enactment and Interpretation*, United Nations Publications (New York), 2014, para. 121.

2 Available at: https://uncitral.un.org/en/case_law.

3 Digest of Case Law on the UNCITRAL Model Law on Cross-Border Insolvency, United Nations Publications (New York), 2021, 34.

tial) stakeholders, notably the creditors, it is vital that publicity is given to the opening of insolvency proceedings, important steps taken during the proceedings and the closure of the proceedings. Creditors, for example, need to be made aware of the possible restrictions that apply in respect of the enforcement of their rights against the debtor, the necessity and modality of filing their claims in the proceeding, the deadlines for the submission of their claims, creditors' meetings, and so on. Third-party debtors need to be put on alert, where the applicable law so provides, that they should pay their debts to the insolvency practitioner and that payment to the debtor itself will not discharge them from their obligations. Banks need to be informed of the opening of insolvency proceedings in order to prevent them from executing payment transactions to the detriment of the estate, and the public at large needs to be informed that insolvency proceedings have been opened so as to prevent parties from entering into transactions with the debtor in ignorance of the changed circumstances. Publicity is required in view of the principle of transparency.[4]

Publicity and access to information regarding insolvency proceedings is crucial **1.14.04**
not only in a purely domestic context, but even more so in a cross-border context, where acquiring the relevant information may be far more difficult and costly for stakeholders. In the specific context of the EU Insolvency Regulation, publicity is particularly important for the efficacy of its system of automatic and immediate recognition of insolvency proceedings.[5] In that light, the EU Insolvency Regulation provides for the mandatory publication of information on the opening and conduct of insolvency proceedings in national electronic insolvency registers that are interconnected and searchable through a single access point, the EU Justice portal (https://e-justice.europa.eu/110/EN/bankruptcy_and_insolvency_registers?clang=en).[6]

2. Forms of Publicity

Jurisdictions provide for various methods of publicity in the context of insol- **1.14.05**
vency proceedings, such as publication in an official government gazette or (local) newspapers, individual notices to creditors, posting notices on court bulletin boards, a combination of such procedures, and, increasingly, the use of online insolvency registers. Unlike the more traditional methods of publicity, the use of online and searchable insolvency registers is an efficient and

4 Cf. Reinhard Bork, Principles of Cross-Border Insolvency Law, Intersentia 2017, para. 3.20 et seq.
5 Cf. Michael Veder, in: Bork and van Zwieten, Commentary on the European Insolvency Regulation (2nd edn), Oxford University Press 2022, para. 24.01 et seq.
6 Cf. Articles 24 et seq. EIR; Veder (n 5), para. 24.06 et seq.

cost-effective mechanism for publicizing the opening of insolvency proceedings, important steps to be taken during the proceedings (such as creditors' meetings) and the closure of the proceedings. Furthermore, such registers can be a useful tool for the dissemination of important information and documents relevant to the proceedings, such as public reports of the insolvency practitioner on the administration of particular proceedings.

C. DUTY TO NOTIFY FOREIGN CREDITORS

1. Relevance

1.14.06 The MLCBI acknowledges that States have varying provisions or practices regarding the methods for notifying creditors and that foreign creditors may not, and typically will not, have access to any local publications where the opening of insolvency proceedings is announced. If complying with the publication and notification requirements for domestic cases would be sufficient, also in relation to foreign creditors, foreign creditors would not be made aware – in a timely manner – of the opening of insolvency proceedings in respect of a debtor. Consequently, foreign creditors would not be able to effectively exercise their right to participate in local insolvency proceedings on the same basis as local creditors pursuant to Article 13(1) MLCBI. This would put foreign creditors in a less advantageous situation than local creditors.[7] Article 14 MLCBI thus imposes a specific duty to notify foreign creditors of the opening of insolvency proceedings, beyond the methods that are commonly used in a purely domestic case.[8]

2. When?

1.14.07 The duty to notify foreign creditors under Article 14 MLCBI is triggered whenever notification must be given to local creditors ('creditors in this State'). The provision thus takes account of the fact that the moment when notice has to be given to creditors varies in different legal systems (for example, at the outset of the insolvency proceedings or at a later stage).[9]

---

7 Cf. Guide to Enactment (n 1), para. 122.

8 Notwithstanding the obligation to publish the opening of insolvency proceedings (whether main or secondary) in interconnected online registers, the EIR provides for individual notices to be sent to foreign creditors (cf. Article 54 EIR).

9 Cf. A/CN.9/433, para. 86. In this light, the wording that notification ought to be given to foreign creditors 'as soon as insolvency proceedings are opened in the enacting State', was deleted. This is different under the EIR. Pursuant to Article 54(1) EIR, known foreign creditors must be informed 'immediately' and 'as soon

3. Who?

The duty to notify foreign creditors under Article 14 MLCBI applies to 'known' creditors that do not have an address in the enacting State. Creditors may be 'known' through, for example, the debtor's books and correspondence and, in the case of debtor-initiated insolvencies, lists of creditors produced by the debtor in the context of a voluntary filing. The duty to inform foreign creditors by way of individual notice under Article 54 EIR also applies to 'known' creditors only.[10] **1.14.08**

Article 14 MLCBI takes account of the fact that the addresses of creditors may not yet be known at the time when notification must be given. Pursuant to Article 14(1) MLCBI, the court may order that appropriate steps be taken with a view to notifying any creditor whose address is not yet known. It seems logical that this also applies to creditors that are not yet known at all, for example because the books and records of the debtor may not be accurate.[11] Essentially, appropriate and reasonable measures should be taken to ensure that all creditors, including foreign creditors, have a reasonable chance of becoming aware of the opening of insolvency proceedings in respect of a debtor. **1.14.09**

4. How?

Pursuant to Article 14(2) MLCBI, foreign creditors, that is, known creditors that do not have an address in the enacting State where the insolvency proceeding has been opened, must be notified individually, unless the court considers that, under the circumstances, some other form of notification would be more appropriate. **1.14.10**

The requirement that foreign creditors should be notified individually was maintained over objections that the notification requirement should be subject to national law, or that the choice of the form of notification should be left to the discretion of the court of the enacting State.[12] While providing for a special form of notification for foreign creditors might be considered to run counter to the idea of foreign creditors being treated on the same footing as local creditors, as reflected in Article 14(1) MLCBI, and might impose additional burden and costs on the proceeding, it was observed that foreign creditors, **1.14.11**

as insolvency proceedings are opened in a Member State' (cf. Katja Lenzing, in: Bork and van Zwieten, *Commentary on the European Insolvency Regulation* (2nd edn), Oxford University Press 2022, paras. 54.11).

10 Cf. Lenzing (n 9), paras 54.05 and 54.06.

11 Cf. A/CN.9/435, para. 161.

12 Cf. A/CN.9/433, paras 89–91.

by not having direct access to local publications of limited circulation, found themselves in a less advantageous situation than local creditors. In those circumstances, it was considered reasonable to require special notification for foreign creditors, so as to ensure that all creditors, both local and foreign, would have an equal opportunity for filing their claims. The solution adopted in Article 14(2) MLCBI seeks to ensure an effective method of notification for foreign creditors. As a general rule, foreign creditors must be notified individually, but the court of an enacting State has sufficient latitude for adopting other methods of notification when the circumstances of a given case do not warrant individual notification, for example in view of excessive costs associated with such individual notification.

1.14.12 Article 14(2) MLCBI has been implemented as such in Australia,[13] New Zealand[14] and the USA.[15] The UK implementation of the MLCBI allows notification to be given to foreign creditors by advertisement in such foreign newspapers as the British insolvency officeholder considers most appropriate for ensuring that the content of the notification comes to the notice of the known foreign creditors, if the notification to creditors in Great Britain is to be by advertisement only.[16]

1.14.13 Article 14(2) MLCBI explicitly mentions that no letters rogatory or other, similar formality is required. This is intended to express that notifications should be effected by expeditious means, without having to adhere to unnecessarily cumbersome formalities. The Guide to Enactment and Interpretation observes in this context that, with regard to the form of individual notifications, States may use special procedures for notifications that have to be served in a foreign jurisdiction (for example, sending notifications through diplomatic channels). In the context of insolvency proceedings, those procedures will often be too cumbersome and time-consuming and their use would typically not provide foreign creditors timely notice concerning insolvency proceedings.[17] This of course, like the observations in the Guide to Enactment and Interpretation on obligations under treaties to which States may be a party that address the service of documents abroad,[18] pre-supposes that sending a notification to foreign creditors can be regarded as the service of a (judicial or extra-judicial) document abroad. Whether this is the case

13 Cf. Insolvency (Cross-Border) Act 2006.

14 *Ibid.*

15 Cf. 11 US Code § 1514.

16 Cf. Article 14(2)(b) Cross-Border Insolvency Regulations 2006.

17 Guide to Enactment and Interpretation (n 1), para. 123.

18 Guide to Enactment and Interpretation (n 1), para. 124.

is doubtful. To the extent that individual notifications to be sent to foreign creditors would be caught by such treaties, and the informal and expeditious process of effecting notification envisaged by the MLCBI would conflict with obligations of a State under such treaties, States must, of course, adhere to the obligations under such treaties.[19]

5. Language

The MLCBI does not specify in which language a notification addressed to foreign creditors must be made. This is left to the enacting States. Various options were considered regarding the language in which notifications to foreign creditors should be issued, such as (i) that the notification be issued in more than one language, including one or more of the official languages of the United Nations; (ii) that the notification contain a statement of its purposes in all official languages of the United Nations; or (iii) that the notification be issued in a standard form to be annexed to the MLCBI.[20] **1.14.14**

The EIR, on the other hand, does contain requirements as to the language in which notifications must be given to foreign creditors and it does provide for a standard form in this respect. Pursuant to Article 54(3) EIR, the information to be provided to foreign creditors as per Article 54(1) and (2) must be provided using a standard notice form.[21] That standard notice form bears the heading 'Notice of insolvency proceedings' in all the official languages of the institutions of the Union. It must be transmitted in the official language of the State of the opening of proceedings or, if there are several official languages in that Member State, in the official language or one of the official languages of the place where insolvency proceedings have been opened, or in another language which that State has indicated it can accept, in accordance with Article 55(5) EIR, if it can be assumed that that language is easier to understand for the foreign creditors. **1.14.15**

Article 55 EIR establishes the procedure for lodging claims by foreign creditors. Foreign creditors may lodge their claims using a standard claims form that bears the heading 'Lodgement of claims' in all the official languages of **1.14.16**

---

19 Cf. Article 3 MLCBI, which in a sense is superfluous as in many jurisdictions, under rules of constitutional law, obligations under treaties to which a State is bound prevail anyway.

20 A/CN.9/433, para. 92.

21 The standard notice form referred to in Article 54(3) EIR is attached as Annex I to Commission Implementing Regulation (EU) 2017/1105 of 12 June 2017 establishing the forms referred to in Regulation (EU) 2015/848 of the European Parliament and of the Council on insolvency proceedings, OJ L 160 of 22 June 2017, 3 et seq.

the institutions of the Union.[22] Pursuant to Article 55(5) EIR, claims may be lodged in any official language of the institutions of the Union. The court, the insolvency practitioner or the debtor in possession may require the creditor to provide a translation in the official language of the State of the opening of proceedings or, if there are several official languages in that Member State, in the official language or one of the official languages of the place where insolvency proceedings have been opened, or in another language which that Member State has indicated it can accept. Member States are obliged to indicate whether they accept any official language of the institutions of the Union other than their own for the purpose of the lodging of claims.

6. Non-compliance with the Duty to Notify Foreign Creditors

1.14.17 Failure to comply with the duty to inform foreign creditors may have serious consequences for those creditors, in particular in States that have strict bar dates and limited remedies available for creditors in case of late filing of claims.[23] The question then arises whether, in case of creditors that have not been duly notified pursuant to Article 14 MLCBI, national time limits for lodging claims start running and the consequences attached to late filing apply.

1.14.18 The MLCBI does not specify the consequences of non-compliance with a duty to inform foreign creditors. This is a matter that must be decided by the applicable national law.[24]

D. INFORMATION TO BE INCLUDED IN THE NOTIFICATION

1.14.19 Pursuant to Article 14(3) MLCBI, the following information must be included in the notification to foreign creditors:

(a) a reasonable time period for filing claims and details as to the place for the filing of claims;[25]

---

22 The standard claims form referred to in Article 55(1) EIR is attached as Annex II to Commission Implementing Regulation (EU) 2017/1105 of 12 June 2017 establishing the forms referred to in Regulation (EU) 2015/848 of the European Parliament and of the Council on insolvency proceedings, OJ L 160 of 22 June 2017, 13 et seq.

23 For some examples under the EIR, see Lenzing (n 9), paras 54.16 et seq.

24 On the consequences of failure to comply with the duty to inform foreign creditors pursuant to Article 54 EIR, see Lenzing (n 9), paras 54.16 et seq.

25 Time limits for the filing of claims are determined by the law of the enacting State. However, it was felt that it would be equitable to afford foreign creditors an extended time-limit to file their claims, as was the case in a number of jurisdictions. But, at the same time, it was observed that it would not be realistic to provide a single time-limit for all jurisdictions. It was thus agreed to require that foreign creditors be given a reasonable time-limit. Cf. A/CN.9/433, para. 96.

(b) whether secured creditors need to file their secured claims;[26] and
(c) any other information required to be included in such a notification pursuant to the laws of the enacting State and the orders of the court.

The information that the notice to foreign creditors must contain pursuant to Article 14(3) MLCBI is similar to what Article 54(2) EIR prescribes. However, Article 54(2) EIR also requires the notification to contain information on the 'penalties' regarding the time limits imposed on lodging claims in the proceeding. This is important, as jurisdictions may have strict bar dates and offer limited remedies for curing the late submission of claims by foreign creditors. Given the severe consequences that may be attached to missing the deadline for the submission of claims, it is unfortunate that the MLCBI does not require such information to be included in the notification to foreign creditors. **1.14.20**

26 In this respect it is observed in the Guide to Enactment and Interpretation (n 1), at para. 126: 'In some legal systems a secured creditor who files a claim in an insolvency proceeding is deemed to have waived the security or some of the privileges attached to the credit, while in other systems failure to file a claim results in a waiver of such security or privilege. Where such a situation may arise, it would be appropriate for the enacting State to include in paragraph 3, subparagraph (b), a requirement that the notification include information regarding the effects of filing, or failing to file, secured claims.'

Chapter III Recognition of a foreign proceeding and relief

Article 15

APPLICATION FOR RECOGNITION OF A FOREIGN PROCEEDING

G. Ray Warner

1. A foreign representative may apply to the court for recognition of the foreign proceeding in which the foreign representative has been appointed.
2. An application for recognition shall be accompanied by:
   (a) A certified copy of the decision commencing the foreign proceeding and appointing the foreign representative; or
   (b) A certificate from the foreign court affirming the existence of the foreign proceeding and of the appointment of the foreign representative; or
   (c) In the absence of evidence referred to in subparagraphs (a) and (b), any other evidence acceptable to the court of the existence of the foreign proceeding and of the appointment of the foreign representative.
3. An application for recognition shall also be accompanied by a statement identifying all foreign proceedings in respect of the debtor that are known to the foreign representative.
4. The court may require a translation of documents supplied in support of the application for recognition into an official language of this State.

A. INTRODUCTION TO ARTICLE 15

1. An Expeditious Process

1.15.01 The MLCBI is designed to facilitate cooperation between jurisdictions to address more effectively insolvency proceedings involving debtors with assets and creditors in more than one jurisdiction.[1] It includes several 'modest but significant' features that promote a uniform approach to cross-border insolvency.[2] One of the four main objectives of the MLCBI is providing a framework for the recognition in one jurisdiction of the opening of an insolvency-related proceeding in a different jurisdiction.[3]

1.15.02 The MLCBI largely separates the question of recognition from the nature of the relief provided. Recognition is a prerequisite for most relief,[4] but recognition is not required for the foreign representation to institute a local insolvency proceeding.[5] And the cooperation and coordination provisions of the MLCBI apply whether or not the foreign proceeding has been recognized.[6]

1.15.03 At the most basic level, recognition is simply a judicial determination that: (1) there is a proceeding in a foreign jurisdiction that is of the type covered by the MLCBI;[7] (2) the foreign proceeding is either a main or non-main proceeding;[8] and (3) the person or body applying for recognition is the authorized representative of the foreign proceeding.[9] In most cases, these determinations should present no difficulty and will likely not be challenged.

1.15.04 However, prior to the MLCBI, existing mechanisms for obtaining assistance from a foreign court often involved cumbersome and time-consuming procedures that made it difficult to provide timely assistance.[10] For example, a formal process of 'legalization' to establish the authenticity of relevant documents may have been required.[11] The legalization process is designed to create a chain of

---

1 *UNCITRAL Model Law on Cross-Border Insolvency with Guide to Enactment and Interpretation*, United Nations Publications (New York), 2014, para 1.
2 *Guide to Enactment* (n 1), para 3.
3 *Guide to Enactment* (n 1), para 24.
4 Interim relief is available after the application for recognition is made, but before the decision to recognize: MLCBI art 19.
5 MLCBI art 11; *Guide to Enactment* (n 1), para 25.
6 *See* MLCBI art 25 *et seq.*
7 MLCBI art 2(a).
8 MLCBI art 2(b & c).
9 MLCBI art 2(d).
10 *Guide to Enactment* (n 1), para 127.
11 *Guide to Enactment* (n 1), paras 127 & 128.

certifications in the foreign jurisdiction where the first authority certifies the issuer of the document and each subsequent authority certifies the previous one up to the foreign jurisdiction's foreign office. The receiving jurisdiction's diplomatic mission in the foreign state could then certify the foreign office's certification and provide a document recognizable in the receiving jurisdiction's courts. This process could require use of letters rogatory or other forms of diplomatic or consular communications and might involve the cooperation of authorities at several different levels in the jurisdiction where the foreign proceeding was pending.[12]

Time is often of the essence when assistance is needed in a jurisdiction different from the one where an insolvency proceeding is pending. Assets may be at risk of dissipation, transfer or concealment unless the court in the receiving jurisdiction acts promptly on any request for assistance.[13] Thus, one of the key objectives of the MLCBI is to establish a simplified process for recognition of qualifying foreign proceedings.[14] **1.15.05**

2. Minimal Requirements

Articles 15, 16 and 17 are designed to work together to create a simple and expeditious recognition process that dispenses with cumbersome technical requirements that might unnecessarily delay the recognition decision.[15] Article 15 sets forth the technical requirements for the application for recognition and the documentation required. Article 17 governs the recognition decision and Article 16 supplies several presumptions that apply to the recognition determination. **1.15.06**

The applicable requirements for recognition are minimal and the MLCBI goals of fostering international cooperation, maximizing stakeholder outcomes and promoting uniformity suggest that States should not encumber the recognition process by adding additional requirements.[16] The receiving court's role is limited to determining whether the application meets the applicable requirements and whether recognition is contrary to public policy.[17] If those standards are met, recognition should be granted as a matter of course,[18] without consid- **1.15.07**

12 *Guide to Enactment* (n 1), paras 128 & 129.

13 *Guide to Enactment* (n 1), paras 135 & 163; *UNCITRAL Model Law on Cross-Border Insolvency: The Judicial Perspective*, United Nations Publications (New York), 2014, paras 38 & 39.

14 *Guide to Enactment* (n 1), para 29.

15 *Guide to Enactment* (n 1), para 127.

16 *Guide to Enactment* (n 1), para 161.

17 MLCBI art 6; *Guide to Enactment* (n 1), paras 30 & 161.

18 *Guide to Enactment* (n 1), para 150; *Judicial Perspective* (n 13), para 41.

eration of extraneous factors.[19] In a straightforward case with no opposition, the recognition process might be completed within a matter of days.[20] While the MLCBI is designed to expedite the evidentiary process, the receiving court is free to require legalization of documents and call for other evidence. While designed to be an expeditious process, resolution of a contested application for recognition process might take months or years.[21]

1.15.08 While the court must recognize a complying foreign proceeding (subject to the public policy limitation), the court generally has discretion to consider a wide range of other factors in deciding whether to grant relief.[22]

1.15.09 Nonetheless, the recognition decision itself has several important consequences. After recognition, the foreign representative may intervene in any proceedings in which the debtor is a party,[23] and may participate[24] in an insolvency proceeding in the receiving State.[25] In addition, without commencing a local insolvency proceeding, the foreign representative has standing to initiate the types of actions available in a local insolvency proceeding to render ineffective acts detrimental to creditors.[26]

1.15.10 More significant consequences flow automatically from the recognition decision if the proceeding is recognized as a foreign main proceeding.[27] Article 20 creates 'breathing space' for foreign main proceedings by suspending the debtor's right to transfer, encumber or dispose of assets and by staying executions against the debtor's assets and the commencement or continuation of most other individual actions and proceedings affecting the debtor.[28] In addition, recognition of a foreign main proceeding generally limits the scope of a later-commenced local proceeding to local assets.[29]

---

19 *Guide to Enactment* (n 1), para 151.

20 *Guide to Enactment* (n 1), para 163; *Judicial Perspective* (n 13), para 38.

21 *Guide to Enactment* (n 1), para 163; *Judicial Perspective* (n 13), para 38; *see In Re PT Bakrie Telecom Tbk,* 628 BR 859 (Bankr SDNY 2021) (US) (recognizing application filed in January of 2018).

22 *Guide to Enactment* (n 1), paras 36 & 65.

23 MLCBI art 24.

24 The foreign representative may institute a local insolvency proceeding without the need for recognition (MLCBI art 11). However, if first recognized as a foreign main proceeding, the foreign representative is aided by a presumption of insolvency (MLCBI art 31). And, as noted in the text, recognition is necessary for the foreign representative to participate further in the local proceedings (*Guide to Enactment* (n 1), para 25).

25 MLCBI art 12; *Guide to Enactment* (n 1), para 34.

26 MLCBI art. 23(1); *Guide to Enactment* (n 1), para 34.

27 *Guide to Enactment* (n 1), para 37.

28 MLCBI art 20; *Guide to Enactment* (n 1), para 37.

29 MLCBI art 28.

Article 15 sets forth the core procedural requirements for an application by a foreign representative for recognition.[30] In furtherance of the MLCBI policy of creating a simple and expeditious process, the requirements are minimal and the court is permitted, but not required, to rely upon documents that have not been legalized. The court may require translation of documents into an official language of the receiving state. Article 15 also requires the foreign representative to disclose other foreign proceedings involving the debtor so that relief can be tailored to accommodate the cooperation and coordination goals of the MLCBI. **1.15.11**

B. APPLICATION FOR RECOGNITION

1. Foreign Representative and Foreign Proceeding

Article 15(1) provides the jurisdictional grounds for an application for recognition. It authorizes the foreign representative appointed in a foreign proceeding to apply for recognition of that foreign proceeding in a court of the receiving state. Since different courts in the receiving state may have competence for the different judicial functions addressed by the MLCBI, Article 4 of the MLCBI specifies the court or other authority to which the application must be made.[31] Article 9 of the MLCBI grants the foreign representative direct access to that court and removes barriers such as licences and consular action that might otherwise delay the recognition process.[32] Nothing in Articles 9 or 15 permits any entity other than the foreign representative to apply for recognition of a foreign proceeding.[33] **1.15.12**

The simple phrasing of Article 15(1) disguises the detail it encompasses. Since both 'foreign representative' and 'foreign proceeding' are defined in Article 2 of the MLCBI, all of the elements required by those definitions must be satisfied before recognition can be granted under Article 17.[34] Although a foreign insolvency-related proceeding might be recognized in the receiving state under some other law or doctrine, it cannot be recognized under the MLCBI unless it is a foreign proceeding as defined in Article 2. Article 2(a) provides: **1.15.13**

30 *Guide to Enactment* (n 1), para 127.

31 MLCBI art 4; *Guide to Enactment* (n 1), para 95. See also Commentary discussion at paragraph 1.4.1 *et seq.*

32 MLCBI art 9; *Guide to Enactment* (n 1), para 108. See also Commentary discussion at paragraph 1.9.1 *et seq.*

33 *Judicial Perspective* (n 13), para 30.

34 MLCBI art 17; *Judicial Perspective* (n 13), para 37.

> 'Foreign proceeding' means a collective judicial or administrative proceeding in a foreign State, including an interim proceeding, pursuant to a law relating to insolvency in which proceeding the assets and affairs of the debtor are subject to control or supervision by a foreign court, for the purpose of reorganization or liquidation.[35]

1.15.14 In addition, since only a foreign representative has standing to apply for recognition, the applicant will need to satisfy the Article 2(d) foreign representative definitional requirements.[36] Article 2(d) provides:

> 'Foreign representative' means a person or body, including one appointed on an interim basis, authorized in a foreign proceeding to administer the reorganization or the liquidation of the debtor's assets or affairs or to act as a representative of the foreign proceeding.[37]

2. Other Issues

1.15.15 Consistent with the goal of providing a simplified procedure for recognition of qualifying foreign proceedings, the receiving court should grant recognition if the jurisdictional pre-conditions specified in Article 2 regarding the nature of the foreign proceeding and the foreign representative are met.[38] Subject to the overarching public policy limitation in article 6, no additional requirements should be imposed for recognition. However, if additional requirements are imposed by a local non-uniform provision of the MLCBI or by judicial decisions, the application may need to include whatever additional information is required under the receiving jurisdiction's law to demonstrate compliance with those provisions. For example, as discussed in connection with Article 17, US case law may require the application to allege that the debtor in the foreign proceeding has property in the US.[39]

1.15.16 Article 15 sets forth only the substantive requirements for the recognition application. The local law of the receiving state governs procedural matters, such as whether notice of the application must be provided to creditors or other interested parties.[40] The standards for notice vary from jurisdiction to jurisdiction, with some states requiring that all affected parties have an opportunity to be heard before recognition is granted and others viewing the need for

35 MLCBI art 2(a).
36 *Judicial Perspective* (n 13), para 36.
37 MLCBI art 2(d).
38 *Guide to Enactment* (n 1), para 29; *Judicial Perspective* (n 13), para 41.
39 See Commentary discussion at paragraph 1.17.12, *et seq.*
40 *Guide to Enactment* (n 1), para 136.

expeditious treatment as inconsistent with the issuance of notice prior to the court decision on recognition.[41]

Often several related entities operate as an integrated business enterprise and may all be subject to foreign proceedings in the same jurisdiction. Although the entities may be closely related, the MLCBI operates on an entity-by-entity basis.[42] Thus, a separate recognition application must be filed for each foreign proceeding for which recognition is sought.[43] **1.15.17**

Additionally, since recognition relates to a particular proceeding pending in a foreign State, it may be necessary to file a new application if the initial foreign proceeding is dismissed in the foreign jurisdiction and recognition is sought for a subsequent foreign proceeding involving the same debtor.[44] However, where the initial recognized foreign proceeding was terminated but a second, although technically different, proceeding followed immediately, Article 17(4) might be used to modify the recognition instead of requiring a new recognition application.[45] **1.15.18**

Neither the MLCBI nor the Guide to Enactment and Interpretation address amendments to the application. While Article 15 suggests the application would be defective if insufficient, it may be possible to amend or supplement the application if the initial submission was lacking or if circumstances change. This would turn in part on the procedural rules of the receiving state. The overarching goal of flexibility, the obligation to advise the court of changes in status of the foreign proceeding or the foreign representative's appointment under Article 18(1), and the modification provisions of Article 17(4), support a liberal approach to amendments and supplementation. **1.15.19**

A foreign proceeding may be recognized even if the decision commencing the proceeding or appointing the foreign representative is subject to a pending appeal.[46] If the foreign decision is later reversed by the appellate court in the **1.15.20**

---

41 *Guide to Enactment* (n 1), para 135.

42 *Judicial Perspective* (n 13), para 68. Enterprise group issues are addressed in the 2019 UNCITRAL Model Law on Enterprise Group Insolvency https://uncitral.un.org/sites/uncitral.un.org/files/media-documents/uncitral/en/19-11346_mloegi.pdf

43 *In Re British American Ins Co Ltd*, 425 BR 884, 889 (Bankr SD Fla 2010) CLOUT 1005 (US).

44 Digest of Case Law on the UNCITRAL Model Law on Cross-Border Insolvency (CLOUT), United Nations Publications (Vienna), 2021, art 15 para 3.

45 *In Re Comair Ltd* 2023 WL 1971618 at *11–12 (Bankr SDNY Feb 12 2023) (US) (noting that requiring a new application would only '*add duration, costs, and complexity*'). The court did, however, treat the motion for amendment like an article 15 application and analysed whether the appropriate documents were included.

46 *Re Garuda Indonesia (Persero) Tbk* [2025] SGHC(I) 1 para 77 (SG); *In Re Gerova Financial Group Ltd* 482 BR 86, 94 (Bankr SDNY 2012) CLOUT 1275 (US).

foreign state, Article 17(4) can be used to modify or terminate the recognition order.[47] However, if the applicant's appointment in the foreign jurisdiction had not yet commenced, for example because the appointment decision was stayed pending an appeal, the applicant would not yet qualify as a foreign representative.[48]

1.15.21 An extreme example of the liberal approach comes from the *British American* case. The documents submitted with the application failed to establish that the foreign legal action was 'for the purpose of reorganization or liquidation' as required by the article 2(a) foreign proceeding definition. That was not a pleading defect but reflected the fact that the foreign action was merely investigative at that time and did not yet qualify for recognition. However, between the time of application and decision, the proceeding had evolved from merely an investigatory process to a reorganization and thus satisfied the foreign proceeding criteria. The application was supplemented with a subsequent foreign court decision and the receiving court found that the application, as supplemented, met the Article 15 requirements. The court noted that denial of recognition would serve only to delay the process since the applicant could simply file a new application for recognition. The court reasoned that the nature of the recognition process allowed it to consider both changes that supported and those that undermined the grounds for recognition.[49]

C. DOCUMENTS REQUIRED

1. Legalization Not Required

1.15.22 Article 15(2) addresses the documentation required for a recognition application. In keeping with the MLCBI's goal of providing a simple and expeditious procedure for recognition, the required documents need only address the two issues relevant to the recognition decision: (1) whether there is a foreign proceeding; and (2) whether the applicant is its foreign representative.[50] Although

47 *Ibid; Judicial Perspective* (n 13), para 57.

48 *Judicial Perspective* (n 13), para 36.

49 *British American* 425 BR at 905–06. Note that article 17(4) authorizes modification *'if it is shown that the grounds for granting it were fully or partially lacking or have ceased to exist'*. The language does not address the situation where a previously unrecognizable proceeding becomes recognizable.

50 MLCBI art 17(1)(a & b). While article 15(2) requires evidence only of the existence of the foreign proceeding and the appointment of the foreign representative, a third issue – whether the foreign proceeding is a foreign main or foreign non-main proceeding – must also be determined as part of the recognition process; MLCBI art 17(2). However, unlike the two preconditions for recognition, no evidence of that issue need accompany the application.

the Article 15 application requirements are minimal and should be easily satisfied, Article 15 applies only to the filing (or pleading) stage of the process and much more evidence may be required to persuade the receiving court to recognize the foreign proceeding under Article 17 or to grant relief.

Article 15(2) dispenses with any requirement that the documents accompanying the application for recognition be legalized. Instead of legalization, a certified copy of the foreign decision commencing the foreign proceeding and appointing the foreign representative or a certificate from the foreign court is sufficient.[51] Subparagraph (c) moves even further away from formal requirements like legalization and permits recognition without a certified copy of the decision or a certificate from the foreign court. It permits submission of 'any other evidence acceptable to the court of the existence of the foreign proceeding and of the appointment of the foreign representative'.[52] **1.15.23**

While article 15 eliminates the need for legalization of documents in connection with the application, article 16 provides presumptions that replace the primary role of legalization in establishing that foreign documents are authentic.[53] Article 16(2) provides that '[t]he court is entitled to presume that documents submitted in support of the application are authentic'.[54] This presumption applies not only to certified copies of the foreign judgment and certificates from the foreign court, but also to any document submitted in support of the application – including the wide array of documents that are permitted under subparagraph (c). Although Article 16 entitles the receiving court to presume authenticity, it is not required to do so and remains free to require legalization if it chooses[55] or if it questions the authenticity[56] of the submitted documents.[57] **1.15.24**

---

51 MLCBI art 15(2)(a & b).

52 MLCBI art 15(2)(c); *Guide to Enactment* (n 1), para 131.

53 Legalization might also be used to establish the capacity in which the signer of a foreign document acted. This concept should be covered in most cases by the presumption of authenticity where the capacity of the signer is clear from the document.

54 MLCBI art 16(2).

55 Nonetheless, some States have added language to article 16 stating that the receiving court 'may' require legalization of documents. The CLOUT Digest notes that Chile and Columbia have this provision. Digest of Case Law on the UNCITRAL Model Law on Cross-Border Insolvency (CLOUT), United Nations Publications (Vienna), 2021, art 16 n 8.

56 *Guide to Enactment* (n 1), paras 127 & 129.

57 The wording of article 15 and the policy of not adding extra requirements suggest that legalization of the copy of the judgment or the certificate of the court referred to in article 15(2)(a & b) should not be required at the application stage, although the court could so require as a prerequisite to deciding whether to recognize the foreign proceeding under article 17. For other documents submitted under article 15(2)(c), the receiving court may require legalization.

1.15.25 Article 15(2) provides three options for supplying the documentation necessary to support the application for recognition. The first is a certified copy of the foreign decision commencing the foreign proceeding and appointing the foreign representative.[58] Unlike the legalization process, which involves diplomatic or consular officials of the receiving State, the certification required by subparagraph (a) is provided by officials in the State in which the foreign proceeding is pending. The MLCBI does not further define what is required, presumably leaving that to the laws and procedures of the foreign State.[59] Of course, if the receiving court is not satisfied with the document's certification, it can require further evidence or legalization of the decision as a precondition to recognition.[60]

2. Certified Court Order or Certificate

1.15.26 While the 'decision' referred to in Article 15 often will be a judicial decision, foreign proceedings include both judicial and administrative proceedings, so the relevant decision might be a certified copy of an administrative agency document.[61] Additionally, two or more decisions may be needed if the commencement of the proceeding and the appointment of the foreign representative are not both included in a single decision. Often, the foreign court's decision expressly authorizes the applicant to act as a 'foreign representative' and confers authority to commence a foreign proceeding in the receiving court.[62]

1.15.27 The second option is to provide '[a] certificate from the foreign court affirming the existence of the foreign proceeding and of the appointment of the foreign representative'.[63] The MLCBI does not indicate what form such a certificate may take, presumably leaving it to the receiving court to decide what is acceptable. The term 'foreign court' is broadly defined to include 'a judicial or other authority competent to control or supervise a foreign proceeding'.[64] Thus, the relevant certificate may be issued by an administrative authority rather than a court. For example, in *Betcorp* the court accepted, as a complying certificate

---

58 MLCBI art 15(2)(a).

59 The Hague Apostille Convention provides a similar procedure of certification by the issuing authority in the originating state, see Convention of 5 October 1961 Abolishing the Requirement of Legalisation for Foreign Public Documents, United Nations, *Treaty Series*, vol 527, No 7625.

60 MLCBI art 2(a); *Guide to Enactment* (n 1), para 129.

61 *See* MLCBI art (2)(a); *In Re Betcorp Ltd*, 400 BR 266, 294–95 (Bankr D. Nev 2009) CLOUT 927 (US).

62 CLOUT Digest art 15 para 4 at 36; *Probe Resources Ltd* 2011 CarswellBC 1043, 79 CBR 5th 148 (BC SC) (CAN); *Oversight & Control Comm of Avanzit SA* 385 BR 525, 534 (Bankr SDNY 2008) CLOUT 925 (US); *Basis Yield Alpha Fund (Master)* 381 BR 37, 46 (Bankr SDNY 2008) CLOUT 789 (US).

63 MLCBI art 15(2)(b).

64 MLCBI art 2(e).

under subparagraph (b), a document showing that the applicant had been appointed as a liquidator by the foreign administrative agency that regulated corporations.[65] Multiple certificates may be required if the appointment of the foreign representative is made by a different authority than the court administering the foreign proceeding.[66]

The minimal documentation required by Article 15(2) works in tandem with the presumptions permitted by Article 16 to allow recognition promptly and summarily on the basis of the application alone where there is no serious question about the status of the foreign proceeding or of the foreign representative. If the decision or certificate submitted pursuant to subparagraph (a) or (b) 'indicates that the foreign proceeding is a proceeding within the meaning of subparagraph (a) of article 2 and that the foreign representative is a person or body within the meaning of subparagraph (d) of article 2, the court is entitled to so presume'.[67] Thus, if the application is accompanied by a certified decision or a court certificate affirming the existence of a foreign proceeding and the appointment of the foreign representative, the Article 16 presumptions can be used to establish the grounds for recognition. This is because Article 16(2) permits the receiving court to presume that the decision or certificate is authentic.[68] Article 16(1) then allows the receiving court to rely, without requiring further evidence, on the representations in the decision or certificate that the foreign insolvency action satisfies the MLCBI definition of a foreign proceeding and that the applicant is its foreign representative.[69] **1.15.28**

The only issue left to decide is whether the proceeding is a foreign main proceeding,[70] but that can also be resolved summarily if the application is accompanied by official documentation showing that the debtor's registered office is in the foreign jurisdiction. This is because of the Article 16(2) presumption of authenticity coupled with the Article 16(c) presumption that the debtor's registered office is its COMI. Thus, if recognition as a foreign main proceeding is sought for a proceeding pending in the jurisdiction of the debtor's registered **1.15.29**

65 *Betcorp* 400 BR at 294–95 (US).

66 For example, in the US the bankruptcy court administering the proceeding does not have authority to appoint bankruptcy trustees, who are appointed by an administrative agency. *See, e.g.*, 11 USC 701(a)(1). However, the US court might issue an order specifically authorizing a different entity to act as foreign representative, in which event the bankruptcy court could issue a certificate affirming both the existence of the foreign proceeding and the appointment of the foreign representative.

67 MLCBI art 16(1).

68 MLCBI art 16(2). See Commentary discussion of Article 16.

69 MLCBI art 16(1).

70 MLCBI art 17(2).

office, the documents submitted with the application may be all that is needed to obtain recognition as a foreign main proceeding.

1.15.30 The foreign decision or court certificate accompanying the application might not sufficiently indicate that the foreign insolvency proceeding meets the MLCBI's foreign proceeding requirements or that the applicant satisfies the foreign representative requirements. For example, the decision commencing the proceeding may simply indicate that a legal proceeding was opened, but may not provide any indication whether that proceeding is 'collective' or was commenced under 'a law relating to insolvency'.[71] While those elements eventually must be established for recognition, presumably either a certified copy of the decision commencing the proceeding and appointing the foreign representative or an appropriate court certificate is sufficient at the application stage.

3. Other Documents Permitted

1.15.31 The third option adds flexibility to the process by giving the receiving court discretion to accept any other evidence of the existence of the foreign proceeding and of the foreign representative's appointment.[72] This furthers the MLCBI's goal of maximizing cross-border cooperation and coordination since it allows recognition where the applicant may be unable to obtain the certified decision or court certificate required under subparagraph (a) or (b) or where the submitted documents fail to meet all the requirements of those subparagraphs.[73] In addition, since the MLCBI includes informal non-judicial proceedings as long as there is supervision by a court or administrative authority,[74] the types of official documents referred in subparagraphs (a) and (b) may not exist.[75] The flexibility provided by subparagraph (c) ensures that recognition would not be denied 'because of noncompliance with a mere technicality'.[76] The three documentary options under Article 15 are separated by the word 'or', suggesting that any of the three would suffice. Indeed, in some cases a combination of documents may be necessary, with different documents satisfying different Article 15(2) criteria.

---

71 These requirements appear in MLCBI art 2(a).

72 MLCBI art 15(2)(c).

73 *Guide to Enactment* (n 1), para 131.

74 MLCBI art 2(a).

75 *Betcorp* 400 BR at 294 (US) (noting that compliance with subparagraphs (a) and (b) might not be possible where there is no formal insolvency proceeding).

76 Guide to Enactment (fn.1), para 131.

A decision or certificate referenced in subparagraphs (a) and (b) would be sufficient for the application even if it did not address each of the required elements of the MLCBI definition of foreign proceeding and foreign representative. However, if the applicant relies upon subparagraph (c), a higher threshold applies, and the evidence submitted must address all elements required for recognition. Presumably the evidence provided under the third option to establish the *prima facie* case for recognition must be documentary in character, although not necessarily from a governmental entity. Article 15 governs the minimum requirements for the application and requires that the application 'shall be accompanied by' the evidence allowed in subparagraph (c). This suggests that the evidence must be in a form that could accompany the petition, which is not surprising since Article 15 applies at the filing stage of the recognition process. A sworn affidavit from a representative of the debtor attesting to relevant facts might be sufficient, if that were acceptable to the receiving court. Even an unsworn statement or other document such as a copy of the foreign state's insolvency law might be adequate as long as it was presented in a form considered 'evidence' under the receiving state's law.[77] **1.15.32**

Like the decision and certificate referred to in subparagraphs (a) and (b), documents submitted under subparagraph (c) need not be legalized.[78] In addition, Article 16(2) entitles the receiving court to presume that any 'documents submitted in support of the application for recognition are authentic' and that includes documents submitted under subparagraph (c).[79] While Article 16 permits the court to presume the documents are authentic, unlike the decision or certificate supplied pursuant to subparagraphs (a) or (b), there is no presumption that the assertions contained in the submitted documents establish that the foreign insolvency action is a foreign proceeding or that the applicant is a foreign representative as those terms are defined in the MLCBI. **1.15.33**

Article 15 establishes a hierarchy of documents, permitting recourse to subparagraph (c) only when the decision or certificate referred to in subparagraphs (a) and (b) are not available. This is suggested by the introductory language to subparagraph (c), which states that other evidence may be used '[i]n the absence of evidence referred to in subparagraphs (a) and (b)'. The Guide to Enactment's discussion supports the view that subparagraph (c) serves as a fallback provision where the applicant is unable to comply with the techni- **1.15.34**

---

77 *Judicial Perspective* (n 13), para 67. An internet link to a webpage containing the relevant information might even be sufficient. *Betcorp* 400 BR at 282–83.

78 MLCBI art 15(2)(c) & 16(2).

79 MLCBI art 16(2); *Guide to Enactment* (n 1), para 131.

cal requirements of subparagraphs (a) and (b).[80] Thus, the applicant may be required to explain why the documents referred to in subparagraphs (a) and (b) are not available.[81]

1.15.35 A wide range of documents could be used to meet the subparagraph (c) requirements. A good example of the flexibility of subparagraph (c) is the *Betcorp* case. There the court relied upon a memorandum to the debtor's equity holders as well as minutes and a resolution of the debtor's directors as evidence that the non-judicial insolvency process had commenced and that it met several of the MLCBI's definitional requirements.[82] The court relied on internet links to copies of foreign statutes and interpretive materials to establish other recognition requirements, although it is not clear whether those links or copies of those materials were included in the application or supplied later as part of the decision process.[83] The court also relied upon a declaration filed by the applicant and statements included in the application, which had been verified.[84]

1.15.36 Other US cases adopt a similarly liberal approach. For example, in *Pro-Fit Holdings* notices of appointment of the foreign representative that were signed by a solicitor were sufficient to show both the existence of the foreign proceeding and the appointment of the foreign representative where no court filing was required to commence that type of insolvency proceeding.[85] Similarly, in *Cell C Proprietary* a copy of a board of directors' resolution was sufficient to show the appointment of the foreign representative and a copy of the notice of a motion made to the foreign court was sufficient to show that the proceeding was a foreign proceeding.[86]

1.15.37 Article 15 merely sets forth the minimum pleading standards for the application and requires at least some evidence in the application of the required elements for recognition. Additional and more persuasive evidence might be needed in order for the receiving court to decide whether recognition should be granted.[87] Those questions, as well as the characterization of the proceeding as a foreign main or foreign non-main proceeding, would need to be determined

80 *Guide to Enactment* (n 1), para 131.
81 *Probe Resources Ltd* 2011 CarswellBC 1043, 79 CBR 5th 148 paras 14–16 (BC SC) (CAN).
82 *Betcorp* 400 BR at 284–85.
83 *Betcorp* at 282–83.
84 *Betcorp* at 271–72.
85 *In Re Pro-Fit Holdings Ltd* 391 BR 850, 858 (Bankr CD Cal 2008) (US).
86 *In Re Cell C Proprietary Ltd* 571 BR 542, 553–54 (Bankr SDNY 2017) (US).
87 *Guide to Enactment* (n 1), paras 129 & 131; *Judicial Perspective* (n 13), para 67.

by the receiving court pursuant to Article 17 using whatever local evidentiary and procedural rules were applicable.

The receiving state may be a party to a bilateral or multilateral treaty on recognition and legalization of documents that establishes a standard different from Article 15.[88] That would present no conflict if the treaty permits laws that abolish or further relax legalization requirements.[89] In case of a conflict between the MLCBI and a treaty, Article 3 of the MLCBI provides that the treaty prevails.[90] **1.15.38**

D. DISCLOSURE OF OTHER PROCEEDINGS

In addition to the documents required by Article 15(2), the application must include 'a statement identifying all foreign proceedings in respect of the debtor that are known to the foreign representative'.[91] This requirement works together with Article 18(b) to impose an ongoing obligation on the foreign representative to advise the receiving court of all other foreign proceedings involving the debtor that it becomes aware of.[92] **1.15.39**

Articles 15(3) and 18(b) expressly impose the duty to inform upon the foreign representative to counteract the incentive not to disclose competing foreign proceedings.[93] Foreign representatives may be primarily concerned with obtaining relief favouring their local proceedings and less concerned about coordinating with other foreign proceedings.[94] There might also be competition between the foreign proceedings for valuable assets or control of the debtor's liquidation or reorganization. Additionally, the foreign representative's role in the foreign proceeding likely would provide it with information about the debtor's operations in third states and other insolvency proceedings involv- **1.15.40**

88 For example, the Hague Apostille Convention (n 59) has been adopted by more than 100 jurisdictions and establishes a simplified procedure for legalization that generally requires only certification by the issuing body in the originating state, much like article 15(2)(a).

89 For example, art. 3(2) of the Hague Apostille Convention (n 59) leaves in force any laws, regulations, practices, or other treaties that abolish or simplify legalization or that exempt documents from the process.

90 Article 3 of the MLCBI provides: 'To the extent that this Law conflicts with an obligation of this State arising out of any treaty or other form of agreement to which it is a party with one or more other States, the requirements of the treaty or agreement prevail.' MLCBI art 3; *Guide to Enactment* (n 1), para 130.

91 MLCBI art 15(3).

92 The article 17(3) disclosure requirement applies at the time of application, with article 18(b) imposing an ongoing disclosure obligation from that time forward (see MLCBI art 18(b)).

93 *Guide to Enactment* (n 1), para 133.

94 *Guide to Enactment* (n 1), para 133.

ing the debtor.[95] The duty to inform is limited to other foreign proceedings known to the foreign representative.

1.15.41 The existence of other foreign proceedings would be an important factor for the receiving court to consider in deciding whether and what relief should be granted.[96] Where multiple foreign proceedings are pending in respect to the same debtor, Article 30 requires the court to seek coordination and cooperation among the proceedings. Further, Article 30 provides rules for coordinating the relief provided when there are multiple foreign proceedings involving the same debtor.[97] In addition, the existence of other proceedings may be relevant to the receiving court's decision whether to recognize the proceeding as a foreign main proceeding or a foreign non-main proceeding.

E. TRANSLATION OF DOCUMENTS

1.15.42 In cases where documents supplied with the application are in a foreign language, Article 15(4) authorizes the court to require a translation of some or all such documents into an official language of the receiving state. The Guide to Enactment notes that Article 15(4) 'entitles, but does not compel, the court to require a translation of some or all of the documents accompanying the application for recognition'.[98]

1.15.43 Curiously, the Guide to Enactment emphasizes the receiving court's discretion to consider the application without the need for translation of the documents if that would facilitate a decision being made at the earliest possible time as directed by Article 17(3).[99] The language of the provision, however, is not phrased in a way that grants discretion to dispense with translation, unlike the discretionary grants regarding other documentation in Article 15(2)(c) or the presumptions permitted by Article 16(1 & 2). If translation into an official language is otherwise required under the applicable local law, then it would be required of the application for recognition regardless of Article 15(4). While the provision does not negate any discretion to forego translation that the receiving court may have under local law, it would appear to have no operational effect unless the local law did not otherwise permit translation of foreign language documents into an official language of the receiving state.

95 *Guide to Enactment* (n 1), para 133.
96 *Guide to Enactment* (n 1), para 132.
97 MLCBI art 30(1–3).
98 *Guide to Enactment* (n 1), para 134.
99 *Guide to Enactment* (n 1), para 134.

Article 16

PRESUMPTIONS CONCERNING RECOGNITION

G. Ray Warner

1. If the decision or certificate referred to in paragraph 2 of Article 15 indicates that the foreign proceeding is a proceeding within the meaning of subparagraph (a) of Article 2 and that the foreign representative is a person or body within the meaning of subparagraph (d) of Article 2, the court is entitled to so presume.
2. The court is entitled to presume that documents submitted in support of the application for recognition are authentic, whether or not they have been legalized.
3. In the absence of proof to the contrary, the debtor's registered office, or habitual residence in the case of an individual, is presumed to be the centre of the debtor's main interests.

A. INTRODUCTION TO ARTICLE 16

1. In General

1.16.01 Effective cross-border assistance often requires prompt action by the courts of the receiving jurisdiction in order to preserve value and prevent the transfer, concealment or dissipation of assets.[1] One of the key objectives of the MLCBI is to establish a simplified process for recognition of qualifying foreign proceedings so that prompt relief can be provided.[2] Articles 15, 16 and 17 are designed to work together to create a simple and expeditious recognition process that dispenses with cumbersome technical requirements that might unnecessarily delay the recognition decision.[3] Article 15 sets forth minimal technical requirements for the application for recognition and the documentation required and Article 17 governs the recognition decision. Article 16 plays a critical role by supplying several important presumptions that apply to the recognition determination. These presumptions can greatly simplify and speed up the evidentiary process in cases where there is no serious challenge to recognition.

1.16.02 The Article 16(2) presumption of document authenticity complements Article 15's elimination of the 'legalization' requirement for the documents submitted with the application to demonstrate that the foreign action is a 'foreign proceeding' and that the applicant is the 'foreign representative'.[4] Article 16 goes further and permits the receiving court to presume that all documents submitted in support of the application are authentic, regardless of the issue they may address. This allows the court to dispense with time-consuming and cumbersome authentication requirements when there is no reason to doubt authenticity.

1.16.03 The other Article 16 presumptions are more substantive, allowing the court to presume that critical factual and legal prerequisites for recognition have been met, even without other evidence. The two primary requirements for recognition are that the foreign insolvency action is a 'foreign proceeding' and that the applicant is the 'foreign representative'. If the applicant has submitted a certified copy of the foreign decision commencing the foreign proceeding

1 *UNCITRAL Model Law on Cross-Border Insolvency with Guide to Enactment and Interpretation*, United Nations Publications (New York), 2014, paras 135 & 163; *UNCITRAL Model Law on Cross-Border Insolvency: The Judicial Perspective*, United Nations Publications (New York), 2014, paras 38 & 39.

2 *Guide to Enactment* (n 1), para 29.

3 *Guide to Enactment* (n 1), para 127.

4 See Commentary discussion at paragraph 1.15.22.

or appointing the foreign representative and if that decision indicates that the foreign action is a foreign proceeding or that the applicant is the foreign representative, then the receiving court is entitled to so presume.[5] This presumption similarly applies if the applicant has, instead, submitted a certificate from the foreign court affirming either of those points.[6]

In addition, Article 17 requires that, as part of the recognition decision, the receiving court must determine whether the foreign proceeding is a 'foreign main proceeding' or a 'foreign non-main proceeding', which are the only types of foreign proceedings that can be recognized under the MLCBI.[7] A foreign main proceeding is one that is pending in the jurisdiction of the debtor's 'centre of main interests' (COMI).[8] In contrast, a foreign non-main proceeding is one pending in a jurisdiction where the debtor merely has an 'establishment'.[9] Significant consequences flow automatically from the recognition decision if the proceeding is recognized as a foreign main proceeding.[10] Most importantly in cases where prompt protection is needed, recognition as a foreign main proceeding automatically suspends the debtor's right to transfer, encumber or dispose of assets and imposes a moratorium staying executions against the debtor's assets and the commencement or continuation of most other individual actions and proceedings affecting the debtor.[11] **1.16.04**

The final Article 16 presumption expedites the main versus non-main determination by establishing a presumption that the debtor's registered office is its COMI.[12] In the case of an individual (human) debtor, the COMI presumption applies instead to the debtor's habitual residence.[13] No similar presumption applies to the determination whether the debtor has an establishment in the foreign jurisdiction. **1.16.05**

---

5 MLCBI art 16(1).

6 ibid.

7 MLCBI art 17(2)(a & b). If the insolvency proceeding is pending in a jurisdiction that is neither its COMI nor the location of an establishment, then it should not be recognized under the MLCBI, although some MLCBI provisions, such as the cooperation and coordination article, would be applicable. Situations that fall into this category might include insolvency proceedings pending in a jurisdiction where the debtor has assets but no operations, or the jurisdiction of its registered office if it has no other presence there (a 'letterbox' company).

8 MLCBI art 2(b).

9 MLCBI art 2(c). '*Establishment*,' as defined in article 2(f), '*means any place of operations where the debtor carries out a non-transitory economic activity with human means and goods or services*.' MLCBI art. 2(f); see Commentary discussion at paragraph 1.2.25.

10 *Guide to Enactment* (n 1), para 37; *Judicial Perspective* (n 1), para 65.

11 Ibid.

12 MLCBI art 16(3).

13 ibid.

2. Nature of Presumptions

1.16.06 Article 16 contains both discretionary and mandatory presumptions. The presumptions in Article 16(1 & 2) regarding document authenticity and the foreign proceeding and foreign representative determinations are discretionary. The MLCBI merely permits, but does not require, the receiving court to indulge in the stated presumptions.[14] The receiving court is free to ignore those presumptions entirely and require legalization of submitted documents and the presentation of other evidence to establish the elements of the MLCBI foreign proceeding definition and the appointment of the foreign representative. In contrast, Article 16(3) establishes a mandatory presumption that the debtor's COMI is located in the jurisdiction of its registered office or, in the case of an individual, its habitual residence.

1.16.07 All of the Article 16 presumptions are rebuttable. So, even if the presumption applies, the receiving court may require additional and more persuasive evidence to decide whether recognition should be granted and whether the foreign jurisdiction is the debtor's COMI.[15] Those questions would need to be determined by the receiving court pursuant to Article 17 using whatever local evidentiary and procedural rules were applicable.

1.16.08 Courts disagree about the strength of the presumptions permitted by Article 16 and the quantity and quality of evidence needed to rebut them.[16] This turns in part on differences in the wording of local MLCBI adaptations[17] and on the local jurisdiction's rules regarding the effect of evidentiary presumptions.[18] At one end of the spectrum, the presumption only operates to establish the relevant point in the absence of any contrary evidence or proof whereas, at the other end of the spectrum, the presumption establishes the relevant point unless the party opposing it carries the burden of presenting sufficient contrary evidence to persuade the court that a different conclusion is warranted.

---

14 *Guide to Enactment* (n 1), para 137.

15 *Guide to Enactment* (n 1), paras 129 & 131; *Judicial Perspective* (n 1), para 67.

16 *Judicial Perspective* (n 1), para 99.

17 For example, the Japanese version of the MLCBI substitutes the principal place of business for the COMI concept and does not include the article 16(3) registered office presumption. *Think3,* case nos. (shou) 3 and 5 of 2011, Tokyo District Court, ch 3, issue 2-2, (2) CLOUT 1335 (JP); J 123 n 160; Ho, Look Chan (ed), A Commentary on the UNCITRAL Model Law, 4th ed, Globe Law & Business (London), 2017, 326 (stating that the COMI concept 'is irrelevant under Japanese insolvency law').

18 *Judicial Perspective* (n 1), paras 99-125.

Many of the reported decisions adopting the weaker view of the presumptions are from the United States[19] and must be read in light of two US-specific factors. Thus, while the United States is a major in-bound recognition jurisdiction and its approach is important for US recognition applications, those cases may not be persuasive authority on the weight that should be given to the presumptions in other jurisdictions. First, with respect to the very important Article 16(3) COMI presumption, the US version of the MLCBI (chapter 15 of the Bankruptcy Code) replaced the MLCBI's language '[i]n the absence of proof to the contrary' with the weaker language 'in the absence of evidence to the contrary'.[20] In light of the United States' general approach to evidentiary presumptions, discussed below, the change from proof to evidence merely conforms the MLCBI Article 16(3) with US practice. **1.16.09**

As importantly, the US evidentiary rules specify that 'the party against whom a presumption is directed has the burden of producing evidence to rebut the presumption. But this rule does not shift the burden of persuasion, which remains on the party who had it originally'.[21] That evidence rule distinguishes between the burden of going forward (that is, of presenting some evidence of the point at issue) and the burden of persuasion. In the US, the applicant bears the burden of persuasion on all elements required for recognition.[22] Thus, the presumption alone would be sufficient to establish the point at issue in the absence of any other evidence. For example, recognition could be granted on the strength of the application and supporting documents alone if there was no opposition. **1.16.10**

However, if any evidence is presented to the contrary, then the presumption is no longer enough to establish the point. For example, in *Bear Stearns* the presumption was rebutted by statements in the application regarding the letterbox nature of the debtor.[23] The US courts disagree on whether the presumption vanishes entirely upon the presentation of contrary evidence (that is, the 'bursting bubble' approach) or whether the presumption can still be considered by the court as part of its fact-finding analysis, with the bursting bubble view being the more accepted approach.[24] Even under the bursting bubble **1.16.11**

19 The most well-known such case is *In Re Bear Sterns High-Grade Structured Credit Strategies Master Fund, Ltd*, 374 BR 122, 129-30 (Bankr SDNY 2007), *aff'd* 389 BR 325 (2008) CLOUT 760 (US).

20 11 USC 1516(c).

21 Fed R Evid 301.

22 *In Re Pirogova*, 593 BR 402, 408 (Bankr SDNY 2018) aff'd 612 BR 475 (SDNY 2020) CLOUT 2018 (US).

23 *Bear Stearns* 374 BR at 129.

24 Paul F Rothstein, Fed Rules of Evidence Rule 301 (2022 ed).

approach, however, the location of the debtor's registered office[25] remains an important part of the COMI analysis, but simply as one of several factors for consideration.

B. FOREIGN PROCEEDING AND FOREIGN REPRESENTATIVE PRESUMPTIONS

1.16.12 Article 15(2) requires that the application for recognition be accompanied by documentation that the foreign insolvency action is a foreign proceeding and that the applicant is the foreign representative.[26] Three types of documentation are permitted. The application may be accompanied by a certified copy of the foreign decision(s) commencing the foreign proceeding and appointing the foreign representative.[27] Alternatively, a certificate from the foreign court that affirms the existence of the foreign proceeding and the appointment of the foreign representative may be submitted.[28] These are the preferred types of documentation. However, in the absence of such a decision or certificate, the applicant may submit other evidence of the existence of the foreign proceeding or the appointment of the foreign representative.[29]

1.16.13 If either a decision or certificate is submitted with the application for recognition, then Article 16(1) permits the receiving court to presume that the proceeding is a foreign proceeding within the meaning of MLCBI Article 2(a) and that the applicant is the foreign representative within the meaning of MLCBI Article 2(d) if the decision or certificate so indicates. No similar presumption applies if the third option is used, even if the documents submitted indicate that the proceeding is a foreign proceeding and that the applicant is the foreign representative.

1.16.14 In cases where foreign recognition and assistance likely will be needed, the court in the jurisdiction where the insolvency proceeding is initiated can facilitate the recognition process by including the Article 16(1) information regarding the nature of the proceeding and the appointment of the foreign representative in the decision opening the foreign insolvency proceeding.[30] For example, the English court in *Worldspreads Ltd.*[31] included in its order

25 Or the habitual residence of an individual.
26 See Commentary discussion at paragraph 1.15.25 et seq.
27 MLCBI art 15(2)(a).
28 MLCBI art 15(2)(b).
29 MLCBI art 15(2)(c).
30 *Guide to Enactment* (n 1), para 139.
31 [2012] EWHC 1263 (ch) para 38 (ENG).

a statement that the English proceeding qualified as a foreign proceeding and the administrator qualified as a foreign representative. Similarly, if a certificate is used, the court making the certification could include in the certificate the information necessary to establish the foreign proceeding and foreign representative requirements. Either approach would entitle the receiving court to presume that the pre-requisites for recognition were satisfied.[32] The recitations in the decision or certificate of the foreign court are not binding on the receiving court and it must independently satisfy itself that the recognition requirements are met.[33]

The MLCBI does not specify the level of detail required for the 'indications' needed to trigger the Article 16(1) presumptions. Presumably either a general conclusory statement in the foreign decision or certificate or more specific statements detailing the required elements of the MLCBI's definitions would suffice. Neither the Guide to Enactment nor Judicial Perspective discusses the point, and use of the term 'indicates' could be read either to require specification or permit a mere suggestion. While the safer practice would be to include a recitation of the required elements, reading Article 16(1) to permit a conclusory statement would be consistent with the goal of providing a simple expedited process of recognition in cases where there is no opposition to the application or no serious doubt. The presumption can be challenged and rebutted, so giving the receiving court discretion to base the presumption on a conclusory statement does little harm. **1.16.15**

The presumptions permitted by Article 16(1) work in tandem with the minimal documentation required by Article 15(2) to allow recognition promptly and summarily on the basis of the application alone where no question is raised about the status of the foreign proceeding or of the foreign representative. Although Article 17(1)(a & b) require the receiving court to determine these points before it may grant recognition, the Article 16 presumptions aid that process. If the application for recognition is accompanied by a certified decision or a court certificate affirming the existence of a foreign proceeding and the appointment of the foreign representative, the Article 16 presumptions can be used to establish the grounds for recognition. This is because Article 16(2) permits the receiving court to presume that the decision or certificate is authentic and Article 16(1) allows the receiving court to rely, without requiring **1.16.16**

32 The CLOUT Digest discusses unpublished opinions utilizing the presumption. Digest of Case Law on the UNCITRAL Model Law on Cross-Border Insolvency (CLOUT), United Nations Publications (Vienna), 2021 art 16 n 6.

33 *Guide to Enactment* (n 1), para 139.

further evidence, on the representations in the decision or certificate that the foreign insolvency action satisfies the MLCBI definition of a foreign proceeding and that the applicant is its foreign representative.

C. PRESUMPTION THAT DOCUMENTS ARE AUTHENTIC

1.16.17 While Article 15 eliminates the need for 'legalization' of documents submitted in support of the application for recognition, Article 16 provides presumptions that replace the role of legalization[34] in establishing that certain foreign documents are authentic.[35] Article 16(2) provides that '[t]he court is entitled to presume that documents submitted in support of the application are authentic'.[36] This presumption applies not only to the certified copies of the foreign judgment and certificates from the foreign court referenced in Article 15(2) (a & b), but also covers the wide array of documents that might be submitted with the application under Article 15(2)(c) or submitted later in support of the application. For example, in *Betcorp* the court accepted as authentic a document showing that the applicant had been appointed as a liquidator by the foreign administrative agency that regulated corporations and a copy of the foreign state's insolvency law to establish elements of the foreign proceeding definition.[37]

1.16.18 The presumption is not limited to official government documents, but has also been applied to private documents, such as a memorandum to the debtor's equity holders and minutes and resolutions of the debtor's directors.[38] The MLCBI does not indicate what constitutes a 'document' to which the article 16(2) presumption might apply, but the *Betcorp* court suggested that an internet link to a webpage containing the relevant information might be sufficient.[39]

1.16.19 Article 16(2) does not limit the authenticity presumption to the documents referenced in Article 15(2) showing that the foreign insolvency action is

34 Although the MLCBI's authenticity presumption is not mandatory, some States have added language to article 16 stating that the receiving court 'may' require legalization of documents. The CLOUT Digest notes that Chile and Columbia have such provisions. Digest of Case Law on the UNCITRAL Model Law on Cross-Border Insolvency (CLOUT), United Nations Publications (Vienna), 2021 art 16 n 8.

35 Legalization might also be used to establish the capacity in which the signer of a foreign document acted. This concept should be covered in most cases by the presumption of authenticity where the capacity of the signer is clear from the document.

36 MLCBI art 16(2).

37 *In Re Betcorp Ltd* 400 BR 266, 282-85 & 294-95 (Bankr D. Nev 2009) CLOUT 927 (US); see also *Judicial Perspective* (n 1), para 67.

38 *Betcorp* at 284–285.

39 *Betcorp* at 282–283.

a foreign proceeding and that the applicant is the foreign representative. Thus, the authenticity presumption should apply to any documents supporting the application for recognition, including documents submitted to show the debtor's COMI is in the foreign jurisdiction or that the debtor has an establishment there. For example, if the applicant submits a copy of the registration certificate issued by the foreign administrative agency that regulates corporations as evidence of the location of the debtor's registered office, the receiving court can assume that it is authentic. Notwithstanding the breadth of the authenticity presumption, it is discretionary, and the receiving court remains free to require legalization if it chooses or if it questions the authenticity of the submitted documents.[40]

Interestingly, the authenticity presumption is limited to documents 'submitted in support of the application for recognition'.[41] Thus, documents submitted in opposition to the application do not benefit from the presumption of authenticity and presumably remain subject to whatever legalization requirements otherwise apply in the receiving jurisdiction. While it is inconsistent to apply different authentication requirements to documents supporting recognition from those undermining it, the rationale for the Article 16 presumptions (and the minimal application standards of Article 15) was to provide a simple expeditious mechanism for recognition in cases where prompt action was needed and there was no serious question whether recognition was proper.[42] The simplified process established by Articles 15 and 16 further the Article 17(3) requirement that the application for recognition 'be decided upon at the earliest possible time'.[43] Working in tandem, these provision may allow recognition in a matter of days where there is no objection.[44] The one-sided authenticity presumption in article 16(2) furthers that objective, as do the one-sided foreign proceeding and foreign representative presumptions in Article 16(1). **1.16.20**

This suggests that article 16(2) authenticity presumption may be limited to documents submitted to support the factors needed under Article 17 for the recognition determination: (1) the existence of a foreign proceeding; (2) the appointment of the foreign representative; and (3) the location of the debtor's **1.16.21**

40 *Guide to Enactment* (n 1), paras 127 & 129. The wording of article 15 and the policy of not adding extra requirements suggest that legalization of the copy of the judgment or the certificate of the court referred to in article 15(2)(a & b) should not be required at the application stage, although the court could so require as a prerequisite to deciding whether to recognize the foreign proceeding under article 17. For other documents submitted under article 15(2)(c), the receiving court may require legalization.

41 MLCBI art 16(2).

42 *Guide to Enactment* (n 1), paras 29 & 127.

43 MLCBI art 17(3).

44 *Guide to Enactment* para 163; *Judicial Perspective* (n 1), para 38.

COMI or an establishment in the foreign jurisdiction.[45] The title of article 16 also suggests the presumptions are limited to matters 'concerning recognition'. Thus, documents addressing other issues, such as preliminary relief under Article 19 or discretionary relief under Article 21, may need to be legalized, even though prompt relief may be needed.

1.16.22 Finally, while Article 16(2) permits the receiving court to presume that certain documents are authentic, unlike Article 16(1), there is no presumption that the assertions contained in the submitted documents establish the points they address. The local law of the receiving jurisdiction will determine whether the statements contained in documents qualify as evidence of the points they support.[46]

D. CENTRE OF MAIN INTEREST PRESUMPTIONS

1. Importance of COMI

1.16.23 Article 15(2) requires that the application for recognition include documents showing that the foreign insolvency action is a foreign proceeding and the applicant is the foreign representative. Article 17(1)(a & b) then requires the receiving court to decide those issues before granting recognition. The Article 16(1 & 2) presumptions permit that decision to be based on the application alone.

1.16.24 Article 17(2) further requires, as part of the recognition process, that the receiving court also decide whether the foreign insolvency action is a foreign main proceeding or a foreign non-main proceeding. A foreign main proceeding is one that is pending in the jurisdiction of the debtor's COMI and a foreign non-main proceeding is one pending in a jurisdiction that is not the debtor's COMI but where the debtor has an establishment. The Article 16(3) COMI presumption expedites this aspect of the recognition process by establishing a presumption that the debtor's registered office is the COMI of legal entities, such as corporations, and the debtor's habitual residence is the COMI of an individual (human) debtor.[47]

45 MLCBI art 17(1)(a & b) & (2).

46 See Commentary discussion at paragraph 1.16.28.

47 MLCBI art 16(3).

Article 16(3) provides that 'in the absence of proof to the contrary' the debtor's registered office[48] 'is presumed to the centre of the debtor's main interests'.[49] Thus, where the submitted documents or other evidence show that the debtor's registered office is in the jurisdiction where the foreign insolvency action is pending, the receiving court can grant recognition as a foreign main proceeding quickly. This is important because the COMI concept is fundamental to the operation of the MLCBI.[50] In a globalized economy where it is relatively easy to move assets quickly across borders, immediate and automatic relief may be necessary to prevent fraud and protect the legitimate interests of parties.[51] **1.16.25**

Recognition as a foreign main proceeding automatically imposes a stay in the receiving jurisdiction of execution against the debtor's assets and against the '[c]ommencement or continuation of individual actions [and] individual proceedings concerning the debtor's assets, rights, obligations or liabilities'.[52] In addition, recognition as a foreign main proceeding automatically suspends '[t]he right to transfer, encumber or otherwise dispose of any assets of the debtor'.[53] Thus, the combined Article 16 presumptions can provide both prompt recognition and prompt relief in the receiving jurisdiction if the foreign insolvency action is pending in the location of the debtor's registered office or habitual residence. No similar presumption applies to the determination of whether the debtor has an establishment in the foreign jurisdiction.[54] **1.16.26**

2. COMI Presumption is Mandatory

Unlike the other Article 16 presumptions, which are discretionary, the article 16(3) COMI presumption is mandatory. Also, unlike the other Article 16 presumptions, the COMI presumption can be used by either the applicant to establish that the foreign jurisdiction is the COMI and the proceeding is a foreign main proceeding or by a challenger attempting to establish that the COMI is elsewhere and the proceeding should not be recognized as a main proceeding. However, like the other Article 16 presumptions, the COMI presumption may be rebutted. The MLCBI requires 'proof to the contrary'[55] **1.16.27**

48 Or the 'habitual residence in the case of an individual' is presumed to be the debtor's COMI. MLCBI art 16(3).

49 MLCBI art 16(3).

50 *Guide to Enactment* (n 1), para 144; *Judicial Perspective* (n 1), para 65.

51 *Guide to Enactment* (n 1), para 37.

52 MLCBI art 20(1)(a & b).

53 MLCBI art 20(1)(c).

54 *Judicial Perspective* (n 1), para 138.

55 The United States version of the MLCBI, chapter 15 of its Bankruptcy Code, substitutes the term '*evidence*' for '*proof*'. The effect of that change is discussed at paragraph 1.16.09. The Japanese version of the MLCBI does not include the COMI presumption. *Judicial Perspective* (n 1), para 124.

in order to rebut the COMI presumption but does not state a standard for rebuttal of the other Article 16 presumptions.

1.16.28 While documents submitted in support of the application to establish the location of the debtor's COMI may benefit from the Article 16(2) authenticity presumption, Article 16 does not create a presumption that the COMI is located where such documents indicate. This is different from the Article 16(1) presumptions that permit the receiving court to presume that the foreign insolvency action is a foreign proceeding and the applicant is the foreign representative. The local law of the receiving jurisdiction will determine whether the statements contained in documents qualify as evidence of the location of the debtor's registered office or habitual residence. The authentication presumption may be sufficient if the local law permits the court to accept as true statements in authenticated public records, such as the certificate of registration issued by the jurisdiction's registrar of corporations.[56]

3. Compared to the European Insolvency Regulation COMI Presumption

1.16.29 While the 'centre of main interests' concept plays a central role in the MLCBI, the MLCBI does not attempt to define it.[57] The COMI concept and the registered office presumption were drawn from the proposed European Union Convention on Insolvency Proceedings[58] and used in the MLCBI to provide consistency between the two international instruments.[59] The Convention subsequently lapsed, but its COMI concept was carried forward into the European Insolvency Regulation (EIR).[60] Thus, COMI interpretations under the EIR may be relevant to its meaning in the MLCBI.[61] Consequently, some courts have applied the principles established under the EIR to recognition

56 For example, if a foreign certificate of incorporation were presented in support of a recognition application in the United States, the article 16(2) authenticity presumption would override the otherwise applicable foreign public document authentication requirements of evidence rule 902(3). FR Evid R 902(3). Having authenticated the foreign certificate, the applicant would be able use the statements in the certificate as evidence that the debtor was incorporated in the foreign jurisdiction. However, that result flows from US evidence rule 803(8), rather than the MLCBI. FR Evid Rule 803(8).

57 '[A] deliberate decision was taken not to define "centre of main interests".' *Judicial Perspective* (n 1), para 94; see *Guide to Enactment* (n 1), para 31.

58 European Union Convention on Insolvency Proceedings opened for signature 23 Nov 1995 [1996] 17 ZIP 976, 35 ILM 1223.

59 *Judicial Perspective* (n 1), para 94.

60 *Judicial Perspective* (n 1), para 95. The original version of the EIR is Council Regulation (EC) 1346/2000 of 29 May 2000 on insolvency proceedings [2000] OJ L160/1. The current version is Regulation (EU) 2015/848 of 20 May 2015 on insolvency proceedings (recast) [2015] OJ L141/19.

61 *Guide to Enactment* (n 1), para 141.

applications under the MLCBI.[62] This is consistent with the MLCBI article 8 admonition to interpret the law in light of its international origin.[63] For example, on appeal in *Stanford Int'l Bank Ltd* the English court, noting the clear correlation between the EIR and the MLCBI, followed EIR case law in interpreting the MLCBI COMI presumption.[64] Australian courts also adopt this approach.[65]

Other courts look to the EIR interpretations for guidance but do not apply identical principles. This is because the COMI concept performs very different functions under the EIR and the MLCBI.[66] The most important difference is that the COMI concept is jurisdictional under the EIR,[67] determining the EU Member State[68] in which an insolvency proceeding may be opened. Thus, under the EIR there can be only one COMI. Further, since the concept is jurisdictional, the debtor's COMI must be determined at the outset of the proceeding by the court opening the proceeding. If the initial court holds that it is located at the debtor's COMI, that determination is binding on other EU courts.[69] **1.16.30**

In contrast, COMI under the MLCBI has a much more limited effect. It is used primarily[70] to determine whether recognition triggers the immediate, automatic relief provided by Article 20, or whether discretionary relief must be sought under Article 22. COMI is not determined at the outset of the foreign proceeding; nor is it determined by the court opening that proceeding. The COMI issue arises later, possibly several years later, when recognition is sought in a different jurisdiction. That determination is made by the receiving court and it is not bound by a previous finding of COMI by a receiving court in a different jurisdiction.[71] **1.16.31**

---

62 For a discussion of the EIR principles, see *Judicial Perspective* (n 1), paras 95–104.

63 MLCBI art 8.

64 [2010] EWCA Civ 137 para 39, CLOUT 1003 (ENG). Singapore adopted a similar approach in a case decided under its common law and before it adopted the MLCBI. *Re Opti-Medix Ltd (in liquidation)* [2016] 4 SLR 312 [25], *discussed at* Ho, Look Chan (ed), A Commentary on the UNCITRAL Model Law, 4th ed, Globe Law & Business (London), 2017, 532.

65 *Ackers v Saad Investments Co Ltd (in official liq)* 118 ALD 498, [2010] FCA 1221 para 49 CLOUT 1219 (AU).

66 *Judicial Perspective* (n 1), para 95, *Guide to Enactment* (n 1), para 141.

67 Of almost equal importance, the EIR also uses COMI for important choice of law issues.

68 The EIR does not apply to Denmark.

69 Case 341/04, *Eurofood IFSC Ltd*, 2006 ECR 1-3813, paras 39, 42, 49 and 52.

70 The MLCBI also gives greater deference to the foreign main proceeding when multiple foreign insolvency proceedings are pending.

71 The court opening the foreign proceeding might include recitations in its orders to aid the foreign receiving court in this determination, but those findings are not binding on the receiving court. *Judicial Perspective* (n 1), para 118.

1.16.32 The 2013 revision to the Guide to Enactment adopts the EIR approach that the debtor can have only one COMI and that the COMI is determined based on the facts at the time that the foreign proceeding was opened[72] – which increases the likelihood that all receiving courts globally might agree on which foreign proceeding is the foreign main proceeding.[73] In contrast, the courts of several jurisdictions, including the US, have adopted a slightly different view that the debtor can have only one COMI at any given time, but that the relevant time is when recognition is sought or granted.[74] While this increases the likelihood that different receiving courts globally may reach conflicting conclusions, minimal harmful consequences flow from that result. The automatic relief under Article 20 that flows from a COMI determination is the same relief that could be accorded in a discretionary manner under Article 21, or even before recognition under Article 19. Since the effects of recognition are limited to the recognizing jurisdiction, no inherent conflict is presented if two different jurisdictions provide local automatic relief to different foreign proceedings. The MLCBI's cooperation and coordination provisions may present an issue since they defer to the foreign main proceeding, but that deference is largely discretionary in any event.

1.16.33 The Article 16(3) COMI presumption is tied to the debtor's registered office or, in the case of an individual, the debtor's habitual residence. Neither term is defined in the MLCBI. The term 'registered office' refers to the place of registration, incorporation or the equivalent for an entity that is not a human.[75] The debtor's registered office ordinarily will be easily determined and not subject to any ambiguity. In the rare case where the debtor has more than one registered office, the presumption does not apply because the COMI must be at a single location and the MLCBI provides no rule for multiple registered offices.[76]

4. Habitual Residence of an Individual Debtor

1.16.34 Although not defined in the MLCBI, 'habitual residence' has a well-developed meaning in other international conventions and instruments that use the term and courts have looked there for its meaning.[77] This approach reflects the

72 *Guide to Enactment* (n 1), para 159.

73 The 2013 Guide to Enactment (n 1), states that '*It is not advisable to include more than one criterion*' for determining COMI since an approach using multiple criteria raise the risk of competing claims for recognition as the main proceeding. *Guide to Enactment* (n 1), para 155.

74 *In Re Fairfield Sentry Ltd* 714 F3d 127, 137 (2d Cir 2013) CLOUT 1339 (US).

75 HR Rep No 109-31 at 113 (2005) (legislative report to US chapter 15).

76 *Legend Int'l Holdings Inc* [2016] VSC 303 para 123 CLOUT 1619 (AU).

77 Digest of Case Law on the UNCITRAL Model Law on Cross-Border Insolvency (CLOUT), United Nations Publications (Vienna), 2021 art 16 para 27.

international origin of the MLCBI, in keeping with the interpretive standard of Article 8. Unfortunately, the habitual residence of a natural person often will be less clear than the registered office of a juridical entity, especially when the individual has multiple residences or often lives in different locations for work or recreation. This may greatly diminish the usefulness of the Article 16(3) presumption since the proof needed to establish the individual's habitual residence may be as extensive as that needed to establish the individual's COMI in the absence of the presumption.[78] Nonetheless, the presumption will permit quick recognition in cases where the individual has a single residence, or one residence is clearly the primary one.

The courts have stated various formulations of the habitual residence concept. **1.16.35** The US court in *In Re Loy* interpreted the term to refer to the debtor's customary or usual residence.[79] The English court in *In Re Stojevic* distinguished between an individual's habitual residence (the settled, permanent home where they lived with their partner and children and to which they returned after business trips) and an 'ordinary residence' where they might live while away from home on business or a holiday.[80] The settled, permanent home was the habitual residence even though the debtor might spend a greater number of days at the ordinary residence. Numerous factual factors are relevant to the determination of the debtor's habitual residence, including the debtor's settled purpose, the length and purpose of the stay, the nature and strength of the debtor's ties to the jurisdiction and the degree of the debtor's assimilation and cultural, social and economic integration in the jurisdiction.[81] Unlike the COMI of juridical entities, where an emphasis is placed on factors that are ascertainable to creditors, several of the habitual residence factors, such as the debtor's subjective intent,[82] are not ascertainable to creditors.[83]

---

78 For a discussion of an individual's COMI, see Cody Vandewerker, 'The Jetsetter's Guide to Bankruptcy: Chapter 15 and Recognition As A Foreign Main Proceeding for Individual Debtors,' 33 Ariz J Int'l & Comp L 451, 472 (2016) (focusing on US cases).

79 308 BR 154, 162 (Bankr ED Va 2007), CLOUT 924 (US).

80 [2007] BPIR 141 para 58 *et seq* (ENG), *discussed at Judicial Perspective* (n 1), para 62.

81 CLOUT Digest art 16 para 28; see also *Williams v Simpson (No 5)* [2010] NZHC 1786 [2011] 2 NZLR 380 para 42 CLOUT 1220 (NZ); *In Re Kemsley*, 489 BR 346, 360 (Bankr SDNY 2013), CLOUT 1274 (US).

82 The court considered the debtor's stated intention to permanently leave their earlier home in *In Re Pirogova*, 593 BR 402, 409 (Bankr SDNY 2018) CLOUT 2018 (US).

83 *Gainsford in the matter of Tannenbaum v Tannenbaum* [2012] FCA 904 para 44, CLOUT 1214 (AU).

5. Rebutting the COMI Presumption

(a) Varying Approaches

1.16.36 Different courts take different approaches to the COMI determination and to the effect of the article 16(3) presumption. As discussed at paragraph 1.16.08 above, the presumption ranges from a strong presumption that can be overcome only by a persuasive showing of proof to the contrary to a 'bursting bubble' presumption that disappears if any contrary evidence is presented. While the COMI determination is a holistic one that does not turn on any single factor, the relative importance given to particular factors varies greatly from jurisdiction to jurisdiction. Finally, even the relevant time for making the determination is in dispute.[84] These differences between MLCBI jurisdictions are further exacerbated by questions of whether COMI shifts should be recognized and how members of enterprise groups should be treated.

1.16.37 The 2013 revision of the Guide to Enactment attempted to resolve some of these differences,[85] primarily by emphasizing the EIR approach to COMI and criticizing contrary approaches, notably the evolving US interpretations. That effort was largely unsuccessful, especially to the extent that it was designed to shift the US interpretations toward the EIR approach. The US approach to COMI, and recognition more generally, reflects a longstanding willingness to recognize and enforce foreign insolvency orders. Long before the MLCBI, US Bankruptcy Code section 304 authorized broad assistance to foreign insolvency proceedings without the COMI and establishment restrictions of the MLCBI.[86] The US cases, and the conflicts they create with cases from some other jurisdictions, must be read in light of that background. In addition, the nature of the US 'bursting bubble' presumption means that some of the important aspects of the EIR rebuttal requirements simply do not apply in US cases.

(b) Factors for Consideration

1.16.38 Rebuttal of the COMI presumption under the EIR requires proof of objective factors that are ascertainable by ordinary creditors and that show the debtor's central administration is somewhere other than the location of its registered office.[87] The 2013 revision of the Guide to Enactment adopts this view, declar-

---

84 See Commentary discussion at paragraph 1.17.21.

85 *Judicial Perspective* (n 1), para 118.

86 11 USC § 304, Pub L 95-598, Nov 6, 1978, 92 Stat 2560, *repealed,* Pub L 109-8, Title VIII, § 802(d)(3), Apr 20, 2005, 119 Stat 146.

87 Case 341/04, *Eurofood IFSC Ltd,* 2006 ECR 1-3813, para 37; *Judicial Perspective* (n 1), paras 102 & 104. The contrary earlier English "head office functions" test was rejected. Ibid at paras 114 & 117.

ing that the principal COMI factors 'are the location: (a) where the central administration of the debtor takes place, and (b) which is readily ascertainable by creditors'.[88] These factors are elevated above all others. Only if 'these principal factors do not yield a ready answer regarding the debtor's centre of main interests, a number of additional factors concerning the debtor's business may be considered'.[89] The English[90] and Australian cases appear to follow the EIR approach.[91] The Canadian court in *Massachusetts Elephant & Castle Group, Inc*[92] similarly focused on a set of principal factors but used three principal factors instead of two, adding the location of the debtor's principal assets or operations as a principal factor.[93] Other factors were of secondary importance.[94]

The requirement that the rebuttal factors be ascertainable to creditors, which plays such an important role under both the EIR and the 2013 Guide to Enactment, is relevant in the US cases but plays a smaller and different role. The US presumption is easily destroyed by any evidence to the contrary, whether obvious to creditors or not, so ascertainability does not play an important role in rebutting the presumption. Ascertainability is important in the US cases,[95] but as part of the multi-factor analysis of determining the actual COMI after the presumption is rebutted, and not as a preliminary hurdle that must be surmounted in order to reach the analysis stage. **1.16.39**

While the EIR, the 2013 Guide to Enactment and some MLCBI cases focus on the place of central administration of the debtor, the US cases use a variety of tests that generally focus on the principal place of business[96] or the 'nerve **1.16.40**

---

88 *Guide to Enactment* (n 1), para 145.

89 *Guide to Enactment* (n 1), para 146.

90 For a discussion of the differing English and US approaches, see Bryan Rochelle, 'Cross-Border Insolvency in the U.S. and U.K.: Conflicting Approaches to Defining the Locus of a Debtor's "Center of Main Interests"', 50 Int'l Law. 391 (2017).

91 *Stanford Int'l Bank Ltd* [2010] EWCA Civ 137 para 39, CLOUT 1003 (ENG); *Ackers v Saad Investments Co Ltd (in official liq)* 118 ALD 498, [2010] FCA 1221 para 49 CLOUT 1219 (AU).

92 2011 ONSC 4201 (Ont SCJ [Commercial List]) CLOUT 1206 (CAN); *accord In Re Lightsquared LP* 2012 ONSC 2994 (Ont SCJ [Commercial List]) CLOUT 1204 (CAN); *see also* Ho, Look Chan (ed), A Commentary on the UNCITRAL Model Law, 4th ed, Globe Law & Business (London), 2017, 102–3.

93 Note that the location of assets does not appear to be sufficient to rebut the presumption under the EIR. *Interedil Srl* [2011] CJEU C-396/09, [2012] Bus LR 1582 para 59 (EU).

94 Discussion at *Judicial Perspective* (n 1), paras 123 & 124.

95 This may explain the confusion of some courts about whether the US applies an ascertainability requirement. See discussion at *Judicial Perspective* (n 1), para 116. As the *Betcorp* court stated, 'That inquiry examines the debtors' administration, management and operations along with whether reasonable and ordinary third parties can discern or perceive where the debtor is conducting these various functions.' 400 BR at 290.

96 *In Re Bear Sterns High-Grade Structured Credit Strategies Master Fund, Ltd,* 374 BR 122, 129 (Bankr SDNY 2007), *aff'd* 389 BR 325 (2008) CLOUT 760 (US).

center'[97] of the debtor's operations. The 'nerve centre' test is similar to the 'head office functions' test that was rejected under the EIR.

1.16.41 Both the US approach and the 2013 Guide to Enactment permit the consideration of many other factors in determining the location of a debtor's COMI. While the 2013 Guide to Enactment relegates other factors to secondary status, the US approach may give them equal or greater weight than the principal factors. The 2013 Guide to Enactment provides a non-exhaustive list of relevant factors that might be considered. The breadth of the list indicates how broad the scope of the COMI inquiry might be. As the Guide to Enactment states:

> The additional factors may include the following: the location of the debtor's books and records; the location where financing was organized or authorized, or from where the cash management system was run; the location in which the debtor's principal assets or operations are found; the location of the debtor's primary bank; the location of employees; the location in which commercial policy was determined; the site of the controlling law or the law governing the main contracts of the company; the location from which purchasing and sales policy, staff, accounts payable and computer systems were managed; the location from which contracts (for supply) were organized; the location from which reorganization of the debtor was being conducted; the jurisdiction whose law would apply to most disputes; the location in which the debtor was subject to supervision or regulation; and the location whose law governed the preparation and audit of accounts and in which they were prepared and audited.[98]

(c) Enterprise Group COMI

1.16.42 The MLCBI's focus is on a single debtor entity that is the subject of a foreign insolvency proceeding. Where the debtor is part of an enterprise group, composed of several related legal entities, the COMI determination should be made separately for each debtor entity.[99] There is no 'group COMI'.[100] This creates a potential problem where the related entities operate as an integrated business enterprise because the COMI of different group members likely will be in different jurisdictions.[101] A successful global restructuring of the business enterprise may require a coordinated restructuring of all critical group members in a single jurisdiction. However, the resulting group restructuring might not easily be recognized and given relief in other jurisdictions because some

97 *In Re Fairfield Sentry Ltd* 714 F3d 127, 138 n 10 (2d Cir 2013) CLOUT 1339 (US).

98 *Guide to Enactment* (n 1), para 147.

99 *In Re Servicos de Petroleo Constellation SA* 600 BR 237, 278-79 (Bankr SDNY 2019) (US); *In Re Lightsquared LP* 2012 ONSC 2994 para 29 (Ont SCJ [Commercial List]) CLOUT 1204 (CAN).

100 *Judicial Perspective* (n 1), para 68.

101 *See* Ilya Kokorin, Stephan Madaus & Irit Mevorach 'Global Competition in Cross-Border Restructuring and Recognition of Centralized Group Solutions' 56 Texas Journal of International Law 136 (2021).

members of the enterprise group might not have their COMI in the foreign restructuring jurisdiction. Worse, some critical group members may not even have an establishment in the foreign restructuring jurisdiction and therefore the foreign proceedings involving those members could not be recognized at all under the MLCBI. The 2019 UNCITRAL Model Law on Enterprise Group Insolvency[102] attempts to address this gap in the MLCBI's coverage,[103] but as of early 2023 it had not been adopted by any jurisdiction.

The 'nerve centre' approach to COMI may permit the receiving court to find the COMI of various group members to be in the jurisdiction of the operating company when the activities of the member are directed from that office, even if the member has no assets or establishment in that jurisdiction. Even if the subsidiary is merely a special purpose entity used for financing, the multi-factor test might permit a receiving court to locate its COMI in the jurisdiction of the operating company. For example, in *OAS* the COMI of an Austrian special purpose financing entity was found to be in Brazil, where the enterprise headquarters and operations were located.[104] Under this approach, the ascertainability analysis shifts from the EIR approach of trying to identify a single jurisdiction where creditors *would expect* the debtor's insolvency proceeding to take place to a notice approach of whether the foreign jurisdiction is one of the locations where creditors *might have anticipated* an insolvency proceeding could be filed.[105] 1.16.43

(d) Moving the COMI

The COMI of a debtor might shift over time. This could result from a change in the debtor's place of registration (or habitual residence for an individual). Such a shift would cause the Article 16(3) presumption to apply to the new location. Alternatively, without moving its registered office, the debtor's operations may shift over time so that a different jurisdiction becomes the centre of the debtor's main interests. Although the MLCBI does not impose a minimum time requirement, when a COMI shift occurs in close proximity to the commencement of the foreign insolvency proceeding, the receiving court may consider the COMI factors more carefully and take account of the debtor's circumstances more broadly.[106] The ascertainability factor may be difficult 1.16.44

102 https://uncitral.un.org/sites/uncitral.un.org/files/media-documents/uncitral/en/19-11346_MLCBIoegi.pdf

103 'Global Competition' (n 101) at 147–50.

104 *In Re OAS SA* 533 BR 83, 101-02 (Bankr SDNY 2015) CLOUT 1629 (US).

105 *In Re Modern Land (China) Co Ltd* 641 BR 768, 788 (Bankr SDNY 2022) (US) (analysing creditor expectations based on statements in offering memoranda for bond debt).

106 *Guide to Enactment* (n 1), para 148.

to satisfy unless the debtor has taken steps to alert creditors and other third parties to the shift.

1.16.45 A COMI shift might be the natural consequence of changes in the debtor's business or might be a strategic move designed to change the outcome of the insolvency process by accessing a different insolvency law in a more favorable jurisdiction. A footnote to the 2013 revision to the Guide to Enactment suggests that such a strategic eve-of-commencement COMI shift might be appropriate if designed 'to give the debtor access to an insolvency process, such as reorganization, that more closely met its needs than what was available under the law of its former centre of main interests'.[107] This is contrasted with a COMI shift 'designed to thwart the legitimate expectations of creditors and third parties'.[108] Several cases reflect this view of modifying the COMI determination to permit foreign main proceeding recognition of 'good' COMI shifts designed to maximize value preservation but not of 'bad' COMI shifts that harm creditors.[109] For example, *Modern Land* states that for recent COMI shifts, 'courts may engage in a more holistic analysis to ensure that the debtor has not manipulated COMI in bad faith'.[110] This approach to the COMI analysis may be at odds with the article 15 and 17 principle that no additional requirements be imposed on recognition. The problem of abusive COMI shifts might alternatively be addressed by applying local abuse of process remedies[111] or modifying the relief provided under article 20.[112]

1.16.46 A closely related issue, upon which there is disagreement, is the point in time at which the debtor's COMI should be measured. The US and Singapore cases analyse the debtor's COMI as of the time recognition is sought,[113] but the 2013 revision to the Guide to Enactment takes the view that the COMI should be measured as of the time of commencement of the foreign insolvency

---

107 *Guide to Enactment* (n 1), para 148 n 33.

108 *Guide to Enactment* (n 1), para 148 n 33.

109 *Re Zetta Jet Pte Ltd and Others (Asia Aviation Holdings PTE Ltd, intervenor)* [2019] SGHC 53 paras 57 CLOUT 1816 (SG) (noting that debtor might legitimately shift its COMI, even after commencing the foreign proceeding, to a 'jurisdiction that will offer the best prospects for achieving an effective restructuring solution'); *In Re Ocean Rig UDW Inc* 570 BR 687, 703 (Bankr SDNY 2017) *affirmed* 585 BR 31 CLOUT 1863 (US) (stating 'COMI shift was done for proper purposes to facilitate a value-maximizing restructuring').

110 *In Re Modern Land (China) Co Ltd* 641 BR 768, 782 (Bankr SDNY 2022) (US); *see Stanford Int'l Bank Ltd* [2010] EWCA Civ 137 para 61 CLOUT 1003 (ENG) (considering the time between commencement of the foreign proceeding and the recognition application to evaluate whether the debtor had manipulated its COMI in bad faith).

111 See Commentary discussion at paragraph 1.17.13.

112 Although the article 20 relief is automatic, local law can be used to modify the relief under article 20(2).

113 The Australian courts adopt a similar approach but focus on the date of the recognition decision.

proceeding for which recognition is sought.[114] The US approach creates the possibility that a COMI shift might occur even after the commencement of the foreign proceeding. In fact, the foreign insolvency proceeding might itself become the centre of main interests of a debtor that previously lacked a sufficient connection to the foreign jurisdiction. In some cases the foreign insolvency proceeding may have been pending for a lengthy amount of time and reached a stage where the only remaining interest of the debtor is the activity of the insolvency administrator. However, the US cases have extended this principle to much less comprehensive proceedings, such as the provisional liquidation in the *Suntech* case.[115]

The US approach offers a solution to several otherwise difficult problems presented by the limitations of the MLCBI. For example, in the case of an enterprise group restructuring, the foreign restructuring proceeding may shift the COMI of every affected group member to the restructuring jurisdiction, permitting a receiving court to recognize all of the related-entity cases as foreign main proceedings. **1.16.47**

(e) Letterbox Companies

So-called letterbox companies present special problems under the MLCBI. Although a letterbox company has its registered office in one jurisdiction, it has no assets or operations there. Thus, its actual COMI is located elsewhere and it has no establishment in the letterbox jurisdiction. The law under which the company is organized may require that it file its insolvency proceeding in the letterbox jurisdiction. However, such a proceeding would be neither a foreign main proceeding nor a foreign non-main proceeding and could not be recognized under the MLCBI.[116] The US approach overcomes that obstacle and permits recognition of the letterbox proceeding as a foreign main proceeding.[117] **1.16.48**

114 See Commentary discussion at paragraph 1.17.21.

115 *In Re Suntech Power Holdings Co* 520 BR 399, 417 (Bankr SDNY 2014) (US).

116 Recognition of letterbox company was refused in *In Re Bear Sterns High-Grade Structured Credit Strategies Master Fund, Ltd,* 374 BR 122 (Bankr SDNY 2007), *aff'd* 389 BR 325 (2008) CLOUT 760 (US).

117 The *Fairfield Century* case is an example of this use of the timing rule to recognize a proceeding pending in a letterbox jurisdiction. *In Re Fairfield Sentry Ltd* 714 F3d 127 (2d Cir 2013) CLOUT 1339 (US).

Article 17

DECISION TO RECOGNIZE A FOREIGN PROCEEDING

G. Ray Warner

1. Subject to Article 6, a foreign proceeding shall be recognized if:
   (a) The foreign proceeding is a proceeding within the meaning of subparagraph (a) of Article 2;
   (b) The foreign representative applying for recognition is a person or body within the meaning of subparagraph (d) of Article 2;
   (c) The application meets the requirements of paragraph 2 of Article 15; and
   (d) The application has been submitted to the court referred to in Article 4.
2. The foreign proceeding shall be recognized:
   (a) As a foreign main proceeding if it is taking place in the State where the debtor has the centre of its main interests; or
   (b) As a foreign non-main proceeding if the debtor has an establishment within the meaning of subparagraph (f) of Article 2 in the foreign State.
3. An application for recognition of a foreign proceeding shall be decided upon at the earliest possible time.
4. The provisions of Articles 15, 16, 17 and 18 do not prevent modification or termination of recognition if it is shown that the grounds for granting it were fully or partially lacking or have ceased to exist.

A. INTRODUCTION TO ARTICLE 17

Prompt recognition and relief is often essential to effectively protect a debtor's assets from dissipation or concealment.[1] A key objective of the ML is to establish a simplified process for recognition of qualifying foreign proceedings so that prompt relief can be provided.[2] Articles 17 works in conjunction with Articles 15 and 16 to create a simple and expeditious recognition process that dispenses with cumbersome technical requirements that might unnecessarily delay the recognition decision.[3] While Article 15 sets forth minimal technical requirements for the application for recognition, Article 17 is the source of the receiving court's power to recognize a foreign proceeding.[4] **1.17.01**

Article 17 sets forth the elements that must be established before the receiving court may grant recognition. In keeping with the goal of prompt recognition, the Article 17 elements are minimal and designed to be the only consideration at the recognition stage. In addition to the basic recognition determination, Article 17 requires the receiving court to determine whether the foreign proceeding is a foreign main proceeding or a foreign non-main proceeding as part of the recognition process. This determination is important because the ML provides automatic, immediate relief if the proceeding is recognized as a foreign main proceeding, but only discretionary relief if it is recognized as a foreign non-main proceeding. Article 17 further requires that the application for recognition 'shall be decided upon at the earliest possible time'.[5] Article 16 **1.17.02**

1 *UNCITRAL Model Law on Cross-Border Insolvency with Guide to Enactment and Interpretation*, United Nations Publications (New York), 2014, para 163; *UNCITRAL Model Law on Cross-Border Insolvency: The Judicial Perspective*, United Nations Publications (New York), 2014, para 38.

2 *Guide to Enactment* (n 1) para 29.

3 *Guide to Enactment* (n 1) para 127.

4 *Judicial Perspective* (n 1) para 42.

5 ML art 17(3).

plays a supporting role by supplying several important presumptions that may expedite the process.

1.17.03 Article 17 sets forth only the substantive requirements for recognition.[6] The local law of the receiving state governs procedural matters, such as whether notice of the application must be provided to creditors or other interested parties.[7] The standards for notice vary from jurisdiction to jurisdiction, with some states requiring that all affected parties have an opportunity to be heard before recognition is granted and others viewing the need for expeditious treatment as inconsistent with the issuance of notice prior to the court decision on recognition.[8]

B. THE RECOGNITION DECISION

1. Recognition Requirements

1.17.04 Article 17(1) lists only four elements that must be determined in order to recognize a foreign proceeding and both the 'shall be recognized' language of Article 17(1) and the related interpretive comments indicate that no additional requirements should be imposed at the recognition stage. Two of the four requirements are procedural in nature and should be simple to satisfy in all cases. These are that the application has been submitted to the correct court in the receiving jurisdiction under Article 4 and that the application satisfies the minimal documentary requirements of Article 15. The receiving court should be able to make those determinations simply by referring to the local version of the ML and reviewing the application.

1.17.05 The remaining two elements are those necessary to establish the grounds for recognition, specifically that the foreign insolvency process is a 'foreign proceeding' and that the applicant is the 'foreign representative', as those terms are defined in the ML. These issues may require a more complicated evaluation, the presentation of evidence or even a lengthy trial. However, the application generally will be accompanied by a foreign court order or certificate establishing both points.[9] If there is no serious question, the Article 16(1) presumptions can be used to satisfy those requirements where the foreign order or certificate

6 *Guide to Enactment* (n 1) para 167. 'Questions of notice to interested persons, while closely related to the protection of their interests, are in general not regulated in the Model Law.' Guide to Enactment para 28.

7 *Guide to Enactment* (n 1) para 136.

8 *Guide to Enactment* (n 1) para 135.

9 ML art 15(2).

indicates that the foreign action is a foreign proceeding and the applicant is the foreign representation.[10] Thus, in the absence of a challenge, the receiving court should be able to grant recognition on the basis of the application alone.

In those cases where the Article 16 presumptions are not applied by the receiving court, or are rebutted, the receiving court must be satisfied that all of the definitional requirements have been met.[11] The ML's foreign representative definition has only a few requirements so the determination of whether the applicant qualifies should be a simple process in most cases.[12] **1.17.06**

The ML's foreign proceeding definition is more complex and requires determination of several sub-issues.[13] The *In re ABC Learning Centres Ltd* court broke the foreign proceeding definitional requirements into seven sub-elements: (a) a proceeding; (b) either judicial or administrative in character; (c) collective in nature; (d) in a foreign State; (e) authorized or conducted under a law related to insolvency; (f) in which the debtor's assets and affairs are subject to the control or supervision of a foreign court; and (g) which is for the purpose of reorganization or liquidation.[14] Determination of these issues may require consideration of the nature of the foreign proceeding at issue, the actions taken in that proceeding and the foreign law governing the proceeding. Where recognition is contested, the recognition decision may require a full trial. For example, in the *PT Bakrie Telecom* case recognition was granted only after a trial on the merits and not until more than three years after the application had been filed.[15] **1.17.07**

2. Imposing Additional Requirements

If the four elements listed in Article 17(1) are met, the application should be granted 'as a matter of course',[16] subject to the overarching Article 6 public policy exception that is incorporated by a specific reference in the chapeau to Article 17(1). That limitation is a narrow one that should be applied rarely to deny recognition of an otherwise eligible foreign proceeding.[17] In most cases **1.17.08**

---

10 ML art 16(1).

11 *Judicial Perspective* (n 1) para 59.

12 The elements of the foreign representative definition are discussed at Commentary paragraph 1.2.31, *et. seq.*

13 The elements of the foreign proceeding definition are discussed at Commentary paragraph 1.2.02, *et. seq.*

14 728 F3d 301, 308 (3d Cir 2013) CLOUT 1338 (US).

15 *In re PT Bakrie Telecom Tbk*, 628 BR 859 (Bankr SDNY 2021) (US) (recognizing application filed in January of 2018).

16 *Guide to Enactment* (n 1) para 150; *Judicial Perspective* (n 1) para 41.

17 *Guide to Enactment* (n 1) para 30. The public policy limitation is discussed at Commentary paragraph 1.6.01 *et. seq.*

involving public policy concerns, those concerns might more appropriately be addressed by limiting or denying the requested relief.[18]

1.17.09 The ML envisages that no limitations beyond public policy and the preconditions of the ML definitions be imposed on the recognition decision.[19] For example, the receiving court should not consider whether the foreign proceeding was correctly instituted under the foreign law.[20] While an enacting state is free to vary the ML, absent a local variation in the text, other factors should not be considered. The ML does not require reciprocity, so a foreign proceeding should be recognized even if the foreign jurisdiction would not recognize an insolvency proceeding originating in the receiving jurisdiction.[21]

1.17.10 Further, the limitations imposed by the receiving jurisdiction's law on domestic insolvency proceedings should not be imported into the recognition process. Nonetheless, additional recognition requirements might be imposed because of the ML's failure to define the term 'debtor', which is used in both the foreign proceeding and foreign representative definitions. While a local insolvency proceeding might be commenced by or against a debtor, the recognition process is not an action to which the debtor is a party but rather a request for assistance involving the foreign representative. The references to the debtor in the definitions raises the possibility that local debtor eligibility limitations for insolvency proceedings might be imported into the recognition process.

1.17.11 For example, *Rubin v Eurofinance*[22] involved an application for recognition in England of a US proceeding involving a 'business trust', a type of trust that was recognized in the US as a legal entity but not under English law. It was argued that recognition should be denied because the trust could not be a debtor under English insolvency law. The English court relied on the international origins of the ML to reject a 'parochial interpretation' of the term debtor.

1.17.12 The contrary view was adopted by a leading US case. The domestic US bankruptcy law requires that a debtor have property in the US in order to

---

18 While the court has no discretion to refuse recognition, the relief provided is largely discretionary. *In re Metcalfe & Mansfield Alternative Invs* 421 BR 685, 697 (Bankr SDNY 2010) (US).

19 *Guide to Enactment* (n 1) paras 29, 151, & 161; Judicial Perspective para 41; Peter M Gilhuly, Kimberly A Posin & Adam Malatesta, 'Bankruptcy Without Borders: A Comprehensive Guide to the First Decade of Chapter 15' 24 Am Bankr Inst L Rev 47, 88 (2016).

20 *Judicial Perspective* (n 1) para 41; *In re Millard* 501 B.R. 644, 650 & 653 (Bankr SDNY 2013) (US) (refusing to consider whether foreign proceeding was properly commenced under foreign law).

21 *Judicial Perspective* (n 1) para 47. A few States have added a reciprocity requirement. The Judicial Perspective lists Mexico, Romania, South Africa, and Uganda as examples. Ibid at para 47 n 69.

22 *Rubin v Eurofinance SA* [2009] EWHC 2129 paras 39–40 (Ch), *on appeal* [2010] EWCA Civ 895, *on second appeal* [2012] UKSC 46 (Eng) CLOUT 1270.

institute a US bankruptcy proceeding.[23] The US courts are split on the question whether the entity subject to the foreign proceeding must have property in the US in order for that proceeding to be recognized.[24] Fortunately, even if a property requirement applies, it is easy to satisfy and presents little barrier to recognition. For example, even the unearned portion of fees paid to the US bankruptcy lawyer or the debtor's rights under a debt instrument governed by US law are sufficient.[25]

A more difficult question is whether local laws and rules designed to address an abuse of the judicial process provide grounds to deny an application for recognition. Although the ML does not explicitly prevent application of domestic law or procedural rules aimed at abuse of process, the policy against adding extraneous factors to the recognition process suggests that such rules should only be applied when the public policy exception is triggered.[26] For example, in *In re Gold and Honey*,[27] the court suggested that a foreign proceeding instituted in violation of the US automatic stay might be void and not recognizable. However, the court ultimately rested its decision on the Article 6 public policy exception. **1.17.13**

Similarly, in *Creative Finance* the recognition application was filed in bad faith and for the purpose of thwarting the only non-insider creditor's attempts to collect a judgment against the debtor. Although a domestic insolvency proceeding could be dismissed for such bad faith, the mandate of Article 17 required recognition since the misbehaviour of a party is not the kind of factor that triggers the public policy exception.[28] The English court in *OGX Petroleo E Gas SA*[29] suggested that, notwithstanding the limited nature of the public policy exception, it had residual discretion to refuse recognition where the applicant was abusing process for an illegitimate purpose. **1.17.14**

---

23 The property requirement is one of several alternative grounds for instituting a bankruptcy case in the US. 11 USC 109(a).

24 *Compare In re Barnet* 737 F3d 238 (2d Cir 2013) CLOUT 1336 (US) (imposing property requirement for recognition) *with Al Zawawi v Diss (In re Zawawi)* 97 F4th 1244 (11th Cir 2024) (US) (debtor eligibility requirements do not apply to recognition).

25 *In re Olinda Star Ltd* 614 BR 28, 40 (Bankr SDNY 2020) (US).

26 *Guide to Enactment* (n 1) para 161.

27 410 BR 357, 368 & 371–2 (Bankr EDNY 2009) (US) CLOUT 1008.

28 *In re Creative Finance Ltd* 543 BR 498, 515–16 (Bankr SDNY 2016) CLOUT 1624 (US); *In re Millard* 501 BR 644, 653 (Bankr SDNY 2013) (US) (rejecting bad faith as a ground for denial of recognition).

29 [2016] EWHC 25 (Ch) para 60 CLOUT 1622 (ENG).

C. THE MAIN VS NON-MAIN PROCEEDING DETERMINATION

1. Recognition of Main and Non-Main Proceedings

1.17.15 In addition to deciding whether the requirements for recognition have been met, Article 17(2) requires the receiving court to determine whether the foreign proceeding is a foreign main proceeding or a foreign non-main proceeding as part of the recognition process.[30] Effectively, Article 17(2) adds a fifth requirement for recognition – that the foreign proceeding be pending in either the location of the debtor's COMI or a location where the debtor has an '*establishment*'. Only those two types of foreign proceedings can be recognized under the ML.[31] 'Proceedings commenced on a different basis, such as presence of assets without a centre of main interests or establishment, would not qualify for recognition under the Model Law scheme'.[32] The establishment requirement has not been imposed by all ML jurisdictions. Canada, for example, simply defines foreign non-main proceeding to include any foreign proceeding that is not at the debtor's COMI, permitting wider recognition of insolvency proceedings.[33]

1.17.16 The distinction between a foreign main proceeding and a foreign non-main proceeding is important and must be decided at the time of recognition because automatic, immediate relief is triggered by the recognition of a foreign main proceeding.[34] This includes the important moratorium on creditor action and suspension of the debtor's ability to dispose of assets provided by Article 20. In contrast, the Article 21 relief available for a foreign non-main proceeding is not automatic relief, but discretionary with receiving court. Other consequences flow from recognition of a foreign main proceeding, such as the Article 31 presumption of insolvency if a local insolvency proceeding is instituted, but these are not as critical as the prompt Article 20 relief that can prevent the dissipation or concealment of assets.

---

30 *Guide to Enactment* (n 1) para 31.

31 *Judicial Perspective* (n 1) paras 45 & 55; *see Williams v Simpson* (no 5) [2010] NZHC 1786 [2011] NZLR 308 para 26 CLOUT 1220 (NZ); *see also* Samuel L Bufford, 'Tertiary and Other Excluded Foreign Proceedings under Bankruptcy Code Chapter 15,' 83 Am Bankr LJ 165 (2009).

32 *Guide to Enactment* (n 1) para 32. Although other types of insolvency proceedings cannot be recognized under the ML, the receiving jurisdiction may have other laws that do allow recognition of such proceedings. An example is section 426 of the United Kingdom Insolvency Act of 1986. Judicial Perspective para 45 n 68.

33 Ilya Kokorin, Stephan Madaus & Irit Mevorach, 'Global Competition in Cross-Border Restructuring and Recognition of Centralized Group Solutions' 56 Texas Journal of International Law 136 (2021); *see also* Janis Sarra 'Northern Lights, Canada's Version of the UNCITRAL Model Law on Cross-Border Insolvency' 16 Int'l Insolvency R 19, 42 nn 101–3 (2007).

34 *Judicial Perspective* (n 1) para 65.

2. Foreign Main Proceedings

The Article 16(3) presumption plays an important role in determining whether the proceeding is a foreign main proceeding. A foreign main proceeding is one pending in the location of the debtor's COMI. That determination is aided by the mandatory presumption that the COMI is located at the jurisdiction of the debtor's registered office.[35] The location of the registered office might be established by documents such as the certificate of registration issued by the foreign jurisdiction's registrar of corporations.[36] If the foreign proceeding is pending in that jurisdiction, the determination that it is a foreign main proceeding might be made on solely the basis of the documents submitted in support of the application, assuming that the receiving jurisdiction's evidence rules permit the court to accept as true the statements in the certificate.[37] **1.17.17**

While the Article 16(3) presumption is mandatory, it is rebuttable. The factors considered in determining the debtor's COMI and the effect of the presumption are discussed in detail in the commentary to Article 16.[38] **1.17.18**

3. Foreign Non-Main Proceedings

A foreign non-main proceeding is one pending in a jurisdiction that is not the debtor's COMI, but where the debtor has an 'establishment'.[39] The ML defines establishment as 'any place of operations where the debtor carries out a non-transitory economic activity with human means and goods'.[40] This requires less connection than COMI, but one significant enough to justify recognition of an insolvency proceeding originating there. The concept was inspired by the similar definition in the EIR, which is used there to identify 'secondary proceedings'.[41] Unlike the COMI determination, the establishment determination is factual and is not aided by a presumption.[42] **1.17.19**

The factors considered in determining whether the debtor has an establishment are discussed in detail in the commentary to Article 2.[43] **1.17.20**

---

35 Or, the habitual residence of an individual. ML art 16(3).

36 The article 16(2) presumption of authenticity can be used to avoid the need to 'legalize' the foreign certificate.

37 See Commentary discussion at paragraph 1.16.28.

38 See Commentary discussion at paragraph 1.16.38.

39 ML art 2(c).

40 ML art 2(f).

41 See Commentary discussion at paragraph 1.2.26; see also Judicial Perspective paras 136–7.

42 See Commentary discussion at paragraph 1.2.26; see also Judicial Perspective paras 67 & 138.

43 See Commentary discussion at paragraph 1.2.25 *et. seq.* For an individual, the concept of establishment might relate to the location of a second residence or a place of employment. Judicial Perspective para 141.

4. Timing of the Determination

1.17.21 The ML does not clearly state the time at which the receiving court should measure the location of the debtor's COMI or the existence of an establishment.[44] This has created a conflict over whether the relevant time is the date when the foreign proceeding was commenced in the foreign jurisdiction or the date when the application for recognition is made or ruled upon in the receiving jurisdiction.

1.17.22 The relevant language of Article 17 is phrased in the present tense: '*is* taking place in the State where the debtor *has*' its COMI or '*has* an establishment'.[45] This led the US courts to measure both the debtor's COMI and the presence of an establishment as of the date when the application for recognition is filed.[46] The trend seems to be towards the US approach. The Singapore courts have followed the US application date approach because it 'provides greater certainty and better accords with commercial realities and the language of the provisions of the Model Law'.[47] In addition, the Australian courts appear to adopt a similar approach, but use the recognition hearing date rather than the application date.[48]

1.17.23 That difference may not matter because the US courts have considered events occurring between the application date and the decision date. For example, in *British American*[49] the foreign process was merely investigative, and thus not capable of recognition, at the time of the application. Nonetheless, the court granted recognition because the process had evolved into a restructuring proceeding by the time of the hearing. Although the US courts focus primarily on the application date, they are not restricted to that date, but can consider events preceding the application if the debtor has manipulated its COMI in bad faith.[50]

44 *Guide to Enactment* (n 1) para 157; Judicial Perspective paras 129 & 143.

45 Article 17(2)(a & b) (emphasis added).

46 *In re Fairfield Sentry Ltd* 714 F3d 127, 137 (2d Cir 2013) CLOUT 1339 (US). The contrary *Millennium Global* decision discussed at paragraph 131 of the Judicial Perspective is no longer good law.

47 *Re Zetta Jet Pte Ltd and Others (Asia Aviation Holdings PTE Ltd, intervenor)* [2019] SGHC 53 paras 52-61 CLOUT 1816 (SG).

48 *Moore, as Debtor-in-Possession of Australian Equity Investors v Australian Equity Investors* [2012] FCA 1002 para 19 CLOUT 1477 (AU). There seems to be some confusion in the Australian cases about what date should be used. *King in the matter of Zetta Jet Pte Ltd* [2018] FCA 1932 paras 11–12 CLOUT 1817 (AU) (discussing conflicting authority).

49 *In re British American Ins Co Ltd*, 425 BR 884, 905–6 (Bankr SD Fla 2010) CLOUT 1005 (US).

50 *Fairfield Sentry* (n 46) 714 F3d at 137.

In contrast, the 2013 revision to the Guide to Enactment adopts the view that the date of commencement of the foreign proceeding is the relevant date for determining both COMI and the existence of an establishment.[51] The Guide explains that the present tense usage in Article 17(2) does not address the question of the relevant date for the COMI and establishment determinations, 'but rather requires the foreign proceeding to be current or pending at the time of the recognition decision'.[52] The Guide supports its view primarily on the basis that it produces a clear test that can 'be applied with certainty to all insolvency proceedings'.[53] Using the date of commencement is also consistent with the EIR approach[54] and addresses the issues that might otherwise arise where the debtor has ceased all business activities or an individual debtor has changed their residence after the commencement of the foreign proceeding or where a reorganizing entity, rather than the original debtor entity, is continuing the business.[55] **1.17.24**

The English courts follow the EIR approach of using the commencement date.[56] The commencement date approach was adopted in the Japanese *think3* case.[57] **1.17.25**

As discussed in the commentary to Article 16, the analysis used to determine COMI is not consistent from jurisdiction to jurisdiction.[58] The commencement date approach would increase consistency because receiving courts in all jurisdictions would be evaluating COMI at the same point in the life cycle of the foreign proceeding, whereas the application date approach might yield different COMI determinations for the same foreign proceeding depending on when recognition was requested in different jurisdictions. **1.17.26**

Use of the application date by the US courts has several interesting implications that are discussed in greater detail in the commentary to Article 16.[59] Primarily **1.17.27**

---

51 *Guide to Enactment* (n 1) paras 159 & 160.

52 *Guide to Enactment* (n 1) para 158.

53 Ibid.

54 *Judicial Perspective* (n 1) para 133.

55 *Judicial Perspective* (n 1) para 134.

56 *Re Videology Ltd* [2018] EWHC 2186 (Ch) para 49 CLOUT 1823 (ENG); *Stanford Int'l Bank Ltd* [2010] EWCA Civ 137 para 30, CLOUT 1003 (ENG). The English view may be shifting towards the application date approach. An English court adopted that view in an unpublished recognition order involving Toisa Ltd. Herman Jeremiah & Kia Jeng Koh, Singapore: Timing Is Everything: Different Approaches To The Relevant Date For Determining COMI In Cross-Border Recognition Proceedings (2019) <https://www.mondaq.com/insolvencybankruptcy/837102/timing-is-everything-different-approaches-to-the-relevant-date-for-determining-comi-in-cross-border-recognition-proceedings>

57 Discussed in paragraph 132 of the Judicial Perspective.

58 See Commentary discussion at paragraph 1.16.36.

59 See Commentary discussion at paragraph 1.16.47.

it means that the debtor's COMI could shift not only shortly before the commencement of the foreign proceeding, but also after the proceeding is opened. Thus, activities taken as part of the liquidation or restructuring process and any changes in the debtor's business resulting from that process become part of the COMI analysis. The foreign proceeding might itself become the main interest of the debtor, thereby shifting the COMI to a jurisdiction that did not have a sufficient connection to the debtor to be recognized at all under the ML. The US courts have used this analysis to recognize proceedings pending in the jurisdiction of organization of letterbox companies and to recognize enterprise group restructurings where not all group members have an otherwise sufficient connection to permit recognition.

D. EXPEDITING THE DECISION

1.17.28 Article 17(3) requires the receiving court to decide on the application for recognition 'at the earliest possible time'.[60] This is in keeping with the ML goal of providing prompt relief. Since recognition is a prerequisite to most relief, the assets of the debtor may be at risk of dissipation or concealment if the foreign representative is unable to obtain early recognition.[61] As discussed above, the receiving court might be able to rule on an uncontested recognition request on the basis of a review of only the application itself. In such a case, recognition might be granted in a matter of days. However, the standard is an elastic one and recognition might take much longer if circumstances warrant.[62] In such a case, interim relief might be provided under Article 19 to protect the interests of the debtor and its creditors.[63]

E. MODIFICATION AND TERMINATION OF RECOGNITION

1.17.29 Article 17(4) permits modification or termination of the recognition decision if the grounds for granting recognition either 'were fully or partially lacking or have ceased to exist'.[64] The provision was added to clarify that the courts of the receiving jurisdiction may review the recognition decision.[65] The US version

---

60 ML art 17(3).

61 *Guide to Enactment* (n 1) para 163; Judicial Perspective para 38.

62 *Guide to Enactment* (n 1) para 163.

63 ML art 19; see Commentary discussion of article 19.

64 Article 17(4).

65 *Guide to Enactment* (n 1) para 164.

of the ML adds language providing a mechanism for closing the recognition proceeding when the underlying foreign proceeding ends.[66]

While this provision may seem awkward in common law jurisdictions, it is necessary in some civil law jurisdictions where recognition of a foreign main proceeding creates a status with the automatic effects set forth in Article 20. Modification of the relief provided under Article 20 might require modification of that status, and not simply modification of the relief.[67] In many jurisdictions, modification or termination of the Article 20(1) automatic stay and suspension might more easily be achieved under the domestic law rules listed in the receiving jurisdiction's version of Article 20(2). **1.17.30**

While Article 17(4) gives the receiving court authority to review its recognition order, it does not affect the domestic appeal procedures applicable to the decision under the receiving State's law.[68] The provision may, however, override the otherwise applicable local rules governing the receiving court's power to review of its own orders.[69] The power to modify the recognition decision is not limited to the Article 17(1) recognition factors but extends to the determination of whether the foreign proceeding is a main or non-main proceeding,[70] as it must in order to achieve the goal of modifying the Article 20 relief in certain civil law jurisdictions. **1.17.31**

Article 17(4) breaks the review into two prongs: one looking backward to determine whether the basis for recognition previously presented to the receiving court was flawed and the other looking forward to whether something has changed since recognition.[71] Examples of changes occurring after recognition that might justify modification of termination of the recognition order include: (i) termination of the foreign proceeding;[72] (ii) reversal on appeal of the order commencing the foreign proceeding;[73] (iii) the nature of the foreign proceed- **1.17.32**

---

66 Peter M Gilhuly, Kimberly A Posin & Adam Malatesta, 'Bankruptcy Without Borders: A Comprehensive Guide to the First Decade of Chapter 15' 24 Am Bankr Inst L Rev 47, 96 (2016). The US version also requires the court to consider prejudice to parties who relied on the recognition order. 11 USC 1517(d).

67 HR Rep No 109-31 at 113 (2005) (US).

68 *Judicial Perspective* (n 1) para 58.

69 *In re Oi Brasil Holdings Coöperatief UA* 578 BR 169, 203 (Bankr SDNY 2017) (US) (applying the discretionary standard of ML article 17(3) instead of the much stricter standard generally applicable to revocation of orders).

70 *Judicial Perspective* (n 1) para 56.

71 *Oi Brasil* 578 BR at 197.

72 *Re Sanko Steamship Co* [2015] EWHC 1031 (ch) (ENG).

73 *Re Garuda Indonesia (Persero) Tbk* [2025] SGHC(I) 1 para 78-80 (SG).

ing has changed; (iv) the status of the foreign representative has changed;[74] or (v) the court becomes aware of another foreign proceeding involving the same debtor.[75] Article 18 works in tandem with Article 17(4) by requiring the foreign representative promptly to inform the court of any change in the foreign representative's status or the status of the foreign proceeding and of any other foreign proceeding that becomes known to the foreign representative.[76] The forward-looking aspect of Article 17(4) is in tension with the Guide to Enactment's use of the commencement date as the relevant time for measuring COMI and the existence of an establishment,[77] but may be necessary in order to permit modification of the automatic relief provided by Article 20.

1.17.33 The Guide to Enactment also suggests that the foreign representative's post-recognition misbehaviour might also justify modification of revocation of the recognition order.[78] This is at odds with the Article 17 policy against considering other factors in the recognition process but also may be necessary in certain civil law jurisdictions.

74 *Guide to Enactment* (n 1) para 165; *Judicial Perspective* (n 1) para 57. Where the recognized foreign proceeding was terminated, but a new, technically different, foreign proceeding followed immediately, the recognition could be modified under article 17(4) instead of terminating the recognition and requiring a new application for the new proceeding. *In re Comair Ltd* 2023 WL 1971618 at *11–12 (Bankr SDNY Feb 12, 2023).

75 In *Oi Brasil*, the court had previously recognized as a foreign main proceeding a Brazilian bankruptcy involving the Dutch special purpose financing affiliate of a Brazilian operating company. It was asked to modify its COMI determination in order to recognize a later-filed Dutch bankruptcy proceeding as a foreign main proceeding. *Oi Brasil* 578 BR at 175.

76 Article 18.

77 *See* Look Chan Ho (ed), A Commentary on the UNCITRAL Model Law, 4th ed, Globe Law & Business (London), 2017, 533.

78 *Guide to Enactment* (n 1) para 165; *Judicial Perspective* (n 1) para 57.

Article 18

SUBSEQUENT INFORMATION

G. Ray Warner

From the time of filing the application for recognition of the foreign proceeding, the foreign representative shall inform the court promptly of:

(a) Any substantial change in the status of the recognized foreign proceeding or the status of the foreign representative's appointment; and
(b) Any other foreign proceeding regarding the same debtor that becomes known to the foreign representative.

A. INTRODUCTION TO ARTICLE 18

Article 18 operates after recognition is granted and imposes on the foreign representative an ongoing duty to inform the receiving court of any substantial changes in the status of the foreign proceeding or of the foreign representative's appointment and of any other foreign proceedings regarding the same debtor that become known to the foreign representative.[1] The provision serves the twin purposes of providing information that might cause the receiving court to terminate the recognition or modify its prior orders and alerting the court to other pending foreign proceedings so that it can maximize the cooperation and coordination policies of the ML.[2] **1.18.1**

1 ML art 18.
2 *UNCITRAL Model Law on Cross-Border Insolvency: The Judicial Perspective*, United Nations Publications (New York), 2014, para 44.

B. CHANGES IN STATUS

1.18.2 Subparagraph (a) addresses changes in status that might necessitate modification of prior orders. This requirement ties into the receiving court's power under Article 17(4) to modify or terminate the recognition when the grounds for recognition 'have ceased to exist'.[3] The Article 18 duty of disclosure is designed to assist the court's ability to modify relief by creating a mechanism that will provide the needed information.[4] The ML definition of foreign proceeding includes interim proceedings and its definition of foreign representative includes those appointed on an interim basis.[5] Article 18 plays a particularly important role when interim proceedings have been recognized since changes in the status of the proceeding or of the foreign representative are expected and may affect the recognition.[6]

1.18.3 The disclosure duty is limited to 'substantial' changes and does not apply to the many changes that typically occur during an insolvency proceeding but that have no impact on the recognition or relief granted in the receiving jurisdiction.[7] For example, approval of a reorganization plan in the foreign proceeding might not require any change in the recognition where the foreign court retains supervisor authority following approval.[8] However, despite the connection between Article 18 and Article 17(4), the disclosure duty is not limited to events that might cause changes in the recognition order, that is, those affecting the automatic relief accorded a foreign main proceeding.[9] Substantial changes might also include events that affect discretionary relief provided under Article 21.

1.18.4 Article 18 may not perform its function very well when the foreign proceeding has been terminated in the originating jurisdiction. Such an event ends the foreign proceeding and should end most ongoing relief provided under

---

3 ML art 17(4).

4 *UNCITRAL Model Law on Cross-Border Insolvency with Guide to Enactment and Interpretation*, United Nations Publications (New York), 2014, para 165.

5 ML art 2(a & d).

6 *Guide to Enactment* (n 4) para 168.

7 *Guide to Enactment* (n 4) para 168.

8 *Oversight & Control Commission of Azanzit SA* 385 BR 525, 533–4 (Bankr SDNY 2008) CLOUT 925 (US). In *Yakushiji* the court noted that the end date of a foreign liquidation proceeding might not have any effect on the recognition or relief previously granted. However, the end date of a reorganization may necessitate termination of the relief granted under article 20 and 21. *Yakushiji v Daiichi Chuo Kisen Kaisha (No 2)* [2016] FCA 1277 para 21 CLOUT 1998 (AU).

9 The court might require regular reports from the foreign representative regarding a variety of matters. *See In re Cozumel Caribe SA de CV*, 508 BR 330, 338 (Bankr SDNY 2014) (US) (ordering the foreign representative to report developments involving the debtor, guarantors, and the affiliates).

Articles 20 and 21.[10] However, in such a case the foreign representative's appointment may also have terminated, so there will be no foreign representative left to perform the Article 18 duties.[11] An interested creditor or the debtor might have to inform the court instead.[12]

C. OTHER FOREIGN PROCEEDINGS

Subparagraph (b) requires the foreign representative to advise the receiving court of other foreign proceedings involving the same debtor that become known to it after recognition.[13] This provision works in tandem with the similar Article 15(3) duty to impose an ongoing obligation on the foreign representative to advise the receiving court of all other foreign proceedings involving the debtor that it becomes aware of.[14] **1.18.5**

The foreign representative's role in the foreign proceeding likely would provide it with information about the debtor's operations in third states and other insolvency proceedings involving the debtor.[15] Articles 15(3) and 18(b) expressly impose the duty to inform upon the foreign representative to counteract the incentive not to disclose competing foreign proceedings.[16] **1.18.6**

Information about the existence of other foreign proceedings is needed by the receiving court in order tailor the relief and further the ML's cooperation and coordination goals.[17] Where multiple foreign proceedings are pending in respect to the same debtor, Article 30 requires the court to seek coordination and cooperation among the proceedings.[18] Further, Article 30 provides rules for coordinating the relief provided when there are multiple foreign proceedings **1.18.7**

---

10 *Re Sanko Steamship Co* [2015] EWHC 1031 (ch) (ENG); *Yakushiji v Daiichi Chuo Kisen Kaisha (No 2)* [2016] FCA 1277 para 21 CLOUT 1998 (AU).

11 *Re OJSC International Bank of Azerbaijan; Bakhshiyeva v Sberbank of Russia* [2018] EWCA Civ 2802 para 97 CLOUT 1822 (ENG). In addition to lacking authority to act, the previous foreign representative may also lack the financial means to inform the receiving court of the change. *Board of Directors of Rizzo-Bottiglieri-De-Carlini Armatori SpA v Rizzo Bottiglieri-De-Carlini Armatori SpA* [2017] FCA 331 para 28 (AU).

12 Digest of Case Law on the UNCITRAL Model Law on Cross-Border Insolvency (CLOUT), United Nations Publications (Vienna), 2021, art 18 para 2. In *Yakushiji* the solicitors who had filed the recognition application advised the court of the termination of the foreign proceeding and the retirement of the foreign representative. *Yakushiji v Daiichi Chuo Kisen Kaisha (No 2)* [2016] FCA 1277 para 7 CLOUT 1998 (AU).

13 *Guide to Enactment* (n 4) para 169.

14 *Guide to Enactment* (n 4) para 133. The article 15(3) disclosure requirement applies at the time of application, with article 18(b) imposing an ongoing disclosure obligation from that time forward.

15 Ibid.

16 Ibid.

17 *Guide to Enactment* (n 4) para 132 & 169.

18 Article 30.

involving the same debtor.[19] In addition, the existence of other proceedings may cause the receiving court to modify its initial decision granting foreign main proceeding recognition.[20]

19 ML art 30(1–3).

20 In *In re Oi Brasil Holdings Coöperatief UA*, the court had previously recognized as a foreign main proceeding a Brazilian bankruptcy involving the Dutch special purpose financing affiliate of a Brazilian operating company. It was asked to modify its COMI determination in the initial recognition order to instead recognize a later-filed Dutch bankruptcy proceeding as a foreign main proceeding. *Oi Brasil* 578 BR 169, 203 (Bankr SDNY 2017) CLOUT 1864 (US).

Article 19

RELIEF THAT MAY BE GRANTED UPON APPLICATION FOR RECOGNITION OF A FOREIGN PROCEEDING

Christopher Symes

1. From the time of filing an application for recognition until the application is decided upon, the court may, at the request of the foreign representative, where relief is urgently needed to protect the assets of the debtor or the interests of the creditors, grant relief of a provisional nature, including:
   (a) Staying execution against the debtor's assets;
   (b) Entrusting the administration or realization of all or part of the debtor's assets located in this State to the foreign representative or another person designated by the court, in order to protect and preserve the value of assets that, by their nature or because of other circumstances, are perishable, susceptible to devaluation or otherwise in jeopardy;
   (c) Any relief mentioned in paragraph 1 (c), (d) and (g) of article 21.
2. [*Insert provisions (or refer to provisions in force in the enacting State) relating to notice.*]
3. Unless extended under paragraph 1 (f) of article 21, the relief granted under this article terminates when the application for recognition is decided upon.
4. The court may refuse to grant relief under this article if such relief would interfere with the administration of a foreign main proceeding.

A. INTRODUCTION TO ARTICLE 19

1. Rationale

1.19.01 Article 19 grants the court the discretion to order provisional relief, when it is urgently needed, from the moment of the application for recognition.[1] As Mason puts it, the rationale is: '[T]o halt the "potential race of the swiftest" to take advantage of local assets, the foreign representative may request the court to grant immediate provisional relief upon filing of the application if relief is urgently needed to protect the debtor's assets or the creditors' interests.'[2] Justice Heath in *Williams v Simpson* captured the rationale when he stated:

> [T]he purpose of art 19 is to provide a mechanism to enable the Court to protect assets or the interests of creditors when concern exists that the assets may perish, be susceptible to devaluation or otherwise be in jeopardy. The emphasis is on flexibility of approach. The framers of the MLCBI could not have anticipated the vast array of circumstances in which interim relief might be required. The provision is expressed in non-exhaustive terms, using the word 'including' before specifying particular types of relief that might be ordered.[3]

1.19.02 He added that the relief must be restricted to urgent and provisional measures for the collective good.[4] It has been said to subserve the principle of universalism and is an article that is flexible so that in each case the judge will

1 For a detailed analysis of Article 19 see Andre J. Berends, 'The UNCITRAL Model Law on Cross-Border Insolvency: A Comprehensive Overview' (1998) 6 *Tulane Journal of International and Comparative Law* 309 at 357–62.

2 R Mason, 'Where Private International Law and Insolvency Law Meet' in *International Insolvency Law: Themes and Perspectives* (P Omar ed) Ashgate (London) 2008, 56.

3 *Williams v Simpson HC Hamilton* CIV 2010-419-1174 [2010] NZHC 1631 [44]. Other examples include *In Re SIVEC Srl*, 2011 Bankr LEXIS 2368; *Vitro v ACP Master Ltd (In Re Vitro)* 455 BR 571 (Bankr ND Tex 2011); *Tucker, in the matter of Aero inventory (UK) Limited v Aero Inventory (UK) Limited* [2009[FCA 1354.

4 *Williams v Simpson HC Hamilton CIV 2010-419-1174* [2010] NZHC 1631 [47].

determine the relief most appropriate to the circumstances of the particular case and address any conditions on which the relief should be granted.

Article 19(3) provides that the interim measure of relief terminates when the application is finally decided upon, although the court may extend the interim relief. Strategically, interim relief can be extremely important where the recognition is 'hotly contested' and will be potentially delayed due to requiring extensive evidentiary support including discovery. **1.19.03**

In New Zealand the court said that while a strong likelihood of the substantive application succeeding was not necessary for the interim relief to be granted, nevertheless the likelihood of substantive success was a relevant consideration in granting the interim relief.[5] **1.19.04**

2. Scope of Application

Article 19(1) confers standing to the foreign representative to apply to the court to provide relief and the scope of the orders is broad, with express mention of (a) staying execution against the debtor's assets; (b) entrusting the administration or realization of all or part of the debtor's assets located in this State to the foreign representative or another person designated by the court, in order to protect and preserve the value of assets that, by their nature or because of other circumstances, are perishable, susceptible to devaluation or otherwise in jeopardy; (c) any relief mentioned in paragraph 1 (c), (d) and (g) of Article 21.[6] However, the scope of the relief is not limited to these or considered 'exclusive', as discussed in para 1.19.15 below, and as interim relief will mean having access to State courts this may then include staying local execution proceedings (a discretionary stay of such matters as enforcing a charge) against the debtor's assets and liabilities and entrusting the foreign representative (or delegate) with the power to administer or realize all or part of the debtor's local assets in the State. It may also include the suspension of the right of the debtor to transfer or dispose of assets as well as the examination of witnesses, the taking of evidence or the delivery of information concerning the debtor's affairs. **1.19.05**

Article 19(1)(b) provides for the foreign representative or 'another person designated by the court' to act, and so the scope with respect to entrusting the administration or realization of all or part of the debtor's assets is not limited to just the foreign representative. In Australia the court decided to entrust **1.19.06**

5 *Whittman v UCI Holdings Ltd* [2016] NZHC 1228.

6 See Commentary in Article 21.

the administration of the debtor's local assets jointly to the foreign liquidators together with a locally based registered liquidator.[7]

1.19.07 There is a timeframe which applies to Article 19. The article commences with 'From the time of filing an application for recognition until the application is decided upon' and so an order for interim relief is only going to be able to be applied for during this period. In New Zealand the period commences from the time of the complete publication of the notice of the fact of filing under Article 19(2).[8] In the US, bankruptcy courts have determined that a formal adversary proceeding need not be commenced to seek preliminary relief pursuant to s1519, which is Article 19. However, one issue with s1519 is whether and at what juncture the US Court may grant preliminary relief in aid of foreign proceedings where the relief requested would not yet be available within the foreign proceeding itself.[9] For example, if a scheme is still being worked on in the foreign bankruptcy then the US court would look at things like the likelihood of success of the creditor approval and court sanctioning in determining whether the US court would grant injunctive relief.[10] Extension for the relief granted under Article 19 is possible, as indicated by Article 19(3). As the Guide to Enactment and Interpretation suggests, the court might wish to grant an extension, for example, to avoid a hiatus between the provisional measure issued before recognition and the measure issued after recognition.[11]

1.19.08 Article 19(1) includes the words 'urgently needed to protect the assets of the debtor or the interests of the creditors'. As has been mentioned by the court in Australia, 'the inclusion of the specific powers in Article 19 does not limit the Court's general power conferred by the prefatory words of that Article to make any orders that are "urgently needed to protect the assets of the debtor or the interests of the creditors"'.[12] Further, in the US, courts have predicated their grant of a stay upon the US Bankruptcy Court's 'inherent power', which would grant relief if it was necessary or appropriate to carry out the provisions of the US Bankruptcy Code.[13]

7 *Ackers v Saad Investments Co Limited (in official liq)* (2010) 276 ALR 508; [2010] FCA 1221.

8 *Williams v Simpson HC Hamilton CIV 2010-419-1174* [2010] NZHC 1631 [42].

9 Selinda A Melnik, 'United States' in Look Chan Ho (ed.) A Commentary on the UNCITRAL Model Law, 4th ed. 2017, Global Law & Business (London) 491.

10 Melnik (n 9), 491.

11 UNCITRAL Model Law on Cross-border Insolvency with Guide to Enactment and Interpretation, United Nations Publications (New York), 2014 para 174. For an example see *Yu v STX Pan Ocean Co Ltd (South Korea), in the matter of STX Pan Ocean Co Ltd (receivers appointed in South Korea)* [2013] FCA 680 [34].

12 *Tucker, in the matter of Aero Inventory (UK) Limited v Aero Inventory (UK) Limited* (2009) 76 ACSR 19; (2009) FCA 1354 [12].

13 US Bankruptcy Code s105(a); This is suggested in Melnik (n 9), 491.

It must be noted that this interim relief is just that, a form of 'pre-recognition relief', and is designed to preserve the position and assets of the debtor for a limited period pending the hearing of the application seeking recognition. Once recognition is accorded then the automatic effects provided for in Article 20 commence and the interim relief is terminated.[14] In Australia the court has suggested that 'accordingly, the provisional orders will cease to operate altogether when recognition is granted. From that time, apart from the consequences of the operation of Article 20, additional orders under Article 21 are required if consequences additional to those accomplished by Article 20 are intended.'[15] **1.19.09**

3. Legislative Background

The legislative process of passing Article 19 was lengthy. The Working Group and the Commission had lengthy discussions about the issue of provisional relief. In this respect, it should be noted that there are two kinds of provisional relief. The first is 'collective provisional' relief. This may include, for instance, a general stay of execution against the debtor's assets, a general stay of commencement or continuation of individual actions concerning the assets and a general suspension of the debtor's right to dispose of the assets. The second kind of provisional relief is 'individual' relief. These measures cover specific assets identified by a creditor. This kind of provisional relief does not prevent a creditor from commencing or continuing an individual action against the debtor's other assets.[16] **1.19.10**

In relation to interim relief it is reported that during the UNCITRAL negotiations there was 'discomfort amongst many of the Working Group members [...] as to the extent of the rights of a foreign representative following his [or her] application for recognition of a foreign proceeding under Article 19 and subsequently upon recognition under Article 21'.[17] **1.19.11**

---

14 See discussion in Commentary on Article 20.

15 *Yu v STX Pan Ocean Co Ltd (South Korea), in the matter of STX Pan Ocean Co Ltd (receivers appointed in South Korea)* [2013] FCA 680 (Buchanan J) [17].

16 Berends (n 1), 357–8.

17 S Chandra Mohan, 'Cross-border Insolvency Problems: Is the UNCITRAL Model Law the Answer?' (2012) 21(3) *International Insolvency Review* 143, 213.

B. PREREQUISITES FOR APPLICATION AND FOLLOW-UP PROCEDURES

1. The Applicant is the Foreign Representative

1.19.12 The application must be made by the foreign representative. This right is not extended to 'interested parties' who do get the entitlement to petition only after the order for recognition. While foreign representatives are extensively covered in other articles, particularly in the Article 2 definition, it is interesting to note some variations in different States to the access for interim relief. In Mexico the foreign representative's right of access to the courts under local legislation, for example, is subject to various restrictions and so if a foreign representative has to make urgent applications for interim relief in that State, he or she can do so only through the local inspector or receiver and cannot make the application directly,[18] and presumably the local receiver must first be satisfied as to the necessity for the foreign representative to make such applications.[19]

1.19.13 Some States have considered other requirements such as the use of a local representative, the need to have an establishment existing locally, and whether the court could itself initiate the application or empower 'other interested parties'. In the United States a debtor applied for relief under Article 19 and the court found that there was insufficient evidence to show the debtor was the foreign representative and therefore no relief could be granted.[20]

1.19.14 Primacy is given to foreign main proceedings and so Article 19(4) provides that relief granted in favour of a foreign non-main proceeding should not interfere with the administration of a foreign main proceeding. The Guide to Enactment and Interpretation suggests that 'in order to foster [...] coordination of pre-recognition relief with any foreign main proceeding, the foreign representative applying for recognition is required, by article 15, paragraph 3, to attach to the application for recognition a statement identifying all foreign proceedings with respect to the debtor that are known to the foreign representative'.[21]

---

18 Articles 298 and 300 of the Mexican Commercial Insolvency Law (2000); Mohan (n 17), 213.

19 For example, see Mexico.

20 *Daymonex Limited* (Bankr. SD Ind, Feb. 7, 2007).

21 *UNCITRAL Model Law on Cross-border Insolvency with Guide to Enactment and Interpretation*, United Nations Publications (New York), 2014 para 175.

2. Notice

Article 19(2) gives the option to an enacting State to detail provisions or refer to provisions in force in the enacting State, relating to notice. For example, in one State the requirement is to provide notification to the debtor as soon as practicable after the local court has granted provisional relief. **1.19.15**

3. Possibilities for Orders of Interim Relief

Article 19(1) provides a list of types of relief that may be granted, but the list is not exhaustive, as mentioned above in 1.19.04. It is heartening to see many aspects featuring in the orders such as a prohibition on commencement or continuation of lawsuits against the debtor, attachment upon the debtor's assets and enforcement of a judgment, the foreclosure of a mortgage, the prohibition on repayment or disposition of the debtor's assets by the debtor, a suspension order for compulsory execution, a conservation order to appoint a provisional trustee, stays being extended to litigation as well as execution, stays of enforcement proceedings extending to enforcement of rights *in rem* and security interests. It is in the nature of discretionary interim relief such as that found in Article 19 that the court may tailor it to the case at hand. **1.19.16**

C. LEGAL CONSEQUENCES

1. Local Law or Article 19

A number of States have chosen not to adopt Article 19. This is in part due to local laws existing which provide other methods that result in similar results, such as appointing receiver/interim receiver.[22] **1.19.17**

2. Relationship to other Articles

Article 22, in dealing with protection of creditors and other interested persons, permits a court to modify or terminate the interim relief granted under Article 19. Article 22 directs courts that, in granting relief under Articles 19, a court must be satisfied that the interests of creditors and other interested persons are adequately protected. To that end, Article 22 provides that a court may grant **1.19.18**

22 See, for example, Canada, where s 61 of the Companies Creditors Arrangement Act (2009) may be used to apply legal and equitable rules regarding the recognition of foreign insolvencies and assist foreign representatives, discussed in S Gollick, M Wasserman in Ho (n 9) 89.

relief under Article 19 subject to conditions and modify or terminate such relief. [23]

1.19.19 Article 29(b) provides that, where the local proceedings commence after recognition or the filing of an application for recognition of foreign proceedings, any relief granted under Article 19 shall be reviewed and modified or terminated if inconsistent with the local proceedings.

3. Insolvency and Maritime Law

1.19.20 Article 19 has been used to seek an application to stay the issue of a warrant for the arrest in a particular State of any vessel owned or chartered by the debtor. In the case of *Yu v STX Pan Ocean Co Ltd (South Korea), in the matter of STX Pan Ocean Co Ltd (receivers appointed in South Korea)*[24] the importance of interim relief in the maritime law context was highlighted. In the Federal Court of Australia the plaintiff had applied for recognition as a 'foreign representative' of STX Pan Ocean Co Ltd (South Korea) and for recognition of proceedings commenced in Korea as a 'foreign proceeding'.[25] The plaintiff desired interim relief to stay any potential maritime claims. The judgment dealt with the potential significance of the fact that ships owned or operated by the defendant pass through Australian waters and may be subject to arrest under the Admiralty Act 1988 (Cth) in accordance with generally accepted maritime conventions. In the judgment, under the heading 'Grounds for provisional relief – Ground 1 arrest of other ships in Australian waters', Buchanan J outlines that he was informed that vessels owned by the defendant that were due to enter Australian waters had been drifting in nearby waters for fear of being subject to arrest or attachment.[26] He was informed that numerous vessels owned by the defendant which were scheduled to call into Australian ports had not been able to enter into Australia due to the threat of arrest and that the arrest and delay of ships in Australia would cause a chain reaction of delays, as the vessels were scheduled to depart Australia to other destinations around the world.[27] The arrest and delay of ships may have led to severe liqui-

23 *Yu v STX Pan Ocean Co Ltd (South Korea), in the matter of STX Pan Ocean Co Ltd (receivers appointed in South Korea)* [2013] FCA 680 (Buchanan J) [12].

24 *Yu v STX Pan Ocean Co Ltd (South Korea), in the matter of STX Pan Ocean Co Ltd (receivers appointed in South Korea)* [2013] FCA 680.

25 *Yu v STX Pan Ocean Co Ltd (South Korea), in the matter of STX Pan Ocean Co Ltd (receivers appointed in South Korea)* [2013] FCA 680.

26 *Yu v STX Pan Ocean Co Ltd (South Korea), in the matter of STX Pan Ocean Co Ltd (receivers appointed in South Korea)* [2013] FCA 680 [31].

27 *Yu v STX Pan Ocean Co Ltd (South Korea), in the matter of STX Pan Ocean Co Ltd (receivers appointed in South Korea)* [2013] FCA 680 [31].

dation damage payments and termination of contracts of affreightments with the defendant's major customers, which was one of the main sources of the defendant's revenue.[28] If these vessels, which were owned by the defendant, were subject to arrest or attachment in Australia, there would be little possibility for the defendant to achieve a successful reorganization in Korea. If the defendant was unable to call into Australian ports, then voyages to other countries would be meaningless since there would be no cargo to deliver.[29] This ground, along with another ground relating to ongoing arrest warrant litigation, was enough to convince Buchanan J to grant interim relief.

4. Protecting Assets

Article 19 (1) expressly mentions 'protecting asset' and this is well illustrated in **1.19.21**
the case of *Tucker in the matter of Aero Inventory (UK) Limited v Aero Inventory (UK) Limited*,[30] where the plaintiffs were appointed as joint administrators of Aero Inventory Plc by order of the High Court of Justice of England and Wales and the defendant was a subsidiary of Aero Inventory Plc. The defendant owned or controlled property in Australia.[31] The defendant's principal activity was providing a comprehensive procurement and inventory management service where they sourced, distributed and sold numerous consumable and expendable parts that are required in the maintenance of commercial aircraft sold in various countries around the world.[32] The defendant had entered into a crucial agreement with Qantas Airways Limited (Qantas) pursuant to which it purchased from Qantas a certain inventory of spare parts, agreed to supply Qantas with certain aircraft parts, and agreed, among other services, to maintain and manage an aircraft parts consignment inventory at certain Qantas locations in Australia. The Federal Court of Australia made orders for interim protection of aircraft parts inventory stored at locations in Australia and controlled by Qantas, on the basis that they might be at risk because of a dispute as to entitlement to the parts.[33] Justice Lindgren observed that the relief was designed to preserve the position and assets of the defendant

---

28 *Yu v STX Pan Ocean Co Ltd (South Korea), in the matter of STX Pan Ocean Co Ltd (receivers appointed in South Korea)* [2013] FCA 680 [32].

29 *Yu v STX Pan Ocean Co Ltd (South Korea), in the matter of STX Pan Ocean Co Ltd (receivers appointed in South Korea)* [2013] FCA 680 [33].

30 *Tucker, in the matter of Aero Inventory (UK) Limited v Aero Inventory (UK) Limited* [2009] FCA 1354; For another example see *Asafuji (in his capacity as the Foreign Representative of the Sanko Steamship Co., Ltd) v The Sanko Steamship Co., Ltd* [2012] FCA 1154 [3].

31 *Tucker, in the matter of Aero Inventory (UK) Limited v Aero Inventory (UK) Limited* [2009] FCA 1354 [5].

32 *Tucker, in the matter of Aero Inventory (UK) Limited v Aero Inventory (UK) Limited* [2009] FCA 1354 [16], [17].

33 *Tucker, in the matter of Aero Inventory (UK) Limited v Aero Inventory (UK) Limited* [2009] FCA 1354 [19].

in Australia for a limited period pending the hearing of the application seeking recognition of the UK proceeding. He held that on the evidence before him it was likely that recognition would be granted and the right to transfer, encumber or otherwise dispose of any assets of the debtor would be automatically suspended. Lindgren J noted that the purpose of the provisional relief sought was to ensure that those effects would not be rendered nugatory.[34]

1.19.22 The protection of assets is very much in the forefront of the judges' thinking in Article 19 cases as illustrated by Heath J in *Williams v Simpson*,[35] who stated: 'The purpose of art 19 is to provide a mechanism to enable the Court to protect assets or the interests of creditors when concern exists that the assets may perish, be susceptible to devaluation or otherwise be in jeopardy. The emphasis is on flexibility of approach. The framers of the MLCBI could not have anticipated the vast array of circumstances in which interim relief might be required.'

5. The Potential Outcome of the Application for Recognition

1.19.23 A New Zealand case depicts the court's concern during deliberations for interim relief of the potential outcome of the application for recognition. In *Whittman v UCI Holdings Limited*[36] Palmer J granted interim relief and in doing so considered whether the substantive application would succeed. UCI Holdings Ltd was incorporated in New Zealand and it was also the parent company of a group which had filed for Chapter 11 bankruptcy in the United States. Whittman had been appointed by the United States Bankruptcy Court as foreign representative of UCI Holdings Ltd and he applied by interlocutory application in New Zealand for interim orders without notice except as to one creditor, Credit Suisse.[37] The interim orders were to last until Whittman's application for recognition in New Zealand of the Chapter 11 proceedings was decided. Justice Palmer in the New Zealand High Court acknowledged and derived assistance that the NZ High Court rules provided for interim freezing orders, and he considered that Whittman would succeed later in the substantive application, although at the present time there was a risk that property would be dissipated.[38] He decided that there was an overall balance of convenience and interest of justice in favour of granting the interim orders, and so he did. The Cayman Islands branch of Credit Suisse was served with a draft copy of the application for interim relief and its position was that any

34 *Tucker, in the matter of Aero Inventory (UK) Limited v Aero Inventory (UK) Limited* [2009] FCA 1354 [22].

35 *Williams v Simpson HC Hamilton CIV 2010-419-1174* [2010] NZHC 1631 [44].

36 *Whittman v UCI Holdings Limited* [2016] NZHC 1228.

37 *Whittman v UCI Holdings Limited* [2016] NZHC 1228 [1].

38 *Whittman v UCI Holdings Limited* [2016] NZHC 1228 [2], [28].

relief granted in New Zealand should be on the express basis that the position of creditors was protected. In particular, Credit Suisse submitted that any temporary relief under Article 19 should be granted on the express condition that UCI Holdings Ltd complied with any order of the bankruptcy court in Delaware and United States bankruptcy law.[39] Whittman submitted that there was a strong likelihood that the NZ Court would make orders recognizing that the UCI Holdings Ltd Chapter 11 proceedings would be either a foreign main proceeding, in which case the stay would come into effect automatically, or they would be a foreign non-main proceeding where a discretionary stay was likely to be issued.[40] However Palmer J rejected that a 'strong likelihood' of the substantive application succeeding was necessary for the interim relief to be granted. Palmer J agreed with Lindgren J, of the Federal Court of Australia in *Tucker, Re Aero Inventory (UK) Ltd* [2009] FCA 1354 at [22], that the likelihood of substantive success is a relevant consideration in granting interim relief. He also added that under the local law the same was true in relation to granting freezing orders in the form of 'a good arguable case'.[41]

39 *Whittman v UCI Holdings Limited* [2016] NZHC 1228 [14].

40 *Whittman v UCI Holdings Limited* [2016] NZHC 1228 [24].

41 *Whittman v UCI Holdings Limited* [2016] NZHC 1228 [25].

Article 20

EFFECTS OF RECOGNITION OF A FOREIGN MAIN PROCEEDING

Christopher Symes

1. Upon recognition of a foreign proceeding that is a foreign main proceeding:
   (a) Commencement or continuation of individual actions or individual proceedings concerning the debtor's assets, rights, obligations or liabilities is stayed;
   (b) Execution against the debtor's assets is stayed; and
   (c) The right to transfer, encumber or otherwise dispose of any assets of the debtor is suspended.
2. The scope, and the modification or termination, of the stay and suspension referred to in paragraph 1 of this article are subject to [*refer to any provisions of law of the enacting State relating to insolvency that apply to exceptions, limitations, modifications or termination in respect of the stay and suspension referred to in paragraph 1 of this article*].
3. Paragraph 1 (a) of this article does not affect the right to commence individual actions or proceedings to the extent necessary to preserve a claim against the debtor.
4. Paragraph 1 of this article does not affect the right to request the commencement of a proceeding under [*identify laws of the enacting State relating to insolvency*] or the right to file claims in such a proceeding.

A. INTRODUCTION TO ARTICLE 20

1. Rationale

Article 20 provides for the application of an automatic stay covering commencement or continuation of individual actions concerning the debtor's assets, rights, obligations or liabilities; a stay of execution against the debtor's assets; and the suspension of any transfer, encumbrance or other disposal of any of the debtor's assets. Article 20 in staying actions or enforcement proceedings provides 'breathing space' until appropriate measures are taken for reorganization or liquidation of the assets of the debtor. **1.20.01**

The Guide to Enactment and Interpretation suggests that the suspension of transfers is necessary because in a modern, globalized economic system it is possible for a multinational debtor to move money and property across boundaries quickly.[1] The mandatory moratorium triggered by the recognition of the foreign main proceeding, as required by Article 20, provides a rapid 'freeze' which is essential to organize an orderly and fair cross-border insolvency proceeding, to prevent fraud and to protect the legitimate interests of the parties involved until the court in the receiving State has an opportunity to notify all concerned and to assess the situation. **1.20.02**

The automatic consequences envisaged in Article 20 are intended to allow time for steps to be taken to organize an orderly and fair cross-border insolvency proceeding, even if the effects of commencement of the foreign insolvency proceeding in the country of origin are different from the effects of Article 20 in the recognizing State. **1.20.03**

With many cross-border insolvencies there is a risk of dissipation of local assets and so Article 20 enables this risk to be avoided and defers the commencement of further actions by all creditors until after the foreign proceeding is resolved. This avoids the local court making orders inconsistent with the foreign proceeding. The effect of the moratorium period does not prevent the commencement of a local insolvency proceeding, as contemplated by Article 20(4), and this will ensure that local interests are protected. **1.20.04**

Article 20 is special in the sense that it provides for an effect or state of affairs which arises by law and does not involve an order of a court, and the relief **1.20.05**

1 *UNCITRAL Model Law on Cross-Border Insolvency with Guide to Enactment and Interpretation*, United Nations Publications (New York), 2014. Para 177.

cannot be described as 'discretionary', unlike the other articles that deal with relief.[2] The stay and suspension are procedural and they do not affect the substantive rights of the creditors.

2. Scope of the Stay and Suspension

1.20.06 The scope of the automatic relief is dictated by Article 20(2), where the enacting State is given freedom to define, modify or terminate the stay and suspension. This results in a 'far from uniform' automatic relief across the world.[3] What Article 20 presents though to enacting States is the possibility of aligning the relief resulting from recognition of a foreign proceeding with the relief available in a comparable proceeding under the local law.

1.20.07 The automatic stay does not operate retrospectively from the date of the foreign main proceeding and the right to transfer assets ceases on the date of recognition, not on the date of the commencement of the foreign proceeding.[4]

1.20.08 One of the important aspects of the scope of the automatic relief is the treatment a particular State gives to the enforcement of security interests. Another important aspect is set-off and whether the local recognition of the foreign main proceeding is to have the same effect locally as the commencement of insolvency proceedings under the laws of the enacting State.[5]

1.20.09 The automatic relief does not apply extraterritorially and so it is important to note that the scope of the automatic stay that arises pursuant to Article 20 is not what the debtor would enjoy in their home jurisdiction. Rather, the scope is the same as what the debtor would receive if the stay arose under whatever jurisdiction the stay is to be exercised in. This requires the local court to assess what local insolvency procedure the debtor's procedure would 'most closely resemble'. It will be the breadth of the stay available under the analogous local procedure that will determine the form of the stay the debtor can enjoy.[6]

1.20.10 While Article 20 does not specify the length of the duration of the automatic stay, it is true that most disputed cases have focused on the time at which the

---

2 *Akers v Saad Investments Co Limited (in official liquidation)* (2010) FCA 1221 [55].

3 Look Chan Ho (ed.), *A Commentary on the UNCITRAL Model Law* (4th ed) Globe Law & Business (London) 2017, p11.

4 *O'Sullivan v Loy (In Re Loy)* 432 BR 551 2010.

5 Scott Atkins & Rosalind Mason, 'Australia' in Look Chan Ho, 'England' in Ho (ed.) *A Commentary on the UNCITRAL Model Law* (4th ed) Globe Law & Business (London) 2017, 37.

6 Angus Stewart & Karen Patch, 'Cross-border insolvency law in Australia and shipping insolvencies: unique challenges or issues of wider significance?' (2018) 19 *Insolvency Law Bulletin* 15.

stay ceases to apply. In a Canadian case,[7] the court declined to make an order that the automatic stay be effective retroactive to the date of commencement of the foreign proceeding. The Legislative Guide described it thus: the automatic relief afforded by recognition of a foreign main proceeding is normally coterminous with the stay applicable in the corresponding foreign proceeding. Accordingly, the court said that absent exigent circumstances, the automatic stay under Article 20 ceases when the foreign proceeding is closed, the purpose of the stay, that is, to allow the debtor time to devise a plan and prevent creditors from pursuing alternative remedies, being no longer applicable.[8] In Australia the court has commented that 'The reach of Art 20 should be understood to be for the currency of foreign main proceedings. If it is a liquidation, it will be unlikely that an end date for the orders will become relevant. For rehabilitation or reconstruction proceedings, an end date for the operation of orders will or may [...] be relevant. Article 20, however, provides not for orders but the effect of operation of the Article. Plainly, however, Art 20 and orders under Art 21 are intended to be limited to the currency or life of the rehabilitation.'[9] The judge concluded: 'I would not read the effect of Art 20 as lasting beyond the end of the foreign proceeding.'[10]

3. Legislative Background

When discussing mandatory stays and suspensions, UNCITRAL decided to include a short list of autonomous effects in Article 20, which were designed to provide immediate protection for locally situated assets and would be triggered automatically by recognition of a foreign main proceeding, while giving courts leeway in Article 21 to grant additional discretionary relief.[11] **1.20.11**

B. ADJUSTMENTS TO AUTOMATIC RELIEF

1. Modifications to the Automatic Relief

When adopting Article 20, most States have provided certain modifications. It **1.20.12**
must be recognized that any modification of the stay imposed by Article 20(1)

7 *Hanjin Shipping Co.*, 2016 BCSC 2213 [paras 24–30].

8 *Hanjin Shipping Co.*, 2016 BCSC 2213 [12].

9 *Yakushiji v Daiichi Chuo Kisen Kaisha (No 2)* [2016] FCA 1277 [21].

10 *Yakushiji v Daiichi Chuo Kisen Kaisha (No 2)* [2016] FCA 1277 [21].

11 Discussion in UNCITRAL and in the Working Group are found at Official Records of the General Assembly, Fifty-Second Session, Supplement No. 17(A/52/17), paras 47–60; A/CN.9/419, paras 137–143; A/CN.9/422, paras 94–110; A/CN.9/433, paras 115–126; A/CN.9/435, paras 24–48.

required an evaluation and balancing of the protection afforded to relevant creditors.[12]

1.20.13 Modifying or terminating relief by the court will depend on the rules governing the power of the court to do so and these vary. In some legal systems the courts are authorized to make individual modifications upon request by an interested party, under conditions prescribed by local law, while in others the courts do not have that power, in line with the principle that, in general, courts do not have the power to set aside the application of a statutory rule of law. If courts are to be given such a power, some legal systems would normally require the grounds on which the court could modify or terminate the mandatory effects of recognition under Article 20(1) to be specified. In view of that situation, Article 20(2) provides that the modification or termination of the stay and the suspension provided in the article is subject to the provisions of law of the enacting State relating to insolvency.

1.20.14 A fine example of the freedom provided to the enacting State to modify the automatic relief is Australia. The Australian legislation has identified the Australian laws on stays and suspensions which are then the laws which will apply to cross-border cases under Article 20. The local Bankruptcy Act and Corporations Act provide a general rule that all actions and proceedings against a debtor are stayed upon the commencement of insolvency proceedings although there are various exceptions and modifications for secured creditors to realize their security in liquidations and there is a statutory moratorium provided in the corporate rescue laws known as voluntary administrations. Because Australia has quite different corporate rescue legislation with a very wide stay and suspension provisions, it may be difficult to identify which of those provisions are the ones intended to provide, under Article 20(2), the modification of the stay and suspension of proceedings concerning the assets, rights obligations and liabilities of a debtor in a cross-border case under Article 20(1).[13]

1.20.15 The United States can be exemplary in Article 20 contemplation due to its long history of automatic stays. The scope of the automatic stay under the US Bankruptcy Code, s1520 (a), which adopts Article 20 and provides that, upon recognition of a foreign main proceeding, the automatic stay is limited

12 *Akers as joint representative of Saad Investment Co Ltd (in Official Liquidation) v Deputy Commissioner of Taxation* (2014) 223 FCR 8 at 38 [126]–[128].

13 Steven Rares, 'Consistency and Conflict – Cross-Border Insolvency' Speech by Justice Rares, September 2015 www.fedcourt.gov.au/digital-law-library/judges-speeches/justice-rares/rares-j-20150904.

to proceedings that could have an impact on the debtor's property located in, or within the territorial jurisdiction of the United States.[14] Under Chapter 15 of the US Bankruptcy Code, application of the stay arises upon recognition of a foreign main proceeding and applies to the debtor for all local purposes and extends to extraterritorial proceedings but only for the purposes of protecting property of the debtor that is located within the USA. The automatic stay does not apply extraterritorially to the debtor in a foreign arbitration proceeding, unless there is a demonstrated relationship between that proceeding and property of the debtor within the USA. Furthermore, the representative of the foreign main proceeding under s1520(a) (3) may operate the debtor's business and may exercise the rights and powers of a trustee in relation to the US-located assets of the debtor. Such far-reaching rights are only connected to the foreign main proceeding and are of huge importance for those proceedings where large parts of the debtor's global assets are located in the USA, as they fall directly under the administration of the foreign insolvency representative, who can use these assets either to continue the business or liquidate it for the benefit of the debtor's creditors.

2. Article 29 and Automatic Relief

Article 20 is negated if the foreign proceeding is recognized as a main proceeding by the operation of Article 29, dealing with the coordination of the foreign and the local proceedings. Under Article 29, if the foreign proceeding is a main proceeding, the automatic effects pursuant to Article 20 are to be modified or terminated if they are inconsistent with the local proceeding. Importantly, the automatic effects from Article 20 do not terminate automatically since they may be beneficial and the court may wish to maintain them.[15] Where a local proceeding is pending at the time a foreign proceeding is recognized as a main proceeding, the foreign proceeding does not enjoy the automatic effects of Article 20.[16] **1.20.16**

14 This incorporates ss 361 and 362 of the US Bankruptcy Code.

15 Article 29(b)(ii) MLCBI.

16 Article 29(a)(ii) MLCBI.

C. LEGAL CONSEQUENCES

1. Maritime Law and Article 20

1.20.17 What is readily observable is that maritime cases are numerous when considering cases on Article 20,[17] and unfortunately there is uncertainty. The common law and legislation provide a long history and established principles of maritime law. English courts take a clear stance in favour of the supremacy of maritime creditors and arrest proceedings. This stance has been adopted in many Commonwealth jurisdictions and has led courts to allow arrest procedures in their harbours despite the fact that insolvency procedures had already been initiated in other jurisdictions.[18] For example, under maritime law a person seeking to enforce a maritime lien or other charge could commence an action *in rem* against the ship and the question then arises whether Article 20 prevents that person from arresting a ship. In the event of any clash of principles between the areas of cross-border insolvency and admiralty law, as a matter of interpretation, admiralty principles should, at the very least, be taken into account.

1.20.18 One Australian judge, writing extrajudicially, has explained it like this: the issues in cross-border insolvencies of shipping companies are not as straightforward as in other cases. A maritime creditor with an existing secured claim, such as a maritime lien, over a ship that sails into the jurisdiction of the forum is in a similar position to a creditor with security over real property in the forum. Ordinarily, the interests of a secured creditor are different to those of unsecured creditors of an insolvent. Indeed, the very purpose of the security is to create such a difference in the assets from which secured and unsecured claims will be met in the event of an insolvency.[19] He went on to observe that when this happens in Australia, courts would order that any application to arrest a ship be brought before a judge in the Federal Court of Australia's Admiralty and Maritime National Practice Area, who could then assess whether it was appro-

---

17 For example, see: *Kim v Daebo International Shipping Co Ltd* [2015] FCA 684; *Tai-Soo Suk v Hanjin Shipping Co Ltd* [2016] FCA 1404; and [2017] FCA 404; *Re Eastwind Maritime Inc.* [2009] Bankr. SDNY, case no. 09-14047; *Kim v SW Shipping Co Ltd* (2016) 113 ACSR 260, [2016] FCA 428; *Yakushiji v Kaisha; Fujita v Star Bulk Carrier Co SA* (2015) 333 ALR 515; [2015]1170; *Yu v STX Pan Ocean Co Ltd (South Korea)* (2013) 223 FCR 189; [2013] FCA 680; *Board of Directors of Rizzo-Bottiglieri-De Carlini Armatori SpA v Rizzo-Bottiglieri-de Carlini Armatori Spa* [2013] FCA 157; [2017] FCA 331; [2018] FCA 680; *Alari (Trustee) Rizzo Bottiglieri-de Carlini Armatori SpA* [2018] FCA 1067; *Hur v Samsun Logix Corporation* [2009] FCA 372.

18 Erik Göretzlehner, *Maritime Cross Border Insolvency – An Analysis for Germany, England and Wales and the USA*, Springer (New York) 2019, 124–5.

19 Steven Rares, 'Consistency and Conflict – Cross-Border Insolvency' Speech by Justice Rares, September 2015 https://www.fedcourt.gov.au/digital-law-library/judges-speeches/justice-rares/rares-j-20150904 [40].

priate to issue an arrest warrant or whether the plaintiff ought simply prove in the foreign main proceeding. If a warrant resulted in the arrest of a ship, the foreign representative would be able to argue for the discharge of the warrant in a contested application in which all relevant considerations would be before the Court, including the exact nature of any stay that ought to apply under the MLCBI and the asserted secured right of the plaintiff.[20]

2. Set-off

There is an issue that arises with Article 20 and its automatic nature of providing a stay and suspension, and it is with set-off. The Article does not expressly provide for a set-off. Philip Wood, in his book *Set off and Netting*, commences[21] by stating: 'Set-off is one of the leading, and most accurate indicators of pro-debtor or pro-creditor attitudes to insolvency. It is a litmus test of jurisdictions and a key comparative criterion of financial law. For example, in most English-based countries set-off is restricted between solvent parties [...] and compulsory on insolvency [...] while in many Napoleonic jurisdictions solvent set-off is liquid between solvent parties [...] but prohibited on insolvency. The contrast could not be more complete.' He goes on to state that 'set-off usually only matters on insolvency'. It is acknowledged that there are different views concerning set-off. Most common law countries restrict set-off between solvent parties and make it compulsory in their legislation in the event of insolvency, civil law countries follow the opposite pattern in that they restrict or prohibit insolvency set-off, but not if the conditions for offsetting had been met before the opening of insolvency proceedings. Discussions of insolvency set-off often include the accusation that it is an exception to the equitable treatment of creditors. **1.20.19**

The different jurisdictions are far from consistent in their treatment of set-off predominantly due to varying local treatment. Some examples demonstrate this. France permits set-off, but only in exceptional cases, for example, if claims were related to each other. Italy permits set-off only if the creditor's claim against the insolvent debtor arose three or six months or one year before the opening of the insolvency proceedings, and in Korea there is uncertainty as to whether the governing law of the set-off is the law that governs the cross-claim or that which governs the claim and the cross-claim. Even in the UK it is opined that the law appears 'wide' compared with many other **1.20.20**

20 Rares (n 19) [43].

21 Philip R Wood, *Set-offs and Netting, Derivatives and Clearing Systems* (3rd ed) Sweet & Maxwell (London) 2019 para 15-001.

countries,[22] yet there is uncertainty, as demonstrated by a potential different treatment of contractual set-off with that of insolvency set-off.[23]

3. Courts Giving Leave that the Automatic Stay does not Apply

1.20.21 Article 20(2) is going to be foundational where a party does not wish an automatic stay or suspension to be applied. The case of *Kim v STX Pan Ocean Co Limited*[24] is representational of cases that challenge the stay. The claimants, Kim, were seeking leave to continue their statutory claims *in rem* under the Admiralty Act 1973 (NZ) against the ship *New Giant*.[25] The respondent, STX Pan Ocean Co. Limited (STX), was the charterer by demise of *New Giant* and was liable *in persona* for the statutory claims. STX was under an administration proceeding in Korea that had been recognized in New Zealand as a foreign main proceeding and that recognition had the effect of staying the claimants' admiralty proceedings.[26] Kim initially argued that the stay of proceedings arising by operation of law in New Zealand on recognition of the Korean rehabilitation as a foreign main proceeding does not apply to the admiralty proceedings. This was based on their contention that *New Giant* was not an asset of the debtor STX. Kim then conceded that the New Zealand stay does cover their claims. The UNCITRAL Legislative Guide on Insolvency Law (Parts One & Two) defines 'assets of the debtor' as 'property, rights and interests of the debtor, including rights and interests in property, whether or not in the possession of the debtor, tangible or intangible, movable or immovable, including the debtor's interests in encumbered assets or in third party-owned assets'.[27] STX operated *New Giant* under the terms of a charter by demise. This gave it the right to possession and control of the ship, including the right to provide the master and crew. STX also had an option to purchase the ship. Gilbert J held that it followed that STX's interest under the charter by demise was an asset of STX for the purposes of the Act and even if this was not the case, the admiralty proceedings concerned STX's 'rights, obligations or liabilities' in terms of Article 20(1)(a).[28]

22 Gerald McCormack, 'Set-off under the European insolvency regulation (and English law)' (2020) 29 *International Insolvency Review* 100-117.

23 Look Chan Ho, 'England' in Ho (ed.) *A Commentary on the UNCITRAL Model Law* (4th ed) Globe Law & Business (London) 2017, 213–15.

24 *Kim v STX Pan Ocean Co Limited* [2014] NZHC 845.

25 *Kim v STX Pan Ocean Co Limited* [2014] NZHC 845 [1].

26 *Kim v STX Pan Ocean Co Limited* [2014] NZHC 845 [2].

27 UNCITRAL Legislative Guide on Insolvency Law (Parts One & Two) para 12 p4.

28 *Kim v STX Pan Ocean Co Limited* [2014] NZHC 845 [14]-[18].

Gilbert J in *Kim v STX Pan Ocean Co Limited* concluded that the admiralty proceedings were covered by the automatic stay which came into effect in New Zealand by operation of law following the High Court of New Zealand's recognition of the Korean administration proceeding as a foreign main proceeding. The court then addressed the question whether leave should be granted, acknowledging that, notwithstanding the automatic stay, the court had a discretion under Article 20(2) to allow a person to commence or continue proceedings. Gilbert J stated that it is clear that Article 20(2) was intended to allow enacting States to grant protection to those classes of people who would normally receive protection in insolvency proceedings in the enacting State. He noted that in the commentary to Article 20(2), the Guide to Enactment and Interpretation of the UNCITRAL Model Law on Cross-Border Insolvency suggests that this clause may be used to allow the enforcement of claims by secured creditors, payments made by the debtor in the ordinary course of business, the initiation of court action for claims arising after the commencement of the insolvency proceeding or following recognition of a foreign main proceeding, or the completion of open financial-market transactions. The Guide notes that Article 20(2) is designed to enable persons adversely affected by the stay to apply to the Court for relief.[29] **1.20.22**

In the New Zealand context, rather than identifying any particular exception in enacting Article 20, the Parliament conferred a broad discretion on the court to grant leave in appropriate cases. This solution was recommended by the New Zealand Law Commission in its report on enacting the MLCBI and was consistent with the general approach taken to stays of execution and proceedings under New Zealand's insolvency regime. The New Zealand Law Commission considered that each of the consequences that flow from Article 20 would occur as a result of most formal insolvency regimes in New Zealand and that the discretion reserved under Article 20(2) should enable the High Court to exercise the same type of discretion to override the consequences of a stay or suspension as it has under other insolvency provisions.[30] **1.20.23**

In *Kim v STX Pan Ocean Co Limited*, before exercising his discretion under Article 20(2), Gilbert J wanted to be satisfied that the commencement of proceedings would not enable a creditor to gain an advantage over other creditors, that the proposed proceeding was the most convenient way of establishing **1.20.24**

29 *Kim v STX Pan Ocean Co Limited* [2014] NZHC 845 [22].

30 Law Commission, 'Cross-Border Insolvency – Should New Zealand Adopt the UNCITRAL Model Law on Cross-Border Insolvency' (NZLC R52, February 1999) at [180] cited in *Kim v STX Pan Ocean Co Limited* [2014] NZHC 845 [23].

the claimed right, and that the claim was at least arguable so that the assets of the company would not be dissipated in wasteful litigation.[31] In considering whether to grant leave, Gilbert J said it was first necessary to examine the nature of the claimants' rights and when they arose. The claimants did not have maritime liens and therefore did not acquire any secured interest in *New Giant* at the time their services were provided. The claimants had only statutory *in rem* rights arising under the New Zealand Admiralty Act.[32] The court considered precedent cases from the UK such as *Re Aro Co. Ltd*, [1980] Ch 196 (CA), where admiralty proceedings had similarly been stayed by a foreign insolvency and which was entitled to pursue a statutory *in rem* claim.[33]

1.20.25 In *Kim v STX Pan Ocean Co Limited*, while granting of leave for the statutory claims *in rem* under maritime law, the court noted that the Insolvency Cross-Border Act (including Article 20) in New Zealand was procedural in nature and was designed to facilitate the management or realization of the debtor's assets in a single jurisdiction in accordance with the pari passu principle. The Act was not intended to deprive creditors of their substantive rights or interests. Consistent with usual practice followed under s 248 of the Companies Act (NZ), where leave would normally be given for secured creditors to commence or continue proceedings to establish their security, the claimants would normally be entitled to obtain leave. This would not give them an unfair advantage over other creditors because their respective rights and interests would normally be determined at the time the rehabilitation proceedings commenced. The judge felt that the continuation of the admiralty proceedings was the most effective way for Kim, the claimants, to be able to establish their secured interest in *New Giant* at that time, and there was no dispute that the claimants had good arguable claims.[34]

31 *Kim v STX Pan Ocean Co Limited* [2014] NZHC 845 [25].
32 *Kim v STX Pan Ocean Co Limited* [2014] NZHC 845 [26].
33 *Kim v STX Pan Ocean Co Limited* [2014] NZHC 845 [27]–[29].
34 *Kim v STX Pan Ocean Co Limited* [2014] NZHC 845 [30].

Article 21

RELIEF THAT MAY BE GRANTED UPON APPLICATION FOR RECOGNITION OF A FOREIGN PROCEEDING

Christopher Symes

1. Upon recognition of a foreign proceeding, whether main or non-main, where necessary to protect the assets of the debtor or the interests of the creditors, the court may, at the request of the foreign representative, grant any appropriate relief, including:
   (a) Staying the commencement or continuation of individual actions or individual proceedings concerning the debtor's assets, rights, obligations or liabilities, to the extent they have not been stayed under paragraph 1 (a) of article 20;
   (b) Staying execution against the debtor's assets to the extent it has not been stayed under paragraph 1 (b) of article 20;
   (c) Suspending the right to transfer, encumber or otherwise dispose of any assets of the debtor to the extent this right has not been suspended under paragraph 1 (c) of article 20;
   (d) Providing for the examination of witnesses, the taking of evidence or the delivery of information concerning the debtor's assets, affairs, rights, obligations or liabilities;
   (e) Entrusting the administration or realization of all or part of the debtor's assets located in this State to the foreign representative or another person designated by the court;
   (f) Extending relief granted under paragraph 1 of article 19;
   (g) Granting any additional relief that may be available to [*insert the title of a person or body administering a reorganization or liquidation under the law of the enacting State*] under the laws of this State.
2. Upon recognition of a foreign proceeding, whether main or non-main, the court may, at the request of the foreign representative, entrust the distribution of all or part of the debtor's assets located in this State to the

foreign representative or another person designated by the court, provided that the court is satisfied that the interests of creditors in this State are adequately protected.

3. In granting relief under this article to a representative of a foreign non-main proceeding, the court must be satisfied that the relief relates to assets that, under the law of this State, should be administered in the foreign non-main proceeding or concerns information required in that proceeding.

A. INTRODUCTION TO ARTICLE 21

1. Rationale

1.21.01 Article 21 authorizes the court, following recognition of a foreign proceeding, to grant relief in addition to the mandatory stay and suspension under Article 20. The relief under Article 21 is discretionary and the types of relief listed in Article 21(1) are typical of the relief most frequently granted in insolvency proceedings. Article 21(1), by using the word 'including', indicates that the list is not exhaustive and the court is not restricted unnecessarily in its ability to grant any type of relief that is available under the law of the enacting State and needed in the circumstances of the case.

1.21.02 The discretionary relief in Article 21 complements the interim relief provided by Article 19 and the mandatory or automatic relief provided in Article 20. The rationale is to facilitate courts granting discretionary relief upon the recognition of a foreign main proceeding and non-main proceeding in order to protect the debtor's assets or the creditors' interests.

The court has the power under Article 21 to grant what is expressed in Article 21(1) as 'appropriate relief', indicating the true discretionary nature of the relief, although it is not an unlimited power.[1] **1.21.03**

2. Scope of Application

While the discretionary relief is only available at the behest of the foreign representative, it has been suggested that Article 21 provides a very broad reservoir of power that enables courts to grant any appropriate relief to assist that foreign representative to effectuate the purposes of the MLCBI and to protect assets of the debtor or the interests of creditors.[2] **1.21.04**

The claim for relief under Article 21 is dependent on the court acceding to the foreign representative's application for recognition of the 'foreign proceeding' as a foreign main proceeding or a foreign non-main proceeding and the jurisdiction to make orders under Article 21 depends on the existence of a 'foreign proceeding'. **1.21.05**

To address the scope of the discretionary relief an application may be made at any time by a foreign representative following recognition of a foreign main or non-main proceeding and up until the foreign proceeding comes to an end, and then there is no scope for further orders in support of the foreign proceeding to be made and any relief previously granted under Article 21 should terminate.[3] **1.21.06**

Different States have addressed the issue of scope. For instance, in one State Article 21(1)(g), which provides for 'additional relief', has been excluded on the grounds that the rest of Article 21 provides wide and non-exclusive grounds and so nothing further is required. **1.21.07**

The scope of the discretionary relief may include matters already addressed in the interim relief under Article 19 or the automatic relief under Article 20. Additionally, Article 6 provides that 'nothing in this Law prevents the court from refusing to take an action governed by this Law if the action would be **1.21.08**

1 *Gladstone (Trustee) v Digrigoli (No 2)* [2016] FCA 1220 [9]; *Re Pan Ocean Co Ltd* [2014] EWHC 2124; *Larsen v Navios International Inc* [2011] EWHC 878 (Ch).

2 Daniel M Glosband & Leif M Clark, 'Ancillary and other cross-border insolvency cases under Chapter 15 of the Bankruptcy Code' Collier Monograph, LexisNexis Mathew Bender (New York) 2008. https://www.lexisnexis.com/documents/pdf/20090109094045_large.pdf

3 *Fibria Celulose S/A v. Pan Ocean Co. Ltd.* [2014] EWHC 2124; *Bakhshiyeva ex rel. Int'l Bank of Azerbaijan v. Sberbank of Russia* [2018] EWCA (Civ) 2802 [95].

manifestly contrary to the public policy of this State' and so this can qualify Article 21, although its use is closely obeyed.[4]

3. Legislative Background

1.21.09 The aspect that raised discomfort among many of the Working Group members was the extent of the rights of a foreign representative following his or her application for recognition of a foreign proceeding under Article 21. To address this discomfort and after much debate, Article 21(2) was drafted, which requires a court to be satisfied that the interests of local creditors are 'adequately protected' before the foreign representative is entrusted with the distribution of the debtor's assets within the State.[5]

B. APPLICATIONS FOR DISCRETIONARY RELIEF

1. Prerequisites

1.21.10 In some States, the foreign representative will apply for discretionary relief by making an interlocutory application which must be served on other parties as directed by the court, such as local judgment creditors. Variations to the discretionary relief would also be approached in this way.[6]

1.21.11 In South Africa the reference to actions and proceedings has been adjusted so that stays will only be applied to 'legal actions' and 'legal proceedings'.[7] In the US the Article 21 adoption, namely Section 1521 (a) of the Bankruptcy Code, has the condition that the court will be satisfied that the relief relates to assets which, under US law, should be administered in the foreign non-main proceeding and that these assets will have some direct connection with the non-main proceeding. South Africa has added an additional provision which requires the court to indicate the laws of the enacting State that will apply, such as laws relating to proof of claims and meetings.[8]

---

4 David Goldman, 'New Frontiers for Australian Cross-border Insolvency' (2011) 23(2) *A Insol J* 20, 26. See the discussion in *Fibria Celulose S/A v Pan Ocean Co. Ltd & Anor* [2014] EWHC 2124 (Ch) at [103]–[104].

5 S Chandra Mohan, 'Cross-border Insolvency Problems: Is the UNCITRAL Model Law the Answer?' (2012) 21(3) *International Insolvency Review* 143, 213.

6 This is the procedure used in both Australia and New Zealand.

7 R Kelly & C vanZuylen, 'South Africa' in Look Chan Ho, 'England' in Ho (ed.) *A Commentary on the UNCITRAL Model Law* (4th ed) Globe Law & Business (London) 2017.

8 *Ibid.*

2. Article X

Whether the recognition and enforcement of insolvency judgments shuld be the subject of discretionary relief has been uncertain. In the US the courts have considered that Article 21 does allow for recognition and enforcement of insolvency-related judgments. The MLIJ in its final article, which does not follow the previous articles' sequence and is thus entitled Article X, clarifies that the intended scope of the MLCBI, and Article 21 in particular, was to be broad and to be inclusive of enforcement of judgments. **1.21.12**

While the adoption and implementation of the MLIJ has not been rapid, jurisdictions that already have the MLCBI or ones that are intending to adopt it have the option of including an amendment pursuant to Article X of the MLIJ. In 2022, the UK Insolvency Service published a consultation on the UK's proposed adoption of the MLIJ.[9] At present the MLCBI does not explicitly regulate how foreign insolvency judgments are to be recognized and enforced. The MLIJ aims to produce a straightforward and harmonised procedure for recognizing and enforcing insolvency judgments in a predictable way. **1.21.13**

The UK wishes only to implement the MLIJ in part, in the form of the MLIJ's 'Article X', rather than a full implementation. This would mean that relief granted would be at the discretion of the UK courts. Therefore, the recognition of insolvency-related judgments becomes a form of assistance that can be granted under the MLCBI. If the UK were to adopt Article X then this would mean that the UK proposal respects the judgment of *Rubin v Eurofinance*, the key Supreme Court decision of 2012, which held that the Cross-Border Insolvency Rules of the UK do not extend to the recognition of a foreign insolvency-related judgments, while allowing the court to exercise a discretion to do just that: recognize a foreign insolvency-related judgment.[10] It has been noted that, depending on prior interpretations of Article 21 in the particular State, it may be helpful to clarify by saying that any 'other relief' includes the enforcement of judgments as well. The result would then be that there will be two laws in a particular State pursuant to which enforcement of insolvency judgments can be sought once the MLIJ has been adopted.[11] **1.21.14**

9 See www.gov.uk/government/consultations/implementation-of-two-uncitral-model-laws-on-insolvency/implementation -of -two -uncitral -model -laws -on -insolvency -consultation #uncitral -model -law -on -enterprise-group-insolvency

10 H Morris & JM Peck, The UK Insolvency Service's New Consultation on the Adoption of Two Insolvency-Related UNCITRAL Model Laws, www .mofo .com/ resources/ insights/ 220916 -the -uk -insolvency-services-new-consultation

11 Irit Mevorach, 'Overlapping International Instruments for Enforcement of Insolvency Judgments: Undermining or Strengthening Universalism?' (2021) 22 *European Business Organization Law Review* 283–315.

1.21.15 It has been suggested that, although an amended Article 21 could note that additional discretionary relief that may be granted includes enforcement of judgments, a fuller amalgamation of the two Model Laws could strengthen the framework. To this end, explicit reference to the recognition and enforcement of insolvency-related judgments could also provide the detail of the procedure and conditions for the recognition and enforcement of judgments as is presently specified in the MLIJ.[12] Article 21 could clarify that the judgment shall be given the same effect it has in the originating country or the same effect it would have had if it had been issued by a court in the recognizing country.[13]

3. Discretional Relief and Article 29

1.21.16 Article 21 must always be considered with Article 29 that preserves the pre-eminence of local proceedings over any foreign proceeding (whether main or non-main). This means that the court will review and modify or terminate relief if it is inconsistent with the proceeding in the local jurisdiction.

4. Main and Non-main Proceedings

1.21.17 It is important to note that Article 21(3), unlike Article 21(1) and (2), is restricted to non-main proceedings, and this has been noted by the courts.[14] Given that the scope of non-main proceedings might be less than all-encompassing, the scope of the foreign proceeding should be considered in fashioning appropriate relief.

C. LEGAL CONSEQUENCES

1. Local Creditors being 'Adequately Protected'

1.21.18 Article 21(2) requires that the court is satisfied that the interests of creditors in the enacting State are adequately protected.[15] This phrase has been much analysed by courts dealing with Article 21. It has been observed that entrusting the distribution of domestic assets to the foreign representative is a particularly

12 Mevorach (n 11).

13 Mevorach (n 11).

14 *Swissair Schweizerische Luftverkehrsaktiengesellschaft* [2009] EWHC 2099 (Ch) [14].

15 In the US, the legislation uses 'sufficient protection'. In Japan there is no phrase as it is anticipated that creditors will be adequately protected by way of court supervision and court orders and the court will be satisfied that there is no likelihood of the interests of creditors in Japan being unreasonably prejudiced.

far-reaching form of relief,[16] since the foreign priorities regime may be significantly different from that of the enacting State and so requiring the creditors' interests to be adequately protected is essential. The phrase 'adequately protected' is not defined in the MLCBI and is left to the interpretation of the local courts.

Akers as a joint foreign representative of Saad Investments Company Limited (in Official Liquidation) v Deputy Commissioner of Taxation[17] provides a detailed judicial discussion on local creditors being adequately protected. The joint foreign representatives were Cayman Islands liquidators of Saad Investments Company Limited (in official liquidation) (a company registered in the Cayman Islands), who appealed to the Full Court of the Federal Court of Australia over treatment of a claim by the Deputy Commissioner of Taxation ('DCT'), Australia's revenue office, that Saad was liable to Australian tax and penalties. Saad was not carrying on any business in Australia and could not be wound up by an Australian court under the Australian Corporations Act 2001 (Cth). The company had funds in Australia and the DCT claimed tax and penalties, although the difficulty for the DCT in the liquidation of the company in the Cayman Islands was that under Cayman Islands law his or her proof would not be accepted, on the basis that to do so would be to enforce foreign revenue laws.[18] Allsop CJ acknowledged that Article 21(2) was important as it contained an express recognition of the need to adequately protect the interests of local creditors. He noted that Article 21(2), together with Article 22(1), must be recalled and taken account of when statements of universalist principles of the MLCBI are being relied on. He said that if this language of characterization is to be employed, then Article 21(2) reflects a degree of modified universalism in the MLCBI and it concerns entrusting the distribution of local assets to the foreign representative, a subject closely related to the subjects of Article 20(1).[19] The DCT submitted in applying Article 21(2) that the focus was upon the DCT's position because it was the creditor whose domestic rights were to be destroyed by the repatriation of the moneys to the Cayman Islands. The DCT submitted that the limitation on recovery which had been ordered by the primary judge put the DCT in a position of parity with other 1.21.19

16 Gerard McCormack & Anil Hargovan, 'Australia and the International Insolvency Paradigm' (2015) 37 *Sydney Law Review* 389, 395.

17 *Akers as a joint foreign representative of Saad Investments Company Limited (in Official Liquidation) v Deputy Commissioner of Taxation* [2014] FCAFC 57.

18 *Akers as a joint foreign representative of Saad Investments Company Limited (in Official Liquidation) v Deputy Commissioner of Taxation* [2014] FCAFC 57 [3].

19 *Akers as a joint foreign representative of Saad Investments Company Limited (in Official Liquidation) v Deputy Commissioner of Taxation* [2014] FCAFC 57 [58].

creditors (assuming equal enforcement). The DCT submitted that adequate protection of all creditors involved the notion of relativity. The posited lack of any enforcement by the DCT in Australia would create a relative injustice among all the creditors. The DCT argued that a windfall would be created for foreign creditors by the remittance to the Cayman Islands of untaxed profits. The application of Article 21(2) could assist local creditors by implementing a cap which would satisfy the adequate protection of all creditors in accordance with Article 22(1).[20] The DCT further submitted that the question of adequate protection was an evaluative consideration within a discretion. In exercising that discretion, and in making that evaluation, the court was entitled to have regard to the Guide to Enactment and Interpretation, in which there is a discussion of the turning over of assets to foreign representatives and its discretionary character. The Guide to Enactment and Interpretation notes that the MLCBI contains several safeguards designed to ensure the protection of local interests before assets are turned over to the foreign representatives and among them is Article 21(2).[21]

1.21.20 In *Akers as a joint foreign representative of Saad Investments Company Limited (in Official Liquidation) v Deputy Commissioner of Taxation* Allsop CJ agreed that Article 21(2) is a two-step process, this being evaluation and then discretion. Using precedent to explore the meaning of 'adequate protection', the judgment noted that in one case[22] a court had analysed what was meant by the term 'adequate protection', suggesting that 'adequate' was a word that imports notions of relativity and had been defined in a dictionary as 'equal to the requirement or occasion; fully sufficient, suitable, or fit'. In other words, the protection as to which the court is required to be satisfied is not protection which is absolute or perfect in all circumstances, but protection which is adequate or suitable considering the circumstances which actually prevail.[23] Allsop CJ also considered *In Re Atlas Shipping A/S, a Danish Corporation*,[24] where the United States Bankruptcy Court was dealing with s1521(b) of the United States Bankruptcy Code, the equivalent to Article 21. He quoted from the case that 'one Court has described "sufficient protection" [...] as embodying three basic principles: "the just treatment of all holders of claims against the bankruptcy estate, the

20 *Akers as a joint foreign representative of Saad Investments Company Limited (in Official Liquidation) v Deputy Commissioner of Taxation* [2014] FCAFC 57 [124].

21 *Akers as a joint foreign representative of Saad Investments Company Limited (in Official Liquidation) v Deputy Commissioner of Taxation* [2014] FCAFC 57 [125].

22 *Debis Financial Services (Aust) Pty Limited v Allied Bellambi Collieries Pty Limited* [1999] NSWSC 935.[14].

23 *Akers as a joint foreign representative of Saad Investments Company Limited (in Official Liquidation) v Deputy Commissioner of Taxation* [2014] FCAFC 57 [126].

24 *In Re Atlas Shipping A/S, a Danish Corporation* (2009) 404 B.R. 726.

protection of US claimants against prejudice and inconvenience in the processing of claims in the [foreign] proceedings, and the distribution of proceeds of the [foreign] estate substantially in accordance with the order prescribed by US law".'[25] He concluded that the notion of sufficient or adequate protection involves an evaluation of the protection afforded to relevant creditors.[26] Allsop CJ summarized that the balancing of the protection of the local creditor under Article 21(2) and the protection of all creditors under Article 22(1) was achieved by recognizing the equality of all creditors, when considering the dealing with, and access to, the funds of the company.[27] Academic commentary has questioned the usefulness of the judgment, in that it does raise the issue of asset transfers abroad, yet its facts were so extreme – that is, the complete denial of the Australian creditors' claim under the law of the main proceedings – that the Full Federal Court was wise to avoid making any general pronouncements on the meaning of 'adequate protection' in Article 21(2).[28]

2. Examinations and Discovery and 'any Additional Relief'

The discretionary relief available in Article 21(1)(d) and (1)(g) moves beyond property and actions and provides for examinations, delivery of information and any additional relief. In the English case of *Akers & Anor v Deutsche Bank AG*[29] these two subparagraphs, namely (1)(d) and (1)(g), were central to large insolvency administration. In the case the applicants who applied for Article 21 orders were the joint liquidators appointed by the Eastern Caribbean Supreme Court of two companies that were incorporated in the British Virgin Islands, Chesterfield United Inc and Partridge Management Group SA. Both of these companies were owned by offshore vehicles which were in turn owned by high net-worth individuals associated with the Icelandic bank Kaupthing hf. Chesterfield and Partridge were incorporated as special purpose vehicles. The liquidators' appointment was recognized by the English High Court. The liquidators made applications for orders that the respondent, Deutsche Bank AG, be required to produce various documents relying upon both Article 21(1)(d) and (1)(g). In the English High Court, Newey J noted that, while it was common ground between the parties that the relief available to a 'British **1.21.21**

25 *Akers as a joint foreign representative of Saad Investments Company Limited (in Official Liquidation) v Deputy Commissioner of Taxation* [2014] FCAFC 57 [127].

26 *Akers as a joint foreign representative of Saad Investments Company Limited (in Official Liquidation) v Deputy Commissioner of Taxation* [2014] FCAFC 57 [128].

27 *Akers as a joint foreign representative of Saad Investments Company Limited (in Official Liquidation) v Deputy Commissioner of Taxation* [2014] FCAFC 57 [139].

28 Gerard McCormack & Anil Hargovan, 'Australia and the International Insolvency Paradigm' (2015) 37 *Sydney Law Review* 389, 416.

29 *Akers & Anor v Deutsche Bank AG* [2012] EWHC (Ch) 244.

insolvency officeholder' can potentially include an order under section 236 of the local Insolvency Act 1986 (UK) for the production of books, papers or other records relating to the relevant company or 'the promotion, formation, business, dealings, affairs or property of the company', it was disputed whether Article 21(1)(g) allows foreign representatives to take advantage of that local section 236. Deutsche Bank contended that, where what is sought is the provision of information, Article 21(1)(d) must prevail. If the position were otherwise, it is said, there would have been no reason to make express provision in Article 21(1)(d) for the delivery of information.[30] Newey J stated that Article 21(1)(d) was intended to set a common minimum standard. A foreign representative is to be able to seek relief under Article 21(1)(d), regardless of whether an officeholder would be entitled to such relief under the local law. If the local law in fact provided for 'additional' relief, a foreign representative could seek that under Article 21(1)(g).[31] Newey J referred to the Guide to Enactment and Interpretation of the UNCITRAL Model Law, which states (in paragraph 154) that the list of types of relief to be found in Article 21(1) is 'not exhaustive' and the court 'is not restricted unnecessarily in its ability to grant any type of relief that is available under the law of the enacting State and needed in the circumstances of the case'.[32] In finding for the liquidators and agreeing to the orders, Newey J rejected that the precise scope of Article 21(1)(d) was important for this case and agreed with the liquidators that, if Article 21(1)(d) is narrower than section 236 of the local law, that is of no consequence. The liquidators could, via Article 21(1)(g), rely on section 236 of the local UK Insolvency Act.[33] While Deutsche Bank claimed Article 21(1) provided for the court to have power to grant relief 'where necessary to protect the assets of the debtor or the interests of the creditors', Newey J did not regard such words as significantly curtailing the court's ability to grant relief under the local section 236 in cases such as this one. A proper case in which to grant relief under the local section 236 is one where an officeholder 'reasonably requires' to see documents to carry out his or her functions[34] and so, if a foreign representative 'reasonably requires' material with a view to establishing whether a company has a valuable course of action, then relief is likely to be 'necessary to protect the assets of the debtor or the interests of the creditors'.[35] The court exercised its discretion and ordered disclosure with Newey J expressing that the

30 *Akers & Anor v Deutsche Bank AG* [2012] EWHC (Ch) 244 [10].

31 *Akers & Anor v Deutsche Bank AG* [2012] EWHC (Ch) 244 [11].

32 *Akers & Anor v Deutsche Bank AG* [2012] EWHC (Ch) 244 [11].

33 *Akers & Anor v Deutsche Bank AG* [2012] EWHC (Ch) 244 [12].

34 *British & Commonwealth Holdings plc v Spicer & Oppenheim* [1993] AC 426 at 439.

35 *Akers & Anor v Deutsche Bank AG* [2012] EWHC (Ch) 244 [13].

order was, 'in the words of Article 21(1), "necessary to protect the assets of the debtor or the interests of the creditors".'[36]

There is some debate as to whether 'any appropriate relief' as expressed in Article 21(1)(g) could be granted by a court if the type of relief was not available under local law.[37] In *Fibria Celulose S/A v Pan Ocean Co Ltd & Anor*[38] Mr Justice Morgan noted that the textbooks appear to favour a limitation on the relief which might be granted under Article 21 to relief which would be available under local domestic law in relation to a local domestic insolvency and he referenced 'Fletcher on Insolvency in Private International Law, 2nd ed. at para. 8.38 and Sheldon on Cross Border Insolvency, 3rd ed. at paras. 3.91–3.100.'[39] Morgan J conducted a detailed exploration into this question. He started with *Rubin v Eurofinance SA*[40] where it was suggested that a judgment of a New York court should be recognized in England pursuant to Article 21. In that case Lord Collins referred to the Guide to Enactment and Interpretation and stated that enacting states could make available 'the type of relief that would be available in the case of a domestic insolvency'.[41] Lord Collins said that it would be surprising if the MLCBI was intended to deal with judgments in insolvency matters by implication and that Article 21 was concerned with procedural matters and, in his view, it should be given a purposive interpretation and should be widely construed in the light of the objects of the MLCBI. 1.21.22

In *Fibria Celulose S/A v Pan Ocean Co Ltd & Anor* Morgan J referenced a number of cases that in some way dealt with the question of scope of Article 21. He noted that in *Re Atlas Shipping A/S*[42] the New York court held that many of the principles from the former Bankruptcy Code remained in effect in relation to Chapter 15 and that the jurisdiction to grant 'appropriate relief' was 'exceedingly broad'.[43] He noted in *Gandi Innovations Holdings LLC*[44] that a Texas court recognized a foreign proceeding in Canada which had made an order under the Canadian legislation prohibiting the termination of execu- 1.21.23

36 *Akers & Anor v Deutsche Bank AG* [2012] EWHC (Ch) 244 [17].

37 See for example the strident criticism by Ho in 'England' in Ho (ed.) *A Commentary on the UNCITRAL Model Law* (4th ed) Globe Law & Business (London) 2017.

38 *Fibria Celulose S/A v Pan Ocean Co. Ltd & Anor* [2014] EWHC 2124.

39 *Fibria Celulose S/A v Pan Ocean Co. Ltd & Anor* [2014] EWHC 2124 (Ch) [92].

40 *Rubin v Eurofinance SA* [2013] 1 AC 236.

41 *Rubin v Eurofinance SA* [2013] 1 AC 236 [28] and cited by Morgan J in *Fibria Celulose S/A v Pan Ocean Co. Ltd & Anor* [2014] EWHC 2124 (Ch) [90].

42 *Re Atlas Shipping A/S* 404 BR 726 (Bankr SD NY, 2009).

43 *Fibria Celulose S/A v Pan Ocean Co. Ltd & Anor* [2014] EWHC 2124 (Ch) [94].

44 *Gandi Innovations Holdings LLC* (Bankr WD Texas, 2009).

tory contracts without the leave of the court. The Texas court acting under s 1521 of the US Bankruptcy Code made its own order to the same extent as the Canadian order.[45] He noted *Re Condor Insurance Co Ltd*,[46] which was a decision of the United States Court of Appeals. The case concerned a Nevis insurance company which was the subject of a winding-up order in Nevis. The United States court recognized the Nevis proceedings as foreign main proceedings. The case raised the question whether there was power under s 1521 of the US Bankruptcy Code to apply foreign law (Nevis Law) for the purpose of avoiding fraudulent transfers. The alternative of opening proceedings in the United States under Chapter 7 of the Bankruptcy Code was not available because the company was a foreign insurance company. Under Chapter 7, the United States court would have had extensive powers to avoid fraudulent transfers. The US court held that it had the power to apply Nevis law because it could grant 'appropriate relief' under s 1521. This decision supported an interpretation of those words which would allow the recognizing court to give effect to an order of the court of the foreign proceedings even if the recognizing court could not itself have made such an order in its own domestic proceedings.[47] Morgan J also referenced *Re Hartford Computer Hardware Inc*,[48] where the Canadian court recognized United States Chapter 11 proceedings. It was pointed out that one part of the United States order could not be made by a Canadian court in relation to a Canadian insolvency under its domestic insolvency provisions yet the Canadian court held that under the adopted Article 21 provision it could make any order which it considered appropriate, and it concluded that the order requested was indeed appropriate.[49]

1.21.24 In *Fibria Celulose S/A v Pan Ocean Co Ltd & Anor* Morgan J was not persuaded that the words 'any appropriate relief' allowed him to grant relief which would not be available to the court when dealing with a domestic insolvency. [50] In reaching this conclusion Morgan J conceded that the non-exhaustive words 'any appropriate relief' were capable of being given a wide literal meaning. However, the very width of their literal meaning made him 'somewhat cautious about construing the words literally' and suggested that it was not intended that the words should be given such a wide literal meaning.[51] Morgan J also considered the reports of the UNCITRAL working group and deter-

45 *Fibria Celulose S/A v Pan Ocean Co. Ltd & Anor* [2014] EWHC 2124 [95].

46 *Re Condor Insurance Co Ltd* 601 F 3d 319 (Fifth Circuit 2010).

47 *Fibria Celulose S/A v Pan Ocean Co. Ltd & Anor* [2014] EWHC 2124 [106].

48 *Re Hartford Computer Hardware Inc* (2012) 94 CBR (5th) 20.

49 *Fibria Celulose S/A v Pan Ocean Co. Ltd & Anor* [2014] EWHC 2124 [100].

50 *Fibria Celulose S/A v Pan Ocean Co. Ltd & Anor* [2014] EWHC 2124 [108].

51 *Fibria Celulose S/A v Pan Ocean Co. Ltd & Anor* [2014] EWHC 2124 [105].

mined that it was not intended that 'any appropriate relief' would allow the recognizing court to go beyond the relief it would grant in relation to a domestic insolvency.[52]

Another important case that considers Article 21 is *Leite v Amicorp (Re Industria De Alimentos Nilza Sa Buglin Participacoes Ltda)* [2020] EWHC 3560 (Ch) and *Cooper, Leite v. Amicorp* [2020] EWHC 3560 (Ch), (2021), 18 ICR, 137 et seq. Leite, a Judicial Administrator of Nilza, Brazil, had been appointed on an interim basis, pursuant to the Brazilian Bankruptcy Law, Civil Code and Stock Corporations Law, pending final determination of the Extension Applications (these are where the Brazilian Court finds evidence of abuse of a company's corporate structure, co-mingling and misappropriation of assets between a bankrupt company and other individuals and entities closely connected to it, then the court has the power to 'extend' the bankruptcy proceedings to these parties in order to make them jointly liable for the bankrupt company's debts). These were found to be collective proceedings pursuant to a law relating to insolvency for the purposes of the Cross-Border Insolvency Regulations 2006 (UK) and considered 'foreign main proceedings'. Such Extension Applications do not have a direct parallel in UK law. **1.21.25**

Leite, as the foreign representative of Nilza, sought relief pursuant to Article 21(1)(e) and 21(1)(g) and/or section 236 of the Insolvency Act 1986 (UK) to order Amicorp (UK) Ltd to disclose documents and information to Leite. **1.21.26**

Mr Justice Burton in the High Court of England and Wales was provided with extensive evidence of a number of other individuals and entities having a likely connection to Nilza and informed that Amicorp was prepared to cooperate but underlined that it was bound by duties of confidentiality to its clients and could only disclose information when required to do so by law, including by court order.[53] Burton J addressed s236(3) of the Insolvency Act 1986 (UK), which provides that the court may require any person known or suspected to have in his possession any property of the company or whom the court thinks capable of giving information concerning the promotion, formation, business dealings, affairs or property of the company ('Relevant Information') to submit an account of such dealings to the court or to produce any books, papers or other records in his possession or under his control relating to the company **1.21.27**

52 *Fibria Celulose S/A v Pan Ocean Co. Ltd & Anor* [2014] EWHC 2124 [107].

53 *Leite v. Amicorp (Re Industria De Alimentos Nilza Sa Buglin Participacoes Ltda)* [2020] EWHC 3560 (Ch) [64].

or which is Relevant Information.[54] Burton J noted that when considering an application under section 236, the court's discretion is unfettered but, as set out in *Re British & Commonwealth Holdings plc* [1993] AC 426, the court will conduct a careful balancing exercise, asking whether the officeholder reasonably requires the information to carry out his task. Burton J observed that '[T]he officeholder's view as to whether information is reasonably required carries a good deal of weight. In carrying out the balancing exercise, the court will be astute to avoid making an order which is wholly unreasonable, unnecessary or oppressive.'[55] The Court was satisfied that if Amicorp held any documents belonging to, or containing Relevant Information concerning, Nilza or its connected entities named Buglin and Endipa, then these documents fell within the scope of section 236 and should be disclosed to Leite.[56] Where there was less direct evidence as to other connected entities, such as a connected entity named Tipuana, Burton J mooted that '[T]he court will not make an order under section 236 which it considers would be unreasonable, unnecessary or oppressive',[57] yet he still found it appropriate to grant relief based upon work already conducted in the Brazilian court. Without close reconciliation between section 236(3) and Article 21(1)(g) in the judgment Burton J concluded it was appropriate to grant relief pursuant to Article 21(1)(g) by making an order requiring Amicorp to disclose to Leite documents and Relevant Information it held.[58]

1.21.28 In *Re Tantleff, Alan* [2022] SGHC 147 the Singaporean High Court considered the use of Article 21, particularly Article 21(1)(g). The Court considered both the US and UK approaches, noting that the US courts are open to recognizing and enforcing foreign insolvency-related orders and judgments from various jurisdictions whereas the UK courts have taken a much more conservative and circumscribed position with regard to interpreting Article 21. The Singaporean court also noted that the Singapore Ministry of Law had expressed its preference for the US approach in relation to Article 21(1)(g) over the UK approach in the Ministry's Response to Feedback from Public

---

54 *Leite v. Amicorp (Re Industria De Alimentos Nilza Sa Buglin Participacoes Ltda)* [2020] EWHC 3560 (Ch) [66].

55 *Leite v. Amicorp (Re Industria De Alimentos Nilza Sa Buglin Participacoes Ltda)* [2020] EWHC 3560 (Ch) [67].

56 *Leite v. Amicorp (Re Industria De Alimentos Nilza Sa Buglin Participacoes Ltda)* [2020] EWHC 3560 (Ch) [68].

57 *Leite v. Amicorp (Re Industria De Alimentos Nilza Sa Buglin Participacoes Ltda)* [2020] EWHC 3560 (Ch) [72].

58 *Leite v. Amicorp (Re Industria De Alimentos Nilza Sa Buglin Participacoes Ltda)* [2020] EWHC 3560 (Ch) [76].

Consultation on the Draft Companies (Amendment) Bill 2017 to Strengthen Singapore as an International Centre for Debt Restructuring.[59] [60]

The Singaporean Court held that the US approach should be preferred, and it is the US jurisprudence which should be persuasive in determining the scope of relief to be granted.[61] The Court accepted the arguments that the Singapore court is empowered under Article 21(1)(g) of the MLCBI to grant recognition of the US Chapter 11 Plan and Confirmation Order in this case as foreign orders, following the proposition found in the US authorities.[62] It did not matter that there was a difference in the language of the enacting provisions in the US and Singapore.[63] Additionally, while the version of Article 21(1)(g) enacted in Singapore contains the modifier 'available to a Singapore insolvency officeholder' after 'any additional relief', the court did not read Article 21(1)(g) to be so restricted, and stated that 'in line with the Ministry of Law's comments' the scope of relief that may be granted should follow the US approach and the US provisions which contain a similar modifier.[64] **1.21.29**

The court in *Re Tantleff* demonstrated how they would take an expansive view of Article 21. For instance, the Court noted that the section heading of Article 21(1) of the MLCBI contains the phrase 'any appropriate relief'. It said that 'invoking the section heading alone would circumvent the issue that the enforcement of a foreign rehabilitation plan is not ordinarily "relief that may be available to a Singapore insolvency officeholder" under Article 21(1)(g) of the Model Law'.[65] **1.21.30**

The outcome of this judgment in granting recognition and enforcement of foreign insolvency judgments and orders was not to be seen, in the words of the Singapore court, as the local court 'merely acting as a rubber stamp'.[66] The court pointed to the guidance laid down in the US case of In *re CGG SA* 579 BR 716 (Bankr SDNY, 2017), suggesting that it 'must carefully scrutinize the circumstances in which the foreign order was granted and ensure that interested parties were given an opportunity to be heard and that the relevant creditors and shareholders are adequately protected'.[67] They noted that this is **1.21.31**

59 *Re Tantleff, Alan* [2022] SGHC 147 [77].
60 See www.mlaw.gov.sg/files/Annex_A-Goverment_ at para 116.
61 *Re Tantleff, Alan* [2022] SGHC 147 [78].
62 *Re Tantleff, Alan* [2022] SGHC 147 [78].
63 *Re Tantleff, Alan* [2022] SGHC 147 [78].
64 *Re Tantleff, Alan* [2022] SGHC 147 [78].
65 *Re Tantleff, Alan* [2022] SGHC 147 [79].
66 *Re Tantleff, Alan* [2022] SGHC 147 [81].
67 *Re Tantleff, Alan* [2022] SGHC 147 [81].

a requirement encapsulated in Article 22(1) of the MLCBI which provides that in granting relief under Article 21, the court must be satisfied that the interests of the creditors and other interested persons, including if appropriate the debtor, are 'adequately protected'.[68]

68 *Re Tantleff, Alan* [2022] SGHC 147 [81].

Article 22

SCOPE OF APPLICATION

Reinhard Bork

1. In granting or denying relief under Articles 19 or 21, or in modifying or terminating relief under paragraph 3 of this article, the court must be satisfied that the interests of the creditors and other interested persons, including the debtor, are adequately protected.
2. The court may subject relief granted under Articles 19 or 21 to conditions it considers appropriate.
3. The court may, at the request of the foreign representative or a person affected by relief granted under Articles 19 or 21, or at its own motion, modify or terminate such relief.

A. INTRODUCTION TO ARTICLE 22

1. Rationale

Article 22 guides the court in the exercise of discretion under Articles 19 and 21. These provisions allow the foreign representative to request a wide range of measures, the granting of which is at the discretion of the court. However, because the relief requested will often affect many persons with different inter- **1.22.01** ests, Article 22(1) imposes a mandatory requirement that the interests of all interested persons be adequately protected when granting, denying or modifying (Article 22(3)) relief. The requirement of adequate protection is the central feature of Article 22. It is not defined in the MLCBI. Methodologically, it requires balancing the often conflicting interests of creditors, the debtor and other interested persons.[1] Such a balance is essential, according to the *Guide to Enactment and Interpretation*, to achieve the objectives of cross-border insolvency legislation.[2] The concrete application, that is, the question of what kind of interests are to be protected and how different interests are to be weighed, is left to the discretion of the court. It is difficult to make general statements here, as the courts in the enacting states could set different priorities. Thus, Article 22(1) is subject to a certain degree of legal uncertainty. Paragraphs (2) and (3) build on the requirement of adequate protection under Article 22(1) and allow the court to impose conditions on the relief and to modify or terminate it later.

2. Scope of Application

1.22.02 Article 22 can be divided into three different provisions according to its paragraphs. All paragraphs must be seen against the objective set out in Article 22(1) that the interests of all interested persons be adequately protected. In this regard, Article 22(1) serves as a general standard. In addition to its mandatory character, it is supposed to provide a useful guidance for the court in exercising its discretion under Articles 19, 21 and 22(3).[3] All these articles have in common that they are discretionary in nature. Article 22(1) was deliberately not intended to refer to automatic relief, as it follows, for example, from

---

1 *UNCITRAL Model Law on Cross-Border Insolvency with Guide to Enactment and Interpretation, United Nations Publications* (New York), 2014, para. 196; *The Judicial Perspective*, United Nations Publications (New York), 2014, para. 157.

2 *Guide to Enactment and Interpretation* (n 1), para. 196; moreover, one of the objectives of the MLCBI, as stated in paragraph (c) of the Preamble, is to promote a fair and efficient administration of cross-border insolvencies that protects the interests of all creditors and other interested persons, including the debtor; according to Wessels and Berends, a further background to the provision could be the fear of abuse of the MLCBI in the opening state of the foreign proceeding. Abuse could result, for example, from the fact that corruption prevails, and the courts are not independent of the government, see Bob Wessels, International Insolvency Law Part I., 5th ed., Wolters Kluwer (Deventer), 2022, para. 10316 citing Andre J. Berends, 'The UNCITRAL Model Law on Cross-Border Insolvency: A Comprehensive Overview' (1998), 6 Tul. J. Int'l & Comp. L., 309, 373.

3 *Guide to Enactment and Interpretation* (n 1), para. 197; 'The reference to the interests of creditors, the debtor other interested parties in paragraph (1) was found to provide concrete elements to guide the court in assessing the impact of relief measures requested to be granted under article 15 or 17 [now Articles 19 and 21]', see UNCITRAL, Report of the United Nations Commission on International Trade Law on the work of its 30th session, A/52/17, United Nations Publications (New York), 1997, para. 84.

Articles 17 and 20.[4] In particular, the recognition of the foreign proceeding (Article 17) had to be predictable and required precise conditions.[5] In contrast to Article 21(2), the protection of Article 22(1) is not limited to local interests.[6] Rather, the provision serves to protect all interested persons, regardless of their nationality or place of business.[7] Nevertheless, a tendency can be discerned in case law that Article 22(1) is applied in particular when the interests of local creditors do not seem to be adequately protected in the foreign proceedings.[8] Article 22(2) permits the court to impose the requested relief under conditions it deems appropriate. This allows the court to tailor the relief to the specific case.[9] According to Article 22(3), the court may subsequently modify or terminate the relief granted. Such modification or termination may be initiated by the foreign representative, or any person affected by the relief. However, the court also has this possibility ex officio, as the provision explicitly states. Article 22 in general shall operate in the context of the procedural system of the enacting state.[10]

B. PROTECTION OF INTERESTS (ARTICLE 22(1))

Article 22(1) applies whenever the foreign representative requests provisional relief under Article 19 or discretionary relief under Article 21, or whenever the foreign representative, an interested person or the court subsequently wishes to amend the relief granted (Article 22(3)). Before deciding, it is mandatory for the court to consider the interests of all interested persons and to strike an appropriate balance.[11] As a result of this balancing test, it must be satisfied that the interests of all persons affected by the relief be adequately protected. The provision uses two phrases in this regard, the understanding of which is crucial to the application of Article 22(1). First is the term 'interested persons', which is decisive to determine the personal scope of the provision. Article 22(1) mentions creditors and the debtor as examples, but this is not exhaustive. Second, **1.22.03**

---

4 UNCITRAL, Report of the Working Group on Insolvency Law of the work of its Twenty-First Session, A/CN.9/435, United Nations Publications (New York), 1997, para. 73; Report A/52/17 (n 3) para. 86.

5 Report A/52/17 (n 3), para. 86.

6 See in detail below para. 1.22.05 et seq.

7 *Guide to Enactment and Interpretation* (n 1), para. 198.

8 See for example, *Jaffé v Samsung Electronics Co. Ltd*, 737 F.3d 14 (4th Cir. 2013); *Ad Hoc Group of Vitro Noteholders v Vitro S.A.B. de C.V*, 701 F.3d 1031 (5th Cir. 2012); *In re Sivec SRL*, 476 BR 310 (Bankr. ED Okla. 2012); *Ackers v Saad Investments Company Limited* [2013] FCA 738.

9 *Guide to Enactment and Interpretation* (n 1), para. 191.

10 As an example, the *Guide to Enactment and Interpretation* lists that the protection of all interested persons is linked to provisions in national laws on notification requirements: see Guide to Enactment and Interpretation (n 1), para. 199.

11 *Guide to Enactment and Interpretation* (n 1), para. 196; *The Judicial Perspective* (n 1), para. 157.

and even more important, is the notion of adequate protection. Neither the MLCBI nor the accompanying legislative materials specify what kinds of interests are to be protected and how different interests are to be weighed. This is left entirely to the discretion of the court in the recognizing state.

1. Interested Persons

1.22.04 Interested persons is the generic term for persons who may be affected by the grant of relief.[12] Article 22(1) distinguishes between creditors, who have a prominent position, and other interested persons, including the debtor.

(a) Creditors

1.22.05 The relief requested by the foreign representative often conflicts with the interests of local creditors.[13] Moreover, Article 22(1) is one of the safeguards in the MLCBI designed to ensure that local interests are protected before assets are turned over to the foreign representative.[14] Nevertheless, the scope of Article 22(1) is not limited to the protection of local creditors. While Article 21(2) explicitly refers to the protection of creditors in the enacting state, Article 22(1) refers to creditors without limitation. Moreover, the Preamble relates its objective of a fair and efficient administration of cross-border insolvencies to all creditors and not only local creditors.[15] Thus, the *Guide to Enactment and Interpretation* advises not to limit the protection to local creditors. There would be no justification for discriminating against creditors solely on the basis of criteria such as nationality or place of business.[16]

1.22.06 Such an understanding is also supported by case law. In the US in particular, courts have dealt with the personal scope of 11 USC § 1522(a) (which

12 *Guide to Enactment and Interpretation* (n 1), para. 196; *The Judicial Perspective* (n 1), para. 157; although the term '*interested persons*' is not defined in the MLCBI, it is used in paragraph (c) of the Preamble and in Article 1(d), in addition to Article 22.

13 *Jaffé v Samsung Electronics Co. Ltd*, 737 F.3d 14, 27 et seq. (4th Cir. 2013): 'In many cases the affected creditors will be "local" creditors', see *Guide to Enactment and Interpretation* (n 1), para. 198.

14 The *Guide to Enactment and Interpretation* expressly states: 'It should be noted that the Model Law contains several safeguards designed to ensure the protection of local interests before assets are turned over to the foreign representative. Those safeguards include the following: the general statement of the principle of protection of local interests in article 22, paragraph 1; the provision in article 21, paragraph 2, that the court should not authorize the turnover of assets until it is assured that the local creditors' interests are protected; and article 22, paragraph 2, according to which the court may subject the relief that it grants to conditions it considers appropriate': *Guide to Enactment and Interpretation* (n 1), para. 192.

15 See paragraph (c) of the Preamble.

16 *Guide to Enactment and Interpretation* (n 1), para. 198; also, giving local interests more weight than is appropriate is endangering the proper functioning of universal insolvency proceedings and undermining the principle of universalism as well as damaging any serious harmonization effort: see Reinhard Bork, Principles of Cross-Border Insolvency Law, Intersentia (Cambridge/Antwerp/Chicago), 2017, para. 2.29.

implements Article 22(1)). In *In re Sphinx Ltd*,[17] the court highlighted two important aspects of the provision. First, Congress would have directed courts to consider the interests of all creditors and other interested persons, not just the interests of US parties. Second, the provision must be interpreted in light of the objective, as stated by 11 USC § 1501(a), which is similar to paragraph (c) of the Preamble, that courts should protect the parties' interests by implementing fair, efficient and cooperative procedures designed to maximize the value of the debtor's assets for distribution.[18] In *SNP Boat Service SA v Hotel Le St. James*,[19] the court addressed the differences in the application of 11 USC § 1522(a) and 11 USC § 1521(b) (which implements Article 21(2)). This was preceded by the question of whether the US court could consider the interests of a Canadian creditor under 11 USC § 1522(a). The court stated that while it must be satisfied that the interests of local creditors are sufficiently protected before allowing a foreign representative to distribute property in a foreign proceeding (11 USC § 1521(b)), though not an express requirement, it would not be precluded from satisfying itself that foreign creditors' interests are sufficiently protected before allowing a foreign representative to distribute property in a foreign proceeding (11 USC § 1522(a)).[20]

(b) Other Interested Persons

Other interested persons are those whose interests, in addition to creditors' interests, may be affected by the relief requested.[21] Article 22(1) mentions the debtor as an example. However, a wider range of persons may be considered.[22] In past cases, such third parties have, for example, included persons against whom an order for delivery of information is sought,[23] licensees that may have to be protected against the loss of their licenses[24] or members of the debtor's group that may be protected against the foreign representative's claim to **1.22.07**

17 *In re Sphinx Ltd*, 351 BR 103 (Bankr. SDNY 2006).

18 *In re Sphinx Ltd*, 351 BR 103, 113 (Bankr. SDNY 2006).

19 *SNP Boat Service S.A. v Hotel Le St. James*, 483 BR 776 (SD Fla. 2012); for this decision, see also below in para. 1.22.16.

20 *SNP Boat Service S.A. v. Hotel Le St. James*, 483 BR 776, 784 (SD Fla. 2012); see also *In re Sivec SRL*, 476 BR 310, 323 (Bankr. ED Okla. 2012), where the court stated: 'To ensure a party's interests are "sufficiently protected", the bankruptcy court should balance the relief sought by the foreign representative against the interests of those affected by the relief, without unduly favoring one group of creditors over another.'

21 *Guide to Enactment and Interpretation* (n 1), para. 196; *The Judicial Perspective* (n 1), para. 157.

22 Instead of the term 'person', the terms 'party' or 'entity' are sometimes used by courts in the enacting states, see *In re Zhejiang Topoint Photovoltaic Co. Ltd*, Case No. 14-24549(GMB), para. 5 (Bankr. DNJ May 12, 2015).

23 *Picard (Foreign Rep. of Bernard Madoff Investment Securities LLC) v FIM Advisers LLP* [2010] EWHC 1299 [para. 22].

24 *Jaffé v Samsung Electronics Co. Ltd*, 737 F.3d 14, 32 (4th Cir. 2013); for details, see below in para. 1.22.10 et seq.

sealed information.[25] In *In re Zhejiang Topoint Photovoltaic Co. Ltd*,[26] a US court interpreted the term more generally. Based on the purpose of 11 USC § 1522(a), the term must be interpreted broadly to include all persons potentially affected by the relief requested by the foreign representative.[27] This interpretation would also be consistent with the interpretation of comparable terms in the Bankruptcy Code, which could be relied upon because of the limited case law on the issue.[28] For example, the term 'party in interest' (in the context of 11 USC § 1109(b)) would have to be 'construed broadly to permit parties affected by a Chapter 11 proceeding to appear and be heard' and courts would have to 'determine on a case by case basis whether the prospective party in interest has a sufficient stake in the proceeding [...]'.[29]

2. Adequate Protection

1.22.08 Adequate protection is the central concept in Article 22. It plays a crucial role not only in the context of Article 22(1), but also in respect of the question whether relief should be granted subject to conditions (Article 22(2)) or subsequently modified or terminated (Article 22(3)). Because the MLCBI does not provide examples of when a person's interests are not adequately protected and how a person's interests might be adequately protected, the interpretation of courts in the implementing states is determinative. However, it is difficult to identify a consistent line there. Rather, there is a similar methodological approach, but the protected interests vary from case to case.

(a) USA

1.22.09 In the United States, Article 22(1) has been implemented by 11 USC § 1522(a). Deviating from the MLCBI, the provision uses the term 'sufficient protection', 'to avoid confusion with [...] "adequate protection", a very specialized term in United States bankruptcy'.[30] American courts have been by far the most involved in interpreting (the US implementation of) Article 22.

---

25 *In re Petroforto Brasileiro De Petroleo Ltda*, 530 BR 503, 514 (Bankr. SD Fla 2015).

26 *In re Zhejiang Topoint Photovoltaic Co. Ltd*, Case No. 14-24549(GMB) (Bankr. DNJ May 12, 2015).

27 *In re Zhejiang Topoint Photovoltaic Co. Ltd*, Case No. 14-24549(GMB), para. 5 (Bankr. D.N.J. May 12, 2015).

28 *In re Zhejiang Topoint Photovoltaic Co. Ltd*, Case No. 14-24549(GMB), para. 5 (Bankr. D.N.J. May 12, 2015).

29 *In re Zhejiang Topoint Photovoltaic Co. Ltd*, Case No. 14-24549(GMB), para. 5 (Bankr. D.N.J. May 12, 2015), citing *In re Amatex Corp.*, 755 F.2d 1034, 1042 (3rd Cir. 1985).

30 H.R.Rep. No. 109-31, pt. 1, at 115; 'The Code uses the term "sufficiently protected" to distinguish § 1521(b) [and § 1522(a)] from "adequate protection" under [11 U.S.C.] § 361.'; 'The standard for the protection is not the [11 USC] § 361 standard [...], there is no definition [of sufficient protection] in the statute.', Louise De Carl Adler, Managing the Chapter 15 Cross-Border Insolvency Case, 2nd ed., Federal Judicial Center (Washington DC), 2014, 33; see also *In re Atlas Shipping A/S*, 404 BR 726, 731 (Bankr. SDNY 2009).

The cases decided in the USA are therefore the main point of reference when seeking a judicial interpretation of adequate protection (or sufficient protection). In this regard, US courts follow a particular methodology to ensure that the interests of all interested persons are sufficiently protected.

(1) Balancing Test

To ensure adequate protection within the meaning of 11 USC § 1522(a), the court must strike a balance between the relief granted to the foreign representative and the interests of those affected by such relief, without unduly favouring one protected group over the other.[31] Such a balancing test is the methodological approach US courts are taking when faced with conflicting interests. This approach is explained in more detail by the Fourth Circuit Court of Appeals in *Jaffé vs. Samsung Electronics Co. Ltd.*[32] There, the court explained that '[11 USC] § 1522(a) requires the bankruptcy court to ensure the protection of both the creditors [or other interested persons] and the debtor. The provision thus requires the court to ensure that the relief a foreign representative requests under [11 USC] § 1521 does not impinge excessively on any one entity's interests, implying that each entity must receive at least some protection. And because the interests [...] are often antagonistic [...], providing protection to one side might well come at some expense to the other. The analysis required by [11 USC] § 1522(a) is therefore logically best done by balancing the respective interests based on the relative harms and benefits in light of the circumstances presented, thus inherently calling for application of a balancing test'.[33] **1.22.10**

The underlying case[34] concerned the liquidation of a German company, Qimonda AG, which specialized in the manufacture of semiconductor memory devices. The bulk of Qimonda's assets consisted of about 10,000 patents, of which 4,000 were US patents. Their use was mainly regulated by so-called cross-licensing agreements. These allowed Qimonda and its competitors to use each other's patents without the payment of royalties. The German insolvency administrator sought to terminate the agreements and to re-license the patents against the payment of royalties. While German insolvency law allowed him to take such an action,[35] this was not possible on the basis of the **1.22.11**

31 *In re Tri-Continental Exchange Ltd*, 349 BR 627, 637 (Bankr. ED Cal. 2006).

32 *Jaffé v Samsung Electronics Co. Ltd*, 737 F.3d 14 (4th Cir. 2013).

33 *Jaffé v Samsung Electronics Co. Ltd*, 737 F.3d 14, 27 et seq. (4th Cir. 2013); see also *In re Sanjel (USA) Inc.*, Case No. 16-50778-CAG, para. 8 (Bankr. WD Tex. Jul. 28, 2016).

34 *In re Qimonda AG Bankruptcy Litigation*, 433 BR 547 (ED Va. 2010); *In re Qimonda*, 462 BR 165 (Bankr. ED Va. 2011); *Jaffé v Samsung Electronics Co. Ltd*, 737 F.3d 14 (4th Cir. 2013).

35 § 103 of the German Insolvency Code allowed the German insolvency administrator to choose non-performance of current license contracts for patents.

Bankruptcy Code (11 USC § 365n[36]). In the following, he applied for recognition of the German insolvency proceeding as foreign main proceeding (11 USC § 1517) and requested that the Bankruptcy Court entrusted to him the administration of all of Qimonda's assets within the territorial jurisdiction of the United States (11 USC § 1521(a)(5)). This request was ultimately refused by the Bankruptcy Court because 'the balancing of debtor and creditor interests required by § 1522(a), Bankruptcy Code, [would] weigh in favor of making § 365(n) applicable [...] to administration of Qimonda's U.S. patents'.[37] The court based its decision mainly on the fact that 'the risk to the very substantial investment [the Licensees] collectively made in research and manufacturing facilities in the United States in reliance on the design freedom provided by the cross-license agreements' was to be weighted highly.[38] Qimonda's patent portfolio on the other hand would be, although losing value, 'by no means rendered worthless'.[39] The Fourth Circuit Court of Appeals affirmed the Bankruptcy Court's decision, holding that it reasonably balanced the conflicting interests.[40] Moreover, it would be aware that it would thus indirectly further the public policy that underlies 11 USC § 365(n).[41]

1.22.12 The decision of the Fourth Circuit Court of Appeals is viewed controversially because by deciding in favour of 11 USC § 365n, the court unforeseeably preferred the *lex causae* to the *lex fori concursus*.[42]

---

36 11 USC § 365(n) basically assigns, in the case of intellectual property licences, the right to decide on non-performance to the licensee.

37 *In re Qimonda*, 462 BR 165, 182 (Bankr. ED Va. 2011).

38 *In re Qimonda*, 462 BR 165, 182 et seq. (Bankr. ED Va. 2011).

39 *In re Qimonda*, 462 BR 165, 182 (Bankr. ED Va. 2011).

40 The German insolvency administrator had argued against the former decision that 11 USC § 1522(a) would merely be a procedural protection that is 'designed to ensure that all creditors could participate in the bankruptcy distribution on an equal footing and thus should not be used to protect parties from the substantive bankruptcy law that would otherwise apply in the foreign main proceeding.' Such public policy considerations, however, would only be possible under narrow circumstances under 11 USC § 1506. The Fourth Circuit Court of Appeals did not follow his argumentation. 11 USC § 1506's public policy exception would not foreclose use of a balancing analysis under 11 USC § 1522. The latter provision would require a particularized balancing analysis that considers the interests of all interested persons. 11 USC § 1506, on the other hand, would be an additional more general protection of US interests that may be evaluated apart from the particularized analysis of 11 USC § 1522(a): *Jaffé v Samsung Electronics Co. Ltd*, 737 F.3d 14, 27–29 (4th Cir. 2013).

41 *Jaffé v. Samsung Electronics Co. Ltd*, 737 F.3d 14, 32 (4th Cir. 2013); for further guidance see, *Bork*, (n 16), para. 4.54; Wessels (n 2), para. 10318; Ho in: Look Chan Ho (ed.), A Commentary on the UNCITRAL Model Law, 4th ed., Globe Law & Business (London), 2017, 278 et seq.

42 In its first decision, the Bankruptcy Court had still opposed the application of 11 USC § 365(n), see *In re Qimonda AG*, 2009 WL 4060083 (Bankr. ED Va. 2009); also, prior to the Fourth Circuit Court of Appeals' decision, the United States submitted an amicus brief arguing for the application of German law, see Brief for the United States as Amicus Curiae in Support of Neither Party, *In re Qimonda AG Bankruptcy Litigation*, 433 BR 547 (ED Va. Sep. 28, 2012) (No. 12-1802) (Doc. No. 25), 2012 WL 4812564; however, the Supreme Court denied the petition for a writ of certiorari in this case: *Jaffé v Samsung Electronics Co. Ltd*, 135 S.Ct. 66

(2) Interests

With regard to protected interests, it is difficult to make general statements. US courts have looked to the case law interpreting the legal predecessor of the Bankruptcy Code and to the principle of due process. Irrespective of this, the interests to be protected are assessed according to the specific circumstances of the individual case. **1.22.13**

When construing provisions in Chapter 15, courts are encouraged to look at case law interpreting its predecessor, 11 USC § 304.[43] Under 11 USC § 1521(b), courts specifically applied three criteria contained in 11 USC § 304(c) to determine which interests must be 'sufficiently protected'.[44] In this context, the court in *In re Artimm S.R.L.*[45] explained that sufficient protection would encompass three factors of former 11 USC § 304(c): 'the just treatment of all holders of claims against the bankruptcy estate, the protection of [...] claimants against prejudice and inconvenience in the processing of claims in the [foreign] proceeding, and the distribution of the proceeds of the [foreign] estate substantially in accordance with the order prescribed by U.S. law'.[46] This interpretation could also be helpful in the context of 11 USC § 1522(a), particularly where the position of creditors in foreign proceedings is affected. It has been invoked by US courts particularly when relief was sought under 11 USC § 1521(a)(5) in combination with 11 USC§ 1521(b).[47] **1.22.14**

(2014); for criticism, see Allan L. Gropper, (2014), The Curious Disappearance of Choice of Law as an Issue in Chapter 15 Cases, 9(1) Brook. J. Corp. Fin & Com. L., 57, 69–72; Andrew B. Dawson, The Problem of Local Methods in Cross-border Insolvencies (2015), 12(1) Berkeley Bus. LJ 45, 69–72; Louise De Carl Adler (n 30), 29; defending Gerard McCormack, US Exceptionalism and UK Localism: Cross-Border Insolvency Law in Comparative Perspective (2016), 36(1) Legal Studies, 136, 157 et seq.; John H. Chung, In re Qimonda AG: The Conflict between Comity and the Public Policy Exception in Chapter 15 of the Bankruptcy Code (2014), 32(1) B.U. Int'l LJ, 89.

43 'The legislative history to Chapter 15 directs courts to use case law interpreting former § 304 in interpreting current Chapter 15 issues, unless the former § 304 is contradicted by the current provisions of Chapter 15': see H.R.Rep. No. 109-31, pt. 1, at 145; although Chapter 15 replaced § 304 of the US Bankruptcy Code, 'many of the principles underlying § 304 remain in effect under chapter 15': *SNP Boat Service S.A. v Hotel Le St. James*, 483 BR 776, 784 (SD Fla. 2012) citing *In re Atlas Shipping A/S*, 404 BR 726, 739 (Bankr. SDNY 2009).

44 Leif M. Clark/Karen Goldstein, Sacred Cows: How to Care for Secured Creditors' Rights in Cross-Border Bankruptcies, 46. Tex. Int'l LJ 513, 524.

45 *In re Artimm S.R.L.*, 335 BR 149, 160 (Bankr. CD Cal. 2005).

46 *In re Artimm S.R.L.*, 335 BR 149, 160 (Bankr. CD Cal. 2005); see also Digest of Case Law on the UNCITRAL Model Law on Cross-Border Insolvency (Vienna), 2021, 69 which suggests that these principles are also relevant in the § 1522 context.

47 *In re Atlas Shipping A/S*, 404 BR 726, 740 (Bankr. SDNY 2009); *In re Lee*, 472 BR 156, 183 (Bankr. D. Mass. 2012); *In re Ennia Caribe Holding N.V.*, 596 BR 316, 321 (Bankr. SDNY 2019).

1.22.15 The concept of interests is further characterized by elements of due process.[48] In *In re Sivec SRL*[49] the court had to decide whether to allow a US creditor to set-off against an Italian debtor. In the previous litigation in the USA, the US creditor was awarded a claim for breach of contract by the Italian debtor. The Italian debtor, in turn, was awarded a warranty retainage claim. However, because the Italian debtor was in liquidation proceedings and these had been recognized by the court as foreign main proceedings, the automatic stay prevented offsetting the claims against each other. Thus, the creditor applied for the stay to be lifted. The Italian debtor, on the other hand, was interested in having the retainage turned over for distribution in the foreign main proceeding. The court weighed the creditor's interests against those of the debtor (11 USC § 1522(a)). It was not persuaded that the interests of the US creditor, who had secured status under US law, were sufficiently protected in the Italian proceedings. The Italian debtor would have 'failed to provide information regarding Italian law, the status of the Italian bankruptcy case, or meet its burden of proof in requesting comity'.[50] It would still not be clear 'what procedure is currently available for assessing the relative priority of [the US creditor's] claim against other creditors, what proceedings have already occurred in that regard, and what further proceedings could and would take place should [the Court] grant comity and award the retainage to [the Italian debtor] to be held in trust in Italy as requested'.[51] Thus, the court declined the request for turnover of the retainage and lifted the automatic stay, allowing to offset the claims. It concluded that in the particular case, 'basic elements of due process [were] lacking and there [would be] a failure to provide protection of a U.S. creditor's interests'.[52]

1.22.16 In *SNP Boat Service SA v Hotel Le St. James*,[53] the question arose whether a Canadian creditor[54] was sufficiently protected under 11 USC § 1522(a) in a French reorganization proceeding. The creditor had previously obtained a default judgment against the French debtor in Canada and had it recognized in the US in order to obtain the French debtor's assets in the US. After

48 'Due process is a concept that is well understood in jurisdictions of all legal traditions. Minimum standards require a transparent process, notification to the parties of any communications that may take place between relevant courts and the ability for parties to be heard on any issues that arise, whether by their physical presence or through an opportunity to make submissions in writing': *The Judicial Perspective* (n 1), para. 22.

49 *In re Sivec SRL*, 476 BR 310 (Bankr. ED Okla. 2012).

50 *In re Sivec SRL*, 476 BR 310, 324 (Bankr. ED Okla. 2012).

51 *In re Sivec SRL*, 476 BR 310, 324 (Bankr. ED Okla. 2012).

52 *In re Sivec SRL*, 476 BR 310, 325 et seq. (Bankr. ED Okla. 2012).

53 *SNP Boat Service S.A. v Hotel Le St. James*, 483 BR 776 (SD Fla. 2012).

54 11 USC § 1522(a) covers not only the protection of U.S. creditors; on this and the distinction from 11 USC § 1521(b), see above para. 1.22.06.

the assets were seized, but before they were sold, the French debtor had the reorganization proceedings recognized as foreign main proceedings and requested that the US assets be entrusted to him. The creditor objected to this, claiming that he was not sufficiently protected in the French proceedings. The Bankruptcy Court then ordered discovery to ensure that the creditor would be afforded due process in the foreign proceeding and conditioned relief on disclosure of the documents. On appeal, however, the District Court stated that such action was an abuse of discretion. It argued that the court's jurisdiction was limited to reviewing whether a creditor's interests were generally protected in the foreign proceeding, not whether a particular creditor was sufficiently protected in a particular proceeding.[55]

(b) United Kingdom

In the United Kingdom, where Article 22(1) has been implemented by Article **1.22.17**
22(1) CBIR 2006,[56] courts have rarely extensively addressed the interpretation of adequate protection.[57] However, Ho suggests that a court might consider one of the factors discussed in *In re Atlantic Computer Systems*,[58] where the court was confronted with a request to lift an administration moratorium and had to balance the interests of the persons concerned.[59] Similarly, in *Chang Chin Fen vs Cosco Shipping (Qidong) Offhore Ltd*, the Scottish Outer House decided that relief in the context of recognition of a Singapore moratorium could not be granted against an opposing creditor who would – according to the rule in *Gibbs*[60] – not be bound by an intended scheme of arrangement whose protection was the aim of the moratorium.[61]

---

55 *SNP Boat Service S.A. v Hotel Le St. James*, 483 BR 776, 786 (S.D. Fla. 2012); this rationale is consistent with the prevailing view during the development of the MLCBI that issues of appeal and recission are outside the scope of the MLCBI, Report A/52/17 (n 3) para. 92.

56 In the UK, the MLCBI is implemented by the Cross-border Insolvency Regulations 2006 ('CBIR 2006').

57 In *Cosco Bulk Carrier v Armada Shipping* [2011] EWHC 216 (Ch) and *Warner v Verfides* [2008] EWHC 2609 (Ch), for example, adequate protection received mention but was not discussed in more detail.

58 *In re Atlantic Computer Systems* [1992] Ch 505 (CA).

59 *Ho* in: Ho (n 41), 276 et seq.

60 *Gibbs v La Societe Industrielle et Commercial des Metaux* [1890] 25 Q.B.D. 399, 406 (CA). Extensively on English law in this context *Dicey/Morris/Collins*, Conflict of Laws, 15th ed., Sweet & Maxwell, 2012, para. 31R-092 et seq. According to the rule in *Gibbs*, a debt will not be discharged where the proper law of the contract is not the law of the jurisdiction in which the discharge proceedings are taking place. It has recently been confirmed in *Gunel Bakhshiyeva (in her capacity as the foreign Representative of the OJSC International Bank of Azerbaijan) v. Sberbank of Russia and others* [2018] EWCA Civ. 2802. For Hong Kong, see *Re Rare Earth Magnesium Technology Group Holdings Ltd* [2022] HKCFI 1686. For the position in the U.S., see *Re Agrokor dd*, 591 BR 163 (Bankr. SDNY 2018); *Re Modern Land (China) Co., Ltd*, 18.7.2022, Case No. 22-10707 (MG) (Bankr. SDNY 2022); *Re SunEdison*, 577 BR 120 (Bankr. SDNY 2017).

61 *Chang Chin Fen vs Cosco Shipping (Qidong) Offhore Ltd* [2021] CSOH 94.

(c) Australia

1.22.18 In Australia,[62] the Federal Court had to deal with the adequate protection of Australian interests in the decision *Ackers v Saad Investments Company Limited*.[63] The case involved the liquidation of a Cayman Islands-based company, Saad Investments, which had assets in Australia. The liquidation was recognized by the Australian court as a foreign main proceeding and the liquidators, as foreign representatives, were entrusted with the administration, realization and distribution of those assets. These orders were opposed by an Australian taxation commissioner who was pursuing a substantial amount of tax owed by Saad Investments. He claimed that the interests he was pursuing as an unsecured creditor were not adequately protected (Article 22(1)) and sought modification of the court's orders (Article 22(3)). The inadequate protection resulted from the apparent inability to enforce Australian tax liabilities in the Cayman Islands, so that the taxation commissioner could not participate in the distribution of assets as an unsecured creditor. The court stated that it would not be fair to a domestic sovereign, its taxpayers and others doing business in its territory, or the international body of the debtor's creditors, for a debtor's estate to be freed of any taxation obligation except in the debtor's centre of main interest. Thus, it concluded that the interests of the taxation commissioner were not adequately protected.[64] The court modified its first order and allowed the taxation commissioner to exercise its rights against Australian assets (up to the pari passu amount that he would be entitled to receive as a dividend).[65]

C. RELIEF SUBJECT TO CONDITIONS (ARTICLE 22(2))

1.22.19 Article 22(2) expressly permits the court to make the relief requested under Articles 19 or 21 subject to such conditions as it deems appropriate. It may thereby tailor the relief to be granted to the specific circumstances of the individual case.[66] The court is thus facilitated in meeting the mandatory requirement of Article 22(1) that the interests of all persons affected by the relief

---

62 In Australia, the Cross-Border Insolvency Act 2008 (hereafter: CBIA 2008) is the gateway for the MLCBI. Section 6 CBIA 2008 provides that, subject to the Act and with modifications set out in Part 2 of the Act, the MLCBI has direct force in Australia.

63 *Ackers v Saad Investments Company Limited* [2013] FCA 738.

64 *Ackers v Saad Investments Company Limited* [2013] FCA 738, [38 et seq].

65 *Ackers v Saad Investments Company Limited* [2013] FCA 738, [53]; this decision was upheld by the Federal Court of Australia after the plaintiffs filed an appeal, see *Akers v Deputy Commissioner of Taxation* [2014] FCAFC 57.

66 *The Judicial Perspective* (n 1), para. 170.

must be adequately protected. As with Article 22(1), the court is given broad discretion in Article 22(2). It is free to decide on which conditions it makes the relief dependent.[67] Also, the MLCBI (in contrast to some implementations in the enacting states) does not give examples of which conditions may be considered.[68] However, it should be noted that Article 22(2) deliberately refers only to discretionary relief and not (beyond the wording) to automatic relief such as recognition of foreign proceedings under Article 17.[69]

In the United States, Article 22(2) has been implemented with few changes by 11 USC § 1522(b). In addition to 11 USC § 1519 and 1521 (which implement Articles 19 and 21), reference is also made to 11 USC § 1520(a)(3), which, upon recognition as a foreign main proceeding, allows the foreign representative to operate the debtor's business and therefore may be conditioned by the court. In deviation from the MLCBI, 11 USC § 1522(b) lists the giving of security or the filing of a bond as possible conditions. This allows the court to reverse its decision if the relief granted turns out to be unjust.[70] However, the recognition of the foreign proceeding cannot be made conditional on a bond.[71] Regardless of these specific examples, the function of 11 USC § 1522(b) is seen as allowing the court to achieve an appropriate balance between the interests of creditors and other interested entities, including the debtor.[72] In this respect, what applies to 11 USC § 1522(1) can be used as a guide. **1.22.20**

Similar to the US version, the English implementation, Article 22(2) CBIR 2006, also mentions the provision of security or caution by the foreign representative as a possible condition for the proper performance of his functions. **1.22.21**

67 *The Judicial Perspective* (n 1), para. 170.

68 According to Fletcher, an example of a condition could be an 'undertaking from the foreign representative to the effect that creditors from the enacting state whose claims would have preferential status under the local insolvency shall not be deprived of that advantage in the process of distribution taking place under foreign law': Ian F. Fletcher, Insolvency in Private International Law, 2nd ed., Oxford University Press (Oxford), 2007, para. 8.41; Berends cites as examples of conditions the requirement of a security or guarantee in case a certain kind of relief turns out to be granted unjustly or the authentication of documents if the court has doubts in this respect, but not sufficient doubt to refuse recognition: Berends (n 2), 309, 375.

69 Report A/CN.9/435 (n 4), para. 73; Berends (n 2), 309, 375.

70 Berends (n 2), 309, 375.

71 'But there appears to be no case [...] where a foreign representative was required to post a bond to obtain recognition (or to enjoy the fruits of recognition)': see *In re Millard*, 501 BR 644, 654 (Bankr. SDNY 2013).

72 *In re Vitro, S.A.B. de C.V.*, 473 BR 117, 121 (Bankr. ND Tex. 2012) citing *In re Tri-Continental Exchange Ltd*, 349 BR 627, 637 (Bankr. ED Cal. 2006).

D. MODIFICATION OR TERMINATION OF RELIEF (ARTICLE 22(3))

1.22.22 According to Article 22(3), the court may subsequently modify or terminate the relief granted under Articles 19 or 21. The foreign representative and persons affected by the relief are entitled to apply. However, the court may also ex officio modify or terminate the relief. When Article 22(3) was created, there was discussion as to whether the provision should also refer to the recognition of foreign proceedings (Article 17). This was ultimately rejected because the question of modification or revision of the recognition of the foreign proceeding would involve issues of appeal and recission of judicial decisions that are outside the scope of the MLCBI.[73]

1.22.23 11 USC § 1522(c), which implements Article 22(3) in the United States, differs little from the MLCBI. Courts have emphasized that 'the plain language of the statute affords courts flexibility in granting or modifying relief by allowing courts to modify relief either on its own motion or upon request'.[74] Furthermore, 'If it later appears that conditions should be either imposed or relaxed, § 1522(c) authorizes a court, on its own motion or upon request, to modify or terminate any discretionary relief it has granted'.[75] How a court subsequently modifies the relief already granted is vividly demonstrated in *In re Sanjel (USA) Inc.*[76] There, a US court had first fully recognized the orders of the court of the Canadian foreign main proceeding and given them full effect in the United States (11 USC § 1521). That included a broad stay, the protection of which the foreign court extended to the debtor's directors and officers. This prevented two of the debtor's employees from pursuing collective actions alleging violations of the Fair Labor Standards Act against the directors and officers in the United States. The claims hereby pursued were in danger of being barred by the statute of limitations. The US court balanced the interests (11 USC § 1522(a)) and concluded that, because of the risk of the statute of limitations and because it would be unreasonable to require the claimants to oppose the stay in the foreign main proceeding in Canada, its prior recognition order should be modified to permit action against the directors and officers in the United States (11 USC § 1522(c)).[77]

73 Report A/52/17 (n 3), para. 91 et seq; agreeing with this, see *Akers v Deputy Commissioner of Taxation* [2014] FCAFC 57, [80].

74 *In re Sanjel (USA) Inc.*, Case No. 16-50778-CAG, para. 6 et seq. (Bankr. WD Tex. Jul. 28, 2016).

75 *In re Tri-Continental Exchange Ltd*, 349 BR 627, 637 (Bankr. ED Cal. 2006).

76 *In re Sanjel (USA) Inc.*, Case No. 16-50778-CAG (Bankr. WD Tex. Jul. 28, 2016).

77 *In re Sanjel (USA) Inc.*, Case No. 16-50778-CAG, para. 5, 11 et seq. (Bankr. WD Tex. Jul. 28, 2016).

Besides the US courts, only Australian courts have dealt more extensively with the Article 22(3) provision. Subsequent amendments have been made to ensure adequate protection of the persons affected by the relief, as required by Article 22(1).[78] 1.22.24

78 See above, para. 1.22.18.

Article 23

ACTIONS TO AVOID ACTS DETRIMENTAL TO CREDITORS

Reinhard Bork

Scope of application

1. Upon recognition of a foreign proceeding, the foreign representative has standing to initiate [*refer to the types of actions to avoid or otherwise render ineffective acts detrimental to creditors that are available in this State to a person or body administering a reorganization or liquidation*].
2. When the foreign proceeding is a foreign non-main proceeding, the court must be satisfied that the action relates to assets that, under the law of this State, should be administered in the foreign non-main proceeding.

A. INTRODUCTION TO ARTICLE 23

1. Rationale

1.23.01 Article 23(1) deals with transactions avoidance law. It grants the foreign representative procedural standing to initiate domestic avoidance actions, that is, actions under the laws of the enacting state to avoid or otherwise render ineffective legal acts detrimental to the general body of creditors. Upon recognition of the foreign proceeding (Article 17), the foreign representative is entitled to bring such actions under a list of specified provisions designated by the enacting state. The aim is to grant the foreign representative the authority to commence avoidance proceedings under the same conditions as if he or she had been appointed in the recognizing state.[1] This allows the foreign representative to seek relief that would otherwise be reserved to a local Insolvency Practitioner in this jurisdiction. Thus, Article 23 overcomes a potential barrier[2] and is in line with one of the main objectives of the MLCBI, to grant the foreign representative access to the courts of the enacting state.[3]

However, it is of great importance that Article 23(1) neither creates a substantive right of avoidance nor contains any choice of law rules.[4] Like the MLCBI as a whole, Article 23 is a purely procedural provision.[5] The effect is limited to the extent that the foreign representative should not be prevented from initiating avoidance actions under the laws of the enacting state simply because he or she was not appointed in this state.[6] Therefore, in each case, the applicable law must be determined under the established rules and practices of the enacting state.[7] Only if domestic avoidance law applies and the requirements of Article 23(1) are met does the provision allow the foreign representative to bring actions based on that law. In this context, the MLCBI differs substantially from the European Insolvency Regulation, which in Articles 7(2)(m) and 16 also regulates the applicable law of avoidance.[8] **1.23.02**

If the foreign proceeding is a foreign non-main proceeding, Article 23(2) contains a special prerequisite. Since non-main proceedings are typically restricted to the assets located in the state where the non-main proceedings have been opened,[9] the court must consider whether the action relates to assets that should be administered in the foreign non-main proceeding. This shows that, **1.23.03**

1 Ian F. Fletcher, *Insolvency in Private International Law*, 2nd ed., Oxford University Press (Oxford), 2007, para. 8.45; *UNCITRAL Model Law on Cross-Border Insolvency: The Judicial Perspective*, United Nations Publications (New York), 2014, para. 185.

2 Fletcher, *Insolvency in Private International Law* (n 1), para. 8.45.

3 *UNCITRAL Model Law on Cross-Border Insolvency with Guide to Enactment and Interpretation*, United Nations Publications (New York), 2014, para. 3.

4 *Guide to Enactment and Interpretation* (n 3), para. 201.

5 *The Judicial Perspective* (n 1), para. 9.

6 See n 4.

7 *The Judicial Perspective* (n 1), para. 185; *UNCITRAL, Legislative Guide on Insolvency Law*, United Nations Publications (New York), 2014, para. 80.

8 For details, see Snowden in: Reinhard Bork/Kristin van Zwieten (eds), Commentary on the European Insolvency Regulation, Oxford University Press (Oxford), 2nd ed. 2022), [7.70] et seq.

9 Cf. Article 3(2)(sentence 2) EIR.

under the MLCBI, the relief for a non-main proceeding is likely to be more restrictive than for a main proceeding.[10]

2. Scope of Application

1.23.04 Article 23(1) confers standing to the foreign representative to initiate actions aimed at challengeable antecedent transactions.[11] The *Legislative Guide* summarizes them generally as 'transactions intended to defeat, hinder or delay creditors from collecting their claims; transactions at undervalue; and transactions with certain creditors that could be regarded as preferential'.[12] However, these are only examples. It does not refer to all provisions from which, in the enacting state, the ineffectiveness of such a transaction could follow. As Article 23(1) expressly states, the standing is linked to the types of actions 'that are available in this State to a person or body administering a reorganization or liquidation'. Hence, the scope extends to all actions that are available to a local Insolvency Practitioner and which, in terms of content, are attributable to insolvency law.[13] Against this background, national legislators are expected to assign the same avoidance rights to foreign Insolvency Practitioners as they have assigned to domestic practitioners. Any reduced assignment (which would be possible under the normative approach of Article 23(1) which requires national legislators to expressly name the applicable rules) would be an insufficient adoption of the MLCBI. However, this is restricted to transactions avoidance law as provided for in insolvency law. Provisions that are subject to general civil law or that entitle only individual creditors are not covered by Article 23(1).[14]

1.23.05 Article 23 specifically addresses the avoidance of antecedent transactions within the MLCBI. In this context, it can be distinguished from Article 21 which generally regulates relief that may be granted upon recognition of foreign proceedings. The predecessor of Article 21 was originally intended to also govern avoidance actions but due to the complexity of this area, it was decided to create a separate article.[15] Thus, Article 23 takes precedence over Article 21 by way of speciality. However, it is controversially discussed whether Article 21(1)(g) allows the application of foreign transaction avoidance law as

10 *Guide to Enactment and Interpretation* (n 3), para. 202.
11 *The Judicial Perspective* (n 1), para. 183.
12 *Legislative Guide on Insolvency Law* (n 7), para. 170.
13 *Guide to Enactment and Interpretation* (n 3), para. 200.
14 See n 13.
15 UNCITRAL, Report of the Working Group on Insolvency Law of the work of its 20th Session, A/CN.9/433, United Nations Publications (New York), 1996, para. 134.

'any additional relief' that may be available to an insolvency administrator in the enacting state.[16] This issue is not addressed by Article 23, as reference is always made to provisions of the enacting state.

3. Legislative Background

The legislative process of passing Article 23 was particularly controversial.[17] The consultation phase was deliberately placed at the end to let the negotiations on the MLCBI not fail altogether.[18] This is because transactions avoidance law reflects to a large extent national public policies.[19] It was argued that the issue of antecedent transactions would not be suitable for a harmonized solution.[20] Such a solution in the MLCBI would result to a high degree of uncertainty about concluded or performed transactions.[21] Regardless, since the protection of the integrity of the assets was considered essential and the granting of standing was seen as the only realistic way to achieve this protection, it was possible to agree on a provision that governs this area in the MLCBI, albeit with the restriction that the provision neither grants a substantive avoidance right nor contains any choice of law rules.[22] **1.23.06**

16 Such a possibility has been affirmed by the US courts in interpreting the US implementation of Article 21(1)(g) in 11 USC § 1521: see *Fogerty v Petroquests Resources Inc, (In re Condor Insurance Co.)* [5th Cir. 2010], 601 F 3d 319, 327–330; *In re Atlas Shipping A/S* [Bankr. SDNY 2009], 404 BR 726, 744 et seq; *Laspro Consultores Ltda. v Alina Corp.* [Bankr. SD Fla. 2017], 567 BR 212. In the UK, on the other hand, the High Court denied the application of foreign law under the British implementation of Article 21(1)(g) in Art. 21 CBIR 2006: see *Fibria Celulose S/A v Pan Ocean Co. Ltd* [2014] EWHC 2124 (Ch), [2014] Bus. LR 1041 [105–108]; see also generally Ian F. Fletcher, The Law of Insolvency, 5th ed., Sweet & Maxwell (London), 2017, para. 32-040; Gerard McCormack/Wan Wai Yee, The UNCITRAL Model Law on Cross-Border Insolvency Comes of Age: New Times or New Paradigms? (2019), 54 Tex. Int'l LJ, 273, 293–5; Look Chan Ho, Applying Foreign Law – Realizing the Model Law's Potential (2010), 25. J.I.B.L.R., 552–67.

17 Bob Wessels, International Insolvency Law Part I., 4th ed., Wolters Kluwer (Deventer), 2015, para. 10320.

18 Klaus Wimmer, Die UNCITRAL-Modellbestimmungen über grenzüberschreitende Insolvenzverfahren, (1997), ZIP, 2220, 2227.

19 *Rubin v Eurofinance SA* [2012], UKSC 46, [2013] Bus. L.R. [15].

20 UNCITRAL, Report of the Working Group on Insolvency Law of the work of its Twenty-First Session, A/CN.9/435, United Nations Publications (New York), 1997, para. 63; UNCITRAL, Report of the Working Group on Insolvency Law of the work of its Thirtieth Session, A/CN.9/436, United Nations Publications (New York), 1997, para. 87.

21 *Guide to Enactment and Interpretation* (n 3), para. 203.

22 Report A/CN.9/435 (n 20), para. 63; UNCITRAL, Report of the United Nations Commission on International Trade Law on the work of its thirtieth session, A/52/17, United Nations Publications (New York), 1997, para. 213 et seq.

B. PREREQUISITES FOR APPLICATION

1. Recognition of the Foreign Proceeding (Article 23(1))

1.23.07 Article 23(1) grants the foreign representative standing to initiate avoidance actions in the enacting state upon recognition of the foreign proceeding. The requirements for the recognition of a foreign proceeding, whether main or non-main, are set by Article 17(1). According to Article 17(1), the foreign proceeding must comply with the legal definition in Article 2(a), the foreign representative must comply with the legal definition in Article 2(d), an application must have been filed in accordance with Article 15(1), respecting the formal requirements in Article 15(2) and (3), and the application must have been submitted to the competent court within the meaning of Article 4. Provided that the recognition does not violate the public policy provisions of the enacting state (Article 6), the competent court or authority (Article 4) shall then recognize the foreign proceeding as foreign main proceeding (Article 17(2)(a)) or foreign non-main proceeding (Article 17(2)(b)), depending on whether the debtor has its COMI or only an establishment in the state of the foreign proceeding.[23] There are no deviations from other provisions in the MLCBI which link their legal effect to the recognition of a foreign proceeding.[24]

2. Suspect Period

1.23.08 National transactions avoidance laws differ significantly as regards the prerequisites for challenging antecedent transactions.[25] This holds particularly true for suspect periods, that is, the time frame in which the transaction subject to avoidance must have been performed. Although this is beyond the regulatory content of Article 23, there are supplementary regulations in the enacting states which address this topic.

1.23.09 In most insolvency laws, avoidance provisions apply retroactively from a particular date for a specific time to overturn past transactions.[26] The reference

---

23 For an informative examination of the recognition requirements in an Article 23(1) context, see *Wild v Coin Co International PLC* [2015], FCA 354, [60 et seq].

24 Articles 12, 20(1), 21(1), 21(2), 24 also require recognition; also, it is one of the key objectives of the MLCBI 'to establish simplified procedures for recognition of qualifying foreign proceedings that would avoid time-consuming legalization or other processes and provide certainty with respect to the decision to recognize', *Guide to Enactment and Interpretation* (n 3), para. 29.

25 For the European Union, see Reinhard Bork and Michael Veder, Harmonisation of Transactions Avoidance Laws, Intersentia (Cambridge/Antwerp/Chicago), 2021, Chapter 4.

26 *Legislative Guide on Insolvency Law* (n 7), para. 150.

date determining this 'suspect period'[27] is often tied to the date of the application for, or commencement of, the 'insolvency proceeding'.[28] If, however, instead of a domestic insolvency proceeding, a foreign proceeding and an ancillary recognition proceeding based on the MLCBI are conducted, the question arises as to which reference date should be referred to determine the suspect period: to the date of the foreign proceeding or the date of the ancillary proceeding. This issue is often addressed by supplementary regulations (which then go beyond the regulatory scope of Article 23) and in case law.

For example, in the UK, the implementation of Article 23 by Article 23 CBIR 2006[29] contains modifications adjusting the reference date in the designated avoidance law. Whenever there is a reference in the enumerated provisions of the Insolvency Act 1986 (England and Wales) or Bankruptcy Act 1985 (Scotland)[30] to the commencement of the proceeding, the rules are modified under Article 23(3)(a)–(c) CBIR 2006 by referring instead to the commencement of the foreign proceeding.[31] Furthermore, Article 23(4) CBIR 2006 provides that the date of the opening of the foreign proceeding shall be determined in accordance with the law of the foreign state. **1.23.10**

The US implementation of Article 23 in 11 USC § 1523 lacks a provision consistent with the English provision. There is no special rule adjusting the reference date in a proceeding under Chapter 15 US Bankruptcy Code (11 USC).[32] In such a proceeding, however, this issue is of particular importance. 11 USC § 1523(a) grants standing to the foreign representative only in a full case under Chapters 7 or 11 of the US Bankruptcy Code.[33] Thus, to determine the suspect period in the avoidance provisions enumerated in 11 USC § 1523(a), various potential commencement dates are under consideration: the date of application for, or commencement of, the foreign proceeding, the Chapter 15 ancillary proceeding or the proceeding under Chapter 7 or Chapter 11. However, US case law suggests that it is not the opening date of the foreign proceeding but the application date of the Chapter 15 proceeding that should govern the reference date. In *O'Sullivan v Loy*,[34] the court decided in a Chapter 15 case **1.23.11**

---

27 Sometimes also called 'look-back period' or 'claw-back period'.

28 See n 26.

29 In the UK, the MLCBI is implemented by the Cross-border Insolvency Regulations 2006 ('CBIR 2006').

30 Which has now been replaced by the Bankruptcy Act 2016 (Scotland), see Parry in: Parry/Ayliffe/Shivji (eds), Transaction Avoidance in Insolvencies, 3rd ed., Oxford University Press (Oxford), 2018, para 20.3.

31 For details, see Fletcher, The Law of Insolvency (n 16), para. 32-042; Parry in: Parry/Ayliffe/Shivji (n 30), para. 21.126.

32 Chapter 15 is the chapter of the US Bankruptcy Code that implements the MLCBI in the US.

33 See para. 1.23.12 et. seq.

34 *O'Sullivan v Loy* [E.D.Va. 2010], 432 BR 551.

that the reference date would be the date of filing the petition of the Chapter 15 case and not the date of the commencement of the foreign proceeding.[35] In this case, the court was confronted with the question whether a transaction entered into after the commencement of the foreign proceeding but before the filing of the Chapter 15 petition falls within the scope of 11 USC § 1520(2), allowing the avoidance of a post-petition transfer,[36], or 11 USC § 1523(a). The court decided for the latter. In *In re Awal Bank, B.S.C.*,[37] a foreign representative sought to avoid a set-off that occurred two weeks before the opening of the foreign main proceeding. The legal basis for the avoidance, on which he mainly relied, was one of the provisions enumerated in 11 USC § 1523(a).[38] To challenge the set-off, the foreign representative opened a further proceeding under Chapter 11 of the US Bankruptcy Code, as required by 11 USC § 1523(a).[39] Thus, the court had to decide whether the Chapter 15 filing date could be used as reference date in a subsequent Chapter 11 case. It concluded that the only relevant reference date could be the filing date of the Chapter 15 proceeding.[40] The foreign representative could open a plenary proceeding under Chapter 11 after obtaining an order of recognition (USC §§ 1511(a)(2), 1511(b)) but this would not be a new case. It would rather be a conversion from one chapter to another.[41] Furthermore, using the Chapter 15 petition date as reference date would give greater effect to 11 USC § 1523(a).[42]

3. Particularities for a Foreign non-main Proceeding (Article 23(2))

1.23.12 Article 23(2) provides additional requirements if the foreign proceeding is a foreign non-main proceeding within the meaning of Article 2(c). In this case, the court must be satisfied that the avoidance action relates to assets that, under the law of the enacting state, should be administered in the foreign non-main proceeding. This provision could be viewed in conjunction with the avoidance of forum shopping which is especially likely to arise in the context of a foreign non-main proceeding. The court might refuse to grant the foreign representative standing to bring avoidance actions in the enacting state if it concludes that the assets in question should not be administered in the foreign

35 *O'Sullivan v Loy* [E.D.Va. 2010], 432 BR 551, 563.
36 11 USC § 1520(2) implements Article 20(1)(c). However, while Article 20 bars post-petition transactions, § 1520 makes them avoidable, *O'Sullivan v Loy* [E.D.Va. 2010], 432 BR 551, 561.
37 *In re Awal Bank, B.S.C.* [Bankr. SDNY 2011], 455 BR 73.
38 11 USC § 553(b).
39 See para. 1.23.13.
40 *In re Awal Bank, B.S.C.* [Bankr. SDNY 2011], 455 BR 73, 91.
41 *In re Awal Bank, B.S.C.* [Bankr. SDNY 2011], 455 BR 73, 89.
42 *In re Awal Bank, B.S.C.* [Bankr. SDNY 2011], 455 BR 73, 90.

non-main proceeding.[43] For example, English law is heading in this direction. A reference in Article 23(5) CBIR 2006,[44] which implements Article 23(2), requires the court to be satisfied that the assets 'under the law of Great Britain' should be administered in the foreign non-main proceeding. According to Article 2(q) CBIR 2006, whenever there is a reference to 'the law of Great Britain' within the CBIR 2006, rules of private international law are to be included. The court might then decline to hear a case, if it concludes that the avoidable transaction has no sufficient connection with the UK.[45]

The 'asset' in question is the object the foreign Insolvency Practitioner seeks to recover. For example, where the debtor transferred goods from its establishment in State A to a buyer in State B, a non-main proceeding is opened in State A and the Insolvency Practitioner challenges the transfer under the laws of State B, he or she aims at a retransfer of the goods to State A where they would be local assets and subject to the non-main proceeding. The same holds true for a payment to a creditor who is situated in State B but is obliged to repay the money to the Insolvency Practitioner in State A where the money is subject to the domestic non-main proceeding. As opposed to this, where the debtor transferred real estate located in State B, this would not be subject to the non-main proceeding in State A, even if the avoidance of this transfer would be possible under the laws of State B. **1.23.13**

C. LEGAL CONSEQUENCES

1. Procedural Standing

As a consequence of recognition, Article 23(1) grants the foreign representative procedural standing or active procedural legitimation[46] to bring actions under the laws of the enacting state to avoid or otherwise render illegitimate antecedent transactions.[47] Hence, the provision is part of a series of rules in the MLCBI which grant as a form of access standing to the foreign representative.[48] He or she is entitled to apply directly to local courts without seeking **1.23.14**

43 Hollander/Graham in: Klaus Pannen (ed.), European Insolvency Regulation, De Gruyter (Berlin), 2007, Part 4, para. 248.

44 See n 29.

45 Fletcher, The Law of Insolvency (n 16), para. 32-042; Ho in: Look Chan Ho (ed.), A Commentary on the UNCITRAL Model Law, 4th ed., Globe Law & Business (London), 2017, 282; see also para. 1.23.19.

46 Report A/52/17 (n 22), para. 211.

47 *The Judicial Perspective* (n 1), para. 183.

48 Such as Articles 11, 12, 15 (1), 19, 21 and 24; see Hollander/Graham in: Pannen (n 43), Part 4, para. 135 and 247.

any additional form of authorization.[49] This allows the initiation of avoidance actions under conditions that, as Fletcher puts it, are 'exactly analogous' to those applicable to an Insolvency Practitioner in the enacting state.[50] However, as the *Guide to Enactment and Interpretation* emphasizes, Article 23(1) is 'drafted narrowly in that it neither creates any substantive right regarding such actions nor provides any solution involving conflict of laws'.[51] Whether an avoidance provision applies needs to be determined under the established rules and practices of the enacting state.[52] Article 23(1) is limited solely to granting procedural standing.[53] Despite the limited effect of Article 23(1), there are significant differences in the individual implementations in the enacting states. A special approach is taken in particular by the implementation of Article 23(1) in the US. In deviation from the MLCBI and other implementations, the US version imposes additional conditions on the granting of procedural standing to the foreign representative.

(a) USA

1.23.15 In the US, Article 23 is implemented by 11 USC § 1523. In paragraph (a) it says that upon recognition of the foreign proceeding, the foreign representative has standing to initiate US avoidance actions but only in a case concerning the debtor pending under another chapter of the US Bankruptcy Code. Hence, if the foreign representative seeks to initiate US avoidance actions, he or she may only do so in a full, plenary bankruptcy proceeding, usually under Chapter 7 or Chapter 11 of the US Bankruptcy Code. If such a proceeding has not already been opened, the foreign representative is entitled to apply for this under 11 USC § 1511, as long as the foreign proceeding is a foreign main proceeding.[54] 11 USC § 1523 has been subject to a number of court decisions. However, the provision has played more of a marginal role.

1.23.16 The most relevant decision is from the US Fifth Circuit Court of Appeal in *In re Condor Insurance Co.*[55] where the court further illustrated the rationale

49 McCormack/Wan Wai Yee (n 16), 273, 277.

50 Fletcher, Insolvency in Private International Law (n 1), para. 8.45.

51 *Guide to Enactment and Interpretation* (n 3), para. 201.

52 *The Legislative Guide* (n 7), para. 80.

53 *Guide to Enactment and Interpretation* (n 3), para. 201.

54 11 USC § 1511 is the implementation of Article 11; see *In re Awal Bank, B.S.C.* [Bankr. SDNY 2011], 455 BR 73, 79.

55 *Fogerty v Petroquests Resources Inc (In re Condor Insurance Co.)* [5th Cir. 2010], 601 F 3d, reversing the decisions of the US District Court for the Southern District of Mississippi, *Fogerty v Petroquests Resources Inc. (In re Condor Insurance Co.)*, 411 BR 314 (SD Miss. 2009) and the Bankruptcy Court, *Fogerty v Petroquests Resources Inc. (In re Condor Insurance Co.)*, 2008 WL 2858943 (Bankr. SD Miss. 2008); see also, evaluating the decision, McCormack, Conflicts, Avoidance and International Insolvency 20 Years On: A Triple

of 11 USC § 1523(a). In the underlying case, Condor Insurance Ltd was declared bankrupt in its place of corporation, St. Kitts & Nevis. The appointed liquidators filed a Chapter 15 bankruptcy proceeding to recover assets that they claimed were fraudulently transferred to affiliates of Condor in the US. The liquidators based their action not on avoidance provisions of US law but on relevant provisions of the law of St. Kitts & Nevis because Condor, as a foreign insurance company, was prohibited from filing a Chapter 7 or Chapter 11 case.[56] Thus, the main question of the case was whether foreign avoidance law can be applied under 11 USC § 1521(a)(7).[57] Nevertheless, the court took the opportunity to set out the conditions under which a foreign representative is entitled to bring avoidance actions in the US, including actions under 11 USC § 1523(a). The court stated, while 11 USC § 1521(a)(7) provides that US avoidance actions are exempt from a Chapter 15 ancillary proceeding, 11 USC § 1523(a) ensures that they generally may be brought by the foreign representative but only in a full case under Chapters 7 or 11 of the U.S. Bankruptcy Code. The provision removes a 'potential standing roadblock for resort to chapters 7 or 11'[58] by granting the foreign representative the role of a trustee under the relevant provisions. Thus, the assertion of US avoidance actions is deliberately intended to be linked to the conduct of a full rather than an ancillary proceeding. This reflects the concerns of the US delegation during UNCITRAL debates that a simple grant of standing to bring avoidance actions neglects to address very difficult choice of law and forum issues.[59] 11 USC § 1523(a), however, does not create any legal right of avoidance nor does it create or imply any choice of law rules.[60] These issues must be resolved in a full case 'where the court would also decide the law to be applied in the distribution of the estate'.[61]

This interpretation was followed by the US Bankruptcy Court in *In re Awal Bank, B.S.C.*[62] In this decision, the court interpreted 11 USC § 1523(a) in a similar manner. It stated that 11 USC § 1523(a) gives the foreign representative (in a Chapter 7 or Chapter 11 proceeding) the power and authority of **1.23.17**

Cocktail (2013), 2 J.B.L., 141, 152 et seq; Segaal Shorr, Avoidance Actions Under Chapter 15: Was Condor Correct? (2016),1. F. I.LJ, 351, 371-383.

56 According to 11 USC § 109 (3).

57 11 USC § 1521(a)(7) is the implementation of Article 21(1)(g).

58 *Fogerty v Petroquests Resources Inc. (In re Condor Insurance Co.)* [5th Cir. 2010], 601 F 3d, 319, 324.

59 *Fogerty v Petroquests Resources Inc. (In re Condor Insurance Co.)* [5th Cir. 2010], 601 F 3d, 319, 325, citing H.R. Rep. 109-31, 109th Cong., 1st Sess., 2005 USCC.A.N., 116.

60 *Fogerty v Petroquests Resources Inc. (In re Condor Insurance Co.)* [5th Cir. 2010], 601 F 3d, 319, 325.

61 H.R. Rep. 109-31, 109th Cong., 1st Sess., 2005 USCC.A.N., 116.

62 *In re Awal Bank, B.S.C.* [Bankr. SDNY 2011], 455 BR 73; see also above para. 1.23.10.

a trustee under the avoidance provisions of the Bankruptcy Code.[63] It emphasized that 'one of the limited but important purposes of § 1523(a) is to place the foreign representative in the shoes of a chapter 7 or chapter 11 trustee for the purpose of pursuing the enumerated avoidance claims'.[64]

(b) United Kingdom

1.23.18 In the UK, Article 23(1) CBIR 2006[65] implements Article 23(1). It grants the foreign representative standing to make an application to the court under several provisions of the Insolvency Act 1986 (England and Wales) and the Bankruptcy Act 1985[66] (Scotland) to initiate avoidance actions. Unlike the US version, Article 23(1) CBIR 2006 grants standing to the foreign representative without requiring a local proceeding to be commenced.[67] This is emphasized by Article 23(2)(a) CBIR 2006 which provides that the enumerated provisions apply whether or not there is a proceeding under British insolvency law.[68]

1.23.19 Furthermore, since Article 23(1) CBIR 2006 grants procedural standing to bring avoidance actions but does not expressly deal with conflict of law issues, concerns arose during the consultation phase of passing the CBIR 2006 that the provision could be used for forum shopping.[69] However, these concerns were rejected because there was no intention to alter conflict of law rules and substantive rights.[70] Hence, the ordinary rules as developed in *In re Paramount Airways Ltd*[71] apply, requiring a sufficient connection between the UK and the allegedly avoidable transaction.[72] Further security measures are established by paragraphs (6)–(8) of Article 23 CBIR 2006. Paragraph (6) provides that if, in addition to the foreign proceeding, a proceeding under British law takes place in respect of the same debtor, (a) a permission of the High Court (England and Wales) or Court of Session (Scotland) is needed to make an application under Article 23(1) CBIR 2006 and (b) the competent court for this application is the court in which the British proceeding is taking place. Paragraph (7) allows the court to consider that UK creditors are adequately protected when

63 *In re Awal Bank, B.S.C.* [Bankr. SDNY 2011], 455 BR 73, 91.

64 *In re Awal Bank, B.S.C.* [Bankr. SDNY 2011], 455 BR 73, 91.

65 See n 29.

66 Which has now been replaced by the Bankruptcy (Scotland) Act 2016, see n 30.

67 *Fletcher*, The Law of Insolvency (n 16), para. 32-40.

68 In this regard, see also Parry in: Parry/Ayliffe/Shivji (n 30), para 21.124; Willson/Perkins in: Moss/Fletcher/Isaacs (ed.), The EU Regulation on Insolvency Proceedings, 3rd ed., Oxford University Press (Oxford), 2016, para. 5.91.

69 *McCormack* (n 55), 141, 153.

70 *McCormack* (n 55), 141, 153.

71 *In re Paramount Airways Ltd* [1993] Ch 223 (CA).

72 See below at para. 1.23.19.

distributing the proceeds and paragraph (8) ensures that British insolvency office holders are still entitled to invoke any of the listed avoidance provisions without restriction.

(c) Australia

Apart from the US decisions, there are two recent decisions of the Federal Court of Australia addressing the standing conferred by Article 23(1). In Australia, the Cross Border Insolvency Act 2008 (hereafter: CBIA 2008) is the gateway for the MLCBI. Section 6 CBIA 2008 provides that, subject to the Act and with modifications set out in Part 2 of the Act, the MLCBI has direct force in Australia. In this regard, Article 17 CBIA 2008 supplements Article 23 by specifying the avoidance provisions to which Article 23(1) refers. In *Wild v Coin Co International PLC*,[73] the court explained that the legal effect of Article 23(1) is to grant the foreign representative standing to initiate actions that would otherwise only be available in Australia to a person appointed as liquidator under Australian law.[74] Thus, it provides that the foreign representative is not precluded from commencing such actions only because he or she was not approved in Australia.[75] In *King v Linkage Access Limited*,[76] the court further pointed out that the function of Article 23(1) is narrow in solely granting standing without having any substantive legal effect.[77] The wording of the provision would demonstrate the purely procedural nature of the article.[78] However, this would not mean that the provision is of no significance. The MLCBI allows that no costly secondary proceeding must be opened in Australia in addition to the foreign proceedings.[79] **1.23.20**

2. Applicable Law

Article 23, as a purely procedural provision, does not cover choice-of-law issues. Typically, domestic courts apply domestic and not foreign transactions avoidance law. In this respect, the already established rules in the enacting state determine whether domestic avoidance law applies. This issue has to be distinguished from the question previously discussed as to whether the foreign office-holder is permitted to challenge transactions under domestic transactions avoidance law. That a foreign Insolvency Practitioner has standing under **1.23.21**

73 *Wild v Coin Co International PLC* [2015], FCA 354.
74 *Wild v Coin Co International PLC* [2015], FCA 354, [72].
75 *Wild v Coin Co International PLC* [2015], FCA 354, [77].
76 *King v Linkage Access Limited* [2018], FCA 1979.
77 *King v Linkage Access Limited* [2018], FCA 1979, [35].
78 *King v Linkage Access Limited* [2018], FCA 1979, [36].
79 See n 78.

Article 23 to enforce transactions avoidance claims under domestic transactions avoidance law does not automatically mean that such claims exist. It may very well be that the applicable domestic transactions avoidance law does not cover transactions performed abroad, no matter whether the law is enforced by a domestic or a foreign Insolvency Practitioner.

1.23.22 In the US, for example, if a bankruptcy case has a foreign element, the principles demonstrated in the leading cases *In re Picard*,[80] *In re French*[81] and *In re Maxwell Communications Corp.*[82] determine whether an action can be brought under the US Bankruptcy Code. This includes long standing principles as the presumption against extra-territorial application of laws,[83] the question of the closest connection to the transaction[84] and comity.[85][86]

1.23.23 In the UK, the leading case, which is still decisive today, is *Re Paramount Airways Ltd.*[87] In this decision, the Court of Appeal interpreted an English avoidance provision (sec. 238 IA 1986 on transactions at an undervalue), concluding that it applied without territorial limitation to any person involved in the potentially voidable transaction.[88] However, if there was a foreign element, the court would need to be satisfied that the defendant is sufficiently connected with the UK 'for it to be just and proper to make the order against him despite the foreign element'.[89] In considering whether there is a sufficient connection with the UK, the court would look at all circumstances of the case.[90]

---

80 *In re Picard*, [2nd Cir. 2019], 917 F.3d 85; on this case, see Zerjal, Non-US Investors in Non-US Entities Beware: You May Be Subject to Clawback under US Law if the Investment is Ultimately with a US Entity (2020) 17 ICR, 51 et seq.

81 *In re French* [4th Cir. 2006], 440 F. 3d 145 [4th Cir. 2006].

82 *In re Maxwell Communications Corp* [2nd Cir. 1996], 93 F. 3d 1036.

83 Meaning that legislation of Congress, unless a contrary intent appears, is meant to apply only within the territorial jurisdiction of the US, *Equal Employment Opportunity Comm. v Arabian American Oil Co.* [1991], 499 US 244, 248.

84 An analysis asking which jurisdiction is most closely connected with a transaction to determine the applicable avoidance law: see McCormack (n 55), 141, 147.

85 'The recognition which one nation allows within its territory to the legislative, executive, or judicial acts of another nation, having due regard both to international duty and convenience, and to the rights of its own citizens, or of other persons who are under the protection of its law': *Hilton v Guyot* [1895], 159 US 113, [163 et. seq.].

86 See generally McCormack (n 55), 141, 147; Jay Lawrence Westbrook, Avoidance of Pre-Bankruptcy Transactions in Multinational Bankruptcy Cases (2007), Tex. Int.'l LJ, 899, 905–9.

87 *In re Paramount Airways* [1993] Ch 223 (CA). See also *Orexim Trading Ltd v Mahavir Port and Terminal Private Ltd* [2018] EWCA Civ 1660.

88 *In re Paramount Airways* [1993] Ch 223, 239 (CA).

89 *In re Paramount Airways* [1993] Ch 223, 240 (CA).

90 *In re Paramount Airways* [1993] Ch. 223, 240 (CA); for an analysis of this case, see Look Chan Ho, Conflict of Laws in Insolvency Transaction Avoidance (2008), SAcLJ, 343, 351; see also *Kazakhstan Kagazy Plc and others v Zhunus and others* [2021] EWHC 3462 para. 230 et seq.

3. Enforcement

An entirely different matter is the recognition of the avoidance judgment. While recognition in the state whose court has issued the avoidance judgment is unproblematic, there may well be difficulties if recognition is required abroad. However, this is not a typical Article 23 problem but depends on the national law of the recognizing state, which ideally has adopted the UNCITRAL Model Law on Recognition and Enforcement of Insolvency-Related Judgments.[91] **1.23.24**

91 On this, see below at para. P2.27.

Article 24

INTERVENTION BY A FOREIGN REPRESENTATIVE IN PROCEEDINGS IN THIS STATE

Reinhard Bork

Upon recognition of a foreign proceeding, the foreign representative may, provided the requirements of the law of this State are met, intervene in any proceedings in which the debtor is a party.

A. INTRODUCTION TO ARTICLE 24

1. Rationale

1.24.01 The purpose of Article 24 is to give the foreign representative the procedural standing[1] to intervene in any non-insolvency proceeding of the debtor in the enacting State.[2] The provision is thereby an expression of one of the main

1 The concept of standing is also known as 'procedural legitimation', 'active legitimation' or 'legitimation', see *UNCITRAL Model Law on Cross-Border Insolvency with Guide to Enactment and Interpretation,* United Nations Publications (New York), 2014, para. 113, fn. 25.

2 *Guide to Enactment and Interpretation* (n 1), para. 204; Hollander/Graham in: Klaus Pannen (ed.), European Insolvency Regulation, De Gruyter (Berlin), 2007, Part 4, para. 252; according to Fletcher, the provision allows the foreign representative to take effective action on behalf of creditors' interests, Ian F. Fletcher, *Insolvency in Private International Law*, 2nd ed., Oxford University Press (Oxford), 2007, para. 8.47; with respect to other insolvency proceedings of the debtor in the enacting State, on the other hand, there is the more substantive right of participation under Article 12. For the distinction, see para. 1.24.08.

features of the MLCBI, to provide the foreign representative with access to the local courts.[3] However, Article 24 does not simply grant a right to intervene, but makes the granting of such a right dependent on the law of the enacting State. The provision thus pursues a narrow objective. It was merely intended to address the circumstance that the foreign representative may not have been considered as a person who could be granted a right to intervene.[4] The foreign representative is therefore not granted a special possibility to intervene, but rather is put on an equal footing with a local person who has a legitimate interest in the outcome of the decision.[5]

2. Scope of Application

Article 24 joins a number of provisions in the MLCBI that grant the foreign representative procedural standing in the courts of the enacting state.[6] With respect to Article 24, the foreign representative is granted standing to intervene in any proceeding in which the debtor is a party. However, the scope of application is limited on the one hand by the fact that the procedural law of this State ultimately determines whether there is a right to intervene.[7] Article 24 expressly presupposes this as a condition for intervention by the foreign representative in addition to recognition of the foreign proceeding in accordance with Article 17. On the other hand, the scope of application is limited by the proceedings eligible for intervention. First, in distinction to Article 12, only individual proceedings as opposed to collective insolvency proceedings are included.[8] Second, only proceedings not subject to the automatic stay under Articles 20(1)(a) and 21(1)(a) are eligible for intervention.[9] Article 24 does not distinguish between main and non-main proceedings. **1.24.02**

3 *Guide to Enactment and Interpretation* (n 1), para. 25.

4 *Guide to Enactment and Interpretation* (n 1), para. 204.

5 Fletcher (n 2), para. 8.47: '[Article 24] is inserted to the effect that all other requirements of the local law must be met, thereby ensuring that the foreign representative's procedural position is exactly equated to that of any internal party who seeks to intervene'.

6 The Model Law grants the foreign representative standing to commence an insolvency proceeding in the enacting State (Article 11), to participate in insolvency proceedings in the enacting State (Article 12), to seek recognition (Article 15(1)), to request preliminary relief (Article 19), to seek appropriate relief (Article 21) and to initiate avoidance actions (Article 23), see *Hollander/Graham* in: Pannen (n 2), Part 4, para. 136, fn. 333.

7 See para. 1.24.05.

8 See para. 1.24.08.

9 See para. 1.24.10.

B. PREREQUISITES FOR APPLICATION

1.24.03 Article 24 stipulates that the foreign proceeding must have been recognized in accordance with Article 17. Moreover, any additional requirements that the law of the enacting State might attach to the existence of a right to intervene must be observed.

1. Recognition of the Foreign Proceeding

1.24.04 The requirements for the recognition of a foreign proceeding, whether main or non-main, are set by Article 17(1). According to Article 17(1), the foreign proceeding must comply with the legal definition in Article 2(a), the foreign representative must comply with the legal definition in Article 2(d), an application must have been filed in accordance with Article 15(1), respecting the formal requirements in Article 15(2) and (3), and the application must have been submitted to the competent court within the meaning of Article 4. Provided that the recognition does not violate the public policy provisions of the enacting state (Article 6), the competent court or authority (Article 4) shall then recognize the foreign proceeding as foreign main proceeding (Article 17(2)(a)) or foreign non-main proceeding (Article 17(2)(b)), depending on whether the debtor has its COMI or only an establishment in the state of the foreign proceeding. There are no deviations from other provisions in the MLCBI which link their legal effect to the recognition of a foreign proceeding.[10]

2. Additional Requirements

1.24.05 In addition to the recognition of the foreign proceeding, Article 24 expressly states that the existence of a right to intervene depends on compliance with the national law of the enacting State. If the latter imposes additional requirements, these must be observed. The background to this is that many procedural laws grant certain groups of persons the possibility of intervention, but tie this to additional requirements.[11] These remain fully intact.[12] However, Article 24 only generally opens up the possibility that a right to intervene depends on

---

10 Articles 12, 20(1), 21(1), 21(2), 23 also require recognition; also, it is one of the key objectives of the Model Law 'to establish simplified procedures for recognition of qualifying foreign proceedings that would avoid time-consuming legalization or other processes and provide certainty with respect to the decision to recognize', *Guide to Enactment and Interpretation* (fn. 1), para. 29.

11 UNCITRAL, Report of the United Nations Commission on International Trade Law on the work of its thirtieth session, A/52/17, (United Nations 1997), para. 121.

12 *Guide to Enactment and Interpretation* (fn. 1), para 206; see also Paul Torremans, Cross-Border Insolvencies in EU, English and Belgian Law, Wolters Kluwer (The Hague/London/Boston), 2002, 205; Fletcher (n 2),

compliance with these provisions. Due to the multitude of potentially existing conditions, it was deliberately refrained from giving concrete examples.[13] Moreover, such conditions could arise from a variety of legal sources, so it has been left to the individual states themselves to decide which additional conditions to establish.[14] An example of an additional requirement that could be attached to the existence of the foreign representative's right to intervene might be the requirement of a legal interest in the outcome of the dispute between the debtor and the third party.[15] This might be desirable because Article 24 is worded in such a way that it refers to any existing proceedings of the debtor. In personal matters that do not have a sufficient connection to the debtor's insolvency (for example, family law matters) this could go too far. [16]

Most states, such as the United Kingdom[17] and Australia,[18] have adopted the wording of Article 24 without attaching specific requirements to a foreign representative's right to intervene. It is then a question of the individual case as to whether there is a sufficient interest by the foreign representative in intervening and whether additional requirements should be imposed. The US version of Article 24, 11 USC § 1524, even refrains from explicitly requiring compliance with their national law as a condition. This does not necessarily mean that no additional requirements are placed on a foreign representative's right to intervene. Procedural problems could arise in particular from the fact that 11 USC § 1524, as a federal statute, expressly refers also to proceedings in state courts, which follow their own procedural rules.[19] The House Report accompanying the provision is limited to emphasizing that 11 USC § 1524 must apply in both federal and state courts and that substitution of the debtor by the foreign representative is not required, although it may be appropriate in certain circumstances.[20] **1.24.06**

para. 8.47; Bob Wessels, International Insolvency Law Part I., 5th ed., Wolters Kluwer (Deventer), 2022, para. 10323.

13 Report A/52/17 (n 11), para. 121.

14 Report A/52/17 (n 11), para. 121.

15 Report A/52/17 (n 11), para. 121.

16 Report A/52/17 (n 11), para. 120 et seq.

17 See Article 24 Cross-border Insolvency Regulations 2006 ('CBIR 2006').

18 In Australia, the Cross Border Insolvency Act 2008 ('CBIA 2008') is the gateway for the Model Law. Section 6 CBIA 2008 provides that, subject to the Act and with modifications set out in Part 2 of the Act, the Model Law has direct force in Australia. Article 24 applies there without modification.

19 Hollander/Graham in: Pannen (fn. 2), Part 4, para. 255.

20 HR Rep. 109-31, 109th Cong., 1st Sess., 2005 U.S.C.C.A.N., 116.

C. LEGAL CONSEQUENCES

1.24.07 As a legal consequence of Article 24, the foreign representative has the procedural standing[21] to intervene in any proceeding in the enacting State in which the debtor is a party.

1. Intervention

1.24.08 An intervention right, as the *Guide to Enactment and Interpretation* describes it in the context of the MLCBI, exists when, in certain cases, a person who shows a legal interest in the outcome of a dispute, without being a party, has a right to be heard in the proceeding.[22] In the context of Article 24, it is assumed that the foreign representative has a legal interest to be heard in any proceeding in which the debtor is a party.[23] If the requirements of Article 24 are met (that is, the proceeding is recognized and the other procedural requirements of the enacting state are met), the foreign representative has the authority to appear in court and make representations in such proceedings.[24] In this respect the provision shows a certain proximity to Article 12, which allows the foreign representative to participate in certain proceedings of the debtor. The difference is that the term 'participation', as used in Article 12, is more substantial[25] and used by the MLCBI in connection with collective insolvency proceedings, while the term intervention, as in Article 24, is used only in connection with individual proceedings of the debtor.[26] Intervention by the foreign representative is therefore possible only in individual proceedings of the debtor.

1.24.09 In the United States, the foreign representative's right to intervene in a debtor's proceedings (11 USC § 1524, implementing Article 24) is closely related to access rights under 11 USC § 1509. Similar to 11 USC § 1524, 11 USC § 1509(b) grants the foreign representative, upon recognition of the foreign proceeding, the authority to sue or be sued in any US court, to directly apply

---

21 See n 1.

22 *Guide to Enactment and Interpretation* (n 1), para. 207.

23 During UNCITRAL debates, the opinion was expressed that the foreign representative would have a legitimate interest to intervene in proceedings of the debtor only if there was a connection with the debtor's assets and that the scope should therefore be restricted. This was not followed in the result because it seemed difficult, especially in the case of natural persons (that is, individual traders or merchants), to make a clear distinction between the debtor's business and personal affairs, while the latter could also have an impact on the debtor's assets and liabilities: see Report A/52/17 (n 11), para. 120 et seq.

24 *Guide to Enactment and Interpretation* (n 1), para. 208.

25 Fletcher (n 2), para. 8.47: participation involves giving the foreign representative the standing to make petitions, requests or submissions concerning issues such as protection, realization or distribution of assets of the debtor or cooperation with the foreign proceeding; see *Guide to Enactment and Interpretation* (n 1), para. 115.

26 *Guide to Enactment and Interpretation* (n 1), para. 208.

for appropriate relief in that court and to obtain comity and cooperation. The provision thus goes significantly further than Article 9 of the Model, on which it is based.[27] The relationship between 11 USC § 1524 and § 1509 was addressed in *CT Investment Management Co. LLC v Carbonell.*[28] Due to the similar scope of application (that is, the access of the foreign representative to non-insolvency courts in the US), the question arose as to the relationship between the two provisions. The case concerned obligations under a guarantee agreement which, in the plaintiff's view, were triggered because a subsidiary of the defendant had opened a voluntary insolvency proceeding in Mexico. The foreign representative sought access to the US court to request, pursuant to 11 USC § 1509(b)(2), that orders of the Mexican court be recognized, and a stay imposed.[29] The plaintiff argued that the foreign representative lacked the procedural standing to make such applications in the US court. 11 USC § 1524 would limit not only the foreign representative's right to intervene but also the right to apply for appropriate relief under 11 USC § 1509(b)(2) to proceedings in which the debtor is a party. Therefore, the foreign representative could seek relief only to the extent that he had a right to intervene under 11 USC § 1524.[30] The court, however, did not follow this reasoning. No part of 11 USC § 1509(b) would suggest that Congress intended the ability of a foreign representative to apply directly to a court for appropriate relief to be limited in cases in which the Chapter 15 debtor is a party. The plaintiff would have offered no case or legislative history supporting the proposition that 11 USC § 1524 was intended to limit 11 USC § 1509(b) in such a way. Instead, the plain language of both provisions would indicate that they are separate grants of authority.[31]

2. Proceedings

Article 24 is initially broad in its wording and names any proceeding in the enacting State to which the debtor is a party as eligible for intervention.[32] In fact, however, Article 24 can only be considered for a narrow scope of pro- **1.24.10**

27 US courts underline the interrelatedness of 11 USC § 1509 and § 1524 by emphasizing the following access rights as a consequence of recognition of the foreign proceeding: 'The foreign representative is able to sue and be sued in US courts [11 USC: § 1509(b)(1)], to apply directly to US court for relief [11 USC § 1509(b)(2)], to commence a non-Chapter 15 case [11 USC § 1511(a)], to intervene in any US case in which the debtor is a party [11 USC § 1524], and US courts must grant comity and cooperation to the foreign representative [11 USC § 1509(b)(3)], *Fogerty v Petroquests Resources Inc. (In re Condor Insurance Co.)* [5th Cir. 2010], 601 F 3d, 319, 324; *Jaffé v. Samsung Electronics Co. Ltd.*, 737 F.3d 14, 24 [4th Cir. 2013].'

28 *CT Inv. Mgmt. Co. v Carbonell*, 10 Civ. 6872 [SDNY Jan. 11, 2012].

29 *CT Inv. Mgmt. Co. v Carbonell*, 10 Civ. 6872 at [6] [SDNY Jan. 11, 2012].

30 *CT Inv. Mgmt. Co. v Carbonell*, 10 Civ. 6872 at [7] [SDNY Jan. 11, 2012].

31 *CT Inv. Mgmt. Co. v Carbonell*, 10 Civ. 6872 at [7 et seq] [SDNY Jan. 11, 2012].

32 Provided that the law of the enacting State does not impose additional requirements: see para. 1.24.05.

ceedings. First, Article 24, as distinguished from Article 12, refers only to individual proceedings and not collective insolvency proceedings.[33] Thus, proceedings within the meaning of Article 24 are only those concerning individual actions against the debtor by a third party or by a third party against the debtor. Second, the foreign representative may intervene in proceedings of the debtor only if they are not subject to the automatic stay under Article 20(1)(a) or 21(1)(a). Since the automatic stay applies to all proceedings concerning the debtor's assets, rights, obligations or liabilities, this leaves only a few proceedings in which the foreign representative could intervene. The practical relevance of the provision is therefore considered to be low.[34]

1.24.11 The phrase 'any proceeding to which the debtor is a party' is intended to include extrajudicial proceedings, according to the *Guide to Enactment and Interpretation*.[35] In the United States, this may be different. 11 USC § 1524, which implements Article 24 there, concretizes the term proceedings to refer to proceedings in federal or state court. Other proceedings outside these courts seem to be excluded.[36]

---

33 See para. 1.24.08.

34 Ho in: Look Chan Ho (ed.), A Commentary on the UNCITRAL Model Law, 4th ed., Globe Law & Business (London), 2017, 282; Andre J. Berends, The UNCITRAL Model Law on Cross-Border Insolvency: A Comprehensive Overview (1998), 6 Tul. J. Int'l & Comp. L., 309, 378; Torremans (fn. 12), 205; in the US, however, cases where the debtor is a plaintiff may be relevant. The automatic stay implemented there by 11 USC § 1520(a)(1) in conjunction with 11 USC § 362(a)(1)–(6) relates to actions against the debtor and its property and not to proceedings originally initiated by the debtor, see Samuel L. Bufford, United States International Insolvency Law, Oxford University Press (New York), 2009, para. 2.24.

35 *Guide to Enactment and Interpretation* (n 1), para. 205.

36 Hollander/Graham in: Pannen (n 2), Part 4, para. 254.

Chapter IV Cooperation with foreign courts and foreign representatives

Article 25

COOPERATION AND DIRECT COMMUNICATION BETWEEN A COURT OF THIS STATE AND FOREIGN COURTS OR FOREIGN REPRESENTATIVES

Stephan Madaus

1. In matters referred to in Article 1, the court shall cooperate to the maximum extent possible with foreign courts or foreign representatives, either directly or through a [*insert the title of a person or body administering a reorganization or liquidation under the law of the enacting State*].
2. The court is entitled to communicate directly with, or to request information or assistance directly from, foreign courts or foreign representatives.

A. INTRODUCTION TO ARTICLE 25

1. Rationale

1.25.01 Articles 25–27 establish the very foundation of cross-border insolvency law. While the MLCBI respects the differences among national procedural laws and does not attempt a substantive unification of insolvency law, it provides a framework for cooperation between jurisdictions.[1] This includes prominently the permission and authorization of the courts of the enacting State in Article 25(1) to cooperate more effectively with foreign courts and foreign insolvency representatives involved in an insolvency matter.[2] The MLCBI permits courts in the enacting State (Article 25) and persons administering insolvency proceedings in the enacting State (Article 26) to seek assistance abroad and respond to requests of assistance from abroad.[3] In order to provide guidance on how to cooperate with courts and representatives abroad, Article 27 sets out some possible means of cooperation in a non-exhaustive list.[4] The objective is to 'maximize returns to creditors (in liquidation and reorganization proceedings) and (in reorganization proceedings) to facilitate protection of investment and the preservation of employment through fair and efficient administration of the insolvency estate'.[5]

The rules on cross-border cooperation are a core element of the MLCBI.[6] More specifically, they form one of four main elements of the MLCBI: access, recognition, relief (assistance) and cooperation.[7] Given the fact that neither the business nor the assets of an insolvent debtor are necessarily confined to a specific jurisdiction, an insolvency case with cross-border aspects is in need of additional, cross-border tools. The courts and insolvency representatives of the country in which the main insolvency proceedings have commenced would need the support of institutions abroad to investigate, freeze or realize assets, to give notice to foreign creditors or to find the best solution for a reorganization of the enterprise. Cooperation with authorities abroad is the only realistic way to prevent the dissipation of assets, organize a coordinated sale of assets or implement a restructuring plan. Courts in the countries where assets or creditors are located require a legal basis that empowers them to respond to such requests and extend cooperation. The power at common law to assist a foreign 1.25.02

1 *UNCITRAL Model Law on Cross-Border Insolvency with Guide to Enactment and Interpretation*, United Nations Publications (New York), 2014, para. 3.

2 *Guide to Enactment and Interpretation* (n 1), para. 3 at lit. d).

3 *Guide to Enactment and Interpretation* (n 1), para. 3 at lit. e).

4 *Guide to Enactment and Interpretation* (n 1), para. 41.

5 *UNCITRAL Model Law on Cross-Border Insolvency: The Judicial Perspective*, United Nations Publications (New York), 2014, para. 154.

6 *Guide to Enactment and Interpretation* (n 1), para. 211; *Judicial Perspective* (n 5), para. 155. See also Allan L. Gropper, Cooperation in Cross-Border Insolvency Cases, Festschrift für Heinz Vallender, RWS (Cologne) 2021, 207: "the heart of the Model Law".

7 Felicity Deane and Rosalind Mason, The UNCITRAL Model Law on Cross-border Insolvency and the Rule of Law, Int. Insolv. Rev., Vol. 25: 138, 147 (2016); Gerard McCormack and Wan Wai Yee, The UNCITRAL Model Law on Cross-Border Insolvency Comes of Age: New Times or New Paradigms? 54 Tex. Int'l L. J. 273, 276 (2019).

court of insolvency jurisdiction does not seem to provide a sufficiently reliable basis for cross-border cooperation.[8] The provisions in Articles 25 and 26 aim at providing a statutory basis for the cooperation of local courts and office holders with foreign courts and office holders in insolvency matters in both directions. They were based on the principle of comity among nations and seize the opportunity to make this principle more concrete by adapting it to the particular circumstances of cross-border insolvencies.[9] In countries where such forms of cooperation are based on the principle of reciprocity, the MLCBI is able to secure reciprocity either by adopting its rules in a bilateral treaty[10] or by enabling the development of case law in countries that gives proof to the reciprocal assistance and cooperation. It should also be noted that the rules on cooperation do not depend on any allegiance to the principle of (modified) universality. Cooperation is just as needed, if not more, where cross-border insolvency rules are developed under a principle of territoriality.[11] Finally, the ability to cooperate in cross-border insolvency cases may also find a statutory basis in countries that have not enacted the MLCBI.[12] Most prominently, Articles 41–43 EI provide for a similar set of rules that are directly applicable within the EU and authorise courts and office holders to communicate directly and to cooperate within the Common Market based on the principle of mutual trust.

2. Scope of Application

1.25.03 'Cooperation is not dependent upon recognition',[13] which means that the ability to cooperate is not limited to foreign courts or insolvency representatives that are acting in foreign proceedings recognized as a foreign main or non-main proceeding pursuant to Article 17. Instead, the foreign courts

---

8 See, for instance, for Bermuda: *Stephen John Hunt v Transworld Payment Solutions UK Ltd (in liquidation)* [2020] Bda LR 17, on one hand, and *Singularis Holdings Ltd v PricewaterhouseCoopers (Bermuda)* [2014] UKPC 36, on the other; see also McCoy, The Singularis Work-around? Overcoming Limitations to the Common Law Power of Assistance for Foreign Insolvency Investigations (2019), 16 ICR, 210 et seq; Omar, Judicial Cooperation in the Post-Singularis World, (2018), 15 ICR, 22 et seq; Zhen Qu/Godwin, Does the Common Law Power to Grant Cross-Border Insolvency Assistance Apply to an Insolvency Winding-Up that is Voluntary? The reaction to *Singularis* from Singapore and Hong Kong, (2019), 28 IIR, 305 et seq. See for England: *Kireeva (Trustee & Bankruptcy Manager in Russia of Bedzhamov) v Bedzhamov* [2022] EWCA Civ. 35 and [2021] EWHC 2281 (Ch), on the one hand, and *Cambridge Gas Transportation Corp v Official Committee of Unsecured Creditors of Navigator Holdings Plc* [2006] UKPC 26, on the other.

9 *Guide to Enactment and Interpretation* (n 1), para. 214. See also Wessels, *International Insolvency Law Part I.*, 4th ed., Wolters Kluwer (Deventer), 2015, para. 10325.

10 *Guide to Enactment and Interpretation* (n 1), para. 216.

11 Reinhard Bork, *Principles of Cross-Border Insolvency Law*, Intersentia (Cambridge), 2017, para. 2.45.

12 See, for instance, §§ 348(2) and 357 InsO for Germany and, even more prominently, Articles 41–43 and 56–58 EIR.

13 *Guide to Enactment and Interpretation* (n 1), paras. 40, 212.

or insolvency representatives may require cooperation in another court at an earlier stage, for instance in the preparation of a request for recognition.[14] Even more, Articles 25 to 27 also apply in cases where recognition is not available for the proceedings in one (or more) of the participating countries because they are neither main nor non-main proceedings under Article 17. Proceedings which commenced on the basis of the presence of assets, including those aimed at recognition of a foreign main proceeding, are able to seek assistance elsewhere accordingly.[15]

The governance of concurring proceedings for the same debtor in two or more countries is further described in Chapter V of the MLCBI. Articles 28 to 30 protect the virtues of cooperation by limiting the effects of territorial proceedings and providing for the need to cooperate, and thereby coordinate the decisions of courts and acts of the administrators in concurrent proceedings. The rules in Chapter V do not derogate from the rules on cooperation in Articles 25 to 27; they even refer to them directly and should be read as a clarification of the need for cooperation in a case with concurrent proceedings. Any decision, in particular any relief granted under Article 19 or 21, shall be taken with a view to concurrent proceedings abroad. **1.25.04**

The MLCBI only deals with insolvency proceedings concerning one debtor. **1.25.05** The rules on cooperation only apply to parallel proceedings over the assets or business of the same debtor (entity).[16] It is obvious, however, that a similar need to cooperate may also arise in the insolvency of an enterprise group when insolvency proceedings commence for several or all group entities as separate debtors. The cooperation of courts and representatives in concurrent main or non-main proceedings of an insolvent enterprise group may nonetheless be covered by a cooperation-friendly interpretation of Articles 25 to 27 into local law. The wording of the rights and duties to cooperate does not limit their scope to foreign proceedings for the same debtor. The protocols referred to in Article 27(d) were mostly developed in group cases. Pending the adoption of the Model Law on Enterprise Group Insolvency[17] with its special provisions on cooperation and direct communication in Articles 9 to 18 in an enacting State, any cross-border cooperation should find a sufficient legal basis in local rules which have implemented Articles 25 to 27 of this Model Law.

---

14 *Guide to Enactment and Interpretation* (n 1), paras. 40, 212.

15 *Guide to Enactment and Interpretation* (n 1), para. 212.

16 Articles 1(c), 28–30.

17 *UNCITRAL Model Law on Enterprise Group Insolvency with Guide to Enactment,* United Nations Publications (New York), 2020.

B. PREREQUISITES FOR APPLICATION

1. Matters as described in Article 1

1.25.06 Article 25(1) introduces the duty to cooperate in matters described in Article 1. These matters include any inbound requests for assistance by a foreign court or a foreign representative in connection with a foreign proceeding, any outbound request for assistance in a foreign State in connection with a local insolvency proceeding, any case of concurrent proceedings and any case where foreign creditors or other interested persons have an interest in requesting the commencement of, or participating in, a local proceeding.[18] The definition of foreign proceedings in Article 2(a) explains that any cross-border assistance or cross-border interest in insolvency proceedings is covered by the provisions on cooperation in Articles 25 and 26.

2. Court

1.25.07 Article 25 provides for the entitlements and duties of a 'court' to cooperate across borders. The corresponding provision for a person or body administering the estate follows in Article 26 (see [1.26.05]). The term 'court' is not defined in Article 2 but a 'foreign court' is described as 'a judicial or other authority competent to control or supervise a foreign proceeding'. This definition should also suffice to argue in favour of a wider, functional approach to the interpretation of the term 'court'.[19]

C. LEGAL CONSEQUENCES

1. Authorization to Cooperate and Communicate Directly

1.25.08 Article 25(1) is intended to fill any gap in national laws by 'expressively empowering courts' to cooperate in insolvency proceedings.[20] It provides a legal basis for cooperation.[21] Hence, the question whether a court is even allowed to cooperate with a foreign court or a foreign representative is answered favourably.

18 Article 1(1) lit. a) to d).

19 More cautious Wessels, International Insolvency Law Part I. (n 9), para. 10326 ('civil or commercial courts').

20 *Guide to Enactment and Interpretation* (n 1), para. 210.

21 *Guide to Enactment and Interpretation* (n 1), para. 213.

Article 25(2) accentuates the ability of the court to 'communicate directly with, or to request information or assistance directly from, foreign courts or foreign representatives'. The communication of information is an 'essential element of cooperation',[22] yet only, as Article 27(b) explains, one of the means of cooperation. The reason to prominently feature the ability of the court to communicate directly with foreign institutions is only understood against the backdrop of traditional, time-consuming forms of communication, which involved communication via higher courts, letters rogatory or other diplomatic and consular channels.[23] The amount of time it takes to communicate through the channels of diplomacy renders any communication in insolvency cases useless. The identification and preservation of assets for the estate and the coordination of proceedings is often driven by a level of urgency[24] and time constraint that simply requires direct communication across borders. Article 25(2) opens direct channels between enacting States and third countries willing to do the same. The provision clarifies[25] that the court is entitled to actively communicate in order to request information or assistance. The court is also allowed to passively receive such requests directly from foreign courts or representatives. **1.25.09**

The legislative option at the end of Article 25(1) allows courts to communicate with foreign courts and representatives through the insolvency practitioner appointed in the case. This option is mindful of the reservation in the judiciary of many countries to communicate directly, especially when this involves the use of a foreign language or a less familiar legal culture. In such cases, the use of the experience, knowledge and resources of the insolvency practitioner may be of great value. In addition, Article 27(a) points at the ability of the court to separately appoint a person or body for the special functions of cross-border communication and cooperation. Such an appointment is particularly useful in cases in which the administrator lacks the resources or whenever such communication should be organized independently for specific reasons (see [1.27.03]). **1.25.10**

22 *UNCITRAL Practice Guide on Cross-Border Insolvency Cooperation*, United Nations Publications (New York), 2010, Chapter II, para. 4.

23 *Guide to Enactment and Interpretation* (n 1), para. 218.

24 *Guide to Enactment and Interpretation* (n 1), para. 218.

25 The adoption of Article 25(1) without 25(2), as in Canada, does not hinder direct court-to-court communication therefore. See Golick, Riesterer and Wasserman in: Look Chan Ho (ed.), *A Commentary on the UNCITRAL Model Law*, 4th ed., Globe Law & Business (London), 2017, 110.

2. Duty to Cooperate

1.25.11 Article 25(1) not only entitles a court to cooperate; it mandates cooperation.[26] Here, the principle of modified universalism shines through[27] because it follows that the court has no discretion as to whether or not to cooperate whenever a cross-border matter arises.[28] The decisions on when and how to cooperate, however, remain in the discretion of the court.[29] Accordingly, the use of means of direct communication remains in the court's discretion. Article 25(2) merely provides a legal basis for this, not a duty. Further guidance on how courts exercise their discretion and where they find their limits (see [1.25.14]) can be provided by court guidelines adopted by the court (see [1.27.27]). The significant level of discretion makes it difficult to conceive that a court's cooperation is enforceable as such.[30]

1.25.12 The implementation of Article 25 in a number of countries does not include a duty of the court to cooperate as suggested in Article 25(1). In the United Kingdom, most notably, the courts 'may cooperate',[31] which is understood to leave cooperation to the discretion of the court as before.[32] Similar implementations are present, for instance, in Poland[33] or Singapore.[34]

3. Content and Limits

1.25.13 Article 25(1) only regulates the cooperation of local courts 'with foreign courts or foreign representatives'. It does not extend the need to cooperate to other stakeholders abroad. The court is not obliged to communicate or otherwise cooperate with, for instance, a foreign creditors' committee or a foreign mediator, examiner or supervisor even if they are formally appointed. Any cooperation would need to be organized through the foreign court or representative.

---

26 *Guide to Enactment and Interpretation* (n 1), para. 213.

27 Bork, *Principles of Cross-Border Insolvency Law* (n 11), para. 2.71.

28 See Wessels, *International Insolvency Law Part I* (n 9), para. 10326 ('no room for an attitude of non-commitment, apathy or reluctance').

29 *Guide to Enactment and Interpretation* (n 1), para. 213; *Judicial Perspective* (n 5), para. 157. See also, in the context of similar rules in the EIR, Michael C. Frege, Verhandlungslösungen in grenzüberschreitenden Insolvenzen: '*Concordia firmat vires*', Festschrift für Christoph Paulus, C.H.Beck (München) 2022, 200.

30 *Allan L. Gropper*, Cooperation in Cross-Border Insolvency Cases (n 6), 211.

31 Article 25(1) Cross-Border Insolvency Regulations 2006, Schedule 1.

32 Ian F. Fletcher, *The Law of Insolvency*, 5th ed., Sweet & Maxwell (London), 2017, para. 32-044. See also Look Chan Ho in: Look Chan Ho (ed.), *A Commentary on the UNCITRAL Model Law* (n 25), 283.

33 Barlowski in: Look Chan Ho (ed.), *A Commentary on the UNCITRAL Model Law* (n 25), 4th ed., Globe Law & Business (London), 2017, 458.

34 Chan, Yeo and Yeo in: Look Chan Ho (ed.), *A Commentary on the UNCITRAL Model Law* (n 25), 550.

Article 25(1) only provides for the ability and duty to cooperate 'to the maximum extent possible'. Following the logic of the MLCBI, it is the law of the enacting State that describes which forms of cooperation are legally possible to a certain extent.[35] **1.25.14**

(a) Procedural Insolvency Matters (Case Management)

The court would need to cooperate when conducting insolvency proceedings or ancillary proceedings in insolvency matters as described in the law of the enacting State. It is the lex fori that provides for all relevant procedural steps and decisions to take. This includes any discretion for the court as well as its limits. For instance, local rules on notice may describe in detail whether creditors are to be informed directly about the decision to commence proceedings or whether the publication of the opening decision suffices. Any need for notice could include foreign creditors and potentially prompt the need for assistance abroad if it was to be done with formality. Similarly, the court may have discretion about the summoning of hearings, sometimes within certain statutory time frames. The existence of parallel foreign proceedings would be a cross-border aspect that triggers the duty to cooperate with the foreign court which would entail the duty to coordinate hearings with the foreign courts within the time limits provided by the law applicable. The duty to cooperate is not able to extend the limits as they exist in the law of the enacting State; it works within its limits.[36] The duty to cooperate cannot override decisions of the national legislators.[37] Possible forms of cooperation are illustrated in Article 27. **1.25.15**

(1) Conflict of Interest

Local rules in insolvency law may contain the duty of the court or representative not to act in a way that is detrimental to the general interest of their estate or creditors.[38] In the context of cross-border cooperation, any communication or coordination by the court or representative would be out of limits if it had the potential to cause harm to the estate if respective rules on conflict of interest were to be broadly interpreted. Cooperation would be limited to matters that benefit the estate by avoiding costs or maximising value or even shifting value from other, less restrictive jurisdictions. Any cooperation would depend on a cost benefit projection. Such a cautious, territorialistic approach certainly contradicts the spirit of cooperation as envisaged by the Model Law. It should **1.25.16**

35 See Article 27(f) asking the enacting State to list additional forms or examples of cooperation.

36 *Guide to Enactment and Interpretation* (n 1), para. 221.

37 Bork, *Principles of Cross-Border Insolvency Law* (n 11), para. 2.67.

38 See, for instance, § 1 InsO (German Insolvency Code).

be mitigated as much as possible. As far as it is allowed in the construction of local law, only certain direct costs or losses due to cooperation should be considered as relevant. The benefits of a coordinated solution for the debtor's assets should not be neglected even if only a share of these benefits can be claimed by the local estate.[39]

(2) Privacy and Confidentiality

1.25.17 Relevant limits can result from the application of various local rules, not only the rules on insolvency proceedings. Most prominently, applicable rules on (data) privacy[40] or confidentiality may hinder a court to share protected information directly. It is a matter of the applicable law whether protected information may be shared under certain conditions, such as confidentiality agreements, or with additional safeguards, for instance via a trusted third party. In this regard, it should be mentioned that the legal culture in handling information about the status of insolvency proceedings including any motions, decisions and dates of hearings varies widely. Some jurisdictions, most prominently the United States,[41] make such information publicly available, even online. Other jurisdictions, including Germany, insist on the principle of confidentiality and limit any access to such information.

(b) Substantive Insolvency Matters

1.25.18 In principle, the ability and duty to cooperate also extends to decisions that materially affect the rights of a party to the proceedings. Where courts order a discharge of debt, sanction a restructuring plan or decide on an avoidance claim or the duty of a person to produce documents relevant to the case, they act based on local law and within the limits of this law. This includes any decision on jurisdiction. The right and duty to cooperate is not able to derogate from the exclusive competence of the local judge by allowing the foreign court to get involved in making the decision on the merits.[42] This does, however, not hinder court-to-court communication and cooperation as such. Instead, the courts involved must act with care.

(1) No Pre-emption of Court Judgments

1.25.19 The communication of information and the coordination of decisions regarding the organization of the proceedings (see 1.25.12) is not limited by concerns

---

39 A similar suggestion is formulated by Ilya Kokorin and Bob Wessels, *Cross-Border Protocols in Insolvencies of Multination al Enterprise Groups*, Edward Elgar Publishing (Cheltenham) 2021, para. 8.48.

40 *Guide to Enactment and Interpretation* (n 1), para. 221.

41 § 107 US Bankruptcy Code.

42 See the Guidelines for Communication and Cooperation between Courts in Cross-Border Insolvency Matters of the Judicial Insolvency Network (JIN Guidelines), Guideline 4(iv) and 5.

regarding any potential direct or indirect effects on substantive rights. This includes any cooperation between courts preparing decisions that concern the constitution of the estate and thereby affect the rights of creditors only indirectly. Courts may and should, for instance, cooperate when allocating assets of the estate, such as crypto assets, even if this allocation is a controversial issue amongst stakeholders. The ability to cooperate typically ends where a court is asked to pre-empt its own decision by accepting the (future) decision of the foreign court, as prepared by court-to-court communication and joint hearings, as binding unless the ability to defer is an option expressively provided for by the law applicable.[43]

(2) Fair Trial

The role of court-to-court cooperation in preparing a decision on the merits may also call for the application of relevant rules of evidence securing a fair trial under the laws of the participating courts. This may include the right of parties to be informed timely, to object to or to be present in oral/video communications or joint hearings.[44] The implementation of Article 25(2) in the United States and British Virgin Islands (BVI), for instance, added reference to the rights of parties by adding that any direct communication of the court is 'subject to the rights of parties to notice and participation at hearings'.[45] **1.25.20**

(c) Cross-border Matters

In a cross-border case, the request of a foreign court or representative for cooperation can aim at an act which, while not explicitly forbidden under local law, is unknown to local law. Here, the mere fact that the requested act or decision is unknown would by itself not hinder cooperation. It is solely a matter of the construction of the law of the enacting State whether the gap in the legislation is to be understood in a way that would amount to a prohibition.[46] Article 25(1) finds limits to the need to cooperate only in local law. The fact that the requested decision or act would also be available as a relief upon recognition (Article 21(1)) to support main or non-main proceedings bears as little relevance as the fact that the requested decision or act would not be available under this rule because the request comes from a jurisdiction where the debtor only **1.25.21**

43 *Re T&N* [2004] EWHC 2878 (Ch) at [25]; *Perpetual Trustee Company Ltd v BNY Corporate Trustee Services Ltd & Anor* [2009] EWHC 2953 (Ch) at [46]. For a critical review, see Look Chan Ho in: Look Chan Ho (ed.), A Commentary on the UNCITRAL Model Law (n 25), 283: 'What vital role should inter-court communication play, if not to attempt to resolve matters of controversy?'

44 *Judicial Perspective* (n 5), para. 160; see also Parbery; in the matter of *Lehman Brothers Australia Limited* [2011] FCA 1449 [paras 53, 59, 62].

45 For the US, see 11 USC § 1525(2). For the BVI see sec. 458(2) of the BVI Insolvency Act. See also Kite in: Look Chan Ho (ed.), A Commentary on the UNCITRAL Model Law (n 25), 79.

46 Bork, *Principles of Cross-Border Insolvency Law* (n 11), para. 2.69.

has assets. The rights and duties under Chapter IV are independent of any recognition under Chapter III.[47] Hence, relief that may not be available upon recognition may nonetheless be legally granted as an act of cooperation to the extent possible under these separate rules of local law. This may potentially even include the enforcement of a foreign judgment pursuant to provisions on cooperation.[48] In countries where a statutory basis for enforcement is missing, the provision on cross-border cooperation may authorize the enforcement in the enacting State provided that no provision limits the ability of the court, such as public policy concerns. It remains a matter of the interpretation of local law as far as limits are to be identified. The enactment of the MLIJ[49] provides clarity by securing the recognition and enforcement of insolvency-related judgments as additional relief pursuant to its Article 13 or as additional relief under Article 21 of the MLCBI (Article X).

1.25.22 The question may also arise vice versa. A foreign court can request the cooperation of a court in the form of a decision available under local law but not available under the law of the foreign court. For instance, the duty of a third party to provide information or produce documents relevant to investigate assets of the debtor's estate may not exist under the foreign law. If such a duty is, however, provided for in the law of the enacting State, a judgment ordering the production of documents could be issued as a form of cooperation.[50] It is a matter of the law on cooperation to identify its limits. The principle of cooperation would certainly need to account for the reasonable, good faith expectations of the affected party. Cooperation may therefore well be limited to cases where the third party is domiciled locally or otherwise submitted to the jurisdiction that contains the relevant duties.

1.25.23 This does not mean, however, that the duty to cooperate ends where the requesting foreign court is under no obligation to reciprocate,[51] in particu-

---

47 *Guide to Enactment and Interpretation* (n 1), para. 212.

48 See *Rubin v Eurofinance SA* [2010] ECWA (Civ) 895, overturned in *Rubin v Eurofinance SA* [2012] UKSC 46 [125]–[128] (appeal taken from [2011] ECWA (Civ) 917). For comments, see e.g. Gerard McCormack and Wan Wai Yee, The UNCITRAL Model Law on Cross-Border Insolvency Comes of Age: New Times or New Paradigms? 54 Tex. Int'l L. J. 273, 279–81 (2019); Fu, Cross-Border Insolvency in Bermuda: Cambridge Gas Revisited, (2018), 31 Insolv. Int., 118 et seq.; Omar, Cross-Border Insolvency and Principles of Judicial Assistance: Recent Themes and Developments, in: Santen/van Offeren (eds.), Tribute to Bob Wessels, Kluwer 2014, 103, 111 et seq.

49 UNCITRAL Model Law on Recognition and Enforcement of Insolvency-Related Judgments with Guide to Enactment, United Nations Publications (New York), 2019.

50 See *PricewaterhouseCoopers v Saad Investments Company Limited* [2014] UKPC 35; *Singularis Holdings Limited v PricewaterhouseCoopers* [2014] UKPC 36.

51 Wessels, *International Insolvency Law Part I.* (n 9), para. 10326.

lar because the MLCBI has not yet been adopted there. Reciprocity is not a requirement for cooperation.

Article 26

COOPERATION AND DIRECT COMMUNICATION BETWEEN THE [*INSERT THE TITLE OF A PERSON OR BODY ADMINISTERING A REORGANIZATION OR LIQUIDATION UNDER THE LAW OF THE ENACTING STATE*] AND FOREIGN COURTS OR FOREIGN REPRESENTATIVES

Stephan Madaus

1. In matters referred to in Article 1, a [*insert the title of a person or body administering a reorganization or liquidation under the law of the enacting State*] shall, in the exercise of its functions and subject to the supervision of the court, cooperate to the maximum extent possible with foreign courts or foreign representatives.
2. The [*insert the title of a person or body administering a reorganization or liquidation under the law of the enacting State*] is entitled, in the exercise of its functions and subject to the supervision of the court, to communicate directly with foreign courts or foreign representatives.

A. INTRODUCTION TO ARTICLE 26

1. Rationale

Article 26(1) extends the duty to cooperate beyond the court (Article 25) to the person or body administering the estate.[1] Article 26(2) mirrors Article 25(2) in authorizing the direct communication of the administrating body or person with foreign courts or representatives. The provisions in Articles 25 and 26 establish a basis for the cooperation of courts and insolvency practitioners in the enacting State with foreign courts and foreign insolvency practitioners. Implemented globally, the cooperation on both ends is supported by the rights and duties under these Articles. 1.26.01

Cross-border communication and cooperation has its roots in the cooperation of insolvency practitioners. It originated in the practical needs of administering the insolvency of multinational enterprises.[2] Non-governmental organizations of insolvency practitioners spearheaded the first initiatives for cooperation guidelines and model provisions.[3] The original European Insolvency Regulation of 2000 only contained a provision on the cooperation of 'liquidators', not courts.[4] The idea of direct cooperation between courts was difficult to process in many jurisdictions, especially with a civil law background.[5] In practice, cooperation between insolvency practitioners is still the backbone of cross-border coordination and success. Korean courts, for instance, are still 'more likely to exchange information through a trustee than by direct communication with a foreign court because of the difficulties in dealing with differences in the legal systems and languages of the foreign courts'.[6] 1.26.02

1 *UNCITRAL Model Law on Cross-Border Insolvency with Guide to Enactment and Interpretation*, United Nations Publications (New York), 2014, para. 219.

2 See, most notably, the global insolvency proceedings following the death of Robert Maxwell in 1991: *Maxwell Communications Corp.* [1992] BCLC 465; 170 BR 800 (Bankr. SDNY 1994); see also Jay Lawrence Westbrook, 'Comment: A More Optimistic View of Cross-Border Insolvency', 72(3) Wash U L Rev 950 (1994).

3 See the 1989 Model International Insolvency Cooperation Act (MIICA) or the 1990 Cross-Border Insolvency Concordat, both developed under the auspices of Committee J of the Section on Business Law of the International Bar Association in 1989. UNCITRAL Practice Guide on Cross-Border Insolvency Cooperation, United Nations Publications (New York), 2010, Chapter I.

4 See Article 31 EIR 2000.

5 The European Insolvency Regulation introduced such duties only in its 2015 Recast, see Articles 42, 43 and 57, 58 EIR, again only supplementing the cooperation among insolvency practitioners.

6 Rim in: Look Chan Ho (ed.), *A Commentary on the UNCITRAL Model Law*, 4th ed., Globe Law & Business (London), 2017, 595.

2. Scope of Application

1.26.03 The scope of Article 26 follows Article 25 (see [1.25.03]). The application of the provision neither depends on the recognition of the foreign proceedings nor is derogated by such recognition. In case of concurrent proceedings, the need to cooperate in order to coordinate proceedings is further detailed in Articles 28 to 30.

B. PREREQUISITES FOR APPLICATION

1. Matters as described in Article 1

1.26.04 Article 26(1) introduces the duty to cooperate in matters referred to in Article 1 just like Article 25(1) (see [1.25.06]). Any cross-border assistance in insolvency proceedings is covered and can be granted or sought based on the need to cooperate.

2. Person or Body Administering the Estate

1.26.05 Article 26(1) assumes that the enacting State is filling the gap left in the text to insert 'title of a person or body administering a reorganization or liquidation under the law of the enacting State'. This provision reflects the essential role of office holders who are appointed to administer assets of insolvent debtors.[7] Accordingly, the enacting State should name all persons or bodies who may be appointed in their insolvency proceedings, especially where there are various types of proceedings. In restructuring proceedings, the administration of the estate may be left to the debtor (debtor in possession), even without the supervision of an office holder.[8] The rules on cooperation would need to include such forms of the administration of the estate.

C. LEGAL CONSEQUENCES

1. Authorization to Cooperate and Communicate Directly

1.26.06 Article 26(1) provides the legal basis for the cooperation of the insolvency practitioner of the estate with foreign courts and representatives. Article 26(2) highlights the ability to communicate with them directly as part of the ability

7 *Guide to Enactment and Interpretation* (n 1), para. 219.

8 See, for instance, Chapter 11 of the US Bankruptcy Code.

to cooperate. The structure of the article follows the structure of Article 25 (see [1.25.08]).

2. Duty to Cooperate

Article 26(1) not only authorizes but mandates cross-border cooperation within certain limits (see [1.26.09]).[9] Where cross-border assistance or coordination is required, the legal duty to cooperate is principally stated by the law. What remains in the discretion of the administrator is the selection of appropriate means and the timing of cooperation. **1.26.07**

3. Content and Limits

Article 26(1) follows the example of Article 25(1) and only regulates the cooperation of local insolvency practitioners 'with foreign courts or foreign representatives'. It does not include the duty to cooperate with other stakeholders in foreign proceedings (see [1.25.13]). **1.26.08**

Just as a court pursuant to Article 25(1), the insolvency practitioner is only obliged to cooperate with foreign courts or foreign representatives 'to the maximum extent possible'. The available means and relevant limits to any act of cooperation are found in the law of the enacting State (see also [1.25.14]). Article 26(1) reflects these limits by stressing that the duty to cooperate is limited to acts taken by the insolvency practitioner 'in the exercise of its functions' as defined by the law of the enacting State. Concerns in enacting States regarding acts of insolvency practitioners in favour of foreign proceedings are significant. In the United Kingdom, for instance, such concerns led to the introduction of the additional safeguard that the British insolvency office-holder shall (only) cooperate to the extent 'consistent with his other duties under the law of Great Britain'.[10] **1.26.09**

The extent of the insolvency practitioner's discretion in selecting available means of cooperation (see [1.26.07]) may be further diminished by the fact that the insolvency practitioner acts under the overall supervision of the court in many countries, sometimes even as an officer of the court. As for any statutory limits in the ability to cooperate (see [1.25.14]), the 'Model Law does not modify the rules already existing in the insolvency law of the enacting State on the supervisory functions of the court over the activities of the insolvency **1.26.10**

9 *Guide to Enactment and Interpretation* (n. 1), para. 213.

10 Article 25(1) Cross-Border Insolvency Regulations 2006, Schedule 1. See also Ian F. Fletcher, *The Law of Insolvency*, 5th ed., Sweet & Maxwell (London), 2017, para. 32-045.

representative'.[11] Any limit issued by the supervising court would need to be respected. The Guide to Enactment and Interpretation also emphasizes that an act of cross-border cooperation that is principally within the latitude of the insolvency practitioner shall not be restricted without good reason. In particular, there is no suggestion in the MLCBI that 'ad hoc authorization would be needed for each communication between the insolvency representative and a foreign body'.[12]

1.26.11 The interplay between the court and the insolvency practitioner identified in Article 26 is of the utmost importance in practical terms when cross-border cooperation is an issue. Articles 25 and 26 enable both to communicate directly and to cooperate to the maximum extent possible. The court may utilize the insolvency practitioner in order to cooperate (see Article 25(1) last part). The court may also instruct the insolvency practitioner as part of the judicial supervision. This may lead to a division of work concerning the cooperation with foreign proceedings in order to coordinate – either ad hoc or as described in guidelines of the court (see [1.27.27]).

11 *Guide to Enactment and Interpretation* (n 1), para. 219.

12 *Guide to Enactment and Interpretation* (n 1), para. 219.

Article 27

FORMS OF COOPERATION

Stephan Madaus

Cooperation referred to in Articles 25 and 26 may be implemented by any appropriate means, including:

(a) Appointment of a person or body to act at the direction of the court;
(b) Communication of information by any means considered appropriate by the court;
(c) Coordination of the administration and supervision of the debtor's assets and affairs;
(d) Approval or implementation by courts of agreements concerning the coordination of proceedings;
(e) Coordination of concurrent proceedings regarding the same debtor;
(f) [*The enacting State may wish to list additional forms or examples of cooperation*].

A. INTRODUCTION TO ARTICLE 27

1. Rationale

1.27.01 Articles 25 and 26 authorize and mandate cooperation between the courts and insolvency practitioners in the enacting State with foreign courts and representatives in insolvency matters. They do not, however, specify how that cooperation and communication might be achieved. The description of the content and limits of cooperation remains in the competence of the enacting State. The MLCBI does not wish to interfere with an established practice of cooperation in many countries, often based on judicial discretion and comity. In countries with a limited tradition of cross-border cooperation, the MLCBI assists by listing 'possible forms of cooperation that might be used to coordinate cross-border insolvency cases' in Article 27.[1] The list is indicative rather than exhaustive and, as Article 27(f) shows, leaves the enacting State an opportunity to include other forms of cooperation.[2]

2. Scope of Application

1.27.02 Article 27 works within the boundaries of Articles 25 and 26. It is meant to merely illustrate available means or forms of cooperation in the enacting State.

B. FORMS OF COOPERATION LISTED IN ARTICLE 27

1. Appointment of a Person or Body (Article 27(a))

1.27.03 The court may find it useful to appoint a person or body for the specific task of communicating and cooperating with one or more foreign jurisdictions. While Article 25(1) indicates that the court may resort to the insolvency administrator to also cover this task (see [1.25.10]), Article 27(a) illustrates that the court may appoint an independent body or person instead. The decision to appoint an independent third person should involve an assessment of the expertise, resources and capabilities required as well as the additional expenses incurred.

1.27.04 Article 27(a) does not detail the specific tasks or functions of the appointee. The Practice Guide explains that such a 'person may have a variety of possible

---

1 *UNCITRAL Practice Guide on Cross-Border Insolvency Cooperation*, United Nations Publications (New York), 2010, Chapter II, para. 1.

2 *UNCITRAL Model Law on Cross-Border Insolvency with Guide to Enactment and Interpretation*, United Nations Publications (New York), 2014, paras. 220, 222.

functions, including acting as a go-between for the courts involved, especially where issues of language are present; developing an insolvency agreement; and promoting consensual resolution of issues between the parties'.[3] The court is able to indicate the terms of appointment and the powers of the appointee.[4] Ideally, the court is able to make use of office holders in the local insolvency laws other than the administrator of the estate, such as examiners[5] or mediators. The rules applicable to them would regulate issues such as remuneration, reporting, supervision or liability.

The Mexican implementation of Article 27(a) extends the ability to use a person or body in order to assist in cross-border cooperation beyond the court and also includes 'the visitor, the conciliator or the receiver'.[6] **1.27.05**

2. Direct Communication (Article 27(b))

Article 27(b) concerns the communication of information. Articles 25(2) and 26(2) authorize the court and insolvency practitioner to communicate directly with foreign courts and representatives (see [1.25.09] and [1.26.06]). The limits and safeguards for such communication are not specified in the MLCBI; they are found in the law of the enacting State (see [1.25.13–1.25.23]; [1.26.09–1.26.11]).[7] Within these constraints, the court as well as the insolvency administrator are authorized to communicate 'by any means considered appropriate by the court' pursuant to Article 27(b). The Practice Guide illustrates that this includes the 'exchange of documents (e.g. copies of formal orders, judgements, opinions, reasons for decisions, transcripts of proceedings, affidavits and other evidence) [...] by mail, fax, e-mail or other electronic means' as much as any 'oral' communication 'by telephone or videoconference'.[8] The use of new communication technologies, such as online means of communication, certainly facilitates direct and cost-efficient communication around the globe. **1.27.06**

---

3 *Practice Guide* (n 1), Chapter II, para. 2.

4 *Practice Guide* (n 1), Chapter II, para. 2.

5 See § 1527(1) US Bankruptcy Code (implementing Article 27(a)).

6 Perezalonso in: Look Chan Ho (ed.), A Commentary on the UNCITRAL Model Law, 4th ed., Globe Law & Business (London), 2017, 369; Luis Manuel C. Mejan, The UNCITRAL Model Law on Cross-Border Insolvency in North American Countries, Festschrift für Christoph Paulus, C.H.Beck (München) 2022, 509.

7 See also the discussion of limits and safeguards for direct communication in the *Practice Guide* (n 1), Chapter II, paras 7–8.

8 *Practice Guide* (n 1), Chapter II, para. 6. See also the experience shared by judges in *UNCITRAL Model Law on Cross-Border Insolvency: The Judicial Perspective, United Nations Publications* (New York), 2014, paras 163–165.

1.27.07 New technologies may mitigate hesitance to communicate directly with foreign courts or representatives, especially when they concern the language of the communication and any consequent need for translation. Translation tools have been made available widely for written documents and can be used as far as there is no need for an official translation under the law. Technical tools for simultaneous translation in online calls are being developed. The willingness to communicate directly is, however, also determined by the legal culture regarding the communication of judges[9] outside the courtroom or the personal attitudes of judges. The relevant safeguards under local law, especially those protecting the parties or the confidentiality of information (see [1.25.15] and [1.25.18]), would need to inform the form of communication that is considered appropriate by the court.

3. Coordination of the Administration of the Debtor's Assets and Affairs (Article 27(c))

1.27.08 The exchange of information is of particular interest in cases with assets or establishments of the debtor in several jurisdictions. The investigation of the debtor's assets in the main proceedings would comprise the investigation of assets located abroad. Foreign assets, once allocated, would need to be secured and, if possible, realized by the insolvency practitioner. In addition, any transfer of assets to a third party abroad would be scrutinized pursuant to applicable avoidance rules. Overall, cooperation is essential in order to trace and recover assets.[10]

1.27.09 The investigation of the debtor's assets abroad relies on the ability to exchange information with a sense of urgency. The means of direct communication as described in Article 27(b) are to be directed to foreign courts and may rely on the fact that cooperation may pre-date the formal recognition of main proceedings in the target jurisdiction (see [1.25.03]). Details are not yet illustrated in the MLCBI or the Guides. UNCITRAL Working Group V is currently considering more detailed explanations for the tracing and recovery of assets.

1.27.10 The recovery of the debtor's assets (or of the proceeds of their sale) from abroad may follow from the recognition of the main proceedings abroad and may be understood and supported as an act or cooperation under Articles 25 and 27(c).[11] A transfer of assets may also be achieved by the recognition and

9 *Practice Guide* (n 1), Chapter II, para. 9.

10 *Practice Guide* (n 1), Chapter II, para. 11.

11 See the decision of the Seoul District Court, (2014) GOOKJI 1 (26 May 2014), as described in the Digest of Case Law on the UNCITRAL Model Law on Cross-Border Insolvency, United Nations Publications (New York), 2021, 80 n 7.

enforcement of a judgment in a successful avoidance action. Often, however, the location of assets or an establishment abroad prompts the commencement of asset-based or non-main insolvency proceedings. In this case, the administration and realization of the debtor's assets is in control of parallel proceedings and should be coordinated whenever such coordination is useful in order to maximize the value of the assets, for instance their going concern value in a coordinated sale, or to achieve a restructuring. The communication of relevant information and the coordination of relevant procedural decisions (issuing or continuing a stay of enforcement actions, scheduling auctions or hearings to discuss and to vote on a coordinated plan) would need to be synchronized by the courts and the insolvency practitioners involved. Article 27(c) indicates that such coordination is possible regarding the administration of assets. Article 27(e) extends it to any relief available in concurrent proceedings (see 1.27.29).

4. Agreement or Protocols (Article 27(d))

Article 27(d) refers to the ability of courts to approve or implement 'agreements concerning the coordination of proceedings'. Such agreements predate the MLCBI. They have been developed in insolvency practice and concluded in larger cross-border insolvency cases in order to create a reliable basis for the exchange of information and the coordination of concurrent proceedings.[12] Insolvency practice has commonly referred to such agreements as 'protocols'. The Model Law does not intend to replace protocols through the enactment of its rules on cooperation and coordination. Instead, it promotes the use and further development of protocols to complement any enactment.[13] **1.27.11**

The text of Article 27(d) distinguishes between the ability of the court to approve an insolvency agreement and their ability to implement such agreements. The text does not assume that courts are a party to such an agreement themselves. The practice of protocols indicates so far that insolvency agreements (protocols) are commonly negotiated and concluded by representatives, not courts (see [1.27.26]). However, some courts have embraced best practices **1.27.12**

12 The first modern 'protocol' was the *Maxwell Protocol* concluded in 1992 with reference to an older tradition of cross-border case management through protocols (see *McFadyen & Co, ex parte Vizianagaram Co Ltd, Re* [1908] 1 KB 675). A list of all (known) protocols and cases was published by Ilya Kokorin and Bob Wessels, *Cross-Border Protocols in Insolvencies of Multinational Enterprise Groups*, Edward Elgar Publishing (Cheltenham) 2021, xviii–xxii. For a detailed history of insolvency agreements, see, for instance, Evan D. Flaschen and Ronald J. Silverman, Cross-Border Insolvency Cooperation Protocols, 33 Tex. Int'l LJ 587 (1998); Anne Nielsen, Mike Sigal and Karen Wagner, The Cross-Border Insolvency Concordat: Principles to Facilitate the Resolution of International Insolvencies, 70 Am. Bankr. L.J. 533 (1996).

13 *Practice Guide* (n 1), Chapter II, para. 13; *The Judicial Perspective* (n 8), paras 167–168.

in direct court-to-court communication by issuing respective guidelines or implementing these practices ad hoc (see [1.27.27]).

1.27.13 To date, the practice of cross-border insolvency agreements or protocols has remained a phenomenon of insolvency practice with a common law background. Courts in jurisdictions with a civil law background continue to be cautious in their involvement, especially with respect to the adoption of general guidelines (as described in [1.27.27]). Their conservative stance has so far outlasted, for instance, initiatives of the European legislator to promote the use of cross-border protocols;[14] they remain a rare phenomenon limited to cases where European insolvency practitioners conclude protocols initiated in common law jurisdictions. Strict procedural rules in civil law countries effectively limit the ability of courts and representatives to accept certain protocol clauses.[15] In addition, the influence of legal culture and, in part, language barriers remains significant and must be considered when protocols are to be negotiated with courts and representatives from civil law jurisdictions.

(a) Agreement or Protocols negotiated by Insolvency Representatives

1.27.14 Insolvency agreements (protocols) are typically negotiated and concluded by the insolvency representatives who are administering the estate or who represent the debtor-in-possession based on their duty to cooperate under Article 26(1) (see [1.26.07]).

(1) The Need for a Protocol

1.27.15 The need to embark on the (costly) effort to negotiate such agreements is certainly not present in every insolvency case with a cross-border component. It arises in cases that include a certain level of continuous cooperation between foreign representatives which may be limited to cases of an insolvent enterprise group with relevant cross-border activities.[16] The geographical separation of operational entities from financing entities and management entities, often driven by tax concerns, is a key factor to negotiate an agreement that secures the coordinated activities of group entities to a certain degree when they

14 The 2015 recast of the EIR recommends the use of protocols in order to cooperate among EU proceedings in its recital 49. Still, there are hardly any EU-based protocols; see the empirical data presented by Stephan Madaus in Daniele Vatermoli, Stephan Madaus, Federica Pasquariello and Andrés Recalde Castells (eds), Transnational Protocols: A Cooperative Tool for Managing Cross-Border Insolvency, Wolters Kluwer (Milano) 2021, 99–111.

15 Oriana Casasola and Stephan Madaus, Cross-border Insolvency Protocols: Cooperation, Coordination, and Communication Duties under the European Insolvency Regulation Recast, (2022), 33, European Business Law Review, Issue 6, 839, 876–7.

16 Kokorin and Wessels, *Cross-Border Protocols in Insolvencies of Multinational Enterprise Groups* (n 12), para. 4.47.

become insolvent. Based on a principal duty to cooperate, protocols are able to detail channels of communications, shared responsibilities and means to coordinate the management of assets and to resolve disputes. Protocols also provide the opportunity of informing other representatives and courts about relevant legal limits as well as any relevant safeguards representatives must obey under the laws applicable to their proceedings (see [1.25.14–1.25.23]).

(2) The Function of a Protocol and of the Approval of the Court

An essential function of insolvency agreements (protocols) is the ability to identify the capacity and legal limits to cooperate among participating representatives. As limitations under the law applicable to their actions are often not fully clear, the approval of the supervising court is useful in order to provide legal certainty and to shield the cooperating representatives from any threat of liability by creditors or other stakeholders at home. The involvement of the supervising court is therefore a key factor for the success of negotiations. In practice, negotiations are frequently assisted by the courts and they may provide the impetus for reaching an agreement.[17] **1.27.16**

(3) The Content of Protocols

While the content of insolvency agreements is certainly case-specific, a common framework of possible content has emerged in practice. Protocols often include provisions on: **1.27.17**

Information sharing (means, languages, schedule, confidentiality, notice),
- Case management (priority of proceedings, use and disposal of asset including coordinated sales, plan proposals, treatment of claims, post-commencement financing);
- Effectiveness (need for approval, amendments, assignment and enforcement of rights or duties, dispute resolution, termination);
- Costs and fees;
- Safeguards (preservation of rights and jurisdiction, limitation of liabilities, warranties).

Further details and clauses are explained in the Practice Guide.[18] Recently, 'Model Protocols' have been developed[19] and may provide a useful tool for **1.27.18**

17 *Practice Guide* (n 1), Chapter III, para. 16.

18 See also *Practice Guide* (n 1), Chapter III, para. 28. More recently, Casasola and Madaus, Cross-border Insolvency Protocols (n 15), 850-870.

19 "European Model Protocol", Annex 1 in Daniele Vatermoli, Stephan Madaus, Federica Pasquariello, Andrés Recalde Castells (eds), *Transnational Protocols: A Cooperative Tool for Managing Cross-Border Insolvency*, Wolters Kluwer (Milano) 2021.

the development of a protocol in practice. To date, the drafting process often seems to be based on the clauses used in successful protocols.

(4) The Legal Effects of a Protocol

1.27.19 Insolvency agreements (protocols) show a unique, even peculiar set of features. They involve a variety of actors. They contain case-specific information, procedural arrangements and substantive rights and duties. They are concluded based on an economic wish to cooperate, sometimes based on a duty to cooperate. And they operate outside the scope of a single jurisdiction on a transnational level with actors bound by the laws of their respective countries. These peculiarities leave a lot of room for questions with regards to the actual legal effects of such agreements. It is helpful to approach these issues separately for each of the relevant effects.

(b) Enforcement

1.27.20 Protocols may provide for the sharing of information or costs or other actions that a party to the protocol shall undertake in general or at a specified due date. It seems natural to conclude that these actions are to be enforced if not performed (in time). However, such enforcement is difficult to conceive in the transnational sphere of protocols. Parties to the protocols hardly ever share the jurisdiction of the same courts. The only remedy is a motion of the party entitled under the protocol to the court supervising the party in default of their obligation. The performance of duties under the protocol could be ordered as part of the supervision by the court. The supervising court would, however, only act based on an assessment of the duties of the supervised representative under the domestic law and this law would define the ability of a protocol to limit the discretion of the representative by the protocol. The law and duty enforced is the national law providing the duty, not the transnational protocol. Any enforcement of duties under the protocol as such would require the provision of an enforcement mechanism in the protocol itself, based on the ability of all parties under their respective national laws to agree to such a mechanism.

(c) Sanctions

1.27.21 The breach of duties agreed to in a protocol may also result in a liability of the party in default. The payment of damages, including punitive damages, can be included in a protocol clause as far as this is agreeable to the parties, especially with regard to their capacity to agree to such arrangements under their national law. Without such a clause, it would be for the law governing the actions of the party in default to decide (1) whether the breach of duties under the protocol also constitutes a breach of duties under this law and (2) under which additional requirements (for example, gross negligence or bad faith) a payment of damages can be sought.[20]

(d) Legally Binding

The pivotal role of the law providing for the capacity and limits of a party to agree to certain clauses in a protocol controls the issue of the binding or non-binding force of protocols as well. Any content in a protocol clause that exceeds the limits of what a party is allowed to do under their law may not be agreed on or must be regarded as non-binding on this party. Further, any agreement or clause that all parties wish to be legally binding among each other does not automatically also entail a right to enforcement or damages in case of a default. The mere legal obligation to cooperate in a specified manner may provide clarity, predictability, trust and good faith among the parties as well as a clear legal basis for each party to discharge their duty to cooperate under domestic law. All these effects are tremendously important in a transnational context. In fact, the statement in the Practice Guide that protocols 'are nearly always intended to be binding on the parties that enter into them'[21] is only true if their binding nature is separated from the matter of enforcement.[22] To date, this separation is not sufficiently reflected in publications analysing protocols.[23] The binding agreement about certain forms of cooperation between all parties, including the duty to perform certain tasks, does not automatically mean that these duties are also enforceable or shall be enforceable, either under the protocol or the law applicable to them or the party in default (see 1.27.19). While such enforcement can be agreed on additionally, it is not to be assumed. Even so, the will of the parties to agree on a binding yet non-enforceable protocol can be assumed and should be respected. **1.27.22**

(e) The Legal Nature of Protocols

The clarification of the typically binding yet non-enforceable quality of protocols also allows for a statement on their typical legal nature. **1.27.23**

20 See Article 8 of the 'European Model Protocol', Annex 1 in Daniele Vatermoli, Stephan Madaus, Federica Pasquariello and Andrés Recalde Castells (eds), *Transnational Protocols: A Cooperative Tool for Managing Cross-Border Insolvency*, Wolters Kluwer (Milano) 2021.

21 *Practice Guide* (n 1), Chapter III, para. 5.

22 Michael C. Frege, Verhandlungslösungen in grenzüberschreitenden Insolvenzen: 'Concordia firmat vires', Festschrift für Christoph Paulus, C.H.Beck (Munich) 2022, 202: Protocols are meant to be binding but not legally enforceable.

23 *Practice Guide* (n 1), Chapter III, para. 31; Kokorin and Wessels, *Cross-Border Protocols in Insolvencies of Multinational Enterprise Groups* (n 12), paras 7.35–7.40.

1.27.24 The fact that protocols operate on a transnational level above and independent from the various lex fora concursus of the parties as well as their binding effect seems to qualify them as 'essentially case-specific, private international insolvency treaties'.[24] They are, however, not concluded by government officials acting on behalf of a sovereign. The representatives, even where appointed as officers of the court, act only on behalf of their estate.

1.27.25 The role of the court's approval would be understood as a backing of the way in which the representative is exercising their discretion to cooperate with foreigners. The role of the court in protocols between representatives is ancillary and not able to shape the character of a protocol.

1.27.26 Negotiation and conclusion of a protocol follows the mechanism of a (multilateral) contract. The protocol only binds those who agree to it. It is a contract or, if the parties wish it to be neither binding nor enforceable, a memorandum of understanding.[25] As they comprise a variety of matters to cooperate on, including matters on procedure, substantive rights or international law, it is difficult to solely identify them as procedural agreements.[26]

(f) Court-to-Court Communication and Cooperation Guidelines

1.27.27 Courts rarely enter into direct (binding) agreements with foreign courts or representatives.[27] Civil law judges, in particular, are reluctant to do so.[28] Courts are nonetheless often legally obliged to cooperate with foreign courts and representatives.[29] In many cases, such duties are discharged through a person or body who is appointed for this task (see Article 27(a); [1.27.03]).

---

24 Cf. Sean Dargan, The Emergence of Mechanisms for Cross-border Insolvencies in Canadian Law 17(1) Connecticut Journal of International Law 107, 124 (2001); Flaschen and Silverman, Cross-Border Insolvency Cooperation Protocols (n 12), 589; Anne-Marie Slaughter, A Global Community of Courts 44(1) Harvard International Law Journal 191, 193 (2003).

25 Cf. Casasola and Madaus, Cross-border Insolvency Protocols (n 15), 877-878; Anthony V. Sexton, Current Problems and Trends in the Administration of Transnational Insolvencies Involving Enterprise Groups: The Mixed Record of Protocols, the UNCITRAL Model Insolvency Law, and the EU Insolvency Regulation 12 Chicago Journal of International Law 811, 818 (2012); Mathias A. Wittinghofer, Der nationale und internationale Insolvenzverwaltervertrag, Gieseking (Bielefeld) 2004, 121–69.

26 See Passas and Saliaris in: Look Chan Ho (ed.), A Commentary on the UNCITRAL Model Law (n 6), 313 referring the Greek lawyers who qualify protocols as 'private law procedural agreements, aimed primarily at preserving, administrating and liquidating the bankruptcy estate and coordinating reorganization measures, as well as granting information and resolving conflicts'.

27 *Practice Guide* (n 1), Chapter III, para. 16.

28 See the empirical data presented by Stephan Madaus in Daniele Vatermoli, Stephan Madaus, Federica Pasquariello and Andrés Recalde Castells (eds), Transnational Protocols: A Cooperative Tool for Managing Cross-Border Insolvency, Wolters Kluwer (Milano) 2021, 108.

29 Article 25(1). See also Articles 42 and 57 EIR.

Courts may implement their own agreements under Article 27(d). While this can be done in a similar way to protocols between insolvency representatives by concluding an agreement with a foreign court ad hoc in a specific case,[30] courts willing to clarify options of direct communication and coordination may opt for a more general approach – the adoption of guidelines. Guidelines for court-to-court communications have been developed along with the practice of protocols in order to enhance the predictability of the courts' cooperation and clarify the means of cooperation and, in particular, direct communication with a court. Today, the ALI-III Global Principles for Cooperation in International Insolvency Cases (ALI-III Global Principles and Guidelines 2012)[31] and the European Union Cross-Border Insolvency Court-to-Court Cooperation Principles and Guidelines ('JudgeCo Principles and Guidelines'),[32] which were developed based on the ALI-III Global Principles and Guidelines and published in 2015, present a detailed model for courts competent to hear cross-border insolvency cases. They form a global standard and inspired the Guidelines for Communication and Cooperation between Courts in Cross-Border Insolvency Matters adopted by courts participating in the Judicial Insolvency Network (JIN Guidelines) since 2016.[33] For Europe, a European Model Protocol for Court-to-Court Communication is available.[34] **1.27.28**

The guidelines for court-to-court communication are designed to be adopted by the court in a manner available under their law independent of any pending proceedings and they should be known to the parties in advance.[35] The content of the guidelines focusses on modalities to receive and share information directly but also include provisions for joint hearings. Their legal effects and nature depends on the modus of adoption available under local law. Guidelines **1.27.29**

30 See, for instance, court orders approving court-to-court protocols such as the LATAM protocol approved by the Grand Court of the Cayman Islands, *In the Matter of LATAM Finance Limited et.al* – FSD 105, 106 and 154 of 2020 (IKJ), or the *Three Arrows Capital Ltd.* protocol approved by the United States Bankruptcy Courts for the Southern District of New York in order to cooperate with courts in the BVI.

31 Available at www.iiiglobal.org/initiatives/projects-sponsored-by-iii/.

32 Available at www.universiteitleiden.nl/en/research/research-projects/law/eu-judgeco-platform.

33 See the list of courts that have adopted the JIN Guidelines available at www.jin-global.org/jin-guidelines.html. The list includes the United States Bankruptcy Courts for the District of Delaware, for the Southern District of New York and for the Southern District of Texas, the Chancery Division of the High Court of England & Wales, the Supreme Court of Singapore and the Supreme Court of New South Wales.

34 See Part Two of the 'European Model Protocol', Annex 1 in Daniele Vatermoli, Stephan Madaus, Federica Pasquariello and Andrés Recalde Castells (eds), Transnational Protocols: A Cooperative Tool for Managing Cross-Border Insolvency, Wolters Kluwer (Milano) 2021.

35 See the Guide to Implementation of Part Two of the 'European Model Protocol' in Daniele Vatermoli, Stephan Madaus, Federica Pasquariello and Andrés Recalde Castells (eds), Transnational Protocols: A Cooperative Tool for Managing Cross-Border Insolvency, Wolters Kluwer (Milano) 2021, 469–70.

have been issued as Practice Notes[36] or Local Rules[37] under the applicable procedural law.

5. Coordination of Concurrent Proceedings (Article 27(e))

1.27.30 Where the existence of assets or establishments of the debtor abroad leads to the commencement of concurrent proceedings with respect to the same debtor, cooperation is of particular importance. The coordination of these proceedings is detailed in Chapter V of the MLCBI (Articles 28–32). In order to coordinate proceedings, acts of cooperation are required. Information must be shared; relief and other decisions must be synchronized.[38] Article 27(e) explains that all relevant forms of cooperation are available to coordinate concurrent proceedings.

C. ADDITIONAL FORMS OF COOPERATION (ARTICLE 27(F))

1.27.31 The enacting State is not bound by the list of forms of cooperation in Article 27. The list is not exhaustive.[39] Other forms of cooperation may be added as Article 27(f) suggests as a place holder.

1.27.32 The Practice Guide explains possible additions which are, however, sensitive to the limits under the law of the enacting State. First, the Practice Guide mentions the allocation of disputes among cooperating courts for resolution.[40] Especially in cases where courts of several countries have jurisdiction to resolve a dispute and the first-to-a-final-judgment rule would apply in case of conflicting judgments, the coordination of efforts including the deferral of one court to another is suggested provided that such deferral is possible under the applicable law.[41] Second, concurring proceedings result in the need to file and verify the same claims against the debtor in multiple proceedings. The cooperation between courts could, therefore, determine a single jurisdiction to file and verify claims or, alternatively, require the insolvency representatives to

36 See, for instance, the Practice Note issued by the Federal Court of Australia, available at www.fedcourt.gov.au/law-and-practice/practice-documents/practice-notes/gpn-xbdr.

37 See, for instance, the Local Rules issued by the United States Bankruptcy Courts for the Southern District of New York, available at www.nysb.uscourts.gov/procedural-guidelines-and-policies.

38 *Practice Guide* (n 1), Chapter II, para. 14.

39 Guide to Enactment and Interpretation (n 2), para. 220.

40 *Practice Guide* (n 1), Chapter II, paras 18–20.

41 *Practice Guide* (n 1), Chapter II, paras 18, 20.

share lists of creditors and claims admitted, and aligning submission deadlines and procedures.[42]

The legislator of the Philippines used the option in Article 27(f) to add forms of relief upon recognition (Article 21) as acts available (also) based on cooperation, in particular for foreign non-main proceedings. The forms of cooperation thereby include: **1.27.33**

- the suspension of proceedings against the debtor;
- limiting the relief to assets that should be administered in a foreign proceeding pending in a jurisdiction other than the place where the debtor has its principal place of business (foreign non-main proceeding) or information required in that proceeding;
- the implementation of rehabilitation or re-organisation plan for the debtor.[43]

42 *Practice Guide* (n 1), Chapter II, para. 21.

43 Diño-Padlan, Gallos and Lim in: Look Chan Ho (ed.), A Commentary on the UNCITRAL Model Law (n 6), 426.

Chapter V Concurrent proceedings

Article 28

COMMENCEMENT OF A PROCEEDING UNDER *[IDENTIFY LAWS OF THE ENACTING STATE RELATING TO INSOLVENCY]* AFTER RECOGNITION OF A FOREIGN MAIN PROCEEDING

Catarina Serra

After recognition of a foreign main proceeding, a proceeding under *[identify laws of the enacting State relating to insolvency]* may be commenced only if the debtor has assets in this State; the effects of that proceeding shall be restricted to the assets of the debtor that are located in this State and, to the extent necessary to implement cooperation and coordination under Articles 25, 26 and 27, to other assets of the debtor that, under the law of this State, should be administered in that proceeding.

A. INTRODUCTION TO ARTICLE 28

1. Framework: Chapter V

1.28.01 Chapter V addresses the 'confusing issue'[1] of concurrent proceedings,[2] that is, the situation where there are simultaneous local and foreign insolvency proceedings involving the same debtor. The issue is expressly mentioned in the provision which delimits the scope of application of the MLCBI. Article 1(1)(c) states that the MLCBI applies when a foreign proceeding and a proceeding under the law of the enacting State in respect of the same debtor are taking place concurrently.

1.28.02 Experience has shown that, in case of concurrent or parallel proceedings, the courts are often reluctant or unable to defer to foreign courts and seldom accept self-limitations in favour of the latter.[3] The purpose of this chapter is to overcome these and other specific difficulties that emerge from the situation and to implement effective coordination.[4] As one scholar rightly put it, '[r]ealistically, Chapter V does not attempt to superimpose a preconceived solution to such difficulties, but rather to create an environment in which there are opportunities for the representatives, and for the courts of the concerned jurisdictions, to try to reach an accommodation through the process of cooperation and dialogue'.[5] There is a direct link to the purpose of the MLCBI itself, which is to provide 'a framework for cooperation between jurisdictions'.[6] It should also be noted that '[c]ooperation among the courts of States where the debtor's assets are located and coordination of concurrent proceedings' is one of the four key

---

1 See Ronald J. Silverman, 'Advances in Cross-Border Insolvency: The UNCITRAL Model Law on Cross-Border Insolvency' (2000) 6 ILSA Journal of International & Comparative Law 265, 271.

2 The expression 'concurrent' was deliberately chosen, in detriment of the alternative 'secondary'. This is clearly explained in UNCITRAL, Report of the United Nations Commission on International Trade Law on the work of its nineteenth session, A/CN.9/WG.V/WP.44, United Nations Publications (New York), 1996, 28: '[t]he title "concurrent proceedings" is utilized rather than the term "secondary proceedings" so as to provide model rules of coordination in as generally applicable and understandable a way as possible, without linking them for all cases to a determination of which of the concurrent proceedings are "main" proceedings and which are so-called "secondary proceedings", as such a distinction may not be universally made, at least not in the same manner.'

3 See UNCITRAL, *Practice Guide on Insolvency Cooperation, United Nations Publications* (New York), 2010, Chapter I, para. 10, and Chapter III, para. 91.

4 And, as a matter of fact, in the opinion of some experts, 'UNCITRAL's Model Law has successfully resolved the problem of inefficient multiple proceedings'. See, referring in particular to Articles 29, 30 and 31, Sara Isham, 'UNCITRAL's Model Law on Cross-Border Insolvency: A Workable Protection for Transnational Investment at Last' (2001) 26 Brook. J. Int'l L., 1177, 1203.

5 Ian F. Fletcher, *Insolvency in Private International Law* (2nd ed., OUP 2005), para. 8.65.

6 *UNCITRAL Model Law on Cross-Border Insolvency with Guide to Enactment and Interpretation*, United Nations Publications (New York), 2014, para. 3.

elements on which the text of the MLCBI is focused.[7] Coordination of concurrent proceedings regarding the same debtor is contemplated (and expressly mentioned) in Article 27(e) as a possible form of cooperation.

Chapter V comprehends Article 28 (commencement of local proceedings after recognition of foreign main proceedings), Article 29 (coordination of local proceedings and foreign proceedings, particularly with respect to relief), Article 30 (coordination of multiple proceedings), Article 31 (presumption of insolvency) and Article 32 (rule of payment in case of concurrent proceedings). According to the Guidance Note on Enacting Two or More of the UNCITRAL Model Laws on Insolvency, Chapter V could be included in the consolidated text combining the provisions of the MLCBI, the MLIJ and the MLEG without change.[8] **1.28.03**

The provisions included in Chapter V have been largely reflected in the majority of the enacting States. The noteworthy exception is Japan, which adhered to the principle 'one debtor, one proceeding', dictating that, when one proceeding is taking place regarding the same debtor, all other proceedings must be stayed and then terminated when the former proceeding is completed.[9] This is to say: 'two proceedings may not coexist; one proceeding must be suspended or terminated'.[10] **1.28.04**

7 *Guide to Enactment and Interpretation* (n 6), para. 24.

8 See UNCITRAL, Guidance Note on Enacting Two or More of the UNCITRAL Model Laws on Insolvency (Prepared by UNCITRAL Secretariat in Consultation with Experts) (2021) para. 26. This Guidance Note contains a series of technical suggestions regarding how specific provisions of each model law could be combined to create a single consolidated enactment.

9 See Kent Andersen, 'Testing the Model Soft Law Approach to International Harmonisation: A Case-Study Examining the UNICITRAL Model Law on Cross-Border Insolvency' (2004) 23 Australian Yearbook of International Law Online 1, 8 http://classic.austlii.edu.au/au/journals/AUYrBkIntLaw/2004/1.html accessed 22 February 2023. The commentator points out that the (distinct) ways in which the Japanese law and the Model Law handle the coordination among concurrent cases is demonstrative of the split, at the substantive, formal and structural levels, between the two laws. He argues that '[t]he failure of the Japanese law and the Model Law to overlap, however, is not necessarily an indefensible result. Japan's new law, while not as forward reaching as the Model Law, is significantly more progressive, detailed, and internationally oriented than its prior law, both in the books and in action', referring to a previous article: Kent Andersen, 'The Cross-Border Insolvency Paradigm: A Defense of the Modified Universal Approach Considering the Japanese Experience' (2000) 21 U. Pa. J. Int'l L. 679, 728–65.

10 In Japan, 'only one proceeding is allowed to commence at a time, and priority is given to the local proceeding with a stay on the recognition proceeding, unless certain exceptions apply'. See Wai Y. Wan and Gerard McCormack, 'Implementing Strategies for the Model Law on Cross-Border Insolvency: The Divergence in Asia-Pacific and Lessons for UNCITRAL' (2020) 36 Emory Bankr. Dev. J. 59, 85.

2. Purpose

1.28.05 Article 28 deals with the effects of recognition of a foreign main proceeding, as defined in Article 2(b), on proceedings under the insolvency law of the enacting State (local proceedings). It clearly sets out that recognition of a foreign main proceeding does not prevent the commencement of a local proceeding in the enacting State.[11] The norm manifests one of the core procedural principles on which the MLCBI is based – the principle that recognition of foreign proceedings does not prevent commencement or continuation of local proceedings,[12] which is also reflected in Article 20(4).[13] The possibility of commencing local proceedings after (and despite) the recognition of a foreign main proceeding is not unlimited or unconditional: a local proceeding may only commence if the debtor has assets in that State, which means that local proceedings are precluded in the opposite case. In this way, Article 28 settles both a right and a restriction to the commencement of local proceedings.[14,15] Apart from establishing a condition for the commencement of local proceedings, the norm is aimed at delimitating the effects of the local proceeding. The effects of the local proceeding shall be restricted to the assets of the debtor located in this State and, to the extent necessary to implement cooperation and coordination with foreign courts and foreign representatives, may extend to other assets of the debtor that, under the law of this State, should be administered in that proceeding.

---

11 It should be noted that the former version of Article 28 provided that '[u]pon recognition of a foreign main proceeding, the courts of this State have jurisdiction to commence a proceeding in this State'. The Commission decided to abandon this formula because 'it might lead to difficulties of interpretation, particularly as it implied that the courts commenced the proceedings on their own motion'. See UNCITRAL, Report of the United Nations Commission on International Trade Law on the work of its thirtieth session, A/52/17, United Nations Publications (New York), 1997, para. 95.

12 Article 28, in conjunction with Article 29, allows the principle to go on: nor does commencement of local proceedings in the enacting State terminate the recognition already accorded to the foreign proceeding or prevent the recognition of the foreign proceeding. See *Guide to Enactment and Interpretation* (n 6), para. 43. This second dimension of the principle is clearly manifested in Article 29. See Commentary on Article 29 [1.29.01 et seq.].

13 Following closely the terms of Article 20(4), the principle may be enunciated from the perspective of local creditors: recognition of foreign proceedings does not prevent local creditors from initiating or continuing collective insolvency proceedings in the enacting State (*Guide to Enactment and Interpretation* (n 6), para. 21). See also *Guide to Enactment and Interpretation* (n 6), para. 188, according to which, considering Articles 11 to 13, the guarantee extends to the foreign representative and foreign creditors.

14 Pottow observes that it is a 'right [that] is constrained'. See John A.E. Pottow, 'Procedural Incrementalism: A Model for International Bankruptcy' (2005) 45 Va. J. Int'l L. 935, 975.

15 The restriction has been criticized since it may prevent a local winding-up which would otherwise be beneficial. See Rosalind Mason, 'Implications of the UNCITRAL Model Law for Australian Cross-Border Insolvencies' (1999) 8 International Insolvency Review 83, 105.

The possibility of commencing a local proceeding after (and despite) recognition of a foreign main proceeding constitutes a deviation from pure universalism and a concession to territorialism; it reflects, in short, the so-called modified universalism.[16] The paradigm encounters its grounds on the (logical) assumption that, in principle, local creditors are better protected in local proceedings than in the framework of a unique proceeding, with universal scope. This is also the approach adopted in the EIR and manifested in Article 3(2) EIR, pursuant to which insolvency proceedings may be opened in Member States other than those where the centre of main interests of the debtor is located.[17] **1.28.06**

With the possible exception of the presumption of insolvency, enshrined in Article 31,[18] the effects that derive from the recognition of a foreign main proceeding by the enacting State are eminently of a procedural nature.[19] It has been held in case law that, for instance, the recognition of a discharge order is beyond the scope of relief available under the MLCBI: creditors' claims are not discharged, nor in any way affected, by the foreign discharge orders and the local creditors are not inhibited from commencing local proceedings.[20] In *HAHAP 20*,[21] a creditor applied for insolvency proceedings of the debtor to the Korean Court. The debtor sought dismissal of the application claiming that it **1.28.07**

---

16 It is often asserted that the MLCBI is based on the principle of modified universalism. See, for instance, Reinhard Bork, *Advanced Introduction to Cross Border Insolvency Law* (Edward Elgar Publishing 2023), 0. According to Jay L. Westbrook, modified universalism was first suggested in the American Law Institute Transnational Insolvency Project in the following terms: '[u]niversalism [is] a system where one central court administers the bankruptcy of a debtor on a worldwide basis. Modified universalism is universalism tempered by a sense of what is practical at the current stage of international legal development.' See, for instance, Jay L. Westbrook, 'Comity and Choice of Law in Global Insolvencies' (2019) 54 Texas International Law Journal 1, 5 https://papers.ssrn.com/sol3/papers.cfm?abstract_id=3417407 accessed 22 February 2023. Other scholars rather say that 'the Model Law offsets this potential adoption of universalism with three powerfully territorialist caveats', one of them being the 'mechanism to preserve the "pre-eminence" of local proceedings over any foreign proceeding (including a foreign main proceeding) under Articles 28 and 29'. See Pottow, 'Procedural Incrementalism: A Model for International Bankruptcy' (n 14), 966. For an analysis of the several competing systems for international cooperation in insolvency cases see Lynn M. LoPucki, 'Cooperation in International Bankruptcy: A Post-Universalist Approach' (1999) 84 Cornell L. Rev. 696.

17 See, on the subject, Gabriel Moss and Tom Smith in Gabriel Moss, Ian F. Fletcher and Stuart Isaacs (eds), *The EU Regulation on Insolvency Proceedings* (3rd ed., OUP 2016), para. 8.163.

18 See Commentary on Article 31 [1.31.07].

19 Going further, Roy Goode and Kristin van Zwieten argue that the Model Law itself 'is a purely procedural law. It contains no rules of substantive law'. See Roy Goode and Kristin van Zwieten, *Goode on Principles of Corporate Insolvency Law* (5th ed., Sweet & Maxwell 2018), paras 16–19.

20 See UNCITRAL, *Digest of the Case Law on the UNCITRAL Model Law on Cross-Border Insolvency Proceedings*, United Nations Publications (Vienna), 2021, in which the references are, mostly, to Korean decisions. As explained in the Digest, the Republic of Korea manages recognition and relief applications with respect to the same foreign proceeding separately, hence the numerous case references with respect to the same recognition application.

21 *HAHAP 20* (28 August 2008), Seoul Central District Court; RA 1524, Seoul High Court (CLOUT case 1000).

had already been discharged from all of its debts in a US insolvency proceeding, which had been previously recognized as a foreign insolvency proceeding by the Korean Court. The Court did not accept the debtor's contention, stating that, as there had not been any specific relief granted under Korean law, the recognition of the court alone did not prevent the opening of the Korean domestic proceeding. In another reference case, *Azabu Building Company Ltd*,[22] the Japanese Court considered that the effect of a discharge of debt in the foreign proceeding could be recognized in Japan only if the discharge satisfied the conditions for recognition of the effect of a foreign judgment under Japanese procedural law. This does not preclude there being different (wider) interpretations.

3. Scope of Application

1.28.08 The norm applies exclusively to cases where there is a foreign main proceeding, as defined in Article 2(b). Conversely, the recognition of a proceeding as a foreign non-main proceeding, as defined in Article 2(c), is excluded from its scope. The focus on foreign main proceedings finds support in the principle that the proceeding pending in the State of the debtor's centre of main interests (main proceeding) is supposed to have the principal responsibility for managing the insolvency of the debtor (*vis attractiva concursus*) regardless of the number of States in which the debtor has assets and creditors,[23] and, therefore, should be the preferential target of coordination procedures. This does not mean that the recognition of a foreign non-main proceeding prevents the commencement of local proceedings; it simply means that the absence of such an impediment is not a result of Article 28.

1.28.09 There are no impediments for a local proceeding to commence when no recognition of the foreign proceeding (be it main or non-main) occurs. In *Bank of Western Australia v Henderson (No. 3)*,[24] the Federal Magistrates Court of Australia concluded that local proceedings could be commenced irrespective of whether there are unrecognized foreign proceedings. The Australian Court considered the application of the MLCBI in some detail, in particular the question whether it would have any effect where recognition was not being sought, and expressed the view that the MLCBI was not intended to introduce automatic recognition and that it did not restrict a local court or creditors from

---

22 *Azabu Building Company Ltd*, 2006 (shou) No. 1, 2007 (mi) No. 5, Tokyo District Court (CLOUT case 1478).

23 *Guide to Enactment and Interpretation* (n 6), para. 1.

24 *Bank of Western Australia v Henderson* (No. 3) [2011] FMCA 840 (CLOUT case 1216).

commencing or concluding a local insolvency proceeding. Again, it must be highlighted that the absence of impediments to the commencement of local proceedings in the mentioned cases is not by virtue of Article 28.

B. COMMENCEMENT OF A LOCAL PROCEEDING

1. Prerequisites for Application

Generally speaking, the application of the norm presupposes the recognition of a foreign main proceeding and the location of assets of the debtor in the enacting State. The two conditions are not, however, at the exact same level: the recognition of a foreign main proceeding is better viewed as a precondition or a triggering event.[25] **1.28.10**

(a) Recognition of the Foreign Proceeding as a Main Proceeding

The recognition of a foreign proceeding as a main proceeding presupposes not only the fulfilment of the general requirements set out in Article 17(1), for recognition of a foreign proceeding (that is, a foreign proceeding of any kind), but also the fulfilment of the specific requirement set out in Article 17(2)(a), for recognition of a foreign main proceeding (that is, a foreign proceeding as a foreign main proceeding). **1.28.11**

(b) Location of Assets in the Enacting State

The norm sets forth one prerequisite for the local proceeding to be commenced in the enacting State after (and despite) the recognition of the foreign main proceeding: the location of assets of the debtor in that State.[26] **1.28.12**

---

25 The question of whether the triggering event should be the recognition rather than the mere opening of the foreign proceeding was much debated in the Working Group and in the Commission. At the end of the day, it was felt that a system based on recognition would provide greater certainty and predictability. See UNCITRAL, Report of the Working Group on Insolvency Law on the work of its nineteenth session, A/CN.9/422, United Nations Publications (New York), 1996, para. 194, and UNCITRAL, Report of the Working Group on Insolvency Law on the work of its twentieth session, A/CN.9/433, United Nations Publications (New York), 1996, para. 175.

26 Notwithstanding the recognition that Articles 28 to 29 deal with the specific problem of coordinating multiple full insolvencies, Westbrook suggests that, limiting the effect of a domestic proceeding to assets located within that State, Article 28 represents a deference to the main proceeding and, as such, manifests the preference for the 'ancillary method' (method which provides for a limited special proceeding whose central purpose is rendering assistance to the foreign main proceeding), as opposed to the 'parallel approach' (there are full domestic insolvencies in each of the countries concerned and the judges merely seek to coordinate and cooperate in their administration). See Jay L. Westbrook, 'Multinational Enterprises in General Default: Chapter 15, the ALI Principles, and the EU Insolvency Regulation' (2002) 76 Am. Bankr. L.J. 1, 9, 10–11.

1.28.13 The expression 'assets of the debtor' should be understood in broad terms. According to the Glossary of the Practice Guide on Insolvency Cooperation, it covers 'property, rights and interests of the debtor, including rights and interests in property, whether or not in the possession of the debtor, tangible or intangible, movable or immovable, including the debtor's interests in encumbered assets or in third party-owned assets'.[27]

1.28.14 The MLCBI is satisfied with the mere presence of assets, and hence does not require the presence of an establishment.[28] The notion of establishment is defined in Article 2(f) as 'any place of operations where the debtor carries out a non-transitory economic activity with human means and goods or services'.[29] Its role is to serve as the criterion for the recognition of foreign non-main proceedings: under Article 17(2), for a foreign proceeding to be recognized as a foreign non-main proceeding, the debtor must have an establishment in the foreign State. According to the Guide to Enactment and Interpretation, the solution adopted in the MLCBI 'was chosen in a context where the debtor is already involved in a foreign main proceeding'.[30] The meaning of this clarification is not absolutely clear. In spite of the undisputed favour to territorialism that the solution represents (facilitating the commencement of local proceedings), it may be seen as a reinforcement of the universal character

---

27 See UNCITRAL, *Practice Guide on Insolvency Cooperation*, United Nations Publications (New York), 2010, para. 13(a). The aim of the Glossary contained in the Practice Guide is to provide orientation for the understanding of the key terms used therein. It is noted that '[s]ince many terms have fundamentally different meanings in different jurisdictions, an explanation of the use of those terms in the Practice Guide may assist in ensuring that the concepts discussed are clear and widely understood' (para. 6). But the utility of the explanation goes beyond the Practice Guide. It is clarified that '[m]any of these terms are common to the Legislative Guide and the UNCITRAL Model Law and their use in the Practice Guide is consistent with their use in those texts' (para. 13).

28 The legislative history reveals that there were doubts as to whether a criterion based on the mere presence of assets would not undermine the purpose of the norm (to limit the opening of local proceedings after recognition of a foreign main proceeding) and that it was suggested that the words 'an establishment' be added before the word 'assets', and both words be placed within square brackets. The prevailing view, however, was that the proposed amendment was excessively restrictive and should not be adopted. The opening of the local proceeding based not only on the location of an establishment of the debtor in the enacting State but also on the location of assets of the debtor in that State was considered as a (more) realistic solution, taking into account that a number of States already allowed the opening of insolvency proceedings based on the mere presence of assets. See UNCITRAL, Report of the United Nations Commission on International Trade Law on the work of its thirtieth session, A/52/17, United Nations Publications (New York), 1997, paras 96–97.

29 The definition was inspired by the definition provided in Article 2(h) of Council Regulation EC No 1346/2000 of 29 May 2000 on insolvency proceedings (*Guide to Enactment and Interpretation* (n 6), para. 88). The current definition, slightly different, is provided in Article 2(10) of Regulation (EU) 2015/848 of the European Parliament and of the Council on 20 May 2015 on insolvency proceedings (recast): 'establishment' means any place of operations where a debtor carries out or has carried out in the three-month period prior to the request to open main insolvency proceedings a non-transitory economic activity with human means and assets.

30 *Guide to Enactment and Interpretation* (n 6), para. 225.

of the main proceeding (a proceeding aimed at encompassing the whole of the debtor's assets).

The fact that the MLCBI is satisfied with the mere presence of assets and does not require the presence of an establishment may also appear surprising if one considers that the presence of an establishment is a requirement for the opening of secondary/territorial proceedings under the EIR (Article 3(2)).[31] It should be noted, however, that there is no straightforward correspondence or equivalence between local proceedings, on the one hand, and secondary/territorial proceedings, on the other hand.[32] The secondary/territorial proceedings of the EIR are necessarily opened on the basis of an establishment whereas the local proceedings under the MLCBI are any proceedings that do not commence on the basis of the location of the centre of main interests of the debtor in that State but on a different basis (either the establishment or mere assets).[33] Ultimately, this means that not all local proceedings qualify for recognition as non-main.[34] **1.28.15**

In spite of all this, the enacting States are free to adopt a more demanding/restrictive solution and allow the commencement of the local proceeding only when the debtor has an establishment in the State. This can be done simply by replacing the words 'only if the debtor has assets in this State' with the words 'only if the debtor has an establishment in this State' when enacting Article 28.[35] The reason for choosing a more demanding/restrictive solution is encountered on the understanding that, when the debtor is not engaged in an economic activity (which, by definition, is carried out on a regular basis), the protection of local interests does not require the commencement of a local proceeding. It should be borne in mind, however, that local proceedings can serve other purposes, namely the efficient administration of assets (when the assets are particularly complex) or respect for the law and for the legal institutions (when the differences between legal systems are so deep that it is difficult to ensure, in the foreign proceeding, the enforcement of the rights of local creditors). **1.28.16**

31 The insolvency proceeding opened locally shall be a secondary proceeding if, at the time of its opening, the main insolvency proceeding was already opened (Article 3(3) EIR). Otherwise, and until the main insolvency proceeding is opened, it will be a territorial proceeding (Article 3(4) EIR).

32 It has been said that '[t]he Model Law also contemplates local full bankruptcy proceedings, but does not call them "secondary"'. See Jay L. Westbrook, 'Priority Conflicts as a Barrier to Cooperation in Multinational Insolvencies' (2009) 27 Penn St. Int'l L. Rev. 869, 874, fn. 13.

33 See Ian F. Fletcher, *The Law of Insolvency* (5th edition, Sweet & Maxwell 2017), para. 32-046. The scholar speaks of 'a less exacting criterion' in the MLCBI.

34 See infra [1.28.19].

35 *Guide to Enactment and Interpretation* (n 6), para. 226.

1.28.17 The enactment of Article 28 free of prerequisites is also a possibility left to the discretion of the States, which is still consistent with the purpose of the MLCBI and its underlying policy. In England, Article 28 MLCBI was enacted omitting the prerequisite of the presence of assets of the debtor in the enacting State (Article 28 CBIR). This allowed the continued application of rules of jurisdiction based on the (far-reaching) criterion of 'sufficient connection'.[36]

2. Objective of the Local Proceeding

1.28.18 There is no word in Article 28 as to the objective of the local proceeding. *A silentio*, it may be concluded that the local proceeding is not necessarily a winding-up proceeding. The advantages are obvious: the commencement of a local proceeding does not jeopardize the restructuring that may be carried out in the foreign main proceeding. It is possible, however, that there may be cases of mismatch of purposes, either because the main proceeding is aimed at restructuring and the local proceeding is not, or because the main proceeding is a winding-up proceeding and the local proceeding is not. These are the situations where rules on cooperation and coordination (Articles 25, 26 and 27) play a decisive role.

3. Recognition of the Local Proceeding

1.28.19 Local proceedings which are opened in the circumstances referred to in Article 28 will not necessarily qualify for recognition abroad. Under the MLCBI scheme, only proceedings commenced on the basis of the presence of the centre of main interests or an establishment of the debtor within the meaning of Article 2(f) are eligible for recognition (Article 17(2)).[37] When the local proceeding commences on the basis of the mere presence of assets, without a centre of main interests or an establishment, it does not qualify for recognition under the MLCBI scheme.[38] In many States the mere presence of assets is insufficient to commence local proceedings, as the law requires an establishment in the aforementioned sense. In such cases, the local proceeding

36 The version of Article 28 which has been enacted in England reflects the tradition regarding, in particular, the winding up of foreign companies, whereby jurisdiction may be exercised, even in the absence of assets, provided the debtor has 'sufficient connection' with the country. See Ian F. Fletcher, '"Better Late Than Never": The UNCITRAL Model Law Enters into Force in GB' (2006) 19 Insolvency Intelligence 86. See also Fletcher, *The Law of Insolvency* (n 33), para. 32-046.

37 Pursuant to Article 17(2), a foreign proceeding can be recognized as either a main proceeding or a non-main proceeding. It should be noted that the classification 'main'/'non-main' is not exhaustive 'because the definition of foreign proceedings does not require them to be either main or non-main'. See Goode and van Zwieten, *Goode on Principles of Corporate Insolvency Law* (n 19), paras 16-33 and 16-34.

38 *Guide to Enactment and Interpretation* (n 6), para. 32.

may be recognized as a foreign non-main proceeding (Article 2(c)) provided the requirements of Article 17(1) and (2)(b) are met.[39]

4. Presumption of Insolvency

Where under the law of the enacting State the debtor must be insolvent to commence an insolvency proceeding, Article 31 establishes a rebuttable presumption that recognition of a foreign main proceeding constitutes proof of the insolvency of the debtor for the purposes of commencement of a local proceeding.[40] Among other things, this reduces the delay and the costs of the local proceeding.[41] Article 34 EIR provides for a similar effect with respect to the commencement of secondary insolvency proceedings.[42] **1.28.20**

C. EFFECTS OF THE LOCAL PROCEEDING

1. Limitation to Assets Located in the Enacting State

As a rule, the effects of the local proceeding are restricted to local assets. However, under two conditions, there may be an extension to assets of the debtor located elsewhere (foreign assets). The imposition of these two conditions means that there is no open-ended possibility to extend the effects of a local proceeding to foreign assets, which would create uncertainty as to the application of the provision and lead to conflicts of jurisdiction. **1.28.21**

In Canada, Section 49 of Part IV CCAA determines that the making of an order recognizing a foreign proceeding does not preclude the commencement or the continuation of proceedings under the relevant law in respect of the debtor company.[43] Some commentators observe that the Canadian legislation 'does not provide that assets located in Canada should be administered in Canada and assets in another state administered by that foreign state', con- **1.28.22**

39 A foreign non-main proceeding is only susceptible of recognition under Article 17(2)(b) if it is commenced in a State where the debtor has an establishment within the meaning of Article 2(f) (*Guide to Enactment and Interpretation* (n 6), para. 85). Otherwise said: the MLCBI does not admit recognition of proceedings commenced in a foreign State in which the debtor has assets but no establishment as defined in Article 2(c) (Guide to Enactment and Interpretation (n 6), para. 156).

40 See Commentary on Article 31 [1.31.01 et seq.].

41 Rachel Morrison, 'Avoiding Inherent Uncertainties in Cross-Border Insolvency: Is the UNCITRAL Model Law the Answer?' (1999) 15 QUT Law Review, 103, 123.

42 The wording is, however, a little different: 'Where the main insolvency proceedings required that the debtor be insolvent, the debtor's insolvency shall not be re-examined in the Member State in which secondary insolvency proceedings may be opened.'

43 It should be noted that it is not possible to find, in the relevant Canadian legislation, a provision that exactly matches Article 28. From the outset, the CCAA is quite different in structure from the MLCBI.

cluding that '[o]ne may assume that the act is silent on this issue so as to give the courts maximum flexibility to make appropriate orders'.[44] Others express the view that the lack of limitation in scope of concurrent proceedings opened following the recognition of a foreign proceeding as a main proceeding means that Article 28 was not adopted in Canada.[45]

1.28.23 Under the EIR (Articles 3(2) and 34), the effects of secondary insolvency proceedings are also limited to the assets located in that State. Yet, unlike the MLCBI, the EIR does not provide for the possibility of an extension. It should be kept in mind that, as explained above,[46] there is no rigorous correspondence between local proceedings and secondary proceedings.

2. Possible Extension to Other Assets

1.28.24 The fundamental condition for the extension of the effects of the local proceeding to other assets is that the extension is justified by the need to ensure cooperation and coordination as understood in Articles 25, 26 and 27 (Chapter IV).[47] The imposition of this condition establishes a link of proportionality between the extension and the aims of cooperation and coordination. The possibility of this extension is particularly important when there is no foreign proceeding necessary or available in the State where the assets are situated.[48] It is, namely, useful to prevent the natural dissipation and the consequent loss of assets and the even worse operation known as 'asset stripping' (whereby the assets are fraudulently transferred abroad from the enacting State). But it is also useful in other situations. If, for instance, the local establishment has an operating plant in a foreign jurisdiction, it will be advantageous to administrate and sell the local assets and the assets abroad as a 'going concern' (as opposed to piecemeal).[49] The ultimate goal is, obviously, to maximize the value of the assets. Finally, it should be kept in mind that cooperation is not restricted to proceedings that are recognized (cooperation is not dependent upon recog-

44 See Steven Golick, Patrick Riesterer and Marc Wasserman, 'Canada' in Look Chan Ho (ed.), *A Commentary on the UNCITRAL Model Law* (4th ed., Globe Law & Business 2017) 111.

45 See Irit Mevorach, 'On the Road to Universalism: A Comparative and Empirical Study of the UNCITRAL Model Law on Cross-Border Insolvency' (2011) 12 EBOR 517, 526, fn 54.

46 See supra [1.28.15].

47 One commentator links the extension simply to the needs of the foreign proceeding. He says: 'Article 28 permits the local proceeding to reach beyond domestic assets, but only to aid foreign proceedings.' See Pottow, 'Procedural Incrementalism: A Model for International Bankruptcy' (n 14), 675, fn. 165.

48 The possibility of extension to other assets was, in fact, added at a later stage of the *travaux préparatoires*, considering, precisely, its fields of use. These and other considerations led to the decision to redraft the provision. See UNCITRAL, Report of the United Nations Commission on International Trade Law on the work of its thirtieth session, A/52/17, United Nations Publications (New York), 1997, para. 98-100.

49 *Guide to Enactment and Interpretation* (n 6), para. 227.

nition), nor even to proceedings that qualify for recognition. Cooperation is available with respect to proceedings commenced on the basis of the mere presence of assets, which do not qualify for recognition under Article 17.[50]

As mentioned, Article 28 imposes a second condition for the extension of the effects of a local proceeding, related, specifically, to its range: the extension may only involve those assets whose administration, according to the law of the enacting State, should be conducted in the local proceeding. The proviso 'under the law of this State' (i.e., under the law of the enacting State) reflects the principle underlying the MLCBI and guiding other provisions, such as Article 21(3), 23(2) and 29(c), that recognition of a foreign proceeding does not mean extending the effects of the foreign proceeding as they may be prescribed by the law of the foreign State; instead, recognition of a foreign proceeding entails attaching to the foreign proceeding the consequences envisaged by the law of the enacting State.[51] Whenever foreign assets are to be administered in a local proceeding, by virtue of the extension permitted in Article 28, the provisions of Articles 25, 26 and 27 shall apply. **1.28.25**

When the two conditions above mentioned are met, the court of the enacting State is vested with the power to claim the administration of certain assets located abroad, including assets unduly exported either from the enacting State or from third countries to the State of the foreign main proceeding. **1.28.26**

The extension of jurisdiction to the local court over foreign assets is oriented to the sole purpose of protecting the property of the debtor and is not to be confused with, nor does it imply, an extension of jurisdiction to the debtor itself. In *Re JSC BTA Bank*,[52] after the recognition, in the United States, of a foreign main proceeding with respect to the debtor bank, a creditor attached property of the debtor in the Netherlands and in Switzerland and initiated an arbitration proceeding in Switzerland. The foreign representative of the debtor sought to prevent the arbitration going forward by bringing a motion for contempt of the US Chapter 15 and violation of the automatic stay applicable upon recognition of the foreign proceeding in the United States. The Bankruptcy Court of the Southern District of New York denied the motion, explaining that the stay might extend to the debtor as to proceedings in other jurisdictions (but only) for the purposes of protecting property of the debtor that was located within the territorial jurisdiction of the United States. **1.28.27**

50 *Guide to Enactment and Interpretation* (n 6), para. 40.

51 *Guide to Enactment and Interpretation* (n 6), para. 194.

52 *Re JSC BTA Bank*, 434 B.R. 334, 343–344 (Bankr. SDNY 2010) (CLOUT case 1211).

Article 29

COORDINATION OF A PROCEEDING UNDER *[IDENTIFY LAWS OF THE ENACTING STATE RELATING TO INSOLVENCY]* AND A FOREIGN PROCEEDING

Catarina Serra

Where a foreign proceeding and a proceeding under [*identify laws of the enacting State relating to insolvency*] are taking place concurrently regarding the same debtor, the court shall seek cooperation and coordination under Articles 25, 26 and 27, and the following shall apply:

(a) When the proceeding in this State is taking place at the time the application for recognition of the foreign proceeding is filed,
  (i) Any relief granted under Article 19 or 21 must be consistent with the proceeding in this State; and
  (ii) If the foreign proceeding is recognized in this State as a foreign main proceeding, Article 20 does not apply;
(b) When the proceeding in this State commences after recognition, or after the filing of the application for recognition, of the foreign proceeding,
  (i) Any relief in effect under Articles 19 or 21 shall be reviewed by the court and shall be modified or terminated if inconsistent with the proceeding in this State; and
  (ii) If the foreign proceeding is a foreign main proceeding, the stay and suspension referred to in paragraph 1 of Article 20 shall be modified or terminated pursuant to paragraph 2 of Article 20 if inconsistent with the proceeding in this State;
(c) In granting, extending or modifying relief granted to a representative of a foreign non-main proceeding, the court must be satisfied that the relief relates to assets that, under the law of this State, should be administered

in the foreign non-main proceeding or concerns information required in that proceeding.

A. INTRODUCTION TO ARTICLE 29

1. Purpose

Article 29 deals with cases where the debtor is subject to a foreign proceeding and a local proceeding at the same time. The principal objective of the norm is to foster coordinated decisions, particularly concerning the aspect of relief.[1] This is to be accomplished, first of all, through cooperation and coordination pursuant to Articles 25, 26 and 27. The norm embodies two more rules. The first (implicit) rule is that commencement of a local proceeding does not prevent or terminate the recognition or the application for the recognition of a foreign proceeding. According to the Guide to Enactment and Interpretation, this is 'the salient principle embodied in Article 29'.[2] The second rule concerns relief granted to the recognized foreign proceeding: it must be consistent with relief granted in the local proceeding, irrespective of whether the foreign proceeding was recognized before or after the commencement of the local proceeding. The availability of relief, so as to assist foreign proceedings whenever necessary for the orderly and fair conduct of a cross-border insolvency, is a basic principle **1.29.01**

1 According to the Practice Guide on Insolvency Cooperation, the norm aims at ensuring 'that the different proceedings can move forward without being unnecessarily suspended by the operation of a stay'. See UNCITRAL, *Practice Guide on Insolvency Cooperation*, United Nations Publications (New York), 2010, Chapter II, para. 14.

2 *UNCITRAL Model Law on Cross-Border Insolvency with Guide to Enactment and Interpretation*, United Nations Publications (New York), 2014, para. 230.

of the MLCBI.[3] Relief may be granted on an interim basis or as a result of recognition. Interim relief is relief available between the making of an application for recognition and the decision on that application at the discretion of the court (Article 19); relief available upon recognition depends on the proceedings: in respect of main proceedings, there are specified forms of relief (Article 20) and, additionally, relief at the discretion of the court (Article 21); with respect to non-main proceedings there is solely relief at the discretion of the court (Article 21).[4]

1.29.02 The root of Article 29 may be found in Article 27, providing examples of the forms of cooperation and singling out, in paragraph (e), coordination of concurrent proceedings regarding the same debtor. To illustrate the utility of coordination, the Practice Guide on Insolvency Cooperation provides the following examples: (1) when the debtor's assets include assets located in a number of different jurisdictions, the investigation of the debtor's assets may be hampered by the operation of a stay in one or more of those jurisdictions; in such cases, relief from the stay might be required; (2) proceedings commenced in one State might be assisted by the application of a stay in another State where no insolvency proceedings have commenced with respect to the debtor but where the debtor has assets; recognition of the stay in that second State would assist in protecting the assets for the benefit of all creditors; (3) in recognizing and implementing a stay ordered by another court, a court might consult with the issuing court regarding the interpretation and application of the stay; possible modification of, or relief from, the stay; and the enforcement of the stay.[5]

1.29.03 Article 29 contemplates two distinct situations: the situation where the local proceeding is pending at the time of the application for recognition of the foreign proceeding (paragraph (a)) and the situation where the local proceeding commences after recognition or the filing of an application for recognition of the foreign proceeding (paragraph (b)). In addition, it establishes a general condition for any granting or modification (extension included) of relief to the representative of the foreign non-main proceedings (paragraph (c)).

1.29.04 According to the Guide to Enactment and Interpretation, Article 29 'maintains a pre-eminence of the local proceeding over the foreign proceeding', but 'avoids establishing a rigid hierarchy between the proceedings since that

3 *Guide to Enactment and Interpretation* (n 2), para. 35.

4 See Commentary on Articles 19, 20 and 21.

5 *Practice Guide on Insolvency Cooperation* (n 1), Chapter II, para. 14.

would unnecessarily hinder the ability of the court to cooperate and exercise its discretion under articles 19 and 21'.[6,7] The pre-eminence or dominance of the local proceeding is noticeable in the first two groups of provisions: relief to be granted to the foreign proceeding must be consistent with the local proceeding (paragraph (a), subparagraph (i)); relief already granted to the foreign proceeding must be reviewed and modified or terminated to ensure consistency with the local proceeding (paragraph (b), subparagraph (i)); if the foreign proceeding is a main proceeding, the automatic effects pursuant to Article 20 are to be modified and terminated if inconsistent with the local proceeding (paragraph (b), subparagraph (ii)); where a local proceeding is pending at the time a foreign proceeding is recognized as a main proceeding, the foreign proceeding does not enjoy the automatic effects of Article 20 (paragraph (a), subparagraph (ii)).[8]

Undoubtedly, the pre-eminence of the local proceeding over the foreign main proceeding has an advantageous effect for domestic creditors and is particularly justified in cases which involve assets that are perishable or immovable or that have local registration requirements or involve legal procedures, making it impossible or at least very difficult for the foreign representative to seize the assets and perform the usual administrative tasks.[9] **1.29.05**

The equivalent of Article 29 in the United States is 11 USC § 1529. The role of the US provision was highlighted in *Bear Stearns High-Grade Structured* **1.29.06**

6 *Guide to Enactment and Interpretation* (n 2), para. 231. See also Rosalind Mason, 'Cross-Border Insolvency Law: Where Private International Law and Insolvency Law Meet' in Paul Omar (ed.), *International Insolvency Law – Themes and Perspectives* (Ashgate 2008) 27, 57.

7 In the *travaux préparatoires*, it was advocated that there should be a certain precedence of the local proceeding, 'which should preclude any relief measure affecting the debtor's assets in the enacting State'. At the same time, it was pointed out that it was desirable not to unnecessarily hinder the ability of the court to cooperate. See UNCITRAL, Report of the United Nations Commission on International Trade Law on the work of its thirtieth session, A/52/17, United Nations Publications (New York), 1997, paras 107–108.

8 According to Westbrook, the provision that the semi-automatic stay of Article 20 will be inoperative or reduced in light of a local full insolvency represents a clear preference for the local proceeding. In any case, the trumping of the foreign proceeding authorized by the norm 'is subject to the opportunity to defer if cooperation and coordination would best be served by deference'. See Jay L. Westbrook, 'Multinational Enterprises in General Default: Chapter 15, the ALI Principles, and the EU Insolvency Regulation' (2002) 76 Am. Bankr. L.J. 1, 8. With a similar view, Pottow says that 'even if Articles 28 and 29 permit the "pre-eminence" of a local proceeding, that local proceeding may well – in the interests of comity that pre-exist and survive the Model Law – ultimately defer to the foreign proceeding, perhaps self-conscious of an inferior regulatory entitlement'. See John A.E. Pottow, 'Procedural Incrementalism: A Model for International Bankruptcy' (2005) 45 Va. J. Int'l L. 935, 974, fn. 162.

9 See Neil Hannan, *Cross-Border Insolvency – The Enactment and Interpretation of the UNCITRAL Model Law* (Springer 2017), 162.

Credit Strategies Master Fund, Ltd (In re).[10] In a case where recognition under Chapter 15 was denied, on the basis that the proceedings in the Cayman Islands (foreign proceedings) were not pending in a country where the debtors had their COMI or where they had an establishment, the US Bankruptcy Court for the Southern District of New York noted that the petitioners were, nevertheless, not left remediless upon non-recognition. It referred to 11 USC § 1529, which mandated cooperation among, and coordination of foreign and domestic proceedings taking place concurrently concerning the same debtor pursuant to 11 USC §§ 1525–1527 [Articles 25–27 MLCBI].

1.29.07 In *Bank of Western Australia v Henderson (No. 3)*,[11] the Federal Magistrates Court of Australia clarified that Article 29 requires the foreign insolvency representative to take action so as to have the foreign proceeding recognized and does not provide remedies that can be sought by individual creditors (creditors are not parties that can seek recognition under the MLCBI). The court observed that '[b]oth the Guide to Enactment (at [189]) and the Explanatory Memorandum to the CBI Act (at [74]) make clear that the "principle embodied in article 29 is that the commencement of local proceedings does not prevent or terminate the recognition of a foreign proceeding" [...] This suggests that the guiding principle behind article 29 is to preserve the rights of foreign representatives, and not to impinge upon the rights of local creditors'.

2. Scope of Application

1.29.08 It should be noted that Article 29 addresses the situation of concurrence between local proceedings and foreign proceedings in general (that is, not exclusively foreign main proceedings). Nevertheless, it sets down two special provisions for cases where the foreign proceeding is a main proceeding (paragraph (a), subparagraph (ii) and paragraph (b), subparagraph (ii)).

B. DUTY TO SEEK COOPERATION AND COORDINATION

1.29.09 Article 29 (caput) establishes the general duty of the court to seek cooperation and coordination under Articles 25, 26 and 27.[12] The duty was given a privileged location in the norm, leading to the inference that cooperation and coordination, far from being a subsidiary instrument (designed for cases or issues

10 *Bear Stearns High-Grade Structured Credit Strategies Master Fund, Ltd (In re)*. First instance: 374 BR 122 (Bankr SDNY 2007) [CLOUT case 760].

11 *Bank of Western Australia v Henderson* (No. 3) [2011] FMCA 840 (CLOUT case 1216).

12 See Commentary on Articles 25, 26 and 27.

not specifically regulated), constitute a certain (imperative) way in which to fulfil the remaining duties. To be sure, the granting or the refusal, maintenance or termination/modification of the relevant measures has significant effects on the foreign proceeding and, therefore, should not be done unilaterally, and, in most cases, makes it convenient to keep an active dialogue with the foreign counterpart.

The duty to seek cooperation and coordination emerges in matters referred to in Article 1. This is the provision that specifies the scope of the MLCBI. It provides, in paragraph (1), that the MLCBI applies in the following cases: when assistance is sought in the enacting State by a foreign court or a foreign representative in connection with a foreign proceeding (subparagraph (a)); when assistance is sought in a foreign State in connection with a local proceeding (subparagraph (b)); when a foreign proceeding and a local proceeding in respect of the same debtor are taking place concurrently (subparagraph (c)); and when creditors or other interested persons in a foreign State have an interest in requesting the commencement of, or in participating in, a local proceeding (subparagraph (d)). The cases may be divided into three groups: *inbound* cases (when assistance is sought in the enacting State or foreign parties are interested in commencing or participating in local proceedings – subparagraphs (a) and (d)); *outbound* cases (when assistance is sought in a foreign State – subparagraph (b)); and in regard to *concurrent* proceedings (subparagraph (c)).[13] **1.29.10**

In the EIR, in order to facilitate the coordination of main, territorial and secondary insolvency proceedings concerning the same debtor, there are specific provisions on cooperation and communication between insolvency practitioners (Article 41 EIR), on cooperation and communication between courts (Article 42 EIR) and on cooperation and communication between insolvency practitioners and courts (Article 43 EIR). Preceding the legislative text, Recital 48 EIR states: '[m]ain insolvency proceedings and secondary insolvency proceedings can contribute to the efficient administration of the debtor's insolvency estate or to the effective realisation of the total assets if there is proper cooperation between the actors involved in all the concurrent proceedings. Proper cooperation implies the various insolvency practitioners and the courts involved cooperating closely, in particular by exchanging a sufficient amount of information.' According to the same Recital, insolvency practitioners and courts should take into account best practices for cooperation in cross-border insolvency cases, as set out in principles and guidelines on communication and **1.29.11**

---

13 See Commentary on Article 1 [1.1.01 et seq.].

cooperation adopted by European and international organizations active in the area of insolvency law, and in particular the relevant guidelines prepared by the UNCITRAL.

C. SPECIFIC CASES PROVIDED FOR IN THE NORM

1. Local Proceeding Pending at the Time of the Application for Recognition of the Foreign Proceeding

1.29.12 Article 29(a) sets out that, where local proceedings are pending at the time of the application for recognition of the foreign proceeding, the relief granted to the foreign proceeding under Articles 19 and 21 must be consistent with the local proceeding and, if the foreign proceeding is recognized as a main proceeding, the relief available upon recognition under Article 20 will not apply. As previously noted, the principle that may be derived from these provisions is that the recognition or the application for the recognition of a foreign proceeding, either as main or non-main, is not precluded by the fact that the local proceeding has already commenced.[14]

(a) Prerequisites for Application

1.29.13 Article 29(a) presupposes that the local proceeding is initiated before the application for the recognition of the foreign proceeding. In other words, there must be a local proceeding pending at the time of the application for the recognition of the foreign proceeding.

(b) Legal Consequences

1.29.14 Article 29(a)(i) is aimed at ensuring that, in the situation mentioned above, the relief granted to the foreign proceeding under Articles 19 and 21 is consistent with the local proceeding. Relief available under Articles 19 and 21 is 'discretionary relief' (that is, at the discretion of the court).

1.29.15 In *Ian Gregory Thow*,[15] the debtor submitted a plan of reorganization under Canadian insolvency law; one month later, the debtor filed for Chapter 7 pro-

14 *Guide to Enactment and Interpretation* (n 2), para. 230. Fletcher expresses the opinion that this principle 'should perhaps have been expressly stated at this point in the text of the Model Law, in the interests of overcoming any preconceptions about whether such recognition is logically possible if, as it is frequently the case, the insolvency law of the enacting State claims universal effect for a proceeding that has been commenced in that jurisdiction'. See Ian F. Fletcher, *Insolvency in Private International Law* (2nd ed., OUP 2005), para. 8.67.

15 *In re: Ian Gregory Thow* (10 November 2005) [CLOUT case 762]. Note that this order has not been published in the United States official reports.

ceedings in the United States and one day later they relocated to the United States. The foreign representative applied to the US court for recognition of the foreign proceeding as a foreign main proceeding and for orders to stay all actions and deadlines in the case, to turn over property of the debtor located in the United States and to direct the debtor to cooperate with the foreign representative. The US Bankruptcy Court for the Western District of Washington at Seattle recognized the foreign proceeding as a foreign main proceeding and ordered, pursuant to 11 USC § 1521(a)(1)–(5) [Art. 21(1)(a)–(e) MLCBI], that (a) the continuation or commencement of individual actions concerning the debtor's assets and execution against the debtor's assets were stayed, except for the insolvency proceedings pending in the United States; (b) the right to transfer or encumber or otherwise dispose of the debtor's assets in the United States was suspended; (c) the debtor should make himself and pertinent records available for inspection and examination by the foreign representative; (d) the debtor's assets in the United States that would be property of the debtor's estate under the United States insolvency law should be administered by the foreign representative; and (e) the debtor should cooperate with the foreign representative with respect to its rights and duties under the order.

Although 'consistency', as imposed by Article 29(a)(i) and other provisions of the MLCBI, appears in UNCITRAL explanatory texts[16] with the meaning of 'non-interference', the best view is to take the term as calling for a considered judgment which focuses or, at least, takes into special account the nature and the objectives of the local proceeding. In *Swissair Schweizerische Luftverkehrsaktiengesellschaft* the debtor (Swissair) was already in liquidation in England (where it had a branch office and had acquired assets and incurred debts) when the Swiss liquidator applied for recognition of the Swiss liquidation. The English court pointed out that Article 29(a)(i) requires the order sought in the recognition proceeding (for remittal of assets) to be consistent with the local proceeding and concluded: 'it is not necessary to examine the precise meaning and limits of this qualification. It is enough to say that in the circumstances of this case the proposed remittal is unquestionably consistent with the English liquidation.'[17] 1.29.16

16 See, e.g., *UNCITRAL Model Law on Cross-Border Insolvency: The Judicial Perspective*, United Nations Publications (New York), 2014, para. 155. What is more, in Article 19(4) the word 'interfere' is actually used, as it seems, as the equivalent of 'inconsistent'. See *Guide to Enactment and Interpretation* (n 2), para. 175.

17 *Swissair Schweizerische Luftverkehrsaktiengesellschaft* [2009] EWHC 2099 [para. 14] (Ch).

(c) Particularities when the Foreign Proceeding is Recognized as a Main Proceeding

1.29.17 Article 29(a)(ii) provides for the special situation where the foreign proceeding is recognized as a foreign main proceeding, determining that Article 20 does not apply. It should be kept in mind that Article 20 provides for 'automatic relief' (that is, available immediately and automatically upon recognition). The risk of inconsistency/incompatibility between the domestic effects of the local proceeding and the effects of the foreign proceeding, whenever recognized as a foreign main proceeding, is thus minimized.

2. Local Proceeding Commencing After Recognition or Application for Recognition of the Foreign Proceeding

1.29.18 Article 29(b) sets out that, if the local proceeding commences after the recognition or the application for recognition of the foreign proceeding, relief in effect under Article 19 or 21 is to be reviewed by the court and to be modified or terminated if inconsistent with the local proceeding and, if the foreign proceeding is a foreign main proceeding, the stay and suspension referred to in Article 20(1) is to be modified or terminated pursuant to Article 20(2) if inconsistent with the local proceeding.

1.29.19 An important conclusion that may be drawn at this point is that 'Article 28, in conjunction with article 29, provides that the recognition of a foreign main proceeding does not prevent the commencement of a local insolvency proceeding concerning the same debtor as long as the debtor has assets in the State'.[18]

(a) Prerequisites for Application

1.29.20 Article 29(b) presupposes that the local proceeding commences after the recognition or the application for recognition of the foreign proceeding.

(b) Legal Consequences

1.29.21 Article 29(b)(i) determines that, in the situation mentioned above, relief in effect under Articles 19 or 21 is to be reviewed by the court and, if inconsistent with the local proceeding, modified or terminated. It is intended that there be no interference with the autonomy of the enacting State. According to the records of the early legislative work, such a provision, mandating adjustment or termination of the relief granted for the benefit of the foreign proceeding, 'should be flexible enough so as to make it possible to take into considera-

18 *Guide to Enactment and Interpretation* (n 2), para. 228.

tion factors such as fairness, the need to coordinate concurrent proceedings, acquired rights, the disturbance caused by preventing approved actions from being carried out and the general principle of leaving in place measures that did not disturb the proceeding in the enacting State'.[19]

(c) Particularities when the Foreign Proceeding is a Main Proceeding

Article 29(b)(ii) determines that, when the foreign proceeding is a foreign main proceeding, the stay and the suspension under Article 20(1) may be modified or terminated if inconsistent with the local proceeding. This reflects, once more, the policy of non-intrusion into the autonomy of the enacting State: it should be a matter for the enacting State, applying the local law, to determine whether the assets to which the relief relates should be administered in the foreign proceeding.[20] **1.29.22**

There is an additional provision in Article 29(b) CBIR – subparagraph (iii), pursuant to which 'any proceedings brought by the foreign representative by virtue of paragraph 1 of article 23 before the proceeding in Great Britain commenced shall be reviewed by the court and the court may give such directions as it thinks fit regarding the continuance of those proceedings'. According to some authors, this is intended to allow the court to manage any conflict between the rights of a foreign representative and a British insolvency office-holder to bring a transaction avoidance action.[21] **1.29.23**

In Canada, Article 29(b) is implemented by means of the provisions in Sections 54 and 48(2) CCAA, with one relevant difference: while under the MLCBI the filing for the application for recognition of the foreign proceeding is sufficient to trigger the effects of the norm, Section 54 presupposes the order recognizing the foreign proceeding. This is viewed favourably by some commentators; they argue that it provides more flexibility to Canadian courts.[22] **1.29.24**

19 See UNCITRAL, Report of the Working Group on Insolvency Law on the work of its twenty-first session, A/CN.9/435, United Nations Publications (New York), 1997, para. 191.

20 Fletcher, *Insolvency in Private International Law* (n 14) para. 8.68, fn. 93.

21 Look Chan Ho, 'England' in Look Chan Ho (ed.), *A Commentary on the UNCITRAL Model Law* (4th ed., Globe Law & Business 2017), 287.

22 According to Steven Golick, Patrick Riesterer and Marc Wasserman, the Canadian legislation 'does not provide that assets located in Canada should be administered in Canada and assets in another state administered by that foreign state […]. One may assume that the act is silent on this issue so as to give the courts maximum flexibility to make appropriate orders'. See Steven Golick, Patrick Riesterer and Marc Wasserman, 'Canada' in Ho (ed.), *A Commentary on the UNCITRAL Model Law* (n 21), 111.

3. Granting Relief or Modifying Relief Granted to a Representative of a Foreign Non-Main Proceeding

1.29.25 Article 29(c) occupies a place of its own. It does not provide, rigorously, for a situation of concurrence of proceedings, but rather manifests the principle that the relief granted to a foreign non-main proceeding should be limited to assets that are to be administered in that non-main proceeding or must concern information required in that proceeding. This principle is expressed in Article 21(3), which deals in a general way with the type of relief that may be granted to a foreign representative, and is restated in the present provision, in the context of coordination of local and foreign proceedings. According to the Guide to Enactment and Interpretation, Article 19(4), on pre-recognition relief, and Article 30, on coordination of more than one foreign proceeding, are inspired by the same principle.[23]

1.29.26 The restriction imposed by Article 29(c) operates, in practice, as providing two alternative conditions for the granting of relief: relief must either relate to assets that under the law of the enacting State should be administered in the foreign non-main proceeding or concern information required in the foreign non-main proceeding. The proviso 'under the law of this State' (meaning: under the law of the enacting State) reflects the principle underlying the MLCBI and also guiding other provisions, such as Articles 21(3), 23(2) and 28, that the recognition of a foreign proceeding does not mean extending the effects of the foreign proceeding as they may be prescribed by the law of the foreign State; instead, the recognition of a foreign proceeding entails attaching to the foreign proceeding the consequences envisaged by the law of the enacting State.[24]

23 *Guide to Enactment and Interpretation* (n 2), para. 232. See also para. 195.

24 *Guide to Enactment and Interpretation* (n 2), para. 194.

Article 30

COORDINATION OF MORE THAN ONE FOREIGN PROCEEDING

Catarina Serra

In matters referred to in Article 1, in respect of more than one foreign proceeding regarding the same debtor, the court shall seek cooperation and coordination under Articles 25, 26 and 27, and the following shall apply:

(a) Any relief granted under Articles 19 or 21 to a representative of a foreign non-main proceeding after recognition of a foreign main proceeding must be consistent with the foreign main proceeding;
(b) If a foreign main proceeding is recognized after recognition, or after the filing of an application for recognition, of a foreign non-main proceeding, any relief in effect under Articles 19 or 21 shall be reviewed by the court and shall be modified or terminated if inconsistent with the foreign main proceeding;
(c) If, after recognition of a foreign non-main proceeding, another foreign non-main proceeding is recognized, the court shall grant, modify or terminate relief for the purpose of facilitating coordination of the proceedings.

A. INTRODUCTION TO ARTICLE 30

1. Purpose

1.30.01 Article 30 deals with cases of multiple proceedings and, in particular, with the granting and the modification or termination of relief.[1] In terms of objectives, Article 30 maintains an unquestionable proximity to Article 29, as they both aim at promoting cooperation, coordination and consistency of the relief granted to different proceedings.[2] However, whereas Article 29 gives relevance or primacy to the local proceeding, Article 30 assigns preference to the foreign main proceeding whenever there is one.[3] This preference is present in subparagraphs (a) and (b), under which relief granted to the foreign non-main proceedings shall be assured only if it is consistent with the foreign main proceeding.[4] With regard to the (distinct) case where there are solely foreign non-main proceedings, subparagraph (c) establishes no hierarchy; the court is simply urged to decide according to what best facilitates coordination. This being said, it is visible that Article 30 does not attempt at defining how the court is expected to deal with the issues it encounters in the context of multi-jurisdictional proceedings. As Ian Fletcher rightly puts it, 'Article 30 does not issue prescriptive instructions'.[5]

2. Scope of Application

1.30.02 In contrast with Article 28 and in line with Article 29, Article 30 applies to all foreign proceedings, whether main or non-main. The provision applies independently of there being a local proceeding pending in the enacting State. If, besides the (two or more) foreign proceedings, there is a local proceeding,

1 According to Pottow, Article 30 is an administrative provision related to international cooperation and communication. He divides the MLCBI's provisions into two broad areas: 'administrative' and 'substantial'. The first area, administrative provisions, could then be divided further into two subcategories: first, provisions related to international cooperation and communication, and second, antidiscrimination rules. See John A.E. Pottow, 'Procedural Incrementalism: A Model for International Bankruptcy' (2005) 45 Va. J. Int'l L. 935, 961.

2 With respect to Article 30 it has been argued that it 'encourages the court which is occupied with recognising foreign (non-main) proceedings and granting relief to the foreign (secondary) insolvency to ensure consistency between the main and second proceedings'. See Reinhard Bork, *Advanced Introduction to Cross-Border Insolvency* (Edward Elgar Publishing 2023), 106.

3 See Commentary on Article 29 [1.29.01 et seq.].

4 *UNCITRAL Model Law on Cross-Border Insolvency with Guide to Enactment and Interpretation*, United Nations Publications (New York), 2014, para. 234.

5 Ian F. Fletcher, *Insolvency in Private International Law* (2nd ed., OUP 2005), para. 8.69. The author adds that '[i]n truth, dogmatic approaches are seldom if ever of value in such situations (…). In cases where reorganization is being attempted, an open and flexible approach on the part of the judiciary under whose jurisdiction the issues are determined greatly enhances the prospects for a commercially satisfactory outcome'.

the court must also take into consideration what is specially provided in Article 29.[6]

Article 30 only applies when there is more than one foreign proceeding. In *British-American Insurance Co., Ltd*, the Bankruptcy Court for the Southern District of Florida denied relief under 11 USC §1530 (the equivalent of Article 30) since only one foreign non-main proceeding had been recognized.[7] **1.30.03**

Article 30 establishes the general duty of the court to seek cooperation and coordination under Articles 25, 26 and 27[8] and provides, in addition, three special rules. The general duty is applicable to all cases of concurrent proceedings. This is actually a restatement of the principle enshrined in Article 29. The special rules are intended to deal with particular cases of foreign concurrent proceedings, namely the case where the foreign non-main proceeding is recognized after the recognition of the foreign main proceeding; the case where the foreign main proceeding is recognized after the recognition or the filing for the application for recognition of the foreign non-main proceeding; and, finally, the case where the foreign non-main proceeding is recognized after the recognition of another foreign non-main proceeding. All in all, it may be argued that '[t]he provisions of Article 30 are essentially a command to the court to follow the dictates of common sense'.[9] **1.30.04**

B. DUTY TO SEEK COOPERATION AND COORDINATION

Like Article 29, Article 30 establishes, first of all, the general duty of the court to seek cooperation and coordination under Articles 25, 26 and 27. Like in Article 29, cooperation and coordination should be envisaged as the primary duty, imposing a certain attitude which is determinant to the way in which the specific duties are to be performed.[10] **1.30.05**

The duty to seek cooperation and coordination emerges in matters referred to in Article 1. This is the provision that specifies the scope of the MLCBI. It provides, in paragraph (1), that the MLCBI applies in the following cases: when assistance is sought in the enacting State by a foreign court or a foreign representative in connection with a foreign proceeding (subparagraph (a)); **1.30.06**

6 *Guide to Enactment and Interpretation* (n 4), para. 233.
7 *British-American Insurance Co., Ltd*, 425 B.R. 884 (Bankr. SD Fla. 2010) [CLOUT case 1005].
8 See Commentary on Articles 25, 26 and 27.
9 Fletcher, *Insolvency in Private International Law* (n 5), para. 8.69.
10 See Commentary on Article 29 [1.29.08].

when assistance is sought in a foreign State in connection with a local proceeding (subparagraph (b)); when a foreign proceeding and a local proceeding in respect of the same debtor are taking place concurrently (subparagraph (c)); and when creditors or other interested persons in a foreign State have an interest in requesting the commencement of, or participating in, a local proceeding (subparagraph (d)). The cases may be divided into three groups: *inbound* cases (when assistance is sought in the enacting State or foreign parties are interested in commencing or participating in local proceedings – subparagraphs (a) and (d)), *outbound* cases (when assistance is sought in a foreign State – subparagraph (b)), and *concurrent* proceedings (subparagraph (c)).[11]

1.30.07 In the EIR, in order to facilitate the coordination of main, territorial and secondary insolvency proceedings concerning the same debtor, there are specific provisions on cooperation and communication between insolvency practitioners (Article 41 EIR), on cooperation and communication between courts (Article 42 EIR) and on cooperation and communication between insolvency practitioners and courts (Article 43 EIR). Preceding the legislative text, Recital 48 EIR states: '[m]ain insolvency proceedings and secondary insolvency proceedings can contribute to the efficient administration of the debtor's insolvency estate or to the effective realisation of the total assets if there is proper cooperation between the actors involved in all the concurrent proceedings. Proper cooperation implies the various insolvency practitioners and the courts involved cooperating closely, in particular by exchanging a sufficient amount of information.' According to the same Recital, insolvency practitioners and courts should take into account best practices for cooperation in cross-border insolvency cases, as set out in principles and guidelines on communication and cooperation adopted by European and international organizations active in the area of insolvency law, and in particular the relevant guidelines prepared by the UNCITRAL. In *Volo Logistics LLC v Varig Logistica SA (In re Varig Logistica SA)*,[12] the debtor (Varig Logistica, SA) had been in a liquidation proceeding in Brazil, which was recognized as a foreign main proceeding by the US Bankruptcy Court for the Southern District of Florida. Some entities related to the debtor, who were involved in malfeasance (breach of fiduciary duties and piercing the corporate veil), brought proceedings in the US Court seeking an anti-suit injunction against the Brazilian proceedings and also filed a chapter 11 case in a New York court. The US Bankruptcy Court for the Southern District of Florida analysed 11 USC §1501, that emphasizes the importance

11 See Commentary on Article 1 [1.1.01 et seq.].

12 *Volo Logistics LLC v Varig Logistica SA (In re Varig Logistica SA)*, 2021 Bankr. Lexis 2992; 2021 WL 5045684 (CLOUT case 2016).

of cooperation between courts, and 11 USC §1525, that requires the US court to 'cooperate to the maximum extent possible with a foreign court'. Citing the case law,[13] the Court refused to issue the anti-suit injunction and decided to defer to the Brazilian Court and dismiss the Chapter 15 adversary proceeding.

C. SPECIFIC CASES PROVIDED FOR IN THE NORM

1. Recognition of Foreign Non-Main Proceeding After Recognition of Foreign Main Proceeding

(a) Prerequisites of Application

Article 30(a) provides for the situation where a foreign main proceeding has already been recognized at the time of the application for relief filed by a representative of a foreign non-main proceeding. **1.30.08**

(b) Legal Consequences

The legal consequence established in Article 30(a) is that relief granted to the foreign non-main proceeding under Article 19 or 21 must be consistent with the foreign main proceeding. As previously noted, the provision pursues the same objective as the one underlying Article 19(4): to assure consistency of relief granted in favour of the foreign non-main proceeding with the foreign main proceeding.[14] **1.30.09**

As observed in respect to Article 29,[15] consistency does not come down to mere non-interference, calling for the further consideration of core aspects of the prevailing proceeding (*in casu*: the foreign main proceeding), such as its nature and its objectives. The pre-eminence of the foreign main proceeding over the foreign non-main proceeding is understandable since the first tends to involve all the assets and all the affairs of the insolvent debtor.[16] **1.30.10**

---

13 Among others, *Re Atlas Shipping A/S* 404 BR 726, 738 (Bankr. SDNY 2009) (CLOUT case 1277), where it was stated: '[o]nce a case is recognized as a foreign main proceeding, chapter 15 specifically contemplates that the court will exercise its discretion consistent with the principles of comity'; and *In re Oi S.A.,4* 587 B.R. 253, 273 (Bankr. S.D.N.Y. 2018), where it was stated '[i]t is simply not this Court's role to second guess the wisdom of the Brazilian courts or overrule their decisions, which would be fundamentally inconsistent with comity'.

14 *Guide to Enactment and Interpretation* (n 4), para. 234.

15 See Commentary on Article 29 [1.29.15].

16 In the framework of the EIR, some authors refer to the 'dominant role of main insolvency proceedings' *vis-à-vis* secondary proceedings. See Margreet B. De Boer and Bob Wessels, 'The Dominance of Main Insolvency Proceedings under the European Insolvency Regulation' in Paul Omar (ed.), *International Insolvency Law – Themes and Perspectives* (Ashgate 2008) 185.

2. Recognition of Foreign Main Proceeding After Recognition or Filing for Recognition of Foreign Non-Main Proceeding

(a) Prerequisites of Application

1.30.11 The situation provided in subparagraph (b) of Article 30 is the opposite of the situation provided for in subparagraph (a): a foreign main proceeding is recognized, not before, but after the recognition, or after the filing of an application for the recognition, of a foreign non-main proceeding.

(b) Legal Consequences

1.30.12 The legal consequence established in Article 30(a) is that the relief in effect under Article 19 or 21 must be consistent with the foreign main proceeding. The norm specifies that the court must review the relief that has been granted and, if it is inconsistent with the foreign main proceeding, modify or terminate it. Even in this case (that is, despite the fact that the recognition of the foreign main proceeding occurs afterwards), the foreign main proceeding is bound to prevail over the foreign non-main proceeding.

3. Recognition of Foreign Non-Main Proceeding After Recognition of Another Foreign Non-Main Proceeding

(a) Prerequisites of Application

1.30.13 Article 30(c) provides, exclusively, for the situation where the recognized foreign proceedings are non-main proceedings, that is, where no foreign main proceeding is recognized or an application for recognition of a foreign main proceeding is pending. If a foreign main proceeding is recognized or pending of recognition, subparagraphs (a) or (b), depending on the case, shall apply.

(b) Legal Consequences

1.30.14 The legal consequence established in Article 30(c) is that the court shall grant, modify or terminate relief for the purpose of facilitating coordination of the proceedings. There is no ground for preferences, as proceedings are at the same level. Hence, the aim is to coordinate relief granted to the proceedings as best as possible.

Article 31

PRESUMPTION OF INSOLVENCY BASED ON RECOGNITION OF A FOREIGN MAIN PROCEEDING

Catarina Serra

In the absence of evidence to the contrary, recognition of a foreign main proceeding is, for the purpose of commencing a proceeding under *[identify laws of the enacting State relating to insolvency]*, proof that the debtor is insolvent.

A. INTRODUCTION TO ARTICLE 31

1. Rationale

Both Article 31 and Article 32 contain additional means of facilitating coordination of foreign and local proceedings. Article 31 determines that, when the insolvency of the debtor is required for the commencement of a local proceeding, the recognition of a foreign proceeding represents, for that purpose, proof that the debtor is insolvent. Ultimately, the norm envisages that there are **1.31.01** no findings regarding the situation of the debtor in the local proceeding that conflict with those in the recognized foreign main proceeding.[1,2]

1.31.02 As its title implies, the norm establishes a (rebuttable) presumption of insolvency, with the typical effect of relieving certain persons from the burden of proof concerning the insolvency of the debtor. The proceeding at the base of the presumption is the foreign main proceeding and the proceeding in which the presumption will be enforced is the local proceeding. The trigger of the presumption is the recognition of the foreign main insolvency proceeding in the enacting State.

1.31.03 From a strictly literal point of view, it may be concluded that the presumption of insolvency is triggered by the recognition of a foreign main proceeding independently of its prerequisites. This is not entirely correct. As explained below,[3] the preferred interpretation of the norm is that only when the insolvency of the debtor has been previously established in the foreign main proceeding does it not have to be ascertained again in the local proceeding.

1.31.04 Beyond the ultimate purpose of avoiding conflicting findings in the relevant courts, the functioning of a presumption of insolvency of the debtor in the local proceeding has several practical advantages that serve both private and general/public interests: first, the immediate relief of those encumbered with the burden of proof of the insolvency, which, in its turn, permits a substantial reduction in time and costs of local proceedings.[4] Bearing in mind that the commencement of local proceedings may be urgently needed for the protection of local creditors, the reduction in time is particularly relevant.[5] In extreme cases, it reduces the risk of dishonest debtors delaying cross-border resolution of their financial demise in order to fraudulently conceal or remove their assets.[6]

---

1 As some explain, 'in order to avoid contradictory decisions and to expedite the proceedings, many cross-border insolvency laws provide that it is not necessary to establish the debtor's substantive insolvency for the secondary insolvency proceedings if it has been established in the main insolvency proceedings'. See Reinhard Bork, *Advanced Introduction to Cross-Border Insolvency Law* (Edward Elgar Publishing 2023), 101.

2 Different insolvency tests may be applied and, even if this is not the case, there is a chance that distinct courts reach dissimilar results. See, though in the framework of the EIR, Reinhard Bork, in Reinhard Bork and Renato Mangano, *European Cross-Border Insolvency Law* (2nd ed., OUP 2022), para 7.33.

3 See infra [1.31.12].

4 See Rachel Morrison, 'Avoiding Inherent Uncertainties in Cross-Border Insolvency: Is the UNCITRAL Model Law the Answer?' (1999) 15 QUT Law Review, 103, 123.

5 *UNCITRAL Model Law on Cross-Border Insolvency with Guide to Enactment and Interpretation*, United Nations Publications (New York), 2014, para. 238.

6 See Hugo-Pierre Gagnon, 'Bill C-55 and the UNCITRAL Model Law on Cross-Border Insolvency: the harmonization of Canadian insolvency legislation' (McGill University 2006), 63 https://escholarship.mcgill

In *Mexico City Federal District Court Proceedings no. 29/2001 bankruptcies of Jacobo Xacur Eljure, Felipe Xacur Eljure and Jose Maria Xacur Eljure*,[7] the foreign representative approached the Mexico City Federal District Court seeking an acknowledgement of the US bankruptcy proceedings and judgments, as well as international cooperation. Referring, among others, to Article 31, the Mexican Court observed that the acknowledgement and the adoption of judgments from other jurisdictions promoted a modern and equitable legal standard to efficiently and effectively address issues arising out of cross-border insolvency, thereby seeking to counter such issues as hiding assets and fraud, while simultaneously protecting the creditors' and debtors' interests and preserving employment. **1.31.05**

Part of the doctrine regards Article 31 as an illustration of the 'way in which the Model Law foments universalism [...] by embracing the paradigm's other theoretical anchor, namely, pushing enacting states into accepting some cession of regulatory sovereignty in the transnational insolvency realm' and makes a point of saying that Article 31 is 'not part of the core provisions of the Model Law [...] that pertain to the stay upon recognition of a foreign proceeding' but rather 'more to the periphery of the Law'.[8] **1.31.06**

Not surprisingly, the presumption of insolvency is not located with the other presumptions concerning the recognition of foreign proceedings, enshrined in Article 16. While it could be argued that the presumption of insolvency is not purely of procedural nature, their separate location cannot be explained by differences in nature of each group of presumptions[9] but rather on the basis that the presumption of insolvency is the direct result of the recognition of the foreign proceeding as a foreign main proceeding, whereas the presumptions in Article 16 are aimed at facilitating the process of recognition of a (any) foreign **1.31.07**

.ca/concern/theses/h702qb62z accessed 22 February 2023. See also Neil Hannan, *Cross-Border Insolvency – The Enactment and Interpretation of the UNCITRAL Model Law* (Springer 2017), 164.

7 Mexico City Federal District Court Proceedings no. 29/2001 bankruptcies of *Jacobo Xacur Eljure, Felipe Xacur Eljure and Jose Maria Xacur Eljure (19 December 2002)* (CLOUT case 693).

8 See John A.E. Pottow, 'Procedural Incrementalism: A Model for International Bankruptcy' (2005) 45 Va. J. Int'l L. 935, 976–7. The author claims (at 979), on the 'theoretical import of Article 31', that it 'is unabashedly universalist: one state should accept another state's assessment that eligibility for bankruptcy filing has been met, even from those jurisdictions that do not invest great stock in a financial distress requirement'.

9 As pointed out by certain authors, some of the presumptions in Article 16 affect purely procedural matters (Article 16(2)) and others are more substantive (Article 16(3)). See, on this, Pottow, 'Procedural Incrementalism: A Model for International Bankruptcy' (n 8), 977. See Commentary on Article 16 [1.16.01 et seq.].

proceeding.[10,11] The presumption of insolvency should not be approximated either to the (automatic) effects of the recognition of a foreign main proceeding enshrined in Article 20 – this time, however, due to their different nature (the latter effects are, eminently, of procedural nature).

2. Scope of Application

1.31.08 The situation provided for in the norm is, *par excellence*, the situation where both proceedings (that is, the foreign main proceeding and the local proceeding) require the insolvency of the debtor. This is the situation where the presumption of insolvency is, simultaneously, reasonable and useful: reasonable, for it does not make sense that insolvency be presumed in the local proceedings if insolvency is not previously required and therefore established in the foreign main proceeding; useful, for the presumption of insolvency is worthless in the local proceeding if insolvency is not required in the local proceeding. While the second postulate is obvious, the first requires a more detailed explanation.

1.31.09 Given the fact that the norm is silent as to the prerequisites of the foreign main proceeding, it could be argued that it applies even when the foreign main proceeding does not presuppose the insolvency of the debtor. Such an interpretation would lead, however, to paradoxical results: even when the foreign main proceeding would be commenced despite the debtor not being insolvent or, worse, when the foreign main proceeding would only be commenced because the debtor was solvent (which is the case when the proceeding is aimed at preventing or avoiding insolvency), the debtor would be treated as insolvent for the purpose of commencing the local proceeding.[12] It would be easier to tackle the problem if it could be assumed that the proceedings to which the MLCBI applies were all proceedings in which the debtor is either insolvent or in an equivalent situation.[13] The Guide to Enactment refers, on the one hand, to 'severe financial distress or insolvency' of the debtors,[14] but on the other hand

---

10 In the Guide to Enactment and Interpretation's own words, the presumptions in Article 16 are 'presumptions that permit and encourage fast action in cases where speed may be essential' and 'allow the court to expedite the evidentiary process'. See *Guide to Enactment and Interpretation* (n 5), para. 137.

11 Straight to the point, Berends asserts that this is because the presumption of insolvency only takes effect after recognition. See André J. Berends, 'The UNCITRAL Model Law on Cross-Border Insolvency: A Comprehensive Overview' (1998), 6 Tul. J. Int'l & Comp. L. 309, 392–5.

12 A similar reasoning was developed around Article 27 EIR 2000. See infra [1.31.13].

13 See infra [1.31.15].

14 In the *Guide to Enactment and Interpretation* (n 5), para. 48, insolvency proceedings are described as 'various types of collective proceedings commenced with respect to debtors that are in severe financial distress or insolvent'. It is clarified that '[a] judicial or administrative proceeding to wind up a solvent entity where the goal is to dissolve the entity and other foreign proceedings not falling within article 2 subparagraph (a) are not insolvency proceedings within the scope of the Model Law. Where a proceeding serves several purposes,

also alludes to 'debtors that are or *will be* generally unable to pay their debts as they mature' and to 'laws that *prevent* or address the financial distress of those debtors'.[15] The latter can only be understood as references to pre-insolvency proceedings; now, by definition, pre-insolvency proceedings require that the debtor, if not solvent, is not in actual insolvency.

The truth is that there is no consensus on the scope of application of Article 31. Certain scholars appear to devalue the substantive situation behind the presumption and consider the presumption an 'eligibility-related presumption', mandating a domestic State – at least to the extent of a rebuttable presumption – to accept a foreign State's decision that the requirements of 'protection worthiness' have been met.[16] Others express the view that Article 31 constitutes the proof that the concept of foreign proceeding is not to be restricted to a proceeding in relation to a debtor who is technically insolvent.[17] There is doubt as to whether this kind of position, departing from the scope of Article 31 to the scope of the MLCBI and then backwards, is indeed able to demonstrate *quod erat demonstrandum*. **1.31.10**

Article 31 has also been invoked in recent case law to support the broader understanding of the scope of application of the MLCBI. In the 2019 decision *In the matter of Sturgeon Central Asia Balanced Fund Ltd (in liquidation)*,[18] Article 31 was used to justify the granting of recognition to a foreign winding up proceeding commenced with respect to a solvent company on just and equitable grounds. The England and Wales High Court of Justice, Chancery Division, Companies Court sustained that the norm indicated that 'recognition is intended to be available in circumstances where insolvency has not been established as well as in cases where an entity is obviously insolvent', hence **1.31.11**

---

including the winding up of a solvent entity, it falls under article 2, subparagraph (a) of the Model Law only if the debtor is insolvent or in severe financial distress'. It is further added (para. 65) that 'the expression "insolvency proceedings" may have a technical meaning in some legal systems, but is intended in subparagraph (a) to refer broadly to proceedings involving debtors that are in severe financial distress or insolvent' and also (para. 73) that '[a] simple proceeding for a solvent legal entity that does not seek to restructure the financial affairs of the entity, but rather to dissolve its legal status, is likely not one pursuant to a law relating to insolvency or severe financial distress'.

15 *Guide to Enactment and Interpretation* (n 5), para. 49 and 67 (emphasis added).

16 See, though in a critical approach, Pottow, 'Procedural Incrementalism: A Model for International Bankruptcy' (n 8), 978–9. The author claims that 'an easy answer is that the presumption is only an inference that can be deflated with "evidence to the contrary" [...] But the easy answer ignores the effects of presumptions in creating evidentiary hurdles to bias preferred outcomes. There is also arguably an expressive function to delineating the *status quo*.'

17 See Look Chan Ho, 'Recognising an Australian Solvent Liquidation under the UNCITRAL Model Law: *In re Betcorp*' (2009) 18 Norton Journal of Bankruptcy Law and Practice 537.

18 *In the matter of Sturgeon Central Asia Balanced Fund Ltd (in liquidation)* [2019] EWHC 1215 (Ch) (CLOUT case 1819).

'the fundamental question is whether those cases should be distinguished from a situation where there is uncontradicted evidence before the court that the entity is (at least currently) solvent, and/or where it is clear that the purpose, or principal purpose, for which liquidation is sought is not to realize assets for creditors – even though it will have that effect – but instead to distribute surplus assets to shareholders'.[19] Despite accepting that 'there is wording in the 2014 version of the Guide to Enactment in particular, and to some extent in the original version, which appears to [...] indicate that the Model Law applies only to companies that are insolvent or in "severe financial distress"', the Court concluded that 'this limitation is not reflected in the text of the Model Law' and, therefore, 'confining recognition under it to entities that are demonstrated to have these characteristics would conflict with the plain meaning of the words used'.

1.31.12 Admitting that the MLCBI can accommodate other proceedings than those requiring insolvency or equivalent situations (in particular pre-insolvency proceedings),[20] it is fair to say that when insolvency is required for the purpose of commencing the local proceeding but was not established in the foreign main proceeding, the presumption enshrined in Article 31 should not apply.

1.31.13 One of the decisive arguments in favour of the submitted interpretation of Article 31 is that it is fully consistent with the interpretation of the homologous norm of the EIR. After a former version which gave rise to misunderstandings and an intense doctrinal debate[21] (Article 27 EIR 2000), the amended (or improved) Article 34 EIR is now absolutely clear in its wording:[22] for the insolvency of the debtor not to be examined in secondary insolvency proceedings, it is necessary that it has been previously established in the main proceeding.[23,24]

---

19 *In the matter of Sturgeon Central Asia Balanced Fund Ltd (in liquidation)* (fn. 18), para. 55.

20 This is a reasonable line of interpretation. See Commentary on Article 2 [1.2.04]. See also Irit Mevorach and Adrian J. Walters, 'The Characterization of Pre-insolvency Proceedings in Private International Law' (2020) 21 EBOR 855, 870–2. The authors say that the definition in Article 2(b) MLCBI (foreign proceeding) 'is intended to be expansive'.

21 See Renato Mangano, in Reinhard Bork and Kristin van Zwieten (eds), *Commentary on the European Insolvency Regulation* (2nd ed., OUP 2022), para. 34.22.

22 See Bork, in Reinhard Bork and Renato Mangano, *European Cross-Border Insolvency Law* (fn. 2), para 7.34.

23 Article 27 EIR 2000 laid down that '[t]he opening of [...] (main proceedings) shall permit the opening in that other Member State [...] of secondary insolvency proceedings without the debtor's insolvency being examined in that other State'. Article 34 EIR now determines that '[w]here the main insolvency proceedings required that the debtor be insolvent, the debtor's insolvency shall not be re-examined in the Member State in which secondary insolvency proceedings may be opened'.

24 Analysing the new Article 34 EIR, some authors conclude that 'the bar on re-examining the debtor's insolvency is now restricted to cases where the main proceedings require the debtor to be insolvent'. See Gabriel Moss and Tom Smith in Gabriel Moss, Ian F. Fletcher and Stuart Isaacs (eds), *The EU Regulation on Insolvency Proceedings* (3rd ed., OUP 2016), para. 8.651.

An entirely different case is when it is the local proceeding and not the 1.31.14 foreign main proceeding that does not require the insolvency of the debtor. In such a case, the presumption of insolvency is, simply, deprived of utility. If nothing else, the normative reference to the fact that the presumption is 'for the purpose of commencing a local proceeding' reinforces the idea that the presumption may only be of interest when the insolvency of the debtor is a condition for the commencement of the local proceeding. The logical consequence is that, in legal systems where proof that the debtor is insolvent is not required for the commencement of insolvency proceedings, the enactment of the norm is pointless.[25]

It flows from what has been said above that the scope of application of the 1.31.15 norm is dependent on what is, or is to be understood by, 'insolvency'. The fact is that Article 2 MLCBI does not include a definition of insolvency.[26] Both the Legislative Guide[27] and the Glossary of the Practice Guide on Insolvency Cooperation[28] describe insolvency as the situation 'when a debtor is generally

25 The pros and cons of a presumption of insolvency and, in particular, its utility were discussed in the *travaux préparatoires*. See UNCITRAL, Report of the United Nations Commission on International Trade Law on the work of its thirtieth session, A/52/17, United Nations Publications (New York), 1997, paras 102–103. It was argued that for those legal systems where insolvency was not required, the presumption would be of little practical consequence and might be misunderstood as introducing a new criterion for opening insolvency proceedings. Yet, the idea was not to introduce new substantive rules of law in the enacting State, but rather to make it possible for the court to open insolvency proceedings on the basis of a presumption of insolvency, without having first to establish that the debtor was insolvent, where such requirement existed; as such, it was a useful provision that might help to simplify and expedite the proceedings in the enacting State. In view of the reservations, however, it was agreed that the Guide to Enactment should indicate that the presumption might not have practical significance in all States and that, in jurisdictions where proof of insolvency of the debtor was not required for the opening of insolvency proceedings, the enacting State might wish not to enact that provision. Accordingly, the Guide to Enactment and Interpretation clarifies that the presumption 'is for use in jurisdictions where insolvency is a condition for commencing insolvency proceedings' (para. 72), applicable only 'where under the law of the enacting State the debtor must be insolvent to commence an insolvency proceeding' (para. 228), 'in jurisdictions where insolvency is a condition for commencing insolvency proceedings' (para. 236) or 'in those legal systems in which commencement of an insolvency proceeding requires proof that the debtor is in fact insolvent' (para 238). It is also observed that '[f]or the national laws where proof that the debtor is insolvent is not required for the commencement of insolvency proceedings, the presumption established in article 31 may be of little practical significance and the enacting State may decide not to enact it' (para. 237).

26 The *Guide to Enactment and Interpretation* (n. 5), para. 65, explains that the definitions generally avoid using specific expressions that may have different technical meanings in different legal systems, and instead the MLCBI adopts a functional approach.

27 Legislative Guide on Insolvency Law, Part 1 and 2, United Nations Publications (New York) 2005, para. 12 (s).

28 UNCITRAL, *Practice Guide on Insolvency Cooperation*, United Nations Publications (New York), 2010, Introduction, para. 13 (m). The aim of the Glossary contained in the Practice Guide is to provide orientation for the understanding of the key terms used therein. It is noted that '[s]ince many terms have fundamentally different meanings in different jurisdictions, an explanation of the use of those terms in the Practice Guide may assist in ensuring that the concepts discussed are clear and widely understood' (para. 6). But the utility of the explanation goes beyond the Practice Guide. It is clarified that '[m]any of these terms are common to the

unable to pay its debts as they mature or when its liabilities exceed the value of its assets'. The definition corresponds to what is otherwise known, respectively, as 'cashflow insolvency' and 'balance sheet insolvency'. Hence, there may be doubts as to the cases where the opening of the local proceeding depends on circumstances which do not exactly match the inability of the debtor to pay debts as they mature/as they fall due or the excess of the debtor's liabilities over the value of its assets, but still configure severe financial distress. The examples presented in the Guide to Enactment and Interpretation include cessation of payments by the debtor or certain actions of the debtor such as a corporate decision, dissipation of its assets or abandonment of its establishment.[29] Does the recognition of the foreign main proceeding, where insolvency was established, give rise to a presumption in these cases? The possibility should not immediately be excluded. It may happen that the circumstance at stake is equivalent, in substance, to insolvency.[30,31,32] Furthermore, in some jurisdictions, circumstances of the type mentioned in the Guide to Enactment and Interpretation (cessation of payments, dissipation of assets or abandonment of the establishment) are listed as circumstantial evidence for insolvency (that is, facts that demonstrate insolvency or severe financial distress).[33] In such cases, it seems only reasonable to apply the presumption on the basis of an argument *a maiore ad minus*: since the relevant circumstance is required in the local proceeding as a means of proving insolvency, all the more reason to accept the *accertamento* of insolvency made in the foreign main proceeding.

Legislative Guide and the UNCITRAL Model Law and their use in the Practice Guide is consistent with their use in those texts' (para. 13).

29 *Guide to Enactment and Interpretation* (n. 5), para. 72 and 235.

30 One paradigmatic example is France, where the keystone of insolvency proceedings is cessation of payments (*cessation des paiements*), which is the situation where the debtor cannot pay its outstanding due debts for lack of sufficient available cash and liquid assets ('*l'impossibilité de faire face au passif exigible avec son actif disponible*' – Article L631-1 *Code de Commerce*).

31 Sometimes the difference is purely terminological. The Guide to Enactment and Interpretation recognizes that 'different jurisdictions might have different notions of what falls within the term "insolvency proceedings"'. See *Guide to Enactment and Interpretation* (n. 5), para. 48. In the same way as there are different realities under the name 'insolvency', there are different words that designate the same reality, that is, insolvency.

32 Taking, apparently, a similar stand, it has been considered that the (Canadian) balance sheet insolvency test and the Dutch cessation of payments test are 'two roads to the same goal of ensuring a state of financial distress has been demonstrated'. See Pottow, 'Procedural Incrementalism: A Model for International Bankruptcy' (n 8), 978.

33 Just to name a few examples: Brazil (Article 24 (I) *Lei da Recuperação de Empresas e de Falência* and, among the European States which have not enacted the Model Law, Germany (§ 17(2) *Insolvenzordnung*), Spain (Article 4(2) *Ley Concursal*) and Portugal (Article 20(1) *Código da Insolvência*), just to name a few.

In England, not surprisingly, the expression 'inability to pay debts' was adopted instead of 'insolvency' (Section 31 CBIR). Under English law, a debtor is insolvent when it is unable to pay its debts.[34] 1.31.16

In Brazil, apart from the set of norms on cross-border insolvency, the term 'insolvency' is not used at all. The only exception is the expression 'insolvency crisis' (in Portuguese: '*crise de insolvência*'), described as the insufficiency of financial resources and assets with sufficient liquidity to allow the debtor to pay its debts.[35] 1.31.17

In 11 USC §1531 the key expression is 'unpayment of debts'. Unpayment of debts is synonymous with cessation of payments. 1.31.18

B. PREREQUISITES FOR APPLICATION

The prerequisites of the norm can be divided in two groups: prerequisites regarding the proceeding at the base of the presumption and prerequisites regarding the local proceeding. 1.31.19

1. Prerequisites Regarding the Proceeding at the Base of the Presumption

The proceeding whose recognition is at the base of the presumption must be a foreign proceeding in the sense of Article 2(a).[36] The fact that the proceeding is aimed at liquidation or reorganization is not relevant for the purposes of the norm.[37] Secondly, the proceeding must be a foreign main proceeding in the sense of Article 2(b).[38] The norm is quite clear on this point and the Guide to Enactment and Interpretation provides a justification: 'an insolvency proceeding commenced in a State other than the State where the debtor has the centre of its main interests does not necessarily mean that the debtor is to be subject to laws relating to insolvency in other States.'[39] The circumstance illustrates the greater importance attributed to foreign main proceedings 1.31.20

---

34 See, for all, Roy Goode and Kristin van Zwieten, *Goode on Principles of Corporate Insolvency Law* (5th ed., Sweet & Maxwell 2018), para. 4-01.

35 Article 51 § 6.º (I) Lei de Recuperação de Empresas e Falência.

36 See Commentary on Article 2 [1.2.02 et seq.], regarding the meaning of 'foreign proceedings'.

37 *Guide to Enactment and Interpretation* (n 5), para. 48.

38 See Commentary on Article 2 [1.2.21 et seq.], regarding the meaning of 'foreign main proceeding'.

39 *Guide to Enactment and Interpretation* (n 5), para. 236. This was discussed in the *travaux préparatoires* by the Commission. See UNCITRAL, Report of the United Nations Commission on International Trade Law on the work of its thirtieth session, A/52/17, United Nations Publications (New York), 1997, para. 104.

vis-a-vis foreign non-main proceedings. Thirdly, the proceeding must be recognized in the enacting State, which presupposes it complies with the core procedural requirements of Article 15.[40] Finally, a last prerequisite, although not explicit, should be considered: that the foreign main proceeding requires the insolvency of the debtor[41] or, at least, an equivalent situation in the terms explained above.[42]

1.31.21 In Canada, the requirement of recognition of a foreign main proceeding was not reproduced in Section 59 CCAA.[43] Instead, a certified copy of a foreign order opening a foreign insolvency proceeding (whether main or non-main) triggers the application of the presumption in the absence of evidence to the contrary. The scope of application is, therefore, considerably widened.[44] Furthermore, the certified copy of the order constitutes proof not only of the insolvency but also of the appointment of the foreign representative made by the order.

2. Prerequisites Regarding the Local Proceeding

1.31.22 With respect to the recipient proceeding, the prerequisites can be narrowed down to one: it has to be a local proceeding, that is, a proceeding that takes place in the enacting State.

C. LEGAL CONSEQUENCES

1.31.23 The consequence of the application of the norm is the presumption of insolvency of the debtor for the (only) purpose of commencing a local proceeding, which simultaneously relieves certain individuals of the burden of proof and

40 See Commentary on Article 15.

41 See supra [1.31.14].

42 See supra [1.31.15].

43 See also the corresponding (almost *ipsis verbis*) norm in the other major piece of legislation that governs insolvency and bankruptcy in Canada: Section 282 BIA. For a table of correspondence of the MLCBI and the cross-border legislation in Canada in the aftermath of Bill C-55 (and in the US after BAPCPA) see Jacob Ziegel, 'Canada–United States Cross-Border Insolvency Relations and the UNCITRAL Model Law' (2007) 32 Brook. J. Int'l L. 1042, 1075.

44 The Canadian variations have been synthesized in this way: '[f]irst, recognition of a foreign main proceeding is not required. Second, any foreign proceedings – whether main or non-main in nature – give rise to the presumption. Third, given that foreign non-main proceedings may be based simply on the presence of assets, this means that all types of foreign proceedings are covered in practice.' See Gagnon, 'Bill C-55 and the UNCITRAL Model Law on Cross-Border Insolvency: the harmonization of Canadian insolvency legislation' (n 6), 123. Still commenting on Bill C-55 (proposing the amendments to the CCAA), that author gives notice of the constitutional reservations to the Canadian norm and approaches the issue of whether such presumption of insolvency (i.e., with such breadth) is constitutionally valid (at 124–5).

prevents the court from re-examining the insolvency of the debtor. The first part of the norm ('[i]n the absence of evidence to the contrary') constitutes a safeguard, leaving no doubt that the presumption of insolvency enshrined in Article 31 is rebuttable or *juris tantum*[45] and that the court of the enacting State is not bound by the decision of the foreign court.[46,47] This means that for the purpose, and in the context, of commencing a local proceeding, it is admissible that there be proof, resorting to local criteria, that the debtor is, actually, not insolvent.[48] Consequently, when under the law of the enacting State the debtor must be insolvent to commence the local proceeding and the presumption is rebutted, the local proceeding may not be commenced.

45 *Guide to Enactment and Interpretation* (n 5), para. 235.

46 It has been observed that the commentary contained in para. 197 Guide to Enactment and Interpretation in its version of 1997 (corresponding to para. 238 of the version of 2014) on the rebuttable nature of the presumption 'seems almost defensive about Article 31's incursion onto sovereignty'. See Pottow, 'Procedural Incrementalism: A Model for International Bankruptcy' (n 8), 978, fn. 179.

47 In England, where Article 31 is implemented by Section 31 CBIR, it is undisputed that the presumption is rebuttable. See Goode and van Zwieten, *Goode on Principles of Corporate Insolvency Law* (n 34), para. 16-45.

48 *Guide to Enactment and Interpretation* (n 5), para. 238.

Article 32

RULE OF PAYMENT IN CONCURRENT PROCEEDINGS

Catarina Serra

Without prejudice to secured claims or rights *in rem*, a creditor who has received part payment in respect of its claim in a proceeding pursuant to a law relating to insolvency in a foreign State may not receive a payment for the same claim in a proceeding under [*identify laws of the enacting State relating to insolvency*] regarding the same debtor, so long as the payment to the other creditors of the same class is proportionately less than the payment the creditor has already received.

A. INTRODUCTION TO ARTICLE 32

1. Rationale

1.32.01 Both Article 31 and Article 32 contain additional means of facilitating coordination between foreign and local proceedings. Since the creditors have the opportunity to submit their claims in multiple/parallel proceedings,[1] it is desir-

1 Note that Article 13(1) grants foreign creditors the same rights regarding the commencement of, and participation in, a local proceeding as local creditors, thus embodying the principle of non-discrimination. See *UNICTRAL Model Law on Cross-Border Insolvency with Guide to Enactment and Interpretation*, United Nations Publications (New York), 2014, para. 119. See Commentary on Article 13 [1.13.01]. According to some commentators, '[t]his is further enhanced by Article 32 applying the hotchpot doctrine'. See Felicity Deane and Rosalind Mason, 'The UNCITRAL Model Law on Cross-Border Insolvency and the Rule of

able that the proceedings be coordinated to make it impossible for one creditor to obtain greater recovery on its claim as compared to other creditors of his class. Article 32 is designed to achieve this goal. It establishes a rule of payment in concurrent proceedings concerning imputation of dividends, incorporating, in essence, the so-called hotchpot rule (also known as 'equalization provision').

The main purpose of the norm is to provide an orderly liquidation procedure under which the creditors receive equal treatment, or, to put it differently, to avoid situations in which a creditor might make claims and be paid in parallel proceedings regarding the same debtor in different jurisdictions, thereby obtaining more favourable treatment than the one given to other creditors of the same class or ranking.[2] It may be argued that it pursues an additional purpose: to reduce forum shopping, as global adherence to the rule is likely to ensure that creditors generally receive proportional dividends regardless of the number of jurisdictions in which they claim.[3] **1.32.02**

In the words of the Guide to Enactment and Interpretation, the rule enshrined in Article 31 is intended 'to avoid situations in which a creditor might obtain more favourable treatment than the other creditors of the same class by obtaining payment of the same claim in insolvency proceedings in different jurisdictions'.[4] An example of the coveted effect is set forth in the Guide to Enactment and Interpretation: when a creditor has received 5 per cent of his claim in a foreign proceeding and then participates in the local proceeding, where the rate of distribution for creditors of his class is 15 per cent, the rule will prevent him from receiving more than 10 per cent in the local proceeding.[5] **1.32.03**

Law' (2016) 25 International Insolvency Review 139, 153, fn. 54. In fact, though being true that the hotchpot rule is restrictive of the right of the foreign creditors (in the words of Westbrook, 'that right is constrained by a rule of fairness'; see Jay L. Westbrook, 'Breaking Away: Global Proceedings and Local Assets' (2011) 46 Tex. Int'l L.J. 601, 617), the hotchpot rule ensures the sameness of rights pursued by Article 13(1).

2 The quest for the *raison d'être* of Article 32 cannot disregard the normative models for international insolvency law (territorialism/universalism). It is well known that no two priority systems are identical (to paraphrase Garrido, 'no two snowflakes the same'; see José M. Garrido, 'No Two Snowflakes the Same: The Distributional Question in International Bankruptcies' (2011) 46 Tex. Int'l L. J. 459). Depending on the normative model adopted, the differences in outcome for creditors may be substantial. For an analysis of distribution rules, including the interactions of universalism vs. territorialism, cross-filing vs. local filing, and hotchpot vs. one hundred per cent dividends see Ulrik Rammeskow Bang-Pedersen, 'Asset Distribution in Transnational Insolvencies: Combining Predictability and Protection of Local Interests' (1999) 73 The American Bankruptcy Law Journal, 385.

3 See Matthew T. Cronin, 'UNCITRAL Model Law on Cross-Border Insolvency: Procedural Approach to a Substantive Problem' (1999) 24 J. Corp. L. 709, 724-725.

4 *Guide to Enactment and Interpretation* (n. 1), para. 239.

5 *Guide to Enactment and Interpretation* (fn. 1), para. 239.

1.32.04 The principle underlying the hotchpot rule is consensually considered to be the principle of equality (equality in distribution) or *pari passu* principle (*pari passu* of distribution), [6,7] determining that all creditors participate in the common pool in proportion to the size of their admitted claims.[8,9] Considering the roots in the principles of fairness and equality,[10] some commentators qualify the hotchpot rule as a 'common-sense device'.[11] The concept of proportionality is helpful to understand why, in the end, the nominal amount paid to the creditor in the foreign proceeding is not decisive. The crucial point is indeed the percentage of the claim already paid to the creditor: he is not supposed to receive, in the local proceeding, a percentage of the claim that, added to the percentage of the claim already paid, amounts to a percentage that is higher than the percentage of payment received, in the local proceeding, by the creditors of the same class.

1.32.05 The hotchpot rule is not, of course, the only instrument conceivable for the ends mentioned above. In the early days, the UNCITRAL Working Group on Insolvency Law, elaborating on the topic of 'equalization of rate of payment

---

6 See Reinhard Bork, *Principles of Cross-Border Insolvency Law* (Intersentia 2017), para. 2.65, 4.7 and 4.13. and Reinhard Bork, *Advanced Introduction to Cross-Border Insolvency Law* (Edward Elgar Publishing 2023), 23 and 104-105.

7 In the countries of the Romano-Germanic legal system the principle is better known as *par conditio creditorum*.

8 Though dominant, this reasoning is not absolutely undisputed. See, e.g., Look Chan Ho, 'On *Pari Passu*, Equality and Hotchpot in Cross-Border Insolvency' (2003) Lloyd's Maritime and Commercial Law Quarterly 95. Using the Privy Council decision in *Cleaver v. Delta American Reinsurance* (see infra [1.32.11]) as a case study, the author attempts to demonstrate that the rationale behind the hotchpot rule has nothing to do with the *pari passu* rule. The author considers that '[b]asing the hotchpot rule on *pari passu* distribution is unjustifiable because it necessitates leaving preferential creditors out of the scope of the rule'. He exemplifies: '[i]magine a frequent situation where even the preferential creditors do not get paid in full and thus creditors subject to the *pari passu* principle by definition get nothing. Suppose an employee-creditor seizes some asset belonging to the insolvent abroad and proves the rest of his claim in an English liquidation. If the hotchpot rule is tied to *pari passu* principle, this employee-creditor would not be subject to the hotchpot rule because he is not subject to the *pari passu* principle. Other preferential creditors would be justifiably outraged by this result. If the hotchpot rule were indeed built on the foundation of *pari passu*, it would have long lost its modern-day traction'. In short, the commentator submits that if the hotchpot rule applies to preferential creditors (who are equalized among themselves), and not only to creditors subject to the *pari passu* (unsecured creditors), then the hotchpot rule cannot be founded on the *pari passu* principle. He concludes that 'the hotchpot rule is an equalisation rule whose *raison d'être* is to prevent the distortion of the policy of distribution that applies to insolvency'. See also Look Chan Ho, *Insolvency Policy and the* Pari Passu *Principle, in: Cross-Border Insolvency Principles and Practice* (Sweet & Maxwell 2016), 288–290.

9 Other scholars also evoke the notion of equity, saying that the rule is derived from the equity maxim: '[h]e who asks for equity must do equity'. See Kurt H. Nadelmann, 'Concurrent bankruptcies and creditor in the Americas' (1947) 96 U. Pa. L. Rev. 171, 172.

10 The principle of fairness mandates differentiation (equals should be treated equally and unequals unequally). To evoke Aristotle in 'Nicomachean Ethics', the just person wants its fair share, not more, not less.

11 See Renato Mangano, in Reinhard Bork and Renato Mangano, *European Cross-Border Insolvency Law* (2nd ed., OUP 2022), para 6.90, commenting the corresponding rule enshrined in Article 23(2) EIR.

of claims', discussed alternative and additional tools for coordinating concurrent proceedings, namely the cross-filing of claims (the possibility on the part of each representative to cross-file claims from his proceeding in other proceedings),[12] disgorgement (return of the benefit received by a creditor of an individual action to enforce a claim on the debtor's assets) and a reference to the principle of 'marshalling' (the principle according to which creditors must exercise rights with respect to assets to the minimum disadvantage of certain other classes of creditors).[13,14]

The scope of the norm is not unrestricted. From the outset, secured creditors and creditors with rights *in rem* are, as a matter of principle, excluded. As explained in more detail below,[15] the caveat is related to the origins of the hotchpot rule and, in particular, its configuration in English common law. **1.32.06**

The provision which corresponds to Article 32 in the EIR is Article 23(2) (known as the 'charge rule' or 'imputation rule'),[16] laying down that '[i]n order to ensure the equal treatment of creditors, a creditor which has, in the course of insolvency proceedings, obtained a dividend on its claim shall share in distributions made in other proceedings only where creditors of the same ranking or category have, in those other proceedings, obtained an equivalent dividend'.[17] For the purpose of interpreting the predecessor norm (Article 20(2) EIR 2000), **1.32.07**

---

12 The possibility of universal cross-filing is a topic debated in literature. According to Westbrook, the universal cross-filing consists of the liquidator in country A filing claims in country B for all creditors in country A. See Jay L. Westbrook, 'Universal Priorities' (1998) 33 Tex. Int'l L.J. 27, 29–30. Garrido sustains that in a system based on cooperative international bankruptcy, creditors should be allowed to participate in the insolvency proceedings opened vis-à-vis the same debtor, irrespective of the jurisdiction. In his view, universal cross-filing is one of the basic manifestations of cooperation, and implies the ability of foreign creditors to prove their claims in the same manner as local creditors. See Garrido, 'No Two Snowflakes the Same: The Distributional Question in International Bankruptcies' (fn. 2), 480. The problem, as Pottow puts it, is that a 'theoretical ability of cross-border participation is unlikely to be distributed uniformly. Sophisticated multinational creditors can likely file claims in either proceeding relatively painlessly compared to their smaller counterparts'. See John A.E. Pottow, 'Greed and Pride in International Bankruptcy: The Problems of and Proposed Solutions to "Local Interests"' (2006) 104 Mich. L. Rev. 1899, 1910.

13 See UNCITRAL, Report of the Working Group on Insolvency Law on the work of the eighteenth session, A/CN.9/419, United Nations Publications (New York), 1996, para. 89-93. See also, on the cross-filing of claims, UNCITRAL, Report of the United Nations Commission on International Trade Law on the work of its nineteenth session, A/CN.9/WG.V/WP.44, United Nations Publications (New York), 1996, 30.

14 There are even other distributional options, as, for example, cross-priority. According to Westbrook, cross-priority is the availability of local priorities to foreign creditors whose claims qualify for priority treatment if they were local creditors. See Westbrook, 'Universal Priorities' (fn. 12), 30-31. Garrido advocates a system of universal cross-filing and universal priorities. See Garrido, 'No Two Snowflakes the Same: The Distributional Question in International Bankruptcies' (fn. 2), 476-488.

15 See infra [1.32.10].

16 See, e.g., Bob Wessels/Gert-Jan Boon, *Cross-Border Insolvency Law – International Instruments and Commentary* (Wolters Kluwer 2015), 26.

17 Miguel Virgós and Etienne Schmit, 'Report on the Convention of Insolvency Proceedings' (1996) [EU Council of the EU Document] (hereafter: Virgós-Schmit Report), para. 175.

the Virgós-Schmit Report enunciated four rules which are also of interest to the understanding of the rule enshrined in Article 32 MLCBI: (i) nobody may obtain more than 100 per cent of his claims; (ii) the total original amount of the claim (100 per cent of its initial value) shall be taken into account, and not the remaining amount (satisfaction obtained in other proceedings is not deducted); (iii) a claim is not taken into account in distribution until such time as the creditors with the same ranking have obtained an equal percentage of satisfaction in these proceedings as that obtained by its holder in the first proceedings; (iv) the ranking or category of each claim is determined for each of the proceedings by the law of the State of the opening.

1.32.08 Article 32 is also mirrored in the Report 'Transnational Insolvency: Global Principles of Cooperation in International Insolvency Cases', submitted for discussion at the 2012 Annual Meeting of the American Law Institute (ALI).[18] In accordance with Global Principle 12, '[w]here there is more than one insolvency case pending with respect to the debtor, the creditor should not receive more through the distributions made in a particular case than the percentage recovered by other creditors of the same class in that case, having regard to distributions already received in other cases concerning the same debtor. A creditor who receives more than one distribution should account for all previous distributions as a condition to participating in a subsequent distribution in another case.' In the commentary to this Global Principle, it is noted that the hotchpot rule is 'especially relevant to the application of the principle of the sharing of value expressed in Global Principle 10'.[19]

2. Origins of the Rule: The Hotchpot Rule

1.32.09 As observed, Article 32 incorporates the hotchpot rule. The hotchpot doctrine 'has long been an important doctrine within common law systems, which have

18 American Law Institute (ALI)/International Insolvency Institute (III), 'Transnational Insolvency: Global Principles of Cooperation in International Insolvency Cases', 2012 <https://www.ali.org/publications/show/transnational-insolvency/> accessed 22 February 2023. It consists of a non-binding document drafted by Ian F. Fletcher and Bob Wessels and commissioned by the two institutes. See, for a brief presentation of the statement, Bob Wessels, 'A Global Approach to Cross-Border Insolvency Cases in a Globalizing World' (2013) The Dovenschmidt Quarterly 16.

19 According to the commentary on Global Principle 10 of the ALI's Report on 'Transnational Insolvency: Global Principles of Cooperation', the Global Principle 10 'seeks to suppress incentives for individual creditors to engage in self-serving tactics that can be both destructive of value and also detrimental to any prospects of a successful reorganization of the debtor, where there might otherwise have been undertaken'. In its turn, Global Principle 12 is considered 'a logical and necessary counterpart of this objective'. Complementing Global Principle 10, the hotchpot rule set out in Global Principle 12 'addresses the concern that individual creditors might obtain an unfair advantage, relative to other creditors of equivalent standing, by multiple filings of the same claim in distributions that happen to take place in different states'.

taken their inspiration from English law'.[20] The framework of the English hotchpot rule sheds light on the reasons why secured creditors and creditors with rights *in rem* are left out of the scope of application of the norm.

(a) The Hotchpot Rule in England

Before it was given statutory status through Article 32 CBIR, the hotchpot rule was a common law rule in England,[21] deriving from cases such as *Selkrig v Davis*,[22] *Banco de Portugal v Waddell*[23] and *Re Doulgas ex parte Wilson*.[24] These paradigmatic cases demonstrate that the hotchpot requirement applies only to assets that, under English law, are regarded as forming part of the estate in liquidation. Consequently, a secured creditor who has realized his or her security before the commencement of the liquidation is entitled to prove for the balance of his or her claim, after deducting the amount realized.[25] That is to say that secured claims and rights *in rem* fall outside the hotchpot rule, as the rule does not extend to receipts resulting from the realisation of the creditors' own property or security.[26] **1.32.10**

20 Ian F. Fletcher, *Insolvency in Private International Law* (2nd ed., OUP 2005), para. 4.58.

21 Look Chan Ho, 'England' in Look Chan Ho (ed.), *A Commentary on the UNCITRAL Model Law* (1th ed., Globe Law & Business 2017), 288, fn 539.

22 *Selkrig v. Davis* (1814) 2 Rose 291.

23 *Banco de Portugal v. Waddell* (1880) 5 App. Cass. 161. In this clear-cut case, two individuals had carried on business in England and in Portugal as wine merchants. They presented a petition for their adjudication in bankruptcy in England in December 1877. Insolvency proceedings were taken in Portugal after the English petition had been presented. The Portuguese Court took possession of the insolvent's assets in Portugal, realized them, and paid a dividend to the Portuguese creditors. These creditors then proved in the English bankruptcy. They were not allowed any dividend in the English bankruptcy until they had accounted for the dividend they had received in Portugal.

24 *Re Doulgas ex parte Wilson* (1872) L.R. 7 Ch. App. 490. In this case, the debtor carried on business in England and Brazil under two different firms. The debtor filed for bankruptcy protection and its assets in Brazil were administered under Brazilian bankruptcy law. After receiving a dividend in the Brazilian bankruptcy proceeding, certain Brazilian creditors filed claims in the English bankruptcy proceedings. The English Court of Appeal held that, despite the fact that the debtor carried on business under two separate firms in two jurisdictions, the debtor's bankruptcy really only involved one estate (i.e., one pool of assets) which was partially administered in England and Brazil. Accordingly, based on the long-standing principle that a creditor cannot make a second recovery from the same estate, the Court ruled that the Brazilian creditors could not make a second recovery in England until all other creditors of the bankrupt's estate had received the same proportional recovery on their claims (the hotchpot rule).

25 See rule 4.88 of the Insolvency Rules 1986.

26 Put in another way: 'secured creditors claim primarily from their rights *in rem*, and it is the value from their rights *in rem* that satisfy their claims. If their claims are not satisfied from their rights *in rem*, they look to repayment of the balance as unsecured creditors'. See Wai Yee Wan and Gerry McCormack, 'Implementing Strategies for the Model Law on Cross-Border Insolvency: The Divergence in Asia-Pacific and Lessons for UNCITRAL' (2000) 36 Emory Bankr. Dev. J. 59, 88.

1.32.11 In *Cleaver v Delta American Reinsurance*,[27] considered the 'most thorough judicial assessment of the doctrine of the hotchpot of modern times',[28] a Cayman Islands insurance company (Transnational) had given, in the course of trading, security to a Kentucky reinsurance company (Delta Re) by means of a standby letter of credit to be issued by Barclays Bank to Delta Re. At a certain point in time, Transnational went into liquidation. Delta Re then obtained a default judgment against Transnational and payment from Barclays under the letter of credit. As the payment received from Barclays left a balance still outstanding, Delta Re submitted a proof of claim in Transnational's liquidation. The liquidators of Transnational required Delta Re to bring into hotchpot the credit received in a foreign jurisdiction, arguing that, having obtained an advantage over the unsecured creditors for the amount secured, the claiming creditor should make available to all creditors the payment already received. The Privy Council held that the payment received had arisen from a letter of credit and had never been part of the insolvent company's estate. Lord Scott of Foscote, speaking for the Privy Council, explained that '[t]he well-spring of the hotchpot rule is the need to ensure that the assets of a liquidation are, subject to prior claims such as liquidation expenses, preferential debts etc., divided *pari passu* among the unsecured creditors. If any of them obtains a share of the liquidation assets by participating in a distribution of liquidation assets in a foreign liquidation, that share must be brought into account before a dividend in the English liquidation can be claimed.'[29] Their Lordships further clarified that rule 4.88 of the Insolvency Rules 1986 not only did not represent an exception to the hotchpot rule but was also entirely consistent with the hotchpot rule. In the present case, as the payment to Delta Re was not made, either directly or indirectly, out of assets of Transnational, the hotchpot rule did not come into play. Independently of Delta Re being, in substance, a secured creditor, it simply was not subject to the hotchpot rule because the sum was not paid out of the liquidation estate.

27 *Cleaver vs. Delta American Reinsurance* [2001] UKPC 6. This judgement was delivered on 1 February 2001, by the Lords of the Judicial Committee of the Privy Council, upon appeal from the Court of Appeal of the Cayman Islands.

28 Fletcher, *Insolvency in Private International Law* (fn. 20), para. 2.99.

29 In a critical approach to this judgement, it has been argued that the rationale behind the hotchpot rule has nothing to do with the *pari passu* rule. See, once again, Ho, 'On *Pari Passu*, Equality and Hotchpot in Cross-Border Insolvency' (fn. 8).

(b) The Hotchpot Rule in Australia

Article 32 has force of law in Australia (Section 19(3) of Part 2 of the Cross-Border Insolvency Act (hereafter: CBIA)), but the hotchpot rule is a longstanding principle applicable to cross-border insolvencies in Australia.[30] 1.32.12

One of the reference cases is *Re Harris, Goodwin & Co*,[31] decided on 13 May 1887. According to the Supreme Court of Queensland, where a firm has been adjudicated insolvent in Queensland and bankrupt in England, the trustee of the English bankruptcy is not allowed to prove in the Queensland insolvency for the English debts, but the English creditors separately may prove in the Queensland insolvency for the amount of their debts after giving credit for the amount received by them in the English bankruptcy. More recently, in *Akers v Deputy Commissioner of Taxation*,[32] the Federal Court of Australia discussed the hotchpot rule in the context of the application of Australian law to the distribution of the English assets in the light of English public policy. It concluded that 'if there were to be a separate liquidation of the English assets in England, all creditors would be entitled to prove. Those Australian (or other foreign) creditors who see an advantage in proving in England after bringing into hotchpot their dividends in Australia would no doubt do so. But the English public policy does not require them to be afforded this facility.' 1.32.13

(c) The Hotchpot Rule in the US

11 USC §1532 tracks Article 32 MLCBI. Prior to the adoption of Chapter 15, the hotchpot rule was codified under former 11 USC § 508(a), which, in its turn, is an adaptation of § 65d Bankruptcy Act of 1898 as originally enacted.[33] 1.32.14

In re Pollmann,[34] a lien was obtained on property of the debtor by a German creditor in Germany, through judicial proceedings, within four months prior to the bankruptcy of the debtor and while the latter was solvent. The creditor realized therefrom payment of a portion of the claim. The New York District Court decided that the creditor was only entitled to prove the remainder as a claim against the estate in bankruptcy in the US if he surrendered the amount 1.32.15

---

30 See Rosalind Mason, 'Hotchpot and Other Tasty Morsels in International Insolvency' (1995) 3 Insolv. L. J. 149.

31 *Re Harris, Goodwin & Co.* (1887), 7, Queensland Law Journal (Notes of Cases), 94.

32 *In Akers v Deputy Commissioner of Taxation* [2014] FCAFC 57 135 [para. 139] (CLOUT case 1332).

33 On 11 USC § 508 see Frank R. Kennedy, 'Partnerships and Partners under the Bankruptcy Code: Claims and Distribution' (1983) 40 Wash. & Lee L. Rev. 55, 85-89, and on § 65d Bankruptcy Act see Kurt H. Nadelmann, 'Revision of Conflicts Provisions in the American Bankruptcy Act' (1952) 1 International & Comparative Law Quarterly 484, 487-488.

34 *In re Pollmann*, 156 F. 221 (S.D.N.Y. 1907).

so received 'so as to place him on equitable equality with other creditors'. There is no doubt that this case 'can be read to permit application of United States law to avoid as a preference a judicial lien obtained by a German creditor against German real property owned by the United States debtor' but it is arguable that it 'really involved the United States "equalization" provision, or "hotchpot" notion, which, like similar provisions in many countries, requires equalization in making distributions to creditors who have partially satisfied their claims in foreign jurisdictions'.[35]

3. Scope of Application

1.32.16 As noted, the rule enshrined in Article 32 is designed to apply primarily to unsecured creditors, leaving out secured creditors and creditors with rights *in rem*. Secured claims are generally considered claims guaranteed by particular assets of the debtor, whereas rights *in rem* designate rights relating to a particular property that are enforceable against third parties.[36] It is acknowledged that a given right may fall within the ambit of both expressions, depending on the classification and terminology of the applicable law, and admitted that the enacting State uses other term for expressing the concepts.[37] The exclusion of secured creditors and creditors with rights *in rem* means that the proportion of the original claim that was realized through the value of the security or the right *in rem* will be ignored for the purpose of dealing with the unsecured balance of the debt.[38] As explained above,[39] the restriction, as a matter of principle, to unsecured creditors is a consequence of the norm's inspiration in the English hotchpot rule.

1.32.17 The Guide to Enactment and Interpretation confirms that the claims of secured creditors and the claims of creditors with rights *in rem* are not affected

35 Jay L. Westbrook, 'Choice of Avoidance Law in Global Insolvencies' (1991) 17 Brooklyn Journal of International Law 499, 524, fn. 98.

36 *Guide to Enactment and Interpretation* (n. 1), para. 241. It is common to find secured creditors referred as subspecies of creditors with rights *in rem*. See, e.g., Neil Hannan, *Cross-Border Insolvency – The Enactment and Interpretation of the UNCITRAL Model Law* (Springer 2017), 165.

37 In the *travaux préparatoires*, proposals were made to replace the words 'secured claims' and 'rights in rem', with reference to 'privileged claims', 'preferred claims' or other expressions with a similar meaning. The proposals were rejected because it was not intended to affect the ranking of claims pursuant to the laws of the enacting State. See UNCITRAL, Report of the United Nations Commission on International Trade Law on the work of its thirtieth session, A/52/17, United Nations Publications (New York), 1997, para. 132.

38 Put in another way: 'secured creditors claim primarily from their rights *in rem*, and it is the value from their rights *in rem* that satisfy their claims. If their claims are not satisfied from their rights *in rem*, they look to repayment of the balance as unsecured creditors'. See Wan/McCormack, 'Implementing Strategies for the Model Law on Cross-Border Insolvency: The Divergence in Asia-Pacific and Lessons for UNCITRAL' (fn. 26), 87.

39 See supra [1.32.09].

by the provision to the extent such claims are paid in full.[40] In any case, as payment in full to these creditors is, admittedly, a matter that depends on the law of the State where the proceeding is conducted, it may be assumed that the enacting States are not prevented from extending the rule to secured creditors and creditors with rights *in rem*. Indeed, some States have implemented Article 32 so that it may apply both to unsecured and secured claims. This holds true for Canada[41] and Japan.[42]

B. PREREQUISITES FOR APPLICATION

The prerequisites for the application of the norm are two: firstly, the creditor must lodge the claim in a proceeding taking place in the enacting State (local proceeding); secondly, the creditor must have received partial payment in respect of the same claim in another proceeding regarding the same debtor (foreign proceeding).[43] **1.32.18**

These two prerequisites represent a certain behaviour on the part of the creditor unfolding into two successive actions: the lodging of the claim in the foreign proceeding, which corresponds to an initial attempt at being paid; and the lodging of the same claim in the local proceeding, which corresponds to a following attempt at being paid for the same claim.[44] **1.32.19**

---

40 *Guide to Enactment and Interpretation* (n. 1), para. 240.

41 In Canada, the hotchpot rule in cross-border proceedings was given statutory form in Part XIII of the BIA: originally, in Section 274; then, following Bill C-55 (which introduced a revised Part XIII to the BIA and a brand new Part IV to the CCAA, both based on the MLCBI), in Section 283. At present, Section 60(2) CCAA prevents creditors from receiving a dividend from the distribution of the debtor's assets until other creditors of equal rank and priority have received a similar percentage. There being nothing more than a general reference to 'creditors', it is reasonable to conclude that the rule applies both to unsecure and secured creditors.

42 There seem to be three differences between the Japanese legislation and the MLCBI in what concerns the hotchpot rule. First, secured creditors are subject to the rule; second, payments outside foreign insolvency proceedings, including payments in execution proceedings or voluntary payments by debtors, are subject to the rule; and third, only payments made after the commencement of local proceedings are subject to the rule. See Wan/McCormack, 'Implementing Strategies for the Model Law on Cross-Border Insolvency: The Divergence in Asia-Pacific and Lessons for UNCITRAL' (fn. 26), 87-88.

43 Just to be clear, local proceeding is the proceeding in which the creditor is lodging the claim at the time of the application of the rule and in which it is supposed to be applied and, correspondingly, foreign proceeding is the proceeding in which the creditor was previously allocated an amount for the same claim.

44 It follows that foreign creditor is the creditor (any creditor) who was previously allocated an amount for the claim (in one or more foreign proceedings) when he submits the claim locally and is absolutely irrespective of the nationality of the person or entity behind. It should be underpinned that '[t]he definition of "local" or "national" creditors is extremely difficult, as there are no elements to suggest that the criteria should be based on nationality, residence, or place of business'. See Garrido, 'No Two Snowflakes the Same: The Distributional Question in International Bankruptcies' (fn. 2), 480. See also Pottow, 'Greed and Pride in International Bankruptcy: The Problems of and Proposed Solutions to "Local Interests"' (fn. 12), 1907

1.32.20 The provision makes no demands as to the type of proceedings at stake. It may be concluded that neither the foreign proceeding nor the local proceeding need to be main or non-main. The only requirement is that the proceedings regard the same debtor.

1.32.21 Interestingly, in the case *In re Nortel Networks Inc*,[45] despite there being multiple debtors, the hotchpot rule was used to support a *pro rata* distribution. In a nutshell, Nortel Networks Corporation, a publicly traded Canadian company, and 130 of its subsidiaries sought bankruptcy protection in the US and in Canada. The parties were able to sell the debtor's global assets in large pieces and the proceeds from the sale were placed into escrow (lockbox funds). The US Bankruptcy Court for the District of Delaware and the Ontario Superior Court of Justice held a joint trial to decide how these sale proceeds should be allocated. One of the creditors (the UK Pension Claimants) claimed that, although the hotchpot rule does not apply where there are separate plenary proceedings for multiple debtors, it applies 'in cases involving highly integrated debtors where the underlying assets available to satisfy creditor claims are in fact from one source and represent joint assets prior to bankruptcy or assets in which multiple debtors have an interest'. In a joint report submitted on behalf the UK Pension Claimants, Judge Leif Clark and Professor Jay Westbrook advocated for 'a single-pool distribution' of Nortel's assets, reminding that 'the hotchpot rule [ ] provides that a creditor with a claim that can be asserted in two countries should not be able to participate on a *pro rata* basis with creditors with claims that can only be asserted in one of those countries until the latter creditors have received a percentage recovery equal to what the two-country creditor received in the other country'.[46,47]

(giving note of the difficulties in identifying the interests of 'local creditors' due to the ambiguity in the range of individuals that the expression includes). Furthermore, it must be kept in mind that the meaning of foreign and local change depending on the perspective: when a foreign main proceeding is opened in State A, for the courts of State A this proceeding is not foreign.

45 *In re Nortel Networks Inc.*, Case No. 09-10138 (KG), 2015 WL 2374351. *Nortel Networks Corporation (Re)* 2015 ONSC 2987.

46 For a general commentary on the case see Jay L. Westbrook, 'Global Insolvency Proceedings for a Global Market: The Universalist System and the Choice of a Central Court' (2018) 96 *Texas Law Review* 1473.

47 Just for the record, although not attributing relevance to the hotchpot argument, the courts decided on the allocation of the sale proceeds on a modified *pro rata* basis determined by the ratio of the claims against each of the estates, stressing, however, that this did not constitute a global substantive consolidation (each entity will still be required to distribute the funds allocated to it in accordance with its own insolvency procedure and with local insolvency laws).

C. LEGAL CONSEQUENCES

By now, the legal consequences of the application of the norm should be reasonably clear: the creditor cannot share in the distribution in the local proceeding until creditors of the same class have obtained, in that proceeding, dividends that are equivalent in percentage to the dividend obtained by that creditor in the foreign proceeding. In practice, the norm requires that, before lodging a claim and receiving payment in a local proceeding, the creditor accounts for what he has already obtained abroad ('contributes to the hotchpot'). **1.32.22**

Evidently, the creditor is not expected to hand over what he or she has received in the foreign proceeding. Previous payments merely limit what the creditor will receive in the local proceeding. Put in other words: the hotchpot rule is not a 'clawback provision';[48] it does not mandate the restitution to the hotchpot of the amounts already received by the creditors in a proceeding regarding the debtor and only affects the creditors who resubmit their claim. **1.32.23**

There should be no doubt as to what is to be understood by 'the same class'. It is a reference to the ranking in distribution assigned to the claim in the local proceeding.[49] It should also be noted that the class which is relevant for the purposes of applying the rule – the 'comparator for the purposes of applying the Hotchpot rule'[50] – is the class or the ranking assigned to the claim under the law of the enacting State rather than the class or the ranking assigned under the law of the State in which payment was previously obtained[51] (the priority regime that applies to every payment is always that of the State from which the payments are made).[52] **1.32.24**

It is clarified in the Guide to Enactment and Interpretation that the rule is not intended to affect the ranking established under the law of the enacting State and is exclusively designed to establish the equal treatment of creditors of the same class.[53] **1.32.25**

---

48 The expression is used in Ho, 'On *Pari Passu*, Equality and Hotchpot in Cross-Border Insolvency' (fn. 8).

49 Classes formed upon the application of criteria like the nature of the economic interests held by the creditors or their degree of vulnerability are generally relevant for other purposes in insolvency proceedings (e.g., voting and approval *quora*) but are irrelevant for the purposes of the norm.

50 See Fletcher, *Insolvency in Private International Law* (fn. 20), para. 8.70.

51 Since different insolvency laws apply to the different proceedings (each is governed by its own national law), the ranking of the same claim lodged in two different proceedings will almost certainly differ. The only ranking or category that shall be taken into account in order to apply Article 32 is the one given to the claim by the law governing the proceeding in which distribution is to be carried out.

52 See Hannan, *Cross-Border Insolvency – The Enactment and Interpretation of the UNCITRAL Model Law* (fn. 36), 165.

53 *Guide to Enactment and Interpretation* (fn. 1), para. 240.

PART II

THE UNCITRAL MODEL LAW ON RECOGNITION AND ENFORCEMENT OF INSOLVENCY-RELATED JUDGMENTS (MLIJ)

MLIJ PREAMBLE

Michael Veder

1. The purpose of this Law is:
   (a) to create greater certainty in regard to rights and remedies for recognition and enforcement of insolvency-related judgments;
   (b) to avoid the duplication of insolvency proceedings;
   (c) to ensure timely and cost-effective recognition and enforcement of insolvency-related judgments;
   (d) to promote comity and cooperation between jurisdictions regarding insolvency-related judgments;
   (e) to protect and maximize the value of insolvency estates; and
   (f) where legislation based on the UNCITRAL Model Law on Cross-Border Insolvency has been enacted, to complement that legislation.
2. This Law is not intended:
   (a) to restrict provisions of the law of this State that would permit the recognition and enforcement of an insolvency-related judgment;
   (b) to replace legislation enacting the UNCITRAL Model Law on Cross-Border Insolvency or limit the application of that legislation;
   (c) to apply to the recognition and enforcement in the enacting State of an insolvency-related judgment issued in the enacting State; or
   (d) to apply to the judgment commencing the insolvency proceeding.

A. BACKGROUND TO AND OBJECTIVES OF THE MLIJ

P2.01 The UNCITRAL Model Law on Recognition and Enforcement of Insolvency-Related Judgments ('MLIJ'), adopted in 2018, aims to complement the UNCITRAL Model Law on Cross-Border Insolvency ('MLCBI') by introducing rules on the recognition and enforcement of insolvency-related judgments. The MLIJ is designed to assist States to equip their laws with a framework of provisions for recognizing and enforcing insolvency-related judgments that will facilitate the conduct of cross-border insolvency proceedings.[1]

P2.02 The MLIJ seeks to fill a lacuna that exists as a result of the fact that existing international treaties that deal with the recognition and enforcement of judgments generally, exclude from their scope matters relating to insolvency and thus recognition and enforcement of insolvency-related judgments.[2] Most importantly, the MLIJ is a response to the uncertainty that had arisen in the context of the application of the MLCBI, in particular Articles 7 and 21 MLCBI, to the recognition and enforcement of judgments in the context of foreign insolvency proceedings, other than the judgment opening the foreign insolvency proceedings.[3] While some jurisdictions interpreted the MLCBI as including the recognition and enforcement of insolvency-related judgments in the context of relief granted to a recognised foreign proceeding,[4] others did not.

P2.03 Most notably, the case *Rubin & Anor v Eurofinance SA*,[5] decided by the Supreme Court of the United Kingdom in 2012, provided a trigger to consider complementing the MLCBI with rules specifically addressing the recognition and enforcement of insolvency-related judgments. In that case, the UK Supreme Court refused to recognize and enforce a judgment of the US Federal Bankruptcy Court for the Southern District of New York, where insolvency

1 Cf. *UNCITRAL Model Law on Recognition and Enforcement of Insolvency-Related Judgments with Guide to Enactment*, United Nations Publications (Vienna), 2019, para. 1.

2 See, for example, Article 1(5) of the Convention of 1 February 1971 on the recognition and enforcement of foreign judgments in civil and commercial matters; Article 2(2)(e) of the Convention of 30 June 2005 on Choice of Court Agreements; Article 2(1)(e) of the Convention of 2 July 2019 on the Recognition and Enforcement of Foreign Judgments in Civil or Commercial Matters. Cf. *Guide to Enactment* (n 1), paras 5–7.

3 Cf. Guide to Enactment (n 1), para. 2.

4 See, for the United States, for example, *In re Metcalfe & Mansfield Alternative Investment,* 421 BR 685 (Bankr. SDNY 2010). Cf. Irit Mevorach, Overlapping International Instruments for Enforcement of Insolvency Judgments: Undermining or Strengthening Universalism?, European Business Organization Law Review (2021) 22, 283–315, 291.

5 *Rubin & Anor. v Eurofinance SA*, [2012] UKSC 46 (on appeal from [2010] EWCA Civ 895 and [2011] EWCA Civ 971); CLOUT case No. 1270.

proceedings had been opened in respect of 'The Consumers Trust', concerning the avoidance of certain transactions, leading to a judgment of approximately US$ 10 million against Eurofinance SA and others. The defendants had not been present before the court in New York, nor had they submitted to its jurisdiction. The court at first instance recognized the US insolvency proceedings, but dismissed the application for enforcement of the judgment in the avoidance action on the ground that the judgment was *in personam* and a fundamental principle of English private international law was that a judgment of a foreign court was not enforceable unless the defendant was present in the jurisdiction, or had in some way submitted to the jurisdiction, of the foreign court.[6] On appeal, the Court of Appeal held that, although the judgment of the New York court had the indicia of a judgment *in personam*, it was nonetheless a judgment 'in and for the purposes of the collective enforcement regime of the insolvency proceedings' and as such was governed by the rules of private international law relating to bankruptcy and not subject to the ordinary private international law rules that would prevent enforcement of these judgments because the defendants were not subject to the jurisdiction of the foreign court.[7]

The question put to the UK Supreme Court was whether, as the Court of Appeal had decided, the US judgment was enforceable at common law. The UK Supreme Court held that it was not. The Supreme Court found that the Cross-Border Insolvency Regulations 2006, which implemented the MLCBI in English law, did not provide for recognition and enforcement of foreign judgments against third parties: 'the CBIR (and the Model Law) say nothing about the enforcement of foreign judgments against third parties' and 'It would be surprising if the Model Law was intended to deal with judgments in insolvency matters by implication'.[8] The Supreme Court held that Articles 21, 25 and 27 MLCBI were concerned with procedural matters and that, while there was no doubt that they should be given a purposive interpretation and be widely construed in the light of the objects of the Model Law, there was nothing to suggest that they applied to the recognition and enforcement of foreign judgments against third parties. According to the Supreme Court, **P2.04**

6 On this so-called Dicey rule, see the opinion of Lord Collins ([2012] UKSC 46), at para. 7 et seq.

7 For a summary of the reasoning of the Court of Appeal, see the opinion of Lord Collins ([2012] UKSC 46), at para. 89.

8 See the opinion of Lord Collins ([2012] UKSC 46), at paras 142 and 143. A different approach is followed by, for example, the US courts, cf. *In re Metcalfe & Mansfield Alternative Investments*, 421 BR 685 (Bankr. SDNY 2010), on which L.C. Ho, Cross-Border Insolvency, a commentary on the UNCITRAL Model Law, 4th edn., Globe Law and Business, London 2017, 167.

the MLCBI is not designed to provide for the reciprocal enforcement of judgments in insolvency-related disputes.[9]

P2.05 While *Rubin v Eurofinance* concerned the enforcement of a judgment ensuing from avoidance actions, it was feared that the impact of the Supreme Court's decision would also extend to judgments of foreign, notably US, courts approving plans of reorganization. As Jay Westbrook put it in the Liber Amicorum in honour of the late Ian Fletcher:

> The United States insolvency community was quite upset about *Rubin*, but the concern was especially strong with regard to the overruling of *Cambridge Gas*. It was a real blow to think that many fraudulent conveyance cases would have to be relitigated to be enforceable in the United Kingdom, but of far greater concern was the possibility that a United States reorganization judgment could be ignored by manipulating corporate shells that would carefully avoid contact with the United States debtor while their sister companies and principals had a full and fair opportunity to object to the United States proceedings. If that were permitted, the judgment arising from approval of a reorganization would be of dramatically reduced value. For example, an off-shore shell that had taken assignment of the debt could sue the reorganized company in England for the full amount originally owed while the rest of the creditors had settled for less. In turn, that prospect would make it far less likely the other creditors would agree to a plan in the first place – the classic holdout problem that both United Kingdom and United States reorganization (or rescue) provisions are designed to overcome. Given the great commercial importance of the United Kingdom, especially to United States-based companies, American reorganization efforts could be crippled by a United Kingdom refusal to give full effect to a United States reorganization judgment.[10]

P2.06 The concerns expressed by Westbrook are underscored by Mevorach, who points out that *Rubin v Eurofinance* has indeed had further repercussions in the UK, where courts have interpreted modified universalism narrowly when required to defer to foreign judgments, including by applying the 'Gibbs rule'.[11]

P2.07 The concerns about the application and interpretation of the MLCBI, in particular its Articles 7 and 21, in the context of the recognition and enforcement of insolvency-related judgments, together with the general absence of an applicable international convention or other regime to address the recognition and enforcement of such judgments, led to the proposal to UNCITRAL in 2014 to develop a model law or model legislative provisions on the recognition

---

9 See the opinion of Lord Collins ([2012] UKSC 46), at para. 144. On the 'obscurity' of the MLCBI on the issue of the enforcement of judgments and orders, see also Irit Mevorach 2021 (n 4), 290.

10 Jay Westbrook, Ian Fletcher and the Internationalist Principle (2015) 3 NIBLeJ 20, paras 10-11.

11 Irit Mevorach 2021 (n 4), 291–3, with references to, inter alia, *Singularis Holdings Ltd v PricewaterhouseCoopers* [2014] UKPC 36, [2015] AC 1675; *Fibria Celulose S/A v. Pan Ocean Co Ltd* [2014] EWHC 2124 (Ch); *Re OJSC International Bank of Azerbaijan* [2018] EWCA Civ. 2802.

and enforcement of insolvency-related judgments.[12] The MLIJ was negotiated between December 2014 and May 2018. The final negotiations on the draft text took place during the 51st session of UNCITRAL, held in Vienna from 25 June to 13 July 2018. UNCITRAL adopted the MLIJ by consensus on 2 July 2018.[13] Subsequently, the General Assembly adopted resolution 73/200 of 20 December 2018 (see annex I), in which it expressed its appreciation for UNCITRAL's finalizing and adopting the MLIJ.

Paragraph 1 of the Preamble succinctly states the basic policy objectives of the MLIJ, i.e. to create greater certainty, to avoid the duplication of insolvency proceedings, to ensure the timely and cost-effective recognition and enforcement of insolvency-related judgments, to promote comity and cooperation between jurisdictions in relation to insolvency-related judgments, to protect and maximize the value of insolvency estates and, where legislation based on the MLCBI has been enacted, to complement that legislation. **P2.08**

B. RELATIONSHIP BETWEEN THE MLCBI AND THE MLIJ

The subject matters of the MLIJ and the MLCBI are closely related. While the MLCBI addresses the recognition of foreign insolvency proceedings in general, the MLIJ deals with the recognition and enforcement of judgments handed down in the context of insolvency proceedings. Both texts use similar terminology and definitions,[14] a number of the general articles of the MLCBI are repeated in the MLIJ,[15] and the Preamble to the MLIJ refers specifically to the relationship between the MLIJ and the MLCBI.[16] The MLIJ is not intended to replace legislation enacting the MLCBI. Rather, it is intended to be complementary to such legislation.[17] **P2.09**

The MLIJ addresses the recognition and enforcement of 'insolvency-related judgments' as these are defined in Article 2(d) MLIJ on the basis of their relationship[18] to an 'insolvency proceeding' as defined in Article 2(a) MLIJ.[19] **P2.10**

12 Cf. Guide to Enactment (n 1), para. 3. See also Official Records of the General Assembly, Sixty-ninth Session, Supplement No. 17 (A/69/17), para. 155.

13 Official Records of the General Assembly, Seventy-third session, Supplement No. 17 (A/73/17), para. 131.

14 The definition of 'insolvency proceeding', for example, draws upon the definition of 'foreign proceeding' in the MLCBI.

15 Articles 3 to 8 MLCBI.

16 Cf. See also Article 14(h) and Article X MLIJ.

17 Preamble to the MLIJ, para. 2(b).

18 See Veder at para. 2.02.17 et seq.

19 See Veder at para. 2.02.02 et seq.

If the insolvency proceeding to which the specific judgment relates does not satisfy the definition of an insolvency proceeding in Article 2(a) MLIJ, the judgment would not be an insolvency-related judgment capable of recognition and enforcement under the MLIJ. The decision opening the insolvency proceeding, which is the subject of the MLCBI's recognition regime, is specifically excluded from the definition of 'insolvency-related judgment' for the purposes of the Model Law.[20] The MLIJ does, however, apply to judgments issued at the time of commencement of insolvency proceedings (and might be included in the judgment opening the proceedings itself), such as the appointment of an insolvency representative, judgments or orders addressing payment of employee claims and continuation of employee entitlements, retention and payment of professionals during the insolvency proceeding, acceptance or rejection of executory contracts and orders approving the use of cash collateral and post-commencement finance. Such judgments would be considered insolvency-related judgments on the basis that they arise as a consequence of the opening of the insolvency proceedings.[21] Where appropriate, the severability provision of Article 16 MLIJ may come into play.[22]

P2.11 Like the MLCBI, the MLIJ seeks to establish a framework for the cross-border recognition of insolvency-related judgments that provides for a clear and simple procedure that avoids unnecessary complexity.[23] As Article 19 MLCBI does in relation to the request for recognition of a foreign insolvency proceeding, Article 12 MLIJ permits provisional relief to be granted by the court where that is urgently needed to preserve the possibility of recognizing and enforcing an insolvency-related judgment between the time at which recognition and enforcement are sought and the time at which the court issues its decision. Like the MLCBI, the MLIJ seeks to establish certainty with respect to the outcome of the recognition and enforcement procedure: if the relevant documents are provided, the judgment satisfies the definitional requirements and those for effectiveness and enforceability in the originating State, the person seeking recognition and enforcement is the appropriate person and there are insufficient or no grounds for refusing recognition and enforcement, the judgment should be recognized and enforced.[24]

P2.12 With respect to States that have enacted legislation based on the MLCBI (or are considering to do so), Article 14(h) MLIJ includes an optional provision

20 Cf. Article 2(d)(ii) MLIJ and Preamble, para. 2(d).
21 Guide to Enactment (n 1), para. 58.
22 Guide to Enactment (n1), para. 37.
23 Guide to Enactment (n 1), para. 38.
24 Guide to Enactment (n 1), para. 38.

that such States may wish to enact, permitting the refusal of recognition of an insolvency-related judgment when the judgment originates from a State whose insolvency proceeding is not or would not be susceptible of recognition under the MLCBI. Under the terms of the MLCBI, a foreign insolvency proceeding may not be eligible for recognition because it was opened in a State where neither the debtor's centre of main interests (COMI) nor an establishment of the debtor is located.[25] However, Article 14(h) MLIJ also provides an exception to that general principle of non-recognition, provided that (i) the judgment relates only to assets that were located in the originating State; and (ii) certain conditions are met.[26]

Both the MLCBI and the MLIJ include a requirement that the interests of creditors and other interested persons, including the debtor, are adequately protected. However, they relate to different situations. In order to ensure that there is a balance between the relief that may be granted to a foreign representative and the interests of the persons that may be affected by such relief, Article 22 MLCBI requires the recognizing court to ensure that the interests of such other parties are considered when granting, modifying or terminating provisional or discretionary relief under the MLCBI. The relevance of the protection of such interests in the MLIJ is more limited. Article 14 (f) MLIJ allows recognition and enforcement of an insolvency-related judgment to be denied where those interests were not adequately protected in the proceeding giving rise to the judgment and where the judgment materially affects the rights of creditors generally, such as the confirmation of a plan of reorganization.[27] **P2.13**

Another important element that underlines the close relationship between the MLIJ and the MLCBI concerns Article X MLIJ. This provision addresses the interpretation of Article 21 MLCBI. Adoption of Article X MLIJ[28] would clarify that the discretionary relief available under Article 21 MLCBI to support a recognized foreign proceeding (covering both main and non-main **P2.14**

25 In such cases the insolvency proceeding would not qualify as a foreign main proceeding, as defined in Article 2(b) MLCBI, or a foreign non-main proceeding, as defined in Article 2(c) MLCBI. On the possibility of obtaining recognition under Chapter 15 in the United States of foreign insolvency proceedings that meet neither of these thresholds, see Ray Warner and Michael Veder, Enterprise Group Restructuring: Dutch Options and United States Enforcement, European Insolvency and Restructuring Journal (EIRJ) 2021/7.

26 See further Rodriguez at para. 2.14.67 et seq.

27 See further Rodriguez at para. 2.14.44 et seq.

28 As was, for example, suggested by the Insolvency Service in the United Kingdom, see www.gov.uk/government/consultations/implementation-of-two-uncitral-model-laws-on-insolvency/implementation-of-two-uncitral-model-laws-on-insolvency-consultation (last accessed: 7 February 2024).

proceedings) should be interpreted as including the recognition and enforcement of a judgment, notwithstanding any interpretation to the contrary.[29]

C. RELATIONSHIP BETWEEN THE MLIJ AND EXISTING LEGISLATION IN AN ENACTING STATE

P2.15 Obviously, the MLIJ will, like any other Model Law, have to be incorporated in the general legislative framework of countries that wish to implement it. It needs to be tailored to fit in with the existing legal framework, in particular also concerning the recognition and enforcement of foreign judgments in general. Paragraph 2 of the Preamble to the MLIJ in that respect clarifies that the MLIJ is not intended to restrict the application of provisions of the laws of an enacting State that would (already) permit the recognition and enforcement of insolvency-related judgments and does not replace (but rather complements[30]) any legislation enacting the MLCBI.

D. GENERAL OVERVIEW OF THE MLIJ

P2.16 The MLIJ addresses the procedure for and effects of recognition and enforcement of insolvency-related judgments, as defined in Article 2(d) MLIJ, that are issued by a court or administrative authority in another State than the one where recognition and enforcement is sought.

P2.17 For the purposes of the MLIJ, an insolvency-related judgment is a judgment that arises as a consequence of or that is materially associated with an insolvency proceeding, whether or not that insolvency proceeding has closed, and that was issued on or after the commencement of that insolvency proceeding.[31] The judgment commencing an insolvency proceeding is explicitly excluded from the scope of the MLIJ. The recognition of decisions opening insolvency proceedings is addressed in the MLCBI, to which the MLIJ forms a complement.

P2.18 The MLIJ sets forth the procedures and conditions for obtaining recognition and enforcement of insolvency-related judgments. One of the conditions for obtaining recognition or enforcement under the MLIJ is that the judgment concerned has effect in the 'originating State', that is, the State where

---

29 As discussed above in para. P2.02 et seq. See further Rodriguez in his commentary on Article X MLIJ.

30 See also Preamble, para. 1(f) MLIJ.

31 See further Veder at para. 2.02.17 et seq.

it was issued, respectively that it is enforceable there.[32] In cases where an insolvency-related judgment is the subject of (judicial) review in the originating State or if the time limit for seeking ordinary review has not yet expired, recognition or enforcement of such judgment may be postponed, refused or made conditional on the provision of such security that the court in the enacting State determines.[33]

Decisions on the recognition and enforcement of foreign insolvency-related judgments are taken by the courts or authorities identified by an enacting State pursuant to Article 4 MLIJ or any other court before which the issue of recognition of such judgment is raised as a defence or an incidental question.[34] Pursuant to Article 11(1) MLIJ, an insolvency representative or other person entitled under the law of the originating State to seek recognition and enforcement of an insolvency-related judgment may seek recognition and enforcement of such judgment in the enacting State. Article 11 MLIJ sets forth the documents that must be submitted to the court (or administrative authority) together with the request for recognition and enforcement. Any party against whom recognition and enforcement of an insolvency-related judgment is sought has the right to be heard. **P2.19**

The MLIJ provides for provisional relief that is available between the time of submitting a request for recognition or enforcement of a foreign insolvency-related judgment and the moment at which a decision is taken on the request. In cases where relief is urgently needed to preserve the possibility of recognizing and enforcing an insolvency-related judgment, the court may, at the request of, for example, an insolvency representative, grant relief of a provisional nature, such as staying the disposition of any assets of any party or parties against whom the insolvency-related judgment has been issued.[35] **P2.20**

Recognition or enforcement of a foreign insolvency-related judgment that meets the conditions of the MLIJ may be refused if (i) recognition or enforcement would be manifestly contrary to the public policy, including the fundamental principles of procedural fairness, of the enacting State, or (ii) where one of the grounds referred to in Article 14 MLIJ occurs. The grounds for refusal referred to in Article 14 MLIJ relate to, for example, the manner in which the judgment was obtained (such as lack of proper notification of the party against **P2.21**

32 Article 9 MLIJ.
33 Article 10 MLIJ.
34 Article 4 MLIJ.
35 Article 12 MLIJ.

whom the proceeding giving rise to the judgment was instituted, or the existence of fraud); inconsistency with earlier decisions (whether handed down in the enacting State or in another country); interference with the administration of the debtor's insolvency proceedings; lack of adequate protection of creditors in proceedings leading to a judgment that materially affects the rights of creditors generally (for example, the confirmation of a restructuring plan); the grounds on which the court in the originating State accepted jurisdiction; and the decision having been issued in a State whose insolvency proceeding is not or would not be recognized under the MLCBI.

P2.22 Pursuant to Article 15 MLIJ, an insolvency-related judgment that is recognized or enforceable under the terms of the MLIJ shall be given the same effect it has in the originating State or that it would have had if it had been issued by a court of the enacting State. Enacting States have an option there.

E. A DIFFERENT APPROACH: RECOGNITION AND ENFORCEMENT OF INSOLVENCY-RELATED JUDGMENTS UNDER THE EIR

P2.23 The general approach of the MLIJ to recognition and enforcement of insolvency-related judgments is in line with the approach to recognition and relief granted to foreign insolvency proceedings under the MLCBI. This approach is rather different from the approach to the recognition and enforcement of insolvency proceedings and insolvency-related judgments in the EU Insolvency Regulation.[36]

P2.24 The EU Insolvency Regulation provides for the immediate and automatic recognition of judgments concerning the opening, conduct and closure of insolvency proceedings that fall within its scope, and of judgments handed down in direct connection with such insolvency proceedings.[37] The immediate and automatic recognition of judgments is based on the principle of mutual trust. The principle of mutual trust that underlies the EU Insolvency Regulation has enabled not only the establishment of a compulsory system of jurisdiction that all the courts within the purview of the EU Insolvency Regulation are required to respect, but also the introduction of a simplified mechanism for

36 Regulation (EU) 2015/848 of the European Parliament and of the Council of 20 May 2015 on insolvency proceedings (recast) ('EU Insolvency Regulation' or 'EIR').

37 See, with further references, Michael Veder, in: Reinhard Bork and Kristin van Zwieten (eds), *Commentary on the European Insolvency Regulation* (2nd edn), 2022, para. 19.01 et seq, and para. 20.01 et seq.; Paul Oberhammer and Florian Scholz-Berger, in Bork/van Zwieten (ibid), para. 32.01 et seq.

the recognition and enforcement of judgments handed down in the context of insolvency proceedings.

Immediate and automatic recognition means that as soon as the judgment opening insolvency proceedings becomes effective, regardless of whether the judgment is final or not, it is recognized in other Member States without any further formalities being required (such as an *exequatur* or publication) and that, in respect of main proceedings opened pursuant to Article 3(1) EIR, the effects attributed to the proceedings by the law of the Member State in which the proceedings are opened immediately and automatically extend to all other Member States (as set out in Article 20 EIR). This ensures the effectiveness of the insolvency proceedings, saves costs and prevents the delays associated with a procedure of formal recognition. **P2.25**

The immediate and automatic recognition of judgments opening insolvency proceedings is addressed in Articles 19 et seq. EIR. Article 32(1) EIR stipulates that this principle of immediate and automatic recognition also applies to certain other judgments handed down in the context of insolvency proceedings,[38] namely: (i) judgments concerning the course and closure of insolvency proceedings, and compositions approved by that court; (ii) judgments that derive directly from the insolvency proceedings and that are closely linked to them;[39] and (iii) judgments relating to preservation matters taken after the request for the opening of insolvency proceedings or in connection with it. With respect to the enforcement of such judgments, Article 32(1) EIR refers to the simplified enforcement regime under the recast Brussels I Regulation.[40] Pursuant to Article 32(2) EIR, other judgments than those referred to in (i)–(iii) above shall be recognized and enforced in accordance with the recast Brussels I Regulation, provided that that regulation is applicable. **P2.26**

---

38 Jurisdiction in respect of such actions is to be determined on the basis of Article 6 EIR. The courts of the Member State where an insolvency proceeding has been opened, in principle – pursuant to Article 6(2) EIR, certain actions may also be brought before the courts of the Member State where defendants are domiciled – have exclusive jurisdiction to hear any action which derives directy from the insolvency proceeding and is closely linked with it (cf. Case C-296/17 *Wiemer & Trachte GmbH, in liquidation v Zhan Oved Tadzher*, ECLI:EU:C:2018:902, para. 36).

39 The scope of what constitutes an 'insolvency-related judgment' is much more narrowly defined under the EIR than the MLIJ; see para. 2.2.17 et seq.

40 Regulation (EU) No 1215/2012 of the European Parliament and of the Council of 12 December 2012 on jurisdiction and the recognition and enforcement of judgments in civil and commercial matters (recast).

F. ADOPTION OF THE MLIJ

P2.27 At the time of writing in January 2024, the MLIJ had not yet been adopted anywhere.[41] The current status of the adoption of the MLIJ can be found at: https://uncitral.un.org/en/texts/insolvency/modellaw/mlij.

41 Wide adoption of the MLIJ is advocated in Irit Mevorach 2021 (n 4), para. 6.1.

Article 1

SCOPE OF APPLICATION

Michael Veder

1. This Law applies to the recognition and enforcement of an insolvency-related judgment issued in a State that is different to the State in which recognition and enforcement is sought.
2. This Law does not apply to [...].

A. REGULATORY CONTENT (PARA. 1)

Article 1 MLIJ addresses its scope of application. The MLIJ applies to the recognition and enforcement of an insolvency-related judgment that was issued in a proceeding taking place in a State other than the enacting State in which recognition and enforcement is sought. In other words, it applies to the recognition and enforcement of insolvency-related judgments in a cross-border context.[1] This is also highlighted by paragraph 2 (c) of the Preamble, which states that the MLIJ is not intended to apply to the recognition and enforcement in the enacting State of an insolvency-related judgment issued in the enacting State.[2] **2.1.01**

It follows from the wording of Article 1 MLIJ that several situations are included in the scope of the MLIJ. Firstly, it covers the situation where both **2.1.02**

1 What constitutes an insolvency-related judgment for purposes of the MLIJ is defined in Article 2(d) MLIJ. For more details, see Veder at 2.2.17 et seq.

2 This observation in the preamble will be self-evident in most jurisdictions. There will be no question of 'recognition' of judgments issued by a court in the same state and enforcement of such judgments will follow the 'normal' rules in place in that jurisdiction.

the proceeding giving rise to the judgment and the insolvency proceeding to which it relates are taking place in another State (not necessarily the same State, though). Secondly, as Article 1 MLIJ contains no requirement that the insolvency proceeding to which the judgment relates is taking place in another State, the MLIJ also addresses situations in which the judgment was issued in another State but the insolvency proceeding to which the judgment relates is taking place in the enacting State in which recognition and enforcement is sought. For the applicability of the MLIJ it therefore suffices that the judgment in respect of which recognition or enforcement is sought was issued in another State than the enacting State. Where the insolvency proceeding to which the judgment relates is taking place is irrelevant for the scope of the MLIJ.

B. EXCEPTIONS (PARA. 2)

2.1.03 Article 1(2) MLIJ indicates that an enacting State might decide to exclude certain types of judgments from the scope of application of the legislation implementing the MLIJ, such as judgments raising public policy considerations or where other specifically designated legal regimes are applicable. The Guide to Enactment refers to the following (non-exhaustive) list of examples: judgments concerning foreign revenue claims; extradition for insolvency-related matters; or family law matters.[3] As the MLIJ is intended to complement legislation based on the MLCBI, Article 1(2) MLIJ may also be used by an enacting State that has implemented the MLCBI, to exclude judgments relating to entities that are excluded from the scope of the legislation implementing the MLCBI.[4]

3 *UNCITRAL Model Law on Recognition and Enforcement of Insolvency-Related Judgments with Guide to Enactment*, United Nations Publications (Vienna), 2019, para. 47.

4 *Guide to Enactment* (n 3), para. 47. Article 1(2) MLCBI allows enacting States to designate certain types of entities to which the legislation implementing the MLCBI will not apply, such as banks or insurance companies; see Commentary to Article 1(2) MLCBI by Mevorach, at 1.1.13 et seq.

Article 2

DEFINITIONS

Michael Veder

For the purposes of this Law:

(a) 'Insolvency proceeding' means a collective judicial or administrative proceeding, including an interim proceeding, pursuant to a law relating to insolvency in which proceeding the assets and affairs of a debtor are or were subject to control or supervision by a court or other competent authority for the purpose of reorganization or liquidation;

(b) 'Insolvency representative' means a person or body, including one appointed on an interim basis, authorized in an insolvency proceeding to administer the reorganization or the liquidation of the debtor's assets or affairs or to act as a representative of the insolvency proceeding;

(c) 'Judgment' means any decision, whatever it may be called, issued by a court or administrative authority, provided an administrative decision has the same effect as a court decision. For the purposes of this definition, a decision includes a decree or order, and a determination of costs and expenses. An interim measure of protection is not to be considered a judgment for the purposes of this Law;

(d) 'Insolvency-related judgment':

(i) Means a judgment that:

a. Arises as a consequence of or is materially associated with an insolvency proceeding, whether or not that insolvency proceeding has closed; and

b. Was issued on or after the commencement of that insolvency proceeding; and

(ii) Does not include a judgment commencing an insolvency proceeding.

A. INTRODUCTION TO ARTICLE 2

2.2.01 Article 2 MLIJ contains a number of definitions relevant to the MLIJ. Its definitions of the terms 'insolvency proceeding' and 'insolvency representative' are derived from Article 2 MLCBI.

B. INSOLVENCY PROCEEDINGS

2.2.02 Article 2(a) MLIJ defines the term 'insolvency proceeding' as 'a collective judicial or administrative proceeding, including an interim proceeding, pursuant to a law relating to insolvency in which proceeding the assets and affairs of a debtor are or were subject to control or supervision by a court or other competent authority for the purpose of reorganization or liquidation'.

2.2.03 This definition, which, inter alia, is relevant for the definition of what constitutes an 'insolvency-related' judgment in Article 2(d) MLIJ, is derived from the definition of 'foreign proceeding' in Article 2(a) MLCBI. Similar to the MLCBI, the term 'insolvency proceeding' in the MLIJ refers to various types of collective proceedings commenced with respect to a debtor that is in severe financial distress or insolvent, with the goal of liquidating or reorganizing that debtor as a commercial entity. The MLIJ is intended to be applicable to foreign judgments related to proceedings addressing the insolvency of both natural and legal persons.[1]

2.2.04 While the term 'insolvency proceeding' is defined in the MLIJ, the term 'insolvency' is not. The use of the term 'insolvency' in the MLIJ is intended to be consistent with its use in other UNCITRAL insolvency texts, specifically the MLCBI and the UNCITRAL Legislative Guide on Insolvency Law.[2]

1 Cf. *UNCITRAL Model Law on Recognition and Enforcement of Insolvency-Related Judgments with Guide to Enactment*, United Nations Publications (Vienna), 2019, para. 23.

2 Cf. *UNCITRAL Model Law on Cross-Border Insolvency with Guide to Enactment and Interpretation*, United Nations Publications (New York), 2014, paras 48–49; *UNCITRAL Legislative Guide on Insolvency Law*, United Nations Publications (New York), 2005, Introduction (B. Glossary), para. 12(s): '"Insolvency": when a debtor is generally unable to pay its debts as they mature or when its liabilities exceed the value of its assets.'

As is made clear in Article 2(a) MLIJ, a particular proceeding can only be considered an insolvency proceeding for purposes of the MLIJ if it has the following attributes. It must be a judicial or administrative proceeding of a collective nature. The proceeding must have its basis in a law relating to insolvency. There must be an opportunity for involvement of creditors collectively. The assets and affairs must be or have been subject to the control or supervision by a court or another competent authority. And, finally, the purpose of the proceeding must be reorganization or liquidation of the debtor. For a proceeding to be considered an 'insolvency proceeding' it must possess all of these elements.[3] **2.2.05**

As the definition of 'insolvency proceeding' in the MLIJ closely follows the definition of 'foreign proceeding' in the MLCBI, reference is made to the discussion by Mevorach of the definition of 'foreign proceeding' (and its various elements) in Article 2 MLCBI.[4] **2.2.06**

The reference in the definition to assets and affairs of a debtor that '*are or were* subject to control' (emphasis added) – which does not occur in Article 2(a) MLCBI – is intended to include within the scope of the MLIJ situations where the insolvency proceeding has closed at the time recognition of the insolvency-related judgment is sought or where all assets were transferred at the start of a proceeding and, while the assets are no longer subject to control by the court or another competent authority, the insolvency proceeding remains open.[5] **2.2.07**

C. INSOLVENCY REPRESENTATIVE

Article 2(b) MLIJ defines the term 'insolvency representative' as: 'a person or body, including one appointed on an interim basis, authorized in an insolvency proceeding to administer the reorganization or the liquidation of the debtor's assets or affairs or to act as a representative of the insolvency proceeding.' **2.2.08**

This definition, which is, inter alia, relevant for the designation of the parties authorized to submit a request for the recognition or enforcement of an insolvency-related judgment pursuant to Article 11(1) MLIJ, is based on the definition of 'foreign representative' in Article 2(d) MLCBI and the **2.2.09**

3 Cf. *Guide to Enactment* (n 1), para. 48.

4 See the commentary of Mevorach on Article 2 MLCBI, at para. 1.2.21 et seq.

5 Cf. *Guide to Enactment* (n 1), para. 48.

term 'insolvency representative' in the UNCITRAL Legislative Guide on Insolvency Law.[6]

2.2.10 As the definition of 'insolvency representative' in the MLIJ closely follows the definition of 'foreign representative' in the MLCBI, reference is made to the discussion by Mevorach of the definition of 'insolvency representative' in Article 2 MLCBI.[7]

D. JUDGMENT

2.2.11 Article 2(c) MLIJ defines the term 'judgment' as: 'any decision, whatever it may be called, issued by a court or administrative authority, provided an administrative decision has the same effect as a court decision. For the purposes of this definition, a decision includes a decree or order, and a determination of costs and expenses. An interim measure of protection is not to be considered a judgment for the purposes of this Law.'

2.2.12 The MLIJ thus adopts a broad definition of what constitutes a judgment for purposes of the MLIJ. While the focus is generally upon judgments issued by a court, it equally includes decisions issued by an administrative authority, provided a decision of the latter has the same effect as a court decision.[8] By including decisions of administrative authorities within the scope of the MLIJ, UNCITRAL acknowledges that in some jurisdictions insolvency proceedings may be administered by specialized authorities and decisions issued by those authorities in the course of insolvency proceedings merit recognition on the same basis as judicial decisions.[9] The MLIJ does not require an insolvency-related judgment to have been issued by a specialized court with insolvency jurisdiction.[10] This is appropriate as not all States have specialized courts or judges for insolvency related matters, and in many instances insolvency-related proceedings may (have to) be brought before courts with general jurisdiction in civil or commercial matters.

---

6 Cf. *Legislative Guide* (n 2), Introduction (B. Glossary), para. 12(v).

7 See the commentary of Mevorach on Article 2 MLCBI, at para. 1.2.31 et seq.

8 Cf. Guide to Enactment (n 1), para. 52.

9 Cf. Guide to Enactment (n 1), para. 52, where it is also explained that the use of the term 'court' in the MLIJ is intentionally broader than the use of that term in the MLCBI or the UNCITRAL Legislative Guide on Insolvency. On the definition of the term 'court' in the MLCBI, see the commentary of Mevorach on Article 2 MLCBI at para. 1.2.33.

10 Cf. Guide to Enactment (n 1), para. 52.

The approach thus taken in the MLIJ is similar to the approach taken in the EU Insolvency Regulation. Although the EU Insolvency Regulation does not define what constitutes a judgment for purposes of recognition and enforcement pursuant to Article 32 EIR, it draws upon the principles developed under the Brussels I^{bis} Regulation,[11] which also provides for a wide notion of 'judgment'.[12] Pursuant to Article 2(6) EIR, the term 'court' may in certain circumstances also be understood to include not only the judicial bodies of a Member State but also any other competent body of a Member State empowered to open insolvency proceedings, to confirm such opening or to take decisions in the course of such proceedings.[13] **2.2.13**

The reference to costs and expenses in Article 2(c) MLIJ is intended to restrict the enforcement of costs orders to those given in relation to judgments that can be recognized and enforced under the MLIJ.[14] **2.2.14**

Pursuant to the final sentence of Article 2(c) MLIJ, an 'interim measure of protection' is not to be considered a judgment that is eligible for recognition and enforcement under the MLIJ. However, the MLIJ does not define what is meant by the term 'interim measure of protection' in Article 2(c) MLIJ. The Guide to Enactment provides some guidance as to what type of measures the term is intended to refer to: **2.2.15**

> Interim measures may serve two principal purposes: to maintain the status quo pending determination of the issues at trial and to provide a preliminary means of securing assets out of which an ultimate judgment may be satisfied. In addition, they may share certain characteristics; for example, they are temporary in nature, they may be sought on an urgent basis, or they may be issued on an ex parte basis. However, if an order for such measures is confirmed after the respondent has been served with the order and had the opportunity to appear and seek the discharge of the order, it may cease to be regarded as a provisional or interim measure.[15]

Under the EU Insolvency Regulation, on the other hand, provisional, including protective, measures ordered by a court pending an insolvency-related **2.2.16**

11 Cf. Paul Oberhammer and Florian Scholz-Berger, in: Reinhard Bork and Kristin van Zwieten (eds.), Commentary on the European Insolvency Regulation (2nd edn.), 2022, para. 32.05.

12 A 'judgment' is defined in Article 2(a)(1) recast Brussels I^{bis} Regulation as 'any judgment given by a court or tribunal of a Member State, whatever the judgment may be called, including a decree, order, decision or writ of execution, as well as a decision on the determination of costs or expenses by an officer of the court'.

13 On the definition of 'court' in the EIR, see Kristin van Zwieten, in: Bork/van Zwieten (n 11), paras 2.19–2.23.

14 Cf. Guide to Enactment (n 1), para. 53.

15 Guide to Enactment (n 1), para. 55.

case may be eligible for recognition and enforcement in accordance with the Brussels I^{bis} Regulation.[16]

E. INSOLVENCY-RELATED JUDGMENT

2.2.17 Article 2(d) MLIJ contains the – crucial – definition of what constitutes an 'insolvency-related judgment' for purposes of the MLIJ. It defines an 'insolvency-related judgment' as:

> … a judgment that:
> a. Arises as a consequence of or is materially associated with an insolvency proceeding, whether or not that insolvency proceeding has closed; and
> b. Was issued on or after the commencement of that insolvency proceeding.

2.2.18 Article 2(d) MLIJ thus defines the scope of the MLIJ. It addresses the important question under which conditions a foreign judgment falls within the scope of the specific regime of recognition and enforcement of (legislation based on) the MLIJ and thus outside the scope of the regime applicable to the recognition of foreign judgments in general in an enacting State, whether stemming from rules of domestic law of the enacting State or international treaties or other binding international instruments. When implementing the MLIJ into domestic law, this interplay of the MLIJ with existing legislation and applicable treaties must be carefully taken into consideration.[17]

2.2.19 The preparatory materials of UNCITRAL's Working Group V show that this provision has given rise to considerable debate, in particular where it concerns the types of claims and actions that ought to be considered 'insolvency-related' for the purpose of applying the rules on recognition and enforcement in the MLIJ.

2.2.20 As the Guide to Enactment clarifies, a judgment needs to meet certain characteristics in order to fall within the scope of the MLIJ.[18] The most important of the criteria mentioned in Article 2(d)(i) MLIJ is that the judgment must arise

16 Cf. Articles 32(2) EIR and 2(a) Brussels I^{bis} Regulation. These types of protective measures are not covered by the third subparagraph of Article 32(1) EIR, as the preservation measures referred to there concern preservation measures ordered after the request for the opening of insolvency proceedings has been submitted, but before a decision to open insolvency proceedings has been taken. They are therefore measures that seek to protect the estate from dissipation of assets ahead of the opening of insolvency proceedings, and not to protect the means of recourse of, for example, the insolvency practitioner in relation to a claim against a third party. Cf. Oberhammer and Scholz-Berger (n 11), para. 32.46.

17 This was acknowledged already in the early stages of the development of the MLIJ, cf. A/CN.9/829, para. 54.

18 Guide to Enactment (n 1), para. 32 et seq.

as a consequence of or be materially associated with an insolvency proceeding. This criterion is intended to express the nexus that must exist between the action giving rise to the judgment and the insolvency proceeding to which it is linked. When looking at the preparatory materials of Working Group V, it becomes clear that during the course of the negotiations on the MLIJ, the formulation of this nexus has undergone considerable change and has in fact become more flexible. In any event, it appears to encompass a wider range of judgments than would be regarded as insolvency-related judgments under the EU Insolvency Regulation.

The initial draft text that formed the basis of the debate in Working Group V **2.2.21** contained the following definition of 'insolvency-related judgment': 'a judgement that is closely related to a foreign proceeding and was issued after the commencement of that proceeding. A judgement is presumed to be "closely related to a foreign proceeding" if it has an effect upon the insolvency estate of the debtor and either: (i) is based on a law relating to insolvency; or (ii) due to the nature and legal basis of its underlying claims, would not have been issued without the commencement of the foreign proceeding.'[19]

Even though phrased as a presumption, this draft article showed a number of **2.2.22** key characteristics that ought to be met in order for a judgment to be regarded as insolvency related. While the criterion that an insolvency-related judgment requires 'an effect upon the insolvency estate of the debtor' may be too broadly phrased, as it in fact seems to encompass all judgments that may directly or indirectly affect the insolvency estate, this is narrowed down by two criteria that show a clear nexus to the insolvency proceeding. Such a judgment must either (i) be based on a law relating to insolvency, or (ii) due to the nature and legal basis of its underlying claims, would not have been issued without the commencement of the foreign proceeding. The approach thus chosen in the initial draft of the MLIJ bears close resemblance to the approach under the EU Insolvency Regulation.

Under the EU Insolvency Regulation, 'insolvency-related judgments' are **2.2.23** notably judgments which concern the course and closure of insolvency proceedings, and compositions approved by the court,[20] and 'judgments deriving directly from the insolvency proceedings and which are closely linked with them'.[21] With respect to the second category of 'insolvency-related judgments',

19 A/CN.9/WG.V/WP.130, 3.
20 Article 32(1), first paragraph, EIR.
21 Article 32(1), second paragraph, EIR.

the CJEU has held that the decisive criterion to identify whether a particular action derives directly from the insolvency proceedings and is closely linked with them is not the procedural context of which that action is part, but rather the legal basis of the action. According to that approach, it must be determined whether the right or obligation which forms the basis of the action has its source in the ordinary rules of civil and commercial law or in derogating rules specific to insolvency proceedings.[22]

2.2.24 The wording that has ultimately made it into Article 2(d)(i) MLIJ is far more open. That a judgment must arise *as a consequence of* an insolvency proceeding seems to establish the necessary close nexus to justify that a judgment is indeed considered insolvency-related. The same cannot necessarily be said for the alternative ('or') in Article 2(d)(i) MLIJ that, also, if a judgment is 'materially associated with' an insolvency proceeding, it is considered insolvency-related for purposes of the MLIJ. The question is, of course, what 'materially associated with' actually means. The non-exhaustive list of examples of judgments that might be considered insolvency-related that is included in the Guide to Enactment[23] suggests that this criterion should not be interpreted restrictively. These examples will be briefly discussed below.

A judgment dealing with constitution and disposal of assets of the insolvency estate, such as whether an asset is part of, should be turned over to, or was properly (or improperly) disposed of by the insolvency estate.

2.2.25 This first example of 'insolvency-related judgments' is quite broadly phrased. In my view, the type of judgments referred to here should not necessarily be characterized as insolvency-related, at least not in all cases. Even when a question concerning the constitution and disposal of assets of the estate comes up in the context of insolvency proceedings, it very much depends on the exact question that is put before the court whether the action giving rise to a judgment may be characterized as being 'materially associated with the insolvency'. A judgment addressing the constitution of the estate may, for example, simply be based on general property law – was an asset owned by the insolvent debtor and therefore part of the insolvent estate? – and should in that case not be considered 'insolvency-related', but rather as pertaining to general

22 Cf. Case C–535/17 BK/BNP Paribas Fortis N.V., ECLI:EU:C:2019:96, para. 28. On the interpretation of 'judgments deriving directly from the insolvency proceedings and which are closely linked with them', see inter alia: Oberhammer and Scholz-Berger (n 11), paras. 32.14 et seq, and Georg Ringe, in: Bork and van Zwieten (n 11), paras. 6.10 et seq.

23 Cf. Guide to Enactment (n 1), para. 60. Earlier drafts of the MLIJ included a list of examples of insolvency-related judgments in the body of the provision. At a later stage it was decided that these examples should be included in the Guide to Enactment.

private law (law of property).[24] Where the allocation of entitlements to assets to either the debtor or a third party is affected by the opening of insolvency proceedings, on the other hand, judgments addressing such allocation may indeed be regarded as insolvency-related judgments. If the allocation of (rights over) assets to either the insolvent debtor's estate or a third party (for example, a secured creditor) only arises in and as a result of the debtor's insolvency, the case is indeed 'materially associated' with the debtor's insolvency and shows a clear nexus with the insolvency proceeding, as insolvency law interferes with the allocation of assets under general property law.[25]

A judgment determining whether a transaction involving the debtor or assets of its insolvency estate should be avoided because it upset the principle of equitable treatment of creditors (preferential transactions) or improperly reduced the value of the estate (transactions at an undervalue).

The second example of 'insolvency-related judgments' in the Guide to Enactment concerns what are generally referred to as avoidance actions.[26] It is quite commonly accepted that judgments in insolvency-related avoidance actions are to be regarded as insolvency-related judgments.[27] This is the type of judgment that gave rise to the decision in *Rubin/Eurofinance* that sparked the development of the MLIJ in the first place. Avoidance actions are also specifically referred to in Article 6(1) EIR as an action that 'derives directly from the insolvency proceedings and is closely linked with them'.[28] **2.2.26**

The Court of Justice of the European Union has held that, for purposes of the applicability of the EIR, it may make a difference whether an avoidance action is pursued by the insolvency practitioner or rather by a creditor or a third party to whom the avoidance claim has been assigned. In the matter of *F-Tex* the court decided that an action brought against a third party by **2.2.27**

---

24 Cf. CJEU Case C-292/08 German Graphics, ECLI:EU:C:2009:544, where the Court of Justice of the European Union held that an action brought by a seller based on a reservation of title against a purchaser who is insolvent, where the asset covered by the reservation of title is situated in the Member State of the opening of those proceedings at the time of opening of those proceedings against that purchaser, cannot be characterized as an action deriving directly from the insolvency proceedings and that is closely linked with them. In that case the court held that the action concerning the reservation of title clause in question constituted an independent claim, as it was not based on the law of the insolvency proceedings and required neither the opening of such proceedings nor the involvement of a liquidator.

25 This may, for example, be the case where, on the basis of rules that are based on the fixation principle, certain dispositions of assets cannot be invoked as against the insolvent estate. On the fixation principle see Reinhard Bork and Michael Veder, Harmonisation of Transactions Avoidance Laws, Intersentia 2022, paras 2.64 et seq.

26 On transactions avoidance in insolvency, see, for example: Bork/Veder (n 25).

27 See also Case C-339/07 Seagon/Deko Marty, ECLI:EU:C:2009:83.

28 Under the EIR, this is not the case where the action against the third party concerned is based on general tort law: cf. Case C-535/17 HK/BNP Paribas Fortis N.V., ECLI:EU:C:2019:96.

an applicant acting on the basis of an assignment of claims which has been granted by an insolvency practitioner appointed in insolvency proceedings, and the subject-matter of which is the right to have a transaction set aside that the insolvency practitioner derives from the national law applicable to those proceedings, is not an insolvency-related matter but should rather be regarded as a general civil and commercial matter.[29]

2.2.28 The Guide to Enactment suggests that a similar reasoning should not be applied to the MLIJ. The MLIJ takes account of the fact that the cause of action giving rise to an insolvency-related judgment may have been pursued by various parties, including a creditor (with approval of the court, where so required) or, if the cause of action was assigned by the insolvency practitioner, by the assignee.[30] It follows from the Guide to Enactment that also in those cases, the judgment should be considered an insolvency-related judgment that would be eligible for recognition and enforcement under the MLIJ.[31]

A judgment determining that a representative or director of the debtor is liable for action taken when the debtor was insolvent or in the period approaching insolvency, and the cause of action relating to that liability was one that could be pursued by or on behalf of the debtor's insolvency estate under the law relating to insolvency, in line with part four of the Legislative Guide.

2.2.29 This example concerns judgments resulting from actions that deal with insolvency-related liability of directors and officers of a company. The approach under the MLIJ appears to be similar to the approach under the EIR. Where an action concerns the liability of the director of an insolvent company and the provisions applicable to such action derogate from the common rules of civil and commercial law, because of the insolvency of that company, the action (and the resulting judgment) is materially associated with the insolvency proceeding and can thus be said to be 'insolvency-related'.[32] The same does not hold true for actions (and resulting judgments) aimed at holding directors and officers liable, where the liability is based in general company law and could also have arisen outside the context of the company's insolvency. In such a case

29 Case C-213/10 F-Tex/Lietuvos-Anglijos UAB 'Jadecloud-Vilma', ECLI:EU:C:2012:215. An important reason for the CJEU to come to this result was that the assignee, when he decides to exercise his right of claim, acts in his own interest and for his personal benefit (cf. para. 44 of the judgment).

30 In some jurisdictions creditors may be allowed to pursue avoidance actions if the insolvency practitioner decides not to pursue such action. Some jurisdictions also allow the insolvency practitioner to assign an avoidance action (or the claim based thereon) to a third party: cf. Bork and Veder (n 25), paras 4.229–4.234.

31 Cf. Guide to Enactment (n 1), para. 61. See also Reinhard Bork, Advanced Introduction to Cross-Border Insolvency Law, Edward Elgar Publishing 2023, 46 et seq.

32 Cf. Case C-295/13 H/HK, ECLI:EU:C:2014:2410; Case C-594/14 Kornhaas/Dithmar, ECLI:EU:C:2015:806.

the judgment cannot be said to arise as a consequence of or be materially associated with the insolvency proceeding.

A judgment determining whether the debtor owes or is owed a sum or any other performance not covered by subparagraph (a) or (b).

The boundaries of what constitutes an 'insolvency-related judgment' are rather stretched in the fourth example given in the Guide to Enactment. According to the Guide to Enactment, a judgment that determines whether the debtor owes a sum of money or any other performance, or, conversely, is owed a sum of money or any other performance, is considered an 'insolvency-related' judgment for purposes of the MLIJ. It is submitted that, generally, judgments in such matters should not be considered insolvency-related judgments as the debtor's or creditor's entitlement does not depend on specific rules of insolvency law but must rather be established in accordance with rules of general private law. Where it concerns claims that could have been brought by or against the debtor itself, outside the context of insolvency proceedings, in my view the action is not 'materially associated' with the insolvency proceeding for the sole reason that the issue arises in the context of an insolvency proceeding and the claim is pursued by or against the insolvency practitioner (or the insolvent debtor as a debtor-in-possession).[33] The same holds true if the action is pursued by an insolvency practitioner or a debtor-in-possession and is based on a contract concluded between a third party and the insolvency practitioner or the debtor-in-possession. The mere fact that a contract is concluded during the course of an insolvency proceeding with the insolvency practitioner or debtor-in-possession does not entail that the claims resulting from such a contract are to be considered claims based in insolvency law, rather than contract law. **2.2.30**

The types of judgments referred to in paragraph 60, under (d), of the Guide to Enactment to the MLIJ would generally not be regarded as 'insolvency-related' judgments under the EIR.[34] However, that would not mean that such judgments would not be eligible for recognition and enforcement within the EU. If a particular action is considered to be outside the scope of the EIR because it does not derive directly from the insolvency proceedings and is not closely **2.2.31**

33 The argument that was apparently advanced during the negotiations in Working Group V, that such actions ought to fall within the ambit of the MLIJ because they are somehow of benefit to the estate (cf A/CN.9/WG.V./WP.140, para. 4), is not persuasive and constitutes false reasoning.

34 Cf the examples of cases discussed by Oberhammer and Scholz-Berger, in: Bork and van Zwieten (n 11), paras 32.14 et seq, and Georg Ringe, in: Bork and van Zwieten (n 11), paras 6.10 et seq.

linked with them, recognition and enforcement will generally be governed by the Brussels I^{bis} Regulation.[35]

2.2.32 In some cases a court may, during the course of an insolvency proceeding, be requested to determine whether a creditor has a claim against the debtor and whether that claim is admissible in the insolvency proceeding. The Guide to Enactment suggests that in both cases a judgment of a foreign court would be eligible for recognition and enforcement under the MLIJ. In my view, that suggestion ought to be approached with some scepticism. If the question addressed in the foreign court's judgment is whether the debtor owes a sum of money or other performance, that matter will generally not be one that has its basis in insolvency law, but rather in general private law, such as contract law or tort law. In such a case, the resulting judgment should not be regarded as an 'insolvency-related judgment' as it is not 'materially associated' with the insolvency proceeding.[36] Rather, it should be recognized and enforced under the rules applicable to the recognition and enforcement of foreign judgments in general. If, on the other hand, the foreign judgment addresses the question whether the creditor's claim is admissible or enjoys some kind of priority in the insolvency proceeding opened in respect of the debtor in that State, this does pertain to insolvency law, as it is for the rules of insolvency law to determine which claims are admissible in insolvency proceedings or enjoy some form of priority, and thus the resulting judgment should be considered an 'insolvency-related' judgment. However, the categories of admissible or non-admissible claims and the preferences granted or denied to certain types of claims differ (greatly) among States. If the court in a particular State determines that a claim is admissible in insolvency proceedings opened in respect of the debtor in that State and that such claim enjoys a certain preference, that should not oblige the courts in another State to recognize and enforce that judgement where, for example, parallel insolvency proceedings have been

35 Regulation (EU) No 1215/2012 of the European Parliament and of the Council of 12 December 2012 on jurisdiction and the recognition and enforcement of judgments in civil and commercial matters (recast), OJ L 351, 20.12.2012, 1–32. Whether a particular action falls within the scope of the EIR or the Brussels I^{bis} Regulation impacts on the jurisdiction of the court. Under the EIR the courts in the Member State where the insolvency proceeding has been opened have, in principle, exclusive jurisdiction to hear actions that derive directly from the insolvency proceedings and are closely linked with them (cf. Case C-296/17 Wiemer & Trachte, ECLI:EU:C:2018:902).

36 It is noted that the CJ EU took a different view in Case C-47/18 Skarb/Riel, ECLI:EU:C:2019:754, where it held that an action for a declaration of the existence of claims for the purposes of their registration in the context of insolvency proceedings was considered to fall within the scope of the EIR as an action that derives directly from the insolvency proceeding and is closely linked with them. Within the scheme of the EIR this primarily impacts on the jurisdiction of the court (in principle, exclusive jurisdiction of the courts in the Member State where the relevant insolvency proceeding has been opened). Recognition and enforcement of judgments in such actions are dealt with on the basis of Article 32 EIR.

opened in respect of the same debtor in the recognizing State and, under the laws of that State, the claim would be either inadmissible or not enjoy a preference at all.

The far-reaching nature of the example given in paragraph 60, subparagraph d is acknowledged in the Guide to Enactment, where it is observed that **2.2.33**

> Enacting States will need to determine whether this category should extend to all such judgments regardless of when the cause of action arose. While it might be considered that a cause of action that arose prior to the commencement of the insolvency proceedings was sufficiently linked to the insolvency proceeding, as it was being pursued in the context of, and could have an impact on, that proceeding, it might also be considered that a judgment on such a cause of action could have been obtained by or against the debtor prior to the commencement of the insolvency proceeding and, thus, lacked a sufficiently material association with the insolvency proceedings. Enacting States may also wish to have regard to the treatment of such judgments under other international instruments.[37]

A judgment (i) confirming or varying a plan of reorganization or liquidation, (ii) granting a discharge of the debtor or of a debt, or (iii) approving a voluntary or out-of-court restructuring agreement.

The judgments referred to under (i) and (ii) in this example may already be covered by the MLCBI, depending on the interpretation that a certain State has given to the extent of the relief available under the MLCBI. **2.2.34**

The judgments referred to under (iii) do not appear to necessarily be 'insolvency-related' in the sense that they arise as a consequence of or are materially associated with the insolvency proceeding. In this respect it is important to keep in mind that the types of agreement referred to under (iii) are typically not regulated by insolvency law and may be reached through informal negotiation to address a consensual modification of the claims of all participating creditors. This is acknowledged in the Guide to Enactment of the MLIJ, which clarifies that reference is being made to agreements of this type that are ultimately referred to the court for approval in formal insolvency proceedings, such as an expedited proceeding of the type addressed in the Legislative Guide.[38] **2.2.35**

37 Cf. Guide to Enactment (n 1), para. 60.

38 Cf. Guide to Enactment (n 1), para. 60.

A judgment for the examination of a director of the debtor, where that director is located in a third jurisdiction.

2.2.36 This example of an 'insolvency-related' judgment, which is not further elaborated on in the Guide to Enactment, should probably be read in connection with the relief available under the MLCBI generally. Pursuant to Article 21(1)(d) MLCBI, the relief granted by a court that has recognized a foreign proceeding may provide for the examination of witnesses, the taking of evidence or the delivery of information concerning the debtor's assets, affairs, rights, obligations or liabilities. It is rather ambiguously phrased. A recognizing State should apparently recognize and enforce a foreign judgment ordering the examination of a director of the debtor, but only where the director is located in a third jurisdiction, that is, one other than the originating or recognizing State. This does not seem to make a lot of sense. Unless this would be manifestly contrary to the public policy in the enacting State, it would make sense to recognize and enforce an insolvency-related judgment ordering the examination of a director where this would have implications in the enacting State.

2.2.37 The words at the end of Article 2(d)(i)a MLIJ – 'whether or not that insolvency proceeding has closed' – are intended to clarify that an insolvency-related judgment issued after the proceeding to which it relates has been closed can still be considered an insolvency-related judgment for the purposes of the MLIJ. In that respect, reference is made to the fact that in some jurisdictions, for example, actions for avoidance may be pursued after a reorganization plan has been approved and confirmed by the court, and that confirmation is considered to be the conclusion of the proceedings.

2.2.38 In line with paragraph 2(d) of the Preamble, Article 2(d)(ii) MLIJ explicitly stipulates that a judgment commencing an insolvency proceeding is not considered an 'insolvency-related judgment' for purpose of the MLIJ. The recognition of the decision opening an insolvency proceeding is covered by the MLCBI.

Article 3

INTERNATIONAL OBLIGATIONS OF THIS STATE

Michael Veder

1. To the extent that this Law conflicts with an obligation of this State arising out of any treaty or other form of agreement to which it is a party with one or more other States, the requirements of the treaty or agreement prevail.
2. This Law shall not apply to a judgment where there is a treaty in force concerning the recognition or enforcement of civil and commercial judgments, and that treaty applies to the judgment.

A. INTRODUCTION TO ARTICLE 3

Article 3 MLIJ addresses the relationship between the MLIJ, as enacted in a State, and treaties or other types of international regulations that are binding on that State. **2.3.01**

B. SUPREMACY OF INTERNATIONAL OBLIGATIONS

Article 3(1) MLIJ expresses the general principle of the supremacy of international obligations of the enacting State over domestic law. **2.3.02**

2.3.03 Article 3(1) MLIJ is identical to Article 3 MLCBI. Hence, reference is made to the commentary to Article 3 MLCBI.

C. TREATIES CONCERNING THE RECOGNITION OR ENFORCEMENT OF JUDGMENTS IN CIVIL OR COMMERCIAL MATTERS

2.3.04 Article 3(2) MLIJ addresses the specific situation where there is a treaty in force for the enacting State which applies to the recognition and enforcement of judgments in civil and commercial matters.

2.3.05 Article 3(2) MLIJ provides that, if the judgment in question falls within the terms of the treaty, then the treaty prevails and should cover its recognition and enforcement, rather than the MLIJ. The Guide to Enactment observes that binding legal obligations issued by regional economic integration organizations that are applicable to members of that organization might be treated as obligations arising from an international treaty and that this provision can also be adapted in national law to refer to binding international instruments with non-State entities, where such instruments could apply to the recognition and enforcement of insolvency-related judgments.[1]

2.3.06 There are a number of such international instruments that address the recognition and enforcement of judgments in civil and commercial matters.

2.3.07 In respect of the European Union, the matter is covered by the Brussels I^{bis} Regulation.[2] The Convention on jurisdiction and the recognition and enforcement of judgments in civil and commercial matters of 30 October 2007 (the Lugano Convention) regulates the free movement of court judgments in civil and commercial cases between the European Union and Iceland, Norway and Switzerland.[3] However, these instruments do not cover the recognition and

1 Cf. *UNCITRAL Model Law on Recognition and Enforcement of Insolvency-Related Judgments with Guide to Enactment*, United Nations Publications (Vienna), 2019, para. 64.

2 Regulation (EU) No 1215/2012 of the European Parliament and of the Council of 12 December 2012 on jurisdiction and the recognition and enforcement of judgments in civil and commercial matters (recast), OJ L 351 of 20 December 2012, 1 et seq.

3 In April 2020, the United Kingdom applied to rejoin (post-Brexit) the Lugano Convention. However, for a third country to accede to this convention, all parties to the convention must give their explicit consent. Whereas this has been the case with Switzerland, Norway and Iceland, the European Commission, acting on behalf of the EU as a party to the 2007 Lugano Convention, has indicated that it is not prepared to grant such consent, effectively blocking – for the moment – the UK's reintegration within the Lugano regime of mutual recognition of civil and commercial judgments (cf. Communication from the Commission to the European Parliament and the Council of 4 May 2021, COM(2021) 222 final; Communication of 22 June 2021 from the European Commission representing the European Union to the Swiss Federal Council as the Depositary of the 2007 Lugano Convention).

enforcement of judgments in insolvency-related matters, as interpreted by the Court of Justice of the European Union. Both the Brussels I^{bis} Regulation and the Lugano Convention exclude from their scope of application: 'bankruptcy, proceedings relating to the winding-up of insolvent companies or other legal persons, judicial arrangements, compositions and analogous proceedings'.[4] This includes judgments in actions that derive directly from the insolvency proceedings and are closely linked with them, that is, insolvency-related judgments.[5] Whether an action meets these criteria must be determined, according to case law of the Court of Justice of the European Union, not by reference to the procedural context of which that action is part, but to the legal basis of the action. It must be determined whether the right or obligation which forms the basis of the action has its source in the ordinary rules of civil and commercial law or in derogating rules specific to insolvency proceedings.[6] Within the EU, the jurisdiction in respect of such insolvency-related actions and the recognition and enforcement of judgments in relation to such actions are governed by the EU Insolvency Regulation.[7]

On a global level, reference can be made to the Convention of 30 June 2005 on Choice of Court Agreements (HCCH 2005 Choice of Court Convention) and the Convention of 2 July 2019 on the Recognition and Enforcement of Foreign Judgments in Civil or Commercial Matters (HCCH 2019 Judgments Convention). **2.3.08**

The HCCH 2005 Choice of Court Convention applies in international cases to exclusive choice of court agreements concluded in civil or commercial matters. It also regulates the recognition and enforcement of judgments given by the courts of a Contracting State designated in an exclusive choice of court agreement that falls within the ambit of the convention. Pursuant to Article 2(2)(e), the convention does not apply to 'insolvency, composition and **2.3.09**

4 Cf. Article 1(2)(b) of both instruments.

5 Cf. CJEU Case 133/78 *Gourdain*, EU:C:1979:49.

6 Cf. CJEU Case C-535/17 *NK v Paribas*, ECLI:EU:C:2019:96, para. 28. See in more detail (with extensive references to further case law of the CJEU): Georg Ringe, in: Bork and van Zwieten (eds), Commentary on the European Insolvency Regulation (2nd edn), Oxford University Press, paras 6.17 et seq; Paul Oberhammer and Florian Scholz-Berger, in: Bork and van Zwieten (eds), Commentary on the European Insolvency Regulation (2nd edn), Oxford University Press, paras 32.14 et seq. The scope of what constitutes an insolvency-related judgment for purposes of the EIR and the Brussels I^{bis} Regulation is thus much narrower than the MLIJ (see also Veder at paras 1.02.17 et seq.).

7 Cf. Articles 6 and 32 of Regulation (EU) 2015/848 of the European Parliament and of the Council of 20 May 2015 on insolvency proceedings (recast).

analogous matters'. Proceedings are excluded from the scope of the convention if they directly concern insolvency.[8]

2.3.10 The HCCH 2019 Judgments Convention seeks to facilitate the effective international circulation of judgments in civil or commercial matters. By setting forth commonly accepted conditions for recognition and enforcement, and agreed grounds for refusal, the Convention seeks to provide legal certainty and predictability to parties involved in cross-border transactions, providing clarity as to whether and to what extent a judgment will be recognised and enforced in another jurisdiction. Article 2(1)(e) excludes from the scope of this convention 'insolvency, composition, resolution of financial institutions, and analogous matters'. This includes insolvency-related judgments, that is, judgments directly concerning insolvency.[9] The Explanatory Report on the Convention clarifies[10] that, similar to the interpretation given to insolvency-related judgments given by the Court of Justice of the European Union, the exclusion applies if the right or the obligation that was the legal basis of the action in the State of origin was based on rules pertaining specifically to insolvency proceedings, rather than general rules of civil or commercial law. If the action derives from insolvency rules, the exclusion precludes the circulation of the judgment under the Convention. But if the action derives from civil or commercial law, the judgment may circulate. The Convention does not apply, for example, to judgments opening insolvency proceedings, concerning their conduct and closure, approving a restructuring plan, or setting aside transactions detrimental to the general body of creditors or on the ranking of claims. The Convention does, however, apply to judgments on actions based on general rules of civil or commercial law, even if the action is brought by or against a person acting as insolvency representative in one party's insolvency proceedings. Thus the Convention, for example, applies to judgments on actions for the performance of obligations under a contract concluded by the debtor, or actions on non-contractual damages.

---

8 Cf. Explanatory Report to the convention by Trevor Hartley and Masato Dogauchi (available at https://assets.hcch.net/docs/0de60e2f-e002-408e-98a7-5638e1ebac65.pdf), para. 57.

9 Cf. Francisco Garcimartín and Geneviève Saumier, Explanatory Report on the Convention of 2 July 2019 on the Recognition and Enforcement of Foreign Judgments in Civil or Commercial Matters (available at: https://assets.hcch.net/docs/a1b0b0fc-95b1-4544-935b-b842534a120f.pdf), para. 51.

10 Garcimartín-Saumier Report (n 9), paras 51–53.

Article 4

COMPETENT COURT OR AUTHORITY

Michael Veder

The functions referred to in this Law relating to recognition and enforcement of an insolvency-related judgment shall be performed by [*specify the court, courts, authority or authorities competent to perform those functions in the enacting State*] and by any other court before which the issue of recognition is raised as a defence or as an incidental question.

A. INTRODUCTION TO ARTICLE 4

Like Article 4 MLCBI, Article 4 MLIJ prompts enacting States to indicate in the legislation implementing the MLIJ which courts or authorities will perform the functions referred to in the MLIJ in relation to recognition and enforcement of foreign insolvency-related judgments. **2.4.1**

In many cases, the jurisdiction of the courts of an enacting State in respect of the recognition and enforcement of foreign judgments will be regulated in other parts of its legislation already, in particular the law of (international) civil procedure. The value of implementing Article 4 MLIJ, thereby explicitly addressing the jurisdiction in relation to the recognition and enforcement of insolvency-related judgments, would be to increase the transparency and ease of use of the legislation for the benefit of, in particular, foreign insolvency representatives and others authorized under the law of the originating State to seek recognition and enforcement of an insolvency-related judgment.[1] **2.4.2**

1 Cf. *UNCITRAL Model Law on Recognition and Enforcement of Insolvency-Related Judgments with Guide to Enactment*, United Nations Publications (Vienna), 2019, para. 66.

2.4.3 Article 4 MLIJ takes account of the fact that the recognition (and enforcement) of foreign judgments may be at the core of not only the proceedings brought before the court, for example where a foreign insolvency representative seeks recourse against assets of the judgment debtor in an enacting State, but also other types of proceedings, for example proceedings brought against the insolvent debtor or the insolvency representative, as a defence or an incidental question that needs to be addressed in order for the court to take a decision on the dispute before it.[2] Article 4 MLIJ makes clear that the identification by an enacting State of the courts or other authorities that will generally entertain requests for the recognition and enforcement of foreign insolvency-related judgments should not unnecessarily limit the jurisdiction of other courts in this respect. It does so by explicitly stipulating that issues of recognition and enforcement of foreign insolvency-related judgments may also be heard and determined 'by any other court before which the issue of recognition is raised as a defence or as an incidental question'.

2.4.4 As Article 4 MLIJ is based on[3] Article 4 MLCBI, reference is made to the commentary to Article 4 MLCBI.

2 Cf. A/CN.9/WG.V/WP.143/Add.1, para. 17; A/CN.9/898, paras 18–20; A/CN.9/WG.V/WP.145 (footnote 12).

3 Cf. A/CN.9/WG.V/WP.143/Add.1, note [16]. The wording has been revised for consistency with the subject matter of the MLIJ.

Article 5

AUTHORIZATION TO ACT IN ANOTHER STATE IN RESPECT OF AN INSOLVENCY-RELATED JUDGMENT ISSUED IN THIS STATE

Michael Veder

A [*insert the title of the person or body administering a reorganization or liquidation under the law of the enacting State*] is authorized to act in another State with respect to an insolvency-related judgment issued in this State, as permitted by the applicable foreign law.

A. INTRODUCTION TO ARTICLE 5

Article 5 MLIJ, like Article 5 MLCBI, seeks to ensure that insolvency representatives or other authorities appointed in insolvency proceedings commenced in an enacting State are authorized to act abroad with respect to an insolvency-related judgment, in particular by seeking recognition and enforcement of such judgment.[1] 2.5.1

1 Earlier drafts of the MLIJ stipulated that the insolvency representative was 'authorized to seek recognition and enforcement of an insolvency-related judgment' (Cf. A/CN.9/WG.V/WP.143). The current wording leaves room for other types of actions, although it is not clear what other types of actions are envisaged by the MLIJ.

2.5.2 The authority to act abroad is granted under Article 5 MLIJ, regardless of whether or not the foreign State where the insolvency representative wants to take action has enacted legislation based on the MLIJ.[2]

2.5.3 Implementation of Article 5 MLIJ in the laws of an enacting State is only necessary to the extent that the laws of an enacting State do not already provide insolvency representatives with the power to act abroad in that regard.[3]

2.5.4 Like Article 5 MLCBI, Article 5 MLIJ stipulates that the insolvency representative is authorized to act abroad, 'as permitted by the applicable foreign law'. This seeks to clarify that the scope of the powers that the insolvency representative is able to exercise abroad will (ultimately) depend upon the laws and courts in the State where action in respect of an insolvency-related judgment needs to be taken.

2.5.5 As Article 5 MLIJ is based on[4] Article 5 MLCBI, reference is made to the commentary to Article 5 MLCBI.

---

2 Cf. *UNCITRAL Model Law on Recognition and Enforcement of Insolvency-Related Judgments with Guide to Enactment*, United Nations Publications (Vienna), 2019, para. 69.

3 However, implementation of this provision in the laws of an enacting State would provide clear statutory evidence of that authority and may assist foreign courts and other users of the law (cf. Guide to Enactment (n 2), para. 68).

4 Cf. A/CN.9/WG.V/WP.143/Add.1, note [16]. The wording has been revised for consistency with the subject matter of the MLIJ.

Article 6

ADDITIONAL ASSISTANCE UNDER OTHER LAWS

Wan Wai Yee

Nothing in this Law limits the power of a court or a [insert the title of the person or body administering a reorganization or liquidation under the law of the enacting State] to provide additional assistance under other laws of this State.

A. INTRODUCTION TO ARTICLE 6

1. Rationale

Article 6 is intended to clarify that the MLIJ does not limit or displace the application of national law in the event that national law provides assistance that is similar or in addition to the powers that are set out under the MLIJ. Hence a foreign insolvency representative who is making an application for recognition and enforcement of the foreign insolvency-related judgment under Article 11 MLIJ is free to ask the receiving court for such assistance as the national law provides (even if the national law is not one that implements MLIJ). **2.6.1**

Article 6 MLIJ is drafted in a similar manner as Article 7 MLCBI (comments at para. [7]). In fact, it could be argued that Article 6 MLIJ is drafted more widely than Article 7 of MLCBI, which provides that nothing in the MLCBI limits the power of a court or an insolvency representative to provide assistance 'to a foreign representative' under the laws of the state, suggesting that it seems **2.6.2** to restrict the assistance to a foreign representative and not to other kinds of assistance, such as to a foreign court.[1] The wider language can be explained by the fact that a person applying for assistance under Article 6 MLIJ is not limited to a foreign representative but is anyone who has standing to apply for enforcement under Article 11 MLIJ, who is determined to be any 'person entitled under the law of the originating State to seek recognition and enforcement of an insolvency-related judgment may seek recognition and enforcement of that judgment in this State'.[2]

B. ENACTMENT AND APPLICATION OF ARTICLE 6

2.6.3 The *Guide to Enactment and Interpretation* makes clear that the applicant for relief under Article 6 extends broadly to any party who is entitled to apply for recognition and enforcement of the foreign insolvency-related judgment, such as a person specified under Article 11 MLIJ, that is, an insolvency representative or other person entitled under the law of the originating State to seek recognition and enforcement of an insolvency-related judgment.[3]

2.6.4 In addition, the *Guide to Enactment and Interpretation* highlights the relevance of Article X, read with Article 6. Article X (comments at para. [2.X.05] below) makes it clear that the relief available under the legislation implementing Article 21 MLCBI includes recognition and enforcement of a judgment.

2.6.5 For guidance as to interpretation of whether Article 6 is a catch-all assistance to provide assistance or relief that is supplemental to other provisions in the MLIJ, the case of *In re Vitro S.A.B. de C.V.*[4] may be instructive. In *Vitro*, a case decided under the US legislation that implements Article 7 read with Article 21 MLCBI (which provides for relief upon the recognition of a foreign proceeding),[5] the foreign insolvency representative applied to confirm a reorganizational plan from Mexico that purported to release the guarantees issued by the subsidiaries of the debtor to the noteholders. The court held that US leg-

---

1 See Article 7 of MLCBI and commentary.

2 See UNCITRAL, *UNCITRAL Model Law on Recognition and Enforcement of Insolvency-Related Judgments with Guide to Enactment and Interpretation*, United Nations Publications (New York), 2019, para. 70.

3 *UNCITRAL Model Law on Recognition and Enforcement of Insolvency-Related Judgments with Guide to Enactment and Interpretation*, United Nations Publications (New York), 2019, para. 70.

4 *Ad Hoc Grp. of Vitro Noteholders v. Vitro S.A.B. de C.V. (In re Vitro S.A.B. de C.V.)*, 701 F.3d 1031 (5th Cir. 2012). For a summary of the case, see UNCITRAL, Digest of Case Law on the UNCITRAL Model Law on Cross-Border Insolvency, United Nations Publications (New York), 2021, 24, fn. 4.

5 US Bankruptcy Code 1978, ss 1507 and 1521.

islation implementing Article 21 MLCBI[6] did not have the effect of discharging the obligations of such non-debtor subsidiaries as such release was not available in the courts of United States Fifth Circuit. However, as such release had been granted by other courts in the United States, such relief was not precluded under the legislation implementing Article 7 MLCBI.[7] While the court acknowledged that Article 7 MLCBI is a catch-all provision, the court made it clear that the assistance requested under that provision is 'extraordinary' as compared with other provisions that provide for the kinds of specific relief in MLCBI (such as Article 21), and the threshold for granting such relief had to be a high one.[8] In a similar vein, in the United Kingdom, while Article 7 MLCBI is implemented in its domestic law,[9] it has been suggested that the common law jurisdiction on assistance continues to exist in parallel to the MLCBI but common law should be subordinate to the MLCBI.[10]

Thus, if a party is seeking to rely on domestic law that exists in parallel to the MLIJ, the party may continue to do so under the domestic law. However, there may nevertheless be a hierarchy within the menu of options of recognition and enforcement of foreign insolvency-related judgments in that jurisdiction. In particular, the courts in that jurisdiction may not permit a party to rely on the parallel domestic law to get around the restrictions for granting relief that are specifically set out in the MLIJ. **2.6.6**

6 US Bankrupcy Code 1978, s 1521.

7 US Bankruptcy Code 1978, s 1507.

8 *Ad Hoc Grp. of Vitro Noteholders v. Vitro S.A.B. de C.V. (In re Vitro S.A.B. de C.V.)*, 701 F.3d 1031, (5th Cir. 2012) at 1057.

9 Cross-Border Insolvency Regulations 2006.

10 See Ho, Look Chan (ed.), *A Commentary on the UNCITRAL Model Law*, 4th ed., Globe Law & Business (London), 2017, 205.

Article 7

PUBLIC POLICY EXCEPTION

Wan Wai Yee

Nothing in this Law prevents the court from refusing to take an action governed by this Law if the action would be manifestly contrary to the public policy, including the fundamental principles of procedural fairness, of this State.

A. INTRODUCTION TO ARTICLE 7

2.7.1 Similar to Article 6 MLCBI,[1] Article 7 MLIJ provides the exception that the receiving court is able to opt out of enforcing the insolvency-related judgment if it is 'manifestly contrary' to the public policy of the State. While the second part of Article 7, that is, the reference to fundamental principles of procedural fairness, is not present in Article 6 of MLCBI, the *Guide to Enactment* made it clear that the addition was only intended to clarify that procedural fairness was part of public policy, especially in States that may take the view that procedural fairness and public policy are distinct concepts.[2]

1 See Article 6 of MLCBI and commentary above.

2 UNCITRAL, *UNCITRAL Model Law on Recognition and Enforcement of Insolvency-Related Judgments with Guide to Enactment and Interpretation,* United Nations Publications (New York), 2019, para [74].

B. ENACTMENT AND APPLICATION OF ARTICLE 7

Article 7 refers to 'manifestly contrary' to public policy. Public policy is not defined in the MLIJ, as is the case in Article 6 MLCBI. Drawing from the experience of Article 6 MLCBI, there are at least three issues that arise in respect of Article 7. **2.7.2**

First, the word 'manifestly' would suggest that the public policy exception should be used restrictively and in narrow circumstances.[3] English case law has held that these circumstances include where there is a breach of natural justice and procedural fairness.[4] If the case were to arise in the context of the MLIJ, under the second part of Article 7, a lack of procedural fairness in giving the requisite notice would independently be a ground to refuse recognition. **2.7.3**

Second, Article 7 MLIJ is a catch-all provision which covers ground beyond the specific exclusionary grounds set out in Article 14 (which refers to, among others, where the judgment is obtained by fraud).[5] In the context of Article 6 MLCBI, it has been suggested that, given that the public policy exception should only be relied upon sparingly, the exception should be invoked if there is no specific provision that governs its application elsewhere in the MLCBI,[6] and it is likely that the same approach will be used for Article 7 MLIJ. **2.7.4**

Third, jurisdictions have differed in the enactment of the entirety of Article 6 MLCBI,[7] and it remains to be seen whether they would differ similarly in respect of the enactment of Article 7 MLIJ. Many leading common law jurisdictions, such as the United Kingdom[8] and the United States,[9] adopted Article 6 MLCBI, including requiring that the action must be manifestly contrary to public policy before it can be invoked as a ground to avoid recognition. In a similar vein, Article 33 EIR provides that 'any Member State may refuse to recognise insolvency proceedings opened in another Member State or to enforce a judgment handed down in the context of such proceedings where **2.7.5**

3 Ian F. Fletcher, Insolvency in Private International Law, 2nd ed., Oxford University Press (Oxford), 2007, 462.

4 *Cherkasov v Olegovich, the Official Receiver of Dalnyaya Step LLC* [2017] EWHC (Ch) 756.

5 *Guide to Enactment and Interpretation* (n 2), para [98].

6 See UNCITRAL Digest of Case Law on the UNCITRAL Model Law on Cross-Border Insolvency, United Nations, Vienna 2021, 20, citing *Pan Ocean Co. v Fibria Celulose S/A* [2014] EWHC (Civ) 2124, [2014] All ER 03 (Eng.) at [para. 104].

7 W.Y. Wan and G. McCormack, 'Implementing Strategies for the Model Law on Cross-Border Insolvency: the Divergence in Asia-Pacific and Lessons for UNCITRAL' (2020) 36 Emory Bankruptcy Developments Journal 59. See also commentary to Article 6 of MLCBI (para. [1.6.17]).

8 In the UK, the Model Law is implemented by the Cross-border Insolvency Regulations 2006 ('CBIR 2006').

9 In the US, the Model Law is implemented by Chapter 15 US Bankruptcy Code (11 USC).

the effects of such recognition or enforcement would be manifestly contrary to that State's public policy, in particular its fundamental principles or the constitutional rights and liberties of the individual'.[10]

2.7.6 However, several economically significant jurisdictions in Asia, such as Singapore, South Korea and Japan,[11] have not included the word 'manifestly' in their versions of the MLCBI, and in Singapore it has been held that such exclusion was deliberate and that the threshold to invoke the public policy exception is lower than in jurisdictions which have adopted Article 6 MLCBI in full.[12] It would be expected that in these jurisdictions it is likely that the public policy exception is more easily invoked than in the other jurisdictions that have insisted on the requirement that the action must be 'manifestly' contrary to public policy. The choice made by the States on what they view as appropriate thresholds in refusing to recognize or enforce the foreign insolvency-related judgment may run counter to the objectives of MLIJ, which are to create a well-understood uniform framework where there is certainty, predictability and speed in recognizing and enforcing such judgments.

10 EIR, Article 33.

11 See generally, Wan and McCormack (2020), (n 7). In Japan, the Model Law is implemented by Act on Recognition of and Assistance for Foreign Insolvency Proceedings, Act No. 129 of 2000 (allowing a court to refuse recognition of a foreign proceeding if it is contrary to public policy); see also Shin Abe, Japan, in *Cross Border Insolvency: A commentary on the UNCITRAL Model Law* 324 (Look Chan Ho & Freshfields Bruckhaus eds, 4th ed. 2017) (noting that there is no mention of 'manifestly' in the Japanese legislation adopting the Model Law). In South Korea, the Model Law is implemented by Debtor Rehabilitation Act and Bankruptcy Act, Act. No. 7428, Mar. 31, 2005 (providing that the court may dismiss the petition for recognition if the foreign bankruptcy proceeding is contrary to the public policy of the Republic of Korea); Chiyong Rim, South Korea, in *Cross Border Insolvency*, at 585.

12 *Re Zetta Jets Pte Ltd* [2018] SGHC 16 at paras [22]–[23].

Article 8

INTERPRETATION

Wan Wai Yee

In the interpretation of this Law, regard is to be had to its international origin and to the need to promote uniformity in its application and the observance of good faith.

A. INTRODUCTION TO ARTICLE 8

Article 8 MLIJ is drafted in a manner similar to Article 8 MLCBI.[1] **2.8.1**

B. ENACTMENT AND APPLICATION OF ARTICLE 8

The *Guide to Enactment and Interpretation*[2] notes that to improve harmonisation and application on the interpretation of Article 8, the UNCITRAL secretariat publishes the Case Law on UNCITRAL texts (CLOUT) containing summaries of the judicial decisions (and, where relevant, arbitral awards) relating to the conventions and model laws which are promoted by UNCITRAL. **2.8.2**

In line with the promotion of predictability and uniformity of the MLCBL, the *Digest on CLOUT*[3] has noted that aside from the foreign judicial decisions, **2.8.3**

1 See Article 8 MLCBI and commentary [paras 1.8.01–1.8.14].

2 *UNCITRAL Model Law on Recognition and Enforcement of Insolvency-Related Judgments with Guide to Enactment and Interpretation,* United Nations Publications (New York), 2019, paras [75]–[76].

3 See UNCITRAL Digest of Case Law on the UNCITRAL Model Law on Cross-Border Insolvency, United Nations, Vienna 2021, 20, 25.

and the *Guide to Enactment and Interpretation*, the courts have cited various instruments extensively including the *Judicial Perspective*,[4] the *Legislative Guide*,[5] the *Practice Guide*,[6] the reports of UNCITRAL/INSOL/World Bank Multinational Judicial Colloquiums[7] and UNCITRAL Commission reports leading to the preparation of the MLCBI.[8] It would be expected that a similar approach in referring to the above-mentioned documents will be adopted by the courts in interpreting provisions under the MLIJ.

4 See UNCITRAL, *UNCITRAL Model Law on Cross-Border Insolvency: The Judicial Perspective*, adopted in 2011 (currently updated to 2022).

5 *UNCITRAL Legislative Guide on Insolvency Law*, United Nations Publications (New York) 2014.

6 *UNCITRAL Practice Guide on Cross-Border Insolvency Cooperation*, adopted in 2009.

7 Available at https://uncitral.un.org/en/colloquia/insolvency.

8 Available at https://uncitral.un.org/en/commission.

Article 9

EFFECT AND ENFORCEABILITY OF AN INSOLVENCY-RELATED JUDGMENT

Wan Wai Yee

An insolvency-related judgment shall be recognized only if it has effect in the originating State and shall be enforced only if it is enforceable in the originating State.

A. INTRODUCTION TO ARTICLE 9

Article 9 MLIJ deals with the issue of recognition and enforcement of foreign insolvency-related judgments. **2.9.1**

B. APPLICATION AND INTERPRETATION OF ARTICLE 9

An 'insolvency-related judgment' is defined in Article 2(d).[1] The definition is not limited to decisions that are handed down as a consequence of the insolvency proceeding but also takes in judgments that are 'materially associated' with an insolvency proceeding, and it has to be a judgment that was issued on or after the commencement of the insolvency proceeding. The definition of 'judgment' expressly excludes an interim measure of protection. Accordingly, Article 9 excludes any interim or temporary measures that are ordered prior to the commencement of the insolvency proceedings. **2.9.2**

1 See Article 2 MLIJ and commentary above.

2.9.3 Article 9 draws a distinction between recognition and enforcement of an insolvency-related judgment. However, similar to the MLCBI, the MLIJ does not define recognition and enforcement. Instead, it falls to the commentaries to seek guidance as to the distinction between the two concepts. A judgment may be recognized by the originating state as having the effect of determining the rights and liabilities of the parties, but may not be enforceable, such as where there is a stay of execution pending the outcome of an appeal.[2] As pointed out in the *Guide on Enactment and Interpretation*,

> 78. [...] [R]ecognition means that the receiving court will give effect to the originating court's determination of legal rights and obligations reflected in the judgment. For example, if the originating court held that the plaintiff had, or did not have, a certain right, the receiving court would accept and recognize that determination. Enforcement, on the other hand, means the application of the legal procedures of the receiving court to ensure compliance with the judgment issued by the originating court. A decision to enforce the judgment must, for the purposes of the Model Law, be preceded or accompanied by recognition of the judgment.
>
> 79. In contrast, recognition need not be accompanied or followed by enforcement. For example, if the originating court held that one party had an obligation to pay money to another party or that one party had a certain right, the receiving court may simply recognize that finding of fact, without any issue of enforcement arising. If the cause of action giving rise to that judgment was pursued again in the receiving State, recognition of the foreign judgment would be sufficient to dispose of the application.[3]

2.9.4 The issue as to whether a foreign insolvency-related judgment is effective or enforceable is determined by the law of the originating state.[4]

---

2 See also Article 10 MLIJ and commentary below in para. [2.10.06].

3 *UNCITRAL Model Law on Recognition and Enforcement of Insolvency-Related Judgments with Guide to Enactment and Interpretation*, United Nations Publications (New York), 2019, paras 78–79.

4 See *Guide on Enactment and Interpretation* (fn. 3), para. 77.

Article 10

EFFECT OF REVIEW IN THE ORIGINATING STATE ON RECOGNITION AND ENFORCEMENT

Wan Wai Yee

1. Recognition or enforcement of an insolvency-related judgment may be postponed or refused if the judgment is the subject of review in the originating State or if the time limit for seeking ordinary review in that State has not expired. In such cases, the court may also make recognition or enforcement conditional on the provision of such security as it shall determine.
2. A refusal under paragraph 1 does not prevent a subsequent application for recognition or enforcement of the judgment.

A. INTRODUCTION TO ARTICLE 10

2.10.1 Article 10 MLIJ deals with the situation where the insolvency-related judgment is or may be subject to review in the originating State. An 'insolvency-related judgment' is defined in Article 2(d).[1] Article 10 clarifies that the receiving court has a number of options to approach the issue and is not restricted to deciding only whether to recognize and/or enforce the judgment.

1 See Article 2 of MLIJ and commentary above.

B. APPLICATION AND INTERPRETATION OF ARTICLE 10

2.10.2 The use of 'review' in Article 10 MLIJ is broad enough to cover a review by the same originating court that issued the judgment or an appeal to a higher appellate court.[2] 'Ordinary review' is not defined in the MLIJ but the *Guide to Enactment and Interpretation* explains that an ordinary review is to be distinguished from an extraordinary review, such as 'an appeal to a court of human rights or internal appeal for violation of fundamental rights'.[3]

2.10.3 In a proceeding to be considered under the MLIJ where the judgment is the subject of review in the originating State (or if the time for seeking a review has not expired), the receiving court has several options. First, the court may outright refuse to recognize or enforce the judgment. Second, the court may postpone a decision on recognition and enforcement until the period for review expires or it is clear that the judgment will stand. Third, the receiving court may recognize the judgment only but delay enforcement. Fourth, the court may go ahead and recognize and/or enforce the judgment. In such a case, the court may make interim orders, such as an order being conditional on the provision of security by the party seeking enforcement or recognition pending the outcome of the final decision.[4]

2.10.4 If the receiving court refuses to recognize or enforce the judgment on the ground that the judgment is subject of review, the second paragraph of Article 10 clarifies that it is possible to bring a subsequent application.

2.10.5 Article 10 MLIJ may be contrasted with the fourth paragraph of Article 17 MLCBI,[5] which clarifies that a decision to recognize a foreign proceeding will not prevent the modification or termination if the grounds for granting the recognition were fully or partially lacking or had ceased to exist. The decision to recognize proceedings in the MLCBI does not depend on the proceedings being final or non-appealable and Article 17 MLCBI does not expressly provide for conditional orders.[6] However, in the context of the MLIJ, conditional orders will be important given that enforcement is mandatory under

---

2 UNCITRAL, *UNCITRAL Model Law on Recognition and Enforcement of Insolvency-Related Judgments with Guide to Enactment and Interpretation*, United Nations Publications (New York), 2019, para. 80.

3 Guide to Enactment and Interpretation (n 2), para. 80.

4 Ibid.

5 See Article 17 MLCBI and commentary above.

6 See UNCITRAL, *Digest of Case Law on the UNCITRAL Model Law on Cross-Border Insolvency*, United Nations Publications (New York), 2021, 51 (pointing out that courts have characterized the recognition ruling as 'merely a "summary determination"' that is not full and final and thus available for review).

the MLIJ[7] whereas the receiving court will only be recognizing the foreign proceeding under the MLCBI.[8] Further, enforcement (as opposed to only recognition) of the insolvency-related judgment can cause serious prejudice to a defendant if the judgment is ultimately overturned or set aside; the flexibility of granting an interim or conditional order would protect the defendant's interests while the judgment is subject to review.

While Article 10 refers to recognition and enforcement of the insolvency-related judgment, recognition and enforcement are not terms that are defined in the MLIJ (as is the case in the MLCBI).[9] Instead, it falls to the commentaries to seek guidance as to the distinction between the two concepts. A judgment may be recognized by the originating state as having the effect of determining the rights and liabilities of the parties, but may not be enforceable, such as where there is a stay of execution pending the outcome of an appeal.[10] As pointed out in the *Guide on Enactment and Interpretation*, **2.10.6**

> 78. [R]ecognition means that the receiving court will give effect to the originating court's determination of legal rights and obligations reflected in the judgment. For example, if the originating court held that the plaintiff had, or did not have, a certain right, the receiving court would accept and recognize that determination. Enforcement, on the other hand, means the application of the legal procedures of the receiving court to ensure compliance with the judgment issued by the originating court. A decision to enforce the judgment must, for the purposes of the Model Law, be preceded or accompanied by recognition of the judgment.
>
> 79. In contrast, recognition need not be accompanied or followed by enforcement. For example, if the originating court held that one party had an obligation to pay money to another party or that one party had a certain right, the receiving court may simply recognize that finding of fact, without any issue of enforcement arising. If the cause of action giving rise to that judgment was pursued again in the receiving State, recognition of the foreign judgment would be sufficient to dispose of the application.[11]

7 See Article 13 MLIJ.

8 See Chapter 3 MLCBI.

9 For the distinction between recognition and enforcement in the MLIJ, see Article 9 and its commentary above.

10 See also Article 9 MLIJ and commentary in para. 2.9.03.

11 Guide to Enactment and Interpretation (n 2), paras 78–79.

Article 11

PROCEDURE FOR SEEKING RECOGNITION AND ENFORCEMENT OF AN INSOLVENCY-RELATED JUDGMENT

Rodrigo Rodriguez

1. An insolvency representative or other person entitled under the law of the originating State to seek recognition and enforcement of an insolvency-related judgment may seek recognition and enforcement of that judgment in this State. The issue of recognition may also be raised as a defence or as an incidental question.
2. When recognition and enforcement of an insolvency-related judgment is sought under paragraph 1, the following shall be submitted to the court:
   (a) A certified copy of the insolvency-related judgment; and
   (b) Any documents necessary to establish that the insolvency-related judgment has effect and, where applicable, is enforceable in the originating State, including information on any pending review of the judgment; or
   (c) In the absence of evidence referred to in subparagraphs (a) and (b), any other evidence on those matters acceptable to the court.
3. The court may require translation of documents submitted pursuant to paragraph 2 into an official language of this State.
4. The court is entitled to presume that documents submitted pursuant to paragraph 2 are authentic, whether or not they have been legalized.
5. Any party against whom recognition and enforcement is sought has the right to be heard.

A. INTRODUCTION TO ARTICLE 11

1. Scope and Purpose

Article 11 provides for the cornerstones of an expeditious procedure for the recognition and enforcement of insolvency-related judgments.[1] It establishes essentially three things: (1) Who has standing to apply for recognition and enforcement of an insolvency-related judgment under this model law (paragraph 1); (2) what formal requirements the request must fulfil: documents required (paragraph 2 subparagraph b), translation requirements (paragraph 3), issues of proof (paragraph 4); and (3) that the proceedings must respect the defendant's procedural right to be heard (paragraph 5). **2.11.01**

Under the wording of the MLIJ (article 13), where the procedural conditions are met, the judgment 'shall' be recognized and enforced. Unlike the MLCBI, there is no discretion regarding the recognition and enforcement of judgments in the MLIJ. However, whilst enforcement is mandatory, it is also subject to a larger range of refusal grounds (see articles 7, 13 and 14 MLIJ) than available under the MLCBI.[2] **2.11.02**

2. Implementation in the MLCBI Context

Article 11 ('Procedure for seeking recognition and enforcement of an insolvency-related judgment') is very similar to article 15 MLCBI ('Application **2.11.03**

1 Jose Carles, 'Jurisdiction and Recognition of Insolvency-Related Judgments: A Comparison between the European Insolvency Regulation and the UNCITRAL Model Law', INSOL Technical Papers 53, October 2022, 14.

2 Irit Mevorach, 'Overlapping International Instruments for Enforcement of Insolvency Judgements: Undermining or Strengthening Universalism?', European Business Organization Law Review (2021), https://doi.org/10.1007/s40804-021-00204-4, 299.

for recognition of a foreign proceeding'). For jurisdictions having enacted the MLCBI, the UNCITRAL Secretariat's Guidance Note on Enacting two or more of the UNCITRAL Model Laws on Insolvency recommends that both provisions be consolidated in a single article 15, with MLCBI article 15 being paragraph 1, and MLIJ article 11 being paragraph 2.[3] Such change would also require a change to the title of the article, with the addition of the phrase 'or an insolvency-related judgment'.[4]

B. STANDING TO APPLY FOR RECOGNITION AND ENFORCEMENT

2.11.04 Recognition and enforcement of an insolvency-related judgment can be sought by either an insolvency representative or a person authorized to act on behalf of an insolvency proceeding within the meaning of article 2, subparagraph (b).[5] According to that provision, it may also be sought by any person entitled under the law of the originating State to seek such recognition and enforcement. Such a person might include a creditor whose interests are affected by the judgment.[6]

C. REQUESTING RECOGNITION AS A DEFENCE AND INCIDENTALLY

2.11.05 The second sentence of paragraph 1 is borrowed from article 4 MLBCI, noting that the question of recognition may also be raised by way of defence or as an incidental question in the course of a proceeding. A defendant may find himself faced with a claim against him by a creditor for the full amount of a claim that has been modified, reduced or even discharged by a foreign insolvency-related decision.[7]

2.11.06 The sentence in question makes clear that the defendant may request the recognition of that foreign decision as a defence or as an element of his

3 In respect of states also implementing the UNCITRAL Model Law on Enterprise Group Insolvency (MLEG), the Note suggests that some states 'may wish to include MLEG Article 21 ("Application for recognition of a foreign planning proceeding") as paragraph 3 of consolidated article 15, but it may also be included as a separate provision in the chapter on "enterprise group insolvency"'. See MLEG Guide N 139–52.

4 UNCITRAL Guidance Note on Enacting two or more of the UNCITRAL Model Laws on Insolvency 2021, available from https:// uncitral .un .org/ sites/ uncitral .un .org/ files/ media -documents/ uncitral/ en/ v2104338_guidance_note_uncitral_model_laws_on_insolvency.pdf, N 20. See also MLCBI Guide N 127–36; MLIJ Guide N 83–92.

5 See 1.2.08 ff

6 MLIJ Guide, N 84.

7 MLIJ Guide, N 84.

defence in the court proceedings relating to a claim raised against him – that is, without having to start separate recognition proceedings before a separate court. 'As an incidental question' refers to proceedings where the recognition and enforcement is not the subject of a formal request by any of the parties but is an essential question to resolve the formal claim (for instance, a claim for payment of a sum in disregard of a foreign discharge). The recognition and enforcement will not become part of the decision but part of the reasoning leading to the decision.[8]

Even where the issue arises in those circumstances, the requirements of article 11 (2)–(3), and of course the substantial conditions of articles 7, 13 and 14, need to be met in order to obtain (incidental) recognition of the judgment. As to the standing for raising this issue as a defence, the person raising the question in that manner should be a person referred to in the first sentence of article 11(1).[9] **2.11.07**

D. FORMAL REQUIREMENTS

1. Overview

Article 11 (2) lists the documents or evidence that must be produced by the party seeking recognition and enforcement of an insolvency-related judgment in the recognition proceedings (as a main question, as a defence or as an incidental question),[10] these being: **2.11.08**

- a certified copy of the judgment (to be recognized); and
- any documents necessary to establish that the judgment is effective and enforceable in the originating State, including information as to any pending review of the judgment,[11] which could include information concerning the time limits for review.

8 Most procedural laws limit the res iudicata effect of a court decision to its conclusions while it does not extend to the factual and legal reasoning leading to these conclusions, that is, to the incidental questions. Parties may raise a particular issue as a main question, however, when there is an interest to obtain a conclusion with res iudicata effect on that particular question (for instance, to raise the recognition as a defence in a different proceeding).

9 MLIJ Guide, N 84, see 2.11.03, as well as 1.2.08 ff (on Article 2).

10 See 2.11.05 f.

11 This assertion is important for the application of Article 10, under which 'the court has various approaches' it can adopt when addressing a non-final judgment, see MLIJ Guide, N 81 and 2.10.03.

2. The Certified Copy (Subpara. a)

2.11.09 Article 11 paragraph 1 is inspired by the identical provision in article 15(2) MLCBI.[12] Further similar provisions can be found in articles 36 et seq. of the Brussels I Regulation[13] and articles 33 et seqq. of the Lugano Convention.[14] What constitutes a 'certified copy' is to be determined by reference to the law of the State in which the judgment was issued (subparagraph a). Despite it being modelled on existing texts, the requirement of subparagraph a of a 'certified copy' is a questionable provision in a model law intended at encouraging recognition, as it would preclude an implementing state from allowing a simple copy to suffice (at least in a situation where the authenticity of the copy is not questioned by any party). Given the non-binding character of the MLIJ and its overall purpose of facilitating cross-border recognition, this requirement would not necessarily have to be implemented by states that already accept a lower standard of formality. Certification refers to a confirmation (by an authority or any person authorized to do so) that the copy is identical to the original document. Such a certification is not identical to a legalization[15] (see paragraph 4), the latter referring to a complete 'chain of certifications' by generally public authorities of public documents. In the (many) states that are members of the 1961 Hague Apostille Convention[16] a legalization is heavily simplified and may *de facto* be as simple to obtain as a certification.

2.11.10 Although not explicitly cited in the law, it must be assumed that an original copy (or 'the original') of the decision will, *a fortiori*, also fulfil the formal requirements of that provision (without any reference to national law).

3. Any other Documents (Subpara. b)

2.11.11 Subparagraph 2 (b) requires the provision of 'any documents necessary to satisfy the condition that the judgment is effective and enforceable in the

---

12 See 1.15.02 ff MLCBI (Warner).

13 Regulation (EU) 1215/2012 of the European Parliament and of the Council of 12 December 2012 on jurisdiction and the recognition and enforcement of judgments in civil and commercial matters (recast) [2012] OJ L 351/1 (Brussels I recast Regulation).

14 Convention on jurisdiction and the recognition and enforcement of judgments in civil and commercial matters [2007] OJ L 339/3 (Lugano Convention).

15 According to the 2023 Apostille Practical Handbook on the Operation of the Apostille Convention (https://assets.hcch.net/docs/a19ae90b-27bf-4596-b5ee-0140858abeaa.pdf), legalization refers to 'the process of certifying a public document for production abroad. It generally comprises multiple discrete authentications, including by the Embassy or Consulate of the place in which the document is to be presented'.

16 Hague Convention of 5 October 1961 Abolishing the Requirement of Legalisation for Foreign Public Documents (1961 Apostille Convention); see for the convention text and materials www.hcch.net/en/instruments/conventions/specialised-sections/apostille.

originating State, including information as to any pending review of the judgment, which could include information concerning the time limits for review'.[17] Generally, the claimant will obtain from the court that issued the decision to be recognized a written confirmation of enforceability after the term for raising an appeal has elapsed or such appeal has been refused (by an, in turn, enforceable) decision. This information is necessary for the recognizing court in order to assess its options under Article 10 paragraph 1.[18] Unlike many other instruments on recognition and enforcement of decisions, that article of the MLIJ does not require the foreign decision to be recognized to be final, but allows for the recognizing court to tailor the consequences of recognition to the effects of the foreign decisions and to further developments, for instance by postponing recognition and enforcement until it is clear whether the judgment is to be affirmed, set aside or amended in the originating State or proceeding to recognize the judgment, but postponing enforcement.[19]

4. Absence of Evidence (Subpara. c)

Subparagraph c addresses the situation where the applicant cannot submit the documents required under subpara. b, mainly because the applicant cannot provide a certified copy of the decision to be recognized (as for the proof of the effects of the decision, the text of subparagraph b already provides for the necessary flexibility in respect of possible documents to submit). An identical provision can be found in Article 15(2)(c) MLCBI.[20] **2.11.12**

5. Further Evidence

The Guide to Enactment[21] recommends that a copy of the decision commencing the insolvency proceeding to which the judgment is related be submitted to the recognizing court as evidence of the existence of the insolvency proceeding to which the judgment is related. This indeed makes sense in view of Article 14 h), which requires that the judgment does not originate from a State 'whose insolvency proceeding is not or would not be recognizable'. Neither the Model Law nor the Guide to Enactment specify whether the copy of the decision needs to be 'certified' or subject to any other formalities. It must thus be assumed that the general principles on evidence of the State where recognition **2.11.13**

17 MLIJ Guide, N 85.
18 See 2.10.03 ff.
19 MLIJ Guide, N 81.
20 Further guidance can be found in the commentary to that provision, see 1.15.31 ff. MLCBI (Warner).
21 MLIJ Guide, N 85.

is sought will apply. Under those, generally a simple copy should suffice as long as no doubts about its authenticity are raised.[22]

E. TRANSLATION (PARA. 3)

2.11.14 Paragraph 3 of article 11 entitles, but does not compel, the court to require a translation of some or all of the documents submitted under paragraph 2. Where that discretion is compatible with the procedures of the court under the laws of the recognizing court, it may facilitate a decision being made on the application at the earliest possible time.[23] The provision is inspired by article 15(4) MLCBI.[24]

F. PRESUMPTION AND LEGALISATION (PARA. 4)

2.11.15 Paragraph 4 of Article 11 is largely identical with article 16(2) MLCBI.[25] Accordingly, also under the MLIJ there is a presumption that documents submitted in support of recognition and enforcement need not be authenticated in any special way, in particular by legalization, and the court is entitled to presume that those documents are authentic whether or not they have been legalized.[26]

2.11.16 Wherever an implementing state would insist on requiring a legalization or the certification of the copy (under paragraph 2(a)) is replaced by a legalization, the 1961 Hague Apostille Convention[27] would in most instances apply.[28]

G. THE RIGHT TO BE HEARD (PARA. 5)

2.11.17 Article 11(5) establishes the right of the party against whom the relief provided in the judgment is sought to be heard in the proceedings following the application for recognition and enforcement. To ensure that the right is meaningful and can be enforced, the party against whom that relief is sought will require

22 See 2.11.15.

23 MLIJ Guide, N 87 and MLCBI Guide, N 134.

24 Further guidance can be found in the commentary to that provision, see 1.15.43 f MLCBI (Warner).

25 Article 11(4) MLIJ is limited to 'documents submitted pursuant to paragraph 2'. Article 16(2) is not limited but refers in general terms to 'documents submitted in support of the application'.

26 See N 88 of the MLIJ Guide and N 128 of the MLCBI Guide. On the meaning of 'legalization' (and renouncing to it) see 1.16.17 ff. MLCBI (Warner).

27 See fn 16 and 15.

28 See N 90 of the MLIJ Guide and N 130 of the MLCBI Guide.

notice of the application for recognition and enforcement and of the details of the hearing.

A party's 'right to be heard' is a core element of due process, and is enshrined in most constitutions (for the US see the 5th and 14th Amendments)[29] and conventions (see article 6 of the European Convention on Human Rights)[30] and implemented in the procedural laws of the States. The 'right to be heard' as a procedural element of due process generally does not merely cover the right to be given proper notice of a proceeding, but also the possibility for the party concerned to meaningfully state its position in the proceedings, such as the existence of grounds for refusal under articles 13 and 14, and to submit evidence to support its allegations. **2.11.18**

Whether article 11(5) is a provision useful to implement in such general (and probably redundant) terms in the context of a national law on recognition of insolvency-related proceedings is questionable. The laws implementing the MLIJ will more likely directly apply this principle by stating how specifically the parties affected by the decision are involved in the proceedings in a meaningful way and enabled to submit their points of view as well as any evidence. This may be the case in the law implementing the MLIJ or, more likely, within the procedural laws applicable to court proceedings in general. Where the rules of civil procedure that apply to the recognition proceedings already apply these principles – as will generally be the case in all states applying the rule of law – there appears to be no necessity to copy the wording of article 11(5) into the national law. It can be read as a programmatic provision aimed at setting a minimum standard of procedural fairness in recognition procedures. There is no parallel provision to that paragraph in the MLCBI. **2.11.19**

The MLIJ leaves it up to the law of the enacting State to determine not only how notice should be provided,[31] but also at what point in time. It implies, however, that the notice should be limited, in principle, to the party against whom recognition and enforcement is sought.[32] The concept of proper notice is similar to the one used as the basis of the ground for refusal of Article 14(a) **2.11.20**

29 U.S. Government Information, www.govinfo.gov/content/pkg/GPO-CONAN-1992/pdf/GPO-CONAN-1992-7.pdf.

30 Convention for the Protection of Human Rights and Fundamental Freedoms (European Convention on Human Rights) (ECHR).

31 MLIJ Guide N 92.

32 This concept is narrower than that of any party *adversely affected* under Article 20 of the MLCBI, see MLCBI Guide N 185. The narrow approach is justified in the MLIJ because of the nature of the decisions, which will be generally decisions against one of a few specified parties with an *inter partes* effect (as opposed as decision with a *erga omnes* effect such as the opening of an insolvency proceeding). Even where the recognition is

and is rooted in the principles of due process.[33] Based on that parallelism, notice should be given timely and with the necessary information to the adverse party to present a proper defence. However, the provision – open as it is formulated – should not be read as to exclude *ex parte* applications and *ex parte* proceedings, especially where provisional measures are required together with the recognition. In such cases the right to be heard is granted after the hearing and the decision based on it, and an effective remedy must still be available for the party against whom the recognition decision was issued, essentially under the same conditions as in ordinary proceedings.

likely to affect indirectly further parties, the right to be given notice should be limited to the party(ies) against whom recognition is formally sought.

33 See 2.14.05 ff.

Article 12

PROVISIONAL RELIEF

Rodrigo Rodriguez

1. From the time recognition and enforcement of an insolvency-related judgment is sought until a decision is made, where relief is urgently needed to preserve the possibility of recognizing and enforcing an insolvency-related judgment, the court may, at the request of an insolvency representative or other person entitled to seek recognition and enforcement under article 11, paragraph 1, grant relief of a provisional nature, including:
   (a) Staying the disposition of any assets of any party or parties against whom the insolvency-related judgment has been issued; or
   (b) Granting other legal or equitable relief, as appropriate, within the scope of the insolvency-related judgment.
2. [Insert provisions (or refer to provisions in force in the enacting State) relating to notice, including whether notice would be required under this article.]
3. Unless extended by the court, relief granted under this article terminates when a decision on recognition and enforcement of the insolvency-related judgment is made.

A. INTRODUCTION TO ARTICLE 12

1. Scope and Purpose

2.12.01 Article 12 deals with 'urgently needed' relief that may be ordered at the discretion of the court and is available from the moment recognition of an insolvency-related judgment is sought, until a decision on the recognition and, if appropriate, enforcement is made.[1] Like its counterpart (from which it is copy-pasted), Article 19 MLCBI, Article 12's purpose is to preserve the possibility that, once and if the judgment is recognized and enforced, assets will still be available to satisfy the enforcement claimant.

2.12.02 According to the Guide to Enactment,[2] the assets that can be secured by way of an interim order can be either the assets of the judgment debtor or the assets of the debtor in the insolvency proceeding to which the judgment is related. In our view, the second option (securing assets of the debtor of a 'related' insolvency proceeding that would not belong to the defendant under the insolvency-related judgement recognized) does not seem to be explicitly covered by the wording of article 12 para 2(a). Where an implementing state would indeed want to allow for both categories of assets to be covered, the provisions implementing Article 12 should specify this more explicitly. In fact, in order to secure assets of the debtor of foreign insolvency proceedings, it would appear more appropriate to request provisional measures against that debtor under Article 19 of the MLCBI (that is, its implementation in national law). The first option (secure the assets of the judgement debtor), in turn, seems unproblematic.

2.12.03 As opposed to Article 19 MLCBI, Article 12 MLIJ extends the standing to request such measures from the (obvious) insolvency representative to any 'other person entitled to seek recognition and enforcement under article 11, paragraph 1'.[3] That provision, in turn, refers to Article 2(b). That provision would cover any person entitled under the law of the originating State to seek such recognition and enforcement under the MLIJ and might include a creditor whose interests are affected by the judgment.[4]

1 MLIJ Guide, N 93; Gabriel Moss, 'UNCITRAL Model Law on recognition and enforcement of insolvency-related judgments', Insolv Int 32, 4.

2 MLIJ Guide N 93.

3 See also 1.19.11 on Article 19 MLCBI (Symes).

4 MLIJ Guide N 84.

2. Implementation in the Context of the MLCBI

As a general matter of legal drafting, it does not make sense to regulate the provisional measures that are available in the context of decisions under the MLIJ separately from those under the MLCBI (where both are being implemented or the latter has already been implemented). Consequently, the UNCITRAL Secretariat proposal for a Consolidated Text of the UNCITRAL Model Laws on Cross-Border Insolvency, Recognition and Enforcement of Insolvency-related Judgments and Enterprise Group Insolvency (2021)[5] (and N 22 of the Guidance Note hereto) recommends to incorporate Article 12 MLIJ into the proposed Article 19 of the consolidated proposal (see MLCBI Guide paras 150–188; MLIJ Guide paras 93–95),[6] expanding its substantive scope to cover provisional measures taken in the context of an application for recognition under the MLCBI as well as the MLIJ. A specific paragraph could address the extension of the standing to request the measures.[7] **2.12.04**

B. AVAILABLE RELIEF

1. The Stay

Subparagraph 1(a) cites the most important available measure: the stay of the disposition of assets.[8] The extent of the stay is limited to the assets of any party against whom the judgment was issued.[9] **2.12.05**

The provision leaves all procedural and some substantive requirements and modalities up to the implementing jurisdictions to elaborate. While some jurisdictions may focus the measure on the attachment of particular assets (measures *in rem*), other court orders may focus on the defendant (measures *ad personam*) and astrain the defendant to refrain from particular acts (disposing of assets). **2.12.06**

Under the measure applied, any disposal of the assets concerned should be void of legal effects, with a narrow exception for bona fide third parties. The **2.12.07**

5 See https://uncitral.un.org/en/consolidated-text-uncitral-model-laws-cross-border-insolvency-recognition-and-enforcement accessed 9 July 2023.

6 UNCITRAL Guidance Note on Enacting two or more of the UNCITRAL Model Laws on Insolvency 2021, available from https:// uncitral .un .org/ sites/ uncitral .un .org/ files/ media -documents/ uncitral/ en/ v2104338_guidance_note_uncitral_model_laws_on_insolvency.pdf N 22.

7 See 2.12.03.

8 Moss (n 1), 4.

9 MLIJ Guide N 93.

amount or value of the assets thus secured should not exceed the amount to be secured under the recognized decision. The MLIJ does not allocate the burden of proof in respect of the assets to be secured. The implementation of the measure should not impose an undue burden of proof on the claimant in this respect and provide for assistance to the claimant in order to find and identify assets – within the limits of the need to secure the assets. National laws may also provide for security for any possible damage caused to the defendant by an unjustified measure to be provided by the claimant; however, only in exceptional cases, where the measure in question has the potential to cause significant damage. The provision of subparagraph 1(a) being substantially identical to those of Articles 19 and 21 MLCBI, it makes sense that the same measures and procedures for their issuance are made available.[10]

2. Any other Relief

2.12.08 Subparagraph 1(b) provides for other relief, both legal and equitable, to be granted provided it is within the scope of the judgment for which recognition is sought. Reference is made here to the measures applicable under Article 19[11] and those enumerated in Article 21 para 1 of the MLCBI.[12]

C. NOTICE REQUIREMENTS (PARA. 2)

2.12.09 Paragraph 2 contains a placeholder for the implementing state to include, at that point, requirements for notice to be given (either by the insolvency representative upon the order of the court or by the court itself) when relief of the type mentioned in Article 12 is granted. The Guide to Enactment itself refers to the possibility to provide for *ex parte* proceedings. [13] In those cases, notice would only be given to the defendant once the court order intended to secure the assets has been issued and enforced. It will be from this moment on that the defendant will be informed and put in the position to defend him- or herself against the measure, if it considers it to be unjustified. *Ex parte* proceedings should be granted where swift action is needed (and thus no time is available for a hearing) and/or a communication to the defendant would jeopardize the effect of the measure, that is, a 'surprise effect' is necessary. The placeholder of Article 12(2) can be found in identical wording in Article 19 MLCBI.

10 See 1.19.15 on Article 19 MLCBI (Symes), and 1.21.04–1.21.22 on Article 21 MLCBI.
11 See 1.19.22 on Article 19 MLCBI (Symes).
12 See 1.21.04 and 1.21.20 on Article 19 MLCBI (Symes).
13 MLIJ Guide N 94.

Accordingly, reference is made to comments on that provision,[14] which apply *mutatis mutandis* to the present context.

D. NATURE OF THE REMEDY (PARA. 3)

Article 12(3) specifies why (and in what respect) the remedy available under Article 12 is *provisional*. This is, namely, 'in that, [...] it terminates when the issue of recognition and, where appropriate enforcement, is decided, unless extended by the court'. As to the latter option (to extend the effect beyond the entry into force of the decision), the Guide to Enactment[15] specifies that the 'court might wish to do so, for example, to avoid a hiatus between any provisional measure issued before recognition and any measure that might be issued on or after recognition'. In order to avoid this, paragraph 3 should be read as the measure taking an end once the decision (on the recognition of the insolvency-related judgment) is actually effective (the term 'is made' lacks that specificity). **2.12.10**

14 See 1.19.14 on Article 19 MLCBI (Symes).

15 MLIJ Guide N 95.

Article 13

DECISION TO RECOGNIZE AND ENFORCE AN INSOLVENCY-RELATED JUDGMENT

Rodrigo Rodriguez

Subject to Articles 7 and 14, an insolvency-related judgment shall be recognized and enforced provided:

(a) The requirements of Article 9 with respect to effect and enforceability are met;
(b) The person seeking recognition and enforcement of the insolvency-related judgment is an insolvency representative within the meaning of Article 2, subparagraph (b), or another person entitled to seek recognition and enforcement of the judgment under Article 11, paragraph 1;
(c) The application meets the requirements of Article 11, paragraph 2; and
(d) Recognition and enforcement is sought from a court referred to in Article 4, or the question of recognition arises by way of defence or as an incidental question before such a court.

A. INTRODUCTION TO ARTICLE 13

The purpose of Article 13 is to establish clear and predictable criteria for recognition and enforcement of an insolvency-related judgment as defined in Article 2 (d)[1] under the MLIJ (that is, its implementation in national law). For the purposes of that assessment, the court may have due regard to any decisions and orders made by the originating court and to any information that may have been presented to the originating court. Such orders or decisions – or the characterizations made therein – are not binding on the receiving court in the enacting State, which is only required to satisfy itself independently that the insolvency-related judgment meets the requirements of Article 2.[2] **2.13.01**

Article 13 and the articles it further refers to (Article 7 and, especially, Article 14) are key provisions of the MLIJ.[3] Article 13 fulfils a similar function to Article 17 MLCBI. However, while the recognition proceedings and the formal requirements for recognition under the MLIJ are very similar if not identical to those of the MLCBI, the substantial requirements of recognition differ considerably. This is particularly evident from a comparison of Article 14 MLIJ with Article 17 MLCBI. **2.13.02**

The (negative and positive) conditions referred to in Article 13, that will be addressed hereinafter, must be met *cumulatively* – and apply in addition to those resulting from the reference to Articles 7 and 14.[4] **2.13.03**

B. CONDITIONS FOR RECOGNITION

1. The Decision is Final and Enforceable (Article 9)

The judgment to be recognized must be effective and enforceable in the originating State as provided for under Article 9.[5] The proceedings and the evidence required to make that determination are dealt with in Article 11. **2.13.04**

---

1 See 2.2.17–2.2.38 as well as Rodrigo Rodriguez, 'The New UNCITRAL Model Law on Recognition and Enforcement of Insolvency-Related Judgements', in: Ballesteros Barrion/Bovio (eds), Insolvency Law in International Instruments and Comments, Aranzadi 2023, 111–31.

2 MLIJ Guide N 97.

3 John A. Churchill Jr., 'Please Recognize Me: The United Kingdom Should Enact the UNCITRAL Model Law on Recognition and Enforcement of Insolvency-Related Judgments' (2020) 46(1) Brooklyn JIL 215, 238: 'Article 13 gets to the heart of recognition and enforcement'.

4 Churchill (n 3), 239. Though Article 17 MLCBI would appear to be the more complex provision than art. 17 MLIJ, the latter article's references, especially to Article 14 MLIJ, make the recognition proceedings under the MLIJ considerably more challenging than under the MLCBI.

5 See 2.9.02 ff.

2. Documents and Evidence Required are Submitted

2.13.05 Subparagraph (d) requires that the documents or evidence required under Article 11(2), have been provided in the form and manner which that same provision requires.[6]

3. The Person Requesting Recognition has Standing

2.13.06 Under Subparagraph (b), the request for recognition must be made by either

- an insolvency representative within the meaning, of Article 2 (b), or
- another person entitled to seek recognition and enforcement of the judgment under Article 11 (1).[7]

4. A Competent Court is dealing with the Request

2.13.07 The request shall be addressed to a competent court under Article 4[8] of the MLIJ, except when the question of recognition has been raised by way of defence or as an incidental question. In that case, such court or authority shall also be entitled to decide. The MLIJ does not specify the consequences of submitting a request to the wrong authority.

5. Lack of Grounds for Refusal

(a) Violation of Public Policy (Article 7)

2.13.08 Recognition of the judgment (that is, the judgment and/or the effect of its recognition) may not be manifestly contrary to (formal and substantial) *public policy* (or *ordre public*), as evidenced and reiterated by the reference to Article 7.[9]

2.13.09 Article 7 MLIJ is substantially identical to Article 6 MLCBI[10] and states the general public policy (or *ordre public*) reservation, both in respect of substantive and procedural violations of public policy, that can be found in most

---

6 See 2.11.08 ff.

7 See 2.11.04 f.

8 See 2.4.01 ff and the respective national implementation of this provision.

9 See, in particular 2.7.02 ff on the definition of public policy under the MLIJ (and the references therein to Article 6 MLCBI) and, specifically, 2.14.26 on the public policy exception in the context of the 'fraud' exception of Article 14(b) as to proceedings and means of evidence see 2.11.08 ff.

10 MLIJ Guide, N 74. For relevant cases under the MLCBI see, for example, UNCITRAL, *Model Law on Cross-Border Insolvency: The Judicial Perspective* (Updated 2022) (Vienna: United Nations 2022), available from https://uncitral.un.org/sites/uncitral.un.org/files/media-documents/uncitral/en/mlcbi_judicial_perspective_2021_advanced_copypdf, N 49–58.

instruments of international law on recognition and enforcement of decisions; for instance, in Articles 34 n. 1 of the Lugano Convention, 45(1)(a) of the Brussels I regulation or 6(c) of the Hague Choice of Court or 7(1)(c) of the Hague Judgements Convention.[11] Although the Guide to Enactment refers to different national interpretations of the public policy concept,[12] the term 'manifestly' and the terminology used advocate for a strict standard to be applied to any decision (or the proceeding leading to that decision) for it to be flawed in a manner as to fulfil the requirement of Article 7. The second part of that provision, referring explicitly to procedural fairness, was drafted to accommodate those States with a relatively narrow concept of public policy (and which treat procedural fairness and natural justice as being distinct from public policy), but without intending that the approach to public policy in the MLIJ would differ from that of the MLCBI or that the idea of procedural fairness would not be included under the public policy exception in Article 6 MLCBI.[13]

(b) Grounds for Refusal of Article 14

The long and intricate list of grounds for refusal of recognition and enforcement in Article 14 can be summarized and structured as referring to the following sets of situations: **2.13.10**

- Improper notification of the defendant (a);[14]
- Fraud in how the insolvency-related decision was obtained (b);[15]
- Inconsistency with an internal decision (c)[16] or a foreign decision recognized earlier (d);[17] or
- Interference with the administration of the insolvency debtor's estate in the recognizing country;[18] or
- Adverse effect on the interests of creditors either generally or in an unfair manner (f);[19] or
- Improper assertion of jurisdiction by the origination court in the light of the criteria of Article 14 (f).[20]

11 See the references in fns 24 to 27.
12 MLIJ Guide N 72.
13 MLIJ Guide N 74.
14 2.14.05 ff
15 2.14.23 ff.
16 2.14.29.
17 2.14.30 f.
18 2.14.39 ff.
19 2.14.44 ff.
20 2.14.49 ff.

2.13.11 The long list of grounds for refusal, resulting from the application of Articles 7, 13, but particularly Article 14 with its complex and intricate indirect competence provisions – is one of the main differences between the MLIJ and the MLCBI. While the MLCBI focuses on the COMI as main criterion for indirect competence, the MLIJ is open to several alternatives requiring complex provisions in Article 14(g).[21] The relative openness of the MLIJ in respect of its substantive scope[22] has also led to the need for additional safeguards in the form of decision-specific grounds for refusal (Article 14 (e) and (f)).[23]

C. NO FURTHER GROUNDS FOR REFUSAL AND NO *'RÉVISION AU FOND'*

2.13.12 Article 13 establishes (by reference) a *numerus clausus* (or rather a maximum) of grounds for refusal under the MLIJ. This would exclude, for example, for a national implementation to require reciprocity from the originating State as an additional precondition. The MLIJ also precludes the receiving court from embarking on a consideration of the merits of the foreign court's decision to issue the insolvency-related judgment or issues related to the commencement of the insolvency proceeding to which the judgment is related.[24]

D. PROOF AND DOCUMENTS

2.13.13 When making its determination on recognition and enforcement under Article 13, the receiving court is entitled to rely, pursuant to the presumption in Article 11(4), on the authenticity (not necessarily on the veracity of their content) of the certificates and documents provided in support of the request for recognition.[25] The burden of proof for the facts and documents cited in Article 13 is basically upon the requesting party.[26]

21 See 2.14.49 ff.
22 See 2.14.49 ff as well as, in extenso, 2.2.17 ff, especially 2.2.30 ff.
23 See 2.14.39 ff and 2.14.44 ff.
24 MLIJ Guide N 97.
25 See 2.11.09 ff.
26 On the substantial grounds for refusal of Article 14, see 2.14.15 ff.

Article 14

GROUNDS TO REFUSE RECOGNITION AND ENFORCEMENT OF AN INSOLVENCY-RELATED JUDGMENT

Rodrigo Rodriguez

In addition to the ground set forth in Article 7, recognition and enforcement of an insolvency-related judgment may be refused if:

(a) The party against whom the proceeding giving rise to the judgment was instituted:
   (i) Was not notified of the institution of that proceeding in sufficient time and in such a manner as to enable a defence to be arranged, unless the party entered an appearance and presented their case without contesting notification in the originating court, provided that the law of the originating State permitted notification to be contested; or
   (ii) Was notified in this State of the institution of that proceeding in a manner that is incompatible with the rules of this State concerning service of documents;

(b) The judgment was obtained by fraud;

(c) The judgment is inconsistent with a judgment issued in this State in a dispute involving the same parties;

(d) The judgment is inconsistent with an earlier judgment issued in another State in a dispute involving the same parties on the same subject matter, provided the earlier judgment fulfils the conditions necessary for its recognition and enforcement in this State;

(e) Recognition and enforcement would interfere with the administration of the debtor's insolvency proceedings, including by conflicting with a stay or other order that could be recognized or enforced in this State;

(f) The judgment:
   (i) Materially affects the rights of creditors generally, such as determining whether a plan of reorganization or liquidation should be

confirmed, a discharge of the debtor or of debts should be granted or a voluntary or out-of-court restructuring agreement should be approved; and

(ii) The interests of creditors and other interested persons, including the debtor, were not adequately protected in the proceeding in which the judgment was issued;

(g) The originating court did not satisfy one of the following conditions:

(i) The court exercised jurisdiction on the basis of the explicit consent of the party against whom the judgment was issued;

(ii) The court exercised jurisdiction on the basis of the submission of the party against whom the judgment was issued, namely that that party argued on the merits before the court without objecting to jurisdiction or to the exercise of jurisdiction within the time frame provided in the law of the originating State, unless it was evident that such an objection to jurisdiction would not have succeeded under that law;

(iii) The court exercised jurisdiction on a basis on which a court in this State could have exercised jurisdiction; or

(iv) The court exercised jurisdiction on a basis that was not incompatible with the law of this State;

[States that have enacted legislation based on the UNCITRAL Model Law on CrossBorder Insolvency might wish to enact subparagraph (h).]

(h) The judgment originates from a State whose insolvency proceeding is not or would not be recognizable under [insert a reference to the law of the enacting State giving effect to the UNCITRAL Model Law on Cross-Border Insolvency], unless:

(i) The insolvency representative of a proceeding that is or could have been recognized under [insert a reference to the law of the enacting State giving effect to the UNCITRAL Model Law on Cross-Border Insolvency] participated in the proceeding in the originating State to the extent of engaging in the substantive merits of the cause of action to which that proceeding related; and

(ii) The judgment relates solely to assets that were located in the originating State at the time the proceeding in the originating State commenced.

A. INTRODUCTION TO ARTICLE 14

1. General Remarks

Article 14 states the grounds for refusal of recognition that apply in addition to the public policy exception of Article 7. It provides a set of safeguards to the overall objectives of the Model Law to assist States to equip their laws with a framework of provisions for recognizing and enforcing insolvency-related judgments that will facilitate the conduct of cross-border insolvency proceedings. The long and intricate list of refusal grounds of Article 14 can be summarized and structured as referring to the following sets of situations: **2.14.01**

- Improper notification of the defendant (14.a);[1]
- Fraud in the obtainment of the insolvency-related decision (14.b);[2]

1 See 2.14.05.

2 See 2.14.23 ff.

- Inconsistency with an internal decision (14.c)[3] or a foreign decision recognized earlier (14.d);[4] or
- Interference with the administration of the insolvent debtor's estate in the recognizing country (14.e);[5] or
- Adverse effect on the interests of creditors either generally or in an unfair manner (14.f);[6] or
- Improper assertion of jurisdiction by the origination court in the light of the criteria of Article 14.g and h.[7]

2.14.02 Article 14 is a key provision of the MLIJ, probably the most distinctive of the MLIJ. Its complexity stands in sharp contrast to the simplicity of Article 17 MLCBI. The complexity of Article 14 is mainly due to the large substantive scope of the MLIJ. As stated in the commentary on Article 2,[8] the MLIJ covers both typical *ad personam* decisions arising from typical adversarial proceedings – such as avoidance claims – as well as decisions affecting a large number of parties ('*erga omnes*') arising from collective proceedings, such as a discharge decision.[9] The comprehensive scope established by Article 2 calls for different types of guarantees, cautions, reservations and – ultimately – grounds for refusal to apply cumulatively – with the result that the present, complex provision contains no fewer than eight possible exceptions to recognition and enforcement.[10] As a consequence, legislators implementing this provision should be well aware of its discretionary character ('may be refused').[11] They may – or even should, depending on whether and how their existing legal system already addresses certain types of decisions, with their own precautions

3 See 2.14.30 ff.

4 See 2.14.33 ff.

5 See 2.14.39 ff.

6 See 2.14.39.

7 See 2.14.52 ff. and 2.14.63 ff.

8 See 2.2.24 ff.

9 The difference is also relevant in the context of Article X and the jurisprudence that was at the origin of that article: see 49.01 ff. See also Rodrigo Rodriguez, 'The new UNCITRAL Model Law on Recognition and Enforcement of Insolvency-Related Judgements', in: Ballesteros Barrion/Bovio (eds), *Insolvency Law in International Instruments and Comments*, Aranzadi 2023, 101-111.

10 Lia Metreveli, 'Toward Standardized Enforcement of Cross-Border Insolvency Decisions: Encouraging the United States to Adopt UNCITRAL's Recent Amendment to its Model Law On Cross-Border Insolvency' 51 Columbia JL and Social Problems 315 (on the draft Article 13, later Article 14) highlights that at least the eight exceptions need to be considered to be an exclusive limit to judicial discretion for non-recognition, which is supported by the Guide (N 196). The long list of grounds for refusal stands in a sharp contrast with the EIR's Article 32, which relies only that it stems from the jurisdiction whose main proceedings are being recognized; see Bob Wessels and Iliya Kokorin, *European Union Regulation on Insolvency Proceedings: An Introductory Analysis* (4th edn), American Bankruptcy Institute 2018, § 5.2.

11 John A. Churchill Jr., 'Please Recognize Me: The United Kingdom Should Enact the UNCITRAL Model Law on Recognition and Enforcement of Insolvency-Related Judgments' (2020) 46(1) Brooklyn JIL 215, 239.

– refrain from implementing at least some of the grounds of refusal. Where they adopt them, they should apply them in a restrictive manner.

2. A *Numerus Clausus* of Grounds for Refusal

The reference to Article 7 (public policy exception) in Article 14 is already contained in Article 13 and thus redundant in Article 14 from a systematic point of view. Articles 7, 13 and 14 have to be read together to list all requirements for recognition. This list, however, is a comprehensive one: no additional grounds for refusal (such as a reciprocity requirement) should be introduced.[12] **2.14.03**

3. Burden of Proof

While the claimant will have the burden of proof in respect of all facts to be established and documents to be submitted under Article 13, the burden of proof regarding the existence of a ground for refusal under Article 14 will generally be on the defendant. The obligation to submit the documents required under Article 13 will imply basic information on whether and how, for instance, the notifications were made to the defendant, in particular regarding the documents instituting the proceedings.[13] The principle '*negativa non sunt probanda*' relating to the difficulties in proving that something – such as a notification – did *not* happen, calls, in the case of the lack of proper notice, for the claimant to submit evidence of the notice in the request. **2.14.04**

B. IMPROPER NOTIFICATION OF THE DEFENDANT: 14(A)

1. General Scope

Article 14(a) permits the court to refuse recognition and enforcement if the defendant in the proceeding giving rise to the insolvency-related judgment was not properly (under the rules of his or her jurisdiction)[14] notified of that proceeding.[15] Proper notice requires sufficient time for a defence to be arranged. Appearance at a hearing without contesting the sufficiency of notice is a waiver of rights to object under this provision. **2.14.05**

---

12 See n 8.

13 See also [13.05].

14 Metreveli (n 10) exposes why, for this reason, subparagraph (a) would not alter the outcome of Rubin (see, in extenso, P1.03, as well as 2.14.72 ff in respect of jurisdictional rules in this circumstance).

15 MLIJ Guide, N 99.

2. Prevailing International Conventions

2.14.06 The criteria for proper transmission and service of the notification will only apply as long as no overriding provisions of applicable international treatises apply.[16] Many states are party to bilateral or multilateral treaties on judicial cooperation, which often contain provisions on procedures for communicating judicial or extrajudicial documents to addressees abroad. The most important multilateral treaty of this kind is the Convention on the Service Abroad of Judicial and Extrajudicial Documents in Civil and Commercial Matters of 1965[17] adopted under the auspices of the Hague Conference on Private International Law. This treaty is applicable to a large number of states.[18] In some cases, other multilateral or bilateral treaties may apply.[19]

2.14.07 The substantive scope of the Hague Service Convention[20] is a wide one and likely to include most, if not all, of the decisions covered by the MLIJ. In the context of Article 14(a), its applicability and, where applicable, its proper application is relevant in the context of subparagraphs (a) (i) and (ii). In respect of subparagraph (a)(i), respecting the provisions of the Hague Service Convention will displace (and clarify) the criteria of that subparagraph whenever that convention was applicable to the notification initiating the proceedings to be recognized. The Hague Service Convention will also displace any other provisions of the national law of the recognizing state (except for issues not regulated in this convention), as the convention will have become part of the 'rules of this State', thus also by virtue of subparagraph (a)(ii), whenever

16 This is automatically the case in States with a monistic system as soon as the treaty in question is ratified. In States with a dualistic system the transposition into national law would still depend upon the enactment of specific national legislation.

17 Convention on the service abroad of judicial and extrajudicial documents in civil or commercial matters (with annex) (opened for signature at The Hague on 15 November 1965, entered into force 10 February 1969) 9432 UNTS 658 (Hague Service Convention).

18 See the list of states and the proceedings/reservations applicable to each under www.hcch.net/en/instruments/conventions/status-table/?cid=17 (accessed 26 March 2023). [For its application in the US under Rule 4 (k) FRCP see Collier on the Rules of Civil Procedure, 57 (with an example of its application in a service of process to the UK). In at least one case cited therein (Trask v Service Merchandise Co. Inc. D. Mass. 1991 135 FRD 17), non-compliance with the Convention and absence of good faith to comply with it made the court provide the plaintiff with a new chance for proper service.

19 For instance, the Hague Convention of 1 March 1954 on civil procedure (www.hcch.net/en/instruments/conventions/full-text/?cid=33 accessed 11 July 2023). Bilateral agreements may apply in addition to, and complementing, the multilateral agreement.

20 The HCCH, *Practical Handbook on the Operation of the Service Convention* (4th edn 2016) para. 60, refers to the case Arcalon v Ramar of the Supreme Court of the Netherlands, HR 21 February 1986, NJ 1987, 149, which held that a request for evidence issued by a California bankruptcy court was within the ambit of 'civil or commercial matters' for the purposes of the Convention. According to the Supreme Court, the Convention's objective and scope justify an extensive construction of its Article 1.

the defendant was domiciled in the state where recognition is sought and the convention was applicable.[21]

In the framework of Article 14, the correct application of the treatises is examined *ex post*, that is, at the point of deciding on the recognition of the decision. Where the treaty in question is applicable directly in the recognizing state, for instance, because the defendant had its domicile in that same state at the time the proceedings were instituted, the recognizing state will apply the treaty directly and will refuse recognition where such treaty has been breached (also by virtue of (iii)).[22] However, in situations where the treaty did bind the original parties, for instance, where the defendant had its domicile in a contracting party but enforcement is now sought in a non-contracting party, the treaty will not apply directly. Its possible violation should, however, be considered in the determination of whether the defendant's rights under (i), discussed hereinafter, were affected in a manner to justify non-recognition. **2.14.08**

3. Inability to Enable a Defence: (i)

Subparagraph (a)(i) addresses the failure of the originating court to have notified the defendant in sufficient time and in such a manner as to enable a defence to be arranged in view of the proceedings. This ground for refusal actually specifically addresses a subset of the rights protected by the procedural public policy clause,[23] under which the right to be effectively defended constitutes one of the 'truly fundamental rights' protected by the public policy clause.[24] Nevertheless, the particular practical relevance of the proper service for an appropriate defence in virtually all multilateral[25] and bilateral instruments as well as national recognition regimes has created a need for a specific ground for refusal in this respect, thereby also lowering the threshold for a defendant to build a ground for refusal.[26] **2.14.09**

---

21 Where the defendant was in a third State and the Convention was applicable, it will only be indirectly applicable, its respect or non-respect being a central (but necessarily the sole) criterion for determining if the conditions of subparagraph (a) were met or not.

22 See 2.14.19 ff.

23 See also 2.14.26 to 2.14.27.

24 Peter Mankowski, 'Article 45 Brussels Ibis Regulation' in Ulrich Magnus and Peter Mankowski (eds), ECPIL: European Commentaries on Private International Law, vol 1 (2nd edn, Dr. Otto Schmidt KG, 2022) 28–9, see also Case C-7/98 Krombach v Bamberski, ECLI:EU:C:2000:164.

25 See 2.14.10.

26 With the threshold of violation of public policy being a very high one – see 1.7.3 – the comparatively low threshold of improper service of process has led to a certain degree of abuse (with minor formal mistakes in the service of process being abusively raised to avoid recognition) which, in more recent instruments, has in turn led to formulating this ground for refusal in stricter terms, for instance requiring a negative effect on the defendant's rights (not a mere violation of a procedural provision) and, in some instances (see the articles cited in 2.14.12), requiring the defendant to have used all available means in the originating state to appeal

2.14.10 According to the Guide to Enactment,[27] this provision encompasses notification not only of the fact of the commencement of the proceedings, but also of the essential elements of the claims made against the defendant in order to enable a defence to be arranged. This requirement is in line with other sources such as Article 45.1.b Brussels Recast Regulation, Article 34.2 Lugano Convention and Articles 9.c.i. and 7.1.a of the 2005 Hague Court Agreements and HCCH 2019 Judgments Conventions,[28] which generally refer to the 'document instituting the proceedings or the equivalent document'.[29]

2.14.11 The use of the word 'notified' (as opposed to, for instance, 'served' or 'summoned') has no technical legal meaning, and simply requires the defendant to be placed in a position to inform her or himself of the claim and the content of the documentation relating to the institution of the proceedings.[30]

2.14.12 Similar provisions can be found in Article 45.1.b of the Brussels Recast Regulation, Article 34.2 Lugano Convention and Articles 9.c and 7.1.a of the

---

against a violation of any provisions on proper service of documents ('unless the party entered an appearance and presented their case without contesting notification in the originating court, provided that the law of the originating State permitted notification to be contested') – interestingly, this limitation of the ground for refusal can only be found in respect of this particular ground. On its application in the context of the Brussels Recast Regulation, see Mankowski (n 24) N 57 ff; see also 2.14.18.

27 MLIJ Guide, N 100.

28 Regulation (EU) No 1215/2012 of the European Parliament and of the Council of 12 December 2012 on jurisdiction and the recognition and enforcement of judgments in civil and commercial matters (recast), OJ L 339, 21.12.2007, 3–41, http://data.europa.eu/eli/reg/2012/1215/oj; Convention on jurisdiction and the recognition and enforcement of judgments in civil and commercial matters, OJ L 351, 20.12.2012, 1–32, http://data.europa.eu/eli/convention/2007/712/oj; (Hague) Convention of 30 June 2005 on Choice of Court Agreements, www.hcch.net/en/instruments/conventions/full-text/?cid=98; (Hague) Convention of 2 July 2019 on the Recognition and Enforcement of Foreign Judgements in Civil or Commercial Matters, www.hcch.net/en/instruments/conventions/full-text/?cid=137.

29 'Or the equivalent document' was added to the EU/EFTA instruments as an enlargement of the concept due to the accession of the UK and Ireland (Peter Schlosser, 'Report on the Convention on the Association of the Kingdom of Denmark, Ireland and the United Kingdom of Great Britain and Northern Ireland to the Convention on jurisdiction and the enforcement of judgments in civil and commercial matters and to the Protocol on its interpretation by the Court of Justice', OJ C 59/71, 125, 128. In accordance with this open definition, the CJEU opted for functional approach according to which 'the document or documents which must be duly and in due term [be] served on the defendant in order to enable him to assert his rights before an enforceable judgement is given in the State of origin' (Case C-474/93 Hengst Import BV v Campese, ECLI:EU:C:1995:243). This concept seems also appropriate for the MLIJ in view of the wording and its scope. See also Mankowski (fn 24) N 38 ff. In the US, Rule 4 of the US Code 28 (Rules of Civil Procedure) deals extensively with the 'summons': subparagraph (a) with the contents, subparagraph (c) with the service itself and subparagraph (k) with the territorial limits of service – and implicitly, personal jurisdiction; see www.law.cornell.edu/rules/frcp/rule_4 (with the comments of the advisory committee on rules). In the UK, a judgment will not be registered under the Administration of Justice Act 1920 (for judgments falling under that instrument) if the judgment debtor was not duly served, and did not appear, in the original foreign proceedings. Similarly, the registration of a judgment under the Foreign Judgments (Reciprocal Enforcement) Act 1933 would be set aside if the judgment debtor did not receive notice of the original foreign proceedings in sufficient time to enable it to defend the proceedings and did not appear.

30 MLIJ Guide, N 100.

2005 Hague Court Agreements and HCCH 2019 Judgments Conventions.[31] In accordance with those provisions, particular importance must be given to the notification of the writ instituting the proceedings. Once this writ has been properly served, thus allowing for a preparation and defence, special provisions such as an obligation to establish an address for notification or a person entitled to receive notification on behalf of the defendant in the country of the proceedings may be established by the procedural rules of the originating country.

The test of whether notification has been given in sufficient time is a question of fact that depends on the circumstances of each case. The procedural rules of the originating court may afford guidance as to what might be required to satisfy the requirement, but would not be conclusive. Unfamiliarity with the local law and language and problems in finding a suitable lawyer may require a longer period than is prescribed under the law and practice of the originating State. The notification should also be effected 'in such a manner' as to enable the defendant to arrange a defence, which may require documents written in a language that the defendant is unlikely to understand to be accompanied by an accurate translation (at least of the parts that are essential for a proper defence).[32] The criterion in question can also be found in Article 34.2 of the Lugano Convention.[33] **2.14.13**

While the claimant will have the burden of proof in respect of all facts to be established and documents to be submitted under Article 13,[34] establishing a ground for refusal under Article 14 will generally be the responsibility of the defendant. He or she would have to show not merely that, for example, the notice was insufficient, that procedural requirements under the applicable laws or treaties – such as the submission of a translation – were not met, but also that this insufficiency deprived her or him of a substantial defence or evidence.[35] **2.14.14**

The Guide to Enactment[36] further indicates that the defendant must provide proof that the insufficient notice 'as a matter of certainty and not merely of speculation, would have made a material difference to the outcome of the orig- **2.14.15**

31 See n 28.

32 See Mankowski (n 24) N 41 citing Case C-14/07 Weiss & Partner GbR v IHK Berlin, ECLI:EU:C:2008:264.

33 'if the defendant was not served with the document which instituted the proceedings or with an equivalent document in sufficient time and in such a way as to enable him to arrange for his defence, unless the defendant failed to commence proceedings to challenge the judgment when it was possible for him to do so'. The Brussels Recast Regulation renounced to such a ground for refusal (unlike its predecessors, the Brussels Conventions and the Brussels I Regulation).

34 MLIJ Guide, N 100.

35 MLIJ Guide, N 100.

36 MLIJ Guide, N 100.

inating litigation. If that is not the case, it cannot be argued that the defendant was not enabled to arrange a defence.' This strictness is not necessarily in line with practice under other instruments and would not appear to be covered by the text of the provision.

4. Appearance of the Defendant (ii)

2.14.16 The rule in subparagraph (a)(i) does not apply if the defendant entered an appearance and presented their case without contesting notification, even if they had insufficient time to prepare their case properly. The purpose of this rule is to prevent the defendant raising issues at the enforcement stage that they could have raised in the original proceeding.[37] To 'enter an appearance' requires the defendant to have submitted an answer on the merits without questioning the jurisdiction, proper notice or any other requirement for the proceedings to take place before the court in question. The lack of any response to the notification of the claim (and, in consequence, the lack of any participation) is not an 'appearance' and does not trigger the applicability of subparagraph (i).

2.14.17 In any situation where the defendant was in a position to raise the issue of the irregular notification in the proceedings, the obvious remedy would have been for the defendant to seek a remedy in the course of that proceeding or to appeal the decision for violation of procedural rules. If the defendant failed to do so, he should not be entitled to put forward the lack of proper notification *ex post* as a ground for non-recognition of the ensuing judgment.[38]

2.14.18 However, this rule shall not apply if it was not possible to contest the notification in the court of origin.[39] The same rule can be found in Article 45(b) of the Recast Brussels Regulation and Article 34 Nr. 2 of the Lugano Convention. The CJEU had an opportunity to pronounce itself on that rule in practice in respect of the Brussels (recast) Regulation. In case C-283/05 *ASML Netherlands BV v Semiconductor Industry Services GmbH (SEMIS)* of 14 December 2006[40] the CJEU states that the conditions for enforcement are only fulfilled if a defendant actually has 'the possibility' to 'appeal against a default judgment'. According to the CJEU, this will be the case only if he or she has

---

37 MLIJ Guide, N 101, see also Article 45.b, last sentence of the Brussels Recast Regulation and Article 34.2, last sentence of the Lugano Convention.

38 MLIJ Guide, N 101.

39 MLIJ Guide, N 101.

40 Case C-283/05 ASML Netherlands BV v Semiconductor Industry Services GmbH (SEMIS), ECLI:EU:C:2006:787.

actually gained knowledge of its contents through (more or less proper) service; mere knowledge that this decision exists is not sufficient. Service must still be effected in sufficient time to enable him or her to arrange for a defence before the court of the State of origin (that is, to file an appeal). The conclusions of the CJEU should certainly also apply to the interpretation of this provision of the MLIJ, as its rationale is ultimately ensuring the effectiveness of the defendant's right to arrange a defence in all situations.

5. Violation of Mandatory Local Rules on Notification (iii)

Subparagraph (a)(ii) addresses notification given in a manner that was incompatible with rules of the receiving State concerning service of documents, where (and if) the receiving State is the State in which that notification was given.[41] This provision means that this ground for refusal is not applicable to a situation where the defendant was domiciled in a third State at the time when the proceedings leading to the decision to be recognized were initiated (and therefore summoned in that State), but enforcement is now (for any reason, including a change of domicile of the defendant) sought in the recognizing State. **2.14.19**

Such an incompatibility with local rules may be given where a notification happened directly by a party or a party representative. Some States have no objection to the service of a foreign writ on their territory without any participation by their authorities. This situation is generally the case in jurisdictions where no authorities participate in the service of documents also in internal cases (most common law jurisdictions). In such states, a foreign person (or local mandated private person) can serve a writ in those jurisdictions simply by going there and handing it to the relevant person. Other States, however, mostly in the civil law area,[42] take a different view, considering that the service of a writ is a sovereign or official act (as it generally is also in the internal context) and thus service on their territory without permission is an infringement of their sovereignty. Permission would normally be given through an international agreement laying down the procedure to be followed, such as provided for in Article 10 b of the Hague Service Convention – and provided no reservation has been made in respect of this provision.[43] In turn, such States would be unwilling to **2.14.20**

41 MLIJ Guide, N 102.

42 The list of reservations made against Article 10 of the Hague Service Convention (see www.hcch.net/en/instruments/conventions/status-table/?cid=17, column RES/N/D/DC) gives a good indication as to the degree of sovereignty considerations that states attach to the service of documents.

43 This can be consulted in the status table under www.hcch.net/de/instruments/conventions/status-table/?cid=17.

recognize a foreign judgment if the writ was served without participation of the local authorities (under the applicable laws) and/or in disregard of provisions of applicable treatises. The act of service would even be regarded as an infringement of their sovereignty.[44] In any event, virtually all jurisdictions will require the submission of *evidence of service* to obtain recognition.

2.14.21 Accordingly, subparagraph (a)(ii) provides that the court addressed may refuse to recognize and enforce the judgment if the writ was notified to the defendant in the receiving State in a manner that was incompatible with the rules of that State concerning service of documents.[45] According to the Guide (N 102), procedural irregularities that are capable of being cured retrospectively by the court in the receiving State would not be sufficient to justify refusal under this ground.

C. FRAUD IN THE OBTENTION OF THE INSOLVENCY-RELATED DECISION (B)

1. General Remarks

2.14.22 Article 14, subparagraph (b), sets out the ground of refusal that the judgment was obtained by fraud, which refers to a fraud committed in the course of the proceedings giving rise to the judgment.

2.14.23 According to the Guide to Enactment,[46] a case falling under this provision can be a fraud as to the jurisdiction of the court, though more often, it may be a fraud practised deliberately by one party to the proceedings on the court or on the other party. Examples include producing false evidence or deliberately suppressing material evidence. Further examples cited in the Guide to Enactment[47] include cases where the plaintiff deliberately served the writ, or caused it to be served, on the wrong address; where the requesting party (typically the plaintiff) deliberately gave the party to be notified (typically the defendant) incorrect information as to the time and place of the hearing; or where either

44 MLIJ Guide, N 102. In some countries this act is subject to criminal prosecution. This is the case for Switzerland with Article 271 of its criminal code: see Philipp Fischer and Deborah Hondius, 'Article 271 (1) of the Swiss Criminal Code: Myth or Reality?' (Jusletter 4. April 2022) www.lalive.law/wp-content/uploads/2022/04/Jusletter-Article-271-1-of-the-Swiss-Criminal-Code_-myth-or-reality_.pdf (accessed 11 July 2023); for an English translation of the provision see www.fedlex.admin.ch/eli/cc/54/757_781_799/en#art_271 (accessed 11 July 2023).

45 See the similar provisions in Art. 9.c.ii. and 7.1.a.ii. of the 2005 Hague Court Agreements and 2019 Judgments Conventions.

46 MLIJ Guide, N 104.

47 MLIJ Guide, N 103.

party sought to corrupt or mislead a judge, juror or witness, or deliberately conceal key evidence.

This provision is problematic in many jurisdictions: first, because it implies a 'revision au fond' of the decision itself, a second-guessing on the procedural behaviour of the parties by the recognizing court.[48] Mainly, however, it is problematic because of its unclear relationship or, more specifically, its overlap with the procedural *ordre public* (see hereinafter). **2.14.24**

2. Redundancy where Public Policy Clause Applies

In most legal systems fraud will be considered as falling within the scope of the public policy provision, in particular within the formal or procedural *ordre public* (public policy clause), which generally refers to major flaws (in the sense of major violations of internationally recognized legal principles) that are not necessarily found in the decision itself but could also be found in how the *proceedings* that led to the decision were conducted.[49] In *Pellegrini v Italy*,[50] the European Court of Human Rights saw a violation of Article 6 of the ECHR in the recognition of a foreign award that would – through its recognition – have the effect of such a violation. Under the EU Instruments, the ECJ, as well as national courts, have developed the concept that public policy implies a substantive as well as a procedural aspect.[51] There is, however, a considerable potential for overlap between the violation of procedural public policy and the notion of fraud in Article 14 (b) MLIJ.[52] **2.14.25**

48 According to the CJEU, an exception to that rule is admissibly applying the *ordre public* clause where 'the infringement would [...] constitute a manifest breach of a rule of law regarded as essential in the legal order of the State in which enforcement is sought or of a right recognised as being fundamental within that legal order' (CJEU Case C-302/13 flyLAL-Lithuanian Airlines, ECLI:EU:C:2014:2319 N 49, cited by Mankowski (fn 24), N 17 f. with further references.

49 See 1.6.12 on Article 6 of the MLCBI, and Articles 9.d and 7.1.b of the 2005 Hague Choice of Court and 2019 Judgments Conventions.

50 Pellegrini v Italy App no 30882/96 (ECtHR, 20 July 2001). For a list of protected procedural rights see Tanja Domeij and Paul Oberhammer, 'Article 34 Lugano Convention' in Anton K. Schnyder and Miguel Sogo (eds), *Lugano-Übereinkommen zum internationalen Verfahrensrecht* (2nd edn, DIKE 2023) N 23; Mankowski (n 24), N 27

51 See Mankowski (n 24), N 20–32, specifically on fraud (as a procedural ordre public violation); see N 27, citing Schlosser (fn 29) N 192. Mankowski discusses whether an alleged fraud in the first instance can still be a ground for refusal if there were ways to appeal the decision in the originating court. Such a requirement (to appeal if possible) would probably restrict the ground for refusal beyond what is intended by the provision in the MLIJ, particularly as paragraph (b) does not contain a reservation such as subparagraph (a)(i) in finem.

52 Metreveli (n 10), 343 argues that in countries 'where fraud falls within the public policy exception, [14](b) will narrow the exception', as its presence as a 'standalone basis for denying recognition' would 'almost always preempt denying recognition on more amorphous public policy grounds'. This argument appears unconvincing, as the grounds would either overlap or still be covered by the ordre public exception in its further fields of application.

2.14.26 Accordingly, those States in which the respect of elementary procedural rules (or of 'procedural fairness') is already part of their public policy exception and thus examined within the application of Article 7 MLIJ should consider making a policy decision not to include this ground for refusal in their national implementation of Article 14. They may do so whenever it appears to be clear from their law, jurisprudence and doctrine that the concept of fraud of this provision is indeed covered by the *ordre public* clause.

2.14.27 According to the Guide to Enactment,[53] however, this redundancy seems not to apply to all legal systems. In those other jurisdictions, this provision is recommended to be included as a form of clarification, namely where the notion of public policy is so narrow as to not include procedural fairness. Only in such jurisdictions will this clarification be necessary. In all other jurisdictions a clarification, in the sense that the fraud situations cited by the guide are covered by the procedural component of public policy,[54] together with renouncement of the inclusion of this ground for refusal, would be the preferable option for legislators.

D. INCONSISTENCY WITH ANOTHER DECISION: C AND D

1. General Scope

2.14.28 Article 14 (c) and (d) concerns the situation in which there is a conflict between the judgment for which recognition and enforcement is sought and another judgment given in a dispute *between the same parties* (or their legal successors). Both subparagraphs are satisfied where two judgments are inconsistent, but they operate in different ways.[55]

2. Inconsistency with a Judgement of the Receiving State: (c)

2.14.29 Article 14 (c) is concerned with the case where the foreign judgment is inconsistent with a judgment issued by a court in the receiving State. In such a situation, the receiving court may give preference to a judgment issued in its own State, even if that judgment was issued after the issue of the inconsistent

53 MLIJ Guide, N 104.
54 See 1.6.12 on Art. 6 MLCBI.
55 See 1.6.12 on Art. 6 MLCBI.

judgment in the originating court[56] – but before the request for recognition of the foreign decision.[57]

For this provision to be satisfied, the parties must be the same (or their respective legal successors), but it is not necessary – unlike under the examples cited in para. 2.14.38 – for the cause of action or subject matter to be the same[58] (on the different situation in subparagraph (d) see para. 2.14.33 ff). The standard is thus a slightly lower one than under (d) and the concept of 'irreconcilable' decision that underlies that provision (and most international instruments such as the Brussels/Lugano and Hague instruments).[59] Still, there must be an 'inconsistency' between the judgments. According to the Guide to Enactment[60] these inconsistencies between the judgments occur when findings of fact or conclusions of law, which are based on the same issues, are different – even if they are part of a broader claim and even a different subject matter. **2.14.30**

This ground for refusal exception is highly problematic if interpreted too widely. As a ground for refusal, the provision should be limited to situations where the facts (and the parties) underlying the conclusions are the same or part of the same complex of facts, even where the grounds that were the basis of the claims are different and/or one of the decisions covers a broader set of facts. If the provision was, instead, to be interpreted as to apply to further contradictions between judgments (for instance, in the way the law is applied to a particular fact), this interpretation would result in a multiplicity of possible grounds for refusal. Enacting States seem thus better advised to follow the example of the Hague Conventions and of (d): see 2.14.33. In other words, a mere 'inconsistency' should not suffice, but a risk of *contradictory* decisions concerning fully or partly the same matter should be demonstrated. Considering that Article 14 is a discretionary list that could (and should) be adapted to the scope of the implemented MLIJ as a whole,[61] implementation **2.14.31**

56 See 1.6.12 on Art. 6 MLCBI.

57 The request for recognition should trigger the *lis pendens* in respect of the parties and the litigation involved and thus exclude a later proceeding. It should be possible to raise the *lis pendens* exception of the foreign decision in the course of the local proceedings, provided the foreign decision has been filed before and can be recognized in the receiving country (see the examples of such provisions in Article 45.1.c of the Brussels Recast Regulation, Article 34.3 Lugano Convention and Articles 9.f and 7.1.e of the 2005 Hague Court Agreements and 2019 Judgments Conventions). Under the Brussels and Lugano Instruments the situation itself should not even arise thanks to the provision on the lis pendens rule contained in Article 29 (Mankowski (n 24), N 61a on situations where the rule discussed here is nevertheless necessary) and 27 (Lugano). The MLIJ does not provide for such rules (as it does not regulate direct competence).

58 MLIJ Guide, N 105.

59 See para. 2.14.38.

60 MLIJ Guide, N 105.

61 See 2.14.01 ff.

of this provision in national law should follow the stricter approach and be modelled on the provisions cited in 2.14.38.

3. Inconsistency with A(nother) Foreign Judgment (d)

2.14.32 Article 14 (d) concerns foreign judgments, where the judgment for which recognition and enforcement is sought is inconsistent with an earlier judgment issued in another State. In that situation, a judgment may be refused recognition and enforcement only if the following cumulative conditions are given, as discussed in the Guide to Enactment[62] referring to conditions (a) to (d):

(a) the judgment to be recognized was issued after the conflicting judgment

2.14.33 This condition requires that the decision of the receiving country which might be inconsistent with the one to be recognized has been 'issued' before the foreign decision, so that priority in time is a relevant consideration. According to that text, in respect of both decisions, the time of the 'issuing' of the decisions (and not, for instance, when recognition is sought or when the proceedings had been initiated) is relevant. A decision can only create an 'inconsistency' once it is final. Accordingly, the moment when it is 'issued' should refer to the day each decision becomes enforceable, that is, when no appeal with suspensive effect is (any longer) available or it has been dismissed.[63] Unlike the Brussels or Lugano regimes,[64] the MLIJ does not regulate direct jurisdiction and does not mandate to its internal courts the respect of foreign *lis pendens*.[65] Instead it gives priority – in recognition – to the internal decisions, even where the foreign proceeding would have been initiated earlier.[66]

(b) the parties to the dispute are the same

2.14.34 The second condition (b) establishes that the parties to the dispute must be the same. 'The same' encompasses any legal successors (as a consequence of, for instance, a merger (of legal persons), or, for natural persons, of the succession through inheritance, as well as any other legal succession).[67] This provision is

62 MLIJ Guide, N 106.

63 See 2.14.30.

64 Referring to the Instruments cited in n 28.

65 See Mankowski (n 24), N 61 and the analogous provisions in the provisions cited in n 29.

66 Mankowski (n 24), fn 381 in N 71 on a (failed) proposal to modify this situation in the BXL Ibis context. Where the MLIJ is implemented in the framework of a more comprehensive codification of rules of international civil procedure, such rules would incorporate a lis pendens rule (addressing the internal courts), and these situations should only rarely occur.

67 Trevor Hartly and Dosato Dogauchi, 'Explanatory Report to the Hague Choice of Court Convention 2005, Off-print of the proceedings of the 20th session, Tome III, Choice of Court Agreements' (2005) https://assets.hcch.net/docs/0de60e2f-e002-408e-98a7-5638e1ebac65.pdf, 831 n. 231: 'This also applies under

to be interpreted in line with the similar provisions found in other multilateral instruments and case law developed in respect of European (Brussels/Lugano) and Hague instruments.[68]

(c) the subject matter of both decisions is the same

The third condition requires that the subject matter of both decisions is the same. Unlike under the reservation cited under Article 14(c),[69] the inconsistency here must go 'to the central issue of the cause of action'.[70] This notion is consistent with that of similar provisions found in instruments such as those cited in 2.14.10. **2.14.35**

(d) and the earlier conflicting judgment fulfils the conditions necessary for recognition in the enacting State, whether under this Law, other national law or a convention regime.[71]

The last condition (d) (for the inconsistency to establish a valid ground for refusal) requires that the (earlier, conflicting) judgment fulfils the conditions necessary for recognition in the enacting State, whether under national law (implementing the MLIJ) or an applicable convention regime.[72] **2.14.36**

Similar provisions to Article 14 (d) exist in Articles 45.1.d of the Brussels Recast Regulation, 34.4 of the Lugano Convention and Articles 9.d and 7.1.f of the 2005 Hague Court Agreements and 2019 Judgments Conventions.[73] In order to provide a consistency of concepts and terminology, this provision should be applied and interpreted in the same manner. **2.14.37**

E. INTERFERENCE WITH THE ADMINISTRATION OF A LOCAL INSOLVENCY PROCEEDING: (E)

Subparagraph (e) of Article 14 addresses the possible interference of the foreign decision (to be recognized) with the conduct and administration of a local insolvency proceeding over the same debtor/defendant. Its purpose is **2.14.38**

sub-para. f). The requirement that the parties must be the same will be satisfied if the parties bound by the judgments are the same even if the parties to the proceedings are different, for example where one judgment is against a particular person and the other judgment is against the successor to that person.'

68 In particular the ECJ's case law and doctrine developed in respect of Articles 33 and 29 of the Brussels Ibis Recast Regulation (see Mankowski [n 24] N 7 on article 29).

69 See 2.14.11 ff.

70 MLIJ Guide, N 106.

71 MLIJ Guide, N 106.

72 MLIJ Guide, N 106.

73 See n 28.

to preserve the primacy of main proceedings in the recognizing jurisdiction.[74] This ground for refusal is quite specific to this model law. As a consequence, the main source for its interpretation is its materials.

2.14.39 According to the Guide to Enactment,[75] proceedings affected by this provision would be the proceedings to which the judgment is related or other insolvency proceedings (that is, concurrent proceedings) concerning the same insolvency debtor. Helpfully, given the broadness of the concept of 'interference', the provision itself gives examples of what might constitute such interference.

2.14.40 The first example given is inconsistency of the foreign decision with a (local) stay. According to the Guide to Enactment,[76] this situation would typically arise where the stay permitted the commencement or continuation of individual actions to the extent necessary to preserve a claim, but did not permit subsequent recognition and enforcement of any ensuing judgment. It could also arise where the stay did not permit the commencement or continuation of such individual actions and the proceeding giving rise to the judgment was commenced after the issue of the stay (and was thus potentially in violation of the stay).[77]

2.14.41 A further example refers to instances where recognition of the insolvency-related judgment could upset cooperation between multiple insolvency proceedings or result in giving effect to a judgment on a matter or cause of action that should have been pursued in the (local) jurisdiction of the insolvency proceeding (for example, because the insolvency proceeding is the main proceeding or is taking place in the State in which the assets that are the subject of the judgment are located). One possible instance would be the case where the (generally main) insolvency proceedings would provide for all claims against the debtor to be submitted in that proceeding in order to establish a schedule of claims. It will generally imply that disputes over the admission and ranking of claims will be drawn (by the *vis attractiva concursus*) to that same jurisdictions' courts. A concurring, and possibly contradicting claim abroad – and the recognition of the resulting decision in the jurisdiction of the main proceedings – would clearly create an 'inconsistency' with the claims schedule and any local court proceedings regarding that schedule. Such instances should, however, be limited to

74 Metriveli (n 10), 12 f. discussing how such a provision could have modified the outcome of some decisions.
75 MLIJ Guide, N 107.
76 MLIJ Guide, N 107.
77 MLIJ Guide, N 107.

situations where the insolvency preceded the proceedings abroad and where the contradiction is unavoidable.[78]

The mere fact that recognition of a foreign decision would deplete the value of the debtor's insolvency estate should not – *per se* – be a sufficient ground for refusal.[79] **2.14.42**

F. ADVERSE EFFECT ON CREDITORS OR OTHER THIRD PARTIES (F)

Subparagraph (f) of Article 14 applies (only) to judgments that materially affect the rights of creditors and other stakeholders in the manner referred to specifically in that subparagraph. The provision allows the receiving court to refuse recognition of such judgments where (i) the judgement materially affects the rights of creditors generally, and (ii) the interests of creditors and other interested persons, including the debtor, were not adequately protected in the proceeding in which the judgment was issued. **2.14.43**

The provision is drafted in a manner and with the purpose to replicate Article 22 MLCBI so as to apply to the kind of judgments that might also be subject to the MLCBI.[80] It is a typical result of the 'overlap' between the MLCBI and the MLIJ as a consequence of the broad substantial scope of the MLIJ.[81] In a consistent implementation, where the judgments covered by this provision would also be covered by the implementation of the MLCBI, this provision would appear redundant and would not need to be implemented (again).[82] **2.14.44**

As to the judgments covered by Article 14(f)(i), the Guide to Enactment (N 107) cites judgments that materially affect the rights of creditors, giving the example of 'determining whether a plan of reorganization or liquidation should be confirmed, a discharge of the debtor or of debts should be granted or a voluntary or out-of-court restructuring agreement should be approved'. **2.14.45**

---

78 Reference is made here to the litigation in the cases of Sabena vs. Swissair, see Rodrigo Rodriguez, 'Switzerland on Airline Insolvencies – High Noon at The Hague Called Off' (2011) 4 IILR 423–31, and the decisions of the Swiss Federal Court 137 III 268 and 140 III 320 (see www.bger.ch) confirming non-recognition of Belgian claims. The case briefly led to proceedings before the International Court of Justice in the The Hague, initiated (and later withdrawn) by the Kingdom of Belgium, see Dr. Bart-Jan van het Kaar & Gilad Kaplan, 'Airline Dispute Lands in ICJ: A Commentary on the Swissair/Sabena Case' www.haguejusticeportal.net/Docs/Commentaries%20PDF/Commentary_Sabena_EN.pdf. accessed 12 July 2023.

79 MLIJ Guide, N 107 *in finem*.

80 See N 1.2.02 ff. MLCBI.

81 See, on the scope of the MLIJ, 1.2.11 ff.

82 See Churchill (n 11), 236 on the potential conflict of provisions for recognition in the MLCBI and the MLIJ.

2.14.46 The cumulative condition for the application of this provision is that the 'creditors and other interested persons, including the debtor' were not 'adequately protected'. This provision only has a separate relevance insofar as it would protect creditors or 'other interested persons' that were not a party in the proceedings to be recognized. Where the rights of any party to the proceedings (typically of the debtor) was not 'adequately protected', it would already constitute a ground for refusal under the (procedural) *ordre public* clause[83] and also under the fraud clause of Article 14 (b).[84]

2.14.47 According to the Guide to Enactment,[85] the creditors and other stakeholders referred to would only be those whose interests might be affected by the foreign judgment. A creditor whose interests remain unaffected by, for example, a plan of reorganization or a voluntary restructuring agreement (for example, because their claims are to be paid in full) would not have a right to oppose recognition and enforcement of a judgment under the provision. Subparagraph (f) would further not apply to other types of insolvency-related judgments that resolve bilateral disputes between two parties where the effect of such judgments on creditors and other stakeholders (if any) is only indirect (for example, via the judgment's effect on the size of the insolvency estate).[86]

G. IMPROPER ASSERTION OF JURISDICTION BY THE ORIGINATING COURT: (G) AND (H)

1. General Purpose and Method of Subparagaphs (g) and (h)

2.14.48 Article 14(g) permits refusal of recognition and enforcement if the originating court exercised jurisdiction solely on a ground other than the ones listed in subparagraphs (i) to (iv) (the 'safe harbours').[87] Subparagraph (g) works differently to the other subparagraphs of Article 14. While those provisions are freestanding discretionary grounds on which the court may refuse recognition

---

83 See Article 7 MLIJ.

84 See 2.14.23.

85 Guide, N 108.

86 MLIJ Guide, N 109: 'In those instances, permitting a judgment debtor to resist recognition and enforcement by citing third-party interests could unnecessarily generate opportunities for wasteful re-litigation of the cause of action giving rise to the judgment. For example, if a court in State A determined that the debtor owned a particular asset and issued a judgment against a local creditor resolving that ownership dispute, and the insolvency representative then sought to enforce that judgment in State B, the creditor should not be able to resist enforcement in B by raising arguments about the interests of other creditors and stakeholders that are not relevant to that dispute.'

87 MLIJ Guide, N 196. See also Metreveli (n 10), 13 and Rodriguez (n 9), 126.

and enforcement of a judgment, under subparagraph (g) one of the grounds *must* be met or recognition and enforcement of the judgment can be refused.[88]

The Guide to Enactment[89] refers to the accepted grounds of jurisdiction as safe harbours that render any provision refusing recognition on the grounds of jurisdiction inapplicable if the originating court satisfies any one of the safe harbours. The originating court does not need to have explicitly relied on or made findings regarding the relevant basis for jurisdiction, so long as that basis for jurisdiction existed at the relevant time (that is, when the claim was filed). The originating court's reliance on additional or different jurisdictional grounds (for instance, a place of performance, which, however, happens to coincide with the defendant's domicile or the agreed forum) does not prevent one of the safe harbours from applying, if it covers the same forum. **2.14.49**

Similar (generally less complex) provisions on 'indirect competence' can be found in virtually all international instruments on cross-border recognition of judgements.[90] **2.14.50**

2. Explicit Consent to the Exercise of Jurisdiction: (g)(i)

Subparagraph (g)(i) of Article 14 provides that the originating court's exercise of jurisdiction must be accepted if the judgment debtor *explicitly consented* to that exercise of jurisdiction. **2.14.51**

As opposed to most other relevant legal instruments on recognition and enforcement,[91] the text of Article 14 implicitly (and the Guide to Enactment[92] explicitly) allows for expressing such consent not only in writing but also *orally*. Where an oral agreement is accepted, no particular form will be required either for the written agreement (writing, fax, email, messaging). The existence of explicit consent is a question of fact to be determined by the receiving court, generally on the basis of the documents submitted in accordance with Article 13. **2.14.52**

According to the Guide to Enactment,[93] the consent could be addressed to the court (for example, the judgment debtor informed the court that no objections to jurisdiction would be raised) or to the other party (for example, **2.14.53**

88 MLIJ Guide, N 110.
89 MLIJ Guide, N 110.
90 See the sources cited in n 28.
91 See 15.51.
92 N 112.
93 MLIJ Guide, N 112.

the judgment debtor agreed with the other party that the proceeding should be brought in the originating court) either in advance of, at the beginning of, or even during the proceedings. An 'implicit' consent would be addressed by subparagraph (g)(ii), hereinafter.

3. Submission to Jurisdiction without Objection (g)(ii)

2.14.54 Subparagraph (g)(ii) of Article 14 provides that the originating court's exercise of jurisdiction must (also) be accepted if the judgment debtor submitted to the jurisdiction of the originating court by presenting their case without objecting to jurisdiction or the exercise of jurisdiction within any time frame applicable to such an objection, unless it was evident that such an objection would not have succeeded under the law of the originating State.

2.14.55 The wording of this clause appears to be inspired by Article 45.1.b of the Brussels I (recast) Regulation, Article 34.2 Lugano Convention and Articles 9.c.i. and 7.1.a of the 2005 Hague Court Agreements and 2019 Judgments Convention. Accordingly, it would appear appropriate to also draw inspiration from any case law developed by courts (for instance, by the ECJ in respect of the Brussels I (recast) Regulation) or doctrine. Under those principles, a valid submission requires an answer on the merits from the defendant without at the same time (or separately) having raised the lack of jurisdiction of the court. 'Playing dead', that is, not answering a claim at all, cannot be considered a submission. Neither so when the defendant answers on the merits but states clearly that he contests the court's jurisdiction (and the answer on the substance is nevertheless submitted in the event that the court disregards the defendant's opposition and accepts the claim).[94]

2.14.56 In the above circumstances, the judgment debtor cannot oppose recognition and enforcement by claiming that the originating court did not have jurisdiction. The method of raising the objection to jurisdiction is a matter for the law of the originating State. A receiving court, in an appropriate case, may make inquiries where matters giving rise to concern become apparent.

4. Coherence with own Grounds (*'Spiegelbildprinzip'*): (g)(iii)

2.14.57 Subparagraph (g)(iii) of Article 14 provides that the originating court's exercise of jurisdiction must be accepted if it was exercised on a basis on which the

94 Mankowski (n 24), N 57 on Article 45.

receiving court could have exercised jurisdiction itself had an analogous dispute taken place in the receiving State.

This provision enshrines the principle of reciprocity or '*Spiegelbildprinzip*' ('mirroring principle' in German),[95] that is, of mirroring its own grounds for direct competence and establishing the same principles as acceptable grounds for recognition. Despite a certain logic, consequent implementation of this principle in national international private law rules is rather uncommon. A State willing to implement this provision will have to apply some restraint in respect of its own jurisdictional rules in order to avoid having to recognize decisions based on exorbitant grounds of jurisdiction, which at least gives that provision a positive 'restraining' effect on legislation. **2.14.58**

5. Grounds Incompatible with National Law (g)(iv)

Subparagraph (g)(iv) of Article 14 applies to jurisdictional grounds which, while not explicitly grounds upon which the receiving court could have exercised jurisdiction (as provided for under iii), would nevertheless not be incompatible with the law of the receiving State. **2.14.59**

The purpose of subparagraph (g)(iv) is to discourage courts from refusing recognition and enforcement of a judgment in cases in which the originating court's exercise of jurisdiction was not unreasonable (in the eyes of the receiving state), even if the precise basis of jurisdiction would not be available in the receiving state (see iii).[96] According to the Guide to Enactment,[97] this recognition should generally be the case whenever that exercise was not incompatible with the central tenets of procedural fairness in the receiving State. **2.14.60**

Considering the discretionary character of the provisions of Article 14,[98] the implementation of this provision in a particular national regime would highly be conditioned by that particular jurisdiction's legal tradition. In jurisdictions pertaining to legal traditions where legal certainty and clearly defined jurisdictional criteria play an essential role – such as, generally, civil law jurisdictions – the provision of (g)(iv) appears difficult to apply and – in the light of the very 'generous' subparagraph (iii) – probably *unnecessary*. For jurisdictions pertaining to legal traditions with a more open approach to jurisdictional criteria, **2.14.61**

95 See § 343 of the German Insolvenzordnung (InsO); see www.gesetze-im-internet.de/inso/__343.html (accessed 12 July 2023).

96 MLIJ Guide, N 115.

97 *Ibid.*

98 See 2.14.02.

where, for instance, any limitations are deduced from constitutional principles (of 'due process', such as, for instance, in the US),[99] an implementation of subparagraph (iv) would make more sense. As a general guideline, the grounds of jurisdiction of (g) (i)–(ii) and a (closed) list of non-exorbitant long-arm jurisdictional grounds will generally be 'the central tenets of procedural fairness on the receiving state'.[100]

6. Recognition of the Insolvency Proceedings and Judgements Originating in Certain States: (h)

(a) Recognition of Judgements from Related Proceedings' COMI

2.14.62 Subparagraph (h) of Article 14 is tailored to jurisdictions that have implemented or are in the process of implementing the MLCBI (together with the MLIJ).[101] It is, however, just as pertinent to all other jurisdictions that apply the criterion of COMI as their main jurisdictional attachment point for the purposes of main proceedings – as is the case under the EIR and under national provisions that are inspired by the EIR (more than by the MLCBI).[102]

---

99 See the constitutional basis in the US in 2.14.05 and 2.14.14. The US Supreme Court constant case law bases jurisdictional limitations to the due process clauses cited therein, (See International Shoe Co. v. Washington, 326 US 310 (1945). Collier on the Rules of Civil Procedure, Rule 4. Summons, FRCP (24, with further references) recalls that '[t]here remain constitutional limitations on the exercise of territorial jurisdiction by federal courts over persons outside the United States'. These restrictions arise from the Fifth Amendment, which requires that any defendant have affiliating contacts with the United States sufficient to justify the exercise of personal jurisdiction over that party (Wells Fargo & Co. v Wells Fargo Express Co., 556 F.2d 406, 418 (9th Cir.1977)), and that there also may be a further Fifth Amendment constraint in that a plaintiff's forum selection might be so inconvenient to a defendant that it would be a denial of 'fair play and substantial justice' required by the due process clause, even though the defendant had significant affiliating contacts with the United States (See World-Wide Volkswagen Corp. v Woodson, 444 U.S. 286, 293–4 (1980).

100 MLIJ Guide, N 115. John A. Pottow, 'The Dialogic Aspect of Soft Law in International Insolvency: Discord, Digression, and Development' (2019) 40 Michigan JIL 479, 501 sees a 'thinly veiled' rebuke of Rubin in this note of the Guide. It does, however, not result from the discussions that Rubin was an issue during the discussions of this provisions (irrespective of the outcome), given that a different article was dedicated to that issue (Article X).

101 The MLIJ Guide (N 116) speaks of an 'optional provision' – that is, a 'more optional' provision than the other provisions. However, this provision is an essential one. The 'optionality' lies primarily in the attachment to the COMI criterion, but not in the attachment to the recognition of the foreign proceedings to which the decision is related.

102 Several jurisdictions, particularly in Europe, have adapted their autonomous provisions on recognition of foreign insolvency proceedings (applicable to situations where a debtor had its COMI outside the EU or in Denmark) to the EIR and have implemented the COMI as their main criterion for indirect jurisdictions. Even where jurisdictions have not formally adopted the MLCBI, their provisions are often very similar to its key provisions (recognition of COMI-based main proceedings, standing of the foreign administrator, remedy available in accordance with national law, that is, directly or through ancillary proceedings). However, jurisdictions that have not implemented the MLCBI will generally only recognize foreign main proceedings, but will not grant any cross-border effect or recognition to non-main proceedings.

The key principle under that provision is that recognition of an insolvency-related judgment can be refused when the judgment originates from a State whose insolvency proceeding (the one to which the judgment of which recognition is sought is related) is not or would not be susceptible of recognition under the MLCBI. **2.14.63**

In States that have implemented the MLCBI, the reason why a main proceeding may not be recognizable may be because the originating State is not the insolvency debtor's COMI (in the case of a main proceeding) or there is not an establishment (in the case of a non-main proceeding and a decision relating to that proceeding).[103] In States that only provide for the recognition of main proceedings (generally at the debtor's COMI), that is, that have only partly implemented the MLCBI and/or are following the model of the EIR, a decision stemming from a different jurisdiction (that the related proceedings at the debtor's COMI) may be refused. **2.14.64**

The Guide to Enactment[104] states that the language in the chapeau of the Article does not require an insolvency proceeding to have actually commenced in the originating State.[105] Though such a situation is conceivable, it is difficult to imagine specific cases, given the limited number of insolvency-related judgments that could qualify as such before an insolvency proceeding would even have opened.[106] **2.14.65**

(b) Exceptions

Subparagraph (h) of Article 14 addresses the exceptional recognition of judgments issued in a State that is not the related insolvency proceedings' COMI (or, in some cases, establishment) under the preceding paragraph. **2.14.66**

---

103 MLIJ Guide, N 117.

104 MLIJ Guide, N 117.

105 '[O]nly that, were such a proceeding to commence in that State, recognition and enforcement could be refused if the proceeding would not be susceptible of recognition.' The Guide further states the following Example: '[A]n insolvency debtor has its COMI in State A and an establishment in State B, but only a main proceeding in A has commenced and no non-main insolvency proceeding has yet commenced in B. Some other litigation in B results in an insolvency-related judgment that is relevant to the insolvency estate. The insolvency representative from A wants to seek recognition or enforcement of the insolvency-related judgment from B in State C, which has enacted the Model Law and the MLCBI. The court in C would see that the judgment comes from a State whose insolvency proceeding would be recognizable under the MLCBI (i.e., the debtor has an establishment in B and a non-main proceeding could thus be commenced), even though no such recognizable proceeding has yet commenced in B. The receiving court thus cannot refuse recognition on the basis of article 14, subparagraph (h).'

106 See, on possible candidates 1.2.16 (n 16).

2.14.67 Those exceptions generally relate to the situation where the judgment concerns only assets that were located in that state at the time the proceeding giving rise to the judgment commenced. The Guide to Enactment[107] highlights that in those circumstances it may be useful for that judgment to be recognized because, for example, it resolves issues of ownership that are relevant to the insolvency estate and that could only be resolved in that jurisdiction, rather than in the jurisdiction of the debtor's COMI or establishment. These provisions are intended to assist in the recovery of additional assets for the insolvency estate, as well as the resolution of disputes relating to those assets – essentially by not hindering the recognition of favourable awards obtained abroad. At the same time, the exceptions should not result in undermining the Model Law framework by encouraging the resolution of issues that should have been resolved in the State where the debtor has or had its COMI or an establishment in a different jurisdiction.[108] This difficult weighing of interest is achieved by the following criteria.

2.14.68 Subparagraphs (h)(i) and (ii) outline two conditions that must be met cumulatively in order to establish an exception to the general principle of non-recognition of subparagraph (h).

2.14.69 Subparagraph (h)(i) requires the insolvency representative of an insolvency proceeding that is or could have been recognized under subparagraph (h) (paras 2.14.63 to 2.14.66) in the enacting State (that is, the insolvency representative of a main or non-main proceeding) to have participated in the proceeding giving rise to the judgment. Such participation must have involved engaging with the substantive merits of the cause of action being pursued.[109] According to the Guide,[110] participation shall mean that the insolvency representative was a party to the proceedings as a representative of the debtor's insolvency estate or had standing to intervene in those proceedings by appearing in court and making representations on the substantive merits of the case. The proceedings might have been instituted by the insolvency debtor against a third party or have been instituted against the debtor.

2.14.70 Subparagraph (h)(ii) adds to the requirement in subparagraph (h)(i) and requires the judgment in question relates solely to assets that were located in the originating State at the time of commencement of the proceeding giving

107 MLIJ Guide, N 118, See Rodriguez (n 9), 126 f.
108 MLIJ Guide, N 118.
109 MLIJ Guide, N 119.
110 MLIJ Guide, N 119.

rise to the judgment (*forum rei sitae*). With regard to the reference to 'assets of the debtor' (meaning the insolvency debtor), the Guide to Enactment[111] refers to the UNCITRAL Legislative Guide on Insolvency, according to which '"Assets of the debtor" are: property, rights and interests of the debtor, including rights and interests in property, whether or not in the possession of the debtor, tangible or intangible, movable or immovable, including the debtor's interests in encumbered assets or in third party-owned assets'[112] and cites as a further example intellectual property registered in the originating State where it is neither the debtor's COMI nor a state in which the debtor has an establishment.

7. A Fix for *Rubin*?

One of the purposes of the MLIJ was to address (or, more specifically, reverse) the UK High Court's decision in *Rubin*.[113] The article in the MLIJ specifically intended to achieve that objective is Article X (see on this consequently [2.X.01 ff]. Views are split on whether the MLIJ actually achieved that purpose or not (one could argue whether that was a legitimate purpose at all).[114] **2.14.71**

Some doctrinal views have raised the question whether Article 14 is the provision with the potential to reverse *Rubin*.[115] These views focus on section (g) and, mainly, section (h) of Article 14.[116] Section (g) has the potential to reverse *Rubin* in situations where national law would provide direct grounds for jurisdiction in a (reversed) *Rubin*-situation (that is, against a foreign-domiciled defendant not having agreed neither tacitly not explicitly to the jurisdiction of the court in an insolvency-related proceeding, see paras 2.14.58 ff). **2.14.72**

---

111 MLIJ Guide, N 120.

112 Legislative Guide, Introd., para. 12(b).

113 Rubin v Eurofinance SA [2012] UKSC 46, see P2.03 ff. as well as, in the particular context, Rodriguez (n 9), 112, as well as Article X.

114 If one is to agree that the principles established in Rubin (see, on this particular issue, 2.X.06 and 2.X.31) may be reasonable from a jurisdictional standpoint, as they may appear particularly to civil law views, the question is justified as to why this decision needed to be reversed at all. Against that background, it can come as no surprise that the negotiated MLCBI did not finally – without the assistance of the optional Article X – reverse Rubin. Pottow (n 100), at 501, argues that Article 14 (g)(iv) might have done 'the job' after all. This will depend on the implementing jurisdiction.

115 Pottow (n 100), 499 ff., see further references in 2.X.01 ff.

116 Churchill (n 11), 242 identifies another necessary 'fix' to Rubin in Article 14(a)(ii) by allowing service of process in the UK for the adverse party to submit or make an appearance. This 'fix' may appear necessary under US law but would not by itself be sufficient to fulfil the (further) requirements of Rubin (see also Pottow (n 100), 501). See also the criticism of Rubin from the standpoint of the MLIJ by Metreveli (n 10), 21 and Irit Mevorach, 'Overlapping International Instruments for Enforcement of Insolvency Judgements: Undermining or Strengthening Universalism?', European Business Organization Law Review (2021), https://doi.org/10.1007/s40804-021-00204-4, 300.

2.14.73 A second chance for Article 14 to 'fix' the *Rubin* issue '*en passant*' is offered by section (g)(iv).[117] As explained under paras 2.14.60 ff, this provision provides for the recognizing State to recognize further grounds for indirect jurisdictions (in addition to those covered by (g)(i) to (g)(iii)) provided these grounds are 'not incompatible' with national law. The unchartered territory of 'incompatibility' leaves the implementing state a wide margin of appreciation – leading from virtually not going beyond (g)(i) to (g)(iii) to limiting the 'incompatibility' to outright unconstitutional exorbitant jurisdictions.[118] The second approach may in many jurisdictions allow for a *Rubin* 'fix' – but possibly not in those jurisdictions where it was most needed. After all, *Rubin* itself notes an incompatibility, which would have to be re-qualified in the light of (g)(iv)) – with uncertain outcome. Some views argue that Article 14, or more precisely a more specific national implementation, would at least add some predictability to the recognition of insolvency-related judgments.[119]

2.14.74 On a more general point, when implementing Article 14 (g)(iv), the legislator will be well advised to specify which are the boundaries of a 'compatible' exercise of jurisdiction abroad. The standard of 'compatibility' is, in our view, lower than that of a constitutional issue (certainly covered by that provision, see fn 47 on the US jurisprudence on 'minimum contacts') or a violation of jurisdictional public policy.[120] Especially civil law states, where the defendant's forum plays just as important a role as the limitation of exorbitant jurisdictions,[121] will still find in section (h) sufficient grounds to uphold – as they always did – the jurisdictions ground for refusal found in *Rubin*. However, section (g)(iv) can be a door-opener to recognition in a *Rubin* situation in jurisdictions with a more flexible approach to jurisdictional principles (generally the common law area). The ball is thus again in the implementing states' court.

---

117 See Pottow (n 100), 501 and 2.X.09 *in finem*.

118 As Pottow (n 100), 499 puts it: 'There are two opposed concerns: the excessive reach of states with exorbitant exercises of jurisdiction on the one hand, and the need to bind recalcitrant defendants who seek to evade legitimate exercises of jurisdiction on the other.'

119 Metreveli (n 10), 13. The UK consultation on the possible implementation of the MLIJ (see www.gov.uk/government/consultations/implementation-of-two-uncitral-model-laws-on-insolvency/implementation-of-two-uncitral-model-laws-on-insolvency-consultation, accessed 12 July 2023) proposes to implement Article X as well to partly implement Article 14 (through court practice), though still retaining a margin of discretion for the courts.

120 See 1.6.01 ff. Pottow (n 100) leaves the question open ('arguable'), p.501, fn 105.

121 See, for instance, Article 2 of the Brussels Recast Regulation and the Lugano Convention, building the main axis of the jurisdictional system. Article 3 of the Lugano Convention (identical to Art. 3 of the predecessors of the Brussels Recast Regulation) highlights the importance for its jurisdictions to eliminate exorbitant fora. The Hague Judgements Convention of 2019 cites the defendant's domicile as the first 'acceptable' ground.

H. FINAL REMARKS

Together with the definition of 'insolvency-related judgment' in Article 2, the list of grounds for refusal in Article 14 is one of the two key provisions of the MLIJ. As stated previously, the length and complexity – and the sheer number – of grounds for refusal create the impression of a MLIJ being more about impeding recognition than about enabling it. This was certainly not the drafters' intention, but is an undeniable result of the complexity of the task that the MLIJ is deemed to fulfil. Two main factors contributed to the over-complexity of Article 14. **2.14.75**

- First was the concept of the MLIJ as a stand-alone instrument. As a consequence of this conception, the MLIJ needs to implement (and repeat) all necessary elements of a model law about recognition and enforcement of foreign decisions. This must include reservations such as the public policy clause but also procedural provisions and even general provisions on the interpretation of the law (see Articles 15 and 16 of the MLIJ).
- Second was the broad substantive scope of the MLIJ, covering both typical insolvency-related judgements *inter partes*, such as avoidance actions,[122] but also actual proceedings or decisions closing proceedings with an *erga omnes* effect, such as discharges.[123] The result of this broad scope is a cumulation of precautions in the form of grounds for refusal, both those conceived against *inter partes* decisions and those to protect the interests of third parties, typical to the effect *erga omnes* proceedings. [124]

Enacting States have the possibility to address the issue cited in the previous note and to improve the chances of this model law really encouraging recognition by taking a clearer stance on the scope, for instance, limiting it to the decisions referred to in Article 2 (d),[125] leaving other decisions to be clearly subject to the MLCBI (through Article X). This choice should, in turn, allow to reduce the number of grounds for refusal in Article 14, for example by renouncing to lit. e and f.[126] **2.14.76**

Another alternative may consist in implementing Article 14 as proposed by the MLIJ but with a clear message that its grounds for refusal are to be applied restrictively. In turn, despite being the only provision explicitly referred to as **2.14.77**

122 See 2.2.26.

123 See 2.2.34 ff.

124 See also the similar criticism of Rodriguez (n 9), 131.

125 See 2.2.17 ff, in particular 2.2.17–2.2.33.

126 See 2.14.39 and 2.14.44.

'optional', an attachment of the decision to be recognized to a recognizable COMI-based main proceedings (or registered seat-based, if that is a main or alternative criterion in the jurisdiction in question) would be an essential requirement, irrespective of whether the MLCBI has been already implemented or not.[127]

127 The UNCITRAL Secretariat's proposal for a Consolidated Text of the UNCITRAL Model Laws on Cross-Border Insolvency, Recognition and Enforcement of Insolvency-related Judgments and Enterprise Group Insolvency (2021), https://uncitral.un.org/sites/uncitral.un.org/files/media-documents/uncitral/en/v2104338_consolidated_text.pdf> (accessed 11 July 2023), does not explore this possibility by a specific drafting of Article 14, but reminds that 'It is important that enacting States consider the relationship between subparagraph 14(f) (article 14(f) of the MLIJ) and article 22 of the MLCBI'.

Article 15

EQUIVALENT EFFECT

Rodrigo Rodriguez

1. An insolvency-related judgment recognized or enforceable under this Law shall be given the same effect it [has in the originating State] or [would have had if it had been issued by a court of this State].[1]
2. If the insolvency-related judgment provides for relief that is not available under the law of this State, that relief shall, to the extent possible, be adapted to relief that is equivalent to, but does not exceed, its effects under the law of the originating State.

A. INTRODUCTION TO ARTICLE 15

Article 15 addresses the important question of how to give effect to the foreign decision in the enacting state after the decision's recognition (subparagraph 1) and offers different options to the enacting legislator. Subparagraph 2 addresses the situation where the foreign judgment provides for relief that is not available under the law of the enacting state. The MLCBI has no corresponding provisions. **2.15.01**

1 The enacting State may wish to note that it should choose between the two alternatives provided in square brackets. An explanation of this provision is provided in the Guide to Enactment in the notes to Article 15. MLIJ Guide, N 121.

B. THE EFFECT TO BE GIVEN TO THE RECOGNIZED AWARD (PARA. 1)

2.15.02 Article 15(1) provides that an insolvency-related judgment recognized and enforceable under the MLIJ can be given effect in the enacting State in two different ways. This choice is given to the legislator when implementing/enacting the MLIJ; that is, the implementing state has to choose between one of the options (as highlighted in a footnote to the subparagraph). This choice gives the implementing state the chance to follow its existing legal traditions and to be coherent with the approach on recognition in respect of other types of decisions.[2] This unusual legislative technique (of options within a model law) was the result of a lack of consensus in UNCITRAL's Working Group V on whether to prioritize one option over the other.[3]

1. Extension of the Foreign Judgement's Effect

2.15.03 According to the Guide to Enactment,[4] the rationale of the first choice offered (paragraph 1) is to give the judgment the same effect in the receiving State as it had in the originating State (that is, the effect in the originating State is exported to the receiving State).

2.15.04 This approach is (also) known as the extension of effects and is the one adopted for instance by the Court of Justice of the European Union ('*Wirkungserstreckung*') in the Framework of the EU instruments such as the BXL Ibis Regulation.[5] According to the Jenard Report on the 1968 Brussels

2 Despite Article 15's 'tolerance' towards national rules on the enforcement of judgements, neither of both options would appear to allow for the English courts to continue to apply the *Gibbs* rule (Antony Gibbs & Sons v La Société Industrielle et Commerciale des Métaux (1809) LR 25 QBD 399, upheld in a decision of the Court of Appeal of December 18, 2018, Bakhshiyeva v Sberbank of Russia [2018] EWCA Civ 2802) in the context of a hypothetical implementation of the MLIJ. The Gibbs rule states that English courts will not enforce a foreign insolvency judgment discharging or modifying the terms of English law-governed debt (see Mevorach, 291 with a reference to an exception where the defendant has submitted to the foreign jurisdiction, in n 56; see also 2.X.15 and n 35 hereto). Intriguingly, the relevance of the Gibbs rule has not been discussed in this context, but in that of the proposed implementation of Article X (see 2.X.15 f).

3 The discord around these provisions and how they led to the current text are described *in extenso* by John A. Pottow, 'The Dialogic Aspect of Soft Law in International Insolvency: Discord, Digression, and Development' (2019) 40 Michigan JIL 479, 494.

4 MLIJ Guide, N 121.

5 Case 145/86 Hoffmann v Krieg, ECLI:EU:C:1988:61 and Case C-420/07 Apostolides v Orams ECLI:EU:C:2009:271, see Marek Zilinsky, 'Mutual Trust and Cross-Border Enforcement of Judgments in Civil Matters in the EU: Does the Step-by-Step Approach Work?' Netherlands International Law Review (2017), https://doi.org/10.1007/s40802-017-0079-0, 123 and Patrick Wautelet, 'Article 36 Brussels Ibis Regulation' in Ulrich Magnus and Peter Mankowski (eds), *ECPIL: European Commentaries on Private International Law*, vol 1 (2nd edn, Dr. Otto Schmidt KG, 2022), N 4–5.

Convention[6] (the formal predecessor of the Brussels I and [Recast] Ibis Regulations), the recognition of a judgment rendered in one Member State must have the same effect in the other Member States. As a consequence of this approach, the focus of recognition lies on the substantive effects of the decision to be recognized. This means that a judgment recognizes the legal relationship between the parties, including basic procedural effects of a judgment, such as the *res iudicata* effect.[7] In a ruling of 8 June 2023[8] the ECJ stated that 'recognition must have the result of conferring on judgments the authority and effectiveness accorded to them in the State in which they were given' and therefore 'a foreign judgment which has been recognized pursuant to [the BXL Ibis Regulation] must in principle have the same effects in the State in which recognition is sought as it does in the State of origin'.[9] From a methodical standpoint, if follows from the ECJ case law that, where recognition of a judgment is relied on [the BXL 1bis Regulation], it is necessary, in principle, first 'to refer solely to the legal rules of the [...] State of origin in order to determine the effects which that judgment must have in the [...] State addressed and, second, to confer on such a judgment the authority and effectiveness accorded to it in the [...] State of origin'. The decision 'is incorporated into de legal order of the [recognizing] state and its procedural rules apply'[10] and those procedural rules (of the recognizing state) should not hinder the effectiveness of the foreign decisions in the state of recognition.

Basically the same approach underlies Article 15. However, unlike under the BXL Ibis Regulation, the effect given to the foreign decision under Article 15 can be modified to some extent by paragraph 2, which does not oblige the receiving State to provide a form of relief that is not available under its own law. This comes to confirm that paragraph 2 is actually conceived to be applied when the first option under paragraph 1 is chosen and is probably redundant under the second. **2.15.05**

2. Granting the Foreign Judgment the Same Effect

The second option offered by the MLIJ to legislators is to give a (recognized) foreign judgment the same effect as it would have had if it had been issued **2.15.06**

6 P. Jenard, 'Report on the Convention of 27 September 1968 on jurisdiction and the enforcement of judgments in civil and commercial matters', OJ C 59/1, 43.

7 Pottow (n 3), 495 (see ref. in Fn 81 on the US – internal – position); Zilinsky (n 5), 122.

8 *BNP Paribas SA v TR*, 567/21, EU:C:2023:452, paragraphs 47–48.

9 N 47, referring to the ECJ judgment of 15 November 2012, *Gothaer Allgemeine Versicherung and Others*, C-456/11, EU:C:2012:719, paragraph 34.

10 *BNP Paribas SA v TR* (n 8), paragraph 53.

in the receiving State (that is, the effect would be equivalent to that of such a judgment issued in the receiving State).

2.15.07 According to the Guide to Enactment,[11] the rationale of the second choice is based upon maintaining equality, fairness and certainty as between domestic and foreign judgments. The main reason for this alternative approach may reside in practical difficulties that a court in the enacting State may encounter in determining the precise 'effects' of a judgment under the law of the originating State and a need to specify its effects (in the recognizing country) in legal categories and effects of that jurisdiction for the purposes of its enforcement.[12]

2.15.08 This second approach is likely to reduce the situations where paragraph 2 (see hereinafter) would need to be applied. Under the second option, paragraph 2 may be limited to situations where even an equivalent effect cannot be granted, but at least one that gets as close as permissible under national law.[13]

C. EQUIVALENT EFFECT (PARA. 2)

2.15.09 Article 15(2) provides that where the judgment to be recognized provides for relief that is not available or not known in the receiving State, the court should provide a form of relief that has equivalent effects, and give effect to the judgment to the extent permissible under its national law.[14] As stated in the previous note, this provision is of particular relevance in jurisdictions that have implemented the first option cited in paragraph 1.[15]

2.15.10 The receiving court is not required to provide a form of relief that is not available under its national law, but is authorized, as far as is possible, to adapt the form of relief granted by the originating court to a measure known in the receiving State, but not exceeding the effects the form of relief granted in the judgment would have under the law of the originating State.[16] This provision enhances the practical effectiveness of judgments and aims at ensuring the

11 MLIJ Guide, N 122.

12 See the example cited in n 14. Further examples may involve foreign decisions awarding an amount as a percentage of the income (which is usual for alimony awards in some jurisdiction) while the recognizing jurisdiction requires a specific amount for enforcement. Other examples involve orders 'ad personam' referring to the disposal of assets (such as a Mareva Injunction under English law) while the recognizing jurisdiction only know attachments 'in rem' of specified assets.

13 See 2.14.07.

14 MLIJ Guide, N 122.

15 See 2.15.03.

16 See on the identical text that is incorporated in the wording of art. 54 para 1 subpara 2 of the Brussels Ibis (recast) Regulation, Xandra Kramer, 'Article 54 Brussels Ibis Regulation' in Ulrich Magnus and Peter

successful party receives meaningful relief[17] – especially where the receiving state has implemented the first option of paragraph 1.[18]

The wording of paragraph 2 appears to be inspired by Article 54(1) of the BXL Ibis Regulation.[19] Accordingly, literature and existing case law on that provision may serve as guidance on the interpretation of this paragraph.[20] **2.15.11**

While Article 54(1) of the BXL Ibis Regulation applies to (provisional) 'measures', Article 15(2) MLIJ seems to cover all kinds of judgments.[21] However, also under the MLIJ, the main field of application of the 'equivalent effect' clause might indeed probably lie in the adaptation of provisional orders in jurisdictions where such orders are unknown.[22] **2.15.12**

Mankowski (eds), *ECPIL: European Commentaries on Private International Law*, vol 1 (2nd edn, Dr. Otto Schmidt KG, 2022) 12 ff.

17 MLIJ Guide, N 122.

18 MLIJ Guide, N 122; see 2.15.05.

19 'If a judgment contains a measure or an order which is not known in the law of the Member State addressed, that measure or order shall, to the extent possible, be adapted to a measure or an order known in the law of that Member State which has equivalent effects attached to it and which pursues similar aims and interests. Such adaptation shall not result in effects going beyond those provided for in the law of the Member State of origin.' The prior version of the Brussels Regulation (https://eur-lex.europa.eu/legal-content/EN/TXT/HTML/?uri=CELEX:32012R1215&from=EN) had no so such provision but the following comment in Reasoning 28: 'Where a judgment contains a measure or order which is not known in the law of the Member State addressed, that measure or order, including any right indicated therein, should, to the extent possible, be adapted to one which, under the law of that Member State, has equivalent effects attached to it and pursues similar aims. How, and by whom, the adaptation is to be carried out should be determined by each Member State.'

20 The background of that provision is of particular interest. According to Kramer (n 16) N 2, the ECJ had laid the basis for this provision in its decision in Case C-235/09 *DHL Express France* [2011] ECR I-2801. In that decision – in the context of a trade mark infringement – the question was raised as to how to enforce an 'astreinte' under French law (a periodic penalty, generally due for as long as the violation is ongoing) in a jurisdiction that did not know this legal instrument. The court established that the objective pursued by that measure had to be attained by having recourse to the relevant provisions of the national law (of the recognizing jurisdiction) which were such as to ensure that the prohibition was complied with in an equivalent manner.

21 In turn, Article 54 regulates more comprehensively some procedural questions, such as the standing and the modalities to challenge an adaptation (paras 2 and 3).

22 See n 8. When it comes to the cross-border effect of provisional measures, an alternative to recognition (which may always face difficulties in recognition where they are issued 'ex parte', see [2.14.49 ff], or show certain particularities, see n 8) may be the obtention of a new provisional measure under the law of the recognizing jurisdiction, as the facts justifying the original measure may also justify the obtention of a measure in another state where assets of the defendant lie. This may, however, involve higher costs and a higher burden of proof than a recognition proceeding.

Article 16

SEVERABILITY

Rodrigo Rodriguez

Recognition and enforcement of a severable part of an insolvency-related judgment shall be granted where recognition and enforcement of that part is sought, or where only that part of the judgment is capable of being recognized and enforced under this Law.

A. INTRODUCTION TO ARTICLE 16

2.16.1 In some instances, recognition and enforcement of a judgment as a whole might not be possible. This may be the case where some of the orders included in the judgment fall outside the scope of the MLIJ, where they are contrary to the public policy of the receiving State or where they are interim orders that are not yet enforceable in the originating State. The inclusion of non-recognizable punitive damages in an award may also be an example.[1] It may also be the case that only some parts of the judgment are relevant to the receiving State.[2] Article 16 addresses this situation.

1 This will only apply in jurisdiction where punitive damages could not be recognized or where a regime under which such decision (if they are not insolvency-related) would be recognized is not available. See the sources cited in n 10 and 11.

2 MLIJ Guide, N 125. For instance, where some assets are not in the recognizing country any more, or even one of several parties concerned has left the jurisdiction or a relevant legal person has been dissolved.

Article 16 is inspired by similar provisions found in other international instruments.[3] Its inclusion in the MLIJ may be useful, as many national laws may not know such a provision.[4] 2.16.2

B. SEVERABILITY IN THE MLIJ

An important condition to be fulfilled for Article 16 to be applicable is that (at least) one part of the judgment is capable of standing alone.[5] The Guide to Enactment[6] specifies that that assessment would usually depend on whether recognizing and enforcing only that part of the judgment would significantly change the obligations of the parties.[7] Where that question raises issues of law, they would be determined by the law of the receiving State. 2.16.3

The consequence of the application of Article 16 is that the receiving court would not be able to refuse recognition and enforcement of one part of the judgment solely on the basis that another part is not recognizable and enforceable, and that the severable part of the judgment should be treated in the same manner as a judgment that is wholly recognizable and enforceable (Article 15 MLIJ). 2.16.4

C. SEVERABILITY IN THE HAGUE CONVENTIONS

Provisions that are almost identical to Article 16 MLIJ can be found in Article 15[8] of the Hague Choice of Court Convention of 2005 and in Article 9 of the Hague Judgments Convention of 2019. The commentaries in the Explanatory Report to the Hague Choice of Court Convention 2005[9] on that provision are also almost identical to the Guide to Enactment to the MLIJ on Article 16. Accordingly, as to the interpretation of this provision, reference can be made 2.16.5

3 See [2.16.05]. However, a similar provision found in Article 48 of the Brussels I Regulation was eliminated in the revised Brussels Ibis (Recast) Regulation.

4 Where a national law does not know such a provision at all, it may make sense to include in the national law as a general rule, not limited to the decisions covered by the MLIJ.

5 MLIJ Guide, N 125.

6 MLIJ Guide, N 125.

7 See also n 4.

8 'Recognition or enforcement of a severable part of a judgment shall be granted where recognition or enforcement of that part is applied for, or only part of the judgment is capable of being recognised or enforced under this Convention.'

9 Trevor Hartly and Dosato Dogauchi, 'Explanatory Report to the Hague Choice of Court Convention 2005, Off-print of the proceedings of the 20th session, Tome III, Choice of Court Agreements' (2005) https://assets.hcch.net/docs/0de60e2f-e002-408e-98a7-5638e1ebac65.pdf accessed 9 July 2023.

to doctrine and jurisprudence still to be developed in respect of those conventions. One example cited in the materials refers to the case where 'an award of punitive damages is not enforced [...], the remainder of the award must be enforced [...]'.[10]

10 Hartly and Dogauchi (n 9), N 217: 'Article 15 provides for the recognition and enforcement of a severable part of a judgment where this is applied for, or where only part of the judgment is capable of being recognised or enforced under the Convention. For example, if an award of punitive damages is not enforced by reason of Article 11, the remainder of the award must be enforced if it satisfies the requirements of Article 8. In order to be severable, the part in question must be capable of standing alone: this would normally depend on whether enforcing only that part of the judgment would significantly change the obligations of the parties. In so far as this depends on a rule of law, the law of the court addressed must be applied.' This explanatory report, in turn refers to the previous 'Preliminary draft Convention on jurisdiction and foreign judgments in civil and commercial matters, adopted by the Special Commission and Report by Peter Nygh & Fausto Pocar', Prel. Doc. No 11 of August 2000 drawn up for the attention of the Nineteenth Session of June 2001.

Article X

RECOGNITION OF AN INSOLVENCY-RELATED JUDGMENT UNDER [*INSERT A CROSS-REFERENCE TO THE LEGISLATION OF THIS STATE ENACTING ARTICLE 21 OF THE UNCITRAL MODEL LAW ON CROSS-BORDER INSOLVENCY*]

Rodrigo Rodriguez

Notwithstanding any prior interpretation to the contrary, the relief available under [insert a cross-reference to the legislation of this State enacting Article 21 of the UNCITRAL Model Law on Cross-Border Insolvency] includes recognition and enforcement of a judgment.

A. INTRODUCTION TO ARTICLE X

The MLIJ owes its existence[1] to a large part to the legal uncertainty about the court's ability to recognize and enforce *ad personam* judgments against third parties under the MLCBI in the course of insolvency proceedings that the **2.X.01**

1 See, on the general background, P2.01 ff.

Rubin case[2] had created in the UK (and certain other common law jurisdictions).[3] For example, judgments issued in avoidance proceedings under Article 7 or 21 of the MLCBI were not able to be enforced unless certain factors were also met. Though *Rubin* addressed the situation under English law, due to the relevance of English jurisprudence for the common law community, the concern in the international insolvency community was that the English court's determination that the MLCBI lacked explicit authority to recognize and enforce insolvency-related judgments would be regarded as persuasive authority in other States with legislation based upon the MLCBI. Article X is therefore the international communities' response to the concern of 'contagion' of the *Rubin* jurisprudence.[4]

2.X.02 Article X can also be read as UNCITRAL's acknowledgment that the MLIJ does not (at least not to the full extent) neutralize the effect of the *Rubin* decision.[5] Article X and the MLIJ address similar – and to a large part, overlapping – issues in a different manner: While Article X clarifies or (depending on the pre-existing interpretation)[6] expands the scope of the MLCBI, the MLIJ sets up a completely new set of rules for the recognition of insolvency-related decisions.[7]

---

2 Rubin v Eurofinance SA [2012] UKSC 46, see also P2.03.

3 See John A. Churchill Jr., 'Please Recognize Me: The United Kingdom Should Enact the UNCITRAL Model Law on Recognition and Enforcement of Insolvency-Related Judgments' (2020) 46(1) Brooklyn JIL 215, 239 as well as John A. Pottow, 'The Dialogic Aspect of Soft Law in International Insolvency: Discord, Digression, and Development' (2019) 40 Michigan JIL 488, referring in p.485 to the concerns expressed by the Korean delegation (in UNCITRAL's working group V) in this sense. See also Min Han, 'Recognition of Insolvency Effects of a Foreign Insolvency Proceeding: Focusing on the Effect of Discharge', in *Trade Development through Harmonization of Commercial Law* (New Zealand Association of Comparative Law, Hors serie vol XIX, 2015). Rubin found some harsh criticism, to Moss (p.232) it as perceived as a blow to international co-operation via recognition and enforcement of foreign judgments., see also Irit Mevorach, 'Overlapping International Instruments for Enforcement of Insolvency Judgements: Undermining or Strengthening Universalism?', European Business Organization Law Review (2021), <https:// doi .org/ 10 .1007/s40804-021-00204-4>, 291.

4 See Rodrigo Rodriguez, 'The new UNCITRAL Model Law on Recognition and Enforcement of Insolvency-Related Judgements', in: Ballesteros Barrion/Bovio (eds), Insolvency Law in International Instruments and Comments, Aranzadi 2023.

5 Pottow (n 3), 501, however, rightly acknowledges, that it does so to a considerable extent through its complex, but ultimately generous provisions on indirect competence in Article 14(g)(iv) MLIJ.

6 There is ample jurisprudence in the US Jurisprudence on recognition and enforcement under the MLCBI (that is, under its implementation: Chapter 15 of the UBSBC).

7 As to the overlaps see 2.X.08.

B. ARTICLE X AND THE MLCBI

From a formal standpoint, as Article X relates to the application and interpretation of the MLCBI, it is not intended that it be included in legislation enacting the MLIJ. According to the Guide to Enactment,[8] 'to do so might lead to it being overlooked by parties seeking to make use of the MLCBI or by courts interpreting the MLCBI'. Where this provision is enacted, it must be so as part to the legislation giving effect to the MLCBI. **2.X.03**

From a substantial standpoint, Article X overlaps with the MLIJ.[9] Implementing both the MLIJ and Article X (as part of the MLCBI) with no further adaptation and clarification would lead to overlaps and to contradicting legal consequences in respect of the modalities (that is, the conditions and the consequences of the recognition of insolvency-related judgments), but these may be overcome. These overlaps and contradictions – and how to avoid them – are expanded in 2.X.08 and 2.X.16ff. respectively. **2.X.04**

C. PURPOSE AND EFFECT OF ARTICLE X

The MLCBI provisions on the type of relief that can be granted (principally Article 21) make no specific reference to recognition and enforcement of insolvency-related judgments (see, in extenso, N 1.21.15 ff. on Article 21 MLCBI) but the focus is rather on proceedings. According to the Guide to Enactment, the purpose of Article X is to make it clear to States enacting (or considering enactment of) the MLCBI that the relief available under Article 21 of the MLCBI should include recognition and enforcement of an insolvency-related judgments and that such relief may therefore be sought under Article 21.[10] States enacting (or considering enactment of) the MLCBI are thus invited to rely upon Article X to achieve that purpose, irrespective of any prior interpretations of Article 21 to the contrary (that is, as was the case in the UK). The enactment of this provision would consequently not be necessary in jurisdictions where the MLCBI is already interpreted as covering the recognition and enforcement of insolvency-related judgments – except for purposes of additional legal certainty.[11] **2.X.05**

---

8 MLIJ Guide N 127.

9 See 2.X.08.

10 MLIJ Guide, N 126.

11 Ibid.

2.X.06 As the legislative history of Article X shows,[12] the provision was intended to 'fix Rubin' and was addressed mainly to the common-law jurisdictions on which the cited decision might have a determining influence on the interpretation of the MLCBI.[13] The main consequence of the *Rubin* decision for the purposes of jurisdiction was the English Court's denial of recognition of a foreign *in personam* judgment (emanating from and thus related to an insolvency proceeding) using the generous recognition rules of the MLCBI, instead requiring that recognition be based on the originating court establishing its jurisdiction in a manner compatible with established rules on recognition of judgements in England, notably the *Dicey* rules.[14] In short, the *Dicey* rules state that a foreign judgment *in personam* will be only recognized under English law if the person against whom the judgment was given was (i) at the time the proceedings were instituted, present in the foreign country; (ii) claimant, or counterclaimant, in the proceedings in the foreign court; or (iii) it had submitted to the jurisdiction of that court by voluntarily appearing in the proceedings or had, before the commencement of the proceedings, agreed, in respect of the subject matter of the proceedings, to submit to the jurisdiction of that court or of the courts of that country.[15] These conditions were not met in the case underlying *Rubin* and recognition of the judgment was denied.

2.X.07 The effect of Article X is to extend the scope of relief available under the MLCBI to substantive relief as well as procedural relief. Formal and substantial requirements, as well as the consequences of recognition of insolvency-related judgments, would be regulated by the provisions of the MLCBI as adopted into national legislation. For the relevant purposes of recognition of foreign insolvency-related judgement, the main consequence would be that the conditions of Article 17 MLCBI would apply, instead of the *Dicey* rules or of those of Article 14 MLIJ.[16] The *Dicey* conditions are obviously stricter than the provisions of the MLCBI, which essentially 'asks no questions' as to the grounds

---

12 See 2.X.01.

13 Mevorach (n 3), 291, Pottow (n 3), 484 ff. The Rubin decision obviously had a determining influence in England; it was feared that other common law jurisdictions (such as the Republic of Korea) could follow that approach: see Pottow (n 3), 485. See also the references in n 3.

14 Referring to the successive editions of Lord Collins of Mapesbury (ed), Dicey, Morris and Collins on the Conflict of Laws, in which principles on proper exercise of jurisdiction 'in an international sense', and thus acceptable for the purposes of recognition (in continental doctrine partly referred to as 'indirect competence'), have been established (see above). See, *in extenso*, Peter Kutner, 'Recognition and Enforcement of Foreign Judgments – The Common Laws Jurisdiction Requirement' (2017) 83(1) Rabels Zeitschrift 1–76. https://ssrn.com/abstract=3065296 accessed 8 August 2023, referring also to exceptions to the rule and its development over time.

15 Kutner (n 14), 3.

16 Pottow (n 3), 485.

for jurisdiction under which the foreign court had assumed jurisdiction.[17] On the other side, unlike the MLIJ, recognition under the MLCBI (with Article X) would remain, in principle, discretionary.[18]

D. RELATIONSHIP BETWEEN THE MLIJ AND ARTICLE X

1. Overlaps and Contradictions

There is an obvious methodical contradiction in UNCITRAL's approach of establishing a 16-article-long, elaborate model law on the recognition of insolvency-related judgments and at the same time proposing an alternative article that 'solves' the same question (recognition of insolvency-related judgments) by adding an additional sentence to the MLCBI.[19] There is no obvious solution to this contradiction. Some options are presented in the following: **2.X.08**

2. Option 1: Implement only the MLIJ

The *prima facie* most obvious solution is to give priority to the MLIJ and renounce to implement Article X in view of its potential redundancy. As becomes evident by looking at Article 14 of the MLIJ, the rules on indirect competence and further possible grounds for refusal are more elaborate than those of the MLCBI. The MLIJ is tailored to the recognition and enforcement of insolvency-related judgments,[20] as opposed to the MLCBI, which was not developed with the conception that it would be used to recognize and enforce judgements but rather to recognize insolvency proceedings.[21] These more elaborate provisions on indirect competence and grounds for refusal found in Article 14 – the elaboration of which took a considerable time of Working Group V's discussions – evidence that the international consensus on the appropriate grounds of jurisdiction and grounds for refusal for the recognition of insolvency-related judgments that exists today should be more complex than the original approach taken in Articles 17 and 21 of the MLCBI. As the *Rubin* decision points out, there are some essential differences between an insolvency proceeding and a judgment regarding a specific litigation between **2.X.09**

17 See [1.17.04] on Article 17 MLCBI.

18 Mevorach (n 3), 299. This will only be relevant in jurisdictions (generally of the common law tradition) where judicial discretion in the field of recognition is a relevant factor. Implementations in civil law jurisdictions would tend to minimize the room for discretion.

19 According to Mevorach (n 3), 298, Article X admits that the MLCBI and the MLIJ overlap. It actually exacerbates this (limited) overlap to a full overlap.

20 This is further evidenced by its procedural provisions in Articles 11 to 13.

21 See Mevorach (n 3), 293 (and *Rubin*, n 2, para. 63).

two parties that may only loosely be connected to an insolvency. It is these differences that the international community has recognized call for a specific approach to recognition.[22] The MLIJ takes this approach by adopting specific procedural norms to address the recognition of judgements (Articles 11 to 13 MLIJ) and substantial provisions elaborating the grounds for which refusal or recognition may be justified (Article 14), taking into account the different types of judgments. The recognition rules of the MLIJ are more generous that the *Dicey* rules[23] to which *Rubin* referred (see, for instance, Article 14(g)(iii) and (iv))[24] – making the MLIJ at least a partial 'fix' for *Rubin*.[25] An implementation of the MLIJ can thus justly be seen as a major improvement in comparison to applying the *Dicey* rules or applying no regulation at all. The MLIJ does 'fix' some of the consequences of *Rubin* (the application of the strict *Dicey* rules),[26] thanks to complex but ultimately generous rules on indirect jurisdiction (Article 14(g)(iii) and (iv)[27]), rather than bluntly assimilating any insolvency-related judgments to insolvency proceedings as Article X – if read literally – would do.

2.X.10 It is for those reasons that an implementation of the MLIJ (possibly with some suggested amendments, see 2.X.18 *in finem*) appears preferable to incorporating Article X in the MLCBI.

3. Option 2: Implementation of only Article X?

2.X.11 An alternative option for States, particularly those having already implemented the MLCBI (or planning to implement it simultaneously), to address the overlaps and contradictions exposed in paragraph 2.X.08 consists in implementing only Article X. If the substantial scope of Article X is to be considered the same as the one in the MLIJ, then an implementation of Article X renders the MLIJ redundant and unnecessary (on the UK government's proposal in that sense, see 2.X.14f). The consequence of such implementation (and assuming that the term 'insolvency-related judgments' would cover all decisions defined

22 See Churchill (n 3), 236 (and *Rubin*, n 2, para. 143).
23 See 2.X.06.
24 See 2.14.58 and 2.14.60 ff, respectively.
25 See n 39.
26 See n 35.
27 See 2.14.58 and 2.14.60 ff.

in Article 2 of the MLIJ)[28] would be to submit all those decisions to 'the MLCIB's expansive relief provisions'.[29]

Article X's approach of submitting – inter alia – *in personam* judgments to the MLCBI regime (art. 17 ff) would directly contravene the decision in *Rubin* and, thus, in the eyes of its critics, 'fix' the problem with the *Rubin* court's interpretation of the MLCBI which excluded these decisions from the possibility of being recognized.[30] The advantages of such an approach are obvious: no need to characterize a decision as to whether it falls under the MLIJ or the MLCBI, and hardly any grounds for refusal other than public policy. Article X does – at least literally read – not even require that the proceedings to which the decision is related to, is or could be recognized in the recognizing state (see, in contrast, Article 14(h) MLIJ).[31] **2.X.12**

On the other hand, the mere implementation of Article X leaves the MLCBI without any specific procedural rules addressing the different nature of judgments – as opposed to proceedings[32] – and leads to a wide recognition of foreign decisions made in a jurisdiction that may not be the ones expected by parties to become the *forum* of the litigation, for instance when the originating court ignored a *choice of forum* agreement and have had only a loose connection to the insolvency proceeding.[33] This bears the risk of contradictory decisions where the 'proper' courts (the court designated in the contract by the parties) are also seized with the same or a similar claim. **2.X.13**

Furthermore, Article X omits any explicit reference to the recognition of the insolvency proceeding to which the judgment is related. While the MLIJ sets the clear condition that such proceeding must be recognized or recognizable (Article 14(h)), with very limited exceptions, this question is left open under Article X. That Article X would 'imply' such a requirement within the MLCBI is far from obvious, given the complexity of the explicit provision of Article 14(h) with its subparas (i) and (ii) MLIJ. Consequently, Article X could lead to the recognition of a judgment issued in a jurisdiction that asserted its juris- **2.X.14**

---

28 The alternative approach presented under 2.X.17 f suggests that Article X's substantial scope is explicitly limited to a particular set of judgments: see 2.X.19.

29 n 2. Pottow (n 3), 485 suggests that Rubin could be read more broadly to have rejected the notion that any sort of judgment (as opposed to an insolvency proceeding) could be available.

30 Pottow (n 3), 485; on the Dicey Rules see 2.X.06.

31 See 2.14.63 ff, in particular 2.14.72 ff.

32 Mevorach (n 3), 298 considers the differences in treatment to be surmountable through case law.

33 Mevorach (n 3), 300, refers also the concern expressed in Rubin that such generous unilateral recognition rules 'would only be to the detriment of UK businesses without any corresponding benefit' (Rubin, n 2, para. 130) .

diction merely on the basis of its connection to an insolvency proceeding that might not even be recognizable under the MLCBI. Such inconsistencies and legal uncertainties speak against an implementation of Article X as it stands.

4. The UK Consultation

2.X.15 On 7 July 2022, the UK launched an open consultation on the partial implementation of the MLIJ in the UK[34] (together with the UNCITRAL Model Law on Enterprise Group Insolvency).[35] The consultation closed on 29 September 2022. The implementation proposed by the UK focused on the adoption of Article X and did not contemplate the adoption of the MLIJ. In the course of the consultation some raised the idea of adopting the MLIJ in full or at least to a larger extent than merely Article X.[36] Others expressed doubts as to whether Article X would really enhance legal certainty or, more specifically, address difficulties relating the *Gibbs* rule.[37]

2.X.16 The UK government's conclusions from the responses on Article X were that 'significant impacts could flow from the recognition of judgments in the UK under the model law framework, and [that it was] doubtful that the [UK government's] proposed approach to implementation would be sufficient to avoid difficulties'. It went on to say that responses had also highlighted 'the adverse effect that a lack of clear conflict of law rules could have on those who rely on UK law for legal predictability' – referring to the ongoing and unsolved issues around the Rule in *Gibbs*[38] in a recognition context. The UK went on to 'consider further how the technical detail of the proposal can be adapted to address the issues',[39] that is, to halt the implementation for the time being.

---

34 See www.gov.uk/government/consultations/implementation-of-two-uncitral-model-laws-on-insolvency [3.8.2023].

35 See https://uncitral.un.org/en/MLEGI [3.8.2023].

36 See Mevorach (n 3), 305 ff as well as the responses to the consultation, see n 32.

37 *Antony Gibbs & Sons v La Société Industrielle et Commerciale des Métaux* (1890) LR 25 QBD 399, upheld in a decision of the Court of Appeal of December 18, 2018, *Gunel Bakhshiyeva v Sberbank of Russia & Ors* [2018] EWCA Civ 2802. The Gibbs rule states that English courts will not enforce a foreign insolvency judgment discharging or modifying the terms of English-law-governed debt: see Mevorach (n 3), 291 (with a reference to an exception where the defendant has submitted to the foreign jurisdiction, in n 56). Views may differ and reach more elaborated conclusions as to the influence of the MLIJ or Article X on the Gibbs Rule (see Mevorach (n 3), 291 ff). However, it is obvious that nothing in the text of Article X indicates anything as to directing the courts to modify their approach as to the consequences and extent of the effect of recognition. This is evidenced by the differing views and expectations made in the consultation: see n 32. Still, some doubts remained as to a possible effect of Article X on the Gibbs Rule, which prompted the UK government to further examine that issue. It is surprising that the discussion on the effects recognition takes place around Article X and not around, for instance, Article 15 MLIJ (see [2.15.01]).

38 Cited in the preceding fn. See also Mevorach (n 3), 291 ff.

39 See www.gov.uk/government/consultations/implementation-of-two-uncitral-model-laws-on-insolvency/outcome/implementation-of-two-uncitral-model-laws-on-insolvency-summary-of-consultation-responses-and-government-response accessed 8 August 2023.

5. A Proposal for a Combined Implementation

Unlike the MLCBI, the MLIJ is a model law specifically tailored to the characteristics – procedural and substantial – of insolvency-related judgments. It should thus be given legislative priority over an extension of the scope of the MLCBI.[40] **2.X.17**

Important parts of the reasoning of *Rubin* are highly relatable: *ad personam* judgements that are not necessarily part of the insolvency proceedings and that involve expectations and agreements (as to the forum of litigation) that are not necessarily linked with the insolvency proceedings (but only affected by it, for instances in terms of the standing) should remain subject to the jurisdictional rules that are applicable to them irrespective of the event of insolvency. A too-wide scope for the MLCBI (in terms of recognition) leads to disregard of jurisdictional restraint in favour of including all related litigation remotely associated with the insolvency proceeding under an overstretched jurisdictional 'vis atractiva concursus'.[41] *Rubin* has prevented this so far, probably at the price of too strict a standard instead. However, much speaks in favour of the right balance in terms of grounds for refusal actually being achieved by Article 14 of the MLIJ, with provisions that take a middle ground between the *Rubin/Dicey* approach and the MLCBI.[42] **2.X.18**

Against that background, one issue that remains open is that of the treatment of certain judgments that are so closely interconnected with an insolvency proceeding – or could be seen as such – that they should not, or should never have been, considered as not falling under the MLCBI. This would lead us to consider a third option, a modified Article X with a much more limited substantial scope. Under the problematic 'mind the gap' approach[43] that led to the wide scope of the MLIJ, that scope was extended to cover even decisions 'determining whether a plan of reorganization or liquidation should be confirmed, a discharge of the debtor or of debts should be granted or a voluntary or out-of-court restructuring agreement should be approved' (see Article 14(f)(i)). Such decisions (that follow a proceeding or are part of it) should clearly be **2.X.19**

40 See n 25. As to the divergence between the MLIJ and the MLCBI see Mevorach (n 3), 301.

41 See 2.X.12.

42 See Pottow (n 3), 500 and Churchill (n 3), 243, both admitting that Article 14, at least in its paragraph (g) (for Pottow essentially subpara (iv)) does essentially 'fix' the Rubin issues.

43 Some UNCITRAL delegations from common-law jurisdictions were worried that certain proceedings might be considered by courts as falling neither under the MLCBI nor under the MLIJ. Furthermore, the conception of the MLIJ as a possible stand-alone instrument for countries that might have not adopted the MLCBI led to a problematic 'the more the merrier' approach in respect of its substantial scope: see Mevorach (n 3), 293 f.

covered by the MLCBI.[44] Instead of the wide scope of Article X proposed by the MLIJ, a more restricted version addressing specifically these kinds of decisions could be added to the MLCBI.[45] As a very positive side effect, this would allow for deleting section (f) of Article 14, thereby considerably simplifying this overly complex provision.

44 Assuming the states in question have adopted it. See [2.02 ff] on Article 2 MLCBI.

45 Such a provision could read: 'The relief available under [insert a cross-reference to the legislation of this State enacting Article 21 of the UNCITRAL Model Law on Cross-Border Insolvency] includes recognition and enforcement of a judgment determining whether a plan of reorganization or liquidation should be confirmed, a discharge of the debtor or of debts should be granted or a voluntary or out-of-court restructuring agreement should be approved.' See, for a different proposal focusing on English law consequences in respect of the Gibbs Rule, Mevorach (n 3), 310.

BIBLIOGRAPHY

American Law Institute and the International Insolvency Institute, *Transnational Insolvency: Global Principles for Co-operation in International Insolvency* (American Law Institute, 2012).

Andersen, Kent, 'Testing the Model Soft Law Approach to International Harmonisation: A Case-Study Examining the UNICITRAL Model Law on Cross-Border Insolvency' (2004) 23 Australian Yearbook of International Law Online 1, 8 http://classic.austlii.edu.au/au/journals/AUYrBkIntLaw/2004/1.html accessed 22 February 2023.

Andersen, Kent, 'The Cross-Border Insolvency Paradigm: A Defense of the Modified Universal Approach Considering the Japanese Experience' (2000) 21 U. Pa. J. Int'l L. 679.

Atkin, Scott and Mason, Rosalind, 'Australia' in Ho, Look Chan, *Cross Border Insolvency: A Commentary on the UNCITRAL Model Law* 3rd ed. Globe Law & Business (London) 2012.

Bang-Pedersen, Ulrik Rammeskow, 'Asset Distribution in Transnational Insolvencies: Combining Predictability and Protection of Local Interests' (1999) 73 The American Bankruptcy Law Journal 385.

Berends, Andre J, 'The UNCITRAL Model Law on Cross-Border Insolvency: A Comprehensive Overview' (1998) 6 Tulane Journal of International and Comparative Law 309.

Bork, Reinhard, *Advanced Introduction to Cross-Border Insolvency Law*, Edward Elgar Publishing (Cheltenham), 2023.

Bork, Reinhard, *Principles of Cross-Border Insolvency Law*, Intersentia (Cambridge/Antwerp/Chicago), 2017.

Bork, Reinhard, 'The European Insolvency Regulation and the UNCITRAL Model Law on Cross-Border Insolvency' (2017) 26 Int'l Insolvency Rev 246.

Bork, Reinhard and Mangano, Renato, *European Cross-Border Insolvency Law*, 2nd ed., Oxford University Press (Oxford), 2022.

Bork, Reinhard and Veder, Michael, *Harmonisation of Transactions Avoidance Laws*, Intersentia (Cambridge/Antwerp/Chicago), 2021.

Bork, Reinhard and van Zwieten, Kristin (eds), *Commentary on the European Insolvency Regulation*, 2nd ed., Oxford University Press (Oxford), 2022.

Bufford, Samuel L., 'Tertiary and Other Excluded Foreign Proceedings under Bankruptcy Code Chapter 15' (2009) 83 Am Bankr LJ 165.

Bufford, Samuel L., *United States International Insolvency Law*, Oxford University Press (New York), 2009.

Carles, Jose, 'Jurisdiction and Recognition of Insolvency-Related Judgments: A Comparison between the European Insolvency Regulation and the UNCITRAL Model Law', INSOL Technical Papers 53, October 2022.

Casasola, Oriana and Madaus, Stephan, 'Cross-border Insolvency Protocols: Cooperation, Coordination, and Communication Duties under the European Insolvency Regulation Recast' (2022) 33(6) European Business Law Review 839.

Chandra Mohan, S., 'Cross-border Insolvency Problems: Is the UNCITRAL Model Law the Answer?' (2012) 21(3) International Insolvency Review 143.

Chung, John H., 'In Re Qimonda AG: The Conflict between Comity and the Public Policy Exception in Chapter 15 of the Bankruptcy Code' (2014) 32(1) B.U. Int'l L.J. 89.

Churchill Jr., John A, 'Please Recognize Me: The United Kingdom Should Enact the UNCITRAL Model Law on Recognition and Enforcement of Insolvency-Related Judgments' (2020) 46(1) Brooklyn JIL 215

Clark, Leif M. and Goldstein, Karen, 'Sacred Cows: How to Care for Secured Creditors' Rights in Cross-Border Bankruptcies' (2011) 46 Tex. Int'l L.J. 513.

Clift, Jenny, 'The UNCITRAL Model Law on Cross-Border Insolvency – A Legislative Framework to Facilitate Coordination and Cooperation in Cross-Border Insolvency' (2004) 12 Tulane Journal of International & Comparative Law 307.

Cronin, Matthew T., 'UNCITRAL Model Law on Cross-Border Insolvency: Procedural Approach to a Substantive Problem' (1999) 24 J. Corp. L. 709.

Dargan, Sean, 'The Emergence of Mechanisms for Cross-border Insolvencies in Canadian Law' (2001) 17(1) Connecticut Journal of International Law 107, 124.

Das, I., 'The Need for Implementing a Cross-Border Insolvency Regime within the Insolvency and Bankruptcy Code, 2016' (2020) 45(2) Vikalpa 104.

Davies, Martin, 'Cross-Border Insolvency and Admiralty: A Middle Path of Reciprocal Comity' (2018) 66 The American Journal of Comparative Law 101.

Davis, R., Madaus, S., Marcucci, M., Mevorach, I., Mokal, R., Romaine, B., Sarra, J. and Tirado, I., *Financial Institutions in Distress: Recovery, Resolution, Recognition* (Oxford University Press 2023).

Dawson, Andrew B., 'The Problem of Local Methods in Cross-border Insolvencies' (2015) 12(1) Berkeley Bus. L.J. 45.

De Carl Adler, Louise, *Managing the Chapter 15 Cross-Border Insolvency Case*, 2nd ed., Federal Judicial Center (Washington DC) 2014.

Deane, Felicity and Mason, Rosalind, 'The UNCITRAL Model Law on Cross-Border Insolvency and the Rule of Law' (2016) 25 International Insolvency Review 139.

Derrington, Sarah C., 'The Interaction between Admiralty and Insolvency Law' (2009) 23 ANZ Mar LJ 3.

Digest of Case Law on the UNCITRAL Model Law on Cross-Border Insolvency (CLOUT), United Nations Publications (Vienna), 2021.

Fisher, Richard and Al-Attar, Adam, 'The UNCITRAL Model Law' in Sheldon, Richard (ed), *Cross Border Insolvency* (3rd ed) Bloomsbury Professional (London) 2011.

Flaschen, Evan D. and Silverman, Ronald J., 'Cross-Border Insolvency Cooperation Protocols' (1998) 33 Tex. Int'l L. J. 587.

Fletcher, Ian F., '"Better Late Than Never": The UNCITRAL Model Law Enters into Force in GB' (2006) 19 Insolvency Intelligence 86.

Fletcher, Ian F., *Insolvency in Private International Law: National and International Approaches*, 2nd ed Oxford University Press (Oxford) 2005.

Fletcher, Ian F., *The Law of Insolvency*, 5th ed., Sweet & Maxwell (London) 2017.

Frege, Michael C., *Verhandlungslösungen in grenzüberschreitenden Insolvenzen: 'Concordia firmat vires', Festschrift für Christoph Paulus*, C.H.Beck (Munich) 2022, 191.

Gagnon, Hugo-Pierre, 'Bill C-55 and the UNCITRAL Model Law on Cross-Border Insolvency: the harmonization of Canadian insolvency legislation' (McGill University 2006) https://escholarship.mcgill.ca/concern/theses/h702qb62z accessed 22 February 2023.

Garrido, José M., 'No Two Snowflakes the Same: The Distributional Question in International Bankruptcies' (2011) 46 Tex. Int'l L. J. 459.

Garza, Michael A, 'When Is Cross-Border Insolvency Recognition Manifestly Contrary to Public Policy' (2015) 38(5) Fordham International Law Journal 1587.

Gilhuly, P.M., Posin, K.A. and Malatesta, A.E., 'Bankruptcy without Borders: A Compehensive Guide to the First Decade of Chapter 15' ABI Law Review (2016) 47.

Glosband, Daniel M. and Clark, Leif M., 'Ancillary and Other Cross-border Insolvency Cases under Chapter 15 of the Bankruptcy Code' Collier Monograph LexisNexis Mathew Bender (New York) 2008.

Goode, Roy and van Zwieten, Kristin, *Goode on Principles of Corporate Insolvency Law*, 5th ed. Sweet & Maxwell (London) 2018.

Gopalan, Sandeep and Guihot, Michael, 'Recognition and Enforcement in Cross-Border Insolvency Law: A Proposal for Judicial Gap-Filling' (2015) 48(5) Vanderbilt Journal of Transnational Law 1225.

Gordon, J.C., 'Crossing the Line in Cross-Border Insolvencies' (2019) 27 ABI Law Review 17.

Göretzlehner, Erik, *Maritime Cross Border Insolvency – An analysis for Germany, England and Wales and the USA*, Springer (New York) 2019.

Gropper, Allan L., *Cooperation in Cross-Border Insolvency Cases*, Festschrift für Heinz Vallender, RWS (Cologne) 2021, 207.

Gropper, Allan L., 'The Curious Disappearance of Choice of Law as an Issue in Chapter 15 Cases' (2014) 9(1) Brook. J. Corp. Fin & Com. L. 57.

Hafeez-Baig, Mohammud Jaamae, 'Navigating the Waters between Admiralty and Cross-border Insolvency: A Comparison of the Australian, German and French Positions' (2018) 28 Lloyd's Maritime and Commercial Law Quarterly 142.

Hannan, Neil F., *Cross-Border Insolvency: The Enactment and Interpretation of the UNCITRAL Model Law*, Springer (Singapore) 2017.

Hannan, Neil F., 'International Commercial Arbitration and Cross Border Insolvency' (2014) 17(1) International Trade and Business Law Review 447.

Ho, Look Chan (ed), *A Commentary on the UNCITRAL Model Law*, 4th ed, Globe Law & Business (London) 2017.

Ho, Look Chan, 'Applying Foreign Law – Realising the Model Law's Potential' (2010) 25 Journal of International Banking Law and Regulation 552.

Ho, Look Chan, 'Applying Foreign Law under the UNCITRAL Model Law on Cross-Border Insolvency' (2009) 24 Journal of International Banking Law and Regulation 655.

Ho, Look Chan, 'Conflict of Laws in Insolvency Transaction Avoidance' (2008) 20 SAcLJ 343.

Ho, Look Chan, 'Insolvency Policy and the Pari Passu Principle' in Ho, Look Chan, *Cross-Border Insolvency Principles and Practice* (Sweet & Maxwell) 2016.

Ho, Look Chan, 'On Pari Passu, Equality and Hotchpot in Cross-Border Insolvency' (2003) Lloyd's Maritime and Commercial Law Quarterly 95.

Ho, Look Chan, 'Recognising an Australian Solvent Liquidation under the UNCITRAL Model Law: In re Betcorp' (2009) 18 Norton Journal of Bankruptcy Law and Practice 537.

Ho, Look Chan, 'Smoothing Cross Border Insolvency by Synchronising the UNCITRAL Model Law: In re Samsun Logix Corporation' (2009) 24 Journal of International Banking Law and Regulation 395.

House of Representatives Report 109-31, 109th Congress 1st Session, 2005 United States Code Congressional and Administrative News (H.R. Rep. 109-31, 109th Cong., 1st Sess., 2005 USCCAN).

Isham, Sara, 'UNCITRAL's Model Law on Cross-Border Insolvency: A Workable Protection for Transnational Investment at Last' (2001) 26 Brook. J. Int'l L. 1177.

Jeremiah, Herman and Koh, Kia Jeng, 'Singapore: Timing Is Everything: Different Approaches To The Relevant Date For Determining COMI In Cross-Border Recognition Proceedings' (2019) www.mondaq.com/insolvencybankruptcy/837102/timing-is-everything-different-approaches-to-the-relevant-date-for-determining-comi-in-cross-border-recognition-proceedings.

Ji, Jesse, 'Cross-Border Rehabilitation: An Impediment to Ship Arrest in Singapore?' NUS – Centre for Maritime Law Working Paper 17/04 NUS Law Working Paper No. 2017/003 National University of Singapore (NUS) – Faculty of Law.

Jokubauskas, R. and Świerczyński, M., 'The Coordination of Main and Secondary Insolvency Proceedings in European Union Insolvency Law' (2022) 8(1) Int'l Comparative Jurisprudence 1.

Keeper, T., 'Applications for Aid and Assistance in Respect of Foreign Insolvency Proceedings in New Zealand since the Enactment of the Insolvency (Cross-Border) Act 2006 (NZ)' https://openaccess.wgtn.ac.nz/articles/journal_contribution/Applications_for_Aid_and_Assistance_in_Respect_of_Foreign_Insolvency_Proceedings_in_New_Zealand_since_the_Enactment_of_the_Insolvency_Cross-Border_Act_2006_NZ_/12845114?file=24397433.

Kennedy, Frank R., 'Partnerships and Partners under the Bankruptcy Code: Claims and Distribution' (1983) 40 Wash. & Lee L. Rev. 55.

Kim, Minjee, 'Cross-Border Insolvency and Debt Restructuring Law Reform in Singapore: Reflections on the Hanjin Shipping Case' (2019) 19 Australian Journal of Asian Law 233.

Kokorin, Ilya and Wessels, Bob, *Cross-Border Protocols in Insolvencies of Multinational Enterprise Groups*, Edward Elgar Publishing (Cheltenham) 2021.

Kokorin, Ilya, Madaus, Stephan and Mevorach, Irit, 'Global Competition in Cross-Border Restructuring and Recognition of Centralized Group Solutions' 56 Texas Journal of International Law 136 (2021).

Kwang, Hyun Suk, 'Choice of Law Rules in the Cross-border Insolvency under Korean Law' (2008) 4 JURIS 143.

Kwang, Hyun Suk, 'Private International Law Issues concerning Set-off in Judicial Proceedings between Claims Governed by English Law' (2016) 57 Seoul Law Journal.

LoPucki, Lynn M., 'Cooperation in International Bankruptcy: a Post-Universalist Approach' (1999) 84 Cornell L. Rev. 696.

Mason, Rosalind, 'Hotchpot and Other Tasty Morsels in International Insolvency' (1995) 3 Insolv. L. J. 149.

Mason, Rosalind, 'Implications of the UNCITRAL Model Law for Australian Cross-Border Insolvencies' (1999) 8 International Insolvency Review 83.

Mason, Rosalind, 'Where Private International Law and Insolvency Law Meet' in Omar, P. (ed.) *International Insolvency Law: Themes and Perspectives*, Ashgate (Farnham) 2008.

Mason, Rosalind, Atkins, Scott and Maiden, Stewart, 'The Emerging Framework of Cross-Border Insolvency in and around Australia: Saad Investments, Japan Airlines and Lehman Brothers' (2011) 8 International Corporate Rescue 262 and 329.

McCormack, Gerard, 'Conflicts, Avoidance and International Insolvency 20 Years On: A Triple Cocktail' (2013) 2 J.B.L. 141.

McCormack, G., *EU Insolvency Law: Cross Border Insolvency Law in Comparative Focus*, Edward Elgar Publishing (Cheltenham) 2022.

McCormack, Gerard, 'US Exceptionalism and UK Localism? Cross-border Insolvency Law in Comparative Perspective' (2016) 36 Legal Studies 136.

McCormack, G., and Hargrove, A., 'Australia and the International Insolvency Paradigm' (2015) 37 Sydney LR 389.

McCormack, Gerard and Wan, Wai Yee, 'The UNCITRAL Model Law on Cross-Border Insolvency Comes of Age: New Times or New Paradigms?' (2019) 54 Tex. Int'l L. J. 273.

McCoy, Noel, 'The Singularis Work-around? Overcoming Limitations to the Common Law Power of Assistance for Foreign Insolvency Investigations' (2019) 16 ICR 210.

Mejan, Luis Manuel C., *The UNCITRAL Model Law on Cross-Border Insolvency in North American Countries*, Festschrift für Christoph Paulus, C.H.Beck (Munich) 2022, 501.

Metreveli, Lia, 'Toward Standardized Enforcement of Cross-Border Insolvency Decisions: Encouraging the United States to Adopt UNCITRAL'S Recent Amendment to its Model Law On Cross-Border Insolvency' 51 Columbia JL and Social Problems 315.

Mevorach, Irit, 'Beyond the Search for Certainty – Addressing the Cross-border Resolution Gap' [2015] Brooklyn Journal of Corporate, Financial & Commercial Law 202.

Mevorach, Irit, 'Modified Universalism as Customary International Law' (2018) 96 Tex. L. Rev. 1403.

Mevorach, Irit, 'On the Road to Universalism: A Comparative and Empirical Study of the UNCITRAL Model Law on Cross-Border Insolvency' (2011) 12 EBOR 517.

Mevorach, Irit, 'Overlapping International Instruments for Enforcement of Insolvency Judgements: Undermining or Strengthening Universalism?', European Business Organization Law Review (2021), https://doi.org/10.1007/s40804-021-00204-4, p. 299.

Mevorach, Irit, 'Insolvency Standards, Model Laws, and Cooperation in Cross-Border Insolvency: The Role and Impact of UNCITRAL's Instruments' in R Gulati, T John and B. Koehler (eds) *Elgar Companion on the United Nations Commission on International Trade Law*, Edward Elgar Publishing (Cheltenham) 2023.

Mevorach, Irit, *The Future of Cross-Border Insolvency: Overcoming Biases and Closing Gaps* (OUP 2018).

Mevorach, Irit and Walters, Adrian, 'The Characterization of Pre-insolvency Proceedings in Private International Law' (2020) 21 European Business Organization Law Review 855.

Mills, A., 'The Dimensions of Public Policy in Private International Law' (2008) 4 Journal of Private International Law 201.

Mohan, S.C., 'Cross-border Insolvency Problems: Is the UNCITRAL Model Law the Answer?' (2012) 21 Int'l Insolv Rev 199.

Morres, H.P., G. Moss, F.M. Mucciarelli and C.G. Paulus, 'Cross-border Insolvencies after Brexit: Views from the United Kingdom and Continental Europe', British Institute of International and Comparative Law (Waterloo), 2018 (Brexit: The International Legal Implications, delivered at the Centre for International Governance Innovation).

Morrison, Rachel, 'Avoiding Inherent Uncertainties in Cross-Border Insolvency: Is the UNCITRAL Model Law the Answer?' (1999) 15 QUT Law Review 103.

Moss, Gabriel, Fletcher, Ian F. and Isaacs, Stuart (eds), *The EU Regulation on Insolvency Proceedings*, 3rd edn, Oxford University Press (Oxford), 2016.

Moss, Gabriel, 'UNCITRAL Model Law on recognition and enforcement of insolvency-related judgments', Insolv Int 32, 4.

Nadelmann, Kurt H., 'Concurrent Bankruptcies and Creditor in the Americas' (1947) 96 U. Pa. L. Rev. 171.

Nadelmann, Kurt H., 'Revision of Conflicts Provisions in the American Bankruptcy Act' (1952) 1 International & Comparative Law Quarterly 484.

Nielsen, Anne, Sigal, Mike and Wagner, Karen, 'The Cross-Border Insolvency Concordat: Principles to Facilitate the Resolution of International Insolvencies' (1996) 70 Am. Bankr. L.J. 533.

Omar, Paul, Cross-Border Insolvency and Principles of Judicial Assistance: Recent Themes and Developments, in: Santen and van Offeren (eds), *Tribute to Bob Wessels*, Kluwer (Alphen aan den Rijn) 2014.

Omar, Paul (ed.), *International Insolvency Law – Themes and Perspectives*, Ashgate (London) 2008.

Omar, Paul, 'Judicial Cooperation in the Post-Singularis World' (2018) 15 ICR 22.

Pannen, Klaus (ed.), *European Insolvency Regulation*, De Gruyter (Berlin) 2007.

Parry, Rebecca, Ayliffe, James and Shivji, Sharif (eds), *Transaction Avoidance in Insolvencies*, Oxford University Press (Oxford) 2018.

Piñeiro, Laura Carballo, '"Brexit" and International Insolvency beyond the Realm of Mutual Trust' (2017) 26(3) International Insolvency Review 241.

Pottow, John A.E., 'Greed and Pride in International Bankruptcy: The Problems of and Proposed Solutions to "Local Interests"' (2006) 104 Mich. L. Rev. 1899.

Pottow, John A.E., 'Procedural Incrementalism: A Model for International Bankruptcy' (2005) 45 Va. J. Int'l L. 935.

Pottow, John A.E., 'The Dialogic Aspect of Soft Law in International Insolvency: Discord, Digression, and Development' (2019) 40 Michigan JIL 479

Rares, Steven, 'Consistency and Conflict – Cross-Border Insolvency' Speech by Justice Rares September 2015 www.fedcourt.gov.au/digital-law-library/judges-speeches/justice-rares/rares-j-20150904.

Rares, Steven, 'Maritime Liens, Renvoi And Conflicts Of Law: The Far From Halcyon Isle' (2014) 2 Lloyd's Maritime and Commercial Law Quarterly 183.

Rares, Steven, 'Ship Arrests, Maritime Liens and Cross-border Insolvency', paper presented by Justice Rares at the BIT's 6th Annual World Congress of Ocean 2017 in Shenzhen, China, 3–5 November 2017. www.fedcourt.gov.au/digital-law-library/judges-speeches/justice-rares/rares-j-20171103.

Rochelle, Bryan, 'Cross-Border Insolvency in the U.S. and U.K.: Conflicting Approaches to Defining the Locus of a Debtor's "Center of Main Interests"', 50 Int'l Law. 391 (2017).

Rodriguez, Rodrigo, 'The new UNCITRAL Model Law on Recognition and Enforcement of Insolvency-Related Judgments', in: Ballesteros Barros, Angel and Morán Bovio, David (Ed.), *Insolvency Law in Uncitral: Instruments and Comments*, Aranzadi (Pamplona) 2023, pp. 111–131.

Rodriguez, Rodrigo, 'Zuständigkeiten im internationalen Insolvenzrecht - Der 11. Titel des IPRG im Rechtsvergleich mit der europäischen Insolvenzverordnung und dem UNCITRAL-Modellgesetz', Bern

Rothstein, Paul F., Fed Rules of Evidence Rule 301 (2022 ed).

Sachdev, Varoon, 'Choice of Law in Insolvency Proceedings: How English Courts' Continued Reliance on the Gibbs Principle Threatens Universalism' (2019) 93(2) American Bankruptcy Law Journal 343.

Sarra, Janis, 'Northern Lights, Canada's Version of the UNCITRAL Model Law on Cross-Border Insolvency' 16 Int'l Insolvency R 19 (2007).

Sexton, Anthony V., 'Current Problems and Trends in the Administration of Transnational Insolvencies Involving Enterprise Groups: The Mixed Record of Protocols, the UNCITRAL Model Insolvency Law, and the EU Insolvency Regulation' (2012) 12 Chicago Journal of International Law 811.

Sheldon, Richard (ed.), *Cross Border Insolvency*, 3rd ed. Bloomsbury Professional (London) 2011.

Shorr, Segaal, 'Avoidance Actions Under Chapter 15: Was Condor Correct?' (2016) 1 Fordham International Law Journal 351.

Silverman, Ronald J., 'Advances in Cross-Border Insolvency: the UNCITRAL Model Law on Cross-Border Insolvency' (2000) 6 ILSA Journal of International & Comparative Law 265.

Slaughter, Anne-Marie, 'A Global Community of Courts' (2003) 44(1) Harvard International Law Journal 191, 193.

Soars, Julie, Cross-border Insolvency and Shipping – a Practical Guide www.fedcourt.gov.au/law-and-practice/national-practice-areas/admiralty/admiralty-papers/julie-soars-2015.

Stark, B., 'Chapter 15 and the Advancement of International Cooperation in Cross-Border Bankruptcy Proceedings' (2006) 6 J Global L & Bus 203.

Stewart, Angus and Patch, Karen, 'Cross-border Insolvency Law in Australia and Shipping Insolvencies: Unique Challenges or Issues of Wider Significance?' (2018) 19 Insolvency Law Bulletin 15.

Torremans, Paul, *Cross-border Insolvencies in EU, English and Belgian Law*, Wolters Kluwer (The Hague/London/Boston) 2002.

UNCITRAL Case Law on UNCITRAL Texts (CLOUT) 2007.

UNCITRAL, Digest of Case Law on the UNCITRAL Model Law on Cross-Border Insolvency, United Nations Publications (New York) 2021.

UNCITRAL, Guidance Note on Enacting Two or More of the UNCITRAL Model Laws on Insolvency (Prepared by UNCITRAL Secretariat in Consultation with Experts) (2021), https://uncitral.un.org/sites/uncitral.un.org/files/media-documents/uncitral/en/v2104338_guidance_note_uncitral_model_laws_on_insolvency.pdf accessed 22 February 2023.

UNCITRAL, Legislative Guide on Insolvency Law, Part 1 and 2, United Nations Publications (New York) 2005.

UNCITRAL, Legislative Guide on Insolvency Law, United Nations Publications (New York) 2014.

UNCITRAL Model Law on Cross-Border Insolvency (1997) with Guide to Enactment and Interpretation (2013), United Nations Publications (New York) 2014.

UNCITRAL Model Law on Cross-Border Insolvency: The Judicial Perspective, United Nations Publications (New York) 2014.

UNCITRAL Model Law on Enterprise Group Insolvency with Guide to Enactment, United Nations Publications (New York) 2020.

UNCITRAL Model Law on Recognition and Enforcement of Insolvency-Related Judgments, United Nations Publications (New York) 2018.

UNCITRAL Practice Guide on Cross-Border Insolvency Cooperation, United Nations Publications (New York) 2010.

UNCITRAL, Practice Guide on Insolvency Cooperation, United Nations Publications (New York) 2010.

UNCITRAL, Report of the United Nations Commission on International Trade Law on the work of its Thirtieth Session, A/52/17, United Nations Publications (New York), 1997.

UNCITRAL, Report of the United Nations Commission on International Trade Law on the work of its Nineteenth Session, A/CN.9/WG.V/WP.44, United Nations Publications (New York), 1996.

UNCITRAL, Report of the Working Group on Insolvency Law on the work of the Eighteenth Session, A/CN.9/419, United Nations Publications (New York), 1996.

UNCITRAL, Report of the Working Group on Insolvency Law on the work of its Nineteenth Session, A/CN.9/422, United Nations Publications (New York), 1996.

UNCITRAL, Report of the Working Group on Insolvency Law of the work of its Twentieth Session, A/CN.9/433, United Nations Publications (New York), 1996.

UNCITRAL, Report of the Working Group on Insolvency Law of the work of its Twenty-First Session, A/CN.9/435, United Nations Publications (New York), 1997.

UNCITRAL, Report of the Working Group on Insolvency Law of the work of its Thirtieth Session, A/CN.9/436, United Nations Publications (New York), 1997.

UNCITRAL, Updates to 'UNCITRAL Model Law on Cross-Border Insolvency: The Judicial Perspective' A/CN.9/WG.V/WP.180.

Vandewerker, Cody, 'The Jetsetter's Guide to Bankruptcy: Chapter 15 and Recognition as a Foreign Main Proceeding for Individual Debtors' (2016) 33 Ariz J Int'l & Comp L 451.

Vatermoli, Daniele, Stephan Madaus, Federica Pasquariello and Andrés Recalde Castells (eds), *Transnational Protocols: A Cooperative Tool for Managing Cross-Border Insolvency*, Wolters Kluwer (Milano) 2021.

Veder, Michael, *Cross-Border Insolvency Proceedings and Security Rights. A comparison of Dutch and German law, the EC Insolvency Regulation and the UNCITRAL Model Law on Cross-Border Insolvency* (diss. Nijmegen), Series Law of Business and Finance, Volume 8, Deventer: Kluwer Legal Publishers 2004.

Virgós, Miguel and Schmit, Etienne, 'Report on the Convention of Insolvency Proceedings' (1996) [EU Council Document].

Walters, Adrian, 'Modified Universalisms & The Role of Local Legal Culture in the Making of Cross-Border Insolvency Law' (2019) 93 American Bankruptcy Law Journal 47.

Wan, Wai Yee and Gerard McCormack, 'Implementing Strategies for the Model Law on Cross-Border Insolvency: The Divergence in Asia-Pacific and Lessons for UNCITRAL' (2020) 36 Emory Bankr. Dev. J. 59.

Warner, G.R., 'Comparative Collectivity – EU and US Approaches' (International Insolvency Review 2023).

Warner, G.R., and Veder, M., 'Enterprise Group Restructuring: Dutch Options and United States Enforcement' (2021) 7 EIRJ.

Wee, Meng Seng, 'The Belt and Road Initiative, China's Cross-Border Insolvency Law, and the UNCITRAL Model Law on Cross-Border Insolvency' (2020) 8 Chinese Journal of Comparative Law 116.

Wessels, Bob, 'A Global Approach to Cross-Border Insolvency Cases in a Globalizing World' (2013) The Dovenschmidt Quarterly 16.

Wessels, Bob, *International Insolvency Law Part I.*, 4th ed., Wolters Kluwer (Deventer) 2015.

Wessels, Bob and Boon, Gert-Jan, *Cross-Border Insolvency Law – International Instruments and Commentary*, 2nd ed. Wolters Kluwer (Deventer) 2015.

Wessels, Bob, Markell, Bruce A. and Kilborn, Jason J., *International Cooperation in Bankruptcy and Insolvency Matters*, Oxford University Press (Oxford) 2009.

Wessels, Bob and Kokorin, Ilja, 'European Union Regulation on Insolvency Proceedings: An Introductory Analysis' (4th ed), American Bankruptcy Institute 2018.

Westbrook, Jay L., 'A Global Solution to Multinational Default' (2000) 98 Mich L Rev 2276.

Westbrook, Jay L., 'An Empirical Study of the Implementation in the United States of the Model Law on Cross Border Insolvency' (2013) 87(2) Am Bankr L J 247.

Westbrook, Jay L., 'Avoidance of Pre-Bankruptcy Transactions in Multinational Bankruptcy Cases' (2007) 42 Tex. Int.'l L.J. 899.

Westbrook, Jay L., 'Breaking Away: Global Proceedings and Local Assets' (2011) 46 Tex. Int'l L.J. 601.

Westbrook, Jay L., 'Chapter 15 At Last' (2005) 79(3) American Bankruptcy Law Journal 713.

Westbrook, Jay L., 'Choice of Avoidance Law in Global Insolvencies' (1991) 17 Brooklyn Journal of International Law 499.

Westbrook, Jay L., 'Comity and Choice of Law in Global Insolvencies' (2019) 54 Texas International Law Journal 1 https://papers.ssrn.com/sol3/papers.cfm?abstract_id=3417407 last accessed 22 February 2023.

Westbrook, Jay L., 'Comment: A More Optimistic View of Cross-Border Insolvency' (1994) 72(3) Wash U L Rev 950.

Westbrook, Jay L., 'Global Insolvency Proceedings for a Global Market: The Universalist System and the Choice of a Central Court' (2018) 96 Texas Law Review 1473.

Westbrook, Jay L., 'Multinational Enterprises in General Default: Chapter 15, the ALI Principles, and the EU Insolvency Regulation' (2002) 76 Am. Bankr. L.J. 1.

Westbrook, Jay L., 'Priority Conflicts as a Barrier to Cooperation in Multinational Insolvencies' (2009) 27 Penn St. Int'l L. Rev. 869.

Westbrook, Jay L., 'Universal Priorities' (1998) 33 Tex. Int'l L.J. 27.

Wimmer, Klaus, Die UNCITRAL-Modellbestimmungen über grenzüberschreitende Insol-venzverfahren, (1997), Zeitschrift für Wirtschaftsrecht (ZIP), 2220.

Wittinghofer, Mathias A., *Der nationale und internationale Insolvenzverwaltervertrag*, Gieseking (Bielefeld) 2004.

Wood, Philip R., *Principles of International Insolvency* 3rd ed Sweet and Maxwell (London) 2019.

Wood, Philip R., *Set-offs and Netting, Derivatives and Clearing Systems* 3rd ed. Sweet & Maxwell (London) 2019.

Yamamoto, K., 'New Japanese Legislation on Cross-border Insolvency as Compared with the UNCITRAL Model Law' 11 Int'l Insolvency Rev. 67 (2002).

Yamauchi, Keith D, 'The UNCITRAL Model Cross-Border Insolvency Law: The Stay of Proceedings and Adequate Protection' (2004) 13(2) International Insolvency Review 87.

Zechel, Jan-Uwe S, 'Germany's Insolvency Act: An International Approach with the UNCITRAL Model Law on Cross Border Insolvency in Mind' LLM thesis Fordham University School of Law 2000 www.zechel.net/downloads/germanys_insolvency_act.pdf.

Zhen Qu, Charles and Godwin, Andrew, 'Does the Common Law Power to Grant Cross-Border Insolvency Assistance Apply to an Insolvency Winding-Up that Is Voluntary? The Reaction to Singularis from Singapore and Hong Kong' (2019) 28 IIR 305.

Ziegel, Jacob, 'Canada–United States Cross-Border Insolvency Relations and the UNCITRAL Model Law' (2007) 32 Brook. J. Int'l L. 1042.

Zwieten, Kristin van, *Goode on Principles of Corporate Insolvency Law* 5th ed. Sweet and Maxwell (London) 2019.

INDEX